137-½

CONFRONTING**AMERICA**

The New Cold War History   *Odd Arne Westad, editor*

CONFRONTING AMERICA

The Cold War between
the United States and the
Communists in France
and Italy

ALESSANDRO BROGI

The University of North Carolina Press   CHAPEL HILL

© 2011 THE UNIVERSITY OF NORTH CAROLINA PRESS
ALL RIGHTS RESERVED
MANUFACTURED IN THE UNITED STATES OF AMERICA

Designed by Kimberly Bryant and set in Miller with Gotham display by Tseng
Information Systems, Inc. The paper in this book meets the guidelines for permanence
and durability of the Committee on Production Guidelines for Book Longevity of the
Council on Library Resources. The University of North Carolina Press has been a
member of the Green Press Initiative since 2003.

Library of Congress Cataloging-in-Publication Data
Brogi, Alessandro.
Confronting America : the Cold War between the United States and the communists in
France and Italy / Alessandro Brogi.
p. cm. — (The new Cold War history)
Includes bibliographical references and index.
ISBN 978-0-8078-3473-2 (cloth : alk. paper)
1. United States—Foreign relations—France. 2. France—Foreign relations—
United States. 3. United States—Foreign relations—Italy. 4. Italy—Foreign relations—
United States. 5. United States—Foreign relations—1945–1989. 6. Communism—
France—History—20th century. 7. Communism—Italy—History—20th century.
8. Anti-Americanism—France—History—20th century. 9. Anti-Americanism—Italy—
History—20th century. 10. Parti communiste français. 11. Partito comunista italiano.
I. Title.
E183.8.F8B724 2011
327.73044—dc22 2010052563

15 14 13 12 11   5 4 3 2 1

Contents *Acknowledgments vii   Abbreviations x*

Illustrations

Acknowledgments

At first, I thought I could write this book quickly and without much aid. Of course, like most academics caught in the passion of discovery, I was mistaken. The scope of the research would not have been possible without the assistance of several institutions and individuals. I have also benefited from the critical insights of colleagues who read my first drafts. To all these people and institutions I am truly indebted, although, of course, the views expressed herein are my own.

My first acknowledgment goes to the Fulbright College of the University of Arkansas, and more specifically to the History Department, for allowing considerable leeway with my teaching load, and for showing trust and encouragement through a number of travel grants, a generous summer research stipend, and additional support during my off-campus assignments. History Department Chairs Jeannie Whayne, David Sloan, and especially Lynda Coon have been my strongest advocates with the college administrators. This has been true until the finish line, when, in times of budget cuts and restrictions, Professor Coon not only offered a subsidy from the History Department's own account but also obtained one from the office of Fulbright College Dean William Schwab to help cover the printing costs of this sizeable manuscript.

I am also deeply obliged to the Nobel Peace Institute of Oslo, Norway, which is to be singled out, among the external institutions, as the most supportive and encouraging one for my project. My six months there in 2007 as a research fellow were not only the most productive in the whole time span of this work; they were also the most insightful, thanks in part to the frequent discussions I was privileged to have with an elite group of historians. With the Nobel Institute's director, Geir Lundestad, I continue to have fruitful discussions. Geir and I may agree on many things and agree to disagree on many others. What matters most is that he, like the other members of the Nobel fellowship, perfectly fulfills the program's mission: as Geir constantly reminded each of the institute's fellows, our task was to push one another to the limit, with candid and sometimes brutal criticism, as we faced the difficult tasks of adopting an interdisciplinary as well as truly international approach to history, and of writing on many issues that may still be controversial. Swiss historian Benedikt Schoenborn and the genuinely Norwegian Asle Toje, the other two recipients of this fellowship so fortunately resumed that year, patiently considered my arguments, and discussed matters of anti-

Americanism with me. Joining us at the end, the renowned Dutch director of the European Association of American Studies, Rob Kroes, helped ease my "pain" in dealing with the rather elusive notion of Americanization. The Nobel Institute is also exemplary in its library staff: I especially thank Anne C. Kjelling and Bjørn H. Vangen for their help finding rare source material.

My research in the United States, which included visits to presidential libraries stretching from New England to Kansas, would not have been possible without the additional support I received through a George C. Marshall/Baruch Research Grant from the George C. Marshall Foundation and through Truman Library and Ford Library travel grants. All three archives also must be recognized for their remarkably helpful staffs, comparable to that I once experienced at the Eisenhower Library. The Ford Library offered perhaps the most enthusiastic support, showing me the treasure of material on international relations in this frequently overlooked archival source. The Carter Library, too, should be noted for its prompt and effective release of material through its electronic resource access. My research experience in the United States also bears the memory of the iconic archivist at the National Archives and Records Administration, Sally Kuisel. I concur with the list-server H-Diplo, who recently so admiringly paid homage to Sally's memory.

In France, despite the restrictions still applied to the French Communist Party's documentation, archivist Pascal Carreau directed me to unexpectedly informative files and paper collections of some of the party leaders, a discovery that prompted me to extend my stay in Paris. At the Gramsci Institute in Rome I was even more fortunate to gain access to documents of the Italian Communist Party (PCI) up to the late 1970s. My special thanks go to Giovanna Bosman, and to my colleague and fellow Florentine Silvio Pons, the institute's director. Silvio has been not only supportive but enthusiastic about discussing with me the PCI's international record from his masterfully knowledgeable point of view. Simona Granelli, from the Gramsci Institute in Bologna, helped me find some of the most appropriate Italian images for the book's illustrations. From France, Frédérik Genevée also assisted me through the difficult process of acquiring the copyrights for the PCF's propaganda posters.

I was fortunate and honored to have another opportunity for extended research in Italy, thanks to the Johns Hopkins University's offer of a visiting professorship at its Bologna Center in 2004–5. The advantage of being at its renowned School of Advanced International Studies (SAIS) was not simply logistical. John Harper, amid our discussions on the U.S.-European "rift" during the 2004 presidential elections, also took time to discuss my project while it was at its most difficult developing stage. The brilliant students at SAIS also were a source of inspiration—a class later matched in brilliance by my fall 2009 undergraduate and graduate students in Cold War history at the University of Arkansas. At its embryonic stage, this project also benefited from the support and equally inspiring environment of the Institute for Strategic Studies at Yale University. As an Olin fellow there, I had the wonderful opportunity to brainstorm about my tentative topic with Paul Kennedy, with co-Olin fellows Jeffrey Engel, Andrew Preston, and Mary Kathryn Barbier, and, of course, with my long-time mentor, John Lewis Gaddis.

While the drafting of the manuscript was in full swing, several distinguished scholars gave careful consideration and useful recommendations. David Ellwood offered important critical insights on my drafts of chapters 3 and 4; Irwin Wall did the same on chapters 8 and 9; two colleagues at the University of Arkansas, Richard Sonn and Evan Bukey, proofread all the rest, with patience and thoughtful advice. Through frequent correspondence or long conversations, other colleagues patiently listened, encouraged, and lent their insights. In no particular order of importance, they are Richard Kuisel, Mario Del Pero, Federico Romero, Leopoldo Nuti, Kaeten Mistry, Marc Lazar, Frédéric Bozo, Charles Maier, Olav Niølstad, Vladislav Zubok, Günther Bischof, Jessica Gienow-Hecht, Jeremi Suri, Patricia Weitsman, Marc Selverstone, Alonzo Hamby, and my University of Arkansas colleagues David Chappell and Randall Woods. Thanks also to the three (yes, three) anonymous readers selected by the University of North Carolina Press for their endorsement and cogent advice. It has also been a pleasure to work with such an efficient staff at UNC Press. I understand why so many authors are proud to be part of this team.

There is finally one "emerging" reader who perhaps gave the most valuable support. For my seven-year-old son Samuel, this book has literally taken a lifetime. At the end of the long process, whenever stress seemed to be taking over, I only had to look at his smile to be reminded of my ultimate motivation for the work.

Abbreviations

The following abbreviations are used throughout this book.

ACUE   American Committee on United Europe
ADA   Americans for Democratic Action
AFAP   Association Française pour l'Accroissement de la Productivité
AFL   American Federation of Labor
ARCI   Associazione Ricreativa Culturale Italiana
CCF   Congress for Cultural Freedom
CERM   Centre d'Etudes et des Recherches Marxistes
CESPE   Centro Studi di Politica Economica
CGIL   Confederazione Generale Italiana del Lavoro
CGT   Confédération Générale du Travail
CIA   Central Intelligence Agency
CIF   Confederazione Italiana Femminile
CIO   Congress of Industrial Organizations
CISL   Confederazione Italiana Sindacati Lavoratori
CLN   Comitato di Liberazione Nazionale
CPSU   Communist Party of the Soviet Union
CPUSA   Communist Party of the United States of America
CU   Bureau of Education and Cultural Affairs
DC   Democrazia Cristiana
ECA   Economic Cooperation Administration
ECSC   European Coal and Steel Community
EDC   European Defense Community
EEC   European Economic Community
ENI   Ente Nazionale Idrocarburi
ERP   European Recovery Program
EURATOM European Atomic Energy Community
FGCI   Federazione Giovanile Comunista Italiana
FLN   Front de Libération Nationale
FO   Force Ouvrière
IACF   International Association for Cultural Freedom
ILGWU   International Ladies Garment Workers Union
IRBM   Intermediate Range Ballistic Missiles
IRI   Istituto per la Ricostruzione Industriale
JCR   Jeunesse Communiste Révolutionnaire

JCS	Joint Chiefs of Staff
KGB	Komitet Gosudarstvennoy Bezopasnosti
LCGIL	Libera Confederazione Generale Italiana del Lavoro
MDAP	Mutual Defense Assistance Program
MLF	Multilateral Force
MPEA	Motion Picture Export Association
MRP	Mouvement Républicain Populaire
MSA	Mutual Security Administration
MTV	Music Television
NATO	North Atlantic Treaty Organization
NCL	NonCommunist Left
NSC	National Security Council
OCB	Operations Coordinating Board
OECD	Organization for Economic Cooperation and Development
OEEC	Organization for European Economic Cooperation
OSP	OffShore Procurement
OWI	Office of War Information
PCE	Partido Comunista de España
PCF	Parti Communiste Français
PCI	Partito Comunista Italiano
PDS	Partito Democratico della Sinistra
PPS	Policy Planning Staff
PS	Parti Socialiste
PSB	Psychological Strategy Board
PSDI	Partito Socialista Democratico Italiano
PSI	Partito Socialista Italiano
PSIUP	Partito Socialista Italiano di Unità Proletaria
PSLI	Partito Socialista dei Lavoratori Italiano
PSU	Parti Socialiste Unifié
RAI	Radio Televisione Italiana
RDF	Radio Diffusion France
RDR	Rassemblement Démocratique Révolutionnaire
RPF	Rassemblement du Peuple Français
SDS	Students for a Democratic Society
SEATO	South East Asian Treaty Organization
SFIO	Section Française de l'Internationale Ouvrière
SIFAR	Servizio per le Informazioni e la Sicurezza Militare
SPD	Sozialdemokratische Partei Deutschland
UDI	Unione delle Donne Italiane
UEC	Union des Etudiants Communistes

CONFRONTING**AMERICA**

INTRODUCTION

At the onset of the Cold War, Palmiro Togliatti and George F. Kennan shared a particular vision of America. The leader of the fastest growing Communist Party in the West and the architect of America's containment strategy against Soviet Communism, from their opposite points of view, nurtured a similar pessimism about the U.S. role as leader of the Western world.[1] Togliatti's indictment of the United States was occasioned in May 1947 by former Undersecretary of State Sumner Welles's press statements that the Partito Comunista Italiano (PCI) was an insurrectionary party funded by the Soviet Union. These declarations coincided with the political crisis that a few days later led Prime Minister Alcide De Gasperi—allegedly under pressure from Washington—to expel the PCI from the government's national coalition, which had been in place since the last year of the war.

The general secretary's response to Sumner Welles was an emblematic editorial in the 20 May issue of the party's daily *L'Unità*, titled "Ma come sono cretini!" ("What Idiots They Are!"). It was a clever retelling of the old dichotomy between mature, wise, committed, refined Europe and young, crass, hedonistic, naive America—dangerously naive at that, for its stupidity was now matched by its power and arrogance. Only in America, Togliatti wrote, "could a party buy prestige and influence with money"; and, no doubt, Washington treated Italy like "a territory inhabited by competing tribes, instead of parties that naturally emerged from its national traditions." This should not have surprised any European, since at heart, the Americans were still "slaveholders," who now wished to buy entire nations the same way. They also did so, Togliatti judged, because "they [were] not intelligent" and "lacked historical experience and mental finesse." Americans were like "the majority of their films, with all their luxury, their technology, the legs and all the rest of those beautiful actresses"; after watching them for a while, one was "overwhelmed with irritation and boredom, realizing that it [was] only a dehumanized exhibition, a mechanical repetition of gestures and situations deprived of the spontaneous vibrating of souls and things."[2]

Previous foreign rulers had dominated the country, and at times had even influenced its national identity, but not its very soul and intellectual resourcefulness. Italy, the Communists averred, was now engaged in a double resistance: to defend the country's national sovereignty *and* national intelligence against, in Togliatti's words, the "massive wave of plain idiocy" of the Yankee invader.

Two years later, Kennan's judgment of America's world leadership was equally scathing. As director of the State Department's Policy Planning Staff, and still revered for having masterminded containment, he was highly influential at the White House. He was, however, an iconoclast, where the "icon" was modern America as an acquisitive society characterized by its mass phenomena in production, consumption, and culture. His intellectual background associated him with the organicist conservatism dating back to Edmund Burke's condemnation of the French Revolution, a legacy that continued through thinkers such as Ferdinand Tönnies, Oswald Spengler, Max Weber, Henry and Brooks Adams, and Walter Lippmann. They all abhorred the relentless rationalization that subordinated every aspect of life, the logic of material achievements and money making, turning most of the qualitative into quantitative, and transforming the "organic" community into a mechanized, atomized society of passive consumers.[3] Conscious of his position as a policy maker and defender of the system, Kennan for the time being expressed his insightful critique only within small circles. His letter to a staff member from 17 October 1949 offers a fine example of his agonizing reflections.

While Kennan would not have given credit to any communist indictment, he nevertheless took the cue for his own critique of American society and foreign policy from his reflections on the communist adversaries. He did so often with regard to his area of expertise, the Soviet Union. In this case he focused his thoughts on Western Communism. He acknowledged that its strongest drive was emotional, nationalist, and intellectual: the "desire to win appreciation, attention and power [was a] much more important component of Communism than desire to better a material condition." The point was not how many followers communism could thus obtain. Kennan believed (rather incorrectly with regard to Italy and France) that it was a "movement" without "popular appeal" in advanced countries. But since it was a development not only imported from Moscow but also deeply rooted in Western civilization, it could not be regarded as an anomaly. Its "emotional appeal" induced Kennan to stigmatize some "fundamental flaws" in the "complicated civilization" of the West. The main problems stemmed not from fear of material deprivation; they originated "rather from the disintegration of basic social groups in which the individual found the illusion of security through the sense of belonging—namely, the family, the local community, the neighborhood, the recreational group." And since America best represented the evolution of this modern society, Kennan turned his analysis to the problems "within":

Millions of Americans are today bewildered and anxious because they are trying to solve as individuals problems which they could solve only by a collective approach. But what is causing these groups to disintegrate is the urbanization of life—that is, the revolution in living wrought by modern technology, rather than just complexity. As this urbanization fragmentizes social groups, it centralizes the media of psychological influence (press, radio, television, movies) and makes recreation passive and vicarious rather than active and immediate. At the same time that it breaks up the groups in which the individual found scope for the development of leadership, self-respect and self-development, it provides a vast fog of recreational stimuli which demand nothing of the individual, develop nothing in him and tend to atrophy his capacity for self-expression. The result of all this is a gradual paralysis of the sense of responsibility and initiative in people.

Thus lamenting this "drifting" condition of the average American, Kennan concluded "not being the masters of our own soul, are we justified in regarding ourselves as fit for the leadership of others? All our ideas of 'world leadership,' 'the American century,' 'aggressive democracy,' etc. stand or fall with the answer to that question."[4]

This was no admission of communist superiority. The fact remained that all these insecurities of the "Western man," all these conditions of atomized passivity, what philosopher Herbert Marcuse later would call "one-dimensional" society, had already, in Kennan's opinion, "softened up great masses of people for the acceptance of totalitarian rule." The enslavement of the individual would be thus complete.[5] Kennan's alternative was attuned with his self-professed "dirigisme," as opposed to socialism, and reflected his advocacy of minority rule by an enlightened elite: he recommended abandoning "the evils of a *laissez-faire* attitude toward technological advances" and preached a cure through "a high degree of paternalism."[6]

Kennan's position within the U.S. leadership elite has been recognized as that of a "pessimist by nature, one whose pessimism was rendered so much deeper by the ritualistic optimism of official American culture."[7] His ideas, as both an insider of and, later, an academic outsider to U.S. foreign policy, are so often heavily scrutinized because they cast a critical light on conventional America, penetrating its surface, clarifying its idiosyncrasies, its will to power, and making sense of its world role.

These reflections from two rival political positions announced the terms of the cultural and political Cold War in Western Europe. Western Communists would attempt to redefine society and even national identity with the crucial assistance of their virulent, at times dogmatic, and at other times multidimensional and ambiguous anti-Americanism. Americans—not only the iconoclasts—were forced into self-analysis by the cultural and political struggle against communism in allied countries. Western Communism, even more than the Eastern, Soviet brand of communism, compelled U.S. policy makers, diplomats, and influential intellectuals to reconsider the image America projected abroad, and even to ponder the general meaning of American liberal capitalist culture and ideology. Many of those representatives soon had to concede to Kennan and other critics that they could not simply dismiss the political and cultural ascendancy of the Italian and French Communist Parties as an aberration in the Western world. Their reactions to this reality ranged from sober reassessment of America's diplomacy, or even way of life, to radical and at times rabid countervailing anticommunism.

Indeed, the Western European Communists and their anti-Americanism stimulated among American leaders and intellectuals both self-criticism and instinctive patriotism. Sometimes the two feelings were present within the same individual, and both frequently originated from a conviction that America was and should remain "exceptionalist" vis-à-vis Europe. In many respects, this phenomenon was mirrored among French and Italian Communists: their anti-Americanism remained indiscriminate for the most part; but the process of modernization they identified with American capitalism and culture also prompted them at critical times to pursue cultural and political variations of it in order to forge a distinctly European—and often, in the early Cold War, Soviet-inspired—brand of modernity.

Togliatti's and Kennan's anxieties also signified the totality of the conflict between two antagonistic and universalistic models. The United States would gradually realize that economic determinism, the assumption that economic recovery would by itself curtail communist power in France and Italy, was flawed. While economic conditions seemed to provide the main breeding ground for communism in Western Europe, it soon became apparent that the appeal of the PCI and of the Parti Communiste Français (PCF) was emotional as much as economic. By identifying capitalist oppression with American domination, that appeal combined a promise of material improvement with a defense of national independence and indigenous culture. As the Cold War struggle in the Third World would later confirm, nationalism was a crucial component of communist confrontation with America. Beginning in the last year of World War II, the French and Italian Communists' capacity to reconcile patriotism and proletarian internationalism was further corroborated by their organizational power, with an ability to seize key economic and political institutions, and by their intellectual magnetism, since most Marxists understood that the cultural challenge to the established order was as critical as the political dimension. Together, these components of communist influence offered a powerful resistance to American hegemony.

The main purpose of this book is to examine the resilience of that appeal throughout the Cold War, and to assess how effectively the United States countered it by selecting among America's various economic, diplomatic, cultural, and covert options. In particular, this clash induced Washington to test constantly its own flexibility at home and with its European allies. In part this is a story of how the French and Italian Communists confronted American influence—or even its cultural manifestations defined under the broad and often misleading term "Americanization." But in confronting this very influential brand of anti-Americanism, the United States was also encouraged to confront itself, its foreign policy, and its own social structure and overall culture. Today the capacity to confront international problems with ideological, diplomatic, and cultural appeal is known as "soft power"—in contrast to "hard power," consisting mainly of coercion or economic inducements.[8] During the Cold War the most perceptive American officials realized that their resort to soft power could be a formidable complement to America's economic, strategic, and political approaches to Europe; but if misused, this power of persuasion could easily backfire, especially among the most troublesome Western European allies.

While this is ultimately a study of U.S. foreign relations, it is also a work of international history, encompassing perceptions and choices from all three sides of this story. Only from this multiple perspective can we fully reveal how the French and the Italian Communists responded to American hegemony. If this battle for hearts and minds became a basic component of America's handling of the Western alliance, it was an even more fundamental issue for the two parties captive in a hostile "empire"; and through their experiences, it was a crucial part of the two countries' general response to U.S. influence. Several recent studies have focused on the French and Italian Communists' interaction with Eastern Europe, especially with their main frame of reference, the Soviet Union. I am indebted to the literature that has clarified the degree of coordination between Moscow and Western European Communists, as well as the combination of myths and realities in this often tormented relationship.[9] But my study is founded on the assumption that the ultimate confrontation for any Communist party, but especially for those in Western Europe, was with capitalism, consumerism, modernization, and mass culture.[10] The confrontation with America, even when implicit, or used primarily for domestic purposes, was the critical test for the French and Italian Communists. It was a struggle for their own legitimacy and existence.

Toward a Definition of Communist Anti-Americanism in Western Europe

Western Communist anti-Americanism was crucial to understanding U.S.-Western European relations for other reasons as well.[11] It should not be taken for granted as a feeling or a strategy based on ideological aversion and political expediency. Stemming from traditions of Western European perceptions of America, the two parties' views of the United States bore a far larger meaning and far deeper implications than simple mirror opposition. Since they tapped such a vast repertoire of others' cultural constructs and specific denunciations of American policies or the U.S. social landscape, those views also reflected previous realities, contradictions, and irrationalities. By trying to universalize the threat coming from overseas, they also confirmed the elusiveness of the concept known as anti-Americanism.

Some forms of anti-Americanism are about what the United States does; others are about what the United States is. In more than two centuries of U.S. history it has also become gradually clear that there are as many forms of anti-Americanism as there are ways to be American. The various ideological, cultural, nationalist ways of being anti-American thus reflect the very plurality and complexity of the American nation. Several authors have even questioned whether we can clearly identify such a broad sentiment as anti-Americanism.[12] For our purpose it is important to note that in its most radical forms, anti-Americanism is an utter rejection of American policies, society, values, and culture. A resentment so thorough, the most perceptive analyses have pointed out, can only in part result from the disproportionate power of the United States. It is also, and above all, a matter of representations—in some cases of mystifications, too. Todd Gitlin, an American intellectual who has repudiated his radical leftist past, quipped that "anti-Americanism is an emotion substituting for an analysis." The irrational nature of such a feeling can be overstated. Gitlin added that "when the hatred of foreign policies sputters into a hatred of an entire people and their civilization, then thinking is dead and demonology lives. When complexity of thought devolves into caricature—and all broad-brush hatred of any nation, whatever its occasions, is caricature—intellect is on its way to reconciling itself to mass murder."[13] Such reflections are caricatures in themselves, for they confirm the increasingly polemical tones of those who take sides with or against the United States.[14] These polemics show that this discourse has been not about a nation, but about a worldview, a faith, an encryption of everyone's fears and hopes, a frame of reference that acts on the conscious and subconscious levels of every people. No other nation has enjoyed this status.

This is because, as Rob Kroes has put it, "America was invented before it was discovered." Then the republic, from its origins, became a "beckoning beacon poised as counterpoint to Europe."[15] However it was interpreted, America represented a chance for renewal, a tabula rasa on which Europeans could reinvent themselves, shed their burdens of rank, status, subjugation. It follows that the expectations, the standards by which the new land was measured have been far higher than those of any other part of the world. Europeans first forged this conception of American uniqueness. It then became a core element of American identity, for the United States defined itself in opposition to Europe. Forming its own generalized representation of Europe as "imperfect," the United States upheld its own claim to distinctiveness, to what became known as "exceptionalism." The term signified the regeneration of decadent European social, political, and international norms into a perfectible national experience, made possible by the "American promise" of universal freedom, and enshrined in the Declaration of Independence. In the early twentieth century, Americans reiterated this claim to universality and codified their national identity based on this creed: reformulated as *Americanism*, the exceptional traits of the rising world power were, in Theodore Roosevelt's words, "the virtues of courage, honor, justice, truth, sincerity and strength—the virtues that made America."[16]

In the most general sense then, anti-Americanism can be explained as the expression of repeated disillusionment after ever rising expectations about the New World, and as the mirror opposite of the "American creed," of the U.S. pretense to universalism and perfectibility. As will be shown, the communists' resistance to America emanated from their own equivalent assertion of universality and perfectibility. Moreover, several prominent Western European Communists, especially in the early Cold War, nurtured animosity against America in part because their expectations about a progressive, radical America had been shattered.

Western European Communism also incorporated the Old World's notion of the New World as the challenging path to its own modernization. Anti-Americanism became fully formed between the 1920s and 1930s. At that point the United States foreshadowed Europe's future, rekindling endemic fears about modernity. Anti-Americanism thus became a codeword for all the internal tensions within each nation undergoing rapid transformation.

Most such transformations depended only in part on American influence. But when, after World War II, the U.S. presence in Europe became dominant in every field, those fears became more comprehensive and less symbolic. According to the most negative perceptions of this influence, modern capitalism, in its managerial, "Americanized" form, subsumed a mechanized world immersed in materialism, consumerism, mass culture, all of these together projecting the worst visions of a homogeneous, conformist, and spiritually and intellectually hollow society. Italian and French Communists, while echoing and amplifying those fears, also portrayed the Soviet model of modernization as the alternative, serving instead of enslaving humanity.

All the above indicates that, among the various ideologies, communism expressed the greatest coherence in combining the distinct components—political, social, and cultural—of anti-Americanism. Communists in Western Europe were also the most adept at utilizing the intersection between politics and culture to manifest their opposition to the United States and their alleged defense of national independence. Next to the Cold War, these were the main reasons why right-wing anti-Americanism, which had prevailed in the interwar period, was eclipsed by the intellectual and political Left starting in the mid-1940s.[17] Even the prominence of Charles de Gaulle and the significance of his conflicts with the United States must be considered against the backdrop of leftist dominance of the anti-American discourse. Consistency, however, did not always mean rigid, obtuse, and even irrational resistance. Alongside the virulent, all-embracing, dogmatic, and often deceptive communist judgments of America at the peak of the Cold War, we find the ebb and flow of more discerning forms of Marxist anti-Americanism in Western Europe.

The coherence, effectiveness, and cunning of French and Italian communist anti-Americanism can also be assessed against that of the Soviet Union. Power made a difference. The Soviet Union could at crucial junctures compromise with the United States, thanks to the recognition it received as a superpower. For much of their Cold War experience, the French and Italian Communist Parties were powerless—especially on the world stage. Their anti-Americanism consequently often surpassed that of the Soviets in thoroughness, if not consistency. The two parties, however, enjoyed another source of recognition and empowerment: the electorate. Thanks to the relative connection between communist voters and their leaders, the anti-Americanism of the party apparatus did not appear as orchestrated as it was in the Soviet Union.[18] Furthermore, the PCI and PCF could work as magnets for all sorts of discontent regarding the U.S. presence and American policies: for example, in the early 1950s, the Stockholm Peace Appeal, which was coordinated from Moscow, gathered far more consensus in France and Italy than the size of the two parties would indicate. Whenever we consider the alacrity with which French and Italian Communists stepped in line with Moscow, we must also take into account their ability to adapt their Cold War allegiance to national realities. This was especially true in their resistance to American influence.

Approach, Sources, and Broader Questions

It should be clear from the start that my approach to all these themes from a triangular perspective cannot be comprehensive. This is not a thorough history of Western communist politics, culture, and international choices; nor is it a detailed account of U.S. Cold War politics and culture, or of every U.S. intervention against Western Europe's Communists. A survey of that sort would be either too diffuse or, if it accounted for most details, too lengthy. Filtering the enormous literature on all these subjects has helped me to contextualize my broad yet targeted themes. This is a work of discovery and reinterpretation more than a synthesis of existing literature. As an interpretive account, it focuses more on the "why" than on the "how" questions. The discovery, while grounded in archival sources, grows from an analysis that interweaves cultural with traditional diplomatic and economic themes. This relatively rare combination of methods[19] emphasizes deep connections between cultural constructs, issues of national identity, and high policy. Only in this way can we illuminate the multidimensional nature of anti-Americanism and of American management of the Western alliance.

While following a chronological structure, and highlighting the main crises that characterized the multidimensional confrontation between Western European Communism and the United States, I do not pretend to deal with each one of them comprehensively. Nevertheless, I also eschew broad generalizations in favor of the systematic, nuanced discussion that these themes deserve. The analysis does linger on episodes, debates, or reflections by intellectuals and leaders that help trace the nature, logic, trends, and finally the unraveling of the confrontation.

This broad perspective further benefits from its comparative framework. Prompted by pathbreaking works that have conjoined the political or intellectual histories of the French and Italian Communist Parties,[20] I extend this comparison and redirect it "westward" to include the two parties' coping with the Atlantic alliance, and America's own understanding of their parallels and differences. As I did with my previous work on diplomatic relations among the three countries, I use a comparative analysis to show developments and characteristics in U.S. relations with France and Italy that tend to remain hidden or ignored in separate treatments of U.S. bilateral relations with either one of them.

It is by exploring the interconnectedness of diplomacy and cultural constructs that I test my main broad questions. The first regards America's management of the Western alliance. I submit that the American response to the communist threat in France and Italy, and even the effects of Americanization broadly speaking, were most successful when the United States combined its "psychological warfare" with a more subtle use of diplomatic actions that only indirectly helped modify the political balance in each of the two allied countries. Particularly effective was the U.S. emphasis on European integration and Western interdependence as a rising trend against the traditional balance of power. This helped undermine the impact of communist anti-Americanism in many ways; most important among these, European mastery of interdependence helped supersede the most traditional nationalist arguments from any political source, including the Communists; it also defused the communist appeal by shaping a European continent increasingly emancipated from American control.

The same reasoning applies to my second broad question about the effectiveness of communist anti-American campaigns. The two Communist Parties enjoyed their greatest leverage when they conflated their own "psychological warfare" with actions that enhanced their international presence. This was particularly true immediately after the war, when they profited from the artificial extension of the wartime Grand Alliance, and during the pacifist campaigns they orchestrated between the birth of NATO and the debate over the European Defense Community in the early 1950s. It was finally true with regard to the Eurocommunist experiment of the 1970s, with which the PCI especially tried to reverse the trend of Western interdependence away from its pro-American direction, while also staying clear of heavy Soviet influence.

This focus on the diplomatic and international dimensions further prompted me to reexamine previously overlooked differences between French and Italian Communists. Orthodox in most respects, the PCF was also more concentrated and militant than the PCI on foreign affairs. This was in part because of the centrality of France in international developments—including Vietnam, Algeria, the German question, the Gaullist approach to NATO—and in part because of the party's intensive debate and soul-searching regarding French national identity. And yet, the generally more flexible PCI displayed a rather astute understanding of international realities. The diminished relevance of Italy in the international arena made it a detached observatory of others' grand diplomacy. Further, the country's diplomatic weakness increased the international prominence of the Communist Party. This became particularly evident when the PCI positioned itself to subvert the alleged deleterious effects of U.S.-Soviet détente in the 1970s.

Drawing attention to the diplomatic framework can cast some light on the intricacies of specific campaigns and episodes. But the most overarching theme of this book remains that of the coming of the American model of modernization. My third broad question, which addresses both American capacity to project that model and communist ability to resist it, has received considerable attention. Stephen Gundle in particular has elucidated how the challenge of mass communications, commercial cultural industries, and consumerism together undermined the power of the Italian Communists. Furthermore, he has pointed out the irony that the PCI, which excelled in the cultural sphere, best adapted to and survived in the competition with mass media and commercial culture but in so doing also undercut its own attempt at cultural hegemony.[21] While concurring with those conclusions, I propose that a wider perspective including comparative aspects and a closer look at the decision-making process in Washington as well as in the two Communist Parties' political bureaus further illuminates the whole issue of "Americanization" in both countries. That issue must be reformulated, taking into full account the correlation among international events such as Algeria, or Vietnam, and the coming of consumer society. It also needs to be placed in context with the redefinition of oppression by the American civil rights, feminist, and student movements. That very redefinition nourished but also undermined communist orthodoxy, protest, and power in France and Italy, as shown in this book's final three chapters.

Moreover, America's self-perception and changed image by the late 1960s as less exceptionalist, less naively optimistic, more vulnerable in every way, showed the superpower's true weaknesses but also highlighted its pluralistic and multifaceted character. It thus inspired further adaptations and permutations of communist anti-Americanism in France and Italy. It also reignited subtlety and ambivalence in the Communists' assessments of America that echoed and refined their ambiguities of the immediate postwar period. But especially those assessments reflected America's own ambivalence, proved its cultural dominion and confirmed its role as harbinger of Europe's future.

To show the correlation of cultural constructs, economic realities, and political and diplomatic action, I have privileged archival sources—of the two Communist Parties, the U.S. State Department and presidential libraries— and complemented them with significant commentaries by media and intellectuals. Most accounts of anti-Americanism have focused on the latter, without fully establishing the connection between those commentaries and actual decisions and strategies by party leaders. Some scholars have gone in the opposite direction. They decry the elitist approach to the study of anti-Americanism and stress the importance of identifying the phenomenon by social strata. Accounting for the variety of audiences, they favor poll and statistical data.[22] For my purpose, the grassroots response is useful but remains in the distant background. The archival sources reveal how party leaders in France and Italy, or policy makers in the United States, assessed, followed, or guided the voices from below. They also allow me to compare and contrast mutual perceptions of all three sides' political outlooks and to evaluate their accuracy. Intellectual writings, which constitute my other main primary reference, require scrutiny and interpretation in order to reveal the complexity of the anti-American phenomenon. But the examination of the debates among party, government, and embassy officials entails even more careful deciphering. For even their most straightforward pronouncements connote attitudes, preconceptions, and cultural and ideological constructs. I thus found that, especially in such a highly ideologized encounter, the archival documents gave me the best clues to the crosscurrents of politics, diplomacy, and culture.

1 THE COMMUNISTS AND NATIONAL REBIRTH IN FRANCE AND ITALY, 1944–1946

America's confrontation with Western European Communism was as meaningful as its clash with Soviet Communism. Although the postwar growth of the French and Italian Communist Parties highlighted economic distress and quickly induced American policy makers to seek economic solutions, the leftist appeal was broader than simply economics, though this was not always immediately apparent to outsiders. In the first postwar years French and Italian needs for reconstruction entailed a redefinition of national politics and identities. The postwar experience for the two profoundly traumatized nations came to be formulated in terms of national rebirth and renewal, offering, as might be expected, a chance for radical solutions. Communist anti-Americanism and American anti-Communism remained carefully restrained and relatively muted while the two parties remained included in government coalitions, and until the wartime Grand Alliance irretrievably broke down in the spring and summer of 1947. But the very legitimacy acquired by the communist forces in France and Italy in 1944–46, especially when further justified by a public desire for radical renewal, was in most respects more threatening to the emerging Western cohesion than their strong opposition in the first decade of the Cold War.

The Two Parties' Strengths, Differences, and Contradictions

During the last years of World War II, the strength of the French and Italian Communist Parties grew not only from economic distress, but also from their capacity to reconcile passionate patriotism with proletarian internationalism. It was buttressed by organizational power and ability to seize key economic and political institutions, as well as by intellectual magnetism. The two parties' leaders understood that cultural transformation was as critical as political change. All these sinews of communist influence—nationalist, organizational, cultural—became the essential components of a powerful resistance to American hegemony.

At the time of the Liberation, the Grand Alliance yielded immediate results for the French and Italian Communist Parties. In both cases, the Soviet Union gained political influence over the two countries: in March 1944 it was the first of the great powers to recognize Italy's provisional government that had deposed and ousted Benito Mussolini a few months earlier; it was also the first to welcome Charles de Gaulle, then interim prime minister, at a power summit in Moscow that December for a treaty of friendship. These diplomatic moves led to the return from Soviet exile of party leaders Palmiro Togliatti and Maurice Thorez, and to the formation of broad coalition governments including the PCI and PCF.[1] These developments constituted more than a revival of the Popular Front of the mid-1930s, for the two parties received popular acclaim for breaking the political impasse, defending the nation, and giving the masses hope of economic emancipation.

With their participation in the provisional governments, the PCF and PCI transformed themselves from conspiratorial, sectarian cliques into mass parties, adopting parliamentary politics and democratic means to reach power. Their membership skyrocketed in the last year of the war: in France from three hundred thousand in 1939 to more than eight hundred thousand by the end of 1945; in Italy, the underground party of a few thousand became by the end of the war a mass organization of 1.7 million (reaching 2.5 million in 1947), second only to the Communist Party of the Soviet Union (CPSU). Equally staggering was the number of affiliates to the communist-dominated and highly politicized trade unions, reaching in the early Cold War years 3.8 million in the Confédération Générale du Travail (CGT) and a slightly lower figure in the Confederazione Generale del Lavoro Italiana (CGIL), founded in 1944.

While similarities prevailed, significant differences divided the two parties, differences that have been amply examined and reassessed. Many will emerge in the course of this study. Suffice it here to mention the most outstanding ones. A renowned, though a bit overstated distinction casts the PCF as genuinely bolshevized, more doctrinal, and more cohesive than the PCI.[2] To some extent that difference reflected the respective political traditions of Italy and France. In the former, where the state's weakness remained endemic, "partitocracy," or rule by parties, undermined a strong executive—with the notable exception of the discredited fascist years—and also favored the search for constant mediation and even "transformism" (as Italian political culture described party back-channeling), the Communists reinforced their tendency to assimilate and compromise.[3] In the latter, where the state was strong and centralized, where societal conflict was more inscribed in its evolution and even enshrined in the French Revolution, unassailable ideological faith could be more easily conflated with national identity.[4] International status also mattered. In France a strong national identity depended on the obsessive maintenance of a strong international role; no less sensitive to prestige, vanquished Italy was much weaker and severely handicapped by fragile national unity and the disgrace of the fascist experiment. Communist nationalism needed to be calibrated to these different situations.

Because ideological intransigence and national identity could be more closely aligned in France, the French Communists became more subordinate to Soviet dictates than their Italian counterparts. While recent research has revealed that Italian comrades also maintained a strong intimacy with Moscow, at least until the Prague Spring of 1968,[5] the PCI's long experience as a clandestine group under Fascism kept its cadres alert to possible political backlash. A more subtle explanation has also highlighted the need to replace a reactionary *mass regime* with a strong revolutionary *mass organization* deeply inserted in society and with an appeal beyond that of the working class. Fear of being marginalized, as in 1920–21, also informed Togliatti's conduct in "refounding" the PCI in 1944 as a *partito nuovo*, a new national, mass party able and willing to participate in a coalition government. In contrast, the experience in the Popular Front of the mid-1930s gave the PCF more confidence in its capacity to maneuver the system.[6] Furthermore, the rapid growth of the PCI in 1944, the sheer number of new members, "precluded systematic indoctrination in Soviet-style Marxism Leninism," notwithstanding Togliatti's determination to do so, whereas Thorez found it relatively easy to impart the "Marxist-Leninist formation of the party's new adherents." Even at the highest party levels, Thorez retained more control than Togliatti. The latter experienced difficulty persuading the Central Committee to confirm his March 1944 Svolta (turn), a move—mostly decided by Stalin, as we now know—that temporarily set aside the party's antimonarchy stance and subordinated revolutionary goals to the necessity of national unity against Germany and Fascism.[7]

The prominence of intellectuals was notable in both parties. Nevertheless the PCI fielded a more highly educated leadership than the PCF: the intellectual sophistication of founding leaders such as Antonio Gramsci and Palmiro Togliatti had not isolated the party from the masses; in fact it more frequently allowed it to exert an effective control of its rank and file—thus tempering the effects of rapid, "undisciplined" growth—as well as of its most radical leaders, since Togliatti fully exploited his privileged access to Gramsci's legacy. Their French counterparts brandished their modest backgrounds as badges of honor but also maintained less control of fellow-traveling intellectuals. If this was potentially and ironically one of the French Communists' major weaknesses, the Italian Communists found a main obstacle in the countervailing faith of the Italian masses: the Catholic Church.[8]

Relevant as these differences may have been, the two Communist Parties followed remarkably parallel paths, at least until 1956, and for this reason

America's attention focused on those similarities. Immediately the analogies emerged with the two parties' spectacular ascendancy in 1944–46. The Catholic novelist Georges Bernanos had famously claimed that "a poor man with nothing in his belly needs hope, illusion, more than bread." The two Communist Parties demonstrated that, in countries which had experienced material and spiritual loss, the dream of national reassertion could be as important as the need for material restoration.

NATIONALISM

Mass discontent caused by economic dislocation, and the natural craving for change after a devastating wartime period, largely explained communist success. But no less important during the Liberation and postwar period was the overwhelming credit and prestige—among *both* the middle and working classes—that the "red" partisans received from having led the Resistance against Nazi Germany and the fascist forces. Militants in both parties profited from their clandestine record, from the experience many of them had in the Spanish Civil War, and from the discipline and devotion they could muster under intense pressure. Even death brought them luster. Frequent setbacks did not tarnish the Resistance myth, for defeat could also forge a strong sense of national solidarity: in most respects being the *parti des fusillés* for the French Communists or holding the majority of the thirty-five thousand casualties of the Resistenza for the Italian Communists added to their reputation as martyrs of fascist and Nazi repression. Later, the Communists could cite that record to reinforce their claim that the Resistance, the chance for genuine national revival and independence, had been betrayed by the Anglo-American allies and by the other partisan forces. The myth of the heroic battle for national liberation and the partisan propaganda became so effective that communist consent to Stalin's purges or to the Russian-German entente of 1939–41 soon disappeared into public oblivion.[9]

Heroism was not enough, however. The two parties reinforced their patriotic credentials by embracing the rhetoric of national prestige. Even before being readmitted as a legitimate political force, the PCF declared in its 1943 *Charte du Conseil National de la Résistance* that the main task for the Communists was "to defend the political and economic independence of the nation and to restore France's power, grandeur, and universal mission." At the 1945 Party Congress Thorez began to emulate Charles de Gaulle, declaring that "the independence of France and the restoration of its *grandeur*, sacred vow of all our heroes, must be the leading principle of the future foreign policy of the country." Significantly, as a follow-up, the party issued an anthology of Thorez's most prominent speeches titled *Une politique de gran-*

deur française. A year later, with de Gaulle no longer at the helm of the provisional government, and with the PCF at the height of its power, in a highly symbolic gesture, the military parade of 14 July took place for the first and only time at the site of the Bastille instead of at the Arc de Triomphe. As the Christian Democrat prime minister, Georges Bidault, proclaimed, "14 July is the feast of workers, not of the bourgeois. We are going to celebrate it with the people!" For the first time in French history, the Communists were no longer just "communards": under the Resistance, the protection of national greatness seemed perfectly attuned to the socialist promise. Party historian Annie Kriegel even coined the term "National-Thorezism" to explain this strong appeal.[10]

While the French bourgeoisie had temporarily lost its primacy in representing the connection between grandeur and the Revolution, the Italian bourgeoisie appeared more permanently damaged by its historical failure to make Italy one of the great powers. Fascism had left a desire for international respect, a legacy that persisted after humiliating defeat. In his first speech after returning to Italy, Togliatti called for his party to lead the nation and to restore national pride among the youth after "the vacuum created by the collapse of fascism"; under the ideological opposite of fascism, Italy could thus become again "great, strong, respected."[11] In a country where artificial pomp had so often replaced civic and democratic integration, such claims of *grandezza* might have seemed irrelevant and counterproductive. But for the PCI the point was to reclaim a strength and vitality that other movements had failed to project. Writing to his comrade and member of the Comitato di Liberazione Nazionale (CLN) Mauro Scoccimarro in 1944, Togliatti recommended emphasis on the rhetoric of national unity and national grandeur in order to "further help cast our policy as truly national." For defeated Italy, finally, restoring *grandezza* meant nurturing patriotic more than nationalist feelings. The Communists suggested that, thanks to their government participation, the vanquished would never become a client nation.[12] This argument also implied that the arrogance of the winners could reignite revanchist nationalism in Italy.

The message of patriotism remained clear for both Communist Parties: national grandeur should not only be bent on restoring great power status; it would also lead to moral resurrection. The recovery of moral standing after World War II had become a crucial source of international prestige: the French were still reeling from the Vichy experience; the Italians were pervaded by a sense of guilt for having consented to the shames of tyranny — which, on top of being oppressive, had failed miserably in mastering aggression. "To be nationalist today in Italy," Togliatti proclaimed in 1943, "is to be antifascist." The PCF echoed with the slogan, "L'anti-communisme, c'est l'arme de l'anti-France."[13] In countries exhausted, humiliated, and ashamed by defeat and collaboration, a commitment to national independence became perfectly reconcilable with pacifist rhetoric. Besides contributing to national liberation, the Resistance, like most patriotic movements, enjoyed an aura of moral purity, of which the Communists claimed to be the incarnation. Jean-Pierre Rioux noted that the PCF "set itself up as spokesman of the poor and the pure, wielding a moral advantage worth more than all theories." The Italian Communists also found stronger appeal on moral than on doctrinal ground. They contended that the Resistance was not a mere civil war: since the Resistance contributed to the Allied war effort, they argued, it was the best ground for a fair peace treaty and for international recognition of the country's moral rebirth.[14]

By recasting nationalism as democratic and anti-imperialist, the two parties also justified their ambivalence on issues such as the unresolved Trieste dispute between Italy and Yugoslavia, or France's insistence on retaining its overseas empire. In the immediate postwar months Togliatti argued that a nationalist frenzy over the Northeast borderlands would only work to the advantage of reactionary groups who dreamed of a neofascist revival, just as had happened after World War I. Furthermore, he construed, a recrudescence of Italian imperialism, as recent history had shown, would *weaken* Italian independence and grandeur: colonial adventures by a relatively poor country would be a drain on national resources and would also alienate the great powers to the point of reducing Italy to a "vassal imperialist" (of the Anglo-Americans).[15] The PCF was naturally more ambiguous on the French imperial mission, which in North Africa (not ripe for "socialist emancipation") still seemed acceptable. But certainly it lost no opportunity in 1945 to distinguish itself from de Gaulle, responsible, according to Thorez, for "unlatching" reactionary, imperialist ventures (at that point, referring to the bombing of Damascus).[16] All these arguments, from both parties, naturally served Soviet interests; but they also helped the two parties cast an image of moral patriotism. Downplaying chauvinism helped them to further discredit the extreme Right and to uphold the politics of the Grand Alliance. These politics could especially prevent Anglo-American control of their nations, while also validating a communist role in the coalition governments.

Above all, democratic nationalism signified the right of the proletariat to represent national interests, as opposed to the decadent bourgeoisie, which was responsible for the March on Rome, Munich, and Vichy. For the French Communists there was a spiritual equivalence between their leader, former miner Maurice Thorez, who, underscoring his humble origins, proclaimed himself a *fils du peuple* (son of the people), and the historic *fille du peuple*, Joan of Arc. Evoking the feats of one paladin established a link between the party's personality cult and patriotism, while the national mission of the French proletariat became clearer by stressing the ideal continuity with the Revolution of 1789. National grandeur and workers' internationalism were even more intertwined for France than for the Soviet Union, and the eighteenth-century Phrygian cap, symbol of republican liberty, abounded in the iconic propaganda of wartime and postwar French Communism. That myth, confirming that the Left was born in France long before Marxism, granted the PCF an additional emblem of honor, even as it pledged its allegiance to Moscow.[17]

Likewise, the Italian communist partisans, fighting under the banner of the Garibaldi Brigades, claimed continuity between the most progressive traditions of the Italian Risorgimento and the renewed task of the country's working class. The PCI's mission was to complete that revolution, which had remained unfinished under the combined pressure of the bourgeoisie and the monarchy, guilty of collusion with fascism. Further, this reasoning suggested that, since fascism had precipitated Italy's decline, the only hope for a restored role in the world was through the most advanced social transformation, just as had happened before in Britain, France, and Russia. That was the true meaning of a resumed Risorgimento, the nineteenth-century "reawakening" that had restored Italy's ability to contribute to modern civilization, and to aspire to equal status with the other European powers. Togliatti repeatedly argued that Italy could attain real *grandezza* only if it "let its most progressive forces, that is, the working class and its vanguard, lead the nation." And in 1946 *Rinascita*, the communist journal that best reflected the theoretical debate within Italian Marxism, contended that of all parties, the PCI was the one with "the broadest and most accurate vision of the nation's interests," and the journal attributed to the working masses "the strongest will to bring about Italy's rebirth."[18]

Besides seeking legitimacy from the past, the two Communist Parties tried to lay their strongest claim on the present, for their grandeur did not appear as "borrowed" as that of their government coalition partners. Following a pattern later popularized as "'empire' by invitation," the leaders de Gaulle, Pietro Badoglio, and their immediate successors repeatedly wooed the Americans in order to boost their own status through financial assistance and diplomatic support. At the Liberation parade in Paris, de Gaulle asked General Dwight Eisenhower to lend him two American divisions so that he could impress his fellow French and firmly establish his authority. A few months earlier Badoglio had been even more explicit, as he tried to avert

America's isolationist impulse by asking Washington to "assume in Italy and the Mediterranean a leading part vis-à-vis all the other Powers." Only next to the U.S. power, he reminded Roosevelt, could Italy hope for an "honorable place in the world."[19] Even moral resurrection seemed subordinated to Italy's return into the "family" of great powers next to the new Western hegemon, as the Christian Democrat leader Alcide De Gasperi told Secretary of State Jimmy Byrnes in August 1945. According to de Gaulle, France could continue to be a beacon of Western democracy if it could work in harmony with the other beacon, the United States. While none of these diplomatic exchanges were public, Anglo-American efforts to boost the prestige of the two countries' conservative leaders was manifest to everyone. Dependence on America's goodwill was also evident for the French in seeking respectively a seat in the U.N. Security Council, and for the Italians in requesting a milder peace treaty.[20] The main problem with these appeals was that not only the grandeur but even the very nationalism of the two countries' leadership appeared vicarious, linked to a rising U.S. hegemony. This appearance was false, particularly for France, but the Communists continued to exploit that impression.

Success was mixed. The fact remained that the other Resistance forces, especially Charles de Gaulle and Italy's Christian Democrats (DC), vied with the Left for the monopoly in the debate over national resurrection. The United States was rather quick to grasp the renewed importance of the Catholic groups in Italy, though less keen on the formidable appeal of the French general, whom most American policy makers continued to mistrust.

In Italy in 1943 the king had fled Rome. The pope, however, remained, thus restoring the Church's prestige (and also overshadowing Pius XII's previous record of support for Mussolini). The Christian Democrats, under De Gasperi, were perceptive enough to use their Vatican credentials to match the mass appeal of the Socialists and Communists, and also to secure control of the state in order to better protect the Church from the anticlericals. But the Christian Democratic Party also was, unlike its predecessor, the Popular Party, conceived as a government force, with strong interclassist appeal and thus able to elude the strictest controls from the Church.[21] The same happened with the pressure from Washington: from the very start of the Cold War the Christian Democrats resisted U.S. demands for a firmer hand against the Communists. A stalemate with the Communists in fact justified the DC's hegemonic role in the government. But its resistance of the United States was also partly rooted in the mistrust that the most doctrinal elements of the party—at first coinciding with its left elements—nurtured of America's putative materialism, hedonism, and militarism.[22]

While establishing its grip on the state apparatus, the DC also represented its fragmentation: its best leverage was at the community, parish level. In this sense the Christian Democrats profited from Italy's particularism and weak state structure even more than the Communists did. Philosopher Benedetto Croce, whose legacy the centrist parties were trying to claim, warned in 1944 that statist "totalitarian" nationalism had been an aberration in the Italian experience, and the country should do all it could to avoid its repetition. These arguments helped reconcile Catholic power with the Risorgimento. Like the Red partisans, the Church also found its renewed role and prestige in upholding the nation's moral rebirth. The "Grande Italia" of post–World War II, according to historian Emilio Gentile, conjoined "Italianism" and "Catholicism" thanks to a spiritual mystique that exalted the "humble pride," the value of the "cathartic experience which, through pain and humiliation, purifies and uplifts." Under Pius XII and De Gasperi's party, the path to national redemption at first seemed to secure the same moral prestige as that pursued by the Communists.[23]

In France, the nationalist appeal of the PCF faced an even stiffer competition from Charles de Gaulle. Given the General's extraordinary record of service, it was he who ultimately managed to dominate the French discourse on national pride and independence. But at first this was by no means clear. As Pierre Nora has best demonstrated, immediately after the war there were commonalities between Gaullists and Communists. Both claimed to represent France, "all of France the true France." They "shared the most deeply rooted traits of French political culture and tradition: a Jacobin patriotism, a haughty nationalism, a heroic and sacrificial volunteerism, a sense of the state, an understanding of the tragic in history, and a shared hostility to American modernity and world of capitalism and cash."[24] While the emphasis on a Gaullist rejection of modernity was, as well known, questionable, a strong sense of the superiority of French civilization informed the rhetoric and beliefs of both leading factions of the Resistance. Claims of legitimacy by de Gaulle and the Communists, despite arguable democratic credentials, were indeed founded on their promise of rebirth, on their ability to capture the imagination of a recumbent nation: by proving that they personified French history and traditions, they could also redraw those traditions (with competing claims to Joan of Arc, for example) and "cloak the diminution of French power" with their mystique of independence and the rhetoric of grandeur. De Gaulle constantly reminded the allies that France "needed" to feel like a great nation in order to become one again.[25] Thorez insisted on moral as well as material "renaissance" to refute those who now ranked the nation as a secondary power. There was even a burgeoning pride felt in the need to start all over again: "Everything is beginning," leftist writer Simone de Beauvoir recorded in her memoir *Force of Circumstance*. The Resistance, she claimed, "was to efface our old defeats, it was ours, and the future it opened up was ours, too."[26]

De Gaulle strongly appealed to the most instinctive emotional sources—the filial and the religious—of French patriotism. There was also a certain monarchic element in his republican vision.[27] The Communists conveyed a mystical appeal in a different way, counting on the enduring myth of the French Revolution. The republican legacy was their strongest weapon, one that stressed the statist, rationalist, secular nature of French patriotism. But in comparative terms, de Gaulle's rhetoric of independence trumped the communist one: unlike his Marxist counterparts, he needed no dialectic paradigm to prove connections between workers, the party, Stalin the liberator, and the French. He simply declared that "La France est la France."[28] The General never stigmatized the PCF's revolutionary credentials, for he recognized the revolutionary nature of France; instead he assaulted communist separatism. He argued that the PCF failed to represent the nation, not on account of its Marxism, but because of its allegiance to the Soviet Union.[29] The Italian Christian Democrats, while they were still relatively autonomous from the United States, failed to use the same argument.

For all their emphasis on national identity and grandeur, the two Communist Parties could not disavow their allegiance to Moscow. Strong guidance from the Kremlin, they contended, was necessary. An additional problem was that even the abolition of the Comintern in 1943, and the consequent homage to "national paths" to socialism, made the two parties' rhetoric of nationalism appear commanded. Without knowing how closely Stalin had instructed Togliatti and Thorez in Moscow, or how much he had pressed them to act with moderation in order to gain credentials as leaders of national parties with a mass following,[30] the Western allies had little doubt that Soviet support of governments of national unity with the Left in France and Italy was meant to contain Anglo-American strategic and political expansion.[31]

The PCF and the PCI made no secret of their close identification of their nations' interests with those of the Soviet Union. This symbiosis became immediately apparent. According to the communist newspaper *L'Humanité* in 1942, "the Soviet Union *was* France even *before* France would become the Soviet Union"; the French Communist youth three years later affixed posters announcing that "France is only our country, but the U.S.S.R. is our *patrie*." Thorez made it even clearer that at stake was much more than French national identity; by fusing Jacobinism and Bolshevism, he claimed an international mission for the PCF, declaring that "everyone has two fatherlands, France and the Soviet Union."[32]

Most intellectuals affiliated with the PCI acknowledged, in Miriam Mafai's words, that Italian comrades had "simultaneously two motherlands: Italy and the U.S.S.R."; they "celebrated every holiday of both countries" and placed the genius of Stalin above that of Togliatti. The PCI even began to elaborate a myth of "doppiezza," or double choice, which, in its most favorable rendering, signified a renewed pragmatic national, democratic, parliamentary approach while maintaining faith in Moscow and in the forthcoming revolution. Italy had another peculiarity: for the Italian state, which had never fully achieved national unity, the U.S.S.R. appeared as a strong model of the perfect state apparatus serving the working class. That reference became logical for the Italian masses since, as Resistance member Antonio Giolitti later reflected, the Soviets represented the antithesis of fascism. After the March on Rome, marking the beginning of Mussolini's regime, the U.S.S.R. offered double liberation for the Italian proletariat: from capitalist and fascist oppression. In the postwar period, Togliatti further explained in 1946, loyalty to the Soviet Union and national reassertion were still inextricably linked, for the "unity of the democracies" was in itself a "guarantee of peace and independence."[33]

This point was crucial, as it showed that the identification with the Kremlin was intrinsically part of a dialectic process that confirmed the connection between democratic nationalism and proletarian internationalism. Moreover, the French and Italian Communist Parties derived additional credibility from the triumphs of the Red Army in Central Europe. Stalin assumed mythical status among the rank and file of both parties to the point that Togliatti's and Thorez's prestige as national leaders became dependent on it. Some authors have even contended—with regard to the PCI, but the same can be said about the PCF—that the total acceptance of Soviet truth was a deliberate deception by the party leadership to an extent that it became self-deception, that is, a "mechanical and hierarchical list of priorities to which all was subordinated."[34] This almost instinctive reverence of Moscow, as we will see, determined an almost equally mechanical condemnation of Washington, distorting some of the national themes behind Western communist anti-Americanism.

But toeing the Soviet line was not as counterproductive as has been argued. Precisely because France and Italy were in the Western camp, the Communists in both countries enjoyed the advantage of not having to confront their promise of an alternative world with everyday reality. It was relatively easy for them to project, especially at the mass level, an idealistic image of a Soviet-dominated world and overemphasize the oppressive nature of the American presence. Finally, the PCI was more adept than the PCF at concealing its obedience to Moscow. At the peak of Cold War antagonism, recent accounts have shown, the Italian Communists deflected some Soviet pressures, though not as strongly as the Christian Democrats "contained" the American ones. Other accounts have argued that this ostensible autonomy was actually closely coordinated with the Kremlin, in order to better implement communist subversive designs in the West.[35] Whichever is the case, large sections of the Italian public, even outside the PCI's control, did not question the party's nationalist credentials at least until its insurrectionary strikes against the Marshall Plan. But as we will see, even at the peak of the Cold War, the PCI's anti-American propaganda had considerable influence outside its ranks.

Nationalism, no matter how contradictory, remained, next to difficult economic times, the most apparent factor driving communist strength immediately after the war. But the two parties also sought power through their institutional presence and their cultural magnetism.

INSTITUTIONAL POWER

According to a Marxist-Gramscian assumption, the bureaucracy was intrinsically neutral; what really mattered was who controlled it. So as part of their pursuit of legitimacy, but also to increase their organizational power, the French and Italian Communists became interested in maintaining many of the existing bureaucratic structures. The purges were certainly more *sauvages* in France against former Vichy collaborators than in Italy against fascist administrators, as the PCF initially worked in earnest to create "vacancies" to be filled by party members. But overall in both countries, and especially in Italy, the main targets remained the former regimes' top hierarchs, in part because of Gramsci's bureaucracy thesis. This relative mildness also found its justification in the argument that Fascism and Vichy had been a brief parenthesis, an aberration in the two countries' continuous democratic growth—as the then popular thesis of Benedetto Croce put it.[36] By exonerating collective guilt, the two nations would achieve a quick, if superficial moral rehabilitation. Yet with the distinction between ruled and rulers thus sharpened, and the tradition of democracy thus confirmed in both countries, the two Communist Parties could present themselves as stewards of national resurrection *and* reconciliation.

The pursuit of legitimacy in 1944 induced Thorez to commit the party to national unity and to productivity goals, while reminding its rank and file that current sacrifices would allow the Communists to secure the bases— mainly control of the state economic bureaucracy—for future democratic progress. Tactical compromises would also make the party strong enough to contain Anglo-Saxon hegemonic ambitions. The first, most relevant of such compromises was the "battle for production," increasing production goals and limiting strikes—*L'Humanité* presented this policy above all as a way to fight the parasitic trusts and to conduct an independent foreign policy—but for the time being it also meant siding with the economic liberalism of the Christian Democratic forces of the Mouvement Républicain Populaire (MRP) against the reform program of the Radicals' leader, Pierre Mendès-France, in 1945. The second compromise was the consent to de Gaulle's decision to integrate the Forces Françaises de l'Intérieur into the regular army and to dissolve the PCF-dominated *milices patriotiques*. Explaining this decision at a historic meeting of the party's Central Committee in January 1945, Thorez claimed the necessity of "one state, one army, one police" and dismissed the dreamers who "believe[d] they [could] attain all tasks [of renewal] with a machine gun strapped on their chest or banging fists on the table." At the same time, the party concluded that, if it played its cards well, such and integrated army trained in the Resistance could become genuinely democratic and radicalized under its influence.[37]

A more immediate result of the policy of unity was the winning of key posts in the first provisional governments, such as the ministries of the Air Force (Charles Tillon), Industrial Production (Marcel Paul), Labor and Social Security (Ambroise Croizat), and National Economy (François Billoux), all four allowing, through bureaucratic appointments, an enduring influence over defense and other industries (Thorez was also minister in charge of administrative reforms, and Billoux became minister of defense in 1947). Also, the battle for production was no mere concession, for it allowed the PCF to retain control of several state enterprises and to introduce reforms, including a system of social security for workers.[38] The Communists, like their Gaullist rivals, failed to retain influence over the drafting of the 1946 Constitution, which empowered the Christian Democrats of the MRP and the Socialists of the SFIO. Thorez also failed to win the candidacy for premiership that year. But in the elections for the first Legislative Assembly of the Fourth Republic in November 1946, the PCF reached its historic peak with more that 28 percent of the vote, becoming the largest party in the country. Also, the gradual conquest of the CGT between 1945 and 1947 remained one of the fundamental instruments of pressure over the industrial *patronat* and national industry in general. Finally, as in Italy, tactical cooperation with the Christian Democrats was not immediately ruled out, despite the PCF's strong anticlerical traditions. In a February 1945 interview with the Catholic weekly *Temps présent*, Thorez made sure to specify that "Marxism was not a dogma," and that it would adapt to national and cultural circumstances. This was the beginning of a strategy described as the *main tendue*, a hand outstretched to the Catholic masses. In appealing to the "Republican Christian masses" against the Church hierarchy, philosopher Roger Garaudy specified, the PCF upheld rather than attacked France's spiritual traditions. In early 1946 the party directorate finally established that the *main tendue* strategy would help prevent political cooperation between the SFIO and the MRP.[39]

Even more than the French Communists, the PCI refused to make economic reform its top priority in the immediate postwar period, concentrating its energies on the constitutional battle against the monarchy. One reason for this approach was that the party, a captive of its own success as the dominant force of the Resistance, excessively emphasized the necessity to shepherd unity within the antifascist coalition. Also, remembering how divisions among the democratic forces had favored the advent of Fascism in 1922, the PCI now saw a parallel between that failure and the possibility of a "capitalist" dictatorship through the Allied forces. Like the PCF, the Italian Communists aimed to seize control of the state and economic bureaucracy legally, and more than the PCF they hesitated to promote nationalization measures, fearing these could restore fascist-style corporatism.[40] Even the PCI's pressure for higher productivity, though not comparable to the PCF campaign, was justified as an antithesis to the fascist policy of autarky, which had plagued the economy with high costs of production and low living standards. At this stage the PCI was even willing to absorb lessons from overseas: "We have to devise a sort of New Deal," Togliatti told the party directorate in July 1946, "a program that would enable the party to coordinate the main national economic sectors." At the same time, Togliatti reached the maximum institutional compromise when, as minister of justice in 1946, he granted a general amnesty that included former fascist bureaucrats: the gesture was explained to the public mainly as a celebration of "republican unity" right after the country had voted out the monarchy, and to the party as a need to reassure the vast ranks of the bourgeoisie that the PCI was not about to wage a revolution.[41]

In the provisional governments, the PCI held key posts, such as the vice premiership (Togliatti) and the ministries of Finance (Antonio Pesenti and Mauro Scoccimarro), Occupied Italy (Scoccimarro), and Foreign Affairs (held in 1946 by the close ally and leader of the Socialists, Pietro Nenni). The PCI's contribution to the Costituente (the Constitutional Assembly) was essential to redefine the party itself as "constitutional." Even after the Cold War drove the party into a kind of internal exile, its leaders kept referring to themselves as key components of the Arco Costituzionale (Constitutional

Arch of democratic parties) in the parliament—suggesting the exclusion of the neofascists and, from the late 1960s, the extreme Left.[42]

The Communists had to reconcile themselves to the combined influence of the Church and the Christian Democrats. "The Liberal state," Gramsci had written, "has had to come to terms with the spiritual power of the Church, and the workers' state will have to do likewise." Following this injunction, the PCI accepted the Lateran Pacts (signed in 1928 between the fascist regime and the Vatican) as well the new constitution that confirmed the Church's special role in the state. Prior to the parliamentary elections of 1948, the dichotomy between communism and Christianity did not appear so sharp in Italy, and even after those historic elections, the Left would continue to appeal to many devout Catholic workers and peasants. As commander of the Garibaldi Brigades, Gian Carlo Pajetta urged maximum mobilization in the summer of 1945 to persuade Catholic farmers that the Christian Democrats were not their only choice. An independent Catholic fringe known as the Christian Left Party advocated common action with the Communists. Under pressure from the Vatican, this party was dissolved in December 1945, but many of its members joined the PCI. Even though the PCI won only 19 percent of the vote in the election for a Constituent Assembly in June 1946 (compared to 20.7 percent for their socialist comrades, and 35 percent for the Christian Democrats), the party was fast growing and would soon control the Left. The Referendum for the Republic held at the same time marked a triumph of the Left, with the defeat of the country's monarchist forces. Also, simultaneously with the electoral showing of the PCF a few months later, the communist-socialist alliance increased its vote share by one third in local elections in the South (with the PCI now surpassing the Partito Socialista Italiano di Unità Proletaria [PSIUP], as Nenni's party had been renamed in 1943). And, like its French counterpart, the PCI came to dominate the Marxist Left by gradually seizing control of the CGIL, the union still formally shared since 1944 with socialist and Catholic factions.[43] The Communists in both countries had thus confirmed their resurgence as national mass organizations.

The organizational success of the two Communist Parties and its significance in promoting anti-Americanism soon drew Washington's attention. And yet one basic fact seemed to elude both Western communist expectations and American perceptions: the PCI and PCF imitated the institutional strategies of the "peoples' democracies" (the prelude to the dictatorship of the proletariat) in Eastern Europe, without the benefit of the Soviet presence.[44] The bureaucratic strength of the Western Communists, while extraordinary, would eventually be overestimated in Washington, thus precipitating severe contradictions in the American response to the rise of anti-Americanism in both France and Italy.

Intellectual clout also became essential to the communist advance. In the early Cold War, most American officials failed to grasp fully the relevance of the battle for hearts and especially for minds. At a hearing of the House Un-American Activities Committee in March 1947, Motion Pictures Association Director Eric Johnston reiterated the thesis that "Communism hunts misery, feeds on misery, and profits by it," and that "revolutions plotted by frustrated intellectuals at cocktail parties won't get anywhere if we wipe out the potential causes of Communism." This statement could perhaps apply to a certain romantic tradition within the American intellectual Left. Extended to the whole Western world, it reflected both the American underestimation of communist intellectual appeal, and the superficial nature of policy advisors that George Kennan so keenly loathed. By contrast, as one of the prominent Italian communist thinkers, Luciano Cafagna, put it, intellectuals in Europe may not have "number, or mass, but they are like the Pope: while not having divisions, they work as multiplying factors, becoming organizing cadres, or occupying strategic positions such as cafés, university halls, mass media." In frequent commemorations of Gramsci's legacy, Togliatti went further, referring to intellectuals as "the connecting tissue" of the nation.[45] In this sense they not only would serve the progressive cause but even reevaluate and redesign national identity. The PCF simply summarized its cultural role as that of being the *parti de l'intelligence*. Since the 1930s it had counted a great number of distinguished adherents, to which many more were added in the postwar period. The party also controlled numerous key organizations, including the French University Union and the National Committee of Writers.[46] Communist intellectual ascendancy in Europe immediately after the war was all the more extraneous to American cultural understanding because it was at this time that the Soviet myth died among most American intellectuals, as did their adherence to the orthodox CPUSA.

The communist appeal to many liberal intellectuals in Italy and France was consistent with the movement's effort to project a self-image of legality and moderation. It confirmed that Marxism-Leninism was not merely materialistic but also deeply cultural and ethical; it helped tame the party rank and file, reinforced their reorganization from the vanguard model to a mass, popular outlook; it provided the workers with a sense of dignity as they participated in a counterculture and sometimes turned into self-made intellectuals; it reflected above all, and especially in Italy, an attempt to mold and monopolize a new national culture. The nationalist stance blended with the legacy of Antonio Gramsci and his tenet that control of the *superstructure* of culture, the shaping of organic intellectuals—often drawn from the working classes—fully aware of art's social role and of the progressive orientation of culture, were essential to the transformation of the economic *structure*, and the basic prelude to revolution. The ruling classes would gradually lose dominance of the intellectual elite, according to Gramsci, if the party could seduce and assimilate the traditional intellectuals, thus establishing its "cultural hegemony." As Stephen Gundle has noted, this "well-directed strategy aimed at achieving a hegemonic position within national thought and culture was virtually without precedent in the history of the European working-class movement."[47] In France, a strong statist tradition and its philosophical expression in the Enlightenment created a deep connection between government institutions and the intellectual world—above all through a network of schools training public servants—thus offering the PCF opportunities to merge cultural and bureaucratic influence.[48] For both parties, a cultural prominence based on traditions going back to the idealist Risorgimento tradition (in Italy) and to the French Revolution, or even the scientific revolution of the seventeenth century (in France), could also enhance their autonomy vis-à-vis the Soviet Union.

The PCF had started to consolidate cultural power during the Popular Front years, suffered several defections after André Gide's denunciation of the Soviet purges and after the Nazi-Soviet Pact, then regained cultural ascendancy during the Liberation—in spite, and some would say in part because, of the communist-led *épuration* of several intellectuals through questionable trials. In fact, the dialectic between culture and politics in France had traditionally been broader and more autonomous than in most other European countries, a legacy that prevented the PCF from exerting as strong a cultural hegemony as the PCI. The Italian Communists also benefited from Italy's relative bipolarization between leftist culture and political conservatism, whereas in France notable sections of the intellectual radical Left created their own "third force" position between the political opposites.[49]

Overall, however, the intellectual environment of postwar France favored the Communists. The two main "third force" groups that emerged after the war were the Catholic idealists of the review *Esprit* and the existentialists of *Les Temps modernes*. Both were convinced that "Marxism had laid down the indispensable conditions for the humanization of society." Existentialism especially became crucial. Dominating the postwar intellectual debate, it was never closely associated with the PCF, except for a brief period in the early 1950s. Regardless of how strong or tenuous that association was, in the postwar period, as Tony Judt has best shown, existentialism remained quite benevolent toward—even captivated by—communism and the Soviet Union.[50]

Existentialism, to be sure, strongly opposed any determinism, upholding freedom and the uniqueness of the individual; under the tenet that existence precedes essence—which meant that individuals define themselves by their own actions, that they are sources of values and creators of possibilities—it called for commitment and maximum responsibility. And yet the foremost proponents of existentialism, Jean-Paul Sartre, Simone de Beauvoir, and Maurice Merleau-Ponty, did not use their principles to deny the relevance of communism. In fact their postwar polemics with the PCF revolved around their critique of historical determinism and their notion that Marxism stressed the importance of human subjectivity interacting with the material world in order to change it radically.[51] It was at this time that Sartre declared himself "a convinced Socialist but an anti-hierarchical and libertarian one, one in favor of direct democracy." After this sharp veering to the left, some intellectual contributors to *Les Temps modernes*, most notably Sartre's former friend Raymond Aron, left the journal. Sartre's friendship with Albert Camus also began to fade.[52] But these "defections" were still far from creating a climate of opinion as influential as that of the now strongly pro-Marxist Paris intelligentsia. In the final analysis, from the American point of view, it did not matter how many intellectuals actually joined the PCF or the PCI; the problem was the emergence of a cultural milieu dominated by the Marxist or pro-Marxist Left.

Being a leftist had always been a sort of badge of honor among French intellectuals. In the aftermath of the fascist experience, it played a similar role for many Italians as well. Furthermore, the PCI had the additional advantage of having been led by intellectuals from the start. With right-wing nationalism discredited, the PCF, and, even more, the PCI attracted many more intellectuals who were eager to reject their bourgeois past as the main culprit for Europe's recent tragedy. The young generation of intellectuals dominating the postwar debate experienced less atonement than discovery. Their worldview was shaped by a war that had excluded any moral relativism and compromise: it had been a genuine struggle of Good versus Evil, of Resistance versus Collaboration. In both countries the wartime experience had further convinced leftist intellectuals who had not formally joined the communist ranks to assume an activist role, to commit to political choices, and to be *engagé* in History instead of simply witnessing its unraveling. Traumatized by defeat and by the Occupation regime, France was, in de Beauvoir's words, ready for "radical re-modeling." *Esprit*'s editor, Emmanuel Mounier, could confidently state that "if we call ourselves revolutionaries it is not just hot air or being overdramatic. It is because an honest analysis shows us that France is in a revolutionary situation." For Sartre, "revolution was a categorical imperative[,] . . . [an] a priori existential requirement." Like many French intellectuals who resented not only the experience of Vichy but also the mediocrity of the Third Republic, Sartre was in a revolutionary "mood," thinking, through the power of his philosophy, about re-creating "a new collective situation in which revolutionary action sustain[ed] the authenticity of the individual." In Italy, the best evidence of a radical turn came from the media and literary explosion, mostly of the realist kind that put the writer in immediate contact with the people, a sort of "primordial need" after so many years of repression. Even for those literati who skirted political activism, the communist ascent assumed an aura of renewal. Umberto Saba, one of the revered poets of Italian hermeticism, mourned his "dead mother, the Bourgeoisie." He favored communism because it was the best antidote to literary hubris and because it was "socially indispensable."[53]

Marxism also proved attractive because it fulfilled the intellectuals' search for certitude, for a response to multiple questions in a time of profound change. Sartre, even as he questioned the optimism of Marxist orthodoxy, argued that "radicalism meant applying the techniques of truth to lies and illusions." When Pablo Picasso joined the PCF in 1944, he credited Marxism with even greater qualities: It was the only ideology that helped "deepen human knowledge" and that by doing so "would progressively make us more free." Roger Garaudy elaborated on the notion that the scientific truths of Marxism offered empowerment and therefore a more mature sense of liberty. Without knowledge, he argued, freedom would be caprice, like that of a mistaken mathematician, "an engineer without a grasp on things, a powerless engineer, who is therefore a slave." Science and faith were thus conflated. According to some sociological analyses, post–World War II communism possessed the attractive power of a secular religion. But for intellectuals the need for devotion was always complemented by an assertion of strong national identity and public service. As with the nationalist appeal, the certainties were coined through a mixture of universalist and patriotic elements. In France, the poet Louis Aragon, one of the most Stalinist communist intellectuals, proclaimed that Maurice Thorez had made him a true patriot.[54]

The PCI counterposed Marxism-Leninism to the tradition of bourgeois philosopher Benedetto Croce. Idealist thought, best personified in Italy by the Neapolitan philosopher, needed to be transcended rather than destroyed. Togliatti attacked Croce, but not the national traditions of humanism that he represented, and this helped the PCI absorb many men of letters who wished to reinvigorate the country's democratic culture. Croce, from his neo-Hegelian standpoint, had first inspired many Italian intellectuals to assume the role of public servants, fully aware of the most genuine national traditions but detached from the politics of the Fascist regime, as well as alerted to the perils of communism. In the PCI's view, Gramsci provided the next logical step in the intellectual's public role. Only thanks to Marxism-Leninism could intellectuals complete their evolution from autonomy to full commitment to progress. Ideological certitude and sense of public service helped those who joined the PCI break from their insularity.[55]

But the sense of service, the idealization of a doctrine and of the class it represented also had utilitarian purposes: intellectuals needed the informal networks for professional advancement that the two Communist Parties excelled in providing. Furthermore, intellectuals considered themselves "organic," not only because they assumed the role of avant-gardes of the proletariat. Some were members of the proletariat themselves. As literary critic Mario Alicata noted at the PCI's Fifth Congress in 1946, "Many intellectuals in the country's South are starving"; the party assisted and empowered them, creating a "new humanism reconciled with modern conscience and technology." In France, the Communists emphasized that modern capitalism undermined and devalued intellectual work, reducing its financial autonomy and perverting its spirit.[56]

Intellectuals also fancied that their own importance reflected—or produced, depending on the circumstances—international prestige for themselves and the cultural and political traditions they represented. Postwar Paris offers a telling example of such expectations. The French capital, as Tony Judt has noted, revived its fame after the war as the "only one place for properly *European* intellectual life." Hosting as ever many foreign thinkers, it continued to be "the natural European home of the disinherited intellectual, a clearing house for modern European thought and politics." Judt adds that ironically French intellectuals remained parochial, reinterpreting the world "in light of their own obsessions," while a "narcissistic self-importance of Paris within France was projected un-self-critically onto the world at large."[57] It was precisely this combination of cosmopolitan and parochial attitudes that formed the essence of leftist intellectual anti-Americanism in France. Like most Manichean struggles, cultural opposition to America was founded on a binary approach that claimed to defend both France's national traditions and its universalist claims, including the claim that the country's intellectual preeminence entitled it to remain strong on the world stage. Cold War polarism instead confirmed Italy's low-key international position, but it also helped its academics and opinion-makers to achieve greater international stature. Considering the crucial role of intellectuals in shaping Italy's modern national identity in the nineteenth century, cultural recognition became an essential component in recovering Italy's international prestige after World War II as well. Given the two nations' twin intellectual distinction, it is no wonder that their Communist Parties fought for minds as a means of achieving both domestic and international power. Gramsci, for example, had argued that the key to Italian revival lay in the intellectual as a "producer of civilization" who carried on the Italian people's "natural inclination toward a modern form of cosmopolitanism."[58]

There can be no doubt that the gravitation of many influential intellectuals toward communism increased the two parties' political clout. But it did not substantially change national culture, first because party leaders continued to place pursuit of legitimacy above the creation of a genuine counterculture. Second, the leaders' allegiance to Stalinism would alienate many intellectuals by the mid-1950s. Finally, and most consequential in the confrontation with America, the enormous importance attributed to the role of intellectuals turned out to be outdated. The two newly reinvented mass parties fatally neglected mass culture, the main emerging vehicle of social integration and legitimization in modern societies.

Even so, intellectual magnetism mattered enormously at the peak of the cold war of ideas. Washington at first underestimated Gramsci's project of "cultural hegemony" and the determination of Togliatti (and to a lesser extent of Aragon, Garaudy, and other French Communists) to fulfill it. With anti-Americanism so entrenched among intellectuals in both Italy and France, the Communists found precious allies and the fiercest guardians of national cultures and aspirations. As consensus-builders, intellectuals also helped construct a certain image of the enemy.

Ambivalence of Prewar and Postwar Communist Anti-Americanism

Anti-Americanism has had a long and eloquent tradition in France. According to most authors, after a long phase that dated from pre-1776 and marked the elitist judgment of America's artificiality, cultural wasteland, and conformist nature by writers such as Cornelius de Pauw, Joseph de Maistre, Stendhal, Charles Baudelaire, Daniel de Léon, Frédéric Gaillardet, and even the generally laudatory Alexis de Tocqueville, a more multifaceted contemporary French anti-Americanism emerged in the 1920s.[59] By then it already articulated Europe's fear of America's modern, materialist, consumer culture, of its "anticulture" altogether, but it became fully formed and crystallized only in the early Cold War, with the tangible presence of U.S. hegemony in Western Europe.[60] In the interwar period the most vocal critics of America came from the center-right, but after World War II the Left dominated this discourse. Still, as the intersection of de Gaulle's and the Communists' rhetoric also demonstrated, each side could borrow anti-American themes from the other, as well as address common popular grievances against the American presence.

A similar development occurred in Italy, with the first open diffidence toward America expressed in the mid-nineteenth century by left-wing patriot Giuseppe Mazzini. Right-wing intellectuals such as Ugo Ojetti and Giuseppe Prezzolini dominated this critique by the turn of the century, a critique that eventually centered around fascist propaganda.[61] Although Catholic suspicion of American materialism and modernism lingered during and after World War II, the Christian Democrats shared this view with the PCI much less than the Gaullists did with the PCF. The Italian Left soon monopolized the anti-American discourse; and since these themes also reflected the sharp rift between social-communist and Catholic forces, the Christian Democrats and the Church quickly reached across the Atlantic for common ideological ground.[62]

Similarities and connections linking the anti-Americanism of the French Right, Italian Fascism, and Communism in both countries can be easily exaggerated. Nevertheless Cold War leftist thought had a vast repertoire it could tap from various images and *topoi* of America dating from the interwar period. Works such as André Siegfried's *America Comes of Age* (1927), Jean-Louis Chastanet's *Uncle Shylock* (1927), Georges Duhamel's *America the Menace* (1931), and Emilio Cecchi's *Bitter America* (1939) all echoed Mussolini's campaign against American plutocracy, even in the way they transmuted generous Uncle Sam into the reviled usurer of Western tradition.[63] They also predated communist denunciation of the conditions attached to the first American interim post-World War II loans, as well as of racist U.S. cultural crudity.

The specter of a Europe in decline, eclipsed by America—the "machine civilization" according to Duhamel—may have contradicted the energetic optimism of fascist propaganda, but it certainly resembled its condemnation of the advancing "mechanical hell." From the machine derived a sort of "social dictatorship" defined by impersonal market forces; consumerism threatened to replace the organic unity best represented by the state.[64] The destruction of everything that was so organically interconnected would also bring about standardization, and ultimately submerge the spiritual traditions of Europe (however they were conceived from various shades of opin-

ion) and history altogether—for America was the ahistoric nation by definition. According to André Siegfried, "The old European civilization did not
really cross the Atlantic."[65] The emphasis by Siegfried or by various Italian
fascist authors on artisanship and frugality, as opposed to American mass
production and hedonism rang truest after the 1929 crash and would also become a leitmotiv in later communist struggles against America's "easy life" or
even against the "civilization of abundance."[66] Siegfried's utter alienation of
Europe from America was transformed by the Great Depression into an indissoluble and unfortunate link, a real "cancer" as Robert Aron and Arnaud
Dandieu argued in their influential essay, *Le Cancer américain*. Europe in
this case *had* crossed the Atlantic, but, merging its rationalist thought with
the Yankee spirit, it had committed the ultimate error: America was Europe's
sin, "its degenerate descendant" coming back to haunt and infect it. With
the supremacy of its materialism and "scientific management," it brought
not only physical and economic but also spiritual decadence. While the two
authors had a clear sympathy for monarchist reactionary thinker Charles
Maurras, and for a while felt the "spiritual" call of fascism,[67] their repudiation of liberal democracy and modern capitalism as well as their symbolism
of America as a spreading disease would resonate in postwar communist
arguments.

The condemnation of a society based on "material happiness" also implied that America was incapable of withstanding adversity and trying to
weaken other nations similarly. America's inability to suffer, to experience
the tragic fully was also a symptom of its deracinated ahistorical experience.
Europeans, in contrast, had fathomed that only the experience and full comprehension of historical tragedy could lead to real self-fulfillment, real deep-
ening of one's soul. A nation constantly focused on the present, the future,
and "new frontiers" was, per force, shallow.[68] The accent on austerity, on self-
sacrifice, on commitment to the cause already characterized the communist
representation of the Resistance much as it had informed fascist autarky,
comradeship, and abnegation during wartime.

All these arguments often reflected desires to reconcile individual fulfillment and faith in organic cohesion—both interpreted in different ways
according to each idea or ideology. America, the beacon of modernity, had
apparently destroyed both: its path to modernization, irreverent toward any
tradition, lacked perceptiveness, sensibility, and quality; the individual there
was hypnotized by material abundance, gadgets, advertising, and a commercial, complacent spirit that killed all romance, originality, quality of living,
and eccentricity. So the nation harbinger of freedom and equality actually

displayed the hollowest conformity. Hollywood films, Duhamel wrote in 1931, were "a pastime for slaves, an amusement for the illiterate," spectacles that demanded "no efforts" and raised "no questions."[69]

The focus on defending national identity from the 1920s to the 1930s, the exaltation of wisdom and historicism over power and modernity, all reflected an awareness of Europe's impotence. The sense of powerlessness and injured national pride naturally reached a peak in both France and Italy during World War II. These feelings in turn stirred a natural mixture of admiration and resentment toward the American "liberators." To the leaders of the communist Resistance the record of mutual diffidence was clear: in France it included de Gaulle's rift with President Franklin D. Roosevelt and difficult relationship with Harry S. Truman; in Italy it comprised a widespread sense of disillusion at being occupied as much as liberated, with consequent military and economic restrictions. For the French political elite, the humiliation of defeat clashed so much with its expectations of grandeur that it became a genuine issue of national identity; and in part this elite's anti-Americanism could be considered "a cry for recognition."[70]

Influential American commentators had for some time sensed the risk of an American preponderance of power. "It is inevitable," wrote Reinhold Niebuhr in 1932, "that men should hate those who hold power over them. They may love the virtuous and admire the brilliant, but they hate the powerful. Hatred is compounded by envy and fear, and power breeds both. The fear is justified because powerful individuals and nations, even when they make benevolent pretensions, are not as generous as their pretensions or even as their intentions." By contrast, after the war, the criticism of Stalinist autocracy was muted, especially in France. A shared sense of tragedy exempted the Russians from the same scrutiny as the "enriched" United States. Russia fared better, in the words of Le Monde's editor, Hubert Beuve-Méry, because "it [was] poor, it [had] the sense of disinterested effort, of anonymous and communitarian work; thus it would pass the acid test."[71]

By blaming most of their tribulations on American cultural and political hegemony, the critics, from the right, but especially from the left, also established their priorities: the main continuity between the anti-Americanism of the 1920s and after the Second World War was a conviction that *before* tackling the issue of oppression at home, national identity itself had to be rescued from American influence. More than a strategy, this was an instinctive reaction in France, where the legacy of Revolution had conjoined national identity and commitment to social justice. In vanquished Italy, in contrast, the very fact that the national state, the "main generator of cohesive myths and ideologies," had lost much of its authority, made the country acutely receptive to foreign ideologies and symbols, a fact that was in turn "reinforced by the bipolar confrontation of the two superpowers."[72] This meant that, even more than the French, the Italians began to envision matters of modernization or social justice by referring first to the protection or the molding of national identity against one or the other camp in the Cold War.

With all these compelling reasons and precedents added to a natural ideological aversion, it is no wonder that anti-Americanism made an immediate showing among French and Italian Communists during the Liberation. The two parties' efforts to discredit the Anglo-American contribution to the Liberation in France and to the restoration of liberty in Italy immediately paralleled their glorification of the Red Army and of the communist Resistance. Months before Togliatti's return, the PCI's Rome committee, led by Mauro Scoccimarro, already announced a twin struggle for "full national independence," equating fascism and capitalist imperialism. This party line reevoked Georgi Dimitrov's thesis, introduced in the Comintern in 1934–35. In his role of secretary of the organization, the Bulgarian leader had launched the Popular Front campaign, presenting Soviet ideology as mainstream antifascism, while contending that fascism was "the open terrorist dictatorship of the most reactionary, most chauvinistic and most imperialist of finance capital." A termination of the Grand Alliance politics, the PCI thus suggested at the end of the war, would only confirm the collusion of capitalism and fascism.[73]

Capitalist scheming included the cultural dimension as well. Some party leaders, such as Luigi Longo and the orthodox Marxist intellectual Emilio Sereni, advocated the creation of a "Cultural Front" for the defense of national culture against overseas influences as early as the summer of 1945: the strength of such national revival, Longo argued, could best be found in the intersection between intellectual and popular folk traditions. The very Gramscian definition of the "organic intellectual" elicited a renunciation of "cosmopolitanism," often identified as a cultural bourgeois self-indulgence, in favor of native traditions, of an ability to articulate the needs and aspirations of the national masses. The "cosmopolitanism" stigma also evoked the twin ills of capitalism and bourgeois decadence. Before they denounced the collusion between clericalism and U.S. imperialism, the Italian Communists minced no words against the perceived one between American and Italian trusts. In September 1945, citing the case of the country's main automaker, FIAT, and reports of a possible sale of its shares to an American company in exchange for U.S. government assistance, *L'Unità* charged that President Giovanni Agnelli and his administrator, Giuseppe Volpi, would "always sell Italy's independence in order to replenish their safes, and to buy diamonds and fur coats for their mistresses."[74] The potentially corrupting effects of American aid thus included loss of sovereignty, social inequities, and rewards to the lavish and culturally shallow hedonism of the privileged classes.

In France, the communist tendency to minimize the importance of de Gaulle's leadership in the Resistance contained frequent allusions to the proud general being forced to request Anglo-American military assistance. After de Gaulle attempted a departure from that dependency by signing the Franco-Soviet treaty of friendship in December 1944, the PCF began to make a sharp distinction within the Grand Alliance between demanding Anglo-Americans and disinterested Soviets. The latter, in Marcel Cachin's words, would never "from nearby [Britain] or from far away [the United States] impose on France its political regime," and never "advance financial negotiations that would tie her future." For Pierre Hervé the Liberation immediately appeared "betrayed": it was liberty to invade French markets or to control the French press.[75] A year and a half later, the agreements signed by French socialist leader Léon Blum and U.S. Secretary of State James Byrnes for interim financial assistance seemed to confirm all these fears; even worse, with the stipulation virtually preventing limits on film imports from the United States, they added the prospect of a combined control over the French economy and culture. Next, André Marty commented at the Central Committee, America might even dare "request material from the *Armée Française!*"[76] These reactions show that French and Italian Communists from the start fused political and cultural diffidence toward the United States: due to their countries' immediate exposure to America's presence, they sensed the danger of U.S. mass culture earlier than did the still relatively immune Soviets.

Communist anti-Americanism was also rekindled by an even wider leftist reaction against the growing denunciations of the Soviet system and, since the late 1930s, against revelations of Soviet concentration camps. It was this anti-Sovietism that began to prompt French "neutralist" intellectuals to proclaim their "anti-anticommunism." But in their effort to strike a balance, they stressed their solidarity with the PCF and anti-American feelings first. As Sartre declared in October 1946: "I cannot turn my moral values solely against the U.S.S.R. While it is true that the deportation of several million people is more serious than the lynching of a black man, the lynching of a black man is the result of a situation which has been going on for more than a hundred years. So it represents the suffering of just as many millions of black people over the years as there are millions of inhabitants of the Southern Caucasus who have been deported."[77]

But the Grand Alliance did make a difference and was the primary factor prodding a more careful approach to and collaboration with, if not always sincere admiration for, Roosevelt's policies. The very national credentials of the French and Italian Communist Parties depended on their caution toward America; their still fragile presence in the government could be made steadier only if this international reality remained unvaried. Stalin, too, had urged cooperation. As Togliatti explained to the party's directorate in June 1945, this choice was no mere adherence to the Yalta realities. In some ways it was an attempt to combat its superpower logic: for only the Grand Alliance, he said, offered the minor powers margins for autonomy; hence the PCI had to "avoid speculating on the contrasts among the great powers." That was also the message that Maurice Thorez gave his central committee in the spring of 1946, and still sought to convey a few months later in a famous interview with the *Times* of London. In it he denied craven subordination of his party to Moscow and expressed preference for a democratic path to socialism—though undoubtedly France, and the PCF along with it, more deliberately than Italy, used its contacts with Russia to press its own case for equality with the other great powers.[78]

Yalta, however, allowed a mythical reference to wartime cooperation heralded by Stalin and Roosevelt. For at least two years after his death, the American president remained highly respected among Western Communists. They recognized his role as the necessary interlocutor, in some ways—and not always consistently with Togliatti's argument—as their nation's indirect "power access" to Moscow. They also attributed to his New Deal a capacity to alleviate the contrast between capitalism and democracy. Even better, the New Deal allowed them to make a sharp distinction between the political heirs of FDR and the "brutal imperialists" of the Democratic and Republican Right. Except during the height of the Cold War, Communists' perception of a "promising," democratic America was a sign of their ambivalence but also of their sharper focus in combating "threatening," imperialist America.[79]

Another important reason for moderation was the need for reconstruction. Communists in both countries did not spurn American assistance. Sometimes they entertained the hope of juggling aid from both superpowers, as Italian socialist leader Pietro Nenni tried to do as foreign minister at the end of 1946. He opened negotiations for wheat deliveries from the Soviet Union while Prime Minister De Gasperi prepared for his first trip to the United States to discuss a reconstruction loan. Earlier that year Thorez, too, argued at the Central Committee that wheat from Russia, besides showing the equivalence of aid from the East and the West, could have actually induced Washington to make its own assistance less conditional.[80] But both French and Italian Communists were realistic enough to understand the importance and popularity of U.S. assistance. Even in the midst of controversies around the Blum-Byrnes accords of 1946 and the Washington loan De Gasperi managed to obtain in January 1947, the two parties were vociferous only about the "strings attached." Their most public outcries were about two issues of national sovereignty: the humiliating film quota for the French, and Italy's acceptance of some draconian aspects of the peace treaty. They also presumed the loans followed a political motive and a clear anticommunist plan. But they made a clear distinction between exclusively economic and political loans. Some leaders in the PCI outdid their French comrades in viewing U.S. assistance as a potential boost to productivity and to a New Deal approach in Italy.[81]

Despite their skepticism concerning American generosity, these views revealed something more deeply seated than the rather tactical ambiguity of the two parties' pro–Grand Alliance policies. They stemmed from a certain attraction to America's technological and societal innovations, an admiration that Italian communist intellectuals especially had developed in the interwar period. Modernity was not necessarily negative.[82] Indeed, for much of the European Left what distinguished the United States and the Soviet Union, in the period between the 1920s and the years following World War II, was their nature as "young countries," dynamic masters of technology and architects of a new world distinguished from stagnant, decadent Western Europe.[83]

That was how Gramsci first analyzed America, as the place of the most advanced technological *and* societal experimentation. In his essays on Fordism and Americanism he recognized that the United States, first among the capitalist countries, had abandoned "old economic individualism" in favor of a carefully engineered, if not "planned" economy; this marked the abandonment of the last residues of feudalism, explaining the utter opposition to "Americanism" by backward groups in Europe. Placing the manager and the consumer at the center of the capitalist organization, Fordism understood the importance of scientific management and mass consumerism as instruments of efficiency and social control. Under this system the worker was disciplined, rationalized, and "mechanized"; every aspect of his life, from drinking to religion to sexuality was closely monitored. American modern industrialists were "not concerned with the *humanity* or the *spirituality* of the worker, which [were] immediately smashed." But the working class was not opposed to this form of Americanism, since its studiously managed forms of control allowed "coercion . . . to be ingeniously combined with persuasion and consent."[84] As the best interpreters of Gramsci's work have reiterated, this was a portrait of an enemy, perhaps most insidious, but, for that reason, fascinating.[85] At the time Gramsci formulated this analysis, the historic task of that enemy was actually to help defeat the most stagnant and parasitic forms of European capitalism. Gramsci acknowledged the powerful nature of Fordist coercion, also because it was matched by another important factor: the "tradition of strong individual personalities in whom the vocation of work had reached its greatest intensity and strength, men who entered directly, not by means of some army of servants and slaves, into energetic contact with the forces of nature in order to dominate them and exploit them victoriously." Mocking the call for action by Italy's fascist regime, the imprisoned philosopher contrasted its "gladiatorial futility which . . . modifie[d] only the word, not things, the external gesture and not the man inside" to the Americans' "real action . . . which modifie[d] in an essential way both man and external reality (in other words, real culture)." In some respects, the working class in Italy and Europe was closer to Americanism than the European bourgeoisie was, because the workers were best attuned to the "new most modern industrial needs."[86] It was clear that by evoking Fordism to indict the fascist regime's flawed capitalism, Gramsci hoped to increase the possibilities of a socialist takeover in Italy. By also stressing the dehumanized nature of the American worker, he implied that under more auspicious conditions, in the Soviet Union perhaps, the rationalization would be matched with the enhancement of the worker's spirituality.

It was no accident that in the 1920s and early 1930s, the Soviet Union also felt the attraction of American pragmatism and technological prowess. Promoting rapid industrialization, Soviet leaders imitated and even imported America's engineering and planning skills. Vigorous and modernist, the United States at times could be even more than a technological model; its rationalization and its urban energy had a cultural appeal for some Russian leaders and intellectuals.[87] But even without utilizing Gramsci's analysis, the Soviets were weary of Fordism and stayed almost exclusively focused on its technical, not social recipes.

Pointing to the inextricable connection between Fordism and consumerism, Gramsci seemed interested instead in the instruments of political and cultural consensus under the most modern capitalist society. His analysis contained hints of irreverence toward the predominant ideology in Moscow. Even his worst indictments of how modern America had regimented its workers departed from Marxist orthodoxy. Predating some of the 1960s neo-Marxist analyses, this critique also prefigured the dissatisfaction that the youth movement and several communist intellectuals in Italy and France would feel toward their parties' concentration on social oppression and neglect of individual alienation—a theme that found its most articulate expression in America's cultural revolutions of that decade. In the final analysis, for Gramsci, a country so defined by both the most effective tools of consensus and unbridled individuality was also able to generate inspiring forms of internal critique. America's culture and literature had thus left ample room for genuine "organic" intellectuals such as Walt Whitman and Sinclair Lewis.

The founder of the PCI was not the only Italian communist intellectual to be captivated by American literature. As internal and somewhat muffled critics of the Fascist regime, writers such as Cesare Pavese and Elio Vittorini found escape, inspiration, and ultimate intellectual liberation in the works of Ernest Hemingway, Sinclair Lewis, John Steinbeck, William Faulkner, and further back, Walt Whitman, Herman Melville, Nathaniel Hawthorne, Ralph Emerson, and Henry David Thoreau. Reviewing or translating those works, Italian intellectuals discovered an American literature full of energy, youthfulness, informality, and a powerful response to the elitist, rigid academic nature of Europe's bourgeois culture and to the futile pomp of fascist authoritarianism. Whitman, in Pavese's description, was among the first to model "a new language which [shattered] the barrier between things and words." Even better, American culture, Pavese averred, "seemed to us . . . the ideal place for work and experimentation, for painstaking and hard-fought experimentation."[88]

For a short time in the immediate postwar period, Italy's leftist intellectual fascination with America continued. In Italo Calvino's words, to many West European Communists until the mid-1940s Hemingway was "a sort of God"; and modern American literature found its equivalent in modern American music, for jazz was a "banner of untamed cosmopolitanism." Both these art forms reached such transcendental status not because they excelled in sophistication, but because they were vigorous, genuine, closest to reality: Hemingway, Calvino argued, deserved praise because he was "never overblown; he [kept] his feet on the ground."[89] In all its realism, directness, and immediacy, American culture had for more than a decade earned an aura of universality: for Pavese America was "an immense theater where our common drama was played out with greater frankness than elsewhere." Vittorini, who in 1945 had begun to conduct his campaign for cultural innovation and experimentation from his new literary journal *Il Politecnico*, went even further in his tribute to America. As he wrote in his diary in May 1946: "American culture will always have within it the awareness of European culture. It has all the years of human experience within its youth. And because it has all the history of mankind within, it is not a culture limited to America. It marks a new point, but it recapitulates the culture of the entire world at the same moment it marks a new point. . . . Even its originality is thus valid for the entire world."[90] No better description could have been offered of America as the principal place for Europe's reinvention and self-reflection. Even America's contradictions were most fascinating for their heightened truthfulness and immediacy. Communists found it instructive and even alluring to analyze the United States' dualism between conservatism and progressivism, conformity and iconoclasm, philistine attitude and refined nature. Party leader Pietro Ingrao remembered that in the 1930s the American novel "gave us the image of a society where contradictions openly erupted." Even in cinema, the emerging Italian neorealism, while conceived as a counterpoint to Hollywood, also absorbed some of its immediacy, directness and antielitism—or, in some cases, borrowed from American literature a documentary style that also stood against mainstream film productions.[91]

Above all America mattered because, in these intellectuals' view, it was as universal as Marxism was. Their main targets were the stifling provincialism of the fascist regime, or Italy's postwar pressure toward bourgeois "normalcy." Even when cosmopolitanism assumed a negative connotation in the communist jargon, "provincialism" remained the chief villain for most Italian intellectuals. Young Italian radicals shared with many leftist Americans a romantic notion that communism would help them spearhead the war against philistine provincialism. Some of them could even resume the pre-Marxist view of America as the "promised land" of ultimate freedom, a nation that could conceivably attain social equality "without a violent revolution."[92] This prospect of socialism through parliamentary democracy—sometimes distorting expectations about America's "permanent revolution"—would be recurrently appealing to several Italian Communists.

Communist anti-Americanism in France left some room for ambivalence at the broad cultural level, but remained rather adamant on technological or social themes. To the French Communists, even more than to their Italian comrades, Fordism represented the nightmarish enemy. The echo of Siegfried's or Duhamel's revulsion against standardization or "machinism" remained strong for a society that especially prized its humanism, its communitarian ideals and artisanal ways. At the same time, the Communists made an effort to distinguish their critique from the benighted bourgeois condemnation of the machine: the problem was not the machine itself but its political misuse; the indictment was of modernity made in America. As Philip Roger has best summarized, analyzing the work of leading communist intellectual Georges Friedmann, "there was, the Soviets were now saying, a liberating machinism (one used in the context of collective production) and a predatorial and depredating machinism (capitalism and cutthroat competition's)."[93] For a party and an ideology that strove to reconcile historic materialism, Cartesian rationalism, and the legacy of the French Revolution, the idea of progress had to be preserved and reformulated: it had to be divested of the engineering, profiteering, dehumanizing, grossly consumerist qualities that characterized its capitalist version, especially its American technocratic update. Because modernity was so subject to a diametric distinction—emancipatory under the Soviet regime, enslaving under the American and capitalist one—the anti-Americanism of the French Communists was more visceral and systemic than that of their Italian comrades. Only America the menace seemed to remain. Nothing in it portended a new progressive world.

Injured national pride was another factor that promoted unqualified anti-Americanism among all French groups, including the Communists. The political and intellectual elites particularly harbored such resentment from as far back as the clash between Prime Minister Georges Clemenceau and President Wilson at the Paris Peace Conference; the gradual loss of status, and finally the humiliation of defeat in 1940 made things worse. Italy had also felt slighted, blaming Wilson for the "mutilated victory" of 1919. By denying Italy's most ambitious claims to the Yugoslavian borderland, the American president transformed himself from the most admired to one of the most reviled international statesman among Italians. But Fascism temporarily exorcised the slight of Wilsonian diplomacy; and although the national collapse in World War II was also a humbling experience, the nation did not experience it as a decline from its world power status, which had always been questionable in the first place. The year 1940 represented the defeat of the French nation, whereas 1943 to most Italians represented the fall of a fraudulent regime.[94] In its status as permanent ally of the United States, and former great power, France felt the burden of the unbalanced relationship sooner and more intensely than Italy. Furthermore, the French Communists in the interwar period had not had the same political inducement as Italian leftist intellectuals to envision America as an antidote to fascist oppression. On the contrary, their anti-Americanism became one of the main sources of their political strength, further justifying the party's firm position against most things American.

And yet America was not an utterly unredeemable nightmare. It still represented progress, innovation, dynamism, and, even within the framework of its conformity, a multifaceted complexity. Jean-Paul Sartre resembled Calvino as he described "the discovery of Faulkner, Dos Passos, Hemingway, Caldwell, Steinbeck" as "the greatest literary development in France between 1929 and 1939." The American novel, he added, "together with jazz and the movies [was] among the best of importation from the United States." At the Liberation in Paris Simone de Beauvoir was mesmerized by the "tall

[American] soldiers, dressed in khaki and chewing their gum." With their "singing and whistling," their "loud laughs showing teeth as white as children's" the GI's were "living proof that you could cross the seas again"; better still, "to me," de Beauvoir concluded, "these carefree young Americans were freedom incarnate."[95] It was by touring the United States for six months in 1945 as guest of the Office of War Information (OWI) that Sartre developed his mixture of attraction and repulsion toward America. His analysis of individualism best exemplified this ambiguity. While distinguishing French individualism—traditionally defined as the "individual's struggle against society"—from American individualism—which he saw as the individual's pursuit of success—the existentialist philosopher nevertheless recognized that an ethic of success did create "models and examples" for the rest of the world. These exceptional individuals were not just greedy moneymakers: "Ford and Rockefeller, Hemingway and Roosevelt" were men for whom success had become "proof of [their] virtue and intelligence," even—Sartre added tongue-in-cheek—of "divine protection." Ultimately, revulsion prevailed, as Sartre concluded that American individualism, conceived as a struggle to succeed, was "not incompatible with conformism, but, on the contrary, implie[d] it."[96]

But a certain fascination with the land of abundance, resourcefulness, pragmatic ingenuity, individual liberation, and élan vital was not limited to the strongly individualist exponents of leftist existentialism. Several orthodox Communists nurtured a similar ambivalence. Like Sartre, many communist intellectuals had fetishized American jazz since their youth. Beginning in the 1920s Parisian clubs such as Le Boeuf sur le Toit offered Picasso, Louis Aragon, and many other artists a chance to become "organic" intellectuals in new ways: there, jazz was the musical articulation of an avant-garde cultural, artistic elite, who also mingled with "workingmen in sandals come down from Montparnasse."[97] The American music helped break social barriers between bohemians and the proletariat.

The same happened with American literature. While not serving an immediately political purpose (opposing Fascism) as in Italy, the American novels still had a "popular" dimension: for the interwar French avant-garde it was the very humble, nonintellectual origins of the American writers that allowed them to break the conventions, assail the elitism and gentility of Europe's literary traditions, and vividly portray the "vagabonds, inveterate drunkards, the unemployed . . . tough guys stripped of all romanticism—simple victims of economic misfortune." This literary selection, ignoring literati such as Robert Frost, Henry James, F. Scott Fitzgerald, was of course discerning, and even reflected a desire by the French Left to express its highest admiration for those American writers who unveiled the depravity of their own society.[98] But these writers remained a source of inspiration mainly because of their distinctly American way of denouncing their own society: they reflected the force with which the American literary style, even its proximity with the new cinematic form of art, could help break the European even more than the American class structure.

This Marxist ambiguity toward America continued in the immediate postwar period. While the Grand Alliance persisted, the PCF's occasional homage to the United States was not solely instrumental. World War II heroes such as Eisenhower won praise for showing their empathy for the French common man. The PCF may have seen Ike as no match for the *fils du peuple*, but he certainly appeared more genuine and down-to-earth than the haughty de Gaulle. Before the Blum-Byrnes accords, Pierre Courtade had significantly lauded the American secretary of state for continuing Roosevelt's enlightened policies.[99] The United States' appeal was not limited to its contingent political choices or style. Still in November 1946, the party's main literary journal, *Les Lettres françaises*, extolled some unexpected virtues of American society. The article's author, Claude Roy, had toured the United States under the same OWI sponsorship that had brought de Beauvoir, Sartre, and other journalists to America. But unlike those other *Résistants*, Roy was a PCF member.[100] The flexibility demonstrated by certain U.S. officials may have elicited the French Communists' appreciation. Roy went further, describing his captivation with the sense of space, of experimentation, of constant renewal in the land where Europe "could reinvent itself." "America is like the sky," he wrote, "[a] poetry of figures, of statistics, diagrams, curves so fascinating that they flow into the spirit like the waters of Niagara flow into vision and hearing." The marvel of lines and curves was not really a technological, modernist one; it rather reflected the rebellion of the spirit, the American *on the road*, where "the individual himself becomes the road," and where "the road can become a drug, flavorless like *marihuana* [*sic*], this Indian herb that the bad boys smoke in the slums of New York." Infinite space meant infinite possibilities, and, implicitly in Roy's travel log, pursuit of ultimate self-fulfillment. These possibilities could go either way, for America's "pride [was] sometimes tragic and menacing," and "sometimes attractive."[101]

Cold War Alignment and the End of Progressive America, 1946–1947

The Cold War was to erase all this fascination with the new enemy. This transition to a universal and unrelenting anti-Americanism was all but clear cut, especially in Italy. For several intellectuals and party leaders the reappraisal caused considerable agony. They first had to explain to themselves why their own myth of a democratic, pathbreaking America was so rapidly fading. This reevaluation in 1946 and 1947 matters only in part for what it shows about international developments prompting the two parties' ideological alignment. It reveals hopes and fears that the most reflective Marxist thinkers and leaders in the two countries nurtured about how the very notion of progress could be molded by the transatlantic cultural or political dialogue. It also demonstrates these thinkers' underlying interest in themes, such as individual alienation or cultural emancipation, that were only temporarily overshadowed by the Cold War at its peak.

One of the first disappointments with America for many Italian intellectuals was that, in becoming a superpower, it had at the same time lost its aura of discovery, experimentation, human drama, and rebelliousness. The civilization of abundance replaced these spellbinding myths. For Pavese, "without a historically progressive thought to keep alive, no matter how many skyscrapers and cars and armies it may produce, America will not be at the avant-garde of any culture anymore." Worse still, "without progressive political thinking and a progressive struggle, America will rather risk giving itself up to a form of fascism, even if it will do so in the name of its more cherished traditions." American writers also had "lost their miraculous immediacy of expression, that inborn sense of earth and concreteness, the harsh wisdom that made us love them." For Calvino even Hemingway's "political universe and his style" should now be reconsidered as "narrow and easily transformed into mannerism." By mid-1946, as the Cold War was approaching, the PCI actually conducted a concerted effort to debunk the literary myth revolving around Hemingway. The American writer, according to party spokesman Mario Alicata, had committed the main bourgeois sins of formulaic abstraction, individualism, and self-indulgence. Even jazz, now reduced, according to Il Politecnico, to "stereotyped harmonies and melodies," had lost its character as a "powerful educational tool for the masses."[102] The Communists' hopes in a democratic, subversive, experimental America seemed to founder along with the understanding that its maximum subversion—a reconciliation with the Soviet Union under the auspices of the Grand Alliance—had also vanished.

This passage to an intense anti-Americanism mattered even more for its correlation to the party's campaign to rein in any form of intellectual heterodoxy. The polemics within the French and Italian Marxist Left in 1946 were similar, but what distinguished the PCI's feud was that it revolved explicitly around the question of whether America should be a fundamental source for a new Italian culture. Vittorini's Il Politecnico had not abandoned that perception, and despite its disenchantment with much of the American avant-garde, it still gave considerable weight to the works of Hemingway and other American writers. For that reason Mario Alicata first, then Togliatti himself, assailed the journal and finally forced it to cease publication by the end of 1947.[103] As one of the leading intellectuals charged with organizing the party's cultural front, Alicata in the spring of 1946 accused the *Politecnico faction* of "intellectualism," a bourgeois trait of those who had too eagerly embraced cultural eclecticism while neglecting the "productive contact between our culture and the concrete problems and interests of Italy's working class." The journal's self-assigned task of "enlightening" the readers with all the literary and scientific developments that twenty years of fascism had censored had now become arrogant and self-indulgent. Hemingway's discovery of the human was not, Alicata added, even near the ultimate objective of "truth," which coincided with the "achievement of justice and freedom." In such terms American literature was far from deserving the labels of "modern" and "enriching."[104]

Indeed that was Vittorini's main heresy: undertaking a modernist and cosmopolitan path as the party was trying to mold itself as the heir of national, idealist traditions. Vittorini's model was the positivist tradition that found its best Italian representative in the nineteenth-century sociologist Carlo Cattaneo, who also had pursued an international and interdisciplinary approach. A logical connection existed between the Enlightenment/positivist matrix of Vittorini's work and his fascination with that part of American culture that also had reconciled modernist and profoundly humanist approaches. For Togliatti, as I have noted, it was essential to root the party's new cultural project in national traditions, best represented by the idealist philosophy that, through Francesco De Sanctis and Benedetto Croce, had led to Gramsci's reinterpretation of the organic intellectual. In artistic and ideological terms, this at first apparently ecumenical strategy soon translated into a regimented endorsement of realism, the most genuine proletarian art, as Soviet ideologue Andrei Zhdanov had first established at the Soviet Writers' Congress of 1934. No matter how hard Vittorini tried to present cultural openness and experimentalism as beneficial to the party, even as a chance for a truly national path to socialism, he, too, was in the end forced to admit that "to seek in art progress for humanity is nothing compared to struggling for such progress on the political and social ground."[105] Togliatti's final attack on *Il Politecnico* listed its individualistic, abstract, elitist, and cosmopolitan traits, all standing against the party's national popular project.[106]

But while the party thus enhanced its national image, the debate "ultimately impoverished the whole perspective of cultural renewal" and "reinforced the very provincialism the PCI had claimed it wished to see overcome." The party thus limited its own flexibility toward the social changes that rapid economic development would soon bring in the country. But it would be exaggerated to state that Italian Communism immediately lost touch with the needs of the country's intellectuals or even of its society and economy.[107] Since the Christian Democrats fought their own battles against individualistic and cosmopolitan tendencies, the PCI ostensibly continued to embody social and cultural progress. However, that success also implied that one of the party's main propaganda assets, the juxtaposition of American interests and "clericalism," eventually became one of its main faults. That perspective created its own monolithic threat, whereas the anticommunist front was rather multifaceted and divided. Also, by focusing on that collusion, the Communists subordinated their own evaluation of the international enemy, or of foreign policy altogether, to domestic concerns just as much as did the Christian Democrats.

The transition from a muted, subtle anti-Americanism to a virulent, overt one was less traumatic for the French Communists than it had been for their Italian comrades, primarily because their "pro"-Americanism had been faint in the first place. "America is not the New World," *Les Lettres françaises* announced with mixed triumphalism and regret in January 1947. This conclusion was inspired by an interview the journal conducted with writer Richard Wright, whom the French Communists saw as one of the very last political allies in intellectual America, one who not coincidentally was an exile in Paris.[108]

But, as with the Italian case, the controversies that accompanied the passage to a militant anti-Americanism were the most revealing part of this renewed communist struggle. The condemnation of artistic "cosmopolitanism" stormed into the communist press in the fall of 1946. Pierre Hervé and Roger Garaudy, still having qualms about socialist realism, faced the reprimand of Louis Aragon, who declared that realism was "l'esthétique du PCF." Endorsed by the Central Committee in November, Aragon dictated the Zhdanovian line, and at the party's Eleventh Congress in June 1947, Thorez, together with the new director of the party's cultural section, Laurent Casanova, imposed the strictest discipline on its intellectuals. As has been noted, in France, as in Italy, the Communists' "ideological turning point preceded the political one."[109] Even before the Grand Alliance was over, there was the attack on ideological cosmopolitanism and on the relative flexibility it encouraged toward America's society, politics, and culture.

Equally revealing was the polemic between the PCF and the existentialists. On art and literature, Sartre seemed to echo Garaudy when, in his famous essays titled *What Is Literature?*, he railed at the "politics of Stalinist communism," declaring them "incompatible with the honest practice of literary craft." But for the PCF intellectuals, including Garaudy and the party's leading philosopher Henri Lefebvre, there was no possible entente with existentialism. Sartre's concept of the "individual" was, for them, apolitical, ahistorical, and asocial. Garaudy led the attack, sensing the risk coming from existentialism much more than he did from avant-garde art. According to him, Sartre's philosophy held a view of human freedom that, separated from political, social, or historical conditions, was meaningless, and even hostile to human progress: *"uprooted from history,"* he wrote, *"freedom is nothing but an ineffective ersatz."* According to the worst indictments, existentialism appeared idealistic, metaphysical, pathological, pessimistic, self-indulgent, and, not the least, conceptually linked to Nazism "through its association with Martin Heidegger."[110] The other association—with America—was only implied, but it was more consequential. The PCF had reason to fear the appeal of existentialism to French bohemian youth. Leftists in Paris and elsewhere could be captivated by the new philosophy's cosmopolitan aura, just like Italian intellectuals felt the lure of the experimental *Il Politecnico*. Sartre, like Vittorini, could help raise their consciousness, their demiurgic subjectivity, their sense of responsibility for their choices in a given historical context. This mixture of freedom and commitment, as radical, anticapitalist, and even Marxist as it professed to be, was, for that very reason, insidious. It could subvert Marxism from within. Immediately, both the PCF and the PCI highlighted the flaws of those who placed human subjectivity above collective action, choice above historical and material determinism.[111]

In subsequent years, the debate would be increasingly settled in favor of the two parties, primarily because progressive intellectuals of every political shade gave priority to holding the ground against the attacks on communism. At the peak of the Cold War, even those leftists who, such as Sartre, declared neutrality, gradually conformed to the most strident and polarizing forms of anti-Americanism. But three paradoxes emerged from the way anti-Americanism became so consensual.

The first was that the cruder and more sectarian communist anti-Americanism became, the more the two parties enlisted intellectuals. In the ideological cold war, intellectuals became instrumental in the depiction and demonization of the enemy, and in the gathering of consensus around the self-professed nationalism of the two parties. Even radical intellectuals who, especially in France, refrained from joining the party, perceived themselves as protectors of national culture against the overwhelming American presence and guardians of the Marxist faith, which, while imperfect in some of its applications, was, unlike capitalism, perfect in principle.[112]

The second paradox was that, severe as the independent Marxist thinkers or the "anti-anticommunists" might be in their condemnation of America, their set of attitudes, especially their reconciliation of subjectivity and social commitment, was bound to find deep connections with radical thought in the United States. This outlook would characterize much of the intellectual debate within a decade and would influence the leftist youth by the mid-1960s, deeply affecting the French and Italian Communist Parties.

Third, the real issue for many intellectuals developed more out of disenchantment with America than confidence in Soviet Russia or Western Europe. Those who had nurtured hopes about democratic America felt betrayed above all because the "New World" had ceased to be new. Instead of helping to bring liberation to Europe, it imitated and allied itself with Europe's most conservative and stifling political and cultural elements. Pavese best expressed this disillusion: Americans had turned bad only in part because, in their Cold War retrenchment, they appeared now closer to traditionalist American values; actually their main fault was that, in the first years after World War II, they had "undergone a process of spiritual Europeanization," losing "a large part of the exotic and tragic directness that was their essence."[113]

The transition from ambivalent to unquestionable anti-Americanism eclipsed the Communists' keen use of the democratic America versus the reactionary one. Becoming, in this view, the imperialist enemy, the United States lost all its redeeming qualities, but so did the communist denunciation lose much of its depth and discerning quality. It also lost its potential to bring about change at the international level. While framed in the Grand Alliance discourse, Communists' cautious and targeted anti-Americanism could have added room for maneuver for Europe's middle powers, just as Togliatti had hoped. At the onset of the Cold War, the two parties naturally succumbed even more to a bipolarized worldview: their anti-Americanism, so broad and at the same time so instrumental to their own domestic campaigns, accentuated their respective countries' international subordination. This did not mean, however, that the two strongest Communist Parties in the West ceased to stir fears in Washington about their impact at both the domestic and the international levels. Nor should the fault for such a virulent anti-Americanism be attributed solely to the two Communist Parties, or to their regimentation under Moscow and the newly created Cominform in

1947. The United States was at fault, too, not only because of its "imperial" presence, or its government's political entente with French and Italian centrist or conservative groups, but also because of the consensual nature of American society in the early Cold War. Together, these aspects contributed to the Communists' undiscriminating criticism over the next decade.

2 CONFRONTING THE COMMUNISTS IN
GOVERNMENT The American Response, 1944–1947

Utopias

The absolute and overreacting nature of the struggle between the United
States and Western European Communism after World War II soon became apparent to most American officials. The self-assigned identity and
role of the French and Italian Communist Parties clashed profoundly with
the self-image and international role of the United States. Washington's specific options on dealing with the Communists in those two nations came to
be framed in a broader context not only because of the looming Soviet threat,
but also because communist success in the West would test the resilience of
American visions of Europe. In order to comprehend why Western Europe's
communist confrontation with America caused the United States to reflect
on itself, it is necessary to clarify how this clash became one of visions, even
of utopias, affecting the style of U.S. foreign policy and even the definition of
U.S. national security.

Following years of material and moral devastation, France and Italy naturally embraced views that, from either domestic or foreign traditions, promised immediate improvement. The two countries became particularly susceptible to Soviet myths, American dreams, and a renewed faith in human
perfectibility. For all the pragmatic compromises the French and Italian
Communists made to retain power and legitimacy, their appeal remained in
large part anchored to the promise of attaining a socialist society, a utopia
divested of the term's derogatory connotation as "dreamland."

Pragmatism, with its denial of perfectibility, was arguably the main
strength of the United States. But by confronting ultimate promises from
the other side, the United States stressed its own countervailing proselytizing nature, and re-evoked its vision of exceptionalism that combined a sense
of moral superiority, uniqueness, and universalism. It offered the vision of a
promised land, which, under a "permanent revolution"[1] would deliver ultimate freedom and self-fulfillment to its own people and the rest of the world.
The United States' faith in its exceptionalism defined its national identity.
As historian Richard Hofstadter once wrote, "It has been our fate as a nation
not to have ideologies, but to be one."[2] Hence, even before the onset of the

Cold War, anti-Americanism and anticommunism both included utopian elements mirroring opposite images.

Most American officials and intellectuals emphasized the utopian and propagandistic nature of communist influence. Dogma and demagogy were indeed the two sides of the same communist coin: a certain faith that the avant-garde of communism could educate and elevate the masses, together with a keen capitalization on the masses' discontent. Further, that combination expressed a belief that the avant-garde itself, the intellectuals or the party leaders, would, through communism, attain greater, and even purer knowledge, which meant no esoteric endeavor but a capacity to recast their whole existence through a social project, a stronger involvement with everyday realities.

The task was not easy. The pressing need prominent intellectuals and communist leaders felt for certainties involved considerable soul-searching. Perhaps this mood is best illustrated by the reflections of Jean-Paul Sartre, who never enlisted in the party but served the cause of Marxism. In 1945 Sartre described the end of the war as having occurred "among indifference and anguish. . . . it's not peace. Peace is a beginning. But we are living an agony. . . . the future has not started: we no longer believe in the end of wars." As I noted in chapter 1, Sartre denounced orthodox communism for its optimism, determinism, and denial of individual choice. Though he had high praise for the Soviet Union, he did not consider it the workers paradise the PCF made it out to be; nor did he shy from criticizing the Stalinist regime. Nevertheless, Sartre and other existentialists shared with many communist intellectuals the belief that any engaged thinker had to remain aware of the constant struggle for progress. This very commitment proved that they were on the side of progress and History, interpreted as Marxism and the Revolution. Communism had discovered class struggle as the engine that moved History forward.[3] It was during the early Cold War, and in spite of Stalinism, that Sartre saw this project unfolding best. Soviet camps were a bad thing, but in the pages of *Les Temps modernes* both Sartre and Maurice Merleau-Ponty cautioned the public against suggesting a moral equivalence between Stalinism and Nazism, and, even more, between the Soviet Union and America's flawed, imperialist democracy.[4] Existentialist criticism of the Soviet experience, no matter how mitigated, irked the French Communists. They failed to see that Sartre's magnetism, idealization of revolutionary socialism, and condemnation of bourgeois democracy assisted them by encouraging anti-American sentiments in French society. As even leftist critics of the PCF found the Soviet Union not only redeemable but also ideal in principle, Marxism made huge gains in French public opinion.

Italy's leftist intellectuals, recovering from the Fascist regime, reveled in the myth of a rediscovered path to progress with even greater fervor than the French. For many of them the Soviet Union became a myth not only as the land of institutionalized socialism, but also as a nation that, though conscious of its wartime sacrifices, remained proud and combative—an argument that captivated the popular imagination in a prostrate nation such as Italy. As Italo Calvino recalled years later, "Stalin seemed to represent the moment when Communism had become a huge river, now distant from the headlong and uneven course it began with, a river into which the currents of history flowed." Italy's Marxist politicians and writers alike, as Marcello Flores has noted, ascribed mythical proportions to the Soviet "productive efforts, the kindness of the Soviet people and their attachment to Stalin and socialism, the natural beauties and the artistic marvels nourished by the regime," and, not least, to the "supreme sacrifice" Soviet soldiers had been "willing to make to conquer freedom for their land."[5]

In both France and Italy, intellectuals also turned the Soviet dream into one of exactitude, elevating Marxism from social science to mathematical certainty, the perfect tool to attain perfect knowledge and ultimate liberty, according to Roger Garaudy. From the working class's standpoint the utopia was even more immediate. The Soviet dreamland showed that each worker would become master of technology rather than its slave. Indeed, every human being, in this view, would finally become a full participant in life, "fully aware of being both its soul and its engine."[6]

Utopia was further rooted in national myths, and in the peculiar way the two Communist Parties upheld them immediately following World War II. Patriotism in France, ever since the Revolution, had meant much more than mere attachment to the *patrie*. It meant, as Theodore Zeldin explained, "devotion to the ideal of human happiness, to the rights of man. A patriot was, therefore, not a chauvinist, nor a blind follower of any government but a citizen of Utopia, a universal man."[7] While France had during the twentieth century lost its status as universal civilization, the Communists felt they could resurrect this through a renewed utopia, which had its house in Russia but its roots in France. With statism and chauvinism so discredited in Italy, the PCI also reconceived patriotism along the idealist and populist traditions of the nineteenth-century *Risorgimento*. Political and intellectual traditions being more strongly intertwined in Italy than in France, the Italian Communists nurtured even greater determination than their French comrades to dominate national thought. That is why they strove to reabsorb—and, via Antonio Gramsci, supersede—the idealist tradition of thinkers such as Giuseppe Mazzini and Benedetto Croce.

It was less obvious that the political and ideological clash with communism reignited the American utopian vision. I am not referring to the imagery, experience, and even clichés of the American dream as opposed to the Soviet myth. Nor am I addressing the well-known universalist promises of Wilsonian internationalism versus those of Leninist world revolution. Rather, from the evident effort to confront communism and communist anti-Americanism with an alternative combination of demagogy (populism) and pedagogy (elitism), the United States intertwined that combination as thoroughly as did the Western Communists. Furthermore, such inextricable links between demagogic and pedagogic approaches meant that any denunciation of communism as utopian implied an American absolutism that in itself could signify utopia.

The pedagogic inclination was rooted in a long tradition that, from Alexander Hamilton and John Quincy Adams, favored an elitist approach to American foreign policy. The demagogic one evoked the populist tendencies of Jacksonian America. Each of these two approaches fed the Wilsonian vision of interdependence, whereby American national security was connected to global security, and American national identity was correlated to the evolution of a global identity. The United States' rise to global power, together with its political ideas, forging a centralized nation-state out of an immigrant experience, and an economic drive justifying the constant reiteration of its "frontier" experience through market expansion overseas, impelled a proselytizing foreign policy. The task of the elitist was thus to *explain* the complexity of interdependence; whereas that of the populist was to *mobilize* toward international commitments a public opinion still strongly tempted by isolationism. From the pedagogic standpoint it was a matter of "coping with evil," of dealing pragmatically with any sort of threats to world democracy, and of harnessing the most dangerous elements of global interdependence while also finding ways to utilize most of its benefits.[8] Demagogic appeals instead had to promise the "eradication of evil"—as in Woodrow Wilson's decision to enter World War I in order to make it "the war to end all wars." Ideally, the pedagogic approach would have helped temper the demagogic excesses necessary to maximize popular consensus. But America's commitments to an anticommunist crusade escalated instead of clinging to the initially confined idea of containing the communist threat.

This does not simply mean that demagogy trumped the elite. In fact, given the universalist tone of the confrontation with communism, it was often difficult to discern the pedagogic from the demagogic assertions of some of the most elitist policy makers, such as George Kennan, Dean Acheson, and, later, Paul Nitze, Walt Rostow, or, from the conservative side, William F.

Buckley Jr., James Burnham, and Jeanne Kirkpatrick. Particularly significant in the early Cold War were the dilemmas within the Democratic ranks.
Truman's advisers frequently regretted the need to simplify the message and
pound the sense of threat even, or perhaps especially, into the minds of the
country's leaders. As Acheson complained in 1950, "the task of the public
officer seeking to explain and gain support for a major policy is not that
of the writer of a doctoral thesis. Qualification must give way to simplicity
of statement, nicety and nuance to bluntness, almost brutality, in carrying
home a point." Kennan was even more caustic, arguing that "no policy and
no concept . . . will . . . stick in our government unless it can be drummed into
the minds of a very large number of persons, including quite a few whose
mental development has not advanced very far beyond the age which is said
to be the criterion for the production of movies in Hollywood."[9] But these
intellectual elitists were not simply coming to terms with politics. Their very
understanding of the communist threat contained a demagogic undertone.
There is no doubt, for example, that Kennan's seminal Long Telegram, which
set the tone for a containment strategy, displayed an *intellectual*, not populist, rhetoric that demonized the enemy.[10] This point becomes evident when
we consider the reflections of Reinhold Niebuhr, the Cold War's most influential American theologian and philosopher.

As a liberal who embraced the ideas of the Vital Center and as a cofounder of the Americans for Democratic Action (ADA) in 1947, Niebuhr
demonstrated that American intellectuals could be, like their French *engagé* counterparts, profoundly reformist in pursuit of a pragmatic, realist
approach to social and international life. But at the same time he offered a
Manichean vision of the Cold War. After all, the main purpose of ADA was to
counter the soft approach to international communism of many former New
Dealers, and especially of the increasingly dissident Henry A. Wallace. As a
religious man, Niebuhr is best remembered for his accent on inherently sin-
ful and egotistic human nature, and on its effects on power in society. Being
so finite, the argument went, human beings are overwhelmed with anxieties
that foster a "will-to-power" and, ultimately, conflict. Emphasizing the "egotistic corruption in all human virtue,"[11] Niebuhr dismissed those optimists
who, in the tradition of the Enlightenment, believed that science and reason could compensate for the imperfections of the human spirit. He consequently spared no criticism of the American idealists who had conducted
foreign policy in the first half of the twentieth century. As a social guide and
genuine internationalist, Niebuhr also contended that such "imperfectibil-
ity" did not exempt humanity, and, more specifically, imperfect America,
from seeking improvement wherever possible. Both his realist urge in for-

eign policy and his social commitment seemed to suggest *coping* with evil. Indeed, like George Kennan, Niebuhr recommended a restrained policy of containment, and he frequently warned against the opposite temptations of disengagement and arrogance in American foreign policy.

Yet, in confronting the prophets of human perfectibility, Niebuhr, like Kennan, found his own perfect struggle. It was the communist pretension to a perfect solution to all human troubles that turned the relativist Niebuhr into a preacher of absolutes. Most alarming, in his view, was that the communists, through their claim to practice scientific Marxism, intended to optimize humanity by means of social control. Ignoring, or pretending to ignore, human egotism and will-to-power, the communists embodied the worst of all evils, because, unlike the Nazis, they posed "as the liberators of every class or nation which they intend[ed] to enslave"; and they were thus more "consistently totalitarian in every political and historical environment." Their claims of omniscience "reveal[ed] the real pathos of the ideological problem. For the greater the pretension of purity and disinterestedness, the greater the impurity." Such impurity entailed dishonesty, too, as Marxism proved that human egotistical nature would not be tamed by science, but rather would maneuver science into the most unscrupulous power goals. Communism, Niebuhr concluded, was no less than an ominous "organized evil which spreads cruelty throughout the world and confronts us everywhere with faceless men who are immune to every form of moral and political suasion."[12] While all the other political ideas could be improved, there was no hope for this unmitigated evil. It needed not to be *coped* with but *eradicated.*

Domestically, Niebuhr did not serve the reformist impulse well, as McCarthyism could exploit his assertions, adding populist overtones. Internationally, it became difficult to distinguish his call for containment from his appeals for a crusade against communism.[13] Niebuhr, Kennan, Acheson, and several other members of the U.S. foreign policy establishment after them, proved that the complexity of interdependence, and of the Cold War itself, needed not be distilled into a simplistic witch hunt. It was instead the very complexity, ambiguity, duplicity, and pervasiveness of communist "evil" itself that rendered the confrontation so universal and unstoppable.[14]

The debate about the evils of communism was also an internal debate that entailed diverging notions of American exceptionalism. The early Cold War would be the occasion for a great degree of self-doubt for most Cold War liberals, and self-righteousness for most Cold War conservatives. Probably because they were so tempted by a crusading impulse, the former sought to prove that by cultivating enough self-doubt, Americans would "ensure that, unlike the Communists', their idealism never degenerated into fanaticism."

The conservatives, amid uncertainty, sought a renewed faith in America, and argued that only ideological confidence would overcome the opponent's fanatical totalitarianism. According to ex-comrade and militant anticommunist Whittaker Chambers, Americans had to prove that their "faith in God and the freedom He enjoins is as great as Communism's faith in Man." It was in part thanks to this emerging crusade against the red "Anti-Christ" that preacher Billy Graham rose to national prominence: in 1947 he began to denounce the "Sin of Tolerance" toward communism which, in his view, was "masterminded by Satan." It was from some of America's ex-Trotzkyists, James Burnham especially, that, in the early Cold War, came the strongest appeals to "roll back," instead of containing that "demonic" force.[15] Having utterly rejected the ideas of communism with which they had associated themselves in the 1930s, these former radicals—several of whom, including Willi Schlamm, Frank Mayer, Max Eastman, and Suzanne LaFollette, would end up contributing to Buckley's staunchly conservative *National Review*— assumed a special aura of learned converts to the causes of free-market capitalism and American patriotism.

While these apocalyptic—political or religious—debates fully erupted in the first years of the Cold War, the immediate postwar period foretold them, revealing a growing comprehension on both sides of the Atlantic that the pragmatic needs of postwar reconstruction went hand in hand with a capacity and willingness to dream again. France and Italy mattered enormously in this sense, because their need for material restoration matched their need for illusions, and because the Communists in both countries, as I have noted,[16] showed an immediate ability to assert their national presence based on both these needs. Due to these developments, the two countries represented a crucial test of strength for the emerging Western alliance, and they held the potential for the worst Western defeat, by subversion or implosion rather than invasion.

Since Soviet influence in France and Italy merged with Western traditions through the two parties, several U.S. officials soon recognized the terms of this ideological and civilizational battle and were quickly induced to reflect on America's own image and role as well. The first such reflections originated among the two ambassadors and the midlevel staff members at the State Department; they did not immediately evolve into a clear strategy tackling every aspect of leftist influence in France and Italy. And yet it would be too simplistic to say that the U.S. government ignored these analyses, and that at first it ascribed communist advances in the two countries solely to Europe's postwar economic aberration. Moreover, many of these views did lay the ground for America's political strategies in France and Italy.

It is true that the United States refrained from heavy intervention in French and Italian affairs until 1947, planning direct involvement only in case of emergency, such as the never discarded possibility of communist insurrection, and that it otherwise resorted to economic rehabilitation as the best means to bolster the legitimacy of the moderate and conservative parties in both governments. The thesis that communism thrives on economic distress could find no better confirmation than in the elemental struggle between leftist and moderate-conservative forces in war-devastated Western Europe. But this was only the simplest "core" of the problem. Although most American officials recognized the nationalist appeal of the French and Italian Communist Parties, and their institutional clout, they at first largely failed to notice the parties' intellectual power. Recognition of these facts connoted a political and psychological battle that added a margin to the more substantial confrontation based on economic choices. But it was a crucial margin, which the United States needed to master in order to make its aid look less conditional, its political and strategic control less imposing, and to convince the French and the Italians that American hegemony respected pluralism. All this resort to what today would be called "soft power," while still lacking an institutional organization, was however amply discussed between the U.S. administration and the two embassies.

NATION-BUILDING, STATUS, AND DOMINOES

The experience of American history favored a comprehensive approach of "nation-building," a complete restructuring or even overhaul of a country's political and social institutions. The United States, it has been argued, has been attached to this idea more than Western European nations because its own cultural identity was based more on political creed than on a national religion or sense of ethnicity. It was an identity shaped mainly by traditions of constitutionalism and democracy.[17] This fact, in addition to an international environment that emphasized the contrasting utopias, and the realization that the French and Italian Communist Parties might be more dangerous as parliamentary than as insurrectionary opponents, intensified America's determination to help mold the two countries' return to constitutional democracy and to monitor their national resurgence carefully.

These were also the formative years of the political movement of the Vital Center, which combined progressive reform and staunch anticommunism to influence both the domestic and foreign policies of the Truman administration.[18] Throughout the period of the Grand Alliance, even after the war,

American anticommunism remained guarded. But it was never as ambivalent as the anti-Americanism of Italian or French Left extremists. In this view, communism in Western Europe constituted a fifth column of a former wartime ally, a no longer trustworthy ideological foe. Staunch anticommunism of course set its own limits. As a consequence, the United States failed to understand all the elements and subtleties of anti-Americanism, communist and noncommunist, in France and Italy. For Washington, the notion persisted that extraordinary circumstances had created an imbalance in those two countries—now perceived as the new "sick men of Europe."[19] Initial American reactions were thus comprehensive but also tentative, mechanical, and culturally naive.

Americans' own identification of the state as embodied in the nation—based on both their own experience, and on the apparent success of their approach to postwar Western Germany and Japan, prevented a full understanding of the European distinction between state and a national community that could be defined by shared history and culture. The PCI and PCF had in some ways penetrated the state, but had even more seized elements that had bound together their respective nations' histories and cultures. While this discrepancy over what constituted national identity was an overarching reason for the shortcomings of postwar America's anticommunist strategy, even Washington's best conceived moves found immediate obstacles and contradictions.

The most prominent contradiction actually came from the French and Italian leaders themselves. Out of both sincere need for assistance and desire to manipulate their powerful ally, they invited a U.S. role in stabilizing their countries in every way. These appeals began a long pattern of promotion of American hegemony, and amounted to a local endorsement of the Americans' pervasive yet state-focused nation-building approach. Institutional issues were as immediately evident as those of economic instability. Prime Minister Alcide De Gasperi and his ambassador to Washington, Alberto Tarchiani, justified the delay of the elections for a Constitutional Assembly until mid-1946 with the argument that the Italians were "unprepared" for democracy, and pleaded that, without help from the United States, they would have insufficient time to instill these values in the electorate. Charles de Gaulle upheld his country's democratic traditions with more pride, but clearly hinted that, if the old alliance with the United States as a peer were not restored, France might revert to the petty, factionalized system of the Third Republic.[20]

Institutional and political weakness may have been sufficient to prompt American involvement. But from the tone and arguments of those invitations, the problem seemed vaster: it was about saving civilizations more than nations. Much of the "nation-building" approach has originated from the perception that the failure of one democracy might portend the erosion of whole regions, ideologies, and cultures. The first depictions of possible Cold War domino effects came from France and Italy. When Togliatti returned to Italy in March 1944, Carlo Sforza, a post–World War I foreign minister who became a prominent member of the Italian émigré community in the United States during Fascism, evoked fears of continental collapse: communist influence in Rome could usher in the whole "Sovietization of Europe." Tarchiani repeated this appeal several times. Finding a receptive audience in Washington a year later, he finally convinced the president and the State-War-Navy Coordinating Committee that once a weakened and demoralized Italy went "totalitarian," the rest of Europe could also be lost.[21] De Gaulle was both more subtle and more brutal in his warnings. Subtlety characterized his old-fashioned balance of power when he signed a friendship treaty with the Soviet Union in December 1944, fully recognizing the new Cold War power dynamic and using his diplomatic move to obtain more support from the United States. Blunt and brutal was his blackmail, as he reminded the Americans, "If I cannot work with you I must work with the Soviets in order to survive, even if it is only for a while, and even if in the long run they gobble us up, too." And with that "gobbling up" the rest of Europe might go as well. Earlier, de Gaulle had persuaded Eisenhower that if France fell into the Soviet orbit "the other countries of Western Europe w[ould] do the same." De Gaulle's successors continued this litany until the Cold War division of Europe settled in.[22]

The Church added momentum to these invitations with its own depictions of atheistic communism as the West's ultimate civilizational enemy. It is no wonder that Monsignor Tardini, as the Vatican's deputy secretary of state in early 1947, urged the Truman Doctrine's extension from its recipients, Greece and Turkey, to the rest of the politically embattled Mediterranean. It seemed that the United States was readying to join a crusade as much as an alliance.[23]

So these appeals had a double significance. First, following the domino theory, they encouraged its corollary, that immediate action was needed to "nip the problem in the bud."[24] The United States sought preemptive actions to hold the Communists in check, thus begging the question of whether such preemption provoked the very hostility the Americans meant to avert. Second, the appeals anticipated and, to some extent, nurtured the approach Americans were already inclined to follow, a comprehensive one focused on restoring the vitality of the state, of its democracy; and yet they did not understand the national and cultural roots of the problems they confronted. Washington's initial approach to the two countries was more simplistic and haphazard than sensitive and cautious. Certainly it could be accused of being too overtly propagandistic.

THE WINNER'S GENEROSITY

Since injured national pride was the most directly recognizable feeling behind any sort of anti-Americanism, the winner, or liberator, had to show modesty. The United States recognized restoring the national dignity and prestige of France and Italy was as urgent as economic assistance. Such diplomatic gestures in most respects preceded assistance—and they combined an attention to national sensibilities with support of a quick institutional balance favoring liberal democracy.

Following the Italian armistice, the country's new leaders fruitlessly demanded that their status as "cobelligerent" be replaced with one of "allied power." While the United States and, especially, Great Britain, refused to make this concession, Washington immediately discussed ways to rehabilitate the country economically *and* politically. President Roosevelt opposed Winston Churchill's attempt to preserve a monarchical regime in Rome, a solution that might have reduced Italy to a weak and compliant British client, subjugated by a punitive peace treaty, and as a result, also highly unstable.[25] The famous Joint Declaration made by Roosevelt and Churchill at Hyde Park, New York, in September 1944 adjusted Italy's status. It was a "grand gesture"—as the British premier called it—announcing a revision of the armistice clauses, aid through the United Nations Relief and Recovery Administration (UNRRA), and, not the least, the deletion of the word "Control" from the Allied Control Commission, a correction implying greater administrative and diplomatic autonomy for the occupied country. A year later, at Potsdam, President Truman promised the Italians "the dignity of the Free" and the "certainty that no condition essential to their development w[ould] be denied or impaired." He also prodded the British and the Soviets into a joint declaration announcing the Big Three's intention to negotiate a final peace treaty with the Italian government quickly, and to support Italy's application for membership in the United Nations.[26] British General Harold Alexander best summed up the case for a milder treatment of Italy, stating in May 1945, "We cannot afford to keep the Italians down too much and thus leave them no alternative but to go Red."[27]

The pressure to restore France as a great power came from Great Britain first. Thanks mainly to Churchill's concern about reestablishing a balance of power on the continent and to his confidence in de Gaulle's cabinet "despite Communist threats," France obtained membership in the Allied Control Council for Germany, with a concomitant occupation zone, and admission as one of five permanent members of the U.N. Security Council.[28] In Washington the State Department quickly sensed the same urgency. In a briefing book for the Yalta Conference, U.S. officials argued that it was "in the interest of the United States to take full account of [the] psychological factor and . . . to treat France in all respects on the basis of her potential power and influence rather than on the basis of her present strength." Secretary of State Edward Stettinius sharpened the argument, contending that a rejuvenated France would not only help forge a postwar order in Europe but would also make a favorable impression on "other small countries of Europe which profess to fear the results of a peace imposed by non-European powers." In May, Truman even recognized that France should resume "its rightful and eminent place" among the "world powers" (thus implying a restoration of its imperial role) and promised it a portion of America's occupation zone in Germany.[29]

Stettinius's thinking, however, was more consequential. The idea that continental Europe needed to select a guiding power—a champion of European autonomy—would be an enduring one in American Cold War policy. It was not simply a matter of fostering self-reliant allies. Within a few years it would also become part of an American design to supplant its allies' nationalist feelings with a new commitment to interdependence, a plan that also helped undermine the powerful nationalist appeal of the French and Italian Communists.

INTERPRETING COMMUNIST NATIONALISM

Through the first year after the war, America's concessions of status shored up anticommunist forces in France and Italy. They reflected a general understanding of the new patriotic credentials of the two Communist Parties. Jefferson Caffery, a former assistant secretary of state and one of the most respected figures in the State Department, played a crucial role as ambassador in Paris, shaping Washington's views of French political culture. His perceptive analyses drew the State Department's attention to the PCF's "Republican legality." It was relatively easy to comprehend that the party was bent on "persuading the masses and the lower middle classes that the real governing elite of the nation [could] be found only in [its] ranks," hence its moderation, especially after de Gaulle stepped down in January 1946. But Caffery further saw that the party could combine respectability with revolutionary promise. Evoking a similarity with the PCI's *doppiezza*, he depicted the French Communists as "endeavor[ing] to have their cake and eat it too by attempting to prove to the nation that while they [were] not shirking their patriotic duties as a 'government party,' they [had] not been permitted to form a government 'in the image of the nation' which could alone save France from disaster."[30]

The problem with nationalism in France was that, for the time being, it led the nation to clash with its Western allies, and the United States especially, more than with Moscow. Furthermore, Washington also played up its view of the French as cynical, fickle, and intense nationalists. Their lack of a constituency in America, their contempt, politically best personified by de Gaulle, for American utilitarianism and anti-intellectualism, only widened this divide within the West.[31]

France's attitude toward defeated Germany proved particularly troublesome. While the Anglo-Americans contemplated German revitalization starting from their zones of occupation, de Gaulle and his immediate successors insisted on a punitive approach, including the division of the country into small federated states and an autonomous Rhineland under French control. Caffery repeatedly warned of the dangerous implications of France's anti-German policy, which, together with an anti-American stance, would favor French communist nationalism. The specter of a German revival, which still animated France's deepest fears, overshadowed the French Communists' ambiguity between *patrie* and the Soviet "motherland." In the end, Caffery concluded in February 1947, "posing to the average Frenchman as the strongest defender of his fatherland, especially against the German 'menace' and 'international capitalism,' the Soviet 'Trojan Horse' [was] so well camouflaged that millions of Communist militants, sympathizers, and opportunists [had] been brought to believe that the best way to defend France [was] to identify French national interests with the aims of the Soviet Union." In fact, the Soviets were not easy on France, opposing especially a French-dominated Ruhr. But there was a great deal of Anglo-American obstruction, too, in both Germany and in the French colonies. This gave the Communists a chance to deflect public attention away from Soviet vetoes and toward London's and Washington's attempts to supplant French interests everywhere.[32]

Italy, too, encountered resistance from the Anglo-Americans in the drafting of the peace treaty, especially on matters that affected national sentiment, such as those regarding the retention of overseas colonies or the disputed border with Yugoslavia. This is why Ambassadors Alexander Kirk and, with even more determination, his successor, James Clement Dunn, became champions of leniency toward a former enemy that had been converted to the Allied cause. Nowhere more than in Italy could the pride of the winner potentially stir the resentment of the defeated. It was the combination of neglect—as Washington still did not consider Italy a focal point of its diplomacy—and punishment that could either reignite the nationalism of the extreme Right, or reinforce the nationalist credentials of the PCI.[33]

But catering to nationalism in Italy also required more careful balancing of the country's economic needs than it did in France. Italy needed to be kept in its place as a minor power relying on "the International Security Organizations for her security in the future," as Undersecretary of State Joseph Grew explained to President Truman in June 1945. Grew argued that fostering an overly ambitious foreign policy for vanquished Italy would divert efforts from the tasks of reconstruction, thus letting the Communists take advantage of economic distress.[34] Pressures from Ambassador Kirk and General Alexander finally persuaded Eisenhower and even the usually unsympathetic George Kennan that fine-tuning between pride and economic necessity was crucial in Italy. Harsh armistice terms, Eisenhower argued in October 1945, had become "obsolete," and the new American objective was to "strengthen Italy economically and politically so she [could] withstand the forces that threaten[ed] to sweep her into a *new* totalitarianism [*sic*]." No viable democracy could be restored in Italy, Kennan added a few months later, if the Allies failed to upstage the Soviets in accepting Italy as redeemed and recoverable. But, as Alexander summarized the Anglo-American position, there was "no difficulty in reconciling the objective of establishing Italy as a useful and prosperous European state not under Soviet influence with the objective of forcing Italy to drop all pretense of being a great power."[35] Leaders in Rome were somewhat less enthusiastic, constantly warning that any detraction from *both* the country's sense of dignity *and* its economic solvency would generate unprecedented anti-American sentiment among the Italian public. Their invitation for "psychological" as well as material assistance would not yield results until the spring of 1947.[36]

From Paris, Caffery had already attempted to steer Washington in a more subtle direction. He carefully reviewed his accounts of France's resentful nationalism and the appeal to it by the Left. His conclusions anticipated three major approaches in the U.S. diplomacy of stabilization in Europe: he distinguished between manageable and out-of-control anti-Americanism; he suggested dealing with the moderate Left over the conservative parties; and he envisioned tactics to drive wedges between strongly nationalist Communist Parties.

By demonstrating flexibility toward difficult allies, by even accepting a certain dose of anti-Americanism from them, the United States would preempt anti-American campaigns dominated by the extreme Left. Understanding the importance of de Gaulle's nationalist appeal as the counterpoint to communist nationalism, Caffery resigned to dealing with him, the "sour puss" of

French leadership. What mattered most was that de Gaulle was no puppet of the United States, and that his anti-American slant also gave France the confidence it needed to cope with its relative decline: both elements promised to take ammunition away from communist propaganda.[37] To a lesser degree, U.S. diplomats hinted the same with the increasingly demanding, dependent, but hardly subservient De Gasperi, and with other Italian leaders such as Carlo Sforza, who, with experience as foreign minister in the prefascist years, represented an old diplomatic tradition that mitigated the overwhelming reality of outside dominance.[38] This approach would evolve into a deliberate strategy in the following decade.

In the postwar period, however, both de Gaulle and the proudest Italian moderate leaders soon became a liability. Their old-fashioned nationalism meant first that any conflict of interest with the United States was at times too direct, as for example in France's desire for retribution in Germany, or in Italy's demands on Trieste at a time when Yugoslavia's relationship with Moscow remained uncertain. That chauvinism also meant attachment to even more anachronistic claims elsewhere, such as France's effort to keep Indochina thoroughly subjugated, or vanquished Italy's wish to retain most of its African colonies. Such demands were not only unrealistic; they also contradicted the two nations' claims of embracing a "democratic foreign policy"[39] and moral resurrection as new sources of national prestige. Worse still, they surrendered these claims to the Communists, who upheld their *democratic patriotism* against the *imperialist nationalism* of their conservative government partners. That was why it would gradually become critical for Washington to combine encouragement of national pride with the suggestion that Stettinius had first posed of also fostering a new allegiance to continental integration.

One way for the United States to reach both goals was to adopt a more flexible and enlightened approach to the moderate Left in both countries. Caffery urged Washington to depart from its familiar approach with traditional elites and conservatives in France. This opened an enduring U.S. strategy aimed at splitting the Left in both Italy and France. Moreover, moderate Socialists in France and Italy embraced international cooperation that, while ostensibly calling for a European third force between the two superpowers, ultimately favored Western integration. Finally, a split on the Left would also constrain the two Communist Parties' institutional power, especially precluding their monopoly over the trade union movement. Indeed, the main American trade unions—AFL, CIO, and ILGWU—had since the fall of 1944 contacted social democrat leaders in Europe, starting to promote through them a free trade union movement. The AFL set up a Free Trade

Union Committee directed by Jay Lovestone, and Irving Brown became its representative in Paris the following year. The first funding to Socialist and Action Parties in Italy came from the Italian American Labor Council in late 1944.[40] This is not the place to analyze how this support evolved into specific strategies aimed at dividing the French and Italian Lefts. But it is worth noting that the two embassies and Washington quickly realized the advantages of a discerning instead of an indiscriminate anticommunism.

By the time de Gaulle left office in January 1946, Caffery no longer thought the General's chauvinistic policies were France's main asset; he rather welcomed the new MRP-SFIO-PCF coalition because it seemed to curb communist radicalism, while simultaneously prompting a more authoritative role for the Socialists.[41] When the French government sent the historic leader of the Socialists, Léon Blum, as special envoy to the United States to negotiate a massive loan in the spring of 1946, optimism about the choice prevailed in Washington. The ex-premier of the Popular Front did not deny his Marxist credentials, but he had by now rejected any prospect of political alliance with the PCF. He also maintained his popularity among French working-class families. His preference for a cooperative approach to Germany, his old friendship with former U.S. ambassador to Paris William Bullit, his ties with the main Wall Street financial institutions and the Jewish community, and, not least, his imprisonment at Buchenwald all added to his impressive charisma and moral stature, helping him draw public support in the United States. Caffery supported the deal above all to boost the Socialists in the June elections for a Constituent Assembly. What mattered most to the ambassador was that Blum's trip to America helped finalize the divorce between the SFIO and the Communists.[42] Blum confirmed that a prominent section of the Marxist leadership in France would support American policy aims.

While the Christian Democrats seized the role of Italy's most reliable anticommunist bulwark, the United States did not hide its desire for a more center-left coalition. But from the outset, the pursuit of wedge tactics toward Marxists did not work as well in Italy as in France. As early as 1944 American officials contemplated supporting the PSIUP Socialists of Pietro Nenni, who had not yet confirmed a unity of action pact with the Communists. Toward the end of 1946, the State Department still entertained the idea of "knocking off Nenni's ideological blinders" by inviting him to Washington together with De Gasperi for the major loan the Italian prime minister was negotiating.[43] The prime choice for Washington, however, had already become the moderate Giuseppe Saragat. The United States was not involved in the socialist split that in January 1947 gave birth to Saragat's Socialist Workers Party (PSLI), but it did not hesitate to take advantage of it. Saragat immediately established contacts with the AFL and with the American embassy.[44] The Italian social democratic leader may have not been as charismatic as Léon Blum, but he was younger and, like Blum, he became an emblem of a possible American cooperation with progressive forces in Europe. Unfortunately, with his pro-American fervor, he also became the target of an enduring communist/socialist campaign that stigmatized left-wing cooperation with America as the worst betrayal of the workers' and the nation's interests.

But flexibility toward the moderate Left continued in Washington for a while. Throughout 1947, George Kennan insisted that direct assaults on communism would be counterproductive, and that it would be more profitable to rely on "the natural forces of resistance within the respective countries that the Communists are attacking." Those forces were better chosen from the Left, lest the U.S. be associated with "unsavory elements on the right." Kennan further elaborated on this remarkable flexibility. After publicizing his containment policy, he speculated that communists who were forced to cooperate in a government with the moderate Left might continue to bend to government responsibility, become more tractable than if they stayed in "unscrupulous opposition," and finally might even "repudiate the Kremlin's authority."[45]

Indeed, understanding communist nationalism meant also detecting the potential clash *between* Communist Parties with strong patriotic accents. The third approach proposed by Caffery, starting as early as mid-1945, was a still roughly conceived notion of wedge tactics, exploiting conflicting national interests to break the unity of the Communist Parties in Western and Eastern Europe. One additional advantage of supporting moderate Socialists, the ambassador thought, was that their tendency to accept international cooperation would by contrast highlight the most chauvinistic traits of the Communist Parties. The potential for discord between the PCF and the Communist Parties of Germany or Poland was all too apparent. And of course the PCI, while maintaining fraternal ties with its Yugoslavian comrades, could not avoid the contradiction this posed to its call for national resurgence everywhere, including the disputed Trieste borderland.[46] The potential for conflict between the PCF and the PCI was less evident, but it could develop from Franco-Italian postwar border disputes. Walter Dowling, who chaired the State Department Division of Southern European Affairs, subtly noted in early 1946 that French officials, assuming that Germany would look south for commercial or even territorial expansion after being blocked on both its Eastern and Western borders, placed a high priority on securing France's Southern border. In addition, he continued, Foreign Minister Georges Bidault needed a diplomatic triumph to present "before the

Communist colleagues in the French cabinet." He insisted, for example, on satisfying the nation's claims over sections of the Franco-Italian borderland of Val d'Aosta. Dowling concluded that since the PCI was also adamant about retaining Italy's northwestern border, the two Communist Parties would actually profit from their respective nationalist posturing. But Ambassador Caffery and other officials continued to argue that this contrast could benefit U.S. designs: it could at least in part deflect the two parties' anti-American rhetoric toward each other, and debunk their notion that patriotism and proletarian internationalism were reconcilable.[47]

The opportunity to foster such a "fratricidal" clash seemed at hand so long as the two parties pursued national acceptance above anything else. In fact, both French and Italian Communists, politically embattled, confirmed their solidarity. Their pro–Grand Alliance approach prevented an open conflict with any communist party of the East, while it denounced Western preparations for a "Third War [sic] between Slavs and the Occident." Togliatti also worked in the summer of 1945 to avoid a possible divorce between his party and the PCF, by ignoring the French partisans' "ignoble treatment" of Italian prisoners of war, by sending party workers to France to help in the reconstruction effort, and by promising a genuine democratic turnover of Italy's bureaucracy. A year later, from the PCF's Central Committee, Jacques Duclos and Maurice Thorez specified that, though victorious France had to stay above Italy in rank and especially in naval power, the two parties should continue to cooperate on every international matter. Pietro Nenni also posed as a broker, commenting in his *Avanti* newspaper in May 1946 that France and Italy should follow a policy that would "enable them to identify the conception of honor with the common effort for the defense of their common civilization."[48] The appeal fused together democratic nationalism and civilizational solidarity (against the external influence from the United States). America's wedge tactics aimed at isolating the two Communist Parties internationally, never as prominent as Caffery had suggested, would be only mildly repeated after the Hungarian uprisings of 1956 and the Warsaw Pact's invasion of Czechoslovakia in 1968.

IMPACT OF SOVIET MOVES

Isolating or discrediting communist nationalism was difficult also because the Soviet appeal and friendship still retained credibility. Having been the first power to recognize the provisional governments of Italy and to sign a postwar treaty of friendship with France, the Soviet Union not only allowed the triumphal return and government participation of Togliatti and Thorez; it also increased its own diplomatic leverage in two countries outside its sphere of influence. Most important, the Soviet twin diplomatic move had the triple effect of strengthening the two Communist Parties' respectability, endorsing their national posture, and—consistently with Stalin's caution at this stage—harnessing their revolutionary impulse. Only this last aspect was welcome in Washington, since it provided an additional reason for dealing cautiously with the communist presence in the two governments. But further reason for the United States to pursue a policy of caution was that an open attack on the Communists under these circumstances could be construed as an attack on Italy's and France's national interests. Under the aegis of the Grand Alliance, the two Communist Parties had received credit for bridging their countries' political impasse. But the fact that their leaders, prompted by Stalin, chose, in Togliatti's words, to "avoid speculating on the contrasts among the great powers,"[49] also implied that they would indeed speculate on the divisions with their coalition partners.

The point was to shift the blame for the imminent division of Europe to the conservatives in the government. In June 1945, Caffery stressed how Thorez, consistently with his pursuit of "popular frontism," winked at the other mass party, the Catholic Mouvement Républicain Populaire, while attacking de Gaulle's "vain chatter about grandeur." This criticism of de Gaulle did not suggest neglect of national interests, for—the ambassador pointed out—the PCF was striving to demonstrate that it alone had first stood up to "Hitlerism," even during the "phoney war," and that "grandeur" could be attained by turning the Franco-Russian treaty of December 1944 into a true extension of the Grand Alliance.[50] De Gaulle instead had pursued the treaty with Moscow mainly to obtain an equivalent recognition and thus peer status and stricter cooperation with the Anglo-Americans.

The Italian provisional government had also approached the Soviets to obtain concessions from the Anglo-Americans and closer relations with them. Moreover, by June 1945 the cabinet of Ferruccio Parri seemed to switch to a cold war of sorts, as Togliatti noted at a meeting of his party's directorate: Rome was now "squandering its diplomatic achievement" by beginning to oppose Moscow's policies in Poland, and by turning the claim over Trieste into an anticommunist strategy. This, Togliatti reasoned, also undermined the pact for national unity attained the previous year, foretelling a desire to ostracize the PCI.[51] In this light, de Gaulle, the Christian Democrats, and their political allies immediately seemed to promote the division of Europe into spheres of influence, while the Communists came across as champions of nonalignment rather than as Moscow's followers. This argument, as an additional advantage, continued to hold sway over the Socialists, who in both countries included advocates of genuine pacifism and neutralism.[52]

The two governments' approach to Moscow determined American reactions to French and Italian Communism in two ways. First, Washington refrained from moving decisively against the PCI and PCF until the Soviets fully showed the limits of their diplomatic support. By early 1947 both the French and the Italian leaders had soberly reassessed their expectations. French designs over Germany never coincided as much as expected with those of the Soviets; Italy never seemed to Moscow more than a diplomatic pawn to obtain an equivalent recognition from the West of its control over Bulgaria and Romania. Once Moscow consolidated its dominance over Eastern Europe, it was no longer concerned with reciprocal concessions from the West, and it turned more openly hostile toward both countries. With the spheres of influence so determined, the United States felt it had more leeway to confront the French and Italian Communists without risking an irresistible backlash from "proletarian nationalism."

The second outcome of France's and Italy's diplomatic bets was far more ironic. The centrist parties had played a nineteenth-century-style game of balance of power within the emerging reality of a bipolar world. All the diplomatic concessions they obtained from the Anglo-Americans were not so much a result of their pressure as the product of fears in London and Washington that, by opening to Moscow, both governments were in fact increasing their vulnerability to communist subversion. Paris and Rome thus conveyed not the promise of becoming reliable powers and partners but potential imminent collapse, the prospect of being "gobbled up" by the Soviets, as de Gaulle had put it. In other words, the two governments, while trying to avoid strict American tutelage, actually reinforced their condition as captives of Cold War rivalries. Worse still, their attempt to resume realpolitik turned their nations into grounds for greater ideological, civilizational confrontation between America and communism.[53]

PERCEIVING COMMUNIST INSTITUTIONAL POWER
AND POTENTIAL FOR INSURRECTION

The same caution the Americans had used toward the effects of Soviet diplomacy applied more specifically to the institutional dimension of communist power in France and Italy. Immersion in parliamentary tactics increased the two Communist Parties' subversive potential, but it also helped moderate them. An open attack by Washington, through its political allies in France and Italy, on communist institutional power could spark a communist insurrection at the time when the two provisional governments were weakest.

Of course, U.S. union leaders' work toward the creation of a free trade union movement in Europe directly addressed the connection between institutional and political power. Empowering the moderate Left, it eventually became clear, was essential to diminishing communist institutional leverage. But this strategy also had to be harmonized with the need to strike a balance between planning and laissez-faire forces in the French and Italian economies. The State Department, and in particular the pro–laissez faire economic counselor at the U.S. embassy in Rome, Henry J. Tasca, noted that although Italy's recovery required some economic planning, and although the Istituto per la Ricostruzione Industriale (IRI), a huge mixed state and private industrial conglomerate created during Fascism, could help do that job, it was also clear that the Communists were too eager to absorb and expand the public component of this organization for their own purposes. But rather than pressing the Italian government with specific planning recommendations, the embassy simply encouraged Italy's classic liberals and Alcide De Gasperi, prime minister from December 1945, to adopt some planning themselves. Similar concerns, and a similar reticence to intervene, applied to the French modernization plan of Jean Monnet, which the Communists married to their own calls for increased productivity. Washington welcomed Monnet's pro–Americanism and his pursuit of a cure through U.S. assistance rather than through seizing German assets as retribution.[54]

The reality of "partitocracy" in France and Italy also dawned on some U.S. officials. As intelligence reports from the two embassies concluded, parties in France and Italy were thoroughly "dug-in" in most of both countries' social and economic strata. In contrast to the situation in the United States, political parties had a "relatively firm control over agriculture, local administration and social and economic life in general." The elimination of a major party—namely, the Communists—would have been "an invitation to active opposition and political-economic sabotage."[55]

But the possibility of subversion seemed just as high with the Communists in the government. The United States carefully considered the "Trojan horse" factor: the Communists' control of the machinery of the state through nationalized industries, government bureaucracy, and the army could prepare them for insurrection as much as for seizing power legally. According to the second secretary of the U.S. embassy in Paris, Norris Chipman, the Communists' "secret penetration of State institutions" was inseparable from their "clandestine military preparations," simply waiting for Moscow's orders.[56] The United States' own preparation for emergency measures in France and Italy has been amply analyzed, and needs no retelling here. What should be emphasized is that, since most alarms about communist armed factions came from conservative or rightist groups in France and Italy, Washington became acutely aware of the risk of becoming involved by manipulation. If conservatives from the French and Italian side managed to co-opt those U.S. officials, such as Tasca, or Robert Murphy (involved in French affairs since Vichy), who were already inclined toward staunch anticommunism,[57] they would have also corroborated the Communists' depiction of a reactionary conspiracy orchestrated from Washington.

By mid-1946 most U.S. officials had concluded that, while still a possibility, armed insurrection represented only a last resort for the two Communist Parties, whose leaders preferred to "pose as Frenchmen and Italians" in view of forthcoming elections in both countries. The *doppiezza* imposed extreme caution on the American side, since preempting an insurrection probably would have amplified the Communists' nationalist appeal. Unless the Kremlin decided to use its "fifth column" in France and Italy with insurrectionary strikes and even "armed uprisings," Caffery reasoned in May 1946, Washington should refrain from interfering with local politics altogether; for this meddling would only favor the Communists' pursuit of the nationalist "petty bourgeoisie." Later that year, a report by the Central Intelligence Group (which preceded the CIA) confirmed that the risk of upheaval would be greater with the Communists in opposition than if they were participating in government. For the time being, the United States could only hope that democracy would not be eroded from within.[58]

POWER AND LIMITS OF ECONOMIC CURES

When in late 1947 George Kennan made his case for supporting the "natural forces of resistance" in France and Italy, he was mainly summing up the advantages of the Marshall Plan, which had just given birth to the European Recovery Program. General Lucius Clay, chief of the American zone of occupation in Germany, had previously warned there could be "no choice between becoming a Communist on 1500 calories and a believer in democracy on 1000." Long before U.S. officials reached that conclusion, notable French and Italian representatives had pointed out the mass appeal of the "Communism of the belly," as Don Luigi Sturzo, founder of the first Christian Democratic party (Partito Popolare), had called it.[59]

But Kennan's argument was more articulated than the economic determinism exemplified by General Clay. The director of the Policy Planning Staff contended that the strength of U.S. assistance should lie in its combination of economic benefits, political targeting (helping America's political allies), and international coordination (which would reveal to Europe's governments the advantages of interdependence over those of economic and political nationalism). Only such a combination, Washington would come to realize, could help undermine the communist appeal. Moreover, economic assistance, especially if coordinated internationally, presented the advantage of being only an "indirect" interference in each country's political affairs, and thus was less vulnerable to anti-American attacks.[60] Until 1947, U.S. aid policy proved rather ineffective not only because it was a series of insufficient stop-gap measures, but also because it lacked a clear political and international design.

To be sure, even America's immediate postwar assistance—mainly through the United Nations Relief and Rehabilitation Administration for Italy, through the Export-Import Bank for France, and through U.S. government loans for both—was based on the assumption that the American model of productivity, Keynesian reform, and New Deal corporatism should be replicated in Europe. Exporting economic reform would counter backwardness in business practices and in political outlook. It was not meant to abolish concentrations of economic power, for big corporations had proven effective during the last phase of the New Deal, too. Perhaps large private conglomerates *could* reconcile themselves with some necessary government planning and thus co-opt reformist forces from the Left and neutralize the Communists.[61] But the contrast between New Dealers and supporters of free enterprise in Washington or at the Paris and Rome embassies, a parsimonious Congress, and the traditionalist forces in France and Italy, all prevented the transformation of this vision into an immediate strategy. Nevertheless, what counted most in the struggle against *all* aspects of communist power and communist anti-Americanism in France and Italy was that Washington had already established the possibility of turning economic reform into the main instrument of political consensus. Thanks to American-inspired reform, in this view, economic relations in Europe could, as historian Charles Maier best put it, "transcend earlier class conflict," and become altogether "free of conflict."[62]

But in order for economic assistance to appear neutral and apolitical, it had to be conceived first in political terms. It is no accident that the most effective aid measures preceding the Marshall Plan followed a deliberate political plan. This was how Ambassador Caffery championed the loan deal during Léon Blum's visit to the United States; that is, based not on financial solvency but "in terms of its political importance." Undersecretary of State for Economic Affairs William Clayton overcame the objections of those, like Secretary of Treasury Fred Vinson, who still thought in economic terms, and those, like Secretary of Commerce Henry Wallace and Federal Reserve chairman Marriner Eccles, who worried that a "political" loan aimed at influencing foreign elections could backfire and lead to accusations of Yankee "imperialism." Clayton retorted that it was impossible to separate political from economic considerations when thinking about Europe, and that U.S. credit was also a sign of confidence in the French, thus a tribute to their pride, which would counterbalance their resentment of American intrusion.[63] Eccles and Vinson needed no persuasion on Italy. They immediately conceded that political considerations required assistance to this poor new Mediterranean ally "even though it [was] a bad risk" economically. This reasoning prompted a warm welcome for De Gasperi during his visit to the United States several months after the Blum-Byrnes deal. During that visit, John D. Hickerson, director of the State Department's Office of European Affairs, concluded that the loan was above all the "barometer of American confidence in Italy" and that the Italian prime minister felt it "ha[d] acquired an importance far beyond its financial significance."[64]

Indeed, the financial impact was minimal, since the amounts of the two loans were far below what the French and the Italians had requested. But the "political sign," as Ambassador Tarchiani called it, counted far more than the figures. As Marxist economist Antonio Pesenti admitted, De Gasperi's mission thrived amid the Americans' profusion of pro-Italian sentiments. On his return home Blum had been feted with similar fanfare. Moreover, the two statesmen had helped accelerate the formation of a Cold War bipartisan consensus in Washington that let the State Department take the initiative in American foreign economic policy, thus favoring political criteria over economic ones in granting financial assistance abroad.[65]

From Washington's standpoint the twin assistance to France and Italy had the supreme advantage of fostering the forces of modernization and integration in Europe. The Blum-Byrnes agreement had been negotiated partly on the premise that France's planning commissioner, Jean Monnet, had finally prevailed with his "Atlanticist" strategy over the "Nationalists," economists and politicians who had given priority to exacting retribution from Germany. By relying on U.S. assistance as the main source of recovery, France also took its first steps toward accepting a German role in European integration. Leading Italian industrialists, such as FIAT managing director Vittorio Valletta, and steel "baron" Oscar Sinigaglia, had also come up with their own modernization and "Atlanticist" plans. While De Gasperi continued to privilege the laissez-faire forces, he shared with these pro-American "planners" a determination to reconstruct through U.S. aid and an integrated European market.[66] Overall, these developments induced French and Italian statesmen to reconsider the core theme of national rebirth. Departing from a strictly national focus, these statesmen for the first time questioned traditional chauvinism and contemplated a different notion of grandeur, based on managing interdependence. And for the first time also, Washington had managed to calibrate aid with the promotion of interdependence.

But the two agreements, as already noted, came with strings attached that stirred nationalist passions against America's demands.[67] The Blum-Byrnes provision raising the import of Hollywood films was just the most notable example: it hit deep into a cherished national tradition, it showed France's weakness against America's cultural invasion, and it confirmed France's worst fears about America's predatory market forces and cultural shallowness—all aspects that nourished communist anti-American propaganda. According to some U.S. officials, the mass appeal of American films could actually trump that of communist nationalism, further isolating both the PCF and the PCI.[68]

What ultimately prevailed in Washington was a conviction that American aid needed to be complemented by a sagacious resort to psychological means, albeit still broadly and vaguely defined. By early 1947, Ambassador Dunn concluded that the problem in Italy was "fundamentally psychological," and that the United States needed to match material assistance "with adequate propaganda." At the eve of De Gasperi's visit, Walter Dowling put it in starker terms, advocating "a policy so damned pro-Italian that even the dumbest wop would sense the drift, and even the cleverest comrade would have trouble denouncing it." Crude as he might be, the Italian desk officer presented one of the first rough dissections of U.S. Cold War psychological strategy, further explaining:

[This policy] would have to be a judicious mixture of flattery, moral encouragement and considerable material aid. This last needs no advocacy but I might say, as regards the first two elements, that I am sure the Secretary's handshake with De Gasperi at Paris . . . meant as much to the Italians at that moment as all the assistance from UNRRA. . . . This policy would of course require a sustained program for a considerable period. It could not be a one-shot cure, but should consist of a kind word, a loaf of bread, a public tribute to Italian civilization, then another kind word, and so on, with an occasional plug from the sponsors advertising the virtues of democracy American style. Naturally it would not be anti-Communist, nor would it need to be, just pro-Italian. Also, it would cost a lot of money and mean a lot of bother, but if I know anything about Italians, it would pay off handsomely.

Likewise, from Paris, Caffery had earlier favored supplementing financial assistance with thorough publicity campaigns, for the French were reaching "the point where extremists appear to offer the only chance of improvement *in leadership and in material things.*" George Kennan, who had just drafted his Long Telegram defining the strategy of containment against the Soviet Union, further elaborated that an information campaign, based on a genuine "psychological approach," needed to be waged in France. "Our relations with France," he argued, "will be vitally affected by the extent to which the French people get a realistic view of the U.S.S.R." These considerations finally helped shape the Truman Doctrine and the Marshall Plan. Both focused on the division between democracy and authoritarianism, not capitalism versus communism, and, as the president recalled, they showed "that we have something positive and attractive to offer, and not just anti-Communism."[69]

CONFRONTING COMMUNIST CULTURAL POWER

Communists in France and Italy, as I have noted, foresaw the coming of a cultural cold war long before the Americans. The U.S. government indeed had, since World War I, adopted tactics of cultural diffusion. But as means to curb communist influence in the early Cold War, these tactics were even more tentative and haphazard than U.S. economic or diplomatic choices.

In the broadest sense, the confrontation was about political culture, and led the United States to reflect on itself, perhaps especially on the possible distortion of its "permanent revolution." American values could be potentially subverted from within, thanks to a possible political dialogue between dissidents from each side of the Atlantic. Americans' concern about the two strongest Communist Parties in the West never developed into a fear that, by force of example, the Western brand of communism might actually improve the fortunes of communism or left-wing radicalism in the United States, given the rapid decline of the Soviet myth among most leftist American intellectuals. The history of the American Left, according to historian John Patrick Diggins, was "little more than a record of foibles and frustrations." Washington's main worry regarding the PCI and PCF, even during the peak of the American Red Scare, was simply that Western Communism might subvert Western Europe. Yet, as Diggins admits, the reemergence of the Left in Europe could affect political debate in the United States, since, more than anywhere else, the "Left [in the United States] has always identified itself in opposition to the actual state of things and thus affirmed the possibility of hope." To be sure, it was often a betrayed hope and a betrayed ideal, "but the Left's saving remnant is the tension between its promises and its failures." The pursuit of whatever hope and the constant struggle for it were sufficient to leave a deep mark on American society's perception and definition of itself. What was really implied in the Americans' Cold War fears about Western European Communism—even long after the peak of communist power in France and Italy—was that the most insidious forms of left-wing anti-Americanism on *both* sides of the Atlantic could be *mutually* nurtured.[70]

It may then appear strange that the first American cultural moves in post-war France and Italy encouraged populistic themes of national revival that, inadvertently, favored communist propaganda. The first impulse in Washington was to transmit the message of democracy rather than to foster its blossoming from Europe's national realities. The United States showed the benefits of the American way of life, through its most effective instrument of mass culture: Hollywood. All over Europe, including the East, the State Department cooperated with a new cartel, the Motion Picture Export Association (MPEA), to negotiate the distribution of movies from the prewar era, and to establish film quotas favorable to the U.S. industry. The interest was far greater than commercial. Billy Wilder, working in Berlin as an advisor to the Division of Information Control, claimed that the films could best deliver "propaganda through entertainment." The Blum-Byrnes agreements above all seemed to portend an American commercial and cultural invasion. But the State Department ultimately restrained the MPEA and favored, whenever it could, placing film production in the hands of local authorities. An internally reformed cinema seemed the best medium of democratic reeducation, in Germany as in most other European countries.[71]

In France and especially in Italy cinema was presumed to accelerate democracy. If indigenous productions could convey the message better than Hollywood, the State Department was ready to accept compromise. This was particularly important in nations experiencing postwar national rebirth and in need of a restored self-esteem. It would take two years after the Blum-Byrnes accords to convince an obdurate Motion Picture Association that, as Ambassador Caffery admitted, for the French, "to defend [their] movie industry was the same as defending France." The result was a return to quotas and protectionism for the French film industry, for which the Communists above all had tenaciously battled.[72] When many American moviegoers took a break from Hollywood platitudes and flocked to see Roberto Rossellini's *Open City* (1945), and when Vittorio De Sica's *Sciuscià* won an Academy Award in 1946, the sign was clear: Italy's cultural revival and America's positive response to it could nourish the Italians' self-esteem, compensate for the Hollywood "invasion," and consolidate transatlantic cultural ties. An enthusiastic U.S. diplomat described *Open City* as an "excellent work of propaganda" that "would restore self-respect among Italians and Italian-Americans."[73]

But here is where the irony fully arose. As the first film examples of the internationally renowned Italian neorealism, Rossellini's and De Sica's movies also symbolized that movement's penchant for populism, continuing to expose the gap between rulers and ruled, and to advocate a regeneration of the social order. Communist intellectuals virtually monopolized the neorealist movement, making it the spearhead of their own mass cultural campaign against privilege and Hollywood hedonistic vacuity.[74]

The still acerbic U.S. strategy to remold intellectual Europe met similar results. On high culture, however, the ambivalence between genuine exchange with indigenous forces and American unilateralism was immediately even more accentuated than with popular culture. America's cultural penetration of Europe during the interwar period had been uneasily intertwined with the debate over modernization. This penetration, most U.S. officials concluded after World War II, certainly increased America's cultural and economic influence over Europe without the cost of entanglement.[75] But it had also created a lot of mostly intellectual animosity against the American cultural imperium. In order to dispel faulty notions of American culture as a detriment to the Old World, the government had to accept a certain degree of entanglement, and closely monitor cultural activities by private agencies and foundations. Gradually, it had to take more cultural initiative in its own hands. With intellectuals in France and Italy increasingly lured to the Left, the matter seemed urgent.

It is no accident that Sartre and de Beauvoir, who were making a transition from individualism to political commitment and socialism, were both courted by Washington. Their visits to the United States in 1945, followed by those of other leftist intellectuals, such as Vercors (Jean Bruller), and communist Claude Roy, as we have seen, elicited their enthusiasm. Sartre's immediate reaction was however most significant: on his return to France, he acclaimed the possibilities of restoring excellent cultural relations with the Americans; except that he saw the main flow of cultural diplomacy coming from Paris, not Washington or New York. "We must use all possible means," he told a French interviewer, "to promote French culture in the United States. . . . it is the best propaganda."[76] From America's standpoint, restoring pride in French culture and traditions was good, but not at the expense of U.S. cultural diffusion.

The restoration of pride had to be reciprocated. A crucial purpose of cultural information and exchange for the United States, still profoundly affected by a certain intellectual inferiority complex toward Europe, was to forge a sense of common destiny, a sort of permanent mutual feedback among the member nations of Western Civilization. Under the auspices of Senator J. William Fulbright of Arkansas, this cultural exchange policy was attuned to Cold War strategies from its start in 1946, and progressively shed its cultural internationalism and embraced propaganda.

To be sure, Fulbright conceived the program that bore his name as an instrument of peace. By attempting to overcome ignorance, stereotypes, and chauvinism, the cultural exchange of students and scholars "in the fields of education, culture, and science" could "increase mutual understanding between the people of the United States and the people of other countries." The program was extended worldwide. Its first application, in 1947, actually was in China, but Europe soon became its focus. Despite Fulbright's pledge that the "cultivation of ideas" should have nothing to do with propaganda or ideological constraints, he and the rest of the American foreign policy establishment could not resist championing this cultivation's ultimate political purpose in civilizational terms. Presenting his proposal to the Senate Appropriations Committee in June 1946, Fulbright upheld the "identity of interests of all Western Civilizations," and averred, "We are a part of Western Civilization. The British Commonwealth and we are the largest nations. . . . Russia is on the fence, a little of both. I think if we are able to get along on this side of the world, the western part of the world which I call the Christian nations and the others are the orientals—I simply approve of our basic idea of democracy of the emphasis upon the individual as opposed to the way they do it in the Orient. I think it is very essential we help these people get along. I think that is for our own selfish benefit. That is, if we are left alone with out any other strong government to support us we would be in a dangerous position in 20, 30, or 40 years."[77] Fulbright's gospel of cultural tolerance was from the start predicated on a conviction of Western superiority, a confirmation of American exceptionalism, and an attack on the "collectivist" ethic coming from the East. Even granting that such sharp civilizational distinctions might have been necessary to obtain congressional approval, the senator's speech perfectly exemplified the Cold War's fostering of an intertwined pedagogic and demagogic practice in American foreign policy.

From the onset, the Cold War thus transformed America's approach to cultural diplomacy. As several studies have pointed out, the U.S. government may have not commanded the numerous American nongovernmental organizations that took the initiative in managing transatlantic elites after World War II.[78] But undoubtedly the relationship between state and philanthropic patronage became intimate. Before the Fulbright program was shackled within the State Department, the government had already set up instruments of cultural control, most notably by merging the functions of the Office of War Information and the Office of the Coordinator for Inter-American Affairs with those of the State Department's Division of Cultural

Relations, which all came to form the Office of International Information and Cultural Affairs. The government had also helped sponsor specific initiatives, most notably, in early 1947, the Harvard-inspired Salzburg Seminar. Based in Austria, this program was designed to reeducate Germans and Austrians after Nazism and reinvigorate their nations' intellectual life. The seminar became the birthplace of American studies in Europe. Rather than furthering cultural relations based on the exchange of ideas, the United States increasingly adopted a unilateral approach geared to "informing" and to waging propaganda. Two years after the passage of the Fulbright Act, the Smith-Mundt Act specifically authorized the government to use education and propaganda to wage its cultural cold war against the Soviet Union and communist influence worldwide. But the emerging American propaganda was not a mere Cold War tactic. It was a matter of Cold War civilizational visions. As Frank Ninkovich has noted, "it was not that cultural policy was becoming politicized"; on the contrary, "foreign policy issues began to be framed in idealistic cultural terms."[79] It is against this backdrop that we must place the psychological warfare the United States conducted against communism in France and Italy in the following years.

The Expulsion

In France and Italy, never did the interplay between international and political developments run so parallel as during the expulsion of the extreme Left groups from both governments in May 1947. American assertiveness in both countries grew as Soviet influence waned. The Moscow Conference of Foreign Ministers in April sealed the fate of the wartime Grand Alliance, and consequently of the wartime antifascist coalitions in Western Europe. The role of the United States in the ousting of the two parties, it has now been proven, was discreet and cautious. The main initiative was local. In Italy, according to John Harper, De Gasperi "realized that the United States could not rescue him from his sea of troubles, at least not before he had moved decisively *on his own*." In Paris the embassy was even more of a bystander. As Irwin Wall has concluded: "The American response to both crises was improvised, and both American ambassadors were taken by surprise. The myth of American 'orders' should be laid to rest."[80] What remains relevant here is how U.S. officials assessed this parallel situation, and what general impact the event had on communist perceptions of America in both countries.

American sentiments at the peak of the crisis were a mix of relief and fear. The ambassadors worried that the United States might win a political battle but lose the war for hearts and minds. Throughout the spring of 1947 both men expressed increasing frustration with the two anomalous coalition governments. James Dunn had freer rein than Caffery in manipulating the situation. Shortly before the government crisis, he relayed to the secretary of state his idea of a greater "psychological" effort in Italy: "If the large mass of Italian workers . . . had any idea that adoption of Communism in Italy would cut them off from relations with the U.S., I feel sure the vast majority would reject Communist advances. Our practice of holding back from expressing ourselves on ideological views has given all the advantage to the other side and they have not hesitated to use it and abuse it." But the ambassador came to realize that, as Dowling had recommended, shows of being "pro-Italian" and undercover aid to political parties and free trade unions would be more effective than overt anticommunist propaganda. He soon would find himself in a more apt role as greeter of each U.S. aid shipment arriving on Italian shores.[81]

At the peak of the government crisis in Paris, Caffery, who had strived to maintain his detachment, feared that press reports alleging that he had presented U.S. aid as conditional on Paul Ramadier's expulsion of the Communists would intensify public charges of "dollar imperialism." The ambassador suspected the Communists had spread the rumors in an attempt to influence the Socialist Party, still wavering on how strongly it wanted to align with the West. Strongly pro-French, he urged continued U.S. assistance.[82]

But the expulsion could also provoke communist violence and sabotage. A combination of anti-American backlash, public frustration at still dire economic conditions, and, not least, continued communist presence in various bureaucratic and administrative posts even after the expulsion, seemed likely to cause the sort of putsch that soon occurred in Czechoslovakia. The United States dreaded the prospect of a communist act of desperation as much as the Communists' cunning in using all their remaining levers of power. It was in the months preceding the reshuffling of the two cabinets that Washington received the most alarming reports about communist armed factions. And it was at this time that Togliatti, Thorez, and even Italian socialist leader Lelio Basso made their most startling allusions to the need for "direct action." While "armed" action was still improbable, sabotage became a high possibility. By the practice of "partitocracy," the Communists retained many administrative posts. For that reason Washington worried even more about their presence in the military, the police, and the interior ministries of both countries, as well as about their control over the trade unions. In Italy, the national elections, scheduled for October, commanded De Gasperi's prudence and initial preference for a diluted presence of Communists in the government rather than their exclusion. Ramadier had earlier insisted that out of the government the Communists could actually better monopolize the CGT and launch it in a series of insurrectionary strikes. Douglas Mac-Arthur II, the first political secretary of the U.S. embassy in Paris, shared that concern and became one of the early advocates of a thorough action aimed at undermining or neutralizing communist bureaucratic strength.[83] Aggravating the problem, according to both ambassadors, was the fact that the emerging government coalitions favored political polarization between the Right and the Left, instead of co-opting the reformist elements.[84]

Not until the last phases of the government crises did the two Communist Parties denounce America's interference. The internal divorce began much earlier, with the acrimonious debate between the PCI and classic liberal Treasury Minister Epicarmo Corbino in the summer of 1946, and with Thorez's failure to form a cabinet in November.[85] After the formation of the Ramadier government in January, the French communist leaders actually considered not entering the coalition. Once in, they began to fear being ostracized for their opposition to the war in Indochina. But the main theme of the 3 May Central Committee meeting was America's collusion: even the most internal aspect of the crisis, the decision by Renault automaker to clamp down of the CGT's right to strike, was seen as "instigated by the international trusts serving Truman." No archival evidence confirms Caffery's presumption that the Communists might have unleashed rumors of his specific orders to Ramadier in order to restore their relationship with the Socialists. In fact, the Communists were overly concerned about the SFIO's pro-Western drift, and worked more to denounce it than to prevent it.[86]

The PCI expressed similar alarm, especially after the socialist split that, in Togliatti's words, could allow the pro-American Saragat to "assume the role of representative of the working class." But the Italian Communists were more keenly aware than their French comrades of the international context of the cabinet crisis. Given Italy's international weakness and dependence, the party aspired to emerge as a more prominent international actor. Emilio Sereni explained to the political bureau in April that "while Italy [was] not a great power, the Italian Communist Party [was] an international force the Americans must reckon with." Therefore, the bureau concluded, the party needed to show the government that the only way to maintain national independence was to expand trade with Eastern Europe as a counterbalance to the conditional U.S. loan. Through the CGIL and its relative influence over major industries, such as FIAT, the party could work as a broker for more profitable contacts with the East.[87] The following month, the party's hopes were dashed by both the De Gasperi government and Soviet aloofness. And the PCI's worst fears that the United States would use its loan policy to divide

Europe were confirmed. It remained relevant that, in addition to Sereni, Togliatti and party cofounder Umberto Terracini had also seen the potential of using the country's poor international leverage to increase the party's international presence. The PCI would have to wait almost thirty years to reach that goal. Much of its naiveté about its leverage in 1947 depended on its anti-American prejudice and its faith in Soviet resilience and concern about Italy.

The same conclusion applies to the warped French communist view. For not only did the PCF expect for some time to rejoin the governing coalition, but Thorez was also convinced that the United States' "taking the lead of the anticommunist crusade" was "camouflaging its anti-Soviet crusade" and fully expressing "its weakness and fear." Above all, it was America's "mounting fear . . . for the imminent crisis of capitalism" that caused so much political and international havoc. So "instead of being discouraged," the leader concluded, the party should "rally the masses for the defense of national independence." But the connection of Western Europe's proletarian nationalism to Soviet revolutionary internationalism was fading. Moscow, now focused on consolidating its sphere of influence, began to show disdain for the parliamentary tactics of the Western Communists it had hitherto encouraged.[88]

Ironically, the passage to government opposition actually placed Communists in France and Italy ahead of their Soviet comrades in opposition to American influence and foreign policy. Andrei Zhdanov was now developing his theory of the two irreconcilable camps. But the Marxists in France and Italy, having been exposed to American political and cultural presence, began to articulate a full range of anti-American themes before being directed to do so by Moscow and the Cominform. As the anguished intellectual controversies had anticipated a few months earlier, Western Communists were ready to transform their mixed emotions toward America into a raging, demonizing campaign against the "invaders." The expulsion from the governments provided the catalyst. This episode unleashed Togliatti's warning, in *L'Unità*, about the twin threat American dominion posed to Europe's independence and intelligence. An all-embracing condemnation cast America as a tangible presence as much as a metaphor of all the worst vices that could beset Western civilization. The emerging American empire might even destroy Europe physically. Both Communist Parties interpreted Washington's moves, from the Truman Doctrine to the collusion with the conservative groups that had expelled them, as preparations for war. Precisely because of its fears heightened by the imminent capitalist crisis, the two political bureaus declared, the United States had become prone to attack.[89] Through pacifist campaigns, Communists in both countries would continue to highlight and attempt to merge their roles as vehicles for international cooperation (with the East), defenders of national sovereignty, protectors of a cultural patrimony, and paladins of the masses against the rulers.

Under all those banners, even the most strident and obtuse form of anti-Americanism could appear plausible, and could even revamp the popularity of the two parties, victims of Cold War ostracism. Faced with such ideologized and regimented propaganda, the United States temporarily lost sight of the possibility of calibrating its confrontation with Soviet Communism to national characteristics in France and Italy. Even as in the immediate post-war period American representatives in Rome and Paris, or in Washington (most notably, Fulbright), had showed potential for a subtle approach, they had also implied this emerging obsession with a communist monolith.

A Manichean perspective prevailed, even as Washington devised its most enduring and effective strategies for Western Europe. The Marshall Plan and the following steps leading to the integration of Europe came along with the perfection of psychological warfare. Vague and pervasive at once, "psy-war" made America's confrontation with Western European Communism as universalistic as it was cunning. Much of the problem lay in the determination to *eradicate* rather than *cope* with communism in Western Europe. By attacking the problem straight on, the United States too frequently neglected the importance of circumventing it with an approach that coordinated political influence over a specific country with international grand diplomacy. In sum, America's faith in its exceptionalism and universalism grew as it confronted an equally universal anti-American campaign, which, in the specific context of Italy and France, was waged by two parties that the United States nevertheless tried to understand as intricately connected to these two nations' political culture.

3 POLARIZED CONFRONTATION

U.S. Aid and Propaganda versus Cominform in
France and Italy, 1947–1950

Triumph of Economic Determinism? Cominform Choices

America's "permanent revolution," which, according to a 1951 propaganda
book with that subtitle, envisioned a land of ultimate emancipation for every
individual and "for all human spirit"[1] on Earth, had a compelling premise
in another revolution, that of "rising expectations." This was how U.S. economic advisor Harlan Cleveland described the quantitative and qualitative
effects of modernization, mass consumption, and mass democracy that the
United States had experienced since the end of World War I, and was now
supposed to transmit to Europe.[2] The message stressed the universal logic
of the connection between prosperity, democracy and, in general, a sense of
self-fulfillment. Europe's postwar hardship required emphasis on the "quantitative" aspects first. This was how the effects of the European Recovery
Program (ERP), announced by Secretary of State George Marshall on 5 June
1947, and beginning a year later, would be measured at the onset. But the
"qualitative" aspects were actually as important. The United States needed
to restore Europe's self-confidence and sense of limitless possibility for each
individual; through this plan, it was also supposed to inspire social reform
in each of its recipient countries and the formation of a genuinely cooperative international community among them. Under an ideal scenario, the
United States would strike a balance between asserting its role as leader of
an emerging transatlantic community and fostering a truly self-reliant community of European nations. Of course, all this had to appear disinterested
and not exclusively anticommunist. It would not be easy to reconcile all these
purposes, and to avoid charges of hypocrisy.

The communist forces in Western Europe of course exploited the U.S.
contradictions. But, in doing so, they also revealed their own. In a struggle
hinged on material as well as psychological effects, the French and Italian
Communists, together with their Cominform sponsors, became far less consistent than their opponents. Their anti-Marshall campaign almost dissolved
the link they had established after the war between economic promise, national emancipation, and international pacifism. Full alignment with Moscow did not alone cause such mistakes and contradictions. The two parties'

own constructs of America and their interactions with internal dynamics also harmed their strategies—much like U.S. shortcomings could be blamed partly on Washington and partly on government and economic forces in recipient countries.

Most historians now agree that from a strictly economic point of view, the effects of the $13.5 billion aid plan were far from essential.[3] At the political level, too, there was a great deal of resistance from the very government forces the plan intended to benefit.[4] But the impact of the plan was nevertheless fundamental in at least three respects: it provided the "crucial margin" that made European recovery and, by the end of the 1950s, self-help possible;[5] it confirmed most Europeans' desire to emulate the American dream of high productivity, mass consumption, and gratified individuals; and it powerfully reiterated America's reputation of generosity above that of self-interest, especially in contrast with the increasingly gloomier aspects of economic life in the Soviet Union and Eastern Europe. This moral advantage was corroborated by the United States' ostensible offer to extend aid to all of Europe, including the Soviet Union and its satellites, and the Soviets' decision, as expected, to turn it down, and to prevent any of its allies from participating. In due time the plan generated, as its first architect, George Kennan, had augured, the spectacle of a "vigorous, prosperous, forward-looking civilization" across the fence for eyes in Eastern Europe to witness.[6] America's influence through the ERP was so large that it warrants the recent description of the United States as an empire defined mainly by its consumerist lure.[7]

ECONOMIC AND PSYCHOLOGICAL DESIGNS

Historians are not the only ones who have noticed the plan's economic limitations. While the ERP was still in its implementation phase, it failed to deliver the short-term results it had announced. And yet, what mattered most was its psychological effect of increasing Europe's admiration for America as well as "faith in its own potential for renaissance." When George Kennan recommended an aid program for Europe in the spring of 1947 he saw a connection between "the profound exhaustion of [Europe's] physical plant" and that of its "spiritual vigor."[8]

Although self-confidence seemed as important as recovery, the economic situation was so dire in most of Europe, and the distinction between psychological and economic effects was so faint, that many U.S. officials emphasized that economic cures would prevent communist advances. Thus State Department's Soviet expert Charles Bohlen first advocated interim aid for France and Italy in the fall of 1947, to cover the emergency before the implementation of the Marshall Plan the following spring. Starting its work a few weeks later, the National Security Council (NSC) addressed the problem in Italy, pointing out that "prevailing economic distress" caused massive support for the Communists. According to Paul G. Hoffman, head of the Economic Cooperation Administration (ECA), which coordinated the plan, its key effect was that Europeans learned that America "is the land of full shelves and bulging shops, made possible by high productivity and good wages, and that its prosperity may be emulated elsewhere by those who will work towards it."[9] Shortly before the Italian national elections in April 1948, the newly created Central Intelligence Agency, while still uncertain about the electoral results, was optimistic about continued U.S. influence through aid. Even a "Communist-dominated Italian government," the agency stated in one of its analyses, "must do all in its power, short of political suicide, to maintain commercial relations with the West and to avoid a denial of U.S. credits." Marshall had just publicly hinted that U.S. aid would become more difficult if the PCI won the elections. But, in his note to the embassy, he recommended: "avoid material which attributes to U.S. intention (of) unilaterally shut[ting] off ERP aid if Communists win." The Italians were trusted to judge for themselves. From Paris, several months earlier, Ambassador Caffery had anticipated the secretary, urging no public interference in any forthcoming French elections, because the French already knew that if the PCF won, it would mean less U.S. aid.[10] The prospect of getting U.S. assistance was thus enough, in these estimates, to persuade French and Italian opinion *even* among Communists.

In fact, the very pressure the ECA felt to promote the Recovery Plan indicated America's need to penetrate further the hearts and minds of the European masses. With a full-fledged Cold War based on mass ideologies and mass politics, the use of media became as important as the substance of policies. Therefore, in historian David Ellwood's words, the Marshall Plan became "the greatest international propaganda operation ever seen in peacetime." This painstaking effort at "public diplomacy" derived in part from the apparent success of U.S. propaganda in Italy's first postwar national elections.[11] But it is worth noting that it was also a prompt response to communist mobilization and venomous attacks on the plan. Washington's own evaluations of the first anti-Marshall campaigns show that, from the start, U.S. perceptions of communist influence in both countries were not informed solely by economic determinism.

THE COMMUNISTS AND U.S. AID

The French and Italian Communists had indeed opted for a frontal attack on the Marshall Plan. This confrontation, however, did not merely reflect the

"America sends free wheat, coal, gasoline to Italy." Marshall Plan propaganda poster by the Italian Christian Democratic Party (Centro grafico pubblicitario, [1950–55]). Courtesy Archivio Manifesto Sociale, Rome.

ideological polarization. While the two parties' tactics were far from subtle, their broad appeal was heightened by widespread uncertainty about the plan's effectiveness, the overbearing nature of U.S. publicity, and American intentions generally. Facing political isolation, the French and the Italian Communists actually felt considerable self-doubt. But this incertitude, in addition to the need to follow the Soviet line, compelled them to seek refuge in dogmatic anti-Americanism.

The CIA was correct in sensing the Western Communists' torment about U.S. assistance. At first, since Washington had offered aid to all of Europe, the two parties' ambiguity was understandable, at least until Moscow declined the offer. But this was not only about waiting for a signal from the Kremlin. Through the summer of 1947, the French and Italian Communists still nurtured the illusion that they could reenter the government. After the Soviets refused to negotiate American aid and recalled the Czech delegates from the Paris conference discussing the aid proposal in July, the PCI and PCF temporized for three more months. By then the Soviet Union had decided to restore the Communist International, under the name of Cominform, in order to tighten its control on both its Eastern European satellites and the Communist Parties in the West. At the organization's founding meeting in September 1947 in Poland, the Soviet and Yugoslav delegates reprimanded their French and Italian comrades for their parliamentary tactics, urging them to wage militant protest against the Marshall aid offer. It is not necessary here to retell the story of the two parties' regimentation under Moscow's directives.[12] Instead we should highlight the contrast between their initial hesitations and their anti-American rhetoric. While their anti-Marshall campaigns were instigated by Moscow, their anti-Americanism was not.

Tactical reasons of course imposed caution: the PCF pursued a respectable image in view of the municipal elections of October 1947 and even set up negotiations between the Confédération Générale du Travail (CGT) and the Confédération Générale du Patronat Français during the summer. The PCI had the forthcoming national elections in mind.[13] The domestic tactic continued to have as its corollary the continued wartime alliance between the superpowers. Togliatti and Thorez in particular were convinced that a protracted Grand Alliance would not only forestall their political isolation at home, but also, as in the immediate postwar period, give them sufficient international and domestic prominence to conduct flexible political maneuvers. While debating the American offer, both parties continued to nurture the illusion that U.S. aid could and should be matched by a similar offer from Moscow, or at least by expanded trade with the East. This was not only out of economic necessity, but also, as both Umberto Terracini and

Celeste Negarville had anticipated at a PCI directorate meeting in the spring of 1947, "to prevent Truman from luring Poland, Hungary, and other Socialist countries away from the U.S.S.R." The PCI even contemplated using U.S. aid to strengthen the Italian public sector.[14] The French Communists, who had championed their own productivity drive after the war, felt even more "desperate" about the economic situation: at a meeting in June, Thorez gave Andrei Zhdanov the impression that the PCF was "mired in fear that, without American credits, France [would] be ruined." For tactical reasons, too, the party's political bureau instructed as late as February 1948, it was necessary to "specify that our opposition to Marshall plan is not an opposition to U.S. aid nor 'to America in general' but an opposition to the political conditions, which are incompatible with our independence and our national honor."[15]

Even when favoring the use of U.S. aid, the two parties thus followed a logic that was informed primarily by their deep-seated mistrust of Washington. Without discussing American assistance, they thought, they could not prevent the United States from dividing Europe. Even Terracini—who later would cast his dissidence from the Cominform line arguing that for a country in the Western sphere of influence it was impossible "to forsake . . . intense economic relations with America"—never ceased to highlight America's imperialist intentions and the need to mitigate them. It thus became increasingly difficult for the leaders of both parties to explain publicly how a Grand Alliance approach could be reconciled with their intolerance of the United States. Togliatti told his directorate that communist participation in the discussion concerning U.S. aid was "the only way to break the reactionary front."[16] Both French and Italian communist leaders counted on their ability to encourage their nations' governments, or the most enlightened groups within those governments, to place conditions on Marshall aid, preventing the Americans from imposing their own.[17] Only by dividing adversaries, apparently, would it be possible to gain allies. But all this was premised on the two parties' perception of the United States as both overbearing and—because it was so dependent on Europe's markets—vulnerable.

DEMONIZING THE MARSHALL PLAN

By the time the Cominform ordered its French and Italian delegates to resume the class struggle, accept the two camps thesis, concentrate on a systematic denunciation of American imperialism, and, in Zhdanov's words, to hold "aloft the banner of defense of national independence and sovereignty in their countries," the two parties had already on their own fully formed an acutely ideologized depiction of the United States. In fact, as I have noted, given their direct experience with U.S. presence and interference, the virulence of their anti-Americanism predated the Soviets'. The basic theses driving their full-fledged insurrectionary rhetoric in the fall of 1947 had been in place for several months. The Marshall Plan, in their view, was yet another attempt to relieve a crisis in the capitalist mode of production. It also signaled America's intention of dividing Europe and enslaving the West. Even within the Western sphere, they added, Washington clearly adopted a divide and rule approach that ultimately disfavored France and Italy. Disparaging prospects of continental integration, and highlighting national prerogatives, the French Communists dismissed the Marshall Plan as the latest Anglo-Saxon scheme to rehabilitate Germany at the expense of France's industrial potential and grandeur. "The Marshall Plan," Thorez claimed at the party's Central Committee in October, "gives priority to German magnates who operate under U.S. control . . . and aims at reducing France to a colony of the kind of Portugal, or Chile." Similarly, the PCI claimed that the ERP belittled Italy's role in Europe by confirming American hegemony, electing France and Great Britain as America's "second-rate imperialist powers," and casting Italy as the "loser in the scramble for American money."[18] Like the Blum-Byrnes agreements and the loan to De Gasperi, the plan was just another attempt to pry open the two nations' markets, which had to give up any sort of protectionism, "indispensable to their industries."[19] And following the Truman Doctrine, the seemingly benevolent aid plan was, in the Communists' final analysis, another preparation for war. This conclusion was the hardest to prove while American assistance focused on civilian reconstruction and reform. And yet it was the most frequently articulated by both parties' leaders, who sought reassurance in their own economic determinism based on the Leninist thesis that imperialism and war marked the last phase of monopoly capitalism. The PCF displayed more optimism than its Italian counterpart, asserting in July that, while the West was still having trouble integrating, the Soviet Union had succeeded in "consolidating the bloc of progressive democracies." No doubt, the East was consolidated, but Togliatti repeatedly reminded his party that "America's imperialist pirates" had started the integration process from Italy and the Mediterranean (the Truman Doctrine), the best stage for an attack on the East.[20]

Besides condemning U.S. conduct abroad, the two parties began their effort to debunk myths about the society of plenty and happiness. That was the purpose of a studiously planned trip by the PCF's Pierre Courtade to America in the winter of 1947–48. His travel log was published in installments in *L'Humanité* under the title "What Mr. Truman Never Told You." Refuting the Marshall planners' boasts about "the land of full shelves and bulging shops," Courtade noted in one of the articles that the *"grandes bou-*

tiques were no more than bazaars of illusions" for the vast ranks of American poor. "Even the fact that there are probably more telephones, more showers, more refrigerators in Harlem than in all the twenty arrondissements of Paris—he added—means nothing to the Harlem inhabitants who beg for a dime on 144th Street. One can starve to death with a telephone."[21]

America was a land not only of widespread misery but also of repression. The two parties began their equation of American capitalism and fascism as early as the summer of 1947. Given Italy's recent past, the PCI was particularly keen to stress this analogy. "That American policy in Europe is leading to fascism can be no surprise," a September 1947 article in *Rinascita* observed, "to those who already know how the big trusts and their politicians are trying to lead the United States itself into fascism; by attacking Jews and Negroes, by trying to outlaw the Communist Party, by seeking to destroy the trade union movement." Maurice Thorez referred to the ERP Paris Conference as a "new Munich," while Pierre Courtade eventually wrote of "the concentration camp of Marshallized Europe." "Like Hitler," Thorez explained at the Central Committee in October, "the Americans who aim at world domination hide their expansionist, militarist policy behind the screen of anti-communism and . . . present themselves as saviors of order and of capitalist 'civilization.'" Fitting with this argument was the PCF's persistent reference to the specter of German revival under Anglo-American auspices.[22]

The PCI was just as solicitous in rekindling fears of American materialism among Italy's Catholic masses. An editorial titled "God and the Dollar," published first in *Rinascita* in August 1947 and reprinted on several occasions during the following years in other communist periodicals, underlined the incompatibility between the principles of the Gospel and America "the heart of the capitalist jungle." The article was clearly opening a polemic with the Vatican, guilty of allying itself to the country that "based human relations on mere interest" and "measured the value of human personality only with currency." Catholicism, in fact, was under threat, the article continued cunningly, since capitalism was the product of Protestantism, and Masonic lodges (to which President Truman pledged his allegiance) promoted its ideals in Catholic countries like France and Italy. Formally devout but profoundly anti-Christian, the materialist, racist American capitalist would ultimately "prostitute white women, helped by the powerful industry of entertainment and glossy magazines," and would "squander amazing sums of money in a life of luxury, subjugate other nations[,] . . . and foment war." Following Togliatti's reasoning about the "empire of idiots,"[23] the party thus argued that a combination of shallowness and arrogance determined the conformity, hedonism, and warmongering of the American ruling classes.

Solidarity and fraternity instead defined the Soviet Union, the article concluded, the country that followed the principles of the Gospel much more than did the "Christianity of the dollar."[24]

Highlighting the contradictions of American society and proclaiming their solidarity with its victims also helped French and Italian Communists maintain an international profile. The journals *Rinascita*, *Cahiers du communisme*, and *La Nouvelle critique* in particular underlined this point by frequently publishing editorials by American Communists and dissidents such as William Z. Foster, Paul Robeson, James Baldwin, and Howard Fast, or by following the lives of critical icons such as Charlie Chaplin and John Huston. However, the distinction between rulers and victims in America was not comparable to the previous differentiation between New Deal reformists and progressive intellectuals, on the one hand, and reactionary America, on the other. Even to the most discerning among Italian communist leaders only the American extreme Left seemed now redeemable.

All the anti-Marshall rhetoric did not rule out continuing parliamentary tactics. As a frontal attack on national institutions and the U.S. role in Europe, however, it was more consistent with the Cominform instructions to wage extraparliamentary action. Soviet Foreign Minister Vyacheslav Molotov had already scolded PCI leader Eugenio Reale for not reacting to the party's eviction from the government with charges of U.S. interference; Zhdanov specifically enjoined delegates Luigi Longo and Jacques Duclos to take their anti-Americanism from the pages of their journals to the streets.[25] Labeling all their opponents as "American parties" (in the PCF's case the Socialists of the SFIO, too), the French and Italian Communists resumed class warfare. In November the CGIL and CGT launched their insurrectionary strikes against the Marshall Plan and the governments' "policies of starvation."[26] The strikes were particularly violent in France; the PCI remained more cautious until the national elections in spring. But in both countries, the strikes helped bringing the economy to a standstill. Moscow actually had to restrain the most zealous French and Italian comrades. As the PCF's Central Committee declared at the end of December, after Thorez returned with instructions from Stalin, "We must not go too far in the struggle against the Marshall Plan." Likewise, Zhdanov had just dissuaded Pietro Secchia, the militant new vice secretary of the PCI, from starting an armed insurrection unless provoked by the adversary. In some respects, this caution helped the two parties' reputation. The repression, especially in France, after Socialist Interior Minister Jules Moch assumed emergency powers, did "evoke irresistibly the experiences under the German occupation,"[27] making the high casualty rate another occasion for communist martyrdom. But the drawbacks far exceeded the advantages. Moscow had used the two parties' anti-Americanism with the aim of sabotaging the Marshall Plan, but did not expect this would increase their power and popularity. For the Kremlin, the Western European Communists were to a certain extent expendable.[28]

Cominform regimentation prevented the two parties from continuing to exploit divisions among their adversaries. The government forces naturally closed ranks. This replica of the Cold War in internal matters would have happened anyway. But by resuming militant tactics, the PCI and PCF exacerbated this polarization, and isolated themselves, except in the united front of Italian Communists and Socialists. Togliatti rebuked Terracini for fearing isolation, and, at the November meeting of the Central Committee, claimed that the "defense of national independence and honor" would be sufficient to rally the democratic forces around the party.[29] In fact, the Communists' national appeal outside their ranks was damaged, ironically when the two parties heightened their self-professed opposition to their "imperialist foes." At the same time, this emphasis on nationalist rhetoric, merging anticapitalism with anti-Americanism, backfired with the working class. Many workers resented that the insurrectionary strikes hardly focused on their legitimate demands and need for immediate improvements. As historian Annie Kriegel best put it, "Thorez avait voulu être la France, mais les ouvriers voulaient être des ouvriers" (Thorez had decided to be France, but workers just wanted to be workers). This mood fed an already mounting dissidence within the trade union movement, leading to the break of the two parties' monopoly over labor forces and the creation of Léon Jouaux's Force Ouvrière (FO) in December 1947. By the following year, the Free Italian General Confederation of Labor (LCGIL, which eventually became the Italian Confederation of Labor Unions [CISL]), and the Italian Labor Union (UIL), were founded under Catholic and social democratic control respectively.[30]

While the two parties' nationalism was always marred by their devotion to the Soviet Union, this problem became far more explicit after the Cominform decisions. The fight against American imperialism was complemented by a systematic defense of the Soviet Union. The PCF had always been the more sedulous of the two parties in its pro-Soviet celebration. Now in Italy party leaders such as Gian Carlo Pajetta, who had previously insisted on seducing Catholic workers, proclaimed the need to "align with the U.S.S.R." and to multiply the iconography on Stalin. Hard-liner Luigi Longo pledged to promote in his magazine *Vie Nuove* a thorough campaign to "popularize the Soviet Union and all the achievements of the socialist progressive democracies." The brochure series *Propaganda* was also founded on the eve of the 1948 elections with the chief purpose of defending the U.S.S.R. For both parties, national traditions now seemed overshadowed by the Soviet model rather than merged with it. According to Raymond Aron, one of the intellectuals who best opposed the PCF's cultural ascendancy, in those years, Western European Communism, contradicting Marxist theories, made the U.S.S.R. "the sole depository of the historical mission earlier attributed to the proletariat."[31]

The communist campaigns' missing link between patriotism and economic promise was noticed by U.S. officials. "It is significant," Ambassador Dunn observed in November, "that in none of the demonstrations engineered by [the] Communists . . . has there been any cry for bread or employment." The majority of workers were dissatisfied, Dunn concluded, and the political trend in Italy was "unquestionably now away from Communism." This was also the conclusion of a CIA report in October, which stressed that the Italian public increasingly realized that "the Communists' primary loyalty [was] to the U.S.S.R. rather than to the Italian people."[32] The French embassy had at first been less optimistic about the PCF's political isolation, which was mitigated by an atmosphere of national revanchism. As Caffery had noted in July, the PCF sought to rebound from its diminished economic appeal through a "chauvinistic" campaign that fused fears of national economic decline, German revival, and war. Effectively invoking the specter of the nation's previous surrender and collaboration with the enemy, Caffery explained, the Communists contended that the Marshall Plan was a return to a "'Pétainist' policy of rendering France purely agricultural . . . by depriving it of its metallurgical industry while restoring the Ruhr to its prewar position." By December, Caffery noted, much of this patriotism had been drowned in pro-Soviet slogans, while the insurrectionary strikes had alienated much of the French working class.[33] Within a few more months Norris Chipman concluded that "the average French worker welcomed the Marshall aid and did not see it as threat to French independence." The municipal elections of October, furthermore, had rewarded the Gaullists as the true guardians of French chauvinism.[34]

U.S. RESPONSE

Economic disruption caused by the Communists thus tarnished both their nationalist and economic credentials. But the overall systemic economic dislocation of the winter of 1947–48 could naturally rekindle their fortunes. With masses of unemployed, half-starving people, and the breakdown of law and order, the French and Italian Communists were likely to renew their political appeal. Faith in economic cures thus took a firm hold among most U.S. officials: interim aid became essential for both countries, for "the success of the Government in the political sphere," Caffery contended in January, "will be wiped out tomorrow if a reverse is registered in the economic sphere." In the country's dire situation, the PCI's electoral campaign, according to James Dunn, could also effectively revive its anti-imperialist appeal, preying on "intangible factors inherent in the preoccupation of the Italian mentality with 'bella figura.'" But even at the peak of America's economic determinism, very few U.S. officials believed that aid alone could be a panacea. The economic cures depended on the will of the French and Italian governments to carry out reforms that would create the basis for social justice. During the next wave of strikes later that fall, Caffery noted that most French workers were "united in the conviction that they [were] not receiving their fair share of the French economic recovery made possible by the Marshall Plan." In Italy, during the winter of 1947–48, Treasury Minister Luigi Einaudi met the economic situation with austerity measures that penalized the country's working class, and, worse, shifted the blame to America's inadequate credits.[35]

Washington also contemplated the possibility that insurrectionary strikes might be a prelude to armed insurrection. Could the two Communist Parties, scolded by the Kremlin for their parliamentary tactics, go all the way to prove their revolutionary ardor? The general impression at the two American embassies was that inflammatory speeches, such as the one by Togliatti of 7 September at a party rally in Parma, were meant to appease the Kremlin but might end up inciting the party's rank and file out of the leader's control. While the politicized nature of the fall strikes alienated many workers, the rhetoric denouncing America and its servants did not. The resort to scapegoats still worked. The party leaders themselves might be tempted to use violence in case of further political setbacks, as it had appeared they might after their expulsion from the government.[36] As it turned out, most U.S. estimates were correct: Thorez and Togliatti (through his emissary to Moscow, Pietro Secchia) had amply discussed the possibility of insurrection with the Soviet leadership; they concluded that they "had to be ready, but only if the adversary attacked." Stalin had imposed caution on hard-liners such as Secchia partly out of a realistic assessment of the situation and partly out of belief that the "imperialist" forces might commit a foolish act first. In France, where the strikes had been more violent, police reports, on which the U.S. embassy relied, also highlighted communist prudence: "the PCF's paramilitary capabilities have been overestimated," read a report of March 1948 from the Paris Prefecture, but "further repression might revive" violent insurrection.[37]

The United States thus had to fulfill the French and Italian governments' request for logistical support to forestall a violent turn while also avoiding direct involvement that could cause an anti-American backlash. While the first NSC documents on Italy—NSC 1/1 (14 November 1947) and NSC 1/2 (20 February 1948)—recommended intervention as a last resort, the Policy Planning Staff explained the main reasons for caution. One of its memos stated: "The occupation of bases in Italy may be a warning to the Kremlin, but it will also look like intervention in the domestic affairs of Italy. It will look like an attack on Communism as such rather than an attack against international aggression. We will appear to be military aggressors, and as a result we will be placed politically on the defensive." Both the British and the Americans finally decided that any preventive measure and deployment of troops might, as Foreign Secretary Ernest Bevin said on the eve of the Italian elections, "serve to justify Communist action and put our government in the wrong with world opinion."[38]

More than their paramilitary capabilities, it was the institutional presence of the French and Italian Communist Parties that kept worrying American officials. Rather than using the double-edged instrument of the general strike, the PCF was likely to resort to "individual strikes" for sabotage purposes, as the U.S. Labor attaché in London, Samuel D. Berger, warned Charles Bohlen in December 1947. Though still politically "inspired," such targeted strikes were hard to distinguish from legitimate grievances, and "any attack on them [would have invited] the hostility of bona fide labor movements." "It is axiomatic," Berger concluded, "that U.S. financial aid alone cannot defeat the Communists. They can only be permanently defeated if their influence in the trade union movements is broken."[39] The United States began to confront that problem as well with scrupulous attention to America's image. Especially in its effort to undermine the Communists' institutional basis, Washington had to hide its hand. Secretary of State Marshall had already concluded that "any vigorous course of action by the United States would [have raised] the cry of direct interference in French internal affairs" and would have reinforced anti-American attitudes. But while the United States could not "create fifth columns or extensive underground organizations," Marshall continued, "support . . . by a financial nature and funds made available to organizations who are engaged in the unequal struggle against Communist penetration could be quietly supported." The secretary of state thus asked Congress for a "secret fund" to be used with "absolute discretion." What he had in mind in particular was the assistance to "Socialist labor unions fighting Communist control." The National Security Council endorsed this conclusion and included the provision about secretly funding the trade union movement in its first policy document.[40]

Using these "unvouchered funds" as well as the network the AFL and

ILGWU had established in both countries since the end of the war—best exemplified by the activism of the AFL's Irving Brown in Paris—the United States could encourage the secession that led to the formation of Force Ouvrière first and the Catholic and Socialist unions in Italy the following year.[41] While the United States "sealed a division that was probable in any case," it felt particularly proud of its agency. Caffery greeted the union split as "the most important event that ha[d] occurred in France since the Liberation." What mattered most was that a very politicized maneuver helped create an ostensibly apolitical union movement that followed the American model. The Americans' expectation—soon to be foiled—was that, as a consequence of these splits, the reformist forces in France and Italy would be emboldened, and that Marshall planners could thus attain their major goal of making class warfare obsolete in both countries.[42]

Internal reform was to be correlated with the international cooperation required by the Marshall aid stipulation. According to the plan's main proponent, George Kennan, and other State Department advocates of an autonomous, cohesive Western Europe, continental integration would have deep political as well as strategic and economic effects. Early in 1948, when the director of the Office of European Affairs, John D. Hickerson, envisioned this "third force" as "not merely an extension of U.S. influence" and "strong enough to say 'no' both to the Soviet Union and to the United States," he was not speaking solely of self-reliance. This proposition would prove America's art of compromise and influence by mutual accommodation according to its democratic rules; it was also meant to avert polarization within the most politically fragile European nations.[43] Hickerson, who eventually invoked the risk of internal subversion in Italy to champion its access to the Atlantic Pact, already knew how to strike a chord with other U.S. officials who had seen the connection between those nations' regained confidence abroad and sense of mastery at home. Ambassador Caffery later that year explained that in the "tense international situation . . . many Frenchmen [saw] themselves as helpless pawns in an impending conflict between the Russian and American juggernauts," and this "contribute[d] to the prevailing lack of confidence," encouraging "a fatalistic nothingness in non-Communist and non-Gaullist elements."[44] The fate of a "domestic" third force, a centrist coalition able to withstand communist and Gaullist presence, was in sum linked to the evolution of an international third force. Integration thus offered progressive democratic forces in France and Italy the prospect of overcoming not only fears of a revived Germany, but also their own internal Cold War. It would allow them to defuse the nationalism that animated their public opinion's anti-American and anticommunist campaigns, and to manage the modernization process without creating the impression that this was mostly an American import. Furthermore, Marshall aid, if coordinated among its recipients, was better guaranteed to reconcile national honor with the need for assistance: according to the President's Committee on "European Recovery and American Aid," the U.S. contribution "must be viewed not as a means of supporting Europe, but as a spark which can fire the engine."[45]

The Soviets' fatal error was responding to the emerging interdependence with a siege mentality, "conceiving the interests of the U.S.S.R. in terms of separateness, instead of participation in international affairs," and leaving Communists in the West no other option but to reject integration a priori.[46] While French and Italian Communists were ostracized, their resilience in the following years resulted from several factors: the slowness with which the American "promise" of prosperity and social justice materialized, the increased militarization of U.S. aid, and America's alliance with conservative groups in both countries. This last aspect became particularly evident with the Italian elections of April 1948. The event was a catalyst for the establishment of more thorough U.S. covert and propaganda efforts. But the apparent, immediate, and intoxicating success generated some long-term drawbacks for U.S. confrontation with anti-Americanism in both France and Italy.

The Italian Elections of 1948 and the U.S. Adoption of Political Warfare

Italy's first postwar national elections provided the occasion for escalating America's political and psychological warfare.[47] But more than previous episodes exhibiting polarizing visions of Italy (or Europe), they assumed such a civilizational dimension that the attempts at coordination were often contradicted by a crusade-like frenzy. In the United States public mobilization became so intense that Washington almost lost control of its most zealous supporters of a "free" Italy. Highly symbolic was the decision of a group of prominent Italian Americans, led by actor-singer Frank Sinatra, to contact the State Department in mid-March, and offer their "services" to help galvanize the Italian electorate to vote for the Christian Democrats (DC) and the other democratic centrist parties. Sinatra suggested organizing trips to Italy for famous Italian Americans from every field of entertainment, culture and politics—names included Joe Di Maggio, Rocky Graziano, Jimmy Durante, Arturo Toscanini, Frank Capra, and Charles Poletti. These self-made diplomats wished to campaign openly, underscoring the indissoluble links between the two nations. Although "deeply moved" by this initiative, De Gasperi concurred with the State Department that it would not be a good idea.

The borders of Italian sovereignty appeared already too thin to allow for such heavy-handed pressure. A milder demonstration of interest from American media stars would be more appropriate. Sinatra's proposal a few days later became diluted in the famous Voice of America (VOA) and CBS broadcasts of prominent Italian Americans and other star entertainers, an effort that some criticized, in Dunn's words, as "obvious buttering up of Italian listeners."[48]

The whole range of U.S. operations in the electoral campaign combined an established concentration on aid policies, covert support of democratic groups, and a new tendency toward a more aggressive, at times even hysterical anticommunism. Focus thus did not necessarily result in a better understanding and a thorough assessment of communist strength. The apparent success of the first full-fledged CIA covert action also fed complacency, while the perceived interference in Italian affairs hardened the PCI's furious anti-Americanism.

Early in the year, witnessing economic distress and a thorough mobilization of the leftist forces, the U.S. embassy corrected its previous evaluations of communist decline. Rather than an absolute majority at the polls (never a realistic outcome), the United States feared that the Popular Democratic Front—the electoral bloc of the PCI and the Socialist Party (renamed the PSI after the Social Democrats had split from it in 1947)—could garner the sum of the two parties' strength at previous polls, a 40 percent sufficient for them to lay claim to the premiership, or at least to reenter the government from a position of strength. The subordination of the Nenni Socialists to the PCI was at this point unquestionable, raising further alarms about Italy's similarity to the Eastern regimes if the Left won. Despite Togliatti's emphasis on legal tactics, insurrection remained an option for the Communists, whether their conservative opponents rejected their bid for prominent government positions after an electoral success or the Italians turned them down at the polls.[49]

The civilizational dimension of this confrontation was evident: the loss of Italy, and the Vatican surrounded by a communist state, would have had a disastrous psychological effect on the West, starting a chain reaction throughout Europe. In the United States, this result was certain to undermine popular confidence in the Truman administration. Again, the first to evoke the likelihood of a domino effect were the Europeans themselves. In the fall of 1947, the French Socialists had first alerted Washington that a PCI victory would "weaken" France, the next victim in the Soviet "all-out offensive." Paris reiterated this point during the following months. Finally, on 4 March, Foreign Minister Bidault pleaded that "the old and the new world . . . cooperate in strict solidarity for the protection of the only worthy civilization [*sic*]."[50] In Britain, Clement Attlee's Labor government, like the SFIO, believed the PCI-PSI alliance jeopardized European social democracy. Ireland's most devoted Catholics collected private funds to help rescue the Holy See. The Austrians, still uncertain about their future position in the division of Europe, were just as frightened of being next in the chain reaction of "Western collapse."[51]

America's establishment of a National Security apparatus began with addressing Italy as a problem broader than its strategic implications: it was also a matter of saving one of the cradles of Western civilization. The connection between the "cradle" and the "torchbearer" of Western modernity was underlined in the VOA radio broadcasts and other U.S. public relations campaigns. Ambassador Dunn took a pivotal role, greeting the Liberty ships that brought U.S. aid and setting up the dispatch of red, white, and blue "Friendship Trains" distributing goods to the population. The State Department and Hollywood distributed newsreels, documentaries, and movies contrasting Western plenty with Soviet treachery.[52] The government welcomed ingenious private initiatives such as the "Letters to Italy" campaign, first orchestrated by Washington columnist Drew Pearson, then sponsored by the renowned New York–based newspaper *Il Progresso italo-americano*. The campaign involved millions of Italian Americans' writing to their relatives to urge them to vote against the Communists.[53]

Most of the electoral propaganda from both the Popular Front and the Christian Democratic sides also stressed the clash of ideologies and civilizations. Juxtaposed with the respective appropriations of national symbols— Garibaldi for the Popular Front, family and Catholicism for the DC—were the reciprocal accusations of association with the enemy. This collusion, both sides argued, was fatal to the country's traditions and to reemerging democracy. The image of a country enslaved to Stalin was mirrored by the triad of Roman Catholicism, capitalism, and imperialism.[54]

The United States encouraged the Vatican's active role in the elections. Pope Pius XII, having on his own decided to intervene in the campaign since December, and having noticed how his denunciations of atheistic communism were provoking "counterblasts" from the PCI's propaganda, did start questioning the wisdom of his own actions. In late January he asked for advice from Cardinal Francis Spellman, archbishop of New York, and from the U.S. representative at the Holy See, J. Graham Parsons. Their response was that communist reactions were defensive and that he should go on with his speeches. Togliatti's recognition of the Lateran Pacts while he was in the government, the Americans argued, demonstrated the PCI's awareness of the importance of the country's Catholic traditions.[55] Hence persuaded, the pope launched his crusade against the Popular Front, mobilized the Catholic Action against communist trade unions, endorsed political organizer Luigi Gedda's civic committees aimed at mobilizing the Catholic laity, and urged the Catholic clergy to use their pulpits to threaten PCI members with excommunication. The pope even anticipated Hollywood's public relations campaign by giving highly publicized audiences to Italian sports champions and entertainment stars. In the United States the Catholic Church took over the "Letters to Italy" campaign. The U.S. State Department, after discussing the initiative with Ambassador Dunn, gave its own blessing.[56]

The intervention of Italy's most eminent institution was precious for other reasons as well. Activism and the "spiritual" contribution from the Catholic establishment helped to counterbalance the overwhelming presence of American-inspired themes and thus to mobilize Catholics who still harbored misgivings about the "Yankee" culture of materialism and hedonism. It also helped De Gasperi improve his standing in American public opinion, since, as Richard Bosworth has pointed out, "the link with such a revered and age-old institution as the Vatican made [his party] look reliable" to the United States. Moreover, the Church gave the Christian Democrats the opportunity to turn this campaign into their own national crusade. Indeed, the Communists had scored better with anti-Americanism than with anticlericalism. Although De Gasperi found the Vatican's embrace a little too tight, he still stressed his allegiance to Christian values and their national heritage, while persistently denouncing the PCI's enslavement to the Cominform.[57] The confrontation could not be more absolute, but that was what the prime minister wanted: to transform the elections into a referendum on "civilization." He knew that the DC could gain as much from a drama that hit the Italians in their conscience as from the display of American aid that hit them in the stomach.

Having attained such a civilizational dimension, the struggle also led the PCI to reiterate its anti-American themes: at the Sixth Party Congress in February, Secchia first publicly addressed the issue of cultural colonialism. "The great trusts," he contended, "send us not only their riflemen, their spies, their agents, and organizers of sabotage and betrayal, but inundate our country with their books, their films, and their lowbrow ideological rubbish that should serve to weaken, disorient, and corrupt our people." The campaign to regiment the intellectuals behind the anti-American banner gained momentum. In January, Emilio Sereni launched the "Alliance for the Defense of Culture," immediately enlisting many progressive intellectuals. Its stated goal was to combat the twin offensive of "clerical obscurantism" and American "cosmopolitanism."[58] Indeed, this "civilizational" battle helped fuse communist anti-Americanism and anticlericalism. To the Communists, the Church's relentless intervention in the electoral contention was a "spearhead for imperialist interests." The external enemy appeared increasingly ominous because its political and cultural collusion with the enemy within seemed so complete. A few days after the elections, Togliatti instructed all regional party sections to denounce the Vatican's "intervention and [its] religious terrorism."[59] America's overt support of the DC had thus given the PCI the pretext to finalize its divorce with the country's Church establishment, and to suspend its attempts at seducing the Catholic masses. Tracing communism to the evolution of rational thought against clerical "obscurantism," from the Renaissance through the Enlightenment to the Revolutions of France and the Soviet Union, party intellectuals such as Ottavio Pastore and Mario Alicata (a close aide to Togliatti) now contended that in Italy even the liberal-capitalist tradition would be submerged in the antirationalist agenda of its far worse newly found ally, the Church.[60] The question remained whether welding anti-Americanism to anticlericalism could be as profitable for the PCI as it was for the PCF.

The Socialists, who sought in the Popular Front the certainties they had lost after their party split the previous year, rather became eclipsed by both the PCI organizational superiority and the polarization that rewarded unwavering allegiance to the Church or the Soviet Union. To distinguish itself from the PCI, the PSI therefore accentuated its rhetoric of national independence, anti-Americanism, and anticlericalism more than its homage to Moscow. Lelio Basso in particular underlined the connection between class warfare and the struggle against "Washington, the capital of imperialism." Socialist leader Pietro Nenni realized too late in the process that the campaign should have kept the two issues separate. He warned voters that "the electoral discourse [should] not revolve around America or Russia, but on the concrete mistakes committed by the DC in 1947 . . . in its social policies."[61] Fear more than debate underpinned the propaganda war.

Besides providing assistance to Italy's collapsing economy, Washington countered communist anti-Americanism with pro-Italianism more than an equivalent direct attack on the PCI. That Italy would lose Marshall aid if it went communist had to be made clear, but in a subtle way. So when the secretary of state presented this scenario on 15 March, he made sure that the argument did not sound like direct blackmail. After PCI representatives said they would accept aid if divested of its heaviest conditions—especially on the dollar counterpart funds and the heavy intra-European coordination—Charles Bohlen and CIO Secretary Treasurer James B. Carey retorted with a reminder of the strikes the previous autumn. Carey told CGIL Secre-

"18 April 1948—The tombs are uncovered, the dead reemerge: 'Leave Italy, foreigner!'" Christian Democratic poster against the PCI-PSI Popular Front for the 1948 national elections. The poster shows Garibaldi and his troops chasing Togliatti from Italy for defaming his name. Courtesy Archivio Manifesto Sociale, Rome.

tary General Giuseppe Di Vittorio that the ERP "was not a marmalade from which could be picked only the cherries and nuts." Washington argued that it was not American retaliation but rather the PCI's automatic alignment with the Soviet Union that would prevent Italy's participation in the ERP. While countering communist arguments, the American embassy was also trying to reverse Einaudi's economic policy, which had led to an unpopular recession.[62] Pressure for reform remained the lynchpin of America's approach to the election rather than straightforward anticommunism.

The other component of the U.S. pro-Italian display was diplomatic support. After the Soviets announced they would endorse Italy's trusteeship claims over Libyan territories in February, Ambassador Tarchiani did not hesitate to play on American stereotypes about the Italians: aid was not a sufficient show of friendship for the "Latins," who "were always quick to take offense at being slighted. . . . In their present circumstances the Italians were inordinately anxious for indications that they were regarded as equals."

Dunn had noticed that the Communists' nationalist campaign targeted Foreign Minister Carlo Sforza and his "alleged failure to protect Italy's independence from the American imperialists."[63] To remedy this, the United States reiterated its recognition of Italy as a partner during the war and of its promising role in the rebirth of an integrated Europe. Prompted by the French, Sforza on 2 March reminded the American ambassador that public support from the West of Italy's claim to Trieste would expose the Soviets' denial of Italian rights over the city and blunt the PCI's nationalist campaign.[64] On 20 March, Great Britain, France, and the United States issued a joint declaration promising the return of the Free Territory of Trieste to Italian jurisdiction. This diplomatic "masterstroke"[65] may have not been decisive in swaying the Italian electorate, but it certainly proved Sforza's point. It defused the Communists' posturing as defenders of national independence and honor; it exposed their own forced compliance with Soviet whims; and it constrained them to focus on economic issues while the United States was magnifying the benefits of Marshall aid.

But as the NSC already concluded in reexamining the situation a few weeks before the vote, it had become necessary to extend assistance "to the Christian Democrats and other selected anti-Communist parties. . . . by all feasible means." That meant applying the "unvouchered funds" for covert aid that the NSC had authorized in principle since the previous fall, and resorting to clandestine operations, which the CIA had already considered as the best way to fight communism.[66] Recent accounts confirmed that the Soviets also had funded the PCI at least since the previous year, but that the money until early 1948 arrived randomly and at a trickle. In view of the elections, the Soviets did establish a more steady channel through trade agreements and with loyal Italian entrepreneurs as intermediaries; it was, however, a slow operation that gave sizable results only by 1949. At the time of the election the U.S. intelligence on the Soviet funding operations relied mostly on rumors, which Tarchiani promptly exploited to demand action.[67] Even without help from Moscow, the ability of the Left's parties to mobilize grassroots support seemed by itself sufficient to overwhelm the centrist parties' propaganda machine. Apparently that ability had not been tarnished by the coup that in February installed a communist regime in Czechoslovakia. Using a historical cliché, James Dunn noted that the coup had intimidated but also impressed the Italians, who now, as in 1944, saw the Soviet Union "as a powerful and all too close neighbor"; the event even allowed the PCI to play up "with considerable skill and alarming success . . . the Italian propensity to flock to the winning banner."[68]

All these considerations added compelling reasons for CIA covert aid to boost the campaign of the centrist parties. The ensuing operation, under the direction of Secretary of Defense James Forrestal and Secretary of the Treasury John W. Snyder, funneled money to De Gasperi and his allies through the Economic Stabilization Fund established by the War Powers Act of 1941, and with the cooperation of U.S. banks. The complexity of the operation gave it an aura of miracle-working, at least among the officials who managed it. In fact, this contribution added a margin, not crucial, to the array of overt acts of U.S. support, to the appeals from the Church, and to De Gasperi's own campaign skills.[69] In early April, James Dunn credited all these elements for the ebbing communist tide, and added some complacency regarding his own role.[70] At the polls a few days later the Christian Democrats won in a landslide with 48.5 percent of the vote and an absolute majority of seats in the parliament; the Italians gave 31 percent to the Popular Democratic Front and 9.6 percent to the Social Democrats and Republicans combined.

The results, whether attributed to America's hand (visible and invisible) or to the local actors, prompted the Policy Planning Staff (PPS) to inaugurate the concept of "political warfare."[71] As one of its memos, drafted after the Italian elections, stated, "In broadest definition, political warfare is the employment of all the means at a nation's command, short of war, to achieve its national objectives. Such operations are both overt and covert. They range from such overt actions as political alliances, economic measures (as ERP), and 'white' propaganda to such covert operations as clandestine support of 'friendly' foreign elements, 'black' psychological warfare and even encouragement of underground resistance in hostile states."[72] That was how the "holding the line" strategy of containment transmuted into a more active, aggressive form of involvement, in places, such as Western Europe, where actual war was made unlikely by the nuclear deterrent.[73] Notably, the Communists in France and Italy also further downplayed insurrection scenarios by the time the nuclear stalemate between the two superpowers became evident, and the Korean War also showed American willingness to resist localized military aggression. Also confirming the need to harness their paramilitary groups was the instance of the mob violence that followed an assassination attempt against Togliatti in July 1948 and almost escaped the PCI's control.[74] For these reasons, in their own public relations campaign the two parties' strongest weapon became that of the peace appeal.

U.S. policy planners also concluded that political warfare needed a high degree of coordination. Viewing the Kremlin's "conduct of political warfare" as "the most refined and effective of any in history," the PPS criticized the improvised nature of Washington's conduct during the Italian election campaign and warned, "We cannot afford to leave unmobilized our resources for covert political warfare. We cannot afford in the future . . . to scramble into impromptu covert operations as we did at the time of the Italian elections."[75] Communist Party rallies were heavily attended and may have given the impression of effective mobilization, strength, and solidarity; but, as Togliatti admitted months before the polls, they tended to preach to the converted. Washington also overstated Soviet willingness to back the PCI with its full propaganda arsenal. In fact, the Kremlin also had resorted to some ad hoc last minute diplomatic or financial action, fearful rather of creating a precedent for U.S. interference in Eastern Europe.[76] For that reason, too, the PCI felt it urgent after the elections to devise a campaign that could restore its appeal outside its rank and file.

Finally, the fact that overt and covert U.S. support concentrated on the safest anticommunist asset, the Christian Democrats, at the expense of the center-left parties did not bode well for the American goal of superseding Italy's class conflict, with its bipolar mindset of anti-Sovietism and anti-Americanism. American intervention worsened the terms of an electoral battle which already on its own had become heavily conditioned by ideology without much reference to actual programs. In the following years, the United States had to forsake a truly reformist option in Italy. Support and some funding from British Labor and U.S. trade unions were not sufficient to transform Saragat's Social Democrats into a mass party.[77] Covert operations confirmed a client-patron relationship with its typical drawbacks on both ends: in addition to feeding the DC's worst patronage tendencies, dependency on U.S. aid also undermined the Italian leaders' claims of international status within the emerging Western Alliance. The CIA assessment in a postelection report was sober: "Whether we like it or not, now we're intimately involved in Italian politics and the next time the price tag will be considerably higher."[78]

Washington's misgivings about building politically reliable but dependent allies grew, as European leaders persistently called for U.S. protection of and even hegemony over their continent. Of course, the more the Western allies became militarized and dependent on the United States, the stronger became the communist campaign against the warmongering and culturally debased "Yankee empire."

At the PCI's Central Committee the blame for the electoral defeat remained focused on the concerted Washington/Vatican attack.[79] But the rhetoric merging anticlericalism and anti-Americanism prepared the ground for a campaign that stressed not the complementarity of the two aspects but rather the DC's utter subordination to the United States. The "capitalist monolith" thesis was even stronger among the Communists than the communist monolith thesis was in Washington. By emphasizing national enslavement though, the Italian Communists, and, in a parallel way, their French comrades, retained convincing nationalist credentials, reinforced during the birth of the North Atlantic Treaty Organization (NATO) by their pacifist appeal, as well as by the halting pace of economic redistribution.

Between Reconstruction and Rearmament, 1948–1952

By the time the Marshall Plan was implemented, it had become clear that the path to a modernized, consumerist, consensual society in Europe did not depend solely on defeating the Communists. A large majority of French and Italians, as Theodore White said regarding all of Western Europe, may have given an "unequivocal 'No'" to the Soviets, but "an equally steadfast 'Yes' to America was conspicuously missing."[80] According to the New Deal reformist approach dominant in the ECA, the American model based on high productivity and moderate reform, no matter how adapted to local circumstances, was inescapable for all those who wanted to modernize. For these reasons, the ERP's propaganda effort was especially intensified in countries like France and Italy, where the combined resistance from conservative and communist groups might undermine the project. Worse yet, such resistance from opposite directions could be mutually nurturing, either out of shared attachment to national traditions, or because, in response to communist charges, even the pro-American groups found it politically expedient to temper the most direct forms of U.S. influence.

Indeed, the ERP missions in France and Italy topped all the others in the allocation of funds for information and other special projects, such as the productivity drives that invited entrepreneurs and trade unionists to tour U.S. factories. The institutional framework for this public diplomacy was strong, thanks to the set up of an information division within the ECA Office of the Special Representative located in each capital, and—not always well connected with the ECA—the activity of Public Affairs Officers in each U.S. embassy. The propaganda effort accelerated in the summer of 1948, and its range became vast, including radio broadcasts (in conjunction with the VOA), exhibits, printed material and funding of American libraries (in cooperation with the USIS), concerts, essay contests, and ERP trains and ceremonies. While rather heavy-handed, this campaign strived to be multilateral, providing funds to local organizations, such as the Association France–Etats-Unis, the Association Française pour l'Accroissement de la Productivité (AFAP), the Confederazione Italiana Femminile (CIF), the Organizzazione Epoca, Radio Epoca, the Comitato Amministrativo Soccorsi ai Senzatetto, and journals such as *Rapports France–Etats-Unis*, *Réalités*, and *Productivity* (published in Genoa, Italy), to adapt the publicity to the respective cultural milieus.[81] By far the most effective medium, especially in Italy, was cinema.

The inundation of Marshall Plan newsreels and documentaries was the best way to reach the masses, even the "most mentally closed" among the communist workers and peasants. In the words of the deputy director of ECA's Information Division, Andrew Berding, cinema had the advantage of "transmitting information in ways that spectators can understand, believe, and remember."[82] It was not clear which feeling would predominate among the masses watching the films' display of American opulence: emulation or sullen envy. Hollywood films and ECA's images of the American way of life were countered not only by the fading Italian neorealism but, more significantly, by noncommunist sources, such as comedian and filmmaker Jacques Tati, who, with *Jour de fête* (1949) began his series of satires on modernization and productivity. Overall, Hollywood movies still left "much—too much to be desired," as the Motion Picture Association director in Paris, Colonel Frank McCarthy, had admitted in a letter to Marshall in October 1947; "but," he added, "the fact that [*L'Humanité*] devotes a half page twice a week to attacking and condemning them seems to indicate that they are important."[83]

American tourism also was supposed to shape a sort of "consumer diplomacy." Its main advantage was that the connection between government interests and politically un–self-conscious tourists was even less apparent than the one between Hollywood and Washington. Marshall planners intended to transform travel from an elitist pastime to a mass phenomenon "consistent with postwar ideals of a classless society" and to transmit this powerful image to Europeans while also restoring their pride in their own historic traditions and helping them to cover the dollar gap.[84]

As with any propaganda campaign, the main targets of these initiatives were the "undecided" voters within labor or among intellectuals, the two main potential constituencies of Western European Communists. But another general purpose was to address skepticism among conservative groups. Even without getting converts to their own cause, the French and Italian Communists' campaigns elicited alarm in Washington because of their capacity to reignite public mistrust of the United States based on traditions of anti-Americanism in both countries.[85]

Paul Hoffman concurred with the ECA's special representative in Europe that the Marshall Plan was "less successful, less understood, and less appreciated in France than in any other Western European nation." In Italy, after twenty years of fascist propaganda, some U.S. officials speculated, the public had built a certain immunity to any form of publicity from whichever political side.[86] In fact, the April elections had proven that propaganda and ideological discussion were as alive as ever in the Italian political culture. One major problem rather was that, as a memorandum from the State Department's Information Division stated, "the people of third countries [did] not react with shock, anger, or indignation to the charges made in anti-American propaganda as do some Americans." The document then spelled out the main risks of a contagious communist campaign:

> We should bear in mind that anti-American attitudes often exist within strongly nationalist but non-communist groups in third countries who, because of this, are susceptible to Soviet and communist propaganda, but who can and should be won over to a more friendly and sympathetic attitude toward the United States . . . We should bear in mind that the people of most third countries are primarily interested in those United States policies, actions, and internal developments that directly affect their welfare, their immediate economic prospects and their immediate individual interests. . . . We should bear in mind that the people of most third countries are little concerned with pretensions of the righteousness of United States aims or the sincerity of United States motives unless there is concrete supporting evidence that specific United States aims and motives are directly beneficial to their interests.[87]

There was a peculiar dilemma here. Even if Europeans evaluated American aid based on their "immediate economic prospects," Washington could not expect to increase its political leverage simply with economic aid. Recipient nations, while appreciating American generosity, also tailored it to their national and political priorities. The irony was that in order to gain more influence, the United States had to attune its aid policies and campaigns carefully to national sensibilities and specific national cultures. Berding proposed a solution that would reconcile the need to identify U.S. sponsorship with the need to defer to Italian national prerogatives. The ECA, he wrote in a memorandum to be presented in Congress in January 1950, had two objectives.

1. To convince the average Italian "that the Plan is his as well as Mr. Marshall's," in other words to increase the sense of national identification with the plan and to encourage a personal stake in its outcome.

2. To demonstrate the depth and seriousness of Italian-American cooperation: "Thus the signs which the Mission has induced the Italian Government to put up the many hundreds over the ERP Counter-

part fund projects carry the color of both countries, side by side, on the same shield."

Since Italy, after its most unpopular war, especially recoiled from militarism, the sense of shared transatlantic values would be further enhanced by an emphasis on the peaceful purposes of the United States. Therefore the best counterattack against the Communists was, according to Berding, "to avoid direct confrontation with the massive waves of Communist propaganda directed against the plan. Thus, when the Communists said the Marshall Plan was a plan of war, the Mission never said it was not a plan of war but over and over again . . . with every medium at its disposal, the Mission put across the slogan—'ERP means peace and work.'"[88]

The French and Italian governments manifested their resistance on all of the plan's three main levels: economic reform, continental integration, and propaganda. On the economy, more than other recipient nations, they adapted the Marshall Plan to their specific national agendas: in Italy the Einaudi line combined with the Christian Democrats' adaptation of Italian corporatism, and in France Jean Monnet's Modernization Plan diverged from ECA officials' investment priorities.[89] The large ranks of traditionalist businessmen, such as the powerful leader of Italian industrialists association (Confindustria), Angelo Costa, and the head of the French small employers federation, Léon Gingembre, also objected. Many of them in both countries identified national prestige and the protection of national identity with the preservation of ancestral traditions and old practices in the economy—hence their proud resistance to the American "productivist," mass-consumption model. Following this logic, local traditional elites matched the Communists and their denunciations of Americans as "dominateurs."[90] Another problem was that, unlike the Communists, backward-looking entrepreneurs and politicians offered no alternative vision of the future, just tradition. They failed to see that American aid, which they demanded, and American culture, which they shunned, were inseparable; for American culture was partly founded on the twin pillars of market economy and consumerism. Moreover, by basing their nations' legitimacy and prestige on their "historic" value, they unwittingly contrasted past glories with current powerlessness, in fact increasing their nations' dependence on the United States, and giving the Communists additional political ammunition.

The national paths to recovery of course made continental integration more difficult. Even when they did cooperate, the Western European states did not press hard enough toward the "third force" envisioned by U.S. officials. This was in part because they thought that a self-limited military sovereignty (at least toward the United States) was necessary to free up resources for reconstruction. However, from the onset, integration, for all European states, the large ones in particular, juxtaposed interdependence with an old-style balance of power. For each nation-state the Organization for European Economic Cooperation (OEEC—the sixteen-nation council established in April 1948 to oversee and coordinate Marshall aid) was the beginning of a bargaining process that allowed them to recreate themselves as functional units and to retain virtually all power.[91] France immediately championed economic integration, but mainly to keep the initiative and play "arbiter" of German reintegration in Europe's economy. As a memorandum from the French Foreign Ministry put it in 1949, the priority was to make sure "that the recovery of Germany not gain a step upon our own."[92] Other ERP recipients, including Italy, had fewer qualms about Germany's revival, and in 1947 immediately objected to French exclusive focus on the costly Monnet Plan through American aid. British opposition to France's integration plans above all highlighted their limits and further impelled Paris to seek membership in the great power club next to the United States and Britain.[93]

This competition among European nations was potentially a healthy process for each national revival within the framework of interdependence. But its damaging corollary was that it continued to make each large nation vie for America's favor, ultimately increasing their dependence on the United States. As defense minister in 1949, Paul Ramadier proclaimed, with the same counterintuitive logic Jean Monnet used in economic affairs, that within an Atlantic framework guided by the United States France would find "the power to make others respect [its] independence." Italy, after failing to make the OEEC a vehicle for its reentry in the European power club, began, through the negotiations for the Atlantic Pact, to rely on Washington to attain the same goal.[94]

Pro-American propaganda, even when handed to the local authorities, could easily lend itself to communist charges of subservience. This was particularly true for France, where public opinion was rather impermeable to blatantly pro-American publicity and particularly proud of national achievements. Washington did not worry about communist propaganda in its extremist, Cominform-inspired manifestations, but rather about the "chauvinist" connections the PCF was able to establish with proneutralist groups: Hubert Beuve-Méry's *Le Monde*, Jean-Paul Sartre's *Les Temps modernes*, and Emmanuel Mounier's *Esprit* were all leading publications that denounced the government's pro-American slant. Worse still, many proneutral opinion makers appealed to national prestige: "We are just being treated like Liberia," said Beuve-Méry to a group of U.S. embassy officials in 1951, "as an appendage, a satellite." Sartre, in 1948, founded the Rassemblement Démocratique Révolutionnaire, an organization of the "noncommunist" Left which, ostensibly, opposed both capitalism and the "limited" communism in its Stalinist forms; but clearly the organization's main foe was the "rotten" form of capitalist democracy influenced by the United States.[95] Far from weakening the impact of the Communists' rhetoric on national independence, this outlook reinforced their position. It came as no surprise to most U.S. officials that the French government, which, like all other aid recipients, had agreed to allocate some counterpart funds to conduct pro–Marshall Plan publicity, became very reluctant to go through with the agreement. The Italian government was more amenable to carrying on pro–Marshall Plan publicity, but front recruits such as the media group Organizzazione Epoca were too blatant to conceal their sponsors.[96] And even in a country that had cast chauvinism aside, pride reemerged, in part caused by public perception of subservience to the United States. Ironically, a memorandum from the State Department noted in 1950, the "almost miraculous" economic recovery Italy was beginning to experience helped its citizens end the "period of self-vilification" that followed the shameful fascist regime. Even as problems persisted, all parties, Ambassador Dunn observed two years later, "increasingly rel[ied] on [a] nationalist appeal as [a] measure of self-assertion and to distract [the public] from internal difficulties."[97]

The step from nationalist to proneutral sentiments could be a short one. Some Socialists in France and sections of the Christian Democratic Parties in both countries subscribed to the argument that U.S. aid might portend cultural hegemony and a *pax americana*. Prominent French MRP leaders, American officials reported in 1947, argued that U.S. economic power forced them to choose between a "U.S. peace and a Soviet peace," whereas they upheld "Human peace." "We French people," the leaders explained, "will continue to be ourselves only if we persist in defending the value of the spiritual."[98] Among left-wing Italian Christian Democrats, "spiritual" also meant a gradual and selective acceptance of U.S. leadership of the Western world, and avoidance of any risk of war. Some of the most influential DC leaders— Amintore Fanfani, Giorgio La Pira, and Mariano Rumor—had been followers of Cronache Sociali, the party current founded by Giuseppe Dossetti, who combined Catholic devotion, commitment to social welfare (they were early proponents of Keynesianism in Italy), and severe qualms about U.S. society. In 1948–49 the most loyal *dossettiani* also questioned Italy's adherence to NATO. The DC party group led by Giovanni Gronchi also connected Catholic traditions to a sense of social justice and winked at the Nenni Socialists as early as 1949, unwittingly playing, in Dunn's opinion, "the cat's paw of the

Communists."[99] These groups were alarming not only for their cultural *equi-distance* between Russia and America, but also for their *equation* of the two materialist, "war prone" superpowers. Both arguments inadvertently catered to the emerging communist peace campaign.

By 1948 anticommunism and the desire to get a large share of U.S. aid induced French Socialists, as well as left-wing Christian Democrats from both countries, who had toyed with the idea of a truly neutral European third force, to compromise with most aspects of American politics and culture, and to advocate Atlanticism.[100] But most of them, particularly in Italy, continued to reject the "acquisitive" aspects of the American model and remained prone to make their "yes" to America more equivocal than in this time of emergency.

The approval rate for the Marshall Plan was high overall among French and especially Italian public opinion. But the working class in both countries at best suspended its judgment. The masses still shouldered the costs of reconstruction and the slow establishment of a welfare society. As an ERP official in Paris noted in February 1949, "The European worker listens listlessly while we tell him we are saving Europe, unconvinced that it is his Europe we are saving." Almost two years later the same office reported that a "great segment of the European population" kept wondering "whether U.S. policy was aimed at progressive improvement in general living standards" or at shoring up the existing system. The shortcomings in social justice could be thus blamed on the collusion between indigenous "conservative vested interests" and market-driven U.S. capitalism. Some communist local administrators actually welcomed Marshall aid, but they also made sure they got credit for its improved applications. The PCI mayor of Bologna, Giuseppe Dozza, for example, claimed that if his party had run the Marshall Plan nationwide, "it would have worked much better."[101]

General dissatisfaction with the Marshall Plan also meant, as Caffery noted from Paris in November 1948, that the workers continued to have faith in the CGT, while many who had shifted to the Free Trade Union movement lost confidence in "pure" trade unionism.[102] In Italy the trade union split was occurring at this time, but without dramatically curtailing CGIL power. The Marshall Plan had generated widespread benefits for all, but, as a U.S. intelligence report of December 1952 described the situation of the previous years in France, the social gaps only widened. The study noted that "only a rough correlation exists between poverty and adherence to the French Communist Party. What is true, rather, is that the Party rallies those who are discontented with their present living standards, which may not necessarily be the lowest in the country, that they are convinced that only thoroughgoing changes in the social and economic order could possibly improve things for them. . . . to those who share this view, the overall economic improvement of France, which has unquestionably been taking place, does nothing to give them new confidence."[103] Most U.S. officials' immediate impulse was to attribute these setbacks to lack of internal reform and poor application of ECA guidelines. Caffery quickly became disenchanted with the French Socialists, and in 1948 he reconsidered the "Napoleonic" Charles de Gaulle, the strongest alternative to communism. But the general was too abrasive, polarizing, and, most crucial at this point, he seemed inept in economics. Similarly, Washington blamed Italy's traditionalists and the parasitic nature of the country's monopolistic structure for the persistent economic inequality.[104]

These social and political realities hindered the economic and psychological effects of the "revolution of rising expectations." It is true, as Charles Maier and Michael Hogan have pointed out, that the productivity drives helped alleviate the class struggles that arose from scarcity; and a technocratic elite finally emerged as the dominant economic actors in France and Italy by the early 1950s. Scientific management and corporative collaboration did help transform political problems into technical ones, and they diminished the role of class conflict in the French and Italian economies.[105] But the paradox of this "Americanization" lay in its concomitant "rising expectations": those whose gratification was delayed would remain, as Caffery recognized, "sullen, dissatisfied, and distrustful"[106] of their rulers and of America's intentions.

The Marshall Plan ended in 1952, replaced by the Mutual Security Program, but its character had already been distorted by the signing of the North Atlantic treaty and the Mutual Defense Assistance Program (MDAP) in 1949. Both the treaty and the program were designed to assist, not contradict, Europe's recovery efforts. Like the ERP, they primarily raised the morale of fragile governments and thwarted internal subversion. In fact, especially from the start of the Korean War, security and rearmament concerns seemed to prevail, to the detriment of ERP objectives.

From the final phases of the negotiations for a military alliance in early 1949, the aptly named Foreign Assistance Coordinating Committee in Washington emphasized the interconnection between security, recovery, and continental integration. Mutual security, one of its documents argued, would not only prevent Soviet-communist aggression but also "create an atmosphere of confidence . . . within which the chances of economic recovery programs may be enhanced." Furthermore, the MDAP, with the Point IV Program for foreign assistance, could, according to the Truman cabinet, "form the basis for building cooperative relations with other nations on a basis [*sic*] considerably less expensive than the continuation of such programs as [the] ECA." Avoiding military assistance to each country in bilateral form presented not only financial advantages. Bilateralism, as the U.S. ambassador to London, Lewis W. Douglas, explained, would have exposed Washington to the charge of "pursuing [the same] tactics as [the] Kremlin vis-à-vis [its] satellites." This would have "kill[ed] the conception of individual equality in an association of partners which should be [the U.S.] greatest asset." In dealing with defense, coordination and "unity of plans" became even more essential than they were in economic integration. By the fall of 1948, John Hickerson and the Policy Planning Staff already felt that all these issues of confidence and coordination were imperative for countries such as France and Italy. The chief of the State Department's European affairs division particularly urged Italy's inclusion in the Atlantic Pact lest it feel detached from Europe's *economic* integration, demoralized, and therefore prone to neutralism, or even communism.[107]

The goal of strengthening fragile governments' morale ended up hindering that of encouraging their self-reliance. Once military aid was identified as a morale booster, it became difficult to set limits and avoid manipulation by the shaky French and Italian governments.[108] With military self-reliance indefinitely delayed, it became harder to disprove communist charges that an expansionist United States was being obliged by subservient governments. Another problematic aim of military assistance, especially following the Korean events, was that of reconciling France with West Germany. This goal was at odds with Washington's effort to defuse the main PCF argument against rearmament, that it was a prelude to a neofascist U.S.-German entente.

Beginning in 1949 matters in France were further complicated by an inflationary spiral and the added military burden of fighting the Vietminh in Indochina.[109] The strain of rearmament, escalating after the beginning of the Korean conflict and the consolidation of NATO at the end of 1950, coincided with the first serious setbacks in France's colonial war. Not even the government of René Pleven, with the socialist and aggressively anticommunist Jules Moch as defense minister, could ask for rearmament and the extension of the military service while "France [was] being humiliated in Indochina." Although the Korean War had converted many of the French proneutrals into committed Atlanticists, Pleven could not, in the words of U.S. Ambassador David K. E. Bruce, "ask further sacrifices to [a] Communist oriented working class" that had launched the slogan "No national security without social security."[110]

Italy continued to refrain from considerably raising its military expenses.

When De Gasperi introduced the Atlantic Pact in the parliament he significantly described it "not as an act of necessity or submission . . . but as a chance to add to this alliance our thrust for peace . . . and all of [Italy's] vital civilizational contributions." He also immediately inaugurated a long Italian campaign for the application of the pact's Article 2, which emphasized economic cooperation among members of the alliance. During the negotiations for the revisions of the Italian Peace Treaty in 1951, Rome insisted more on its candidacy at the United Nations than on lifting the limitations on its military budget. The Italian government repeatedly argued that the country's living standards were being kept low not by its reform record but by higher military budgets. The Korean War and the prospect of Soviet aggression had no tangible effect on these feelings. For the government of Italy, more than for that of France, the main risk continued to be internal subversion rather than invasion.[111] The basic problem, Ambassador Dunn noted in early 1952, was that accusations of servility to the United States leveled by both Right and Left had the double effect of making the Italian government elusive on military expenses and increasingly inclined to nationalist posturing against any U.S. pressure. In Washington's interpretation, this meant that Italy's "moral recovery" had not yet matched its "astonishing economic recovery."[112]

The French and Italian governments followed a vicious cycle: they used the MDAP to boost their status (for France even its empire in Indochina), their security, and their internal stability, but they also had to reckon with the inevitable subordination that their demands entailed. Therefore they became increasingly sensitive to the superpower's encroachments in their affairs. But the United States presented a similarly contradictory argument, replete with clichés. A State Department memo for the president in January 1951 argued that the Southern European members of the Atlantic Pact (a category that included Belgium and Portugal as well as France and Italy), "by very reason of their Latin nature, suffer from emotional, political, and social instability. They are prone to swing from overoptimism to deep pessimism. . . . They have strong Communist Parties which exercise a corrosive influence on national morale. They are subject to the desire to be 'neutral.' Despite this, their governments have a real desire to move ahead in the building up of the necessary strength." Since these peoples were generally "apathetic" due to their nations' "defenseless condition," the document concluded, the initial drive that would galvanize them would have to come from the United States and more specifically through General Dwight Eisenhower as first Supreme Commander of NATO.[113] But strong U.S. leadership instead hampered the objective of European self-reliance.

A French-guided economic and military continental integration could

"Marshall Plan aid . . . for war." The PCI's anti–Marshall Plan propaganda poster (Roma: La poligrafica, 1948). Courtesy Fondazione Istituto Gramsci Emilia Romagna, Bologna.

solve this dilemma, and Paris had by then already advanced it through considerable U.S. prodding. Washington, however, had to remain only a source of inspiration, as Ambassador Bruce explained in September 1950, "giving the French government opportunity to assert [its] Continental leadership."[114] What Bruce had in mind was the success of the Schuman Plan for a European coal and steel pool, which, a few months earlier, had not only marked the first tangible integration of the French and German economies (also including Italy, Belgium, the Netherlands, and Luxembourg) but in doing so had also made it easier for continental Europe to "face higher military budgets," as the new director of the PPS, Paul Nitze, had argued. These developments, next to higher prestige for France as new leader of Europe, and for Italy as one of its prominent members, were expected to constitute the "best anti-Soviet and anti–PCF-PCI strategy."[115] The problem was that the French government, while ostensibly taking the lead a few weeks later, and proposing a European Defense Community (EDC)—the Pleven Plan as an institutional twin of the coal and steel pool—never felt as in control of military integration as it had with the first move toward economic integration.[116]

The plan indeed seemed too "inspired" by Washington, pressured by NATO's renewed emphasis on military preparedness after the North Korean attack on the South, and too focused on German rearmament, especially after the Americans insisted on amending the original French plan. This kind of pressure, along with atavistic French fears of German revival, reinforced not only the Communists' peace campaign, which had been under way for two years, but also their contagious anti-Americanism.

4 COMMUNIST PEACE CAMPAIGNS AND AMERICAN PSYCHOLOGICAL WARFARE, 1948–1955

Peace Ballots, an Alternative Nationalism, and a Different Europe

The Cold War communist peace campaign officially began in August 1948 with the Wrocław World Congress of Intellectuals for Peace. But the PCF had already mobilized a few months earlier under the drive of Resistance leader Charles Tillon, who, through contacts with prominent French intellectuals, helped found Combattants de la Liberté, later renamed Combattants de la Paix.[1] These initiatives followed Soviet directives. At the Cominform's founding meeting Moscow decided that disarmament propaganda would become its main anti-American offensive in the West. Orchestration from the Kremlin, however, did not exclude a symbiotic relationship that the PCI and especially the PCF sought to establish between their subordination to Moscow and their quest for international prominence. The Soviet Union found Paris, with the PCF's sponsorship, to be the best venue to regroup the pacifist offensive. The World Congress of Peace Partisans gathered in April 1949 in the same Salle Pleyel where the World Congress against Fascism and Imperialist War—under similar orchestration—had taken place in 1933. Back then, Henri Barbusse, Roman Rolland, and Albert Camus had lent their powerful voices to the cause. This time, France's most famous physicist, PCF member Frédéric Joliot-Curie, presided over the assembly.[2] The conference was followed by another Peace Congress in Prague, which adopted Picasso's Dove as symbol of the movement. In September 1949 the PCF introduced the "peace ballot" opposing German rearmament, the war in Vietnam, and nuclear weapons, and calling for a smaller military budget and a united Front of the Left. The appeal came in conjunction with preparations for the third Cominform conference, which in November, under Soviet ideologue Mikhail Suslov, theorized the pacifist strategy. This helped set up a permanent committee of the World Peace Congress in Stockholm in March 1950.[3] Issuing a declaration calling for the banning of nuclear weapons and the punishment as "war criminal" of "any" government that was "first" in using atomic bombs, the Congress clearly targeted the United States and Western European remilitarization. Through the Cominform, it invited all "peace partisans," including "liberals and defenders of free enterprise" to join. The declaration led to an unprecedented mobilization for a peace ballot, gathering 400 million signatures worldwide, including, under the PCF's and PCI's initiative, 9.5 million in France and 16 million in Italy, far beyond the two parties' memberships.[4]

In order to come out of their political isolation and regain domestic prominence and leverage, the two parties needed external exposure. They found it in a campaign that for a while restored their moral and intellectual prestige, and that was aimed at resuscitating Popular Front tactics. This time the front would have to surge from a mass popular movement and remain consistent with a class-conflict approach. The PCI's role at first was less preeminent than that of the PCF (although the formal initiative to appoint a World Committee of Peace Partisans came from Popular Front socialist Pietro Nenni).[5] The Italian party was initially restrained partly because it found German rearmament less urgent and partly because the PCI's isolation was mitigated by its pact with the Socialists. Eventually, however, the party and the astoundingly successful peace ballot benefited from Italy's acquired aversion to statism and war. The PCI also became the largest recipient of Soviet aid for communist activities abroad.[6] Through the Stockholm Appeal, in sum, the two parties assumed an international role comparable to the one they had enjoyed just after the war. Under this common denominator they effectively addressed the broader issues related to American domination.

To be sure, the slogans that characterized all the pacifist campaigns from 1948 to 1952 stemmed from the same battle and the same arguments used against the "Marshallization" of Europe. But with the appropriation of peace, those arguments acquired far greater articulation, intensity, and resonance, which clearly alarmed Washington. By rearticulating issues of Americanization around peace and cultural resistance, the Communists showed awareness that these themes were their greatest assets, and that an economic discourse per se was no longer sufficient to assail a capitalism refurbished by the American promise of widespread affluence.

A MORAL AND ECONOMIC IMPERATIVE

Under their slogan *Lutter pour le pain c'est lutter pour la paix* (fighting for bread means fighting for peace), the French Communists expressed the inextricable link between the true nature of American assistance and the country's economic degradation. From the start, they said, the Marshall Plan had prepared for war. Even the agricultural policy the United States was "imposing" on France, the party's political bureau argued in September 1948, was aimed at "turning her into a supply base for Western occupying troops."[7] From the establishment of the Atlantic Pact, the "bread and peace" slogan signified not only that military expenses siphoned off money needed for reconstruction and social redistribution; it also established a firm connection between economic justice, morality, and patriotism—all three denied by a costly war in Vietnam that served American imperialism.[8] After not voting on most of the peace treaty provisions, the PCI emphasized the damage from the revisions allowing for rearmament, which not only "put the wishes of American warmongers above the needs of Italy's poor and unemployed," but also accepted a double infringement of sovereignty: by conceding airspace and naval bases to the United States, and by closing "natural outlets" for Italian commerce in the East. "At a time when Italy was critically dependent on trade expansion," the economic section of the PCI secretariat argued at the end of 1953, "rearmament has negatively affected all Italian exchanges . . . particularly with the East."[9] In 1950 Togliatti had argued in *Rinascita* that "Italy would not be the poor, backward country it is today . . . if national fanaticism, imperialist wishes, and the blindness of her reactionary rulers or her servants to foreign imperialism had not forced her to war so many times."[10] Only through peace then could Italy attain wealth, real patriotism, and prestige.

Emphasis on economic degradation and the pauperization thesis that was taking hold especially in the PCF merged with the declinist argument about the United States. The Americans would keep resorting to military adventurism, both parties repeatedly claimed, because of their domestic economic difficulties. To gain an international audience, Togliatti explained to the party directorate in September 1949, "we must highlight that militarism originates from the recurrent crisis of international capitalism, and now from the need the United States has to export its capital to Europe." In doing so, he added, the Americans, feigning to support European unity, were in fact "aiming at the disaggregation [*sic*] of Europe."[11] Military escalation in Korea, together with the mixed U.S. attitude toward French colonialism (which it supported only in Vietnam) solidified this conviction that the United States exacerbated economic troubles, colonial oppression, and intraimperialist competition with its Western allies. It also became imperative, a 1948 directive from the PCI explained, "to break America's illusions that it can prevail through war, by illustrating the political, social, industrial, military strength of the U.S.S.R. and of all democratic countries who struggle for peace and for their liberty."[12] *Military* empowerment was thus important for the Soviet camp. The Peace Partisans, while spreading their appeal, maintained a clear distinction from the humanitarian, abstract pacifism of the bourgeois or religious traditions. "We are not a having a meeting of conscientious objectors," said Nenni at the Paris Congress. "We are a world congress of men determined to conduct with any means the struggle against the party of the third war, the struggle against the Atlantic Pact." Both parties made it abundantly clear that peace could be attained only when capitalism was eliminated, through armed struggle if necessary.[13]

Both the economic and the moral issues were at the heart of the peace ballot mobilization. *Pain et paix* was not only a catchy alliteration. It also helped relegitimize the communist trade unions after the failure of the anti-Marshall strikes. The CGT and CGIL galvanized workers by showing them the connection between their welfare and disarmament. By 1952, when the movement was losing steam, the task of the CGT was, according to the PCF's interim secretary Auguste Lecoeur, "to remind workers, who *correctly* understood that the struggle for peace per se would not bring about the liquidation of capitalism," that peace was "not essentially a middle-class issue" (an interesting observation, presaging the party's trouble in reconciling class struggle with broader moral existential questions). For the CGIL, after the first revision of the peace treaty, it was a matter of opposing the industrial reconversion to military production, while pressing for a productivity plan alternative to that of the ERP. The CGIL's plan envisioned nationalization of the service industry and a vast program of public works.[14] But leaders of both parties continued to balance their efforts to restore faith among their rank and file with efforts to extend their appeal "tactically to all groups" likely to question U.S. intentions. The PCI was better at using its own method of "indirection," excluding, according to its carefully crafted instructions, "*specific* institutional connections with organizations or individuals who ha[d] adhered to the peace movement." The ballot had to appear "spontaneous," endorsed by the "most illustrious signers." The goal was to "reach those who [had] voted for the government parties in 1948, and [who were] now dismayed by the missed promises of peace and neutrality."[15]

Another way to heighten the popularity of the movement was to involve the most vulnerable groups. Since the Marshall Plan propaganda had targeted women and young people as the main beneficiaries of U.S. aid in the long term, communist propaganda responded with demonstrations and iconography that illustrated women and children as the principal victims of a total, indiscriminate nuclear war carrying the U.S. label. Sheer horror and the prospect of apocalypse captured Europe's popular imagination during the Korean War. The peace campaigns of the early 1950s owed their success in large part to this collective fear. They invoked either the still recent memories of war devastation or the prospect of certain annihilation in the nuclear age.[16] Both the PCI and the PCF had already developed a pacifist rhetoric by which they portrayed themselves as defenders of the defenseless. The vigor of the peace campaign, the 1948 PCI directive argued, would be "vastly increased by [the party's] combined slogan: Let's save our children from the atomic bomb; let's save the Greek children, victims of fascism and of American imperialism." The PCF posters against NATO and the Korean War tended to merge, on the one hand, international solidarity with the victims of U.S. aggression and, on the other, nationalist assertion: The iconic working-class mothers and children devastated by war were those of World War II France rather than Asia. Besides invoking motherhood and maternalist traditions, the two parties utilized the young to raise tension with U.S. troops. French writer André Stil, who was awarded the Stalin Prize in 1952 for his novel *Le premier choc* exalting the dockworkers' resistance to the disembarkation of U.S. military supplies, also did something more active than writing to "improve" this resistance: he had the PCF's youth organizations send *animateurs* to all locations (bars above all) frequented by U.S. troops, where they were to start clashes that would expose "the scandalous behavior" of the occupants.[17]

The accent on the moral depravity of U.S. foreign policy naturally brought immediate results, unveiling the hypocritical nature of the nation with the highest professed moral standards. For that reason, too, the French unleashed their most venomous protest in 1952 at the arrival in Paris of General Matthew Ridgway, who, according to rumors, had ordered the use of bacterial weapons in the Korean War. But no "genocidal" charges were actually needed to incriminate American occupation. In Italy, the PCI welcomed a visit by the revered General Dwight D. Eisenhower with comparisons to such wartime demons as Rodolfo Graziani and Albert Kesselring.[18]

This formidable mobilization and propaganda apparatus confirmed the two parties' institutional and cultural strength. In fact, uncertainty, sectarianism, and tactical setbacks continued to reduce the scope and reach of the peace campaign. As with the mobilization for the Italian elections, the fervor of party militants had made the demonstrations seem more significant than they actually were: "We seem to gather only people with opinions closest to ours," complained a PCF directive in September 1950. One year after invoking anti-Atlanticism as the main thrust of the movement, Nenni warned that it was dangerous "to alienate those who are with us on the atomic bomb simply because they are not against the Atlantic Pact." The more directly the United States was targeted, the more limited the movement appeared. It is no wonder that the anti-Ridgway demonstrations, a PCF initiative to prove its internal strength, were castigated by the Cominform (for other reasons as well, as I will explain below). At the Central Committee, Lecoeur invited self-

"No, France will not be another Korea!" Anti-NATO poster by the PCF, 1951.
Courtesy Collection du PCF/Archives départementales de la Seine-Saint-Denis.

analysis of such "outrageously sectarian" episodes.[19] The success in gathering signatures was also subjected to a sober assessment: although a powerful statement, it was bound to remain symbolic if, as Emilio Sereni noted, it was not complemented by further press campaigns and other forms of mobilization in parliament and on the streets.[20]

Economic and moral issues galvanized the masses into immediate action. But it was on the themes of national sovereignty and European integration that the PCF and PCI built the movement's most enduring appeal. Even though the two parties' patriotic credentials were not as strong as in the last year of World War II, the effects of their nationalist propaganda reached their peak between 1949 and 1952. The French and Italian governments' drive for European integration allowed the Communists to propose a more assertive definition of their nations' identities and prestige. It was again a brand of moral patriotism, heir of the Resistance, and ostensibly hostile to traditional chauvinism.

The worst trait of bourgeois nationalism, the argument went, was that under the guise of expansionism, it actually protected the privilege of the few. Also, the bourgeoisie would always opt for subservience to more powerful nations, as long as the foreigners secured its class interests. France was littered with examples of such hypocrisy—Lecoeur reminded his party's Central Committee in February 1952—and much as Edouard Daladier, Philippe Pétain, and Paul Reynaud had surrendered to Hitler, so now Robert Schuman, Georges Bidault, René Pleven, and the others were surrendering to America. But while the bourgeoisie's "trahison" of national interests had previously been temporary, now, locked into the institutionalized forms of NATO and especially under the European Defense Community (EDC)—if that project passed the parliamentary vote—it would be a "permanent one."[21] The two parties evoked widespread fears that France would be reduced to providing *fantassins* for a war decided by nuclear weapons, and that Italy would be no more than a *portaerei* (air carrier) *americana*. Nazi and Munich analogies became all the more expedient once the United States began to press for German rearmament—the Communists were not alone arguing that the EDC project would lead to the resurrection of the Wehrmacht. As early as 1949, Charles Tillon had fully developed the argument of a conjoined capitalist-militarist-fascist conspiracy driven by Washington against French national interests. In an open letter to Truman, he said France had "not forgotten that Hitler's aggression was made possible by a growth of German industry fostered by an influx of Anglo-Saxon capital." Of course, in denouncing German resurrection, the PCF especially aimed to capture the support of many bourgeois nationalists; but, Thorez had recommended in 1949, this effort had to go along with the fight against French rearmament so as to exclude "toute orientation chauvine."[22]

Chauvinism was also a code word for Titoism. Thanks to the Soviet

"The United States refuses to sign the ban on bacteriological weapons. Truman declares: 'We have fantastic weapons.' Stop the war criminals! Americans are spreading the plague and cholera in Korea, China. The whole world is threatened!" PCF poster, 1952. Courtesy Collection du PCF/Archives départementales de la Seine-Saint-Denis.

breakup with the Yugoslav dictator in 1948, the PCI could comfortably combine allegiance to Moscow and nationalist claims against Yugoslavia, now even guilty of making deals with NATO.[23] In taking the lead against the Titoist "heresy," the PCI and PCF were also vying for a prominent position within the Cominform. Furthermore, the distinction between the nationalist orientations of Yugoslavia and the purposes of the peace movement underscored the need to place proletarian internationalism (i.e., obedience to Moscow) always above national paths to Socialism. By 1952 the pro-Soviet line of Jacques Duclos and Pietro Secchia prevailed over the opinion of those, such as André Marty, Charles Tillon, Valdo Magnani, and Aldo Cucchi, who wanted to make the peace movement truly independent as well as an instrument of *rapid* emancipation from American control. Consequently, the losers in this diatribe were expelled under the charge that their nationalism was just a form of heretic "Titoism."[24]

One needed not follow these developments to understand the inconsistency of communist nationalism in France and Italy. Under the same pacifist denominator that carried the message of sovereign rights against U.S. domination were also the most controversial declarations by the two parties' leaders. In September 1948 the PCF's political bureau turned a phrase by Maurice Thorez into a memorable slogan: "The French people will not wage, will never wage war against the Soviet Union." A few months later Togliatti announced in the parliament: "There will never be a war against the Soviet Union, the people will prevent you from doing it." While these may have been impromptu declarations, their reiteration in the following years helped focus the two parties' anti-American campaigns, especially after the start of the Korean War.[25] But the slogans also prompted public questioning of the two parties' "patriotic" credentials. The PCF was particularly troubled, fending off accusations of being a "foreign" party. Beginning in the fall of 1948 it even had to conduct a publicity drive to overcome doubts among its rank and file about the declaration.[26] The efforts by both parties were a shrewd campaign to prove that even the nationalist elements attacking communist internationalism were in fact the most emblematic members of the Fascist-American collusion. De Gaulle's Rassemblement du Peuple Français (RPF) triumphed in the 1951 national elections, becoming the second-largest party. The PCF, still the largest vote-getter but declining from the 1946 vote, became keen on exposing the General's authoritarian tendencies as well as his record of subservience [*sic*] to America during the postwar period (Roger Garaudy dug up evidence from Eisenhower's memoirs). In 1953 Italian Prime Minister Giuseppe Pella, who pursued public approval by catering to nationalist sentiments in Trieste, was, in the PCI's jargon, in fact a "mero CEDista" (a mere supporter of the EDC).[27]

The Soviet Union also hindered the nationalist, if not moral appeal of the peace campaign by changing its course from outward opposition to NATO and the EDC to negotiation and coexistence. The Peace Partisans' Berlin Conference of February 1951 endorsed Stalin's proposal for a Five Power Pact. As the Soviet dictator prepared to rearm East Germany and embarked on the H-bomb project, he preferred to deflect attention from this most spectacular arms race. At the same time, he tried to derail the process leading to the EDC: this was the main purpose of his note the following March calling for the neutralization and reunification of Germany. The PCF, which late in 1950 had conducted another ballot against German rearmament and continued to focus on the vilification of the United States, was taken by surprise by the Soviet transition. Anti-Americanism was more intense in France than in Italy. But so was the fear of a strong Germany, even a neutralized one. The PCF's pacifist campaign had until then thrived on a nationalist surge that was largely founded on these twin sentiments. In September 1952 the iconic Joliot-Curie had to announce that the Peace Partisans must follow "the principle of peaceful coexistence . . . and oppose the politics of crusade." The PCI had an easier task keeping its peace campaign distinct from the Cominform diktats.[28] In part for these reasons Stalin attempted to harness Togliatti by offering him the direction of the Cominform in 1951. The Italian leader declined, and the Soviet dictator had better luck controlling the PCF, thanks in part to Thorez's convalescence in Russia for almost three years from the end of 1950.[29] But the main problem with peaceful coexistence was that it moved the axis of confrontation with the United States from military to economic/political plains. Both the PCF and the PCI, despite their accent on disarmament, were troubled by the shift that drew attention to economic competition, even with all the delays and flaws of the two countries' economic redistribution. Their occasional resumption of fierce attacks on American politics and society in part derived from this discomfort as well as from a desire to mitigate their subservience to Moscow.

With all these contradictions, it was not communist nationalism per se that posed a threat to NATO and European integration. Washington rather worried about the appeal of its derived arguments on European integration and, as with communist resistance against the Marshall Plan, about its indirect effects on French and Italian nationalist-neutralist sentiments.[30] While easing the French and Italian Communists from their political isolation, the pacifist campaign hardly portended imminent electoral reversals.

The 1951 polls in both countries actually signaled a shift to the right. Following the vote, the French and Italian governments became keener on their countries' sovereignty and more uncertain about the benefits of European integration, especially military.

While the PCI and PCF continued to exploit nationalist feelings (against the *revanchards allemands* or the unfulfilled Western promises of full redemption for Italy), they appealed to public doubt on European integration in other ways, too. "True" integration should have included the East. It was soon forgotten that the Stockholm Appeal upheld the two-camp thesis. The shift in focus to peaceful coexistence by 1952 implied that Europe's economy would have vastly benefited from trade and, eventually, integration with the East. Even sections of the most anticommunist bourgeoisie, Pajetta told Sereni in early 1954, would join the anti-EDC campaign out of resentment of U.S.-imposed restrictions on trade with the East. Besides economic advantage, under socialism, integration would also be fully compatible with national sovereignty. In 1949 Joanny Berlioz, head of the PCF foreign policy section, had best explained this position in *Cahiers du communisme*, arguing that "Capitalism ha[d] no *patrie*" as it was "detached from the nation, which it betrayed on behalf of class interests." The only true capitalist nationalism in the West was the American one, which, with profits earned in World War II, now aimed at "world domination." Therefore, European integration was nothing but a form of "Americanism." Berlioz concluded: "Proletarian internationalism is the opposite of Americanism, it unites people against their exploiters, the enemies of their peaceful existence, instead of yoking them. . . . It enriches a national sentiment instead of suppressing it, it reinforces it in times when this sentiment has become the prerogative of the working class leading the masses, one of its best weapons against the bourgeoisie, which has no homeland."[31]

In Italy, where nationalism, after the fascist failures, was far less dynamic than in France as a state ideology, pacifism had greater chances of being turned from a subculture to a new national *and* transnational ideology. In fact, much like the Christian Democrats now conceived European integration as "instrument of nation-building," the PCI's pacifist campaign suggested a reconceptualization of Europe. What would distinguish the authentic European integration from the phony one driven by Washington would be its pacifism (under the Soviet aegis). Indeed, more than economic factors, this moral stance could become the paramount distinction between a renewed European identity, now transcending its own recent tragic mistakes, and the "morally backward imperialist America."[32] The PCF took the cue from this argument to portray socialism as the best way to "oppose true

Franco-German reconciliation to false reconciliation." Only socialism would fully convert the Germans to Europeanism instead of fostering their revanchism.[33] The Communists actually had no plausible alternative to offer to Western European integration; their grasp of interdependence was still doctrinal (Leninist) and rudimentary. But the emotional if not the rational appeal could have unsettling effects on Franco-Italian domestic politics and NATO.

INTERPLAY WITH DOMESTIC POLITICS

With all the emphasis on socialist solutions and reverence for Soviet "liberated" Europe, the idea of reaching a proneutralist consensus seemed farfetched. Yet the two parties pursued it relentlessly. The peace movement, while ideologically devout, was also ecumenical in its approach. In Italy, it drew some Christian Democrats, such as Igino Giordani, and Florence Mayor Giorgio La Pira, who beginning in 1952 sponsored annual "Congresses for Peace and Christian Civilization." Indeed, the PCI turned the peace campaign into an instrument to break the Vatican's grip over the conscience of the country's faithful. "We must court the little priests against the big ones," Togliatti told the party's directorate after the Stockholm Appeal. The previous year, in a clever retelling of the argument on "God and the Dollar," *Rinascita* had underlined the collusion between the Vatican and Washington with another editorial titled "God and the Atlantic Pact." Unlike the previous article, which had preceded the 1948 elections, this one took pride in proclaiming the party's atheism. But this did not exclude the appeal to the Catholic masses. What mattered was that the communist embrace of pacifism was still closer to the actual gospel than was the Church's endorsement of Atlanticism. Toward the end of the ratification debate on the EDC, Di Vittorio suggested a renewed emphasis on the imperialist and the "social aspects" of the defense project, because they would have a "sure grip over the Catholic masses."[34] A similar reasoning applied to the French MRP and especially to the left wing of the SFIO, with whom the Communists wanted to restore a unity action pact. Also, in France prominent neutralists continued to fear a pervasive, aggressive United States more than a flawed but redeemable Soviet Union.[35]

By making the World Peace Movement inclusive, the two Communist Parties also fine-tuned their domestic strategies. The PCF endeavored to split the Socialists by exposing the "betrayal" of those among them who were sold out to Atlanticism or those who were mere "humanitarian" pacifists. For the PCI, it became crucial to highlight how the centrist government had betrayed the masses that had elected it in 1948.[36] Indeed, this Popular Front tactic, the PCF specified from the start of its campaign, needed to be diametrically opposed to the 1930s Popular Front choices, which had been "driven from the top at the expense of unity of action at the popular level." The *classe contre classe* method prevailed, and the shift to coexistence, stressing the "will of the people" over their governments, actually accentuated the effort to base the movement on mass mobilization.[37]

Communist propaganda, however, could be disruptive with or without enlisting the dominant parties or groups within them to the communist cause. Although de Gaulle and the PCF felt nothing but antagonism toward each other, against the EDC they both argued for the defense of national independence and against damaging American influence. De Gasperi's Christian Democrats were still crusading against the PCI, but, as Togliatti noted, the pacifist campaign should be partly credited for the prime minister's decision in 1951 to begin advocating the application of NATO's Article 2, which stressed economic over military cooperation.[38]

Under combined pressure from the right and the left, the French and the Italian governments found justification for putting off ratification of the EDC treaty, until Prime Minister Pierre Mendès-France let it founder in the French parliament in August 1954. Worse still, the two governments seemed to lower their guard against the Soviet threat. The French foreign ministry seriously inquired about Stalin's note of March 1952. A year before, Italian foreign minister Carlo Sforza had proposed to test Soviet intentions by announcing a "nonaggression pact." And in the summer of 1954 Mendès-France told the astounded U.S. secretary of state John Foster Dulles that he was considering accepting Molotov's invitation for a summit. In every instance the French and Italian leaders claimed that they intended to "expose" Soviet designs. But all these were sure signs that they were becoming too independent for Washington's comfort, and that they were seeking a way out of the difficult EDC project. As Washington's new Psychological Strategy Board (which I analyze below) noted in 1953, the pursuit of rank through old-style balance of power, together with the twin resilience of their Communists and nationalists, turned the two allies' "understanding and feelings of the immediate Russian danger many degrees below our own."[39]

INTERPLAY WITH CULTURAL FEARS

Neutralist sentiments in France and Italy could also stem from deep-seated fears of the leveling effects of the American presence. That was why communist propaganda encompassed every aspect, linking the cultural to the political connotations of Atlanticism. Intellectual icons, as we have seen, were at the helm of the movement. One of the most emblematic was Jean-Paul

Sartre. In the early 1950s, he became the "model fellow-traveler," and, with his dominance of the French intellectual world, he further strengthened the PCF's cultural appeal. The Soviet Union was, in his view, ultimately bound to peace, and it was only natural for Sartre to become active in the Moscow-orchestrated anti-American "peace offensive." In 1954 he visited the Soviet Union, and later that year he was appointed vice president of the France–U.S.S.R. association.[40]

Intellectuals gave the movement not only luster but also a keen elaboration of the discourse along the theme of the "wasteland"—cultural and physical—portended by the U.S. "empire." At Wrocław, writer Ilya Ehrenburg best evoked the worst fears of Europe's anti-Americans from throughout the Left: "By seizing the countries of Western Europe," he said, "the Yankees bring along not Einstein, Faulkner, Fast, Chaplin, but the standardized thriller novels, the standardized gangster movies, all sorts of opium, that is. They want to narcotize Europe to tie it up and shackle it more easily. It's an attempt against each people's national traits, against their originality, against their diversity." PCI philosopher Antonio Banfi pondered on the troubling "overseas pathetic idealism replete with the Calvinist presumption of pseudo-democratic pedagogism"; next to an "escapist neoromanticism, infected by resentment and impotence"; all these were "manifestations of obscurantism, of a cultural reactionary spirit, bonded together in a destructive endeavor."[41]

Conducting a "grand inquiry" into U.S. military occupation in France, in 1951 *L'Humanité* told its readers that the Americans "loved France's Bourbonnais countryside . . . the mountains, groves, flaky sky, fat silken cow pastures in meadows covered with lucent grass." They "loved" it as did the Nazis who had "shot forty-two patriots" there; and with similar insolence and disregard for the location's beauty, they had now "installed one of their military depots for the coming war." On the occasion of Ridgway's visit to Italy, Togliatti described the general's mixture of biblical devotion and proneness to mass destruction as emblematically American: a "strange, bizarre concoction of the grotesque, tragic, ridiculous that characterizes the primitive nature of the culture and moral stature of the United States of America!"[42] Although this absolute anti-Americanism was somewhat mitigated beginning 1952 by new accents on coexistence, the gist of communist propaganda in France and Italy remained the same: the physical and cultural devastation that the powerful and foolish American empire would bring continued to be interlaced.

Neutralism then might thrive on the antipragmatic intellectual tradition in both France and Italy, which, as the Psychological Strategy Board noted in 1953 with regard to the French, signified not only widespread anti-

Americanism but also an old-fashioned view of power, based on political and cultural more than economic factors.[43] All this meant that the American promise of affluence and rising expectations could be foiled by the necessity of military preparedness in Western Europe, as well as by the combined forces of tradition and Marxism. Historian Yves Santamaria correctly notes that neither the PCI's nor the PCF's "fights for peace" had a "decisive influence" over electoral results; he also questionably concludes that they "did not affect" Italy's and France's contributions to the defense of Western Europe.[44] Both countries' decisions to torpedo the EDC, or to limit their military budgets, were dictated not only by economic and strategic considerations but also by concerns about domestic public opinion.

The recent argument, founded on archival material of the former Soviet Union, that the peace movement was exclusively designed to serve the Kremlin's expansionist agenda is also reductionist; and so is its corollary that it appealed to the most unjustified forms of anti-Americanism, without a lasting effect.[45] For all their orchestration and shortcomings, the communist peace campaigns rekindled public fears about war—especially nuclear—and contributed to the increasing discrepancy between the European and the American governments' views on how to wage the Cold War. What matters most is not how much noncommunist public opinion believed the Communists' arguments about America's ineptitude, imperialism, and "fascist" tendencies, but how much it feared a militarily and economically reckless strategy the United States might impose on its allies.

Overall the pacifist campaigns of the early 1950s allowed Italy's and France's communist leaders to harmonize the various strings of their "grandeur" policies: Togliatti and Thorez seemingly stood at the helm of an international alternative, based on international proletarian solidarity, to the projects of Monnet, Schuman, or De Gasperi; at the same time, the Communists used pacifism to emphasize their commitment to national independence against American imperialism; and, as the "natural" defenders of the economically oppressed, they complemented their patriotism with a display of concern for their countries' welfare, allegedly threatened by a U.S.-imposed rearmament effort. The communist discourse was thus a blend of four different notions of prestige and statesmanship: the internationalist, nationalist, moral, and economic.

Washington Escalates Psychological Warfare, 1950–1953

Facing the convergence of all these sources of communist leverage, the Truman administration thoroughly coordinated its own anticommunist offensive. There was nothing radically new in Washington's conclusion by 1951 that "the doctrine of economic determinism [was] too simple a hypothesis for France and Italy"[46]—except that, as the Communists did with their own campaigns, the United States now intensified and systematized its attack on its opponents' propaganda and institutional power. As containment itself became globalized and more prone to resist any form of communist aggression, so did U.S. resolve not only to exclude French and Italian Communists from power but also to eliminate their influence on every aspect of their nations' life. Improving previous formulations, the new "catchall" definition became "psychological warfare." It was a comprehensive as well as vague notion that, Eisenhower as president explained later, could include anything "from the singing of a beautiful hymn up to the most extraordinary kind of physical sabotage." The very escalation of the Cold War implied a total conflict, in which actual war by traditional military means had become highly deterred, therefore inviting alternative means. "We can reach our objective not solely, not even chiefly by means of military force," read a document from the newly created Psychological Strategy Board in November 1951, "so our intention is to use all other conceivable means to reach our objective; means that are lumped together under the general heading of "'Psychological Operations.'" Clearly, however, the core of "psy-war" consisted of posturing, propaganda, and covert operations.[47]

Thus it was the "uninhibited" Soviet propaganda and the danger of a spreading anti-Americanism in Western Europe, combined with a conservative turn in American politics, that prompted the Truman administration to shift "from a defensive to an aggressive posturing," as a public policy background paper put it in April 1950, in order to "recapture the initiative in the Psychological field." Still alleging that "propaganda," with all its pejorative connotations, simply was "un-American," the United States preferred to launch its psychological warfare in the West (and throughout the countries behind the Iron Curtain), in terms of a "Campaign of Truth," as Truman that same month baptized his program to counteract the Soviet peace offensive. The president also clarified that this would be a "sustained, intensified program to promote the cause of freedom against the propaganda of slavery." To underline this difference, it also had to remain clear that the West's public diplomacy would only complement and never contradict its own actions. "In a free as opposed to a totalitarian society," a document from the United States Information and Exchange Program (USIE) explained two years later, "acts and events have a greater impact on public opinion than propaganda as such."[48] While I analyze the cultural component and the specific complex diplomatic designs of this "counteroffensive" in subsequent chapters, here

I will address the emergence of psychological warfare in its broadest diplomatic, political, and institutional terms.

It may seem peculiar that, in a propaganda revolving around peace, the United States immediately emphasized military preparedness. But America's enduring concern throughout the early 1950s was that the communist peace offensive was designed to deepen apathy in Western Europe. Military strength on *both* sides of the Atlantic was presumed to be a psychological boost regardless of its projected economic benefits. The essence of the pivotal 1950 National Security deliberation known as NSC 68, which tripled the U.S. military budget, was, in Secretary of State Dean Acheson's mind, to "prevent the erosion of European confidence in the U.S." and to "prevent a European sellout" to the enemy. ECA officials concurred that greater NATO coordination, military preparedness, and "greater firmness" toward the Communists all contributed to an "improvement in leadership," particularly in France and Italy.[49] The authors of NSC 68 presumed that Europe would do away with U.S. military assistance in the long term—hence the EDC project. But in the meantime, as the French representative to the Atlantic Council, Hervé Alphand, argued a year later, it was essential to portray NATO to the French people "as a triumph of French diplomacy, which had requested and finally obtained such protection." The French newspaper *Combat* summarized the main problem, not only for France, in this line of thinking: "You cannot combine a hat-in-hand attitude with national dignity."[50] The communist peace appeal, as we saw, intensified a nationalist mood that denounced both the dependence on U.S. aid and the vision of an international third force through Western European integration.

U.S. military assistance needed to be further qualified. From the onset of the military assistance program for Europe, as I have noted, Washington stressed the link between security, recovery, and continental integration. More specifically, America's response to the Soviet peace offensive entailed a systematic campaign, coordinated among the United States Information Service (USIS), radio broadcasts from Voice of America (VOA), and the ECA, to prove that NATO was indeed the best guarantee for peace and for an integrated economic system in Western Europe. "Campaigning for truth" also meant exposing Soviet lies: Moscow's "pretensions of peace" had to "be contrasted with its "repeated obstructions toward peace settlements"; its alleged protection of sovereignty rights "had to be contrasted with its record of domination and exploitation of its satellite states."[51] Moreover, in proposing a global strategy, NSC 68 included nonmilitary aspects. Its key part regarding Western European allies was not rearmament per se but the connection between overt and covert actions "in the fields of economic and political and psychological warfare."[52] No doubt this global strategy was aggressive and potentially overbearing. But its implementation turned out to be more subtle than the new Policy Planning Staff director, Paul Nitze, and other hawkish proponents of NSC 68 envisioned. It combined a quest for greater influence with a promotion of stronger leadership in Western Europe. To obtain both, psy-war had to rely on indirect methods and press French and Italian leaders to exercise statesmanship by taking responsibility against communist subversion and constructing European integration.

Against the communist peace movement, the United States had been following this double approach from as early as 1949, helping to organize parallel pacifist campaigns under the leadership of private pro-Western groups, the most dynamic of which was the Union Démocratique pour la Paix et la Liberté in France. An Italian equivalent with similar strength—publisher Edgardo Sogno's Pace e Libertà—emerged in 1951. The United States followed it closely from the start, though it did not provide secret funds until 1954. The purpose of these organizations became not only to denounce the "deceitfulness" of communist propaganda but also to rally French, Italian, and German public opinion, especially the youth, under the banner of European integration. From as early as the spring of 1948 the former OSS director, William Donovan, together with the then secretary of the Council on Foreign Relations, Allen Dulles, founded the American Committee on United Europe (ACUE). Covert support of the European Movement and its youth affiliations started immediately. In collaboration with the Office of Policy Coordination's assistant director, Frank Wisner, Dulles also helped create the National Committee for a Free Europe as an annex to the ACUE and a magnet for Eastern European defecting intellectuals. According to historian Richard Aldrich, by the early 1950s the CIA had turned the promotion of European unity into its "largest operation in Western Europe," providing funds to the European Movement and to the European Youth Campaign.[53] The United States needed to forestall Soviet "phony" pacifism, and simultaneously tame its own allies' nationalist resurgence, which the PCF and PCI easily brandished for anti-American purposes. By stressing the identification of pacifism with Western integration, Washington also meant to encourage statesmen such as Schuman and De Gasperi to aspire to international prestige as leaders of the European movement rather than as guardians of national prerogatives.[54]

It was no accident that the Truman administration decided to undertake a thorough coordination of its anticommunist offensive at the onset of the EDC debate in the spring of 1951. Uncertainties about European integration, compounded by the still strong electoral prospects of the Communists

"We are building a new Europe." Propaganda poster for the Marshall Plan, 1947. The Marshall Plan propaganda units emphasized how peace and interdependence within Europe and the Atlantic alliance were inextricably linked together. Several pamphlets and posters, like the Communists' propaganda, also used the image of the dove. Courtesy George C. Marshall Foundation, Lexington, VA.

in France and Italy, led the president to authorize the creation of a Psychological Strategy Board (PSB) as an annex to the National Security Council, including the undersecretary of state, the deputy secretary of defense, the CIA director, and the Joint Chiefs of Staff. To insure the new organization's planning authority at all levels, the Office of Policy Coordination, which had previously overseen political warfare, had much of its personnel reassigned to the PSB. To further insure the PSB's broad analytical scope, the White House established links between academia and the government, appointing as its first director Gordon Gray, a former secretary of the Army who had become president of the University of North Carolina. Late in 1951 Gray was succeeded by Raymond B. Allen, who was slated to become chancellor at the University of California at Los Angeles. Although the PSB took offensive action toward Eastern Europe to "roll back Soviet power," its most pressing task was to counter communist propaganda in France and Italy.[55]

U.S. sponsorship of "psychological operations" in the two countries was heavy but had to remain camouflaged, lest the image of the United States and of the two allied governments be tarnished. To avoid leaks, only a handful of officials in Washington and in the embassies had complete knowledge of the operations. The ambassadors were the sole links between the PSB and the governments in Rome and Paris. But even with such frequent exchanges, the two chief diplomats never took their task beyond "discreet stimulation," as James Dunn put it in July 1952.[56] Ideally, under a division of labor, the local governments would assume the main responsibility for repressive measures targeting communist protest and institutional power, while the United States continued to lead the "white" propaganda effort. Most such information aimed at raising French and Italian awareness about the Communists' true nature, while continuing to encourage European integration. It had already been proven that this was a better way to combat anti-Americanism than "taxing [America's] ingenuity in trying to keep up with and refute Communist propaganda and lies." Soon the United States began to defer to local media and activities for this aggressive propaganda as well, minimizing the exposure of the USIE and ECA sponsorship, especially in more sensitive France, much as it did with the Marshall Plan publicity.[57]

Through secretly coded projects ("Cloven" for France, "Demagnetize" for Italy—later renamed "Midiron" and "Clydesdale"), the PSB designed its comprehensive anticommunist assault. On the positive side, it increased U.S. support of the free trade union movement, and it intensified anticommunist propaganda. On the repressive side, it helped the governments in Paris and Rome to take bold measures, such as the removal of Communists from key political, military, and academic offices; the passage of electoral laws that granted a prize to coalition parties; restrictions on the leftist-oriented press; a distribution of Off-Shore Procurement (osp) contracts that discriminated against industries where communist trade unions were predominant; the banning of certain demonstrations; raids on the two parties' headquarters; and the seizure of their paramilitary capabilities. This last measure was important to preclude any insurrection the Communists might have been tempted to wage in case their pacifist campaign failed. Overall, these measures would help diminish the national credentials and eventually the legitimacy of the pci and pcf. It was essential, as the State Department's representative on the psb, Walter Walmsley, argued, to treat the two parties as "foreign" fifth columns.[58]

In its most far-fetched attempt at discrediting the Communists, the psb, inspired by Allen Dulles, then the cia's deputy director, endeavored "to sow discord in Communist party ranks," promoting diasporas and defections in the style of those of Magnani and Tillon. Ambassador Dunn had for some time perceptively noted that the pcf and especially the pci, which had become overnight a mass party, could not for much longer withstand exploitation from the Kremlin against the interests of their nations' working class, and that the "decomposition of Stalinism" could favor the rise of national communist movements "detached from the Cominform." While it remained unclear how American propaganda could effectively promote such divisions, these reflections at least demonstrated that analysis of the French and Italian cases helped the United States mitigate its notions of a communist monolith.[59]

The similarity of—and coordination between—the psb plans for France and Italy was striking. The United States indeed treated the two Communist Parties as equally Stalinist. It also considered them equally threatening, though for slightly different reasons. Washington recognized that the Kremlin gave more importance to the pcf and "held it in tighter rein than the pci" in part because of France's international position. The pcf, which, unlike the pci, could also profit from widespread anti-Americanism across the national political spectrum, could more heavily affect the neutralist debate internationally. Therefore "Cloven" placed emphasis on "building France's military, economic, and political position as a member of nato and a leader of Europe." To reinvigorate European federalism youth groups were also targeted there more than in Italy.[60] The pci, less isolated internally, and more moderate in its propaganda than the pcf, presented a higher risk of internal subversion. Economic distress still mattered for Italy, where in 1953 standards of living remained below the prewar levels, and the psb exerted more pressure on Rome than on Paris for economic reform. One paradox for the

PCI was that, although it had penetrated state institutions, in the PSB's estimate, it also thrived on the "average Italians' traditional attitude of hostility toward government itself," and everything that represented statism. But public indifference or hostility to state institutions also meant more openness to external influences. Thanks to greater public acceptance for American culture in Italy, the propaganda arm of the U.S. psy-war could be more accentuated there than in France.[61]

By 1953 Washington had begun to pay greater attention to Italy's diplomatic importance, after Rome had foiled American attempts at creating a military union between Greece, Italy, and Yugoslavia, and after the first crises of decolonization in North Africa encouraged the Italian governments to play a mediation role between the Arab world and the West. In terms of international influence, distinctions between the French and Italian Communist Parties thus became somewhat blurred for Washington. Furthermore, the PCF's chance to subvert domestic politics began to match that of the PCI, primarily because its domestic isolation was mitigated by the greater government instability of the French Fourth Republic through the whole decade compared to Italy, at least until De Gasperi's death in 1954. By mid-1952, the PSB attributed its lack of full effectiveness in France in part to the difficulty of having to adapt to a new cabinet every few months.[62]

The importance of this restructured U.S. planning, and of its institutional attack against the two Communist Parties, can easily be exaggerated. Some authors, who have not focused on the impact of psy-war in France and Italy, have in fact denied any credit to the PSB, an organism that, in Walter Hixson's words, "produced reams of studies, but failed to marshal the national security bureaucracy behind a coordinated effort."[63] The truth is probably somewhere in between. In many ways, the PSB helped refocus the energy of the United States, as well as of the French and Italian governments, on the organizational and cultural complements to the Communists' social and economic appeal.

The implications of the attack against communist institutional power were actually vaster. In the first draft of Midiron, the PSB recognized that if the French Communists continued to capitalize on the bureaucratic basis they had acquired in 1944–45, the development of the French economy would suffer from hoarding and capital flight. The lack of investment lay "at the heart of . . . France's chronic economic difficulties and inability to support a greater defense effort." In a "war-weary" country this could stir "apathy and fatalism" and, finally, encourage a neutral tendency based on anti-American sentiments. Italy was elusive on military commitments partly and admittedly because of the strength of the CGIL.[64] Having recouped power and prestige through the peace campaign, the communist trade unions represented the crucial connection between a well-orchestrated anti-American propaganda and a strong economic appeal. Leading officials from the Mutual Security Agency (MSA), particularly Averell Harriman and his special assistant, Sam Berger, fully understood this danger. "The decisive area of struggle lies in the trade union movement," Berger wrote in October 1952, "for it is through the trade unions that the Communists maintain a direct hold on the masses and lead and manipulate them for their own purposes." These purposes were to undermine the economy, providing "a cover and cloak for espionage and sabotage," to "intensify class division," and, perhaps worst of all, under the guise of nationalist anti-Americanism "to promote national disunity and confusion." In order to go "beyond the surface," the MSA therefore proposed to "devise a more imaginative approach," expanding the two embassies' connections to "key individuals in the French and Italian Governments and to selected private employers or others in a position to influence their respective governments or the attitude of employers' organizations." Pressing the free trade unions toward unity was another key method. The productivity drives still appeared the best way to "Americanize" the union movement in both countries. They were, according to the MSA, America's "main dynamic idea to offer" to France and Italy and "the major contribution of the United States in the 20th Century to Western Civilization."[65]

Repressive measures helped Italian and French leaders couch the assault on communism in terms of national security and revamp the two governments' image as undisputable guardians of national sovereignty. Raids on Communist Party headquarters revealed the intimate role the Soviet Union played in the PCI's and PCF's strategies, plans, and tactics. The most famous of such raids, during the anti-Ridgway demonstrations in Paris, led to the arrest of PCF leader Jacques Duclos on charges of conspiracy. Three months later the PSB panel in Paris concluded: "By pointing out its pro-Soviet and antimilitarist activities [the peace campaign], the Government has been endeavoring to undermine other principal sources of the [Communist] Party's strength—its guise of being merely a leftist French political party and its false reputation for patriotism. . . . This type of campaign is particularly timely in view of the current resurgence of French nationalistic sentiment." Just as important, exposing the Communists as Soviet pawns allowed the French and Italian governments to strike a middle path between two extreme options: indiscriminate repression of the Communist Parties, which could alienate support from the center-left, and radical reform, which appeared premature, given the growing strength of the right-wing parties.[66]

The PSB offensive on communism had also a profound domestic relevance for the United States. As Sam Berger recognized, the "continued Communist presence in Italy and France" transcended the specific national circumstances, not only because it reinforced neutralist tendencies all over Europe, but also because it reignited an "isolationist sentiment in Congress." The problem of interfering in French or Italian affairs paled in comparison with "*our* responsibility to Congress and to our people, and *our* ability to carry out our present policies with the full confidence of success."[67] In the effort to spread the American message overseas, Washington kept giving priority to overcoming all isolationist resistance at home, even if that meant meddling heavily in others' domestic affairs and risking an anti-American backlash.

This dilemma showed only the tip of the compounded problems incurred by the PSB. First, assessing results remained problematic. Gauging public opinion trends was difficult, given the rudimentary nature of polls at the time. To be sure, by 1953, surveys showed that two-thirds of Italians believed the Americans wanted to "dominate" the world; this may have been an "empire," but it was seen as a benevolent one, for almost 60 percent of Italians still ranked the United States as their favorite foreign nation. In France anti-Americanism had not made considerable advances, and by that same time "on the whole the French viewed the United States as a constructive force."[68] But even America's most fervent psy-warriors admitted their inability to discern how much these trends should be attributed to their own activity and how much to the Communists' mistakes and sectarianism. One thing was certain: the PCI and PCF maintained their electoral strength; the PCI actually looked stronger by 1953.

Second, if the measures needed to unmask communist propaganda were too repressive, their immediate effects could be easily reversed in relatively short time. The arrest of Jacques Duclos was an asset, but his release a few weeks later was a setback: through a well-orchestrated campaign for the release of "political prisoners," the PCF turned the anti-Ridgway demonstrations from a self-segregating episode to a campaign for free speech. This problem, in James Dunn's perhaps too pessimistic view, was compounded by the factional divisions within both countries' governments, in contrast to an extreme Left that profited from its self-discipline and demagoguery.[69]

Third, measures that helped curb communist presence in one area could backfire in another. Discrimination in OSP contracts helped reduce the power of communist trade unions, but, as James Dunn noticed, it also aggravated unemployment, in France especially. This fed the PCF's propaganda against the U.S. "occupation" and the government's "NATO policies."[70]

Fourth, covert operations easily lent themselves to manipulation by their beneficiaries. Rather than creating self-reliant political allies, the strategy of indirection tended to reinforce a patron-client relationship, with all the reciprocal blackmails typical of dependency. By relying so heavily on Washington, the French and Italian governments undermined the primary purpose of psychological warfare, which was to increase their political prestige and legitimacy. This paradox became even more apparent as information about covert operations inevitably slipped out.

A fifth issue hit the PSB at its core: while its attempt to eliminate communist bureaucratic and propaganda power yielded limited results, it also revealed Washington's own bureaucratic wrangling. The State Department in particular refused to submit itself to the PSB authority. In its assault on communist trade unions in France and Italy, American psy-warfare bared the divisions within the U.S. trade union movement. In Italy especially the AFL and CIO clashed over U.S. support of the Catholic CISL, while also straining relationships with the State Department. "By 1953," as James Miller has noted, "the U.S. government, the AFL, and the CIO were carrying out three separate and at times conflicting Italian labor policies."[71]

Psy-War under the "New Look"

The administration of Dwight ("Ike") D. Eisenhower tried to improve America's ability to conduct psychological warfare by restoring the main initiative for psychological strategies to the National Security Council and the State Department in late 1953 with a new Operations Coordinating Board (OCB). To further integrate psychological warfare, the president appointed C. D. Jackson, the managing director of Time-Life Inc. and a former World War II propaganda operations specialist, to the new position of special assistant for psychological warfare. In 1955 Nelson Rockefeller succeeded Jackson.[72] A moribund bureaucratic structure was thus revived. But the problems for the new president lay elsewhere, and during the first years of his term they exacerbated other flaws already inherent in U.S. political warfare against Western European Communism.

It was above all in the overt aspects of psychological warfare that the Republican administration had most trouble. Eisenhower, as well as Congress, recognized that the information service under the Truman administration had been too propagandistic, "unashamedly plug[ging] anti-Communism." The new president therefore set out to project positive themes rather than wage shrill attacks on the enemy. But this conclusion belonged to political campaigning and fit a long-term project more than it reflected a will for an immediate, thorough reform of American propaganda. At first, the Eisenhower cabinet actually assumed a confrontational stance, in part to reawaken the NATO allies against the Soviet peril. The new administration, more than its predecessor, sensed the danger of declining cohesion and morale among the European allies. With NATO relatively secured and the Soviet threat less immediate, Europe could go astray, through "lethargy and inaction."[73] Thus psy-war under the Eisenhower cabinet combined proud celebrations of American democracy and a sophisticated use of the media with even more rigid anticommunist tones than the Campaign of Truth propaganda. The administration's particular emphasis on public posturing was best exemplified by the famous "brinkmanship" of Secretary of State John Foster Dulles. This "New Look" in foreign policy, as it was dubbed during the presidential campaign, entailed a greater reliance on nuclear deterrence, expanding alliances, and covert operations. It also pledged to go beyond containment and "roll back" communism—in the East and, more realistically, in Western Europe.[74] These changes were all designed to regain the initiative against the adversary and to avoid another war like in Korea. This strategy also required a centralized decision-making process complemented by greater unilateralism toward NATO allies.

The PSB had already critically scrutinized overt and "unattributed" propaganda. As the LENAP Committee, which coordinated the French and Italian activities, recognized by the end of 1952, the sheer size of this publicity made average French citizens even more "acutely aware of the presence of America in every field of national activity," leaving them unable to "distinguish between American propaganda and the information programs of international organizations, such as NATO, UNESCO, etc. in which the United States participate[d]." A few months later, the PSB concluded, "The fact that the United States has engaged in a wide array of non attributable activities, directed to mass audiences, has resulted in a situation wherein certain of their programs promise to achieve quite the opposite effect from that intended. . . . The very scale of the effort permits a suspicious and cynical public to recognize the concealed output as U.S. sponsored. As a result, the blatancy of such propaganda contributes to the rise in anti-American attitudes and sentiments."[75] But, despite greater efforts to avoid direct intervention, the Eisenhower administration was undoubtedly more "blatant" than its predecessor. Even the establishment of the United States Information Agency (USIA) in August 1953, a conscious effort to universalize the American message, privileged propaganda over the cultural exchange propounded by the USIE and its affiliate United States Information Service (USIS). The posts overseas retained the old designation, USIS, reflecting Washington's awareness that "Agency" could suggest a covert dimension and the systematic dissemination of propaganda.[76]

More ironically, indiscriminate anticommunism, which was supposed to nurture this effort to project a self-image of resolute universal torchbearer of freedom, called international attention to the interplay between U.S. domestic and foreign policies. The rise of Senator Joseph McCarthy, who led the campaign to suppress domestic communism, had occurred under the critical but rather powerless watch of President Truman. Eisenhower, who had the influence necessary to censor his fellow Republican, appeared too passive, even accommodating. After the execution of Julius and Ethel Rosenberg in 1953 on poorly proven charges of spying on the American atomic project, even mainstream French opinion, as Ambassador Douglas Dillon reported, accused "the world's leading democracy" of indulging in a "behavior which the French associate[d] with dictatorship." Almost one year later Dillon warned that all the work done in psy-warfare could be undone by the "forces of totalitarianism and conformism at home." The consequences could be devastating, the ambassador explained:

> We have long stood in [the] minds of [the] great majority of Frenchmen as bulwark and symbol of representative government, free institutions and tolerance. To the extent it is believed here that we no longer unitedly and resolutely stand for these values, and that forces attacking them in our country are gaining strength, Fr[ench] opinion tends to start looking elsewhere for protection of their national security. Elsewhere is, of course, towards East, which means neutralist search for "reinsurance" by better relations with U.S.S.R. and loosening relations with U.S.[77]

In Italy, McCarthyism was even more tangibly embodied by Eisenhower's chosen ambassador, the playwright and former congresswoman Clare Boothe Luce. A devout Catholic and fervent anticommunist, Luce confronted "atheistic" Marxism in Italy with the tenacity of a crusader. Although her alarm was often exaggerated, she found little obstruction from Washington, not only because of Dulles's own obsession with communism but also because she was in the White House inner circle of "psychological warriors," which, in addition to C. D. Jackson, included media magnate Henry Luce, the ambassador's husband.[78] Clare Luce's public pronouncements on Italian politics became notorious demonstrations of Yankee presumption. As soon as she arrived in Italy, she plunged herself into the campaign for the national elections: during an infamous speech Luce gave in Milan in May 1953, she threatened to cut off U.S. aid in case of victory by either the Left or the extreme Right. This declaration was far more explicit than Secretary Marshall's hint five years earlier. It also addressed an Italian public opinion that had passed the hurdle of its first national election and, compared to 1948, felt less embattled against a civilizational enemy and more impatient with the domineering aspects of American presence. The Communists exploited the ambassador's gaffe to heap scorn on American imperialism and its servants. Although Luce denied responsibility for the Christian Democrats' setback at the polls (the centrist coalition lost votes to both the extreme Right and Left parties), Italian government leaders could not hide their embarrassment and resentment over her unsolicited intrusion in the country's political debate. The ambassador continued to warn, "If there is not soon a reversal of the present trend of the voters towards Communism (especially the young voters of military age) in a few years Italy will be a satellite of Soviet Russia."[79]

From the start, the PSB had considered outlawing French and Italian Communist Parties to be desirable but premature. Under the renewed psywar apparatus, and Clare Luce's influence, and after the relative failure of new electoral laws to limit the Communists' parliamentary power, conditions seemed ripe to drive the two parties underground. After all, Sam Berger had noted, "legality cloth[ed] the Communists with respectability," whereas the Communists themselves had "confessed that driving them underground seriously injur[ed] and hamper[ed] them." Clare Luce established contacts with Italy's strongest supporters of a hard line against the Communists, with the intention of provoking the "Cominform Left" (PCI and PSI) into illegal action. In Paris, Dillon tried to bolster a similar determination from the government of Joseph Laniel, leaning on the strongly anticommunist president of the Republic, Vincent Auriol, but with extreme caution, given France's sensitivity against "anything resembling official pressure." The document NSC 5411/2, approved in April 1954, again took up previously discarded proposals to intervene militarily ("in concert with its NATO allies") if the Communists seized power legally in Italy.[80]

U.S. pressure became more overt and intrusive regarding European integration as well. For Eisenhower, an enthusiastic supporter of the American Committee on United Europe from its early days, Western European integration was a matter of faith as much as a strategic solution. From the time he became the first NATO commander in 1951, Eisenhower thought that America's task was to provide the "enlightened leadership" that would inspire and help rebuild the "European spirit" necessary to achieve integration. For Secretary of State Dulles, the demise of a European defense force in the name of the old-style nationalistic balance of power would prove Europe's "moral decrepitude."[81] The USIA's main task became to encourage European integration and to link it to the notion of an "Atlantic Community" founded on a common heritage and shared interests. The PSB and the OCB revised

"De Gasperi and his associates have brought the foreigners to Italy. With your vote on June 7, let's kick them out! Young man, for peace, and for an independent, democratic Italy, vote PCI." PCI's electoral poster for the 1953 national elections. Courtesy Fondazione Istituto Gramsci Emilia Romagna, Bologna.

Italy's Christian Democratic Party's electoral poster for the 1953 national elections, depicting the party giving the "boot" to Georgii Malenkov. Courtesy Archivio Manifesto Sociale, Rome.

plans to reduce communism in France and Italy, specifically connecting these domestic issues to the need to foster European unity. This connection appeared crucial, particularly after the post-Stalin leadership in the Soviet Union refined its peace offensive with the call for "peaceful coexistence"—a move calculated to weaken Western resolve, as the Eisenhower administration perhaps overemphasized.[82]

This pressure for continental integration also presumed that America's allies would increase their current share of the Cold War burdens. It responded to the president's desire to rely on nuclear deterrence as a financial, as much as a strategic and psychological matter. Reducing conventional warfare spending had broad implications. If the United Sates was turned into a garrison-state, Eisenhower believed, it would not only be debilitated but democracy itself would be impaired. America would lose its credibility as the economic and social model for the free world. Unrestrained spending might also provoke an isolationist mood. The European allies realized that Eisenhower's support for an EDC was largely motivated by his desire to reduce the number of U.S. troops on the continent. The president, naturally, brandished the "third force" argument, telling the Europeans that by sharing defense responsibilities they would gain more independence, self-respect, and a role commensurate with their aspirations.[83] But to European leaders, in Paris and Rome especially, the New Look promised less a genuine third force than the hierarchical division of tasks among allies — nuclear for the Anglo-Americans, conventional for the EDC — that they so obstinately tried to prevent. All of Ike's arguments — the need for Europe to emulate the United States, the fear that America, not Europe, might become a garrison state, the imperative of resuming leadership through nuclear deterrence — showed that the president's, as well as Dulles's commitment to the idea of Europe followed an "exceptionalist" logic that seemed fitting with the dogmatic attitude most contemporaries attributed to both men.

This apparent "unilateralism," particularly when accompanied by Eisenhower's constant appeal for an "Atlantic Community," rekindled the French and Italian governments' will to resist any kind of pressure. Already during the initial phases of institutionalized psychological warfare, the fragile French cabinets as well as the Italian Christian Democrats had shown reluctance to adopt its most daring measures. Outflanked on the right by the Gaullist resurgence, the short-lived governments of Antoine Pinay, René Mayer, and Joseph Laniel at crucial times refused to risk alienating socialist support by assaulting the Communists too indiscriminately. By 1953 this reality, together with the PCF's diminishing references to insurrection, imposed particular caution on the Laniel cabinet.[84]

De Gasperi's tendency to mollify American requests for strong measures against the PCI stemmed from similar considerations. As a centrist, interclassist party, lacking the cohesion of the Right and Left, the Christian Democrats "sought the path of compromise." These compromises involved delicate balancing, especially after the DC's setback in the 1953 elections, with center-left parties or with nationalist pressures coming from both left and right. Also, De Gasperi's successors after 1953 further accentuated the party's already significant ambiguity regarding economic reform. Their compromises led to a growing mix of free-market economics with the preservation of the corporatist structure inherited from fascism — a structure that, according to Luce and the economic expert at the Rome embassy, Henry J. Tasca, indirectly favored the PCI's and CGIL's institutional presence and their

"With the Communists, for the independence of France." Anti-NATO poster by the PCF, 1953. Courtesy Collection du PCF/Archives départementales de la Seine-Saint-Denis.

plans to nationalize several industrial sectors.[85] The PSB had been quick to note that some entrepreneurs and DC leaders clearly preferred a "modus vivendi with the CGIL" in order to keep their trade options open with the East. This further induced Luce to utilize the PSB's discrimination clause on Off-Shore Procurement contracts against FIAT, until the automaker complied by blacklisting many of its CGIL workers. Another general reason for the Italian government's guarded response to U.S. pressure was that the PCI could not be branded as unpatriotic so easily as the PCF was. In Italy there was no episode as spectacular as the arrest of Jacques Duclos; and Italian nationalism was not as strong as its French counterpart.[86]

Above all, as Mario Del Pero has best demonstrated, Italy's Christian Democrats benefited from preserving the political stalemate. The permanence of the communist threat allowed them to increase their leverage on the United States in all respects. In Clare Luce's cynical view, it was "Italy's most profitable business," an "indirect source of U.S. dollars." Internally, the Christian Democrats secured their political hegemony thanks to a tacit understanding that marginalized the PCI but did not exclude it from the country's political life. De Gasperi in particular understood that the legitimacy of his regime rested on the antifascist constitutional agreement that had recognized the PCI as a mass party, more than on the Cold War's increasingly bellicose anticommunism.[87] One of De Gasperi's first objections to the PSB's repressive measures was that "democracy was a young somewhat delicate plant in Italy" and that he could not "go outside the constitution in attempting to suppress the Communists without risking the destruction of democracy." The LENAP Committee noted that the French government likewise proudly upheld its constitutional principles, arguing that it would not allow anything resembling the American "Smith Act," which criminalized any organization advocating the overthrow of the U.S. government.[88] The two governments suggested that since World War II their democratic regimes and their defense of free speech had in some respects surpassed the Americans—therefore they needed no lessons from Washington.

By 1953–54 the Gaullist opposition in France had in many ways superseded the PCF's own nationalist campaigns. But in some respects it had complemented them, too. Gaullism managed to exacerbate the anti-American tones of French nationalism. Certainly, it sowed further uncertainty and divisions in the centrist coalition. MRP leader Georges Bidault, who had eagerly helped launch the Atlantic Pact, as foreign minister in 1953 became increasingly demanding about France's equal status with Britain and the United States.[89] The tension between the United States and France deepened as Radical Party leader Pierre Mendès-France assumed the premiership in June 1954. His combination of nationalist tones with flexibility toward the Soviet threat was anathema to Secretary Dulles. The prime minister not only sank the EDC project, he also liquidated the unpopular war in Vietnam by signing an armistice in Geneva in July. The Eisenhower administration, which had increased assistance to the French effort there, boycotted most of the Geneva agreements. Mendès-France also nurtured a notion of psychological warfare that was less militaristic than the American one. Before entering office he invoked the "magnet" theory, which argued that the West could by way of example draw Eastern Europe away from Moscow's subjugation: "Economic and social progress," he wrote to Prime Minister Laniel, "can become a powerful propaganda weapon abroad; facts and figures illustrating them cross frontiers like missiles which strike the minds." This argument mirrored Eisenhower's concerns about America's own militarization and his pressure for Europe's greater military efforts. It was not too convincing, given the amount of military aid France still received from Washington. Also, rather than maneuvering the Russians, Dulles thought, the French might become their main accomplices in dividing the Western alliance.[90]

Italy seemed to become more compliant than France. In the winter of 1954–55 not only FIAT but an apparently more resolute "cold warrior," Prime Minister Mario Scelba, followed the dictates of Clydesdale. The government approved a series of measures for the removal of public officials "who did not guarantee their allegiance to the democratic state." The outlawing of the PCI seemed imminent. In fact this decision was "largely cosmetic" and "a point more of arrival than of departure" for the Italian government. Never implemented, the announced measures were simply Scelba's ploy to obtain full U.S. assistance for an economic program he presented in competition with the that of former Finance Minister Ezio Vanoni, which had initiated large public investments.[91] Regardless of specific manipulations, the Italian government, like its French counterpart, also kept arguing that Moscow was far more vulnerable to the economic than the military integration of Europe.[92] This version of anticommunism seemed too muted for Clare Luce's standards. It also confirmed the impression in both the Rome and Paris embassies that the Communists' pacifist and anti-American campaigns of the early 1950s might have sown the seeds of neutralism in Europe. The confrontational tones that even the staunchly pro-American Prime Minister Giuseppe Pella had adopted on the Trieste issue late in 1953 did not bode well. The parliamentary appointment of Giovanni Gronchi to the presidency of the Republic in 1955 signaled a potential rift with Washington. A leader of the DC left-wing faction Politica Sociale, Gronchi openly advocated a dialogue with the Nenni Socialists. By 1955 the PSI was no longer pledged to Stalinism;[93] but it had not yet broken with the PCI, and while ostensibly championing neutrality, it still followed a pro-Soviet line. Gronchi also assumed a certain "Gaullist" aura, propounding Italy's right to equal status with the other great powers of Europe.[94] Shortly before Gronchi's election, Clare Luce explained to Eisenhower—with a reasoning which, less colorfully, U.S. officials in Paris applied to France as well—that trying to infuse democracy in Italy was "like trying to infuse blood into the veins of a sick man who was . . . busily engaged in slashing his own wrists." She added: "So long as the Italian constitution permits the C[ommunist] P[arty], Socialists, Neo-Fascists and Monarchists to wield their razors legally on the corpus of the Italian government, the U.S. blood bank—economic and political—can never succeed in bringing roses to the waxen cheeks of Italian 'democracy.'"[95] It almost never occurred to Luce that her abrasive diplomatic style might have induced many Italian rulers to consider American psychological warfare more destabilizing than the attacks from the Communists themselves.

For the Eisenhower administration, so committed to psychological warfare, so able to recognize the centrality of the battle for hearts and minds, it was quite ironic that this battle initially backfired in two of the countries it saw as most central. It was also ironic that a president pledged to projecting America's moral leadership and to making Europe more self-reliant was seen as too rigid, unilateralist, and belligerent even by its closest political allies in France and Italy. The wavering and the apathetic in the two nations remained uncertain. The anti-Americans became more determined and virulent. The loyal, such as Pella or Bidault, made their promotion of American hegemony increasingly conditional, emulating some of the confrontational tones of the neutralists and of the anti-Americans.

The Eisenhower administration could indeed be faulted for its reluctance to consult with its NATO allies, and for its obdurate depiction of a communist monolith. Eisenhower and most of his NSC and OCB advisers did understand the national characteristics and circumstances that determined the strength of the extreme Left in France and Italy. But this did not essentially modify their view of a united communist front. This view was correct in its premise, given the degree of Cominform orchestration. The flaw lay in the ensuing reasoning that, despite specific national circumstances explaining the strong PCI and PCF, communism remained an anomaly in both nations, and as such, it had to be assaulted and extirpated, not contained as in the East. This determination caused frequent backlash in the American psy-war during those years. However, the signs of a gradual recovery from such an approach were already visible in Eisenhower's tendency to merge psychological warfare with watchful grand diplomacy. The evolution of the cultural Cold War, the emergence of the first détente, and the developments associated with decolonization all helped mitigate the administration's rigid anticommunism. They also contributed to the administration's increasing use of diplomatic maneuvering to curtail communist influence and wage the battle for hearts and minds in France and Italy.

5 THE CULTURAL COLD WAR AT ITS PEAK

Mass Culture and Intellectuals, 1948–1956

The Most Insidious Challenge

The Cold War struggle over ideas and mass culture was as crucial as the confrontations in the political, economic, and military arenas. This is now a widely accepted conclusion. The United States strove not only to demonstrate cultural superiority over the Soviet Union but also to defuse widespread anti-Americanism in Western Europe. The French and Italian Communists privileged cultural resistance because they recognized that their leverage was strongest on those issues. By the late 1940s, however, both the Communists and the Americans had come to realize that culture was the most elusive element in their confrontation. Even so, both concluded that a core challenge came from their opponent's "soft power." Recent literature has covered separately each side's actions and debates in the cultural Cold War.[1] The purpose of this chapter is not to revisit these debates in detail but to add perspective to the ideological cultural struggle by juxtaposing and comparing the perceptions and responses from both sides of the Atlantic.

According to the PCI's Gramscian project, cultural hegemony could be achieved by assimilating the intellectual elites and molding a new mass national culture in order to disarm the structural power of the ruling classes. Following the decisions of a national organization conference in January 1947, the party created an intellectuals' section within its propaganda commission. In 1948, the section became a cultural commission, headed by Emilio Sereni. Between 1948 and 1949, the PCF, like its Italian counterpart, created an ideological section within the central committee (directed by François Billoux). That section was divided into three commissions: one for the party schools, a second for general education, and a third for the organization of intellectuals, headed by Laurent Casanova.[2]

Achieving hegemony also meant resisting the most dangerous forms of American influence. Indeed, cultural power was considered most threatening and most insidious. U.S. economic, military, and political presence could be blatant and easier to target than social and cultural seduction. As I noted in chapter 3, in the midst of the 1948 electoral campaign, Pietro Secchia had warned against the combined military, economic, and (lowbrow) cultural threat posed by the American trusts controlling Italy. Three years later, the new director of the cultural commission, Carlo Salinari, still lamented a general mood of "indifference" toward the American "contraband of a pseudo-culture." In contrast to some success on the political and economic level, Salinari added, the party had lowered its guard against the "degradation" of national culture and the "demoralization" of Italian intellectuals. Catholic intellectuals may have unsuccessfully tried to absorb "the Crocean and the decadentist [sic] currents of thought," he continued, but, in alliance with the Americans, they were forging a new combination of provincial and cosmopolitan—all in all, in the party's opinion, superficial and inane—national culture.[3] Repeated communist indignation about indifference, "disorientation," and corruption indicated a growing sense of vulnerability toward a cultural presence that was pervasive at the mass level, and that might even reenlist progressive intellectuals to the capitalist cause.

In beginning its assault against the American film industry, the PCF also recognized the peril of what it called a tempting and tentacular presence. At the Central Committee of Paris in October 1947, Maurice Thorez defined Hollywood as no less than an "enterprise of disaggregation of the French nation, an enterprise of moral corruption and perversion of our young men and women, with such stultifying films, where eroticism competes with bigotry, where the gangster is king; these movies . . . are not meant to prepare a generation of French conscious of their duties toward France, toward the Republic, but rather a troop of slaves crushed by the 'iron heel.'"[4] The Communists considered Hollywood a threat to French youth, most likely because they sensed that American popular culture portrayed a new generational freedom, liberated from parental *and* ideological constraints. Also, for both ideological and nationalist reasons, Thorez felt compelled to portray enslavement to American hedonism or conformity as an aberration from militant service to the country.

European scrutiny, as we have noted, had already pressed the United States to a great deal of self-scrutiny in the years immediately after the war. Now that the Western European Communists, under the guidance and inspiration of Soviet propaganda or, worse, on account of their nations' own cultural traditions, had begun a relentless attack on American cultural imports, the risk for the United States of appearing shallow and overbearing seemed even greater. This sensitivity was yet another manifestation of an enduring cultural inferiority complex.

George Kennan remained among the most vocal critics of the U.S. tendency to project its power in military or mass cultural terms. After ending his five-month-long ambassadorship to Moscow as "persona non grata" in 1952,

Kennan reentered the lecture circuit. In a speech at the New York's Modern Museum of Modern Art in 1955, he deplored the abandonment of the political warfare of the Marshall Plan and urged Washington not to leave the promotion of culture "to the blind workings of commercial interests." By the late 1940s, this kind of critique became diffused in the foreign policy and academic establishment. The influential essayist Dwight Macdonald, widely read on socialist and fascist literature, exemplified this state of mind among several Ivy League academics. In 1953, in a letter to his Italian friend and mentor Nicola Chiaromonte, he wrote: "If the United States doesn't or cannot change its mass culture (movies, radio, sports cult, comics, television, slick magazines) it will lose the war against the U.S.S.R. Americans have been made into permanent adolescents by advertising, mass culture—uncritical, herd-minded, pleasure-loving, concerned about trivia of materialistic living, scared of death, sex, old age—friendship is sending Xmas cards, sex is the wet dreams of those chromium-plated Hollywood glamour girls, death—is not." Reflecting Kennan's elitist views, Macdonald harkened back to a trend first expressed during the First World War within the American intellectual circle of the journal *The Seven Arts*. These cultural elites had first attacked "the fetters of a narrow and provincial 'genteel culture,' the hollow optimism of a commercial spirit, and the bigoted nationalism that wished to close the gates to any more unassimilable aliens."[5] While cosmopolitan and welcoming of a broader, inclusive form of Anglo-Saxonism, these writers and artists aimed to match if not imitate Europe's standards of high culture. They articulated a malaise, if not inferiority complex, as old as the Republic itself.

During the early Cold War, even more consensual thinkers, such as Lionel Trilling from the liberal side and Henry Kissinger from the conservative ranks, reached similar conclusions. They realized that without intellectual rigor or sophistication, without addressing the existential threats to Western civilization, their respective views could be overwhelmed by an inordinate faith in mass consumerist culture. Liberals were particularly concerned that their values could be trumped by the irrational politics of crusading gestures more than ideas.[6]

But by the early 1950s, this attitude was no longer confined to academic circles. The administrators and leaders commanding the country's cultural cold war began to feel similar uncertainties. As assistant deputy administrator for the Economic Cooperation Administration, Richard Bissel in 1951 predicted that only a "profound shift in social attitudes, attuning [the Europeans] to the mid-twentieth century" would move their attention away from the "shallow" and "crude" aspects of American civilization and toward "American labor relations, American management and engineering" which were "respected everywhere." This very focus on the technical and political aspects of U.S. society reflected continued insecurity about the power of America's cultural appeal. From Italy, three years later, Ambassador Clare Boothe Luce, writing to President Eisenhower, even wondered if American propaganda had not "wasted money" making "frauds of ourselves advertising what we haven't got to sell or can't deliver." "What's the 'American way of life,'" she mused, "to a foreigner who can't get an immigrant visa; or the 'free enterprise system' to a foreign businessman who can't trade with America?" The Truman and Eisenhower administrations had tried to back up public diplomacy with actions. But they also waged the battles of words, founding their strategy on campaigns of "truth." And yet, Luce added, "even news information giving the straight-way facts about the world scene doesn't help — not if those facts are what they are: that the U.S.S.R. is still inchworming, tapeworming, and angleworming along to victory."

The ambassador feared the Soviet Union would make political advances in the Western world not so much through its huge propaganda apparatus but rather thanks to the way America's own self-projection would affect its most politically divided allies. "In countries which tolerate a Communist Party," she argued, "the normal voracity of the public appetite for material progress . . . tends to be pathological. Communism is quite literally an economic tapeworm in a nation's system." Democratic leaders made compromises with the "insatiable demands" of this "parasite"; thus most American munificence did not result in "pro-American ideals, or following pro-West policies at the ballot box." Even "American motion pictures," Luce concluded, "and much of the information about the U.S.A. provided by our own information services abroad, which place constantly before the voter the tantalizing picture of the heaven-on-earth which can be his," yielded more votes for the Left, because the Marxist parties gave the "popular mind" the prospect of "controlling the machinery of the State, an "Aladdin's lamp for those who control it."[7]

Luce's hyperbolic statements could be taken with a grain of salt. But the more pondered analyses of the Psychological Strategy Board had also reached an analogous conclusion about intellectuals: an image of a consensual, consumerist society might not positively affect countries such as France or Italy, where the "intellectual liberation" meant primarily a "schism between theory and practice," and "intellectual games [were] more enjoyable in the realm of 'quality' than in the arena of quantitative measurements." As Jean-Paul Sartre had also pointed out, individualism in European countries diverged from the success ethic — hence pressure to fit in — that distinguished the individual in the United States. Influential French or Italian intellectuals stood out for their critical conscience, their anticonformism; for them, the PSB concluded, "freedom to criticize [was] the touchstone of liberty."[8]

For the French and Italian Communists the battle of ideas revealed a challenge to their own cultural elitism; against capitalist modernity they tried to foster their own deep cultural connection with indigenous intellectual traditions and to stem the Americanization of mass culture. For the United States the main task was to diversify its cultural appeal, show sufficient depth and variety, and deflect charges of anti-intellectualism.

Mass Culture and Its Challenges for the Communist and the American Sides

SOVIET APPEAL

By 1954, in President Eisenhower's estimate, the Soviet Union spent "about $2 billion a year on its propaganda," while the United States still spent "only a small amount." In the early 1950s cultural tours of the Soviet Union presented a country with wonderful art, music, theater, and ballet. Especially in the immediate post-Stalin era, "liberalizing trends within the Soviet bloc dulled the image of the Iron Curtain."[9] Adding these elements to its "peace offensive," the Soviet Union appeared moderate, culturally vibrant, and, for that reason, more dangerous. I will analyze the U.S. diplomatic counteroffensive in the next chapter. Here it is important to highlight that the battle for ideas received a jump-start in the East. From the immediate postwar period, the official Soviet newspaper *Pravda*, Radio Moscow, and the agitprop organization led an "unprecedented mobilization of entire populations," among workers at home and Cominform member parties abroad. Subsidized press and media turned this into a "modern cultural warfare." There are no estimates of how much of the Soviet funding to the French and Italian Communists went into their cultural and propaganda apparatus. But the two parties certainly benefited from this emerging cultural myth. Moreover, Soviet cultural emissaries found a receptive audience among French and Italian intellectuals, who believed in a common European cultural heritage, more sophisticated and more attuned to folk traditions than the alien and superficial American adaptations of the same.[10]

Regimentation could be a problem, however. Contrary to Marxist doctrines about proletarian consciousness, the general Soviet approach made the "Party resemble a common room of schoolmasters," in David Caute's words, constantly lamenting "the vulnerability of their pupils to wicked worldly pleasures, idleness, seductions, deviations."[11] While this latter problem did affect to a smaller extent the Communists in the West as well, the dogmas of socialist realism for a while seemed to capture the popular imagination. Better still, the zeal in pursuing those canons promised to unite both intellectuals and the masses. Under the Cominform directives, as I have noted, communist intellectuals and artists hardly enjoyed relative freedom. But Zhdanov's dogmas of socialist realism emphasized a closer connection to popular taste. Art was to be made edifying, optimistic, and more comprehensible to the masses. So while some leftist French and Italian intellectuals initially questioned the uniformity of "communist aesthetics,"[12] they were more inclined to criticize abstract bourgeois art. They did so less from an antielitist viewpoint than from an anticapitalist one. With some exaggeration, they connected marketed, standardized art with the "schematism" of abstraction. This reasoning linked the mechanization of human life to the "mechanization of people's minds," where the "domination of figures, calculations, and statistics" made mental America into the kingdom of abstraction.

In 1948 Simone de Beauvoir noted the paradox of a pragmatic society dominated by abstract literary and visual arts. Such representations did not give the United States intellectual distinction but rather made its "abstract" art mere reproduction, cloned from Europe. Its works were thus "reproduced and reproduced mechanically" and finally "emptied of their contents."[13] Even the most distinctly national forms of American art, from full-blown modernism to abstract expressionism, according to de Beauvoir, did not depart from the characteristics of standardized mass culture. In their "machinism" and mind-manipulation, those art forms were also politically dangerous. And, finally, they were paradoxically unappealing to the taste of commoners. Such was the main justification for socialist realism, the art connecting the intellectuals to the masses, giving both groups an alternative venue between inane mass culture and esoteric literary, artistic expression.

A NATIONAL MASS CULTURE

The Soviet cultural offensive was much less successful in Western Europe than these first impressions, or even Eisenhower's complaints, suggested. In 1949 even the orthodox writer Emilio Sereni recognized that the Soviet Union, while still having a leading role in ideology, suffered a "devaluation in the cultural field." Soviet culture, he admitted, "is something that may poke many people in the eye, and I'm not referring to our adversaries, but also to many of our comrades." Many Western Communists, he mused, found grating the theories of Trofim Lysenko (the Russian biologist whose genetic research had subjected science to ideological celebrations) and were left wondering about the whole value of a strictly regimented science or culture. Sereni, despite his allegiance to the Zhdanovian line, feared that the

PCI might appear "in [the] tow" of the Soviet Union, and proposed reiterating the national-populist nature of the party's culture, and expanding the very definition of cultural work beyond its identification with intellectual work. Popular magazines, more focus on entertainment for workers and to women's issues would, in his opinion, better offset the "obscurantist" clerical-American connection.[14]

The PCI's cultural front thus emphasized national traits, as opposed to meticulous following of the Soviet model. The Alliance for Culture, created in 1948, became a coordinating committee of Communists, Socialists, and independents to protect progressive Italian culture from American "cultural imperialism." That same year neorealist filmmakers, under the party's auspices, initiated a front to defend Italian cinema. This campaign lasted for ten years. The publication of the Gramsci's prison notebooks between 1948 and 1951 under Togliatti's supervision further underscored the indigenous intellectual nature of communist culture in Italy more than its loyalty to Soviet guidelines.[15] But above all, the party waged its nationalist battle against American influences on issues of popular culture.

In August 1949 the cultural commission published a resolution titled "Against Imperialist and Clerical Obscurantism." The document spurred initiatives for the defense of a genuinely "democratic and national popular culture, as opposed to the massified, marketed, contrived and oligarchic version coming from overseas." "In the name of anti-communism," the resolution read, "our country's reactionary groups instrumentalized the foreign invasion, vilifying the actual sense of culture and national independence." Reforming the schools was paramount, for the "obscurantist" offensive intended to keep the public school system under control and heavily disadvantaged ("even unable to overcome widespread illiteracy") compared to private and Catholic schools. Likewise, intellectual work was further reorganized to both include bourgeois intellectuals and spread a "Gramscian outlook."

The "most intensive work" aimed at creating a "mass cultural movement." Most notably in the central and northern regions of the country, a network of Case del Popolo (people's after-work cultural centers) began to develop in the early 1950s. These were the party and entertainment venues for the working class, providing bars, game rooms, libraries, and theaters for plays and movies. The party also increased the publication of Marxist texts for the masses, "to counteract the massive invasion of clerico-American publications." Assuming the regular libraries, even the numerous ones from progressive municipalities, and the Case del Popolo would be insufficient to promote such readership, the party provided traveling libraries. The popular book center, particularly active in the Emilia-Romagna region, was designed to promote literacy and the reading of serious literature, with campaigns such as the "Battle for the Book" in the city of Modena in 1954. Art exhibitions, theater groups, sports associations, and film and music clubs also complemented the work of the Case del Popolo. At the annual fund-raising festivals sponsored by the party's daily—the Feste dell'Unità—propaganda was mixed with, if not submerged by popular entertainment, featuring music, dancing, and theater. In 1948, to restore popular culture to the people, the party launched the "mass theater" initiative, with its main stages in Italy's central regions. Amateur actors, ordinary people wanting to find a collective expression of their experiences, were thus married to the party's propaganda apparatus. After an initial success, this rather contrived venue, excessively celebratory and pro-Soviet, lost popularity and was discontinued in 1952.[16]

The party's magazines strove to combine escapist diversion with educational uplift of the semiliterate, the working-class autodidacts, and even the petits bourgeois. This was the original intent of *Il calendario del popolo* and the glossy women's magazine *Noi Donne*. Beginning in the early 1950s, the already popular *Vie Nuove* ran an increasing number of articles on popular culture, Italian cinema, and eventually, television. The high number of interviewed actors not affiliated with the party ranged from drama actress Anna Magnani to sex symbol Gina Lollobrigida, from heartthrob Amedeo Nazzari to popular comedian Totò. Through the 1950s, the magazine even organized a beauty contest, with prizes including a screen test. Of course, the contestants had better chances of winning if they fit the "typical Italian appearance" of being "healthy and robust" than if they resembled "an American-type cover girl."[17]

The French Communists, as is well-known, prided themselves not only in being the *parti de l'intelligence* but also in reconnecting intellectuals to their working-class origins. Above all, the PCF continued to find its main identity in being the party of workers. Its tendency was not to subordinate workers to intellectuals but vice versa: the worker continued to exert a powerful influence over the intellectual; the party often induced the intellectuals of working-class extraction to maintain full immersion in their original environment. This was immediately apparent after the Cominform meeting of 1947, when the PCF began the battle for the defense of national cinema under an *ouvrièriste* agenda. In conjunction with the anti-Marshall strikes, the party set up committees to protect the French film industry. Under Thorez's plan, the best way to combat the nation's "servility to the United States" was to create a "coalition" of artists, intellectuals, small entrepreneurs, and workers for a united front in defense of both the economy and culture. Most notably, after failing to prevent the ERP policies, the party maintained the organizations to defend the national cinema.[18]

Seizing the public school network for the PCF was even more significant, given the importance, as I noted in chapter 1, of the technical *écoles* for public servants. The highly centralized structure of the French national administration evinced the interconnected bureaucratic and cultural aspects of this leverage. Popular culture was also characterized by the PCF's centralized methods. If the Feste dell'Unità stretched like tentacles through municipalities in Italy, the Fête de L'Humanité, with its origins dating back to the 1930s, became primarily the massive entertainment of the nation's capital. It transformed sections of the Paris *banlieue* into new temporary urban landscapes celebrating the party and providing *loisirs* to its visitors.[19] The PCF's magazines also tried to combine popular entertainment with propaganda. After the war, the Sunday edition of the party's daily, *L'Humanité dimanche*, became notable not only for its varied content, now including more sports, film reviews, and other features with mass-appeal, but also for being sold door-to-door. Activists even attempted to strike up conversations about current events with potential buyers.[20] The party also availed itself of *Almanachs*, popular magazines which since the 1920s had provided a "familiar" reading for the political education of workers and farmers. Its cultural *rubriques* had at least since the 1930s opposed the vigor of progressive art to the "agony" of bourgeois culture. The magazine also closely related to the daily life of the "communist man" and, especially from the late 1940s, evoked the party's connection with both the Jacobin traditions and the "thriving culture of the Soviet Union."[21] While preserving the communist "countersociety," the *Almanachs* also reiterated the revolutionary traditions as part of the nation's heritage. Their propaganda style adopted the expression of popular culture.

PROBLEMS ON THE MASS CULTURAL FRONT

The efforts of the French and Italian Communists to appeal to national folk traditions and combine them with mass-marketing techniques had unintended consequences. As Stephen Gundle points out, the PCI's "ideological purity was diluted in the pursuit of popular support." In part this problem was due to the party's being forced to develop its own version of national popular culture after the void had already been filled by American influence and the Christian Democrats. As a consequence, the PCI "had to partially absorb the values and orientations of a culture industry marked by a propensity for confirming either the specific social and political choices of the DC or

Italy's close alliance with America." The PCF could still rely on its program of anti-Americanism, which had been one of its main assets the 1920s. Yet not even the French comrades were immune to adaptations of "cosmopolitan" culture. It is true that, at the peak of the Cold War, their ethnic-nationalist appeal followed the Zhdanovist canon more closely than the PCI's. The PCF did not "dilute" its ideology. It rather confined itself in a thriving "counter-society," according to Annie Kriegel's definition, "at the heart" of French society but nevertheless "isolated" from the political system.[22]

This result was not foreordained. The debates within the two Communist Parties about folk or mass culture were agonizing in two respects: first, their self-awareness of presenting themselves as elitist clashed with their need to follow popular taste; second, they had to reconcile the provincialism of folk culture to national themes under common, universal denominators that contradicted their urge to forestall "cosmopolitan" influences from the American model.

By the mid-1950s, the PCI's spearhead in popular culture, neorealism, had become either scholastic[23] or diluted into the *commedia all'italiana*, light-hearted comedies displaying the optimism and escapism of workers and petits bourgeois instead of offering enlightened denunciation of impoverished working-class living conditions. Tellingly, the party neglected the visual media for the following two decades. This was a deliberate choice, even though members of the party's press and propaganda section by the early 1950s had acknowledged the growth and influence of Church-affiliated movie theaters (the *cinema parrocchiali*), in cooperation with the YMCA. Instead, the party credited its press for shaping and educating a mass audience.

But in the early 1950s, its main daily, *L'Unità*, was subject to severe scrutiny and charged with being too esoteric for the working-class reader. In September 1952 Felice Platone, one of Togliatti's main collaborators, was invited to discuss these issues at the party's directorate. The paper's Marxist propaganda was a bit lax, he admitted, and its cultural page was dominated by non-Marxist contributors. But since *L'Unità*'s main purpose was to remain a mass-circulation newspaper, more attention was given to the problem of its "intellectualism." The paper's editors, Platone added, had given visiting lectures at the party schools; but, being themselves from petit bourgeois backgrounds, they failed to "understand the workers' main concerns and issues of mass culture." Gian Carlo Pajetta noted that, while aspiring to mass readership, *L'Unità* had devoted more space to the Venice Biennale than to the national congress of retirees, of interest to more than 3 million potential readers. The Monday edition, which extensively covered the Sunday sports events, declined because, according to the party resolution adopted the following month, "the literary virtuosos, ideological gems, eso-teric, incomprehensible commentary" prevailed over reporting: for example, the document noted, on the Tour de France, the readers were stormed with "plenty of poor literature portraying this or that champion" but could not "find out what happened." Furthermore, polling its readers, the newspaper realized it was seen as "too dark, pessimistic," and, as Togliatti himself put it, a bit too "sober and primitive." The party had to learn format, content, and advertising techniques from the bourgeois press while also trying to denounce that press's provincialism and its "corruption under the clerical regime." Together with propaganda, the newspaper increased its attention to lightweight subjects, especially crime reports, because, Platone said, they were "good for sales."[24]

A similar problem haunted the PCF. The main subject discussed at the Central Committee of Saint-Denis in March 1952 was "the battle of the press." Arthur Ramette recommended making the party's dailies and weeklies less "dry" and more "gripping" for the popular reader. The weekly *La Vie ou-vrière*, the main publication of the CGT, was supposed to "break the ground" among socialist and Catholic workers, who seemed to prefer journals such as *Le Parisien libéré* and *L'Aurore*. But it took a few more years for the PCF to tackle the problem fully. In 1955 the party's political bureau acknowledged the sharp decline in sales of a "maladjusted" *L'Humanité*, partly due to the Soviet post-Stalin thaw. To give the daily a more "vivant et humain" content, the party decided to expand its internal politics section, thus "responding to the immediate needs of workers," and to add two sports pages each Mon-day. *L'Humanité dimanche* had taken a turn that was too "intellectual," so the bureau recommended an opening with simple information on political issues of the day. The overarching goal, however, remained improving "the propaganda" impact of the paper "in favor of the Soviet Union."[25] But this dedication to report Eastern European affairs did not necessarily mean a greater focus on foreign policy. While the PCI considered the content of its press too provincial, the PCF, by the early 1950s, regretted that its coverage of foreign affairs was too extensive. The decline in sales of *France nouvelle*, the party's most popular weekly, was attributed to its narrow focus on for-eign policy. These concerns were subsequently reassigned to the more elitist *Cahiers du communisme* and *Paix et démocratie*.[26] With the gradual demise of the peace campaign, foreign affairs were no longer the main propaganda target of the two parties; the first détente had diminished their "populist" appeal and made international coverage more esoteric. Their frequent refer-ence to the interplay between domestic and foreign policy did resume during the high phase of decolonization a few years later; but that propaganda front was never again intertwined with mass politics as much as during the peace campaign of the early 1950s.

In 1951, after many Italian intellectuals objected to the reduction of their role in the cultural commission, Sereni's successor, Carlo Salinari, restored as main cultural priority the reform of the public school system, including universities and scientific research institutes. Salinari also sought to increase influence in the cultural bureaucratic sector. In his report to the commission he made only brief mention of the "need to develop a mass culture."[27] One year later, however, Salinari reevaluated again the party's efforts in the realm of popular culture. Having won the propaganda battle at the political level, he told the national committee on press and propaganda, the party was now subject to a thorough offensive "at the superstructural level." That offensive was more effective at the mass than the high cultural level. Thanks to greater public acceptance of American culture in Italy than in France, Salinari commented, the PCI also needed to make greater efforts than its French counterpart to retain a mass audience. The adversaries did not offer "anything significant in the world of art, science, or philosophy," but the country's film industry was suffering "a colonization" from an ever growing U.S. intervention in the market. USIS reportedly projected more than four thousand films in various small municipalities where movie theaters were absent but where local parishes offered a venue. The conservative women's magazine *Grand Hôtel* sold eight thousand copies a month compared to fewer than three thousand of *Noi Donne*. Local police administrations and the churches used censorship to intimidate the PCI-sponsored events. In order to counter this "preponderance of economic and political power," Salinari recommended the same mobilization methods used for the peace campaign. He also warned against persistent "sectarianism" or "intellectualism" from those within the party who "nurture the illusion that a certain culture can be developed without a quantitative and solely at a qualitative level." It was necessary "to understand that the working class had now a 'national function,' and for this function, it has now absorbed the most progressive traditions of our bourgeoisie." Idealization of the "autodidact worker," and a certain romantic view of his experience ("workers are those who can teach something, . . . telling the nation about their lives, their increasing power"), was thus combined with flexibility toward the country's progressive, non-Marxist currents of thought. The party proceeded to organize a *Centro del libro* (Book Center) and a nationwide *Amici del cinema* (Friends of Cinema) to coordinate local initiatives against illiteracy, and to offset anticommunist censorship with boycotts of American movies.[28]

A scholastic, if not patronizing, approach to mass culture continued to characterize the PCI's cultural commission, which feared the public desire for escapism. It also worried that workers might either drift into the adversaries' ethics or remain confined in a cultural ghetto of the party's mores and rituals. Under the commission's next director, Mario Alicata, the pressure on intellectuals to assume their "organic" tasks and understand the quantitative aspects of culture became even stronger,[29] but too "Zhdanovian," to say the least.

For a party that found its raison d'être in blending *l'intelligence* with a labor ethic, the PCF predictably adopted the scholastic and ideological approach to mass culture much more intensely than did the PCI. At the Fête de L'Humanité it organized huge sales of books through its *batailles du livre*. In the numerous municipal libraries of communist towns it organized *comités d'entreprise* (workers councils) attracting party activists to read or buy its literature. In 1954, following the deliberations of the Central Committee of Arcueil, the party's political bureau increased its effort in sponsoring the *écoles de section*, the *écoles fédérales*, and the *écoles interfédérales*, a vast network of party schools. It also boasted the increasing workers' participation in the courses of the *universités nouvelles* in Paris, Marseille, Bordeaux, and Nice. The bureau carefully instructed its teachers "not to lecture" but simply to present brochures and allow discussion. Deploring "schematism" and "dogmatism," it recommended a populist approach that would highlight the PCF's national role rather than its sectarian nature. After 1956, the *Almanachs* also made an accommodation with de-Stalinization, reaching out to left-wing Socialists. The bureau thus increased the variety of its cultural content and used a "lighter, clearer, more colorful" format.[30] But the party did not agonize as much as its Italian counterpart over the entertaining aspects of its adversaries' culture. Its most consequential efforts to adopt some bourgeois methods remained slight changes in content, style, and advertising in its daily press. And, despite its initiation of the battle for French cinema, the party did not organize actual *ciné-clubs* until the 1970s.

ENDURING AMBIVALENCE AND ELITISM TOWARD AMERICA

The myth of the other America under the New Deal proved enduring. Re-evoking Pavese's disillusionment, Salinari in November 1953 ascribed the decline of American culture to the disappearance of the fascist threat in the world. The United States simply had lost its most "progressive currents of thought." The greatest impact of "Americanism" found in Italian culture was film and the "half-baked knowledge of the readers of the various 'digests.'" But Salinari also recognized that American influence was considerable and should not be neglected. He admitted that the young American generations, especially in colleges, followed new orientations, "less conformist, less inhibited." But, he added, as the clerical exponents adapted American culture, they also turned it into a vehicle of "absolute truths," of "prejudice, superstition, ignorance." Rather than promoting innovation, they fed "provincialism" and encouraged the same stolid, petit bourgeois pursuit of respectability that had led to fascism. Instead of acknowledging the Catholic forces' newfound ability to promote popular culture, Salinari insisted the PCI was the "true steward of cultural inquiry and 'relativism.'"[31]

Prudish bourgeois attitudes also seemed rather selective. Throughout the 1950s Catholic censorship was rigorous on most Italian or communist film productions. But as a 1954 article on *Rinascita* objected, while Rome police had banned the poster of a Soviet film portraying two embracing ballet dancers, they had allowed the city to be "littered" with posters of Howard Hawk's film *Gentlemen Prefer Blondes*. The legs of Marilyn Monroe and Jane Russell apparently passed the Vatican's moral scrutiny. The Italian comrades found a simple reason: American financing and intervention had made this possible. Beyond that, American producers, reportedly in alliance with the American Federation of Labor and Italy's anticommunist trade unions, had become the main agents behind the boycott of Italy's communist filmmakers.[32]

Sometimes elitism could be an asset. The most prominent PCF intellectuals found an audience in and connections with progressive Christians when they denounced, in Aragon's famous words, the "civilization of bathtubs and Frigidaires."[33] This cultural opposition, next to widespread and enduring pacifist feelings in the country, enabled the PCF to confirm its cultural alliance with the progressive *Esprit* and *Le Monde*, as well as Sartre's *Les Temps modernes*. In the early 1950s the neutralist tendencies of these papers reached their peak. Their editors also voiced their culturally assertive opposition to America and the "invasion of *Digests*," the new "pocket-sized . . . drug for little minds," according to Edgar Morin. The party also found new allies in Catholic journals such as *La Quinzaine*, which nurtured a working-class readership. Its purpose resembled that of the Communists: to raise the level of the nation's mass culture against the lowest common denominators from overseas. The PCF thus seemed to confirm its national status in the defense of culture. For a while, as Richard Kuisel has aptly put it, "Marx was on the side of Racine, Rabelais, and the Académie française."[34]

Besides fearing the attraction of escapism for the working class, the two parties began to contemplate the prospect of a generational gap inspired by America's youth mass culture. As leader of the PCI's youth federation, Enrico Berlinguer fought against the invasion of American-style comic books, defining them the new "opium of the youth."[35] The full impact of rock 'n' roll or the beatniks was not felt in France or Italy until the early 1960s. Yet, ironically, rock 'n' roll was demonized by McCarthyist America and Soviet propaganda as a subliminal weapon to undermine the young's adherence to the "correct" ethics—an internal enemy in the case of the United States. Rock music in the 1950s may have signaled the burgeoning Americanization of French and Italian youth. But the two parties found comfort in the various adaptations of the American style of music. In Italy, this adaptation simplified the rebellious generational message into romantic clichés. As Franco Minganti has best explained, "the 'Italian fairy tale' won over the 'American dream,' celebrating the image of the good boy and good girl, with rock and *yé-yé* aesthetics but sound traditional ethics"; the "'versione italiana' would hardly ever match the American original."[36] And if a generational rebellion, existential or hedonistic, was implied in rock 'n' roll's individualistic and irreverent style, the musically conservative party apparatus did not worry so much.

An article from *Vie Nuove* in 1956 exemplified the communist reaction to the "Elvis" phenomenon. This "twenty-one-year-old from Tennessee," the reporter commented, who was "neither good nor bad looking," had attained success mainly through his "lascivious mimicry." In America this caused a sensation, because of its effect in "removing the inhibitions and ancestral fears of the American youth." In the United States *pruderie* was a "pedagogical method," and society was *quacchera e puritana*. In Italy, the article concluded, Elvis Presley would not have the same success, because Italians were "born with malice in their body, so to say, and the devil does not scare anyone . . . even less when it's a little devil made of rhythm and vocalism."[37] This idealized contrast between a mature and uninhibited Europe and a juvenile, repressed America applied just as well to the French youth, although Thorez and Berlinguer kept considering the young vulnerable to American music and pop cultural gadgets. Rock 'n' roll was thus exorcised and reduced to yet another symptom of a dysfunctional society. But its appeal was bound to reach the "uninhibited" French and Italian youth more than the communist cultural guardians expected.

Societies exposed to the mass cultural influence of dominant powers have responded with varying degrees of selection and adaptation. This was the case with French and Italian workers, who often regarded Soviet or American icons as symbols of their everyday life rather than accurate reflections of Soviet or American ethics and societies. In 1954 France's Dourdin Institute reported that, in and around Marseille, workers increasingly attended American movies, and 25 percent of them preferred these films, which in contrast were favored by 15 and 14 percent of people in the middle and upper classes. In 1953, in France's Lorraine region, workers of Italian origin followed the PCF's directives, observing a work stoppage on the day of Stalin's funeral. For the Italian workers, Stalin remained the stern but amiable *baffone* (big moustache). But they also staged moments of public mourning for the deaths of Italian bicycle racer Fausto Coppi and American actor Humphrey Bogart.[38] Sometimes, ethnic pride trumped ideological principles: so, for example, Joe DiMaggio became a model for some aspiring working-class youth in central Italy's new sports centers, where baseball began to take root. In 1953 *Vie Nuove* did not hesitate to celebrate this cultural connection.[39] These examples of adaptations demonstrated the lingering mass fascination with the American entertainment and star system. But they also left room for targeted anti-Americanism.

The Italian and French Communists' attention to American icons of mass culture was selective, praising actors, films, and other popular cultural icons who appeared liberal, or leftist, and who criticized the dominant American values and mass culture. Among filmmakers and actors, Truman Capote, Orson Wells, Buster Keaton, and Marlon Brando were the most featured artists in journals such as *Rinascita, Vie Nuove, L'Humanité dimanche*, and *Les Lettres françaises*. McCarthyist persecution of Charlie Chaplin and the latter's exile back to his native Great Britain sparked a campaign to prove, according to a document from the PCF's secretariat, the "lack of true cultural freedom," the corruption, and generally, the "real nature of American democracy." Reviewing *A King in New York*, the PCI's *Rinascita* exalted the British comedian for showing that even the bad Americans were peculiar victims, "pitiful ones even when they say and do the most horrendous things." The worst thing for the self-righteous American was exactly this illusory sense of empowerment. But the leftist fascination with American cinema crossed political boundaries, and communist reviews celebrated established Hollywood stars such as Clark Gable, Gary Cooper, and James Dean for their larger-than-life depictions of American social contradictions.[40] Thus the two parties kept recognizing the centrality of American mass culture and its frankness compared to its European counterpart. Also, by admitting the degree of dissent allowed to the most "marketed" American stars, the two parties implicitly admitted the pluralism, or even the liberating qualities, of American mass culture.

U.S. TRANSMISSION OF MASS CULTURE AND ITS PROBLEMS

American cultural agents remained generally confident about the impact of U.S. mass culture in Europe. Through music, movies, popular literature, radio, and, eventually, television, the United States conveyed its fulfillment of the masses' rising expectations. As historian Reinhold Wagnleitner has observed, the "presence of American wealth and good life" was "ubiquitous" in the "products of American popular culture, which had an unbeatable allure, especially for the young." In 1950, in the midst of Truman's Campaign of Truth, Congress set most of its allocation for propaganda (ca. $110 million) to fund the main instruments of mass culture—radio, press, publishing, promotion of cinema—and only a relatively small portion of this for cultural exchange. Assistant Secretary of State for Public Affairs William Benton, who first proposed the Campaign of Truth and was connected with the editorial board of *Newsweek* magazine, strongly advocated mass communications (radio, film, and print journalism) over the "slower" cultural media (such as exchanges of books, persons, art exhibits, and classical concert tours).[41]

Besides taking care of cultural exchanges, including Fulbright grants, USIS offices in Europe had a variety of other activities subdivided into branches: from American libraries to press services, from motion pictures to international broadcasting (through the VOA). After 1950 the main USIS programs in France and Italy targeted mass and labor groups, susceptible to communist seduction. The service cooperated with local newspapers and magazines, provided entertainment through the VOA, and movies. USIS also tailored its remedies to local social realities, for example emphasizing audiovisuals in Italy's southern regions, where illiteracy was more widespread than in the North or in France. To be sure, according to a 1951 USIE report, VOA broadcasts, especially its jazz, were effective in France, since *L'Humanité* made repeated efforts to denounce them (the newspaper complained that millions of French listened to *Ici New-York*). "The systematic anti-American propaganda of the PCF," another report inferred, was the best way "to persuade Congress that our informational efforts are not entirely without effect." But USIS also recognized that, unlike movies and radio broadcasts, cultural activities related to art and literature did not cause opposition across the entire political spectrum: French democratic parties "cooperated fully," making "high-pressure driving unnecessary."[42]

These efforts in cultural diplomacy naturally escalated in 1950 as communist propaganda, especially its emphasis on peace versus the American "aggression" in Korea, became relentless. Despite Congress's propagandistic anticommunism under the Smith-Mundt Act, these efforts also reoriented U.S. cultural diplomacy from the unidirectional dissemination of information to a greater emphasis on the common interests of the free world.[43] But this was apparently easier in the areas of high culture. Mass culture and its effects remained rather elusive. There was a high risk that Hollywood and other "pop" culture products projected the image of a mass-marketed, taste-less, superficial, and violent society. The critics from the academic and diplomatic world, as I have noted, kept sounding that alarm. And America's cultural cold warriors took stock of those analyses.

Cinema—a seemingly nonorchestrated means of propaganda—was a case in point. The Motion Picture Association and its affiliates, for example, remained optimistic about the impact of American movies in Italy: a visit by one movie star, as Walter Wanger, chief of the Walter Wanger Pictures Inc. wrote in a 1950 article, was as effective as the visits of twelve statesmen; Hollywood's private initiative, he added, was its strength, its spontaneity. And yet polls conducted by the Common Council for American Unity in 1949 had already suggested that U.S. films brought the nation more negative than positive publicity.[44] Both in France and in Italy, USIS tried to counteract the deleterious effects of the film industry by urging the State Department to distribute documentaries that were, according to a 1951 report, "devoid of violent or highly controversial commentaries" (for example French theater owners had complained about shorts such as *Eisenhower Story* and *One Year in Korea*). Those documentaries also needed to be "extremely short, of newsreel length." Rather than regular movie theaters, USIS recommended venues such as *cinémas éducateurs* for their "quasi-official nature in the French Public School system," or the Service Cinématographique des Armées for the distribution among the French armed forces, and, above all in France, the association France–Etats-Unis, the most active in "proselytizing labor." Films such as *Kidney Function* (for medical faculties), *Ice Patrol*, *Life in a Metropolis*, and Disney's *Defense against Invasion* were made with more recreational than pedagogical intent. Their entertaining quality was proven by the fact that, for example, Colonel Hervé of the French Armed Forces Film Service "declared it was the first time he had known French soldiers to sit through a film on milk and enjoy it." In Italy, the "black" propagandistic nature of the films was more accentuated: films such as *It Can Happen Here*, *Comrade Pulcinella*, *The Man Who Lost Democracy*, and *"Cuckoo" Pictures* (an animated cartoon showing the troubles suffered by its film's characters because of the Communists) all exposed the harsh realities of communism. But they were also balanced with "white" propaganda: for example, *Labor Newsreel* showed the advantages of free trade unionism; *Men in Automobiles* stressed that "everybody owns a car" in the United States. VOA broadcasts, purchased by Radio Televisione Italiana (RAI) and Radio Diffusion France (RDF) also matched this trend, combining attacks on communism with instructional programs focused on productivity—such as the weekly *Agricultural Show* on Italian radio.[45]

During this early phase of USIS activities, the main thrust of American libraries resembled that of the communist book centers. Under the name of "U.S. Information Centers" in France, they targeted especially the youth between age fourteen and eighteen, also providing translation. Likewise in Italy, USIS reported "making special efforts to reach youth groups." Several high schools and universities, especially in central Italy, made agreements with USIS to send students to the American libraries. In Southern Italy, aided first by the Ford Foundation, USIS sponsored the Unione Nazionale per la Lotta contro l'Analfabetismo (Union for the Struggle against Illiteracy, UNLA), assisting rural families in particular.[46] But the effort to address a mass audience and present the most accessible literature had its drawbacks. In France, USIS officials noted, light fiction and thriller literature seemed to be "the sole representatives of American literary activity." These books confirmed to the French "many of the most regrettable notions of American civilization."[47]

Overall, by the mid-1950s, USIS realized that "fast media" were indeed too expensive and did not yield the expected results. The press in France and Italy hardly ever used the news bulletins and magazines produced by their offices. The VOA had a declining audience. The reemergence of French and Italian cinema, plus a growing public *ennui* with Hollywood after the enthusiastic postwar response, led many to question America's most popular mass cultural export.[48] Clearly the influence of American cinema remained strong even on the most leftist directors of the French *Nouvelle vague* and the Italian neorealist *commedia*; but that influence was not as univocal as most U.S. officials would have liked. Many doubts persisted: instead of disproving clichés, most American mass cultural products seemed to confirm them. Moreover, it was difficult to present American mass culture as a form of genuine cultural exchange, or as an expression of the free world's common cause.

In 1952–53 letters from various Italian American associations flooded the offices of the State Department complaining about brash and naive VOA broadcasts. It was also difficult to determine which situations warranted negative or positive propaganda. Most of the pamphlets published for the Italian mass audience derided or denounced communism (cartoons such as *Ridi Pagliaccio*, with jokes targeting communists, or satirical leaflets such as *Baffino e Baffone*, comparing small-moustache Hitler with big-moustache Stalin, were cases in point), but they failed to stir the workers' conscience or strike them as especially funny. In France, a disappointed U.S. consul in Lyon noticed in August 1950 that ECA and USIA pamphlets advertising America's economic affluence and peace record could not match the effectiveness of the PCF's negative propaganda on U.S. conduct in Korea. The consul's conclusion was that "apparently, negative propaganda is more effective than positive."[49]

Culture is also a difficult phenomenon to gauge, measure, and assess financially. As such it was often subject to manipulation. Budgetary fights with Congress and within the State Department were constant. In addition, the various USIS activities, once linked to local agencies, often became a boon for nonbudgeted assistance. In Italy, for example, abuse by such cultural organizations as the Centro Democratico della Cassa per il Mezzogiorno (Democratic Center for Assistance to Southern Italy) in 1956 drew a stern rebuke from Acting Assistant Secretary of State for European Affairs C. Burke Elbrick, who asked the USIA to "break with the custom of the past ten years whereby offices of the Italian government automatically look to the U.S. for all types of minor financial assistance."[50]

Italian or French recipients of U.S. cultural and covert assistance could themselves be manipulative by ironically turning *plus royaliste que le roi*. In Italy, the "civic committees" of the rightist Baron Luigi Gedda, so instrumental in the 1948 elections, soon became unfit, according to a U.S. embassy report, for the "gradual mindset truce" of the "highly religious Italians," which made the public less prone to subscribe to the committees' literature, let alone support their newly formed paramilitary units.[51] In France, the violent turn in the PCF's pacifist campaign had actually preceded the anti-Ridgway demonstrations of 1953, but it was in part attributed to the hard line of the Pinay government. The escalation had resulted in communist raids against USIS offices in Bordeaux and Lille in the summer of 1952. In itself this violence could reflect well on the U.S. image as a victim of intolerance, or even on the effectiveness of USIS work. But within months, USIS officials noted that the government's previous ultra-Atlanticism had morphed into a "griping stage" for French nationalism. A mixture of pride in its renewed economic health and resentment of its continued dependence on U.S. assistance made France in 1953 less amenable to intense American cultural activity. USIS concluded that it should conduct its programs "as unobtrusively as possible because of growing sensitivity in France to the 'American presence.'" Even Italy became less malleable, for similar reasons. The government there, concerned that Marxists or neofascists might capitalize on the public's reawakening nationalism, began to resent unfulfilled American promises, or simply a heavy American presence.[52]

In order to offset these trends, the U.S. cultural agency sought to be more discreet. Ironically, the change occurred under the Eisenhower administration, which had established the USIA to reemphasize the importance of propaganda over cultural exchange. But USIS centers overseas kept operating with "discretion" and a growing use of "indirection." In general, the projection of American mass culture gradually changed from overt propaganda to an instrumentalized world staging of American "ambassadors of good will." These initiatives benefited from an Emergency Fund established by Congress in 1954 to enlist jazz musicians and athletes, or American corporations that participated in exhibits tailored to the European public's tastes and sensitivity.[53] For its part, USIS, instead of distributing propaganda mainly through American centers, or VOA broadcasts, in the mid-1950s increasingly used indigenous networks and molders of public opinion. In December 1951, the Country Plan for France, focusing on written media, urged the fostering of "direct French action, supplemented by indirect USIE action," and the exploitation of the French press's apparently unlimited curiosity "about certain aspects of the American scene."[54] Through Leader and NATO grants—under the Foreign Leader Program, which arranged short-term visits to the United States for individuals or small groups—several French newspapers sent their reporters to experience everyday American life. Those reporters became enthusiastic opinion makers on behalf of America. Le Monde and Le Figaro were particularly targeted for their broad audience and, in Le Monde's case, in order to "neutralize" its neutralist tendencies. By early 1953, thirty-one Italian journalists had been sent to the United States under the same auspices. The result, USIS reported, was over four hundred articles published about their experience and the commonalities between the two countries.[55] Having seen that VOA could not compete with the ratings of the national RDF and RAI broadcasts, USIS began to cooperate more closely with those stations: RDF sent several of its prominent reporters—Michel Droit, Sammy Simon, and Serge Groussard among them—to the United States as Foreign Leader grantees. The radio's Musical Services broadcast hundreds of programs on American music (ready-made by the VOA) for the jazz-avid French audience. Television was first tapped in France to provide a reservoir of American movies previously subject to quotas. USIA media resources saturated the news outlets of French and Italian radio and television.[56]

Indirection also meant a shift toward the cultural "leaders" of France and Italy. Those very contacts with journalists and broadcasters called USIS's attention to the intellectual and academic world. Labor groups had been somewhat impermeable, or just politically neutral, to U.S. mass cultural imports. But influential journalists, teachers, writers, and artists could be the new vehicles for American soft power.

Intellectual Cold War

Most U.S. officials recognized that French and Italian intellectuals had considerable clout over politics and society, that they were consensus builders, and that most on the left were fierce guardians of national cultures and aspirations. Many intellectuals had used a certain image of the enemy to build that consensus.

A "FULBRIGHT DIFFERENCE"?

Part of the Foreign Leader Program was to create a network between talented, influential opinion leaders in Europe and their American counterparts through sponsored visits to the United States.[57] Academia became part of this network, not only in order to encourage the expansion of still embryonic American studies programs, but also to help mold Europe's future political leadership. In France, the Franco-American Commission for Educational Exchange sponsored by the Fulbright Program's Bureau of Education and Cultural Affairs (CU) became most effective after founding in 1952 the Association Amicale Universitaire France-Amérique, which reached a membership of more than twenty-five hundred French alumni of U.S. universities.[58] The study of American literature had relatively deep roots in twentieth-century French universities, but the study of American history elicited little or no interest throughout the 1950s. Likewise, the bureau recognized that history, taught in Italy chronologically and not by country or region, remained a rather Eurocentric discipline. Fulbright lecturers helped stimulate some interest in American fields outside literature. In France, it was not until the mid-1960s that renowned diplomatic historian Jean-Baptiste Duroselle came to express the general realization that it was "silly not to have a chair in American History." As director of the U.S. Educational Commission/France, he managed to establish one at the Fondation Nationale de Sciences Politiques in Paris. Italy had preceded France with the approval in 1960 by the Italian parliament of four chairs in American civilization, one of which was in American history at the University of Florence, held by American specialist Giorgio Spini.

These same academic circles, by the early 1960s, lobbied for the expansion of American studies to include U.S. business history, as well as accounting, financial practices, and sociology. They insisted that the U.S. Educational Commission had been "vital since it reduc[ed] the danger of the exchange program being labeled propaganda." The founding of the Bologna Center of Johns Hopkins University in 1955 was the first example of this wide range and the promising trends from Italian academia. As one official of the Advisory Commission on International Education and Cultural Affairs noted, the center, pulling students from most Western European countries, was "producing part of the future bureaucracy of Europe." The result encouraged Johns Hopkins officials to advocate to "set up centers similar to [theirs] in France and other places in Europe." By the early 1960s this seemed urgent to CU officials because, with "Europe economically and politically" more cohesive, the United States paradoxically "fac[ed] the possibility that the new Europe might turn in on itself." For this same reason, courses in political science and sociology were also geared to encourage the movement toward European integration, but with strong transatlantic connections. The Ford Foundation thus had already for some years helped fund these academic programs in connection with the European Community Movement sponsored by industrialist Adriano Olivetti. Finally, the urgency of funding centers in Paris, Bonn, or London was heightened by their enrollment of "huge groups of students from underdeveloped countries." This presented a "challenging opportunity for USIS."[59] But, for lack of funds and initiative, those centers were never established.

USIS remained active in promoting American art, especially in France. That, according to USIS, seemed a "worthwhile opportunity" to "extend influence in a highly articulate and influential segment of French life,"[60] and, as I have noted, it received the cooperation of French authorities.

Funding for propaganda increased under the Eisenhower administration, but the government's involvement in the intellectual cold war remained by its own admission inadequate. One reason why the State Department did not vigorously engage this battle in France was skepticism. Commenting on the "Plan for Operations for the U.S. Ideological Program" (codenamed D-33) in 1955, embassy counselor Robert P. Joyce reiterated his superiors' "long-time realization" that "an atmosphere of intellectual arrogance precludes effective work with these milieux in Paris," particularly the "fuzzy and unrealistic" neutralist ones. He therefore recommended against making them "our target area, or we will waste a great deal of time attempting to influence them."[61]

This skepticism was not just dictated by political aversion; at the highest levels, it was also frequently related to negative attitudes toward intellectuals in general. McCarthyism thrived not only on anticommunist paranoia but also in the American tradition of anti-intellectualism. Richard Hofstadter's portrait of this climate was not flattering. In his book *Anti-Intellectualism in American Life* (1963), he wrote that during the 1950s "the term *anti-intellectualism*, only rarely heard before, became a familiar part of our national vocabulary of self-recrimination and intramural abuse." McCarthyism, in this sense, was just a symptom of a larger problem that reached its climax in the 1950s. Under the conformist, entrepreneurial, pragmatic atmosphere of that decade, it was common to label prominent liberals, including Eisenhower's opponent in two presidential races, Adlai E. Stevenson, as "eggheads"; and Ike himself was often quoted as saying that intellectuals are "those who use lots of sentences to say what can be expressed in a few words."

This attitude was not confined to the Oval Office. For example, commenting on the Kremlin-inspired peace campaigns in 1950, the refined Charles Bohlen wrote that "only fools and intellectuals support neutrality." Ambassador Dunn left his Rome post in January 1952 with the impression that the voter "supporting the PCI-PSI" wanted "more protection or satisfaction to his personal material interests than is now provided by Commies" and that he was no longer "swayed by metaphysical web-spinning of intellectuals and politicians in Rome." In Paris, Ambassador David K. E. Bruce, who held the post from 1949 to 1952, was known for his vast knowledge of French history and culture. In Rome, Ambassador Clare Luce, with her unusual background as a journalist, playwright, and screenwriter attracted some, mostly conservative, intellectual circles to the Via Veneto Embassy. In both cases, the ambassadors brought a certain panache to the otherwise hackneyed atmosphere of U.S. diplomacy. But Bruce kept his distance from France's most influential intellectuals. For her part, Luce remained obdurate against the traditions that, she recognized, in France and Italy made most intellectuals "spiritually and politically, . . . the descendants of the Jacobins and the 19th-Century Socialists." "Today, as yesterday," she added, "most of them are still men of the Left—that is to say, Marxian Socialists." Unfortunately, Luce explained, "we cannot often enough remind ourselves that for historic reasons—the greatest of which is the French Revolution—present day French and Italian 'intellectuals,' the writers, journalists, professors, scientists, philosophers, and so on, exert far more influence in politics and on public opinion than they do in America or Great Britain."[62] So even the most cultured U.S. officials came to realize that intellectual clout was far greater in Europe, and that it naturally remained a staple of progressive or Marxist thought. It was private foundations, aided by the CIA, that took up the slack of the cultural cold war in Europe. Many officials within the CIA understood the importance of the battle for ideas, but otherwise politicians, both in the executive branch and in Congress, remained reluctant to provide sizeable funds to USIS and cultural exchange.

CCF AND CIA

Already by the late 1940s the U.S. government had realized that exchange programs and academic developments would be insufficient to mobilize pro-

American European intellectuals and to counter communist propaganda. The energy of the communist peace offensive in 1949–50 induced American writers and activists to seek a more permanent alliance with reputable intellectuals of the European moderate Left. The story of the Congress for Cultural Freedom (CCF) has been told extensively, and needs not be revisited in detail here. But by briefly explaining its trajectory, purposes, and achievements as compared with the communist response, we can clearly discern consistencies and contradictions in the intellectual cold war on both sides.

After the communist-inspired peace conferences at New York's Waldorf-Astoria in March 1949 and in Paris the following month, anti-Stalinist intellectuals from the United States and Western Europe—plus some émigrés from the Eastern bloc—convened an alternative forum in Berlin in June 1950, giving birth to the Congress for Cultural Freedom. Several of the American representatives were former Marxists, such as Sidney Hook, Arthur Koestler, James Burnham, and James T. Farrell, who had rejected the Soviet Union. Many of their European counterparts had followed a similar ideological path. Among the most prominent French and Italian intellectuals who joined or sponsored the organization, some, such as Raymond Aron or Benedetto Croce, had never joined the Marxist ranks, and some, such as writers Jules Romains and Ignazio Silone, had previously sympathized with or joined communism. In Rome, Silone had also established contacts with Ambassador Dunn before the founding of the CCF. Thus the main thrust of the CCF was drafting intellectuals "sufficiently left wing that they could not be ignored by their fellow intellectuals, yet they rejected both communism and neutralism."[63]

This opening to the Non-Communist Left (NCL, as it became known) from both continents found common ground with the liberal anticommunist principles of the Vital Center. Arthur Schlesinger Jr. was among the CCF's founding members. After working during the war for the Office of Strategic Services, he remained connected to the State Department. His book *The Vital Center* (1949) warned of the perils of totalitarian extremism from both the right and the left. A similar analysis appeared two years later in *The Origins of Totalitarianism*, by German émigrée Hannah Arendt. In it Arendt conflated Nazism and communism and popularized the term "red fascism," echoing Reinhold Niebuhr's indictment of Marxism's "radical evil." While closer to the ideas of American liberals, Arendt's work, much like Niebuhr's, was used to rekindle a conservative Cold War climate in the United States. Also influential was *The God That Failed* (1949), authored by several former communists who had joined the CCF.

The Vital Center's influence over the CCF—which from 1955 included

Arendt as well—helped adjust the intolerant tones of conservative America. Rather than restricting the debate, Schlesinger invited toleration of "dangerous opinions." Acknowledging the importance of civil liberties, Schlesinger was ready to admit conflict and contradiction as the truly creative aspects of a free society. Loyal to the New Deal legacy, he did not believe that freedom could be harmonious and consensual. But, like most of the CCF participants, he fought utopian or idealist tendencies in American and European political culture and aimed at shaping a nonideological, liberal middle ground.[64] While politicized, the CCF made the powerful point that any progressive democratic society would guarantee cultural excellence only when intellectuals and artists worked completely free from political interference. Culture had to be apolitical.[65]

In most respects, the CCF strove to refute many images and distortions conveyed by American mass culture. European anti-Americanism had been fueled in part by U.S. efforts to present a sanitized version of the American way of life. While in principle agreeing with the transatlantic symbiosis fostered by the Marshall Plan and NATO, the CCF also tried to mitigate the "be like us" attitude of the Marshall Plan propagandists. It was no wonder that Macdonald was among its founding members and that Kennan also joined in 1955. While ostensibly apolitical, the CCF followed an impulse similar to that of the ERP and Atlantic policies to establish a transatlantic community of interests relying on American hegemony. It aimed to restore Western intellectual values and solve "the crisis of the 'European mind' [that] occurred in the wake of fascism."[66]

The best way to solve this crisis was to emphasize the cultural vitality of Western European culture and its commonality with a respectable American culture. The CCF took pains to prove that the United States was not culturally barren. While undoubtedly partisan in its anticommunist rhetoric, the congress rather overplayed its cultural sophistication, endorsing modernist culture, the various examples of the avant-garde that disproved communist accusations of decadence. Its frequent conferences and seminars gave equal honor to American and European thinkers. In 1952 the CCF sponsored a spectacular month-long festival of the arts in Paris, including symphonies, operas, art exhibits, and debates on modern literature. It also underscored the importance of many U.S. cultural magnets, from New York to Chicago, from Boston to San Francisco, where high culture now flourished, and where many artists and intellectuals from around the world had found political refuge.[67]

Sophistication and freedom, the CCF sought to show, went hand in hand. For the congress also strove to project a more human image of America than that portrayed by ERP propaganda: this was an America aware of its strengths but also of its weaknesses, an America that was a beacon, consensual, but also pluralistic and nurturing its inner contradictions. With all its imperfections, CCF sponsors insisted, the American experience had guaranteed social progress and constant improvement of the human condition.

Conscious of the profound influence of Gramscian thought over the Italian and European intelligentsia, the CCF emulated and applied the concept of cultural hegemony. Rather than focusing on intellectuals' individual characteristics, it invested them with social and organizational functions. Operating at the superstructural level, these intellectuals sought to bridge political and civil society. Their ultimate aim was the mirror image of the Gramsci project: to forge a consensus around a shared cultural heritage that ideologically justified Atlanticism and excluded communism. But rather than following strict Atlanticist parameters, the CCF stressed "free-thinking" as the real European tradition. The CCF also helped prove that vibrant European thought could exist outside Marxist influence—hence, its pursuit of recognition by nominating as its honorary presidents some of the most distinguished European and American philosophers: from Bertrand Russell to John Dewey, Benedetto Croce, Reinhold Niebuhr, Karl Jaspers, and Jacques Maritain.[68]

Leftist thought could also be framed in favor of freedom through a reinterpretation of existentialism. The most diffused view of Sartre's philosophy in the United States was reflected in a *Time* magazine article that described it as "another faddist version of Materialism." But the progressives gathered around the Vital Center appreciated existentialism for making "the most radical attempt to grapple with the implications of [modern] anxiety" derived from freedom and the responsibility of choice. Most French participants in the CCF, however, concurred with Aron's critique of Sartre's "elementary" Marxism. These were the years in which Sartre gave his most unconditional support to the Soviet Union, the PCF, and their peace campaigns, while turning his most venomous attacks on McCarthyist America.[69]

The struggle to reinterpret the most influential leftist thinking in France and Italy also testified to CCF priorities. While active in thirty-five countries, the congress paid foremost attention to France and Italy, where communist influence was greatest. The most enduring European organizations born under CCF auspices were the French Amis de la Liberté and the Italian Associazione per la Libertà della Cultura.[70] Like *Encounter* in Britain, other CCF-sponsored periodicals in France and Italy presented liberal views independent of the neutralist opinion-makers of *L'Observateur*, *Esprit*, *Les Temps modernes*, and *Nuovi Argomenti*. In Paris, *Preuves*, the new review edited by François Bondy, and in Italy *Tempo presente*, edited by Chiaromonte, became known for their liberal anticommunist stance and attracted wide readerships.[71]

CCF funding came from several sources. The Free Trade Union Committee and the International Confederation of Free Trade Unions under Irving Brown underwrote the first conferences. The Carnegie, Rockefeller, and especially the Ford foundations provided subsequent support under the CIA's covert sponsorship.[72] The CIA-CCF alliance was mutually sought, first solicited by one of the most fervent anti-Stalinist congress participants, Melvin Laski, editor of the journal *Der Monat*—funded by the U.S. military government in Berlin—and later editor of *Encounter*.[73] Behind the CIA decision was a clear intent to entice the NCL. This became "the theoretical foundation of the Agency's political operations against communism over the next two decades." It also helped alleviate the European elites' main concerns about excessive American political and cultural domination, while still emphasizing the goal of Atlantic unity among intellectuals.[74] Most CCF members were in any case unaware of this connection.

Covert funding gave the whole enterprise an aura of *pax americana*. Exceptionalist assumptions persisted in trying to mold European public opinion rather than letting it develop its response to communism according to its internal dynamics. The Vital Center intellectuals, and the disenchanted American leftists whose faith in communism had been shattered by Stalin's totalitarianism, had an anticommunist drive and still nurtured an exceptionalist outlook on their country. Deception was in itself contradictory with the goal of advancing freedom. It is no surprise that when the magazine *Ramparts* revealed the connection between the CCF and the CIA in 1967, a scandal erupted, and many indignant intellectuals left the organization. The CCF continued with less funding, mostly from the Ford Foundation, and with the different name of the International Association for Cultural Freedom (IACF). But it is plausible to argue that had the revelations occurred in the 1950s, the alliance with the CIA would not have seemed "so outrageous and incomprehensible."[75] More than Americanization, the main concern of CCF members was to combat communist influence.

The main strength of the CCF was its promotion of pluralism to the point of allowing contradictions and open criticism of America. This approach coincided with a gradual evolution within U.S. diplomacy toward tolerating, and, as first suggested by Ambassador Caffery, even encouraging mild forms of anti-Americanism in order to deflect more strident ones. By admitting the NCL's most vocal demonstrations of independence from American control, the CCF conducted its most effective battle against the fellow-traveling Left and its appeal among anti-Americans in Europe and the Third World.

Preuves was a case in point. On its frontispiece, Bondy declared the journal's intention "to defend critical and creative thought against the restrictions of political demands everywhere,"[76] which of course resulted in several essays critical of U.S. politics and society. This openness reached unexpected circles: in the Eisenhower administration the approach to the Center-Left in France and Italy became, as we will see, tactical if not altogether sincere. Even Ambassador Luce, while preferring to interact with conservative politicians and intellectuals, gradually understood the importance of attracting left-of-center Italian intellectuals. By 1955–56 she helped USIS sponsor trips to and lectures in the United States by, among others, Ignazio Silone and Alberto Moravia. The latter's impressions still contained a great deal of criticism. But at least this was a nuanced critique, mixed with ambiguous fascination.[77]

Without denying the CIA's ruthlessness, one must see some merit in Schlesinger's evaluation of the agency's influence as being not always "reactionary and sinister" but actually, at crucial moments, "politically enlightened and sophisticated."[78] In encouraging dissent, the goal was to reduce the influence of and isolate the Marxist Left. But the result was to help inspire the most pluralistic aspects of American intellectual culture.

It is no accident that the CCF's pivotal conferences in Hamburg (1953) and Milan (1955) downplayed its ideological militancy in favor of a more empirical realism espousing the "the end of ideology" popularized by sociologist Daniel Bell. But rather than fostering a conservative consensus, the CCF anticipated Bell's notion that the "repudiation of ideology," in order to be "meaningful, *must mean not only criticism of the utopian order but of existing society as well.*" Two other sociologists, Edward Shils and Seymour Lipset, at the same time argued that Marxism no longer was attuned to social sciences and failed to analyze modern industrial society. The growingly explicit message of the two CCF conferences was that Marxism was obsolete and utopian while capitalism could be reformed. In Milan, Raymond Aron underscored this view proposing the theme of "the end of ideology" for discussion.[79] It is however a bit exaggerated to see this as the turning point that ended the ideological warfare in Western Europe.[80] Implied in "the end of ideology" argument was still a certain dose of American exceptionalism; while perhaps less utopian than the American arguments of the early Cold War, and for all its apparent pragmatism, it was still idealist, or at least complacent.

At the same time, it is true that this turn in the CCF reinvigorated the intellectuals' aversion to dogma, also among many of those who had sided with the communists. While failing to gain the expected number of converts from the Marxist ranks, American cultural diplomacy nevertheless indirectly rekindled a debate about freedom and creativity among Western European Communists. Soviet conduct destroyed their best expectations, and the notion that culture thrived in a progressive democratic society gained further credence in France and Italy.

INTELLECTUAL CLOUT AND "CLOUDS"

Liberalization for French and Italian communist intellectuals did not come swiftly or easily. Pro-Sovietism, or the promise of a national alternative, naturally erased most doubts of those who had joined the two parties' ranks. But there were also those—from Jean-Paul Sartre to Norberto Bobbio—who, without joining, upheld the notion of the working class as the main agent of change and of the Soviet experience as containing the promise of that change. They considered capitalism and NATO mainly at fault, abhorred the United States' consumerist or technologically enslaving aspects, and refused to be "counterrevolutionary."

Anti-Americanism had helped both the PCF and the PCI discipline intellectuals, more so at the peak of this cultural cold war. In 1948 Pietro Secchia had made it clear that intellectuals "must act as militant combatants to the same extent as those on the other side." Those who nurtured the illusion of an ideological "third force" were mere "servants and lackeys" of American imperialism.[81] The two parties' intellectual appeal on both sides of the Atlantic was further proven by the roster of participants in the Marxist-inspired Congress of World Partisans.[82]

The PCF's relationship with existentialism was never easy. But by the early 1950s, Sartre began to stress that no situation could be transcended by individual willpower; only collective struggle was viable. While he was never comfortable with the label of "anti-American," his disenchantment with U.S. society and politics helped his virtual alignment with communism. Sartre and his companion Simone de Beauvoir ostensibly maintained a balance in denouncing both the McCarthyist trials and the purges in the East (such as the Slansky trial in Prague). But their revulsion at the American "witch hunt" revealed which of the two societies now seemed irredeemable. There was something "decidedly rotten in America," Sartre wrote after the execution of Julius and Ethel Rosenberg. What he called "legal lynching" showed a "collective responsibility," an evidence that the United States was the "cradle of a new fascism." For that reason Europe had to "scream: Watch out, America has rabies! We must cut all ties with it or else we shall be bitten and infected next." In Italy, likewise, both the PCI's intellectual and mass media drew a familiar parallel between the Rosenbergs and the Sacco and Vanzetti case of the 1920s.[83]

In general, leftist intellectuals in both countries felt they personally had more at stake than their nation's political independence: their jobs and mission as cultural molders was at risk. Particularly the French thought that America's universal pretensions no longer matched those of their own nation, and that their task was to guard real revolution against the counter-revolutionary, conformist United States.[84]

In contrast to their nationalist credentials, the two parties continued to heed the directives of Andrei Zhdanov, juxtaposing the Cold War to his tenets on socialist realism. With strict discipline the two parties now drew a sharp distinction between proletarian and bourgeois cultures and sciences. The PCI made official its adherence to Zhdanovism at its Sixth Congress in January 1948, only a few months after the PCF immediately endorsed the decisions of the first Cominform meeting.[85] Roger Garaudy, as we have noted, was the first among the French communist intellectuals to question the absoluteness of the "proletarian esthetic." In Italy, Elio Vittorini had extended the polemic to include his endorsement of modernism and American literature.[86]

The real test of the party discipline among intellectuals was to deny Soviet repression. The vicissitudes of Victor Kravchenko are a case in point. A mid-level Soviet bureaucrat who had defected to the United States, Kravchenko had published his memoirs *I Chose Freedom* in 1945. It was the most experimental French communist journal, *Les Lettres françaises* that led the attack against the "heretic." Kravchenko sued the journal for libel, and the ensuing trial in the spring of 1949 paraded some of the most distinguished party intellectuals, from Vercors to Frédéric Joliot-Curie, in defense of the PCF's and the Soviet record. The court awarded Kravchenko only one franc in symbolic damages. A few months later, party intellectuals attacked an "internal" critic, David Rousset, who had been a hero of the socialist Resistance and a cofounder of Sartre's Rassemblement Démocratique Révolutionnaire. Following Rousset's denunciation of Soviet gulags, the party meted out its condemnation: this survivor of Nazi concentration camps had himself become a "fascist."[87] In a similar, though not as consequential controversy in Italy, Togliatti and other intellectuals in 1951 attacked Valdo Magnani and Aldo Cucchi, two party leaders of the Emilian federation, for their support of Titoism against the increasingly repressive Soviet regime.[88] That was the same year in which Vittorini abandoned the party, and together with another restless intellectual, Italo Calvino, founded the journal *Menabò*.

Initially de-Stalinization did not lead many Italian communist intellectuals to criticize Soviet conduct. Ironically, it provoked self-critique for not following the Soviet reform script closely enough. The utopia about the motherland of socialism was now modified and somewhat "humanized." In March 1953, still before de-Stalinization, Salinari suggested responding to adversaries' critique of the Soviet Union and its alleged substitution of culture with propaganda, not by being "defensive," but by retorting that in fact U.S. and Catholic cultures amounted to mere propaganda. But he also admitted that in the U.S.S.R. there were "as many bad writers, painters, etc., as there are good ones." A few months later, the cultural commission acknowledged its failure to be sufficiently self-critical in the cultural field, whereas "in the country of socialism, where the Marxist-Leninist theory has been tempered by thirty years of struggles and experiences, our comrades continue to discuss animatedly about everything . . . from social sciences to experimental [*sic*] linguistics." The commission concluded with an optimistic note: being a little more polemical, not only against the enemy, but also versus certain Soviet positions would actually make the cultural leadership in Moscow feel "more comfortable, and not like reclusive animals from another continent."[89]

For the PCF, the issue was rather how much and how dangerously the new Soviet leadership might depart from Stalin's legacy. So, paradoxically, the French became more prone than their Italian comrades to criticize Moscow, not for what it was but for what it might become, too revisionist perhaps in politics and in the arts: their judgment of the emerging leader Nikita Khrushchev remained suspended. Their self-assigned task was to defend Russian cultural realism against any attack, so as to maintain its link to their own Jacobin traditions. Laurent Casanova, already pledged to the Zhdanovian line, was anointed as the guardian of "national" traditions, tracing Soviet orthodoxy to them.[90]

The malaise among communist and fellow-traveling intellectuals became manifest before the events of 1956 caused many defections. While their distancing was still rather muted, mostly limited to internal debate, they remained skeptical, to say the least, of Stalinist cultural policies.

Among scientists, some, like Marcel Prenant and Luigi Silvestri, were forced to leave because of their objections to Lysenkoism. In France, while the journal *La Nouvelle critique*, founded by Casanova in 1948, was recognized as a publication of "militant Marxism," another review, *La Pensée*, had many clashes with the Cominform. The main problem was with *La Pensée*'s attempts to reconcile Marxism, rationalism, science, and humanism. But the PCF tolerated the journal, mainly because of its reach in the academic community, which could only be seduced with such "eclecticism." In the arts, the party questioned the geniality and loyalty of Picasso after his "doodled" commemorative portrait of Stalin, violating every Soviet canon, was published in *Les Lettres françaises* in March 1953. Louis Aragon, the "reformed surrealist," had conceded too much in his journal. Only fame allowed the Spanish painter to weather this ideological storm and stay in the party.[91] Aragon, however, together with Thorez, ostracized Auguste Lecoeur, responsible for an excessively orthodox and "workerist" attitude toward politics and the arts. At the Thirteenth Party Congress of 1954, Aragon corrected the party's view of Zhdanovism, promoting an art "national in its form, and socialist in its content." At least in culture, nationalism prevailed over loyalty to Moscow. In Italy, consistently with the publication of Gramsci's *Prison Notebooks* between the late 1940s and early 1950s, Togliatti had also reached a similar resolution, urging the cultural commission to nourish "an *Italian* socialist culture." The exegesis of Gramsci's work helped mitigate the effects of Stalinism and Zhdanovism, while stressing the Italian way to socialism; at the same time, it justified Togliatti's firm leadership over cultural and political aspects, and gave the party an "alibi for partial and superficial autocritique."[92]

Still, not all communist artists in Italy felt entirely liberated. The iconic painter Renato Guttuso had closely followed the example of Picasso, exalting the style and message contained in *Guernica*, a painting that symbolized the united front of *engagés* artists against fascism. While opposed to abstractism, the Italian painter and his school never accepted the "neorealist" label; nor did they completely repudiate the bourgeois artistic traditions or the modernism of a Giorgio De Chirico. During the controversy over the Stalin portrait, Guttuso expressed his "filial" solidarity with Picasso. In the cultural commission, from the start he argued that forcing artists to adhere to Marxist canons was tantamount to "ideological terrorism."[93]

Togliatti and Alicata confronted even more challenging opinions from the philosopher Norberto Bobbio and the writer Italo Calvino. Between 1954 and 1955, Bobbio, who offered only external support to the PCI, engaged the party leader in a series of articles defying historic materialism. Against Togliatti's vision of true freedom made possible only by the abolition of economic and social privileges, the philosopher insisted on the "defense of individual liberty against all absolutist regimes." What constituted the "European intellectual tradition," he averred, was "the restless research, the constant doubt, the search for dialogue, the critical spirit," and "the awareness of a complex reality." Bobbio's influence extended to other thinkers, such as economist Luciano Barca and philosopher Ludovico Geymonat, who still belonged to the party.[94]

Calvino, who was fast reaching the peak of his fame as a novelist thanks to his first surrealist folk and fantasy tales, led the ranks of those intellectuals who chastised the provincialism of the party's approach to culture and the sciences. In 1954 he began to invite a more objective analysis of the new social sciences in the United States, especially their impact on industrial relations. The United States was still an enemy, but a respectable one with recognized progressive traditions. Mario Alicata reprimanded these intellectuals for not being "Gramscian" enough. At a meeting of the cultural commission in July 1956, Calvino reiterated his points. Still fascinated with the new social sciences, and struck by the relative Soviet liberalization, he urged the party not only to deal with new trends in sociology and economics but also to allow intellectuals to have full "freedom of inquiry" in "any cultural activity"; for the "objective, historic situations" that had prevented that liberty had now "disappeared." At the meeting, Gianfranco Corsini, an academic who specialized in American studies, echoed Calvino, contending that the main way to "deprovincialize" the PCI's culture was by engaging instead of denying the influence of American culture. The PCI had to "accept its legitimacy, answering the solicitations that this most advanced culture in the capitalist world offers to the contemporary man."[95]

Besides being intrigued by the workings of neocapitalism, intellectuals from both the PCI and the PCF resumed their debate on America's "worthy" literature. Their publications featured new and old heroes, from John Dos Passos to Arthur Miller, from Walt Whitman to Allen Ginsberg. They continued to focus on the contradictions of American democracy. Whitman, just to cite the foremost example, was, according to a 1955 article in *La Nouvelle critique*, the "prophet of American democracy." But the reader of *Leaves of Grass* was also invited to "wonder if this writer was not a 'dupe,'" who "sang the glories of a great nation in full expansion, foreshadowing the endless pride and appetite for conquest by Ford or Standard Oil." But no, the answer was that Whitman's America was, above all, an "Amérique fraternelle," the "America of hard work." After the end of the New Deal, this was a bygone America. Her poet's worthy heirs were elsewhere: Vladimir Mayakovski in Russia, Federico García Lorca in Spain, and Pablo Neruda in Chile.[96] Still, such analyses cast the United States as the birthplace of this cultural solidarity and implied potential guidance by its most enlightened democratic intellectuals.

Although the French and Italian Communists relaxed somewhat their adherence to socialist realism in the arts in the early 1950s, the PCI did not fully abandon Zhdanovism until the end of the decade. A series of conferences at the Gramsci Institute in 1959 discussed "The Problems of Realism in Italy." That marked the beginning of the end of the cultural commission, which had been created in part to impose the Soviet line on such matters. For the PCF the repudiation came later, at the Central Committee of Argenteuil of 1966. On that occasion, Louis Aragon announced that the "experimental requirements inherent in literature and the arts cannot be denied or impeded, for such interference would seriously hinder the development of culture and of the human spirit."[97] The two parties' departure from strict Cominform rules nourished their nationalist tendencies, which naturally translated in greater motivation to resist American influence.[98]

American Society and Its Critics

The Communists' indictment of the American cultural model was tied logically to their depiction of American politics and way of life, especially at the peak of the McCarthy era. If the United States produced a culture that had mass appeal but was oligarchic in the way it was contrived and narrowly controlled[99]—the argument went—this was because American society was experiencing a transition to fascism. Whether the press of both parties deplored the poetry of T. S. Eliot, elevated the myth of Charlie Chaplin, or disparaged the inanity of the *Reader's Digest*, it regularly ascribed these problems to America's betrayed free speech in the years of anticommunist witch hunting.[100] In general, a country that countenanced McCarthyism, conformity, and segregation could not pretend to be morally pure.

Besides establishing a moral equivalence with Soviet repression pointed to by the West, the reference to McCarthyism underscored depictions of a world of conformity and ineptitude. The United States produced a society that, especially in these years, prized family and social cohesion. It was telling that in the United States nonconformity itself was often labeled communistic. It apparently proved Alexis de Tocqueville's thesis that genius would not be possible in a society that valued conformity and made it a requirement to attain social success.

Marxist or *marxisant* intellectuals who called attention to the new social sciences did so in part because in these fields American authors were publishing exposés of their own society. Communist commentators, however, underestimated the consensual nature of many of the critics—such as David

Riesman, Daniel Bell, Vance Packard, Lionel Trilling, and Seymour Martin Lipset—who agreed with or approximated the Vital Center values, and thus foreshadowed the most challenging transformation of leftist thought in the West. These authors focused not on social injustice, as most American radical intellectuals had done in the past. Their subjects were not poverty, minorities, exploitation but rather the psychological and even existential problems of the middle class. They focused on impersonality, uniformity, and manipulation by mass culture. They addressed the moral issues raised by advertising, standardization, alienation, monotonous work, and bureaucratic boredom. In many ways, these subjects anticipated the cultural rebellions of 1960s America. But unlike the dissenters of that subsequent era, the writers of the first postwar decade did not attack the social order. Their ideal was achieving self-determined individualism within the existing order.

These intellectuals also worked in a context in which popular culture largely prevailed, thanks to widespread suspicions of the "brilliant minds" of the New Deal as well as the enduring tradition of anti-intellectualism in America. Consistently, they were reluctant to embrace philosophy for its inherent value, or the world of knowledge for its subversive nature. Some of them followed a spirit of *mens sana in corpore sano*. Riesman's argument in *The Lonely Crowd* (1950) may have resembled many of the existentialist claims about individualism and choice. But his body did not: "Riesman was athletic, well dressed," and, far from highbrow attitude, "he favored fantasy films over intellectual 'message movies.'" Instead of relishing in a bohemian or subversive lifestyle, most postwar American intellectuals gave themselves an aura of "middle-class everyman."[101]

There were important exceptions. John Kenneth Galbraith's *American Capitalism* (1952) was the first analysis that dissected the emerging neocapitalism. It called attention to the oligopolies as a countervailing power to the American "big merger" tradition, but it also underlined the increasing income gaps in America. William H. Whyte's *The Organization Man* (1956) elaborated on Riesman's "Lonely Crowd" arguments, with a greater accent on the declining work-and-thrift ethic under the new corporate norms. Simply put, Fordism had lost its aura of bold entrepreneurship and displayed its worst characteristics: organizational crawl and conformity were now enforced at the expense of individual initiative. Charles Wright Mills's *The Power Elite* (1956) exposed the interwoven interests and self-reproducing power system of the leading military, economic, and political elements in American society. The book poignantly denounced the formal nature of American democracy, demonstrating that the public sector in the United States was not balancing private interests; it was indistinguishable from them. To Western European

Communists, this analysis confirmed the most damaging distortions of the New Deal legacy in America. Mills's work also inferred the imminence of these developments in the U.S.-driven European economic growth since the Marshall Plan years. Most damning of all, the "Power Elite" was bound to be dominated by militaristic and expansionist elements.[102] Generally, these analyses, in the Marxist interpretation, revealed that consumerism generated waste, vast income gaps, social dislocation, suburban uniformity, and even racial discrimination.

References to American racism naturally increased in communist propaganda of the mid-1950s. The emergence of the civil rights movement exposed not so much the coming emancipation but an enduring problem, especially compared to allegedly open-minded Europe. The reaction to American racism was stronger in France, where 66 percent of those polled deplored the treatment of African Americans, than in Italy, where that percentage reached about 35 percent.[103] The leftist press in France and Italy especially stressed that the United States was not entitled to give lessons of democracy while it was still segregating, disenfranchising, or even lynching its black citizens. It could not lecture the French on self-determination in North Africa while it was still suppressing the rights of African Americans. Beyond the most blatant cases in the South, from Montgomery to Little Rock, Communists in France and Italy kept calling the attention to American racial discrimination nationwide. Worse still, not only segregationist groups but the FBI itself frequently connected the civil rights movement to a communist conspiracy: McCarthyism, subdued in mainstream politics, was revived in the South's supremacist agenda.[104] It was not just the legacy of slavery that made the United States so backward. American puritanism and missionary zeal, de Beauvoir observed, together with pervasive ahistoricism and relative immunity from Nazi crimes, especially made Americans impervious to the plight of their blacks.[105]

Coming at the peak of the Cold War, the civil rights movement naturally was exploited by the Soviet Union, as it heaped embarrassment on the United States. By undermining the U.S. anticommunist rhetoric, it also brought Western European intellectuals closer to the Soviet Union. It is no accident that Sartre's play *La putain respectueuse* (*The Respectful Prostitute*, 1946), with its theme of racism in the U.S. South, was performed in the Soviet Union in 1954 (and later in Castro's Cuba). Clare Luce recognized the danger of the Little Rock events in 1957, when Governor Orval Faubus attempted to thwart school desegregation. In a public speech, the former ambassador connected them to the simultaneous scientific triumph of the Russian Sputnik satellite, warning that if the United States did not improve both its technological and democratic records, the uncommitted nations and their neutralist friends in Europe might decide "to hitch their wagon to her [Russia's] Beeping Star."[106]

On women's issues, both French and Italian Communists ostensibly were ahead of the U.S. social model and ethics. As one of France's leading intellectuals and fellow travelers, Simone de Beauvoir spearheaded her country's feminist battles. At the same time, she deplored the social subordination of American educated women. In *America Day by Day*, narrating her experience during her visit in the United States in 1947, she explained that American women, even those she visited with at the elitist Smith and Wesleyan Colleges, were not as free as the myth would have it. For these college girls, the main goal in life remained that of finding a husband. After that, it was all battle of the sexes, whether women tried to assert their independence by "keeping men under their thumb" or, due to puritan traditions, assumed a "frigid" attitude toward their men. In Europe, de Beauvoir observed, "women have understood much better that the moment to affirm themselves as women has passed." They tried to "prove their worth on a universal level, in politics, in the arts or sciences, or simply in their lives."[107] For de Beauvoir, pursuing equality was less about fighting sexism than transcending it. This also helped shift the focus from private matters to political and class conflicts, just as the Marxists would have it.

In Italy Marxists held similar views. While *Vie Nuove* adapted American standards of femininity and glamour to its own beauty contest in order to attract a larger female readership, it also depicted the "struggling" condition of American women. At first glance, their social condition may have appeared more emancipated than that of Italian women—Mike Fioravanti acknowledged in a 1960 article—but their desire to attain equality could not compare to the "social conscience acquired by women in the socialist countries." American middle-class women, the article continued, contributed to their household income out of financial need, or to fill gaps caused by divorce. Both were "anomalous situations" of a dysfunctional society based on acquisition. The job market for educated women was in any case mostly confined to professions—teacher, stewardess, secretary, social worker—traditionally reserved for them.[108]

But beyond women's rights in the workplace, other issues concerning women, from sexism to personal emancipation, did not fit the Marxist script. The two parties either dismissed them or opposed them outright as diversions from the true sexual emancipation under a working-class revolution. Feminist conscience could only be hindered and distorted under a capitalist system that exploited all workers, but especially women.

In its most traditional form, feminism, in both countries, and particularly in Italy, was steeped into the politics of "partitocracy." The Unione delle Donne Italiane (UDI, or Union of Italian Women) drew its strength from its record in the Resistance, and soon became basically the women's arm of the PCI. Given the relative backwardness of Italian legislation on women's rights compared to other Western nations, the PCI did welcome the fast modernization process that, by the early 1960s, as Amendola wrote in a *Rinascita* editorial, accelerated the breakup of "farming communities revolving around the patriarchal family." Amendola admitted that television also fostered this process, inspiring new desires for material self-fulfillment among rural women. Under state monopoly capitalism, he added, this nurtured consumerism. But this emancipation, generated from the bottom of society, had the potential of turning Italian feminism into a mass, rather than elitist movement. Its focus on material desires, the PCI leader concluded, would expose the shortcomings of capitalism, opening further opportunities for socialism.[109]

Women's rights were subject to strict Marxist parameters in the PCF. Ideological orthodoxy mixed with old-style nationalism, praising industrial and demographic growth. In the early 1960s, the party still opposed birth control as a product of reactionary Malthusianism inspired by imperialist capitalism.[110] When de Beauvoir tackled the issue of sexism in her *Le deuxième sexe* (1949) and talked about menstruation, pregnancy, menopause, adultery, abortion, lesbianism, and especially about "womanness" as a cultural constraint in a male-dominated society, the PCF almost unanimously vilified the book.[111] Women's "personal" liberation took second place in its agenda.

It is plausible to argue that once the McCarthyite menace subsided, sociocultural anti-Americanism prevailed over political anti-Americanism. The main focus of most French anti-Americans from the right and the left now turned to the United States as a sociocultural temptation.[112] But this argument insufficiently explains how any sociocultural vision of the United States, especially as seen by the Marxist Left—in both Italy and France— continued to be intertwined with political skepticism, if not even demonization.

Denouncing American society evoked the most damning confluence of consumerism and conformity. French and Italian Communists underscored Jean-Marie Domenach's reversal of political anti-Americanism, making American society the main culprit: "The American state is liberal," Domenach wrote in 1960, "but American society is totalitarian; it is possibly the most totalitarian in the world." The root of the problem was in the United States' "mores and human relations," where "difference is proscribed, not by edict or violence, but naturally, functionally." Even rebellion in such a conformist society was absorbed, commodified. As Domenach quipped: "Try a 1960 Chevrolet. Try Zen. Try Jesus. Try whatever you want. You will feel better and better."[113] The foregone conclusion for the Communists, who through the 1950s held on to a universal anti-Americanism, was that even if American society had its critics, in the end U.S. society and politics were two faces of the same coin.

Even so, there was still room for ambivalence. It is rather compelling, as Pier Paolo D'Attore wrote about Italy, to note that the U.S. model of mass culture and society allowed Christian and communist groups in both France and Italy to shed some of their populist provincialism.[114] While finding their national paths to a consumer society, each group could not avoid a certain contamination from the United States—not even the Communists.

By the early 1960s, as we will see in chapter 7, the consumerist and individualist American model would permeate French and Italian society, at least at the mass level. Both countries' intellectuals, mostly from the left, retained their jaded or alarmist views of the United States, because these very new socializing patterns seemed most threatening to them. But their one-sided critique also morphed again into a nuanced view of American problems, in large part because of Soviet misconduct in 1956. In fact the events of 1956, to many of these intellectuals, showed no misconduct or aberration at all but rather the realities of the Soviet empire.

1956

The content of Nikita Khrushchev's secret report at the Twentieth CPSU Congress of February 1956, denouncing the errors and horrors of Stalin's regime, became immediately known to Togliatti, who reported them at the party's secretariat. An animated discussion followed on the issue, concentrating on the report's possible international repercussions. Togliatti himself, as historians Elena Aga-Rossi and Victor Zaslavsky have noted, never entirely embraced Khrushchev's position, which he thought could undermine the stability of the Eastern bloc, and preferred to maintain a "moderate Stalinist" stance. But the PCI's leadership, as I have noted, initially emphasized the positive potential of the political and cultural debate in the Soviet Union. It also tried to harness its restless intellectuals with appeals for an open discussion. It was only after the publication of the report in the *New York Times* in June, coinciding for the PCI with a slight electoral decline in the 1956 administrative elections, that the party's leadership abandoned its reticence. Significantly, Togliatti chose the nonaffiliated *Nuovi Argomenti* to be interviewed and announce that the Soviet model was no longer an absolute one;

the leader instead proposed a *polycentric* approach for the world's Communist Parties, with greater adaptations to each national set of circumstances. The idea had actually originated in the CPSU Congress, but the Soviet Union soon balked at the prospect of such decentralization. This was particularly true for Italy, where polycentrism also accepted the possibility of reaching socialism without the PCI's being the dominant party. Moreover, the new Italian doctrine emphasized the bureaucratic "degeneration" of the Bolshevik experience more than the cult of personality. This turned the PCI's critique toward structural flaws of the Soviet system rather than toward errors in ideology or personal aberrations.[115] By following this premise, the PCI meant to confirm the key value of its flexible strategies, both internally and internationally. In so doing, it also contradicted its leaders' fears that reform in Moscow itself, if taken too far along Khrushchev's stated intentions, could affect the stability of the Soviet bloc.

At the PCF summit, the reaction was rather muted. Jacques Duclos and the rest of the secretariat, while discussing the personality cult, also recognized Stalin's indispensable "role and merits, as theoretician and leader." Thorez resumed the arguments from his 1946 interview with the *Times* of London, mentioning the different paths to socialism, but without repudiating Soviet guidance or renouncing the possible use of violence. He also immediately distanced himself from Khrushchev, whom the PCF continued to see as a transitional leader. After the June revelations, the party instead focused on denouncing the plot of the bourgeois press.[116]

The following events—the failed reform in Poland and especially the Soviet suppression of the Hungarian revolution in November—caused further reconsiderations in the PCI leadership. While condemning the "Western" "imperialist plot," the party also chastised the Hungarian communist leadership for its errors. But in the end, the PCI fully endorsed—and perhaps Togliatti even encouraged—the Soviet intervention. After its dismissal of de-Stalinization, the PCF gave unqualified approval to the Soviet invasion of Hungary. Its directorate decided to denounce press coverage of the events as a "clearly orchestrated diversion" of the imperialist forces from the Anglo-French invasion of Egypt. The party's ideological connection with Moscow continued to have a nationalist dimension as well. The PCF's chauvinism still recognized and compared itself to the peak of Russian nationalism under Stalin. This also meant confidence in the French superior cultural traditions, which, together with the constant claim that France was the home of the original revolutionary tradition, made the PCF's a particularly "jingoist" brand of Stalinism. "By being more Stalinist," Irwin Wall concluded, "the PCF became more French."[117]

Nationalism and the leader's charisma were also the basis for the party's consolidation of its bureaucracy and intellectuals. Rather than criticize Stalin's excesses, the PCF revived its own cult of personality. The Thorez leadership used that cult and its correlation with intellectuals' deference to the working class to hold a firm grip on possible party defections. Thorez's personality cult was officially relaunched with the second edition of the autobiographical *Fils du peuple* in 1949. But it was especially in 1956 that the party closed ranks in celebration of its popular leader.[118]

Nationalist posturing and revival of the party's leadership—more subtle for Togliatti than for Thorez—helped maintain a sharp distinction between redeemable communism and unquestionably imperialist America. In fact, the events of 1956 caused additional defections among intellectuals, who had always been susceptible to such nationalist, anti-American appeals. Most of the intellectuals who left the two parties had backgrounds in the social sciences. In 1968, after the events in Czechoslovakia, the loss would include a majority of literati and philosophers. This distinction was due in part to the higher Cold War tension in 1956, in part to the different nature of the Czech rebellion, reviving a "human face" of socialism and an antiestablishment outlook, both appealing to many leftist intellectuals. This transition would also reflect a connection with America's own dissent.

The Soviet repression in Hungary was not sufficient to entirely alienate many fellow travelers. Sartre and other existentialists, while critical overall of the Soviet conduct, remained in the fold of "anti-anticommunism." Sartre had denounced the immorality of Stalinism since his play *Les mains sales* (*Dirty Hands*, 1948). He then cooperated more intensely with the PCF in the following years. Early in 1956, while still believing that Marxism "allow[ed] us to understand people, works, and events" and therefore had the "monopoly of Culture" after "the death of bourgeois thought," he also regretted that this was Marxism in ideal terms, while "sadly, we have to see it as it actually is." After Hungary, for all his criticism of Moscow and of the PCF's "total allegiance" to "Soviet intransigence," Sartre still considered the U.S.S.R. essentially "peaceful" but also, "in spite of itself[,] . . . predatory." This contradiction reflected his belief, for some years to come, that the Soviet system was not inherently exploitative and still contained a "dynamic of change," which could be fully applied once the system's abuses were eradicated. Hungary had gone sour because de-Stalinization had not worked there as well as it did inside the Soviet Union. As Tony Judt suggested, albeit with exaggeration, according to Sartre and leftist Catholic Emmanuel Mounier, "the Soviet invasion of Hungary, while bad in itself, was evidence of faults in the Hungarian copy, not the Soviet model." So Marxism was, in Sartre's view, still evolving and redeemable. Capitalism, in contrast, could not be remedied, for it was naturally exploitative, imperialist, and even in "bad faith," because it did not admit its flaws, while Russian bureaucrats had started their self-critique in early 1956. Existentialism had not yet established a close connection with America's social critics and philosophers; nor had the United States yet generated the strong antiestablishment forces that, in the 1960s, would shape a more intimate rapport with existentialism, thanks to their questioning of both the old liberal-capitalist order and Marxist orthodoxy.[119]

Meanwhile intellectuals who officially belonged to the PCF uttered their misgivings, too. On 23 November, ten of them, including Picasso, called for an extraordinary party Congress to express their "profound discomfort" with the events in Hungary. Some of the most famous intellectuals, including Picasso, Garaudy, and Henri Wallon, were allowed to voice their grievances. Others, like historian Emmanuel Le Roy Ladurie, engaged the discussion more polemically, finally leaving the party. Most intellectuals who abandoned the PCF remained rather isolated in the leftist community. More worrisome for the PCF was the appeal of fellow travelers, such as Sartre, de Beauvoir, Vercors, and Jacques Prévert. Their first protest, on 8 November, had encouraged the internal dissent of the following weeks. Furthermore, their document was cosigned by some of the top party writers, Claude Roy, Jacques-Francis Rolland, Claude Morgan, and Roger Vailland, condemning the most blatant forms of Soviet repression.[120]

Italy's intellectuals issued an even more collective protest: on 29 October, a "manifesto" of 101 academics, literati, and philosophers denounced Stalinism and all obstacles to a democratic process in the East; they also demanded an internal revision, with a reevaluation of the rules of democratic centralism within the party. The main "innovators," such as Antonio Giolitti, Luciano Cafagna, Eugenio Reale, and Italo Calvino, abandoned the party after their failed appeal for reform. External supporters—Moravia and Franco Fortini among them—further distanced themselves from the party and became increasingly attracted to the "other" America of dissent. Giolitti and Reale embraced the legacy of the New Deal, welfare, and social democracy. Calvino and another famous novelist, Vasco Pratolini, began contributing to the CCF-funded *Tempo presente*.[121]

Meanwhile the PCI exerted heavy pressure—which included financial, editorial, and other intimidation tactics—on the signers of the "101 Manifesto," getting several of them back into the party's fold. The party, however, did suffer a decline in membership, especially among the young, some of whom would form the basis of the extraparliamentarian Left of the 1960s. Togliatti, in extremis at the Eighth Party Congress in December 1956, recognized that the Cold War had forced the Communist Parties into a "servile" imitation of the Soviet Union.[122] While distancing himself from the Soviet model, the Italian leader thus continued to blame the lack of political and ideological independence mainly on the country's alignment with Atlanticism. Following Soviet attacks on polycentrism, the party's main leaders hastened to qualify that Italy would not choose, in Ingrao's words, a "Yugoslav option," but rather a new, more genuine bond with the Soviet Union, after the demise of the Cominform. In September, at the party's political bureau, Togliatti reiterated that "by finding defects and errors [in the Soviet Union]," the PCI could wage a more effective campaign against the "contradictions of American capitalism." He lamented however that, outside France and Italy, other communist groups in the West were either complacent or defensive. Sereni added that Moscow had in fact lost faith in the French and Italian parties as well.[123]

The events of 1956 also caused a rift between French and Italian Communists. The PCF opposed polycentrism in principle, though in practice it soon found itself pursuing an alliance of convenience with the Socialists. The PCF further accused its Italian counterpart of allowing such open intellectual dissent, thus encouraging similar disputes among its own top thinkers. One of the PCI's prominent intellectuals, Antonello Trombadori, speaking at the cultural commission on 15 November, rebutted that the French Communists were "unforgivably infantile." One year later, Alicata still worried that the quarrel would confirm Moscow's loss of faith in Western Communism and a diminished effectiveness of the anti-imperialist front.[124]

While following this rift, the U.S. embassies in both capitals began to realize that the PCI might quickly restore its legitimacy, and even its international reputation. Rumors circulated in the Italian press by early 1958 that the government encouraged a role for the party in East-West negotiations.[125] At the same time, the Italian Socialists had finalized their break with the PCI, while the internal situation in France lent the PCF an opportunity to participate in an anti-Gaullist popular front. Diplomatic maneuvering became a growing priority in the psychological war against Western Communism.

6 DIPLOMATIC MANEUVERING

Communist and American Interplay of Foreign and
Domestic Policies during the Eisenhower and Kennedy
Administrations

Diplomatic Action, Globalized Cold War,
and Communist Resilience in France and Italy

As U.S. permanent representative at the United Nations, Henry Cabot
Lodge Jr. found himself in a privileged position to detect shifts in the climate
of world opinion. As a seasoned former senator and convinced internationalist, Lodge also understood the interconnection between the diplomacy and
the domestic politics of America's allies. In September 1954 he quickly recognized Moscow's contacts with French Premier Pierre Mendès-France as a
clever subversive move directed against not only European integration but
above all French domestic political stability. He therefore urged Secretary of
State John Foster Dulles to muster all U.S. diplomatic resources to "organize
a countersubversion" that would reckon with the main trends in world public opinion—namely, the decolonization process—and undermine neutralist
tendencies in France, whether these were communist-inspired or not.[1]

From its inception, the Psychological Strategy Board (PSB) included
diplomatic action among all its "conceivable means to reach [its] objectives."
It was a vague definition of diplomatic action to be sure, and, for example,
an early status report on the work of Panel C, which coordinated the PSB's
actions in France and Italy, hesitated to claim that contacts with representatives in the French protectorate of Morocco fell within its competence. But
the PSB recognized that the French—and American—handling of decolonization had "a close relation to the problem of communism in France and
the defense of Western Europe"; "in the realms of psychological strategy,"
the memorandum concluded, "all problems are interrelated."[2] I have already
noted that the demise of the PSB was caused largely by its infringement on
State Department prerogatives. By restructuring the psychological warfare
organization, however, the Eisenhower administration confirmed that such
need for coordination reflected the tight correlation between diplomatic,
economic, covert, and propaganda actions. "Every economic, security, and
political policy of the government," Eisenhower wrote to Nelson Rockefeller

shortly after the first great powers summit of the Cold War, in Geneva in 1955, "manifestly is one of the weapons (or should be) in psychological warfare." This was particularly true for a nation that purported to have an impact on public perceptions through actions more than with words. This emphasis on action reflected the forceful distinction that the United States, since the Marshall Plan and the Campaign of Truth, had sought to make between its sincerity and flexibility, and the Soviets' untruthful, regimented propaganda.[3]

A frontal attack on communism in Western Europe was no longer necessary by the mid-1950s, because the PCF and PCI no longer represented an immediate danger. But, with their staying power and their effects on the other main political forces, the two parties remained an indirect threat, no less insidious than before. As such, they prompted the United States to adopt an equally indirect political and diplomatic response that matched the nuance of its cultural actions. The Operations Coordinating Board (OCB) stopped discussing "psy-war" in Western Europe in the summer of 1955.[4] The most direct forms of psychological warfare in the region were thus dismissed in part due to the lower intensity of the political conflict there, and in part because of the way America's political allies (most blatantly the Italian Christian Democrats) had manipulated them. Diplomatic maneuvering promised to be a more effective form of leverage.

My purpose is not to reduce Washington's diplomatic relations with France and Italy to its anticommunist agenda in both countries. The argument here rather highlights an increasingly refined American perception of the interplay between domestic and diplomatic factors in French and Italian politics. For that reason, while referring to turning points in international politics, we need not retell extensively the story of U.S. strategic and economic goals in Western Europe, the Middle East, and other key areas.

In a total war, with a growing emphasis on war by other means, interference in other countries' internal affairs had become the norm. Less manifest was the establishment of a deliberate connection, beyond the structural one, between American grand strategy and its effects on the local politics of its allies. Focusing on the interplay between domestic and foreign policy in France or Italy, the United States devised some of its most subtle forms of indirect action aimed at curbing communist influence. The combination of the politics and diplomacy of stabilization further helped isolate the Communists. More important, it helped reduce the danger of indirect effects from left-wing anti-Americanism, of rekindled nationalist interests that, in reaction to or cooperation with communism, could foster neutralist tendencies in both countries.

The peak of this discreet manipulation, coinciding with the most intense phase of decolonization, confirmed two salient features of American leadership over Europe: distinguishing itself from traditional Western imperialism with its consensual expansion and highly sophisticated forms of influence, this was, according to a recent definition, an "empire in denial," founded on an anticolonial ideology; but its subtle, pervasive ascendancy was also frequently labeled neocolonial—not only toward the developing world but also toward Europe—by its detractors, and even by many of its allies.[5] French and Italian Communists accordingly exploited the image of neocolonial America and its crusade against communism. They too tried to capitalize on the link between their nations' domestic and foreign policies, and on that same connection in the United States itself, whenever the "torchbearer of the free world" showed glaring discrepancies between its diplomatic rhetoric and its record at home. But whereas the PCI and PCF looked at this interplay as an instrument for their domestic agendas, the United States utilized it at its maximum, monitoring its impact on French and Italian domestic politics, while relying on it for a more effective management of the alliance in Europe and global strategy altogether. While communist anti-Americanism, through the mid-1950s and early 1960s, increasingly looked inward, the United States improved its flexibility and strategic acumen.

A paramount danger persisted: no matter how provincial the two Communist Parties might turn out to be, their anti-Americanism, compounded by slow socioeconomic reform, lower Cold War tensions in Europe, and various reasons for nationalist resentment against the domineering aspects of the New Look, could not only revive neutralism in Europe, but disaffection in Europe could also blend with Third World neutralism. Long before President Eisenhower officially mused about the communist domino effect in Indochina, other U.S. officials had expressed their concern that a chain reaction could start from politically fragile France and Italy and "infect" the developing world. In January 1953 the Head of the Joint Chiefs of Staff, General Omar Bradley, warned that France, incensed by Washington's choice for a peripheral strategy in Europe (which would liberate rather than defend the central part of the continent), might opt for popular frontism with the Communists; this for France would mean dropping Indochina, losing Southeast Asia, and thus forcing Japan to make compromises with China. In Italy, the changing political mood on America's preponderance was best exemplified by Enrico Mattei, the maverick president of Ente Nazionale Idrocarburi (ENI), the state oil company. His rebellion against U.S. influence was not limited to preempting bids from American oil companies to drill the Italian soil. In 1954, Mattei, after being excluded from an oil consortium in Iran, began to defy the "Seven Sisters," as he famously nicknamed the oil cartel dominating the Middle East, and posed as paladin of the exploited Arab nations, offering more favorable contracts to the producing countries. As we will see, Italy's activism in the Middle East, under these auspices, would favor rather than stem the flow of neutralism there.

There was a double irony in these circumstances: the developing nations, while formally neutral, gravitated toward the Soviet Union primarily because of their hostility to Western European imperialism; and the Western European nations became more sensitive to neutralism partly because of their diffidence toward American expansionism and their fear of becoming involved in a nuclear war in the developing world. Late in 1955, French Foreign Minister Antoine Pinay told the American ambassador that there was indeed a strong connection between political developments, especially the rising tide of anti-Americanism in his country, and the Third World nations that had just announced the doctrine of nonalignment at the Bandung Conference. The intention of the conservative leader was undoubtedly to uphold France's imperial role as the best guarantee against this neutral tide. But his warning clearly indicated that America's own "imperialist" tendencies could turn his country neutral, pliable to the PCF's presence in the government, and hostile to the Cold War in the developing world.[6]

Emphasizing domino effects could indeed look like an excuse for expansionism. But treating problems and geographic areas too separately could be just as dangerous. The process of decolonization, gathering steam in the mid-1950s, and marked by anti-Western revolutionary fervor, shifted U.S. attention away from relatively stabilized Western Europe. Given the resilience of the PCF and PCI, this detachment was premature according to some U.S. officials, and to most French and Italian ruling elites. Third World revolutions could stymie U.S. anticommunist strategies in Western Europe also because they revived the economic reading of communism. As a 1959 Congressional report on foreign aid pointed out: "The simple assumption that Communism flows from poverty is so widely accepted in America that it is almost an article of faith." In fact, the burgeoning modernization theory, as interpreted in Washington by the late 1950s, stressed that the best way to prevent Third World nations from falling prey to communism was to combine for each of them self-determination and capitalist development. Nationalism, the theory recognized, was another powerful factor in the Third World rebellion against Western imperialism in all its dimensions—military, economic, and cultural.[7] Under the banner of anti-imperialism, the Communists in Western Europe could thus turn their solidarity with these revolutions into a new, perhaps innovative, anti-American campaign. Even the PCF could profit from France's peculiar condition as that of an exploiter and exploited country, dominator and dominated, and from the overall tension in France between Americanization and decolonization.[8] Living this contradiction, the French people could at least in part suspend their judgment on the PCF's nationalist credentials.

As for the economic factors, the very fact that they were so prominent in Third World radicalism drew a significant contrast with the social conditions in which French and Italian Communism still held its own. In February 1956 Secretary of State Dulles told the National Security Council that the PCI, still strong and dynamic under conditions of relative prosperity, refuted the thesis that communism thrived "only in desperately poor and underdeveloped countries." The French, the secretary of the treasury, Robert B. Anderson, observed two years later, made "more money per capita than any other free world country except the U.S."; this justified American requests that Paris spend more on its military, but the danger was that this kind of pressure, if not balanced with diplomatic concessions, would further revive the surprisingly strong PCF. As we have seen, Clare Luce had lambasted the radical traditions that made most intellectuals in France and Italy "men of the Left." Those cultural peculiarities alerted even the single-minded ambassador to reckon with "the political effect on the French and Italian Socialists and intellectuals of their growing conviction that Communist dogma now makes allowance for the Spirit of Nationalism."[9]

The Eisenhower administration's ability to manipulate the intersection of domestic and foreign policies in Europe was also in part handicapped by the domestic dimension of its foreign policy. A small feud within the OCB apparatus in the summer of 1953 illustrated this problem. Commissioned to investigate the apparent decline of U.S. prestige in Europe, both the PSB and the OCB blamed it primarily on McCarthyism and the arms race. Dulles and psy-war director C. D. Jackson objected to this seemingly oversimplified analysis by indicating the need for a more assertive "Republican" world leadership. The Democratic Party, Dulles grumbled, had been "telling the world for twenty years that Republicans [were] isolationist." At an NSC meeting in October, Jackson chided the OCB report for faulting only the United States and ignoring that this decline in U.S. prestige was also "a function of European neurosis." Actually, since the new administration was "taking a position of world leadership," Jackson added, it was inevitable to "run into [such] difficulties." "We should not expect to be loved overnight," Jackson explained. "In point of fact, we don't want to be loved anyhow but simply to be respected." Eisenhower concurred with his chief psychological warrior, saying that there were too many "New Dealers" and "disgruntled egg-heads in the State Department" who thought that the "only way to recover prestige was to hand out money."[10] This argument not only eerily echoed the McCarthyist attacks on the New Deal; it also signaled the administration's desire to prove, first and foremost, that Republicans would conduct a more audacious foreign policy than their predecessors, yet without alarming or alienating the European allies. In case of escalating tensions with the Soviet Union, this could become a real conundrum.

The Eisenhower administration gradually devised a set of solutions that, under propitious circumstances, might give America's initiative the simultaneous appearance of resolve and ductility. In its global approach to the Cold War, it resorted to a thorough, unscrupulous public diplomacy. Within that framework, it could more easily adopt flexible tactics toward unstable allies such as France and Italy. These tactics included increasingly discerning diplomatic support, a keener encouragement of these governments' choice of interdependence rather than traditional nationalism, and the cultivation of assertive leaders whose criticism of Washington would reduce the appeal of the Communists' more virulent anti-Americanism.

PUBLIC DIPLOMACY

By the mid-1950s, the United States' political warfare had become an intrinsic part of its diplomatic activity. The result, public diplomacy, turned into perhaps its most formidable Cold War weapon. Nowhere was this more apparent than in both superpowers' propaganda efforts to manipulate the psychological effects of the utmost weapon at their disposal: nuclear warheads. Neither side seriously considered taking steps toward a settlement. Each rather hoped to force the adversary into diplomatic submission by exerting pressure through world public opinion. Both launched these diplomatic initiatives to consolidate their influence within their respective spheres, and, if the opportunity presented itself, to provoke dissidence within the enemy camp.

The Soviet Union had preceded the United States in exploiting nuclear fears. The Stockholm Appeal was a skillful fusing together of mass and intellectual appeal to pressure governments. After stressing the gap between rulers and ruled, Moscow dealt with the governments, through various détente proposals regarding Germany, Korea, and disarmament. The State Department was stormed with alarmed reports about the Soviet diplomatic offensive. But from Rome, Clare Luce distinguished herself by dramatizing the main problems in a long memorandum to President Eisenhower in August 1954. On a general level, the ambassador contended that many "good Europeans" believed the "United States was more likely to precipitate a thermonuclear war than Soviet Russia," and worse still, that the Soviet Union appeared to be "winning the political war," even by "capturing the American Dream," that is, the "dream of plenty, and power and peace for the people." Luce sounded apocalyptic as usual, even though Eisenhower himself had warned that it was necessary to avoid bleak or sanguine references to the Cold War; rather one should project "something dramatic to rally the peoples of the world around some idea, some hope, of a better future." The Psychological Strategy Board, a few months earlier had recognized the urgency of "diverting the attention from Soviet propaganda by advancing, where useful, campaigns of our own designed to undermine Soviet credibility and prestige, and to endeavor to reflect a responsible and humanitarian image of the U.S. and the exercise of its power in all areas." The PSB concluded by quoting George Kennan: "We should elevate both the tone of our utterance and the platform of its delivery to a plane which will wholly distinguish it from what is being said on the other side."[11]

Fears of extinction of course haunted the public on both sides of the Cold War. But keeping public opinion under control in the West was far from easy. It was a matter not just of forging public perceptions in a free society but also of taking into account the political and cultural plurality within the Western alliance. In general, the Eisenhower administration needed to inspire public mobilization by balancing fear of the enemy's capabilities with public reassurances of America's peaceful intentions. Evoking too much fear might sap public morale, inducing paralysis or apathy. The threshold between motivation and apathy was lower among NATO allies than it was in American public opinion. In the United States a certain dose of isolationism was compatible with a strategy that, like the New Look, reduced spending for conventional weapons and demanded more from the allies. Across the Atlantic, these very demands, together with hypotheses of nuclear annihilation, as well as the pressure from peace activists and communist propaganda, made fear of nuclear war the "leading cause of neutralism."[12] With the hydrogen bomb first tested by the United States in November 1952 and by the Soviets nine months later, the frightening prospects of a thermonuclear war put an additional burden on the Eisenhower administration, which, under the massive retaliation doctrine, had increased its reliance on the nuclear buildup. The danger loomed that the United States could be seen as not only aggressive but barbaric.

The propaganda of the French and Italian Communists continued to connect the political and cultural depravity of their Cold War enemy. At a

PCI Central Committee meeting in April 1954, Togliatti evoked prospects of thermonuclear holocaust hitting "where civilization has made the greatest progress, that is the regions of the U.S.A. [*sic*], the British isles, Western Europe, the most populous and advanced areas of the Asian continent, the Mediterranean . . . in one word the seat of contemporary civilization." The speech ecumenically included the United States, but mainly to point out that close transatlantic ties would embroil Europe in the self-destructive choices made in Washington—hence Togliatti's conclusion that Europe's salvation would lie in opting for a "third way" between the United States and the Soviet Union. This was no conversion to a genuine third force. With his own public diplomacy move, Togliatti rather reiterated his appeal to the Catholic masses to repudiate the Christian Democrats' international policies and embrace true national independence. In July the PCF's political bureau reached similar conclusions about winning the Socialists over to the anti-NATO campaign: massive retaliation, in this view, was aggravated by the extension of the U.S. alliance system, now including the Southeast Asian nations (through the South East Asian Treaty Organization [SEATO]).[13] The PCF's anti-American appeal could thus evoke nuclear fears at home and among developing nations.

It was therefore with a particular attention to international perceptions that the Eisenhower administration planned its main public diplomacy moves: the president's proposals of a "Chance for Peace" in April 1953, "Atoms for Peace" at the end of that year, and "Open Skies" in 1955. All three initiatives were conceived to steal the thunder of détente from the Soviets, to energize Western opinion against Soviet military might, and to help world opinion adapt to the nuclear age and a protracted Cold War. They were not sincere peace initiatives, as Kenneth Osgood has convincingly argued, but rather skillful acts of "political warfare designed to wrestle the peace initiative away from the Kremlin"[14]—and consequently to blunt the communist-led peace offensive in Western Europe.

The "Chance for Peace" speech was crafty in its emulation of communist propaganda, connecting peace and welfare: the strategic arms race was, in the president's words "a theft from those who hunger and are not fed, those who are cold and are not clothed." "Under the cloud of a threatening war," he added, "it is humanity hanging from a cross of iron." But, mirroring the argument of its communist counterpart, Washington stressed that the cost of rearmament was much heavier for the East, while the West would best secure peace and prosperity by being "ready for the risk of war" against Soviet tyranny. The speech matched communist rhetoric also in highlighting a clash of opposing dogmas. The president, according to one account, depicted the Cold War "as a profound struggle between absolute good and absolute evil, with the enemy's unconditional surrender as the only acceptable result." Eisenhower offered no negotiation but rather a general ultimatum on Korea, Indochina, German reunification under Western control, and even full independence for the nations of Eastern Europe.[15]

But America's divergence with its Western allies became evident. After Stalin's death and the peace offers by Georgii Malenkov in March, the Soviet Union gained credibility. Its departure from dogmatic fervor, while minimal, was nonetheless a striking novelty that persuaded even Eisenhower's most loyal ally, Winston Churchill. The British premier suggested testing Soviet sincerity, and on 11 May he called for a summit. To American eyes, this was a triumph for the Soviet wedge strategies. Earlier in the Cold War, an aggressive, blatantly repressive, and atomically inferior Soviet Union had worked much better in emboldening Western resolve. By August of that same year, Malenkov could merge intimidation—announcing his country's first thermonuclear test—with conciliatory gestures—presenting his new doctrine of peaceful coexistence. At least until the repression of the Hungarian rebellion, military might, political appeal in the emerging Third World, and the process of de-Stalinization, with its seemingly liberalizing trends within the Eastern bloc, converged to empower Soviet political warfare.[16] To inspire the free world, the United States had to depart from overly straightforward demonization of the enemy, lest it appear the more rigid of the two superpowers.

The "Atoms for Peace" speech of 8 December 1953 was designed to do this. Countering the Soviets' campaign to "ban the bomb," it threw the ball into their court by setting a new line of argument: the peaceful applications of nuclear energy would overshadow the destructive power of nuclear arsenals; as Eisenhower famously announced, he would pursue a plan "by which the miraculous inventiveness of man shall not be dedicated to his death, but consecrated to his life."[17] Only after adopting this conceptual reversal, and only after both sides had been completely open about their arsenals, could serious disarmament negotiations start. Eisenhower reassured his advisors that proposing talks would not undermine the New Look's reliance on nuclear deterrence, for the Soviets would never allow inspections of their nuclear capability. Indeed, Soviet intransigence would foster greater public acceptance of the doctrine of massive retaliation. While alerting Americans and Europeans to the Soviet danger, the speech was also contrived to soothe Europe's fears of a pending thermonuclear doom. In addition, by inaugurating bilateral contracts, especially with developing nations, for the installation of power reactors, it offered an alternative to Soviet recipes for fast Third

World industrial progress.[18] The formidable worldwide campaign aimed at crediting the United States for the peaceful applications of the atom relied on the usual media coverage the United States could set up so masterfully. USIA-sponsored exhibits drew large crowds. The one in Rome gained tremendous importance because, as a USIA report explained, it found a most receptive audience among peace-oriented Italians and helped "spread . . . President Eisenhower's message on peaceful uses of atomic energy throughout Italy and well beyond its borders."[19]

With West Germany inducted into the NATO alliance and Europe relatively stabilized by 1955, the prospects for a European Cold War settlement seemed nearer. In fact, the Eisenhower administration dreaded that the Soviet Union might lower Europe's vigilance. This concern motivated the next initiative: the Open Skies proposal. It was the president's public relations coup at the Geneva Summit of May 1955. Suggesting that the two superpowers allow reconnaissance flights over each other's territory, the president called public attention to the crucial relevance of mutual guarantees against surprise attacks and escalation. The main purpose of the announcement was to prevent European détente or neutralist sentiments from getting out of hand: the conference was indeed the result of British and French pressure for a dialogue with Moscow.[20] While regaining the initiative in disarmament negotiations, Open Skies also aimed to expose the Soviets' insincerity about inspections, and to reveal the closed nature of their society. The proposal also justified maintaining strength through talks, and actually negotiating "peace through strength," as the American slogan put it. Eisenhower clearly placed inspection rights before negotiations for reduction of armaments, thus maintaining the necessary level of alertness in the West. Predictably, the Soviets turned down the proposal.[21]

Eisenhower's public diplomacy initiatives did not directly target the Western European Communists. But precisely because these steps were so removed from the specifics of each anti-American campaign, and because they countered Soviet propaganda in such a global way, they constituted an excellent form of indirect intervention in French and Italian affairs.

Naturally, Communists in both countries continued to credit the Soviet Union for the spirit of détente. According to *Rinascita*'s foreign policy editorialist, Renato Mieli, since 1953 Moscow had at least managed to tame the natural aggressiveness of a Republican administration that felt the need to assert its credibility and its distinction from its Democratic predecessor by increasing its reliance on nuclear weaponry—or by seeking improvements of its peaceful use of nuclear energy through an international pool (the "Atoms for Peace.").[22] Far more skeptical about the prospects for détente, the PCF, rather than subscribing to Malenkov's public diplomacy, preferred to side with Molotov, who argued that an atomic war would end American imperialism. In March 1955 Thorez urged his party to stop exaggerating the dangers of atomic warfare. By contrast, the PCI not only continued to support Malenkov's thesis after his eviction from the party, it even argued that "denunciation of warmongering in the United States" could help "define what had gone wrong in the U.S.S.R.": no longer forced by a wartime atmosphere to neglect the material and cultural needs of its population, the Soviet Union had now a chance to tout its social and economic triumphs.[23] After Geneva, the French Communists began to convert to that spirit, partly out of the same faith in Soviet economic progress but also for reasons of their own. Détente offered them common ground with the Socialists, who by 1955 wished to test Moscow's peaceful intentions; it also offered them a cue in the debate on the nuclearization of France. The country, the party deliberated in April 1956, had its greatest chance to combine grandeur and pacifism by taking the lead in the peaceful applications of atomic energy.[24]

The PCI concurred with the PCF that détente should not lead Communists to lower their guard against their internal enemies and American interference. Since détente partly delegitimized anticommunism, the French and especially the Italian governments, in Pajetta's words, felt the "urgency of carrying out an offensive" against the two Communist Parties, "using American assistance" and "American methods typical of gangsterism" (his refer ence was to Scelba's antiunion measures under Clare Luce's supervision). In response, Togliatti concluded, the PCI had to publicize that "Italy [was] the only country in which, without foreign intervention, the bourgeoisie would not be in power." Détente, Togliatti reiterated after Geneva, did not mean compromise with the United States or with the Christian Democrats. In fact, the "Soviet-inspired" peace moves were expected to "end the discrimination against the working class" and to empower the trade unions. The PCI's polemics over the Socialists' will to cooperate with the government (the Opening to the Left) clearly affected its approach to the spirit of Geneva. While remaining pacifist, the party never established a parallel between external and internal détente, and, if anything, it amplified its anti-Americanism.[25]

What is most notable about these reactions is that détente, even within the PCI, did not complement de-Stalinization. The two Communist Parties remained highly diffident toward Washington, yet they found renewed faith in the Soviet Union. That faith was further reinvigorated by the Soviets' technological achievements, particularly the launching of Sputnik in October 1957. In many respects, that success, together with the Soviets' renewed emphasis on détente and economic competition with the West, substantially mitigated the effects of the 1956 communist crises. But it did not reinvigorate the pacifist movement. While ostensibly reorganized during the meeting of the sixty-eight Communist Parties in 1957, and targeting the negotiation for installation of U.S. Intermediate Range Ballistic Missiles (IRBM) in France and Italy, the "peace offensive" in both countries was, by the end of the decade, admittedly "artificial and worn out."[26] The Sino-Soviet split of the late 1950s may have sapped the movement; but certainly Eisenhower's public diplomacy also forced the French and Italian Communist Parties into further self-segregation.

Mastering European Integration and Communist (Modified) Opposition

Within the framework of Eisenhower's public diplomacy lay another level of American manipulation of domestic and foreign policy in France and Italy: its promotion of Western interdependence as an alternative to traditional European nationalism and diplomacy. The United States had frequently proposed that French, Italian, and German national prerogatives could coexist, and would actually be enhanced by the emergence of a genuine European statesmanship. Leaders of Europe could gain more prestige and more tangible rewards from mastering the process of integration than by clinging to unrealistic visions of national grandeur. What was new by the mid-1950s was that Washington's encouragement, while still strong, also grew in flexibility.

FINE-TUNING PRESSURES FOR INTEGRATION

The EDC debate in France and Italy had abundantly demonstrated the residual influences of nationalism from both the right and the left. But in Italy the extreme Left was best positioned to profit from the critique of European federalism, for the PCI and the Socialists of Pietro Nenni dominated nationalist discourse. In France, Charles de Gaulle seemed too polarizing a figure, capable of provoking a countervailing leftist insurgency, inadvertently echoing the PCF's main arguments against the Fourth Republic, or pressing that regime toward nationalist posturing in order to survive. Washington's pressures and "exceptionalist" tones (asking the Europeans to emulate the United States while also maintaining strict control over nuclear deterrence) largely contributed to the French and Italian rejection of the EDC and the indefinite postponement of Europe's military autonomy.

The Eisenhower administration therefore learned to distance itself from the integration debate. While continuing to encourage the next successful integration projects, it basically acquiesced to Europe's, and particularly France's, agenda. Having pushed through a diluted military integration under the Western European Union (WEU) closely coordinated with the Atlantic alliance, and having further tied the United States "militarily" to NATO, that agenda set out to focus on economic integration. The ECSC Messina Conference of June 1955 relaunched Europe, by adopting a functionalist approach which two years later led to the creation of the European Atomic Energy Community (EURATOM) and the European Economic Community (EEC), or Common Market. Still reaping benefits from cooperation with the United States (especially EURATOM), the two organizations could be seen as the basis for the "economic" third force many Europeans, from Jean Monnet to Alcide De Gasperi, had first envisioned. Indeed, American enthusiasm seemed to dwindle. The number of opponents to the EEC grew in the State Department: they viewed with concern the beginning of discriminatory trade practices from the Europe of Six, and worse, the prospect of a "political third force which [could] seek more energetically than either of the great powers to establish the means and modes of coexistence." But these ranks of "Euroskeptics," while occasionally supported by the still prointegration Secretary of State Dulles, remained a minority. Most officials in the Eisenhower administration and, to a lesser extent, the Kennedy administration, understood the advantage of a lower profile American "hegemony."[27]

Washington also realized, as early as during the EDC debate, that if the nationalists were torpedoing America's most cherished French integration project, the point was not to fight all nationalism but to persuade those nationalist forces on the U.S. side that national interests and glory were best served by mastering integration. Already as NATO commander, Eisenhower had tried this political seduction with the wayward de Gaulle, reminding him a few weeks before the signing of the EDC treaty that by taking the flag of European unity, France would prove "her long tradition of bold and imaginative leadership." Such prestige, he added, would also provide security, for France "would never fear the Germans" within a federation that "she had brought about." A year and a half later, Dulles was more blunt, telling Foreign Minister Georges Bidault that France's role as a great power would be commensurate to its role as leader of Europe. In Rome, Clare Luce, whether or not she had a mandate from Washington, was far more explicit in explaining the correlation between national distinction and their acceptance of integration, promising the Italians special regard "when question of allotting commands in EDC arose" or even of "strengthening [the] Italian position on Trieste."[28]

Luce was right in this respect. The whole EDC debate proved that promises of long-term benefits from integration had to be complemented with prospects of more immediate, tangible rewards, calibrating prizes for supranational choices (for example, giving aid priority to EDC countries) with concessions to nationalist feelings in France and Italy. Washington's diplomatic support, as in the immediate postwar period, would help offset charges, from the Communists above all, that Western European integration constituted a mere fulfillment of American imperial designs. It is true that the French in part utilized the EDC negotiations to obtain more American assistance in Indochina, and that Italy similarly secured sovereignty over Trieste, and, ultimately, the long-coveted U.N. membership.[29] America's diplomatic support represented a mixture of substantial concessions and more symbolic gestures. International prestige was more than ever a pressing need for the two European allies suffering from uncertain international status and fragile internal politics. In 1953 Eisenhower toyed with the idea of giving the French NATO's "Central European Command, or even General Ridgway's job"; and while denying France equal status to Britain on nuclear matters, in his second mandate he was willing to give them a privileged position in his NATO "nuclear-share" concept. To placate the Italians' feelings of inferiority, Ambassador Luce insisted on providing "diplomatic mechanisms [that permitted] the smaller nations (especially Italy) to be more 'in' on major military planning and political decisions affecting Europe." At the eve of the EDC ratification debate, the ambassador even suggested rewarding the still ostracized Italians with a permanent seat on the Security Council, replacing Chiang Kai-shek's China.[30]

One problem immediately became apparent with this sort of diplomatic support. It corroborated Washington's worst fears of manipulation by its allies. Luce kept venting her frustration with the Italian Christian Democrats' reliance on American munificence and their relative passivity toward the Communist Party. Shortly before the EDC failure, Eisenhower curtly expressed his impatience with Paris, blurting out at an NSC meeting, "Must we go on forever coddling the French?"[31] Instead of fortifying the two fragile allies, exceptional diplomatic support lent itself to mutual recriminations, which highlighted a relationship of dependency.

By sponsoring Italian or French status policies, the United States also further induced the two nations to look to NATO more than European integration as their main vehicle for self-promotion. Interdependence, for both nations, still meant continuous pursuit of America's special favor, hence their demand for U.S. assistance, which not only prolonged the pattern of dependency, but also undermined the complementarity of NATO and a genuine European third force. The Italian government often exhibited its loyalty to Washington as a badge to enter the great powers club. The French were more defiant than the Italians, but by insisting on a NATO three-power direc-torate, they revealed their need for American assistance and fear of isolation more than their potential as equal partners with the British and the Ameri-cans.[32] In sum, since the prospects of supranationality were still uncertain, and NATO potentially offered more immediate power rewards, the European allies' tendency to promote U.S. hegemony in competition with each other persisted with increasing contradictions, the greatest of all was basing fed-eralist designs on this very competition.

COMMUNIST ATTACKS ON INTERDEPENDENCE

French and Italian Communists perceived these contradictions and focused their attacks on them. The Common Market, in their view, remained an in-strument of capitalist monopolies, a step toward a militarized, nuclearized Germany, and, above all, the crowning of Washington's imperialist design over Europe. The two parties intensified their attacks on Western inter-dependence as "cosmopolitan enslavement" to American capital. But the PCI first also saw the potential contradiction between the EEC and American imperialism. Fear of isolation played a great part in this change. The issue of European integration was a crucial factor, in addition to de-Stalinization, in the Socialist Party's tactical and ideological split with the Communists. At first, the Socialists' virtual acceptance of economic integration as an instru-ment of modernization and social reform free from close American guid-ance induced most PCI leaders to sharpen their criticism of the EEC: these condemnations, as Luigi Longo explained to the party's political bureau in April 1958, would help both "denounce and co-opt the Socialists" back to a united front.[33]

The most noteworthy aspect of this debate within the Italian Left was that the two parties seemed to suggest two alternative paths to emancipate Europe from American tutelage. Communists and Socialists emulated each other in truculent depictions of American imperialism, but whereas the PSI pointed toward European interdependence, the PCI at first accentuated its nationalist tones. Like their French comrades, the PCI leaders portrayed their country's sovereignty as the most endangered of all. They correctly per-ceived the integration process as another "instrument of nation-building" but in a bargaining process in which their nation, under the current regime, would be the loser. They likewise stressed that West Germany would domi-nate the process. Since Germany would assume the greater industrial role, the PCF political bureau contended in January 1957, France was likely to be "deindustrialized" to some extent, leading to "massive unemployment for our factory workers." Germany also would "buy agricultural products where it would be best for her, in the U.S.," making competition unsustainable for France's small farmers. "Salaries," the document added, "will be averaged on the lowest in Europe and . . . even women will suffer setbacks, as only France had the most advanced legislation for women workers." Upholding French grandeur, the PCF also argued that EURATOM would make the country dependent on the United States and weaken its position in scientific research, at that time ranking third in the world. Showing little confidence in Italy's fast-growing economy, most PCI leaders concurred that it was still a "developing country," and that in this new "concert of great powers," it would become, as Mauro Scoccimarro sardonically remarked, using the term for Italy's poor South, "the Mezzogiorno of Europe." Even the doctrine of polycentrism, in this context, suggested that each "Western" European country would choose its own path to social and political progress. But neither party advocated autarky; each rather insisted that without opening trade with the East, Europe would remain subject to a precarious power balance and to the ultimate predominance of American capital.[34]

Nationalism for the PCF, however, became even more a matter of identity, as, in the midst of the 1956 shocks, the party strove to assert its primacy as the essential link between the Stalinist and the French revolutionary traditions—whereas for the PCI nationalism remained a rather ambivalent cause, tempered by the country's traditions of antistatism and "transformism." The Italian Communists did not feel as immune as the PCF from changes in other parties. In order to prevent the Christian Democrats' "opening" to the Socialist Left, "coopting" the PSI became more important than "denouncing" it. As many authors have noted,[35] by the late 1950s the PCI's moderate ranks had begun to challenge the orthodox rejection of European federalism, arguing that, as with the state bureaucracy, European institutions could be best manipulated from within. Nationalism, in their opinion, was no longer sufficient to confront interdependence, lest it appear as backward protectionism. The EEC, in this view, was flawed not in its premise but rather in its · current implementation as an instrument of monopolies and of "capitalistic Americanization." In January 1959 Togliatti concluded simply that "asking to leave the EEC would be mere propaganda."[36] The party, like its socialist counterpart, now felt the need to tie integration to reform. It is no accident that the strongest institutional force within the party, the CGIL, had already started adapting to the new situation, seeking contacts with other European trade unions and, in the fall of 1958, pursuing the creation of a coordinating committee of unions within the EEC as a component of the World Federation of Trade Unions. The purpose of this organization, then endorsed by

Communist Parties of the Europe of Six at their first meeting in 1959, would be to forge a "people's Europe" rather than a "Europe of monopolies." This unfulfilled plan was as ambitious as the CGIL's previous attempts to forge alternatives to the ECA recipes; but it nevertheless signaled the end of the party's decade of neglect and isolation from Europe. Consistently with this view, most PCI leaders also thought that an integrated Europe could help revive the languid peace movement, freeing each national campaign from its provincialism, spurring the disentanglement of EURATOM from NATO, and extending the Peace Partisans' scope through connections with liberation movements from developing countries.[37]

Beginning in 1959, the PCI's position differed only slightly from that of the PSI, demanding internal reform as a necessary precondition to accepting the supranationality features of the Common Market.[38] By the early 1960s, the PCI's renowned economist Eugenio Peggio, while still skeptical of the vitality of American capitalism, recognized that the EEC offered certain economic advantages, most notably accelerated industrial development.[39] This view reflected the party reformers' appreciation of the EEC as the most fertile ground for genuine polycentrism. At the party's Eighth Congress in December 1956, Giorgio Amendola had called for a "liberation from the external nexus [with the Soviet Union]." Three years later he led a party group accepting Western European integration on a temporary basis and inviting a "democratic alternative" from within the EEC.[40]

By 1962–63, the CPSU, while ignoring the autonomist stance of certain Italian comrades, began to understand the destabilizing effects of the PCI's strategy for NATO, and accepted its position, forcing the PCF to reevaluate European integration.[41] A few years later, de Gaulle's proposal for an integrated Europe extending to the Urals also mitigated the PCF's opposition. But both developments attested to the fealty of a party that either complied with Moscow's new line or emulated the French president's eastern diplomacy. The PCI, despite its efforts, was still in a limbo, for its idea of Europe was "irreconcilable with the prevailing one in Western Europe and remote from the established views of integration in the Socialist bloc."[42]

But the two parties' most relevant potential impact was domestic. Their most destabilizing efforts consisted of using the debate over integration to restore the unity of the Left. The PCI's struggle to reform the EEC, in Gian Carlo Pajetta's words, was to "wrestle the masses away from the DC" and to "win back all Socialists and a part of the DC grassroots." The PCF tried to win socialist cooperation in the same sense.[43] Whether or not the two parties stood a chance of reuniting the Left, they might still affect a climate of opinion already increasingly critical of American choices in both countries. Even the most loyal Christian Democrats might swing toward positions akin to the Socialists', while quarrelsome France might veer even more out of control. The Eisenhower administration had already realized that tamed dissent was sometimes better than solicited loyalty. It thus further encouraged mild forms of anti-Americanism.

Managing Defiance: U.S. Encouragement of Mild Dissent in France and Italy

As with the intellectual cold war, tolerance of "dangerous opinions" seemed opportune in the diplomatic sphere as well. Diplomats had an even more detached attitude than the CCF architects' toward mild forms of European dissidence, since their reasoning was generally divested of the crusading impulse and exceptionalist accents displayed by Vital Center cultural cold warriors.

One way to confront European nationalism and its neutralist connotations, some U.S. diplomats argued, was paradoxically to encourage it and then let it burn out quickly. The first of such bold suggestions emerged during the EDC ratification debate. In October 1952 the second secretary of the embassy in Paris, Martin F. Herz—a frequent participant in the Psychological Strategy Board who remained in office under the new administration—devised his cure to rekindle French pro-EDC "dynamism." Having ascertained that "American sponsorship or advocacy of the EDC [was] counterproductive," Herz recommended allowing a measure of anti-Americanism. This, he added, would be more beneficial than threatening France with ostracism and the prospect of separate German rearmament:

> The combination of a certain anti-American sentiment with advocacy of European integration, is, as a matter of fact, the strongest possible basis on which EDC could be sold to the French. Such an attitude accommodates the inferiority feelings of the French on the material plane and their feelings of superiority as far as political acumen and their qualities for leadership are concerned, by making it appear as though Europe collectively would be able to achieve what France alone is unable to obtain, namely a position of substantial equality in its dealings with the U.S. and with the Soviets. . . . If the European idea were sold to Frenchmen as a means to achieve a supranational "greatness" in world politics that France has been unable to find on the national plane, and if above all it were defended as the best means of preventing

alleged American designs for a direct alliance with Germany, such an argumentation would have a large potential appeal here.

This perceptive analysis underscored the fundamental need to reorient the French quest for status toward policies of interdependence—or "supranational 'greatness.'" Of course to do that the United States would have to resume the arguments of John Hickerson and George Kennan in favor of a third force. Would such third force, partly created in the name of "anti-Americanism," set Europe on a neutralist path? Herz's response was optimistic: Since any such union would increasingly become subject to German influence, "France would all the more attempt to strengthen her ties with the U.S. and Britain both in NATO and elsewhere in the world," and it "would no[longer] behave erratically and neurotically." "Therefore," he concluded, "even if the EDC were to be initially endorsed out of an attitude of 'Third Force' sentiment, the prospects are that such a sentiment would lessen as EDC becomes a reality."[44]

After Truman left office, the Eisenhower administration seemed to turn a deaf ear to this tactic. The president not only became the main champion of the EDC plan, despite all French concerns; he also complained about the Europeans' abuse of American generosity: "I get weary," he said to his advisors shortly after taking office, "of the European habit of taking our money, resenting any slight hint as to what *they* should do, and then assuming, in addition, full right to criticize us as bitterly as they may desire. In fact, it sometimes appears that their indulgence in this kind of criticism varies in direct ratio to the amount of help we give them." Both Eisenhower and Dulles felt that through manipulation, criticism, or a combination of both, the Europeans might end up embracing neutralism. From Rome, Clare Luce defined "Europe's neutralism" primarily as an attempt "to make it impossible for America to go it alone and equally possible for her to make America go along with her."[45]

In spite of the EDC failure, it is important to note that Herz's "transgression" was not an isolated instance. Rather, it had an impact on the new administration, which gradually understood the importance of dealing with difficult but manageable allies. While stationed in Paris at the end of 1952, Ambassador James Dunn strongly argued for "treating our partners as truly partners" and using U.S. "strength and influence very gently and tactfully," showing respect for their variance as the best rebuke of "Commie charges that [America] dominate[s] European 'satellites.'" This presented an additional advantage: Dunn noted that since the government of Antoine Pinay had "ostensibly asserted its 'independence' of U.S. interference," it was enabled "to take strong action against the Communists without being vulnerable to the usual criticism of following 'U.S. orders.'" This impression was confirmed by Dunn's successor in the post, the very pro-French David K. E. Bruce.[46]

The Psychological Strategy Board agreed that a French mitigated form of anti-Americanism could overall benefit the alliance: "We do not require subservience nor love," stated one of its analyses in February 1953, "but the cooperation of partners, and the French need from time to time a verbal test of their 'coordinate' rather than 'subordinate' position in the Western alliance." "To a certain extent," the memo concluded, "manifestations of French petulance are a proof of improving morale." The PSB nevertheless warned that fostering the litigious qualities of the French might reinvigorate their anachronistic "commitments assumed under nationalistic and protectionist imperatives of power," which were "much in excess of French capabilities." As France seemed increasingly tempted to bite off more than it could chew, it was imperative to find leaders who could reconcile status and nationalistic concerns with the demands of interdependence. That is what Premier Mendès-France did, as the rather optimistic Herz noticed, first catering to nationalist sentiments and torpedoing the EDC project, then helping to replace it with a more realistic rearmament project which included Germany in both the Western European Union and NATO.[47]

Eisenhower, for his part, had already reached the conclusion that "the indifference of the French people toward their government," not their anti-Americanism, was the main problem. In the president's opinion, they could overcome this "cynical disgust" through a "a sort of evangelical uprising, following a Billy Sunday, or a Pied Piper." While drawing metaphors from America's religious experience, Eisenhower envisioned this quest for leadership as finding someone able to "preach the religion of French renaissance."[48] The notion that a strong French leader, even one critical of certain U.S. policies, would ultimately rescue the Atlantic partnership, gradually became consensual in Washington, finally including the rather "unilateralist" John Foster Dulles.

These unconventional views even inspired Clare Luce to mitigate her approach of applying McCarthyist solutions to the delicate communist problem in Italy and in Europe. The best way to overcome neutralism among the European allies, the ambassador told Eisenhower in her memorandum of August 1954, was to "*tacitly* accept the *spirit* of neutralism in Europe as an understandable, but *undesirable*, fact." "Our diplomatic attitude" she added, "should be 'all is calm tho' all is not right.'" To prove her point, Luce suggested going as far as allowing "the growing desire of many nations to better their relations with Russia,"—which included Churchill's call for a summit, or Europe's desire to trade with both China and the Soviet Union—and permitting "Locarno-type" pacts between France, Britain, and the Soviet Union, provided that they not "attempt to get us to sign similar agreements." Ultimately, Luce argued, following Herz's reasoning, this would help forge a genuine third force, and "put a *friendly* end to the present military and diplomatic situation in which the weakest and most frightened member of our collective defense system dictates the terms" (an argument sure to strike a chord with Eisenhower).[49]

In Luce's opinion, however, Italy's political situation, less fragmented than France's, but far more polarized between the Marxist Left and the Christian Democrats, did not warrant a dose of anti-Americanism as a vaccine. The ambassador almost clashed with Allen Dulles in the aftermath of Gronchi's election to the presidency. The CIA director thought that Gronchi's growing influence might after all be a blessing in disguise: the leader of the Christian Democratic Left was certainly too eager to cooperate with the Nenni Socialists and to open trade with the Soviet Union; but his insistence on greater national assertion, and his clout over his own party's left-wing, could offset the pressures from the extreme right for a more confrontational stance and from the extreme left for an utter rejection of Atlanticism. Luce continued to fear the new president, precisely because, having "nothing Communist in his background," as she put it, he earned credibility in his criticism of American policies. Nevertheless the ambassador, echoing opinions of several European specialists at the State Department, continued to urge a more "respectful" attitude toward Italy's growing national assertiveness.[50]

The Italian government also clearly signaled a need to downplay its NATO orthodoxy. Some leaders of the Christian Democratic Left resumed the emphasis on consultations and, following De Gasperi's championing of NATO's Article 2, they insisted on greater economic cooperation within the alliance; but they also demanded recognition of Italy's right to expand its economic interests autonomously in the Middle East. It is significant that a conservative Christian Democrat, Giuseppe Pella, as foreign minister in 1957, coined the term *neo-Atlanticism* to expound this international vision. "Primarily," he explained at a press conference, "neo-Atlanticism is against anti-Atlanticism." Pella iterated what had become the main party line, dominated by its left-wing factions and by Party Secretary Amintore Fanfani. The new DC leader, at the party congress the following year, chided its conservative ranks and their "blind Atlanticist loyalty" for allowing the Communists to pose as the guardians of national aspirations. The speech summarized the attempts Fanfani and other party reformers had conducted for a few years to wage a more assertive foreign policy, largely responding to status concerns and fending off criticism from the extreme Left. While the range of opinions among these leaders was rather wide, none of them seriously considered neutralism to be an option. They still sought cooperation with Washington, possibly even a special one, which would elevate Italy, making it not a simple follower but a proponent.[51]

For Clare Luce, Fanfani was an "Italian Kerensky," without ideological conviction and with a dangerous inclination to "compromise with the Cominform Left" (Luce thought his "Opening to the Left" would lead straight to co-operation with the Nenni Socialists). For that reason she thought the "devious" Fanfani was even less trustworthy than the straightforward Gronchi.[52] But the developments within the Christian Democratic Party compelled the ambassador to become somewhat more flexible toward Italian politics. Her foremost concession toward the Left was her decision in 1956 "to do anything to strengthen Saragat." Given the ironclad, almost servile Atlanticism of the social democrat leader, bolstering his party certainly did not preclude communist-inspired anti-Americanism. But considering Luce's original support for Monarchists and classic liberals, and her diffidence toward any form of welfare-oriented group in Italy, this was indeed a major sign of increasing U.S. malleability.

The CIA's William Colby, stationed in Rome, strongly advocated covert funding of a potential reform-oriented coalition. The codename for this project, which started in 1953 but began to be seriously implemented two years later, was "Civic Action." Without Luce's rather grudging support, it could not have continued into the late 1950s. Luce actually thought that a left-of-center (namely, the Social Democratic and Republican Parties) with certified pro-American credentials might be useful to prevent the most deleterious consequences of the Opening to the Left, since she agreed with Henry Tasca that the left-wing Christian Democrats were "a group of Catholics infected with Marxism," likely to introduce "a major shift in foreign policy." The effects of the Civic Action program were quite modest: in Italy's national elections of May 1958 the center-left parties were actually weakened, while the Communists maintained their strength. Those who stood to gain were the Christian Democrats, taking votes from the right, and the Socialists, who were rewarded for their autonomous stance. This situation forced the Eisenhower administration to come to terms with those Christian Democrats who were looking further left, toward Nenni. First among those suggesting this flexible approach was, as usual, Allen Dulles, who in January 1959 called the dialogue for a socialist reunification (between the Nenni and Saragat Socialists) "a very interesting development" that showed promise of isolating the Communists.[53]

The Eisenhower administration's decision to countenance mild dissent in France and Italy was therefore far from unanimous. But it constituted an evolving view, especially among the top officials. This change cannot be fully explained without illustrating the intersection of that dissent with the peak of the decolonization crisis in North Africa and the Middle East.

Mediterranean Crises and Reformed Leadership

FRENCH AND ITALIAN VISIONS OF THE ATLANTIC ALLIANCE

At first glance, France and Italy, from their different standpoints on decolonization, represented two diametrically opposite approaches to the Atlantic alliance and the rising U.S. hegemony in the Mediterranean. France had opposed granting full independence to its most precious possession, the *territoire* of Algeria. But while Paris needed Washington's help, it resented American interference in North Africa. As the United States tried to disentangle itself from its collusion with traditional imperial powers, and proposed alternative paths of modernization to developing countries as the best way to steer them away from communism, the clash was apparent. Worse still, the Algerian conflict heightened what has been referred to as the "antagonism born of a competitiveness between the two democratic revolutions," since the French and American claims to universalism collided in North Africa as nowhere else. The most spectacular evidence of this contrast came from a highly symbolic—and politically expedient—speech by Senator John F. Kennedy in July 1957, condemning French colonialism, and earlier from President Eisenhower himself, who, through economic blackmail, forced London and Paris to cease hostilities against Gamal Nasser's Egypt during the Suez crisis of November 1956. U.S. diplomats, claiming the rational pragmatic nature of their country's revolution, came to describe the French as "highly idealistic about the empire," "living in a dream world," and "bordering on the irrational." The U.S. minister to Algiers, Julius Holmes, lambasted the nation of the "Revolution, the Rights of Man, Descartes," for becoming "allergic to change."[54]

Far from contesting American leadership in the Mediterranean, Italy promoted its expansion. Profiting from decolonization, Italy began to proclaim a special competence in Mediterranean affairs, or, as it became known, a "Mediterranean vocation." The premise was rather simple: geographic position, cultural contacts, trade flows, historic traditions, and, not the least, its recent loss of status as an imperial power, made Italy the best candidate for bridging the West and the emerging Arab nations. Of course, Rome tried to use its presumed flexibility toward Arab nationalism as its main credential for a special cooperation with Washington. It also sought the right to participate in great power summits for the region and for European affairs as well. While the French began to consider their rivalry with the United States in the Mediterranean as a prime reason to loosen their ties to NATO, Italian leaders ultimately viewed decolonization as a chance to improve their country's position in Europe *within* a stronger NATO framework.[55]

But French acrimony and assiduous Italian cooperation also hid significant realities. The French foreign ministry did not actually seek a clash with NATO. Posing as stalwart defender of Western freedom and civilization against an "Islamic-communist" tide, French leaders pursued their ideal of NATO solidarity without NATO strings attached. U.S. assistance to France in Algeria, in their view, should have been free of conditions. They hoped rather it would stimulate their cherished project for an Anglo-French-American directorate of NATO.[56] Italy's loyalty was not incontrovertible. Neo-Atlanticism, with its emphasis on commercial advantages and multilateralism, was tightly interlaced with the "Mediterranean vocation" and implied considerable criticism of the United States for its unilateralism, neocolonial tendencies, and military power. All these American proclivities seemed embodied in the Eisenhower Doctrine for the Middle East, approved by Congress in January 1957, an assistance package that included possible armed intervention to help Arab countries threatened by communist infiltration or by Nasser's expansionism. In the course of the following year, the Italian government, for its part, came up with two aid proposals for the Middle East that would be multilateral instead.[57] Oilman Enrico Mattei continued to marry economic opportunism with a tendency to pose as paladin of Arab underdogs against the prerogatives of the Anglo-American companies. President Gronchi and other left-wing Christian Democrats, for their part, wished to utilize the "Mediterranean vocation" and closer relations with Nasser, one of the nonalignment leaders, to reach out to the neutralist Socialists of Pietro Nenni.[58] These ambivalent positions in France and Italy were therefore fraught with perils of neutralism and, worse, replete with opportunities for the Communists in both countries.

CONFLATING ANTICOLONIALISM AND ANTI-AMERICANISM
Following the national consensus on Algeria, the PCF refrained from giving the same unconditional support to the Algerian liberation movement it had given Ho Chi Minh. At first, it justified postponement of emancipation in

North Africa with its own "missionary" argument: the nationalist movements there represented the bourgeoisie and had not yet absorbed Lenin's anti-imperialist message. In fact, both the French and the Algerian Communists (basically a settlers' party until the early 1950s) labeled the Front de Libération Nationale (FLN), the nationalist movement of Fehrat Abbas, as "sectarian and chauvinist." Worse still, Abbas "represented the Islamic bourgeoisie, which wanted to separate Algeria from France in order to bring it into the American orbit."[59] Consistently opposed to the insurrection, from the spring of 1956 the party advocated the "recognition of Algeria as a national fact, [with] the presence of Europeans, whose rights must be respected." The PCF political bureau decided to favor Algerian independence only in January 1957, but it also recommended that Algerian workers continue to be indoctrinated (through the CGT), and it castigated the collusion between the FLN and the United States.[60] By insisting that decolonization would open the door to American neocolonialism, the PCF averted political isolation on the Algerian question. By conflating anticolonialism and anti-Americanism, it reached out to the Socialists, appealing to their resentment of Washington's preponderance, especially after the Suez crisis. Even before that crisis, the socialist prime minister, Guy Mollet, had called the Algerian war "imbecilic." Thorez announced in October 1957 that he would support the Socialists on any platform calculated to bring peace; at the political bureau he urged pressing the Socialists to abandon their allegiance to the United States.[61] Emphasis on that cleavage reinforced the PCF's Leninist conviction that the clash between imperialist powers sapped their energy to resist the working class, and that the demise of capitalism would mainly come at the hands of the "alliance between workers of the Metropole and the slave peoples of the colonies that depend on that same country."[62]

Predictions of an imminent capitalist collapse were, as usual, a matter of faith more than analysis; more accurate was the estimate of the growing communist influence in the decolonization movement. However, the PCF remained straddled between that solidarity and its pursuit of nationalist anti-Americanism in the name of French grandeur. In an effort to wrest its political rivals on the left away from the United States, it also sacrificed internal cohesion: intellectuals and the radical youth resented its lukewarm attitude toward Algerian independence. This precipitated the "first crack in its relations with the student movement."[63]

The PCF's nationalist posturing on colonial issues irked the Italian comrades as well. Aggravating their reciprocal estrangement of 1956, this disagreement made the PCI for once far more "principled" than the PCF. In Rome, condemnation of Western imperialism became unconditional.

Furthermore, the PCI had devised its own "Mediterranean vocation," feeling that it had received a tacit mandate from Moscow to bridge the gap between the Muslim and Socialist worlds. From the early 1950s the PCI had established contacts with North African delegations to the Peace Congresses sponsored by Florence's Mayor Giorgio La Pira. Of course, the other gap to bridge was with the Socialists: if Nasser, admired by most PSI leaders, remained friendly to the Soviet Union, the PCI could improve its dialogue with Nenni. Increased financial support from Moscow starting in 1956 gave the PCI additional confidence that its diplomatic outlook enjoyed Soviet endorsement.[64] These tactics had other potential ramifications. One of the propositions advanced by the doctrine of polycentrism was that socialism could be constructed even in Third World countries that did not have strong Communist Parties.[65] By forging solidarity with the developing nations' upheaval against Western imperialism, the PCI thus enhanced both its own political prospects at home and those for socialist expansion among the nonaligned countries of North Africa.

But because the Italian Communists nurtured the same distorted views of America as the PCF, they circumscribed their diplomatic acumen on these issues. Togliatti believed that the imperialist powers demonized the Hungarian events mainly in order to "conceal their inner contradictions" and "their own suffering in North Africa." The new U.S. ambassador to Rome, David Zellerbach, defined the PCI's reaction to the first applications of the Eisenhower Doctrine in the Middle East as "hysterical." By the end of the decade, Togliatti predicted a new civilizational clash, since "capitalism, which used to fight only Socialist countries," now "fought Islamic ones as well."[66]

These arguments entailed another, far more penetrating and damning critique: that of American racism. The French and the Italian Communists kept exploiting the hypocrisy of a nation that tried to distance itself from European old-fashioned imperialism while lagging far behind Europe in its domestic record of race relations.[67] Like the campaign against nuclear weapons, these arguments gave the Communists extended appeal, for the critique of America's tarnished civil rights record was a matter of virtual consensus in both France and Italy. Western European Communism gained minimal clout among the liberation movements in North Africa; but decolonization still offered both the PCI and the PCF opportunities to rekindle their nations' anti-American feelings and to limit their political isolation.

NEW LEADERS

Decolonization brought with it the possibility of rising neutralism, or, at least of a political polarization from which either the extreme Right or Left could profit. In France the main threat, Washington realized, came from the rightist military ranks, not from the Communists. In the aftermath of the Suez crisis Ambassador Dillon was quick to point out that disgruntled generals in Algeria might create "some type of Fascist movement . . . largely anti-U.S. and isolationist." The CIA had been gathering evidence that the French military had prepared for possible coups d'état since 1953, and Allen Dulles kept warning about the prospect of a military dictatorship, until a coup finally occurred on 13 May 1958 in Algiers.[68] Even more ominously, the State Department wondered if, in reaction to the right-wing resurgence, the Socialists might revert to a Popular Front strategy. Rumors of an improbable plan organized by previously staunch anticommunist Jules Moch, again interior minister in the spring of 1958, for a common resistance with the Communists against the rebels were sufficient to alarm Washington. These charges, artfully circulated by the rebels themselves, illustrated how much the Algerian affair had aggravated the polarization of French politics. The possibility of a Popular Front was taken seriously in Washington. Secretary of State Dulles had already depicted that coalition as one that would be able to "liquidate the Algerian affair," but that unfortunately "was likely to liquidate NATO as well." A French Popular Front could also prove fatal for European integration. Dulles could not forget that the "EDC received its death blow from the left wing government that liquidated the Indochina war."[69]

This reflection did not imply any urgent need to persuade or seduce the French. In times of deep bilateral crisis, allowing a large degree of dissent was still a better option. In the midst of the Suez crisis in October 1956, John Foster Dulles had best expressed his conversion to the idea of encouraging a moderately dissident "third force" in Europe centered on France. The secretary of state did not worry about the moderate criticism of the United States that such a force might produce because "the British and the French [were] more actively hostile to the Soviet Union" than ever before, and, he noted, "they could not mention the Soviet Union without spitting." It was also positive that European and especially French feelings of autonomy derived in part from their understanding that the United States could no longer "pull their chestnuts out of the fire whenever the fire occurred." Dulles concluded that there would be no danger of neutrality in such a more assertive "third force" because "it was weakness, and not strength that led nations to adopt a neutralist policy"—hence his agreement to strengthening Europe's retaliatory capacity by going "as far as possible under the present law to share our knowledge of atomic weapons" with the allies. Practical reasons may have thwarted the neutralist option, but spiritual and ideological reasons mattered even more: the third force led by the quarrelsome French would stay on the U.S. side, in Dulles's opinion, ultimately because Western Europe and the United States were "part and parcel of Western Civilization, with similar religion, culture, and other fundamental affinities." After the Suez crisis, Ambassador Dillon ventured that the "wave of anti-Americanism [might] well subside" because of French "mercurial public and governmental opinion . . . with its special bias and egocentric viewpoint."[70]

Even at the peak of the Fourth Republic crisis, in the spring of 1958, American optimism did not lapse. In fact, Washington came to believe that alienating the French for a while would still cause less damage than alienating their rivals in North Africa. Washington insisted that the French colonial war was not against an already existing Soviet-Arab coalition, but that it might *create* one, rallied behind the banner of national liberation—worse still, such a banner could help redirect communist anti-American propaganda in France, too. Therefore, a rather estranged France might actually allow Washington to cultivate the new friendship with North African leaders, while also preventing a chain effect of subversive anti-Americanism starting from there. Washington confirmed its view that Western European Communism could now mutually nurture its anti-imperialist campaign with those of colonial peoples only if the "domino" effect began in Third World nations. At the height of the Franco-Tunisian crisis, and significantly also during the Fourth Republic's agony in April 1958, State Department legal advisor Loftus Becker thus summarized the situation: "If [the pro-Western Tunisian leader] Bourguiba falls, it is almost certain that North Africa would change its alignment. . . . if we exert more pressure on the French, it is less certain that they would leave NATO." The State Department applied a similar reasoning to the other possible North African strategic anchor for the West, Morocco.[71]

Finally, the United States decided to abandon the regime it had so sedulously shored up, not worrying about an anti-American backlash, mainly because a much more self-confident leader, Charles de Gaulle, was ready to dominate and moderate France's antagonistic position. Indeed, lack of firm leadership, together with a protracted condition of dependency on the United States, continued to be the main problem with the Fourth Republic. Its volatile governments kept compensating for their dependency with nationalist posturing, but they then showed little control over the chauvinism they unleashed in the country and among the French *colons* in Algeria.[72] The Fourth Republic's "resentful nationalism," so accentuated from the Suez crisis, needed to be replaced with a nationalism of pride. The United States did not intentionally undermine the Fourth Republic; but during the May

1958 crisis, it exercised a restraint that ultimately favored de Gaulle's return to power.

De Gaulle was redeemed in Washington for the same qualities for which he had been previously reviled: worshiped by the military, he was most likely to quell their insurrection; thanks to his nationalist posturing, he would be able to restore vision for the French rather than stirring their fears. For both reasons, the returning prime minister was also likely to preempt Popular Front scenarios. De Gaulle also had acquired new traits that increased his appeal among American officials. He dispelled American fears about his inclination toward the extreme Right by immediately establishing contacts with the SFIO and Guy Mollet in particular. His first cabinet contained only two Gaullists and included representatives from the old order. U.S. ambassador Emory Houghton was elated, as were most French left-of-center leaders.[73] De Gaulle appeared now as a "moderate right-wing" leader, rather as than a polarizing figure; although the Eisenhower administration resolved to foster mild dissidence from any political direction in allied countries, it could not hide its predilection for moderate right over moderate left solutions. Charles de Gaulle enjoyed more trust from the Republican administration than he ever did with the Democrats.[74] With complacency and a dose of the usual exceptionalism, the U.S. government and public also welcomed the establishment of the new French presidential republic with the referendum of 28 September, for it seemed to suggest that emulation of the American constitutional model could fix fragile parliamentary situations as in France. Even de Gaulle's mysticism and rhetoric of grandeur, so remote from U.S. political style, appeared immediately alleviated by the new president's pragmatic choices, especially in the economic field, in which, U.S. officials thought, he had previously shown woeful incompetence.[75]

De Gaulle was above all reassuring for his partial conversion to European integration. Indeed, his main reason for liquidating the Algerian war was to focus on French leadership in Europe, and consequently to acquire more self-sufficiency within NATO, both welcome goals in Washington. Besides mastering French nationalism, the new president now also seemed likely to master interdependence. The United States thus accepted a regime and a leader who would be "admittedly difficult." But there was no doubt in Dulles's mind that this man was "all that stands between France and chaos."[76] The "Gaullist solution" appeared the best cure for the unmanageable forms of French anti-Americanism from the right or the left.[77]

Following parallel reasoning, Washington thought that Italy's swings between obedience and insubordination could be best prevented by an improvement in the country's leadership. Amintore Fanfani, who had regained the premiership in June 1958, ultimately seemed to be the leader who could best steer a government through the treacherous waters of neo-Atlanticism. More than de Gaulle, he would have to proceed with American assistance. From the time of the Suez crisis, the DC party secretary had managed to persuade the Eisenhower administration that his moderate reformism and his desire for an active foreign policy—neo-Atlanticist yet, on colonial matters, opportunistically pro-American—would be the perfect alternative to either a stagnant Italy or a neutralist solution.[78]

Through the previous year U.S. diplomats, further elaborating on Herz's and Luce's ideas of fostering independence and mild dissent from the NATO allies, had recommended appeasing the "natural resurgence of Italian national pride," by "consulting the Italians on all matters affecting the Middle East." This would "remove [any] pretext for uncoordinated actions and give the Fo[reign] Off[ice] and other realistic elements ammunition to defend themselves against [the] free wheeling [of] Gronchi [and others]." It seemed therefore wise to be "tolerant, considerate, and sympathetic" toward Fanfani's international activism, even when the premier openly flirted with Arab nationalism. The president's opinion also weighed in. Eisenhower no longer acquiesced to Luce's alarming reports (as the ambassador remained rather fickle even when adopting a more flexible diplomacy). The main reason for her resignation from her post in Rome at the end of the president's first term may be attributed to the increasing dissonance between her highly publicized, shrill pronouncements, and the newer, subtler, more stealthy approach advocated by most U.S. officials in the State Department, the CIA, and the Rome embassy.[79]

Fanfani earned the trust of the Eisenhower administration for other reasons as well. First, his adeptness in concentrating power, was, in this context, welcome in Washington: in addition to retaining his post as party secretary, Fanfani also assumed the portfolio of foreign minister. A Gaullist solution was unthinkable for Italy, given its previous catastrophic experience with authoritarianism. Also, the Italian Republic, unlike the previous French regime, was far from collapsing, even though it had suffered an erosion of consensus since De Gasperi's last government. Virtually every U.S. official knew that Fanfani was hardly a "man of destiny." But they perceived him as an individual skillful in maneuvering and dominating intraparty squabbles, possibly able to overcome Italy's main political problem, which was stagnation.[80] Second, the Republican administration in Washington, in keeping with its affinity for de Gaulle, also welcomed Fanfani's moderate turn following his radical beginnings as party secretary. The prime minister announced his domestic program with the slogan of "Progress without Adventures." It is no accident that Allen Dulles spent three weeks in September between Paris and Rome specifically to assess what seemed to be a twin political turn in the two countries. His conclusion was that both the French and the Italian leaders could forestall opportunities for the extreme Left in the two countries; they both seemed able to isolate the Communist Parties. As he reported to the NSC in October, Italy had "the best government since De Gasperi," and Fanfani was "very astute, very friendly to the United States and strongly anti-Communist." The CIA director stressed another trait that Fanfani shared with de Gaulle: his steadfast pursuit of greater diplomatic initiative and international prestige.[81] As in France, this soon appeared the most influential factor in stabilizing the internal political situation. Driven by the new prime minister, Italy's Mediterranean vocation was meant to keep the Socialists at bay until they fully converted to NATO. Fanfani's very closeness to Gronchi and Mattei seemingly enabled him to bridle their neutralist impulse. He shared with them the goal of restoring Italy's self-confidence in its international image; and he meant to do this without assuming the anti-American tones of a Mattei, or a de Gaulle.[82]

Eisenhower had earlier instructed his secretary of state to find ways to "give the Italians an additional dose of prestige within NATO,"[83] a broad mandate he was able to refine after Fanfani became prime minister. The occasion was a new crisis in the Middle East, which in July 1958 led to a joint intervention by the British and the Americans to rescue the Jordanian and Lebanese governments from pro-Nasser insurrections. Fanfani secured Washington's goodwill by lending Italian bases to stage the U.S. military showdown in Lebanon. He also carried on negotiations undertaken by his predecessors for the installation of IRBMs on Italian territory. But the prime minister's emphasis was less on military matters than on other sources of Italian expertise and prestige. Visiting Washington at the end of July, Fanfani explained that Italy's primary role would be to continue orchestrating economic assistance to the Middle East and to mediate between Egypt and the West as well as between Israel and the Islamic nations in order to promote a nonaggression pact in the region. This accent on economic cooperation or on Italy's ability to shape international compromises certainly followed an international design: it was intended to increase Italy's prestige while also improving NATO cooperation, foiling hierarchies like the one conceived by de Gaulle during those same days. In light of these considerations, Washington finally interpreted the Mediterranean vocation for what it was: not a way for Italy to distance itself from European integration and favor a Third World approach but rather as an attempt by Italy to improve its position within an integrated Europe.[84] This reconciliation of nationalism and mastery of interdependence paralleled de Gaulle's choices. Above all, Washington stayed focused on the internal repercussions of this outlook.[85] Fanfani's flexibility toward Arab neutralism seemingly further tamed Italy's moderate Left; his mild disapproval of American antagonism toward Egypt blunted the usual communist charges of pro-American servility; his appeal on arbitration, enhancing Italy's reputation based primarily on international statesmanship instead of old-fashioned nationalism, also helped refute the Left's accusations that the government pursued vassal nationalist ventures under the U.S. aegis.

Fanfani did not obtain the expected results, in part because of the half-hearted support the Eisenhower administration gave to his overly ambitious good-offices mission to Egypt, and in part because his consolidation of power at home was foiled by opponents within the conservative DC ranks. In January 1959 these leaders plotted his downfall, partly assisted by a U.S. press campaign orchestrated with the media circles of former ambassador Luce and her husband. The Eisenhower administration had overestimated Fanfani's ability to fix Italy's political ills.[86] But the notion persisted in Eisenhower's cabinet, and even more, in the next administration, that diplomatic cooperation with stronger and moderately dissident leaders in Italy could be the best way to isolate the extreme Left and neutralize the effects of its anti-American campaigns.

COMMUNISTS ISOLATED

Whatever the limits of U.S. encouragement of a new partnership with France and Italy, the effects of these political turns on the PCI, and, especially the PCF, were tangible. The Soviets were the first to note that de Gaulle was "the man who defeated the Communists." The PCF plunged for the first time under 20 percent of the vote in the November 1958 elections, and, thanks to the abolition of proportional representation, sent only ten deputies to the National Assembly (compared with the 150 elected in 1956). From this marginal position the party logically spurned parliamentary tactics, privileging street and strike action. Also, since internal reform was unfeasible with such a negligible parliamentary presence, the Communists aimed to regain some exposure by restoring priority to foreign policy issues, particularly Algeria and the peace movement. This international focus was also necessary to "unmask" the nature of the Gaullist regime. Following interpretations put forward by Georgi Dimitrov in the 1930s, the PCF insisted that Gaullism was akin to fascism, that it followed the aspirations of the "most colonialist, chauvinist, reactionary sections of the bourgeoisie," and that it served the monopolies in the same way it served American imperialism. Resuming the claim to moral patriotism, the Communists also charged that de Gaulle's grandeur was a travesty, since its military, colonialist connotations, and its basic dependence on U.S. goodwill (the president's insistence on a three-power NATO directorate), in fact reduced the *rayonnement* of France.[87] On Cold War issues, de Gaulle could even be portrayed as *plus royaliste que le roi*: during the Berlin crisis of 1961, the PCF castigated the president's opposition to any form of negotiated settlement.[88]

Diverging communist interpretations of Gaullist "imperialism" led to another crisis of dissidence within the party. In 1960–61, Thorez repeatedly censored Laurent Casanova and Marcel Servin for arguing that the renewed French imperialism was on a collision course with American imperialism. In fact, the party secretary explained in *L'Humanité* on 5 July 1960, "it would be a grave mistake to attribute genuine nationalist concerns to the monopolist capital or to the government that represents it, for both by nature are integrated with cosmopolitanism." After expelling his two rivals from the Central Committee in May 1961, Thorez proceeded to adopt their theses and to reevaluate the developing "contradictions" between French and American imperial interests, while maintaining with de Gaulle, in Annie Kriegel's words, "a system of strictly controlled reciprocal aggression."[89] Partly induced by Soviet wedge tactics to divide NATO, this new approach would allow the PCF to pursue the same tacit anti-American entente with its internal archenemy as it had done during the early 1950s. In the 1962 elections the Communists recovered strength and quadrupled their parliamentary presence.

In Italy, the PCI faced no "national savior" of de Gaulle's caliber. But the party knew that Fanfani had broken the path toward the opening to the Socialist Left. His Atlanticism, tempered by his pro-Arab positions, rendered that political scenario even trickier for the Communists. It was therefore paramount, as Luigi Longo confirmed after the prime minister's fall from government in January 1959, to show that the Fanfani ranks of the DC aimed at "setting up a clerical regime disguised as social reform," and that, instead of uniting a moderate Left, they provoked a rightist insurrection within their own party assisted by America's reactionary groups around Clare Luce. Echoing their French comrades' depiction of Gaullist monopoly capitalism, the Italian Communists insisted that Fanfani, who had a past in the Fascist youth, intended to "set up a corporative totalitarian regime."[90] This argument referred to the DC's first steps toward the creation of a national energy monopoly under its control. But it also reflected the PCI's fear that partial nationalization of major industries would further co-opt an already "revisionist" PSI. Amendola and other moderates first warned, after the socialist success in the 1958 elections, that the risks of isolation and anticommunist backlash were even greater for the PCI than they were for the PCF.[91] Stressing the inherent contradictions of reform under a Christian Democratic group that profoundly revered the Vatican might not be enough to avert isolation. Beginning in the early 1960s, the Communists were also forced to revise their theses of capitalist collapse, just as they were reconsidering the potential of European integration.

Contradictions in the Diplomatic Approach

Fostering mild dissent could become problematic. The problem was a matter not just of fine-tuning disagreements with challenging leaders but of deeper contradictions in the evolving Western alliance. Strong leaders were more likely than fragile governments to show statesmanship through mastery of European interdependence. But they might also intensify their competition for a privileged partnership with the United States, as both Fanfani and de Gaulle had immediately demonstrated.[92] Persistent "competitive invitations" of U.S. hegemony were not about subservience; they more often reflected manipulative intentions. They offered little advantage to the United States but still fed communist propaganda.

Another inconsistency in the United States' "flexible" approach toward its two troubled allies was its ill-concealed desire to reassert American exceptionalism. The Eisenhower administration ostensibly sought a full symbiosis with its European allies. These allies had to show the necessary self-confidence to become harmonious among themselves (reducing nationalist claims toward each other) and more combative against the common enemy. Both traits would enable them to share burdens with the United States. But there were two problems: first, once Washington convinced them to change their style of foreign policy among themselves, it became rather difficult to have them focus on military preparedness against the Soviets; second, the burden-sharing concept, rather than facilitating transatlantic symbiosis, aimed at preserving American exceptionalism. Eisenhower continued to fear that, without greater mutual assistance with the allies, his country would run the risk of becoming a garrison state, and of losing its distinctiveness as a democracy founded on entrepreneurship and nurtured by consumerism.

The Suez and Hungarian crises combined to evoke a moral equivalence between East and West, which also forced the Eisenhower administration to rethink its own moral role and public diplomacy. Most of Eisenhower's advisors preferred to turn moral issues into opportunities to pursue more energetic political warfare against Soviet Communism. The prevalent mood was actually best exemplified by Henry Kissinger, then a policy critic whose main connection to the administration was his close friendship with Nelson Rockefeller. In the aftermath of the events in Suez and Hungary, the young academic told the psy-war director: "We seem obsessed with risks, they seem conscious of opportunities." For Washington, of course, the missed opportunity was that of fully exploiting Soviet repression in the East the same way the Communists had denounced the ugly face of Western imperialism. Shortly thereafter Kissinger also complained to former Ambassador Adolf Berle about the administration's passivity toward the Hungarian events and its false confidence that "we shall inherit the world without any effort," indicating "a moral weakness rather than an analytical one on the part of the free world." "What really seems to be lacking in us," he concluded, "is a sense of mission."[93] These reflections were attuned to the renewed impulse that had produced the Eisenhower Doctrine, and, following the debate over the missile gap spurred by Sputnik, to an additional nuclear buildup. But the sense of purpose, or "mission," also anticipated the president's growing desire to articulate a more convincing image of the United States.

Eisenhower, while no idealist, was always acutely prone to emphasizing the psychological and moral dimension of the Cold War. It was in conjunction with the crises in the Middle East, and the U.S. intervention in Lebanon, that the president, seeking to leave a legacy of peace, insisted on a more sincere, less manipulative projection of America's image. Eisenhower mused with his speechwriter Emmet J. Hughes that he felt "the need to assert American purposes, before all the world, in terms more proud, and in measures less mean, than sheer material might." Then, with the civilizational emphasis that, under his presidency, especially informed the American view of the Cold War, he added that he was groping for a way "to give practical testimony to the higher kind of power—and the 'spiritual values'— that inspired all civilizations based upon a religious faith." Propaganda and openness to negotiation with America's adversaries in Moscow or in Cairo would be a first step to translate such faith "in the most earthy way possible"; then, many Western leaders would "truly join" Washington.[94] This new conduct, Eisenhower seemed sure, would help refute the main reasons for anti-American sentiment in Europe.

While accelerated by events in the Middle East, and leading to a milder approach toward Nasser, this shift in the president's attitude had begun earlier, reflecting mainly Eisenhower's Eurocentric worry about NATO allies and public opinion at home. It also originated from his long-standing concern that, in the eyes of others, the materialistic, hedonistic, and jingoistic aspects of U.S. culture had overshadowed the nation's spiritual and intellectual achievements. Eisenhower felt acutely the pressure from Western European public opinion to undertake disarmament negotiations seriously, not just to score propaganda points as during his first term. "We need some basis of hope for our own people and for world opinion," he told Secretary of State Dulles in March 1958. "It is simply intolerable to remain in a position wherein the United States, seeking peace, and giving loyal partnership to our allies, is unable to achieve an advantageous impact on world opinion." This resulted in his earnest attempt to negotiate a test-ban treaty with the Soviet Union. And, in the fall of 1959, Nikita Khrushchev became the first Soviet leader to visit the United States, on a loudly trumpeted goodwill tour. Had U.S. pilot Gary Powers not been downed and captured on Soviet territory while on his unauthorized reconnaissance flight the following spring, the U.S.-Soviet summit scheduled in Paris might have reached an agreement on the partial ban.[95]

But the civilizational overtones of Eisenhower's pursuit of a dialogue constituted yet another problem. The president wished to leave a legacy bearing a greater "missionary" impulse than in his first term. His dichotomy stressing that "spiritual values" would help overcome the cynicism of the enemy's materialism evinced a faith in the U.S. capacity to convert others that opened itself to charges of exceptionalism and arrogance. It certainly echoed Eisenhower's double claim that the United States distinguished itself by being a pragmatic nation, driven by its consumerist economy, and also a nation "under God," as in the new pledge of allegiance introduced by his administration. Eisenhower's psychological warriors, from the beginning of his presidency, had warned him that the French were "impatient of any moralistic and legalistic aspects of [U.S.] policies." The French legal tradition, they pointed out, was "different from that of the common law, and their ethics [did] not derive from a Puritan experience," while the United States held that "success is closely linked with goodness." The French considered such an attitude "a form of hypocrisy." Separating mundane interests from spiritual goals, the French were prone to accuse the United States of "sanctimoniousness and preaching."[96] Eisenhower himself seemed to admit American hypocrisy, as in his farewell address he denounced the "military-industrial complex" that threatened the country's "liberties or democratic processes." Although the speech confirmed his aura of statesmanship, it still contained too much preaching for Europeans to bear. Furthermore, Eisenhower admitted losing control of the political, diplomatic, military, and business forces he was supposed to harness.[97] Under his command, the United States had seemed to swing between torpor and brinkmanship.

That was the contrast most heavily emphasized by communist propaganda in light of the failed détente. Hosting editorials by CPUSA secretary Gus Hall, the new French communist journal *Démocratie nouvelle* stressed its own argument about the American military-industrial complex. Pointing to America's mild recession of 1958–59 as evidence, Hall simply argued that the American foreign policy and business establishment had finally refrained from détente out of "fear that it would bring an economic collapse."[98]

Kennedy, Diplomacy, and the Opening to the Left

The Kennedy administration, inspired by the principles of the Vital Center, was determined to assume energetic involvement abroad, to wage social reform at home, and above all, calling for a "New Frontier," to restore vision and sense of purpose in the country. Kennedy's ideas and political style, which perhaps best projected America's combined claim to exceptionalism and universalism, immediately won some admiration among Europe's moderate Left. For the extreme Left, including most Italian Socialists, it was the epitome of arrogant exceptionalism, made worse by the intellectual hubris of "the best and the brightest." Nothing in the Democratic Party's new outlook, from its approach to civil rights reform to its renewed détente policy, mitigated communist perceptions in Western Europe. In fact, as an article in *Démocratie nouvelle* pointed out, if the Eisenhower administration had represented the power of the trusts, the Kennedy administration added an element of intellectual arrogance, conjoining Ivy League and economic privilege, and assuming an even more aggressive posture abroad.[99] The Kennedy myth among the European Left was posthumous; we will thus consider its cultural and political effects on the French and Italian Communists in the next chapter. The focus here is instead on continuity with the previous administration's diplomatic, pragmatic approach toward communism and the risks of neutralism in Western Europe.

While not having the same organizational structure of Eisenhower's public diplomacy, the Kennedy administration counted on personal style and its proverbial mastery of the media. Also, whatever claim to exceptionalism might have irked Europe's leaders was tempered by the Northeastern, Ivy League upbringing of the new president. As his ambassador to Italy Frederick Reinhardt recalled in an interview, Kennedy had a particular ability to communicate with Europeans, for "there must have been something in the way he expressed himself, much nearer to them than the average American."[100] It was under Kennedy that the United States and the Soviet Union negotiated a treaty to ban testing in the atmosphere. And it was under Kennedy that the United States enshrined the notion of Atlantic interdependence, in one of the president's famous speeches. More specifically with regard to France and Italy, Kennedy was aware of the connection between communist anti-American propaganda in the West and the emerging protest against American "neocolonialism" in Third World regions. The administration, for example, paid close attention to the PCI's activism in various Latin American countries. As Italian President Antonio Segni reminded Kennedy in October 1963, "any increase in the strength of Italian Communism would . . . necessarily have repercussions in Latin America."[101]

But the test-ban treaty came in the wake of the Cuban missile crisis and executive brinkmanship. Communist pacifism was weakened, but, particularly in Italy, other political and religious groups had absorbed some of its arguments. This raised Washington's concerns about neutralist trends. It was the pacifist Christian Democrat groups around Florence's mayor, Giorgio La Pira, that had initiated the Italian campaign against nuclear testing.[102] Generally, Kennedy's détente policies were eclipsed by the globalized Cold War approach of his "Flexible Response" strategy—essentially a resumption of NSC 68, with additional emphasis on guerrilla tactics and modernization programs for the Third World. They were no less overshadowed by his "macho" approach to the Cold War enemy. The president's endorsement of a European third force was contradicted by the centralizing features of his Multilateral Force (MLF) project—basically an attempt to contain the Gaullist challenge, putting sea-based nuclear arsenals within a U.S.-controlled transatlantic framework, with the additional aim of giving Germany a sense of greater equality with Britain and France.[103] The New Frontier in general evoked more distinction than a peer attitude toward the Western allies.

But the litmus test of the administration's understanding and flexibility toward Europe's political subtleties was its response to the *apertura*, the "Opening to the Left" operation in Italy. With greater conviction than the previous administration, and thanks to the PSI's final abjuration of its pro-Sovietism, the Kennedy cabinet helped accelerate the center-left experiment: the PSI offered external support to a centrist government in 1962 and, finally, entered a coalition government in December 1963. It is beyond my scope to retell the intense U.S. maneuvering behind this development.[104] But it is worth highlighting the general reasoning behind the decision, its expected ramifications, and communist reactions.

Direct meddling in Italian affairs may have seemed like an old-fashioned remedy, replicating the style of the 1948 intervention, or the "rollback" designs of psychological warfare at its peak. In some respects, such interference was intensified, with the permanence of a secret military apparatus set up by the CIA and Italy's Servizio per le Informazioni e la Sicurezza Militare

(SIFAR, the military intelligence service) in 1956, after the Suez Crisis. Its main purpose was to thwart a possible neutralist turn by a center-left government.[105] But the Kennedy cabinet's decision to give financial assistance and, finally, an official endorsement of a center-left coalition including the Socialists rather reflected a growing understanding by a liberal administration that tamed dissent offered the best opportunities to isolate the Communists and to promote necessary social reforms in Italy.

The effort to "purify" the PSI and convert it to Atlanticism was qualified from the start. In fact, from as early as the summer of 1956, when the Eisenhower administration began to monitor the dialogue for a reunification between the Saragat Social Democrats and the Nenni Socialists, Washington remained rather standoffish, suggesting only adherence to the anti-Soviet positions of the Socialist International as a precondition for unity. One of the most perceptive U.S. diplomats, the chargé at the Rome embassy, John Jernegan, insisted that the best way to take votes from the PCI was to help the Nenni Socialists keep a firm hold on the Left. Trying to force the PSI to move to the right would have backfired. With this in mind, two years later Ambassador Zellerbach authorized his first secretary, George Lister, to inaugurate contacts with the Nenni Socialists.[106] This flexibility was matched by an increasingly diffused diplomatic approach. To persuade the PSI, the United States relied on the British Labor Party, which from 1955 openly cultivated Italian politicians favorable to the Opening to the Left, and soon later began to encourage Nenni's new course. Leopoldo Nuti has best described the "tacit agreement between [the CIA and MI6] on a possible division of labor, with the British assigned responsibility for nudging Nenni's party away from its roughest ideological leanings and directing it toward the goal of social democratic respectability. The United States, for its part, would prevent the release of a premature certificate of good behavior."[107]

Within the Kennedy administration, the main initiative to support the Nenni Socialists came more openly from the president's special representatives, W. Averell Harriman and Arthur M. Schlesinger Jr., and the NSC's staff member, Robert W. Komer. Most notably, following the suggestion of George Lister, the first task toward the Socialists was to overcome their prejudice toward Americans as a people of "fat, happy idiots, who had reached a position of world leadership more out of luck than from sacrifice, intelligence, and determination." Schlesinger and the other Kennedy advisers who had understood the importance of the Congress for Cultural Freedom also were confident they could convince the Socialists that the Americans, especially under the "New Frontier," had the necessary qualities and intellectual acumen to face the Soviet challenges.[108]

Schlesinger and Komer's arguments also crucially qualified American intervention. Financial assistance would not help, they contended, unless it was accompanied by social reform, as well as keen wedge tactics to stir feuds in the Marxist Left. In recommending "active measures to help Nenni" in 1961, Schlesinger reflected that otherwise "the PSI would be cut to pieces by the Communist counteroffensive."[109] The problem with the PSI was that, in its majority, it still upheld neutralist positions. Nenni had returned the Stalin Peace Prize, had accepted the EEC, and in principle NATO, too. But by 1961–62, the party's expectations of a more autonomous foreign policy still included recognition of China, a neutralized Germany, and a disengagement zone in Central Europe. Secretary of State Dean Rusk concurred with Ambassador Reinhardt that this was unacceptable.[110] Komer fended off objections from the State Department that supporting the PSI would induce Fanfani and the other proponents of the *apertura* to "slack off on firm anti-Communism and pro-NATO policy" by weighing the opportunities for reform against the dangers of neutralism. Fears of Italy's going neutral, Komer contended, "were legitimate in the late Forties and early Fifties"; but in the "prosperous Italy of today" further pressure to translate the "economic miracle into meaningful political and social [reform] far outweigh[ed] the risks of undermining the center party or encouraging a neutralist trend."[111] Rather than fearing charges of interference, these advocates of the *apertura* felt that overt support of Nenni by a reformist American administration would give his party an "aura of affluence," not one of "influence" from the United States. There was no doubt that, while being nudged to nonneutralist positions, Nenni, unlike Saragat, would remain quite autonomous from U.S. control—and that was a healthy diversion from the country's polarized politics. Analysts in the State Department's Office of Intelligence and Research went further, envisioning the possibility that the PSI induction into the government might further press the PCI toward a moderate line, if not a "rupture with the Soviet Union."[112]

Enlisting the PCI to the Western cause in the 1960s may have been a pipe dream; but the idea of subduing its revolutionary stance in order to further split the communist movement was notable. Togliatti certainly sensed the danger of being ostracized, as he confided to Nenni: "You are lucky, you are going back to make policy, whereas I, as you can see, will have to continue making propaganda." Since the main financial support for the Socialist Party came from U.S. trade unions—the United Automobile Workers in particular[113]—it is no accident that the PCI's political bureau reconsidered previous alarming reports by CGIL leader Di Vittorio, who had first warned about the wedge tactics of Walter and Victor Reuther. Besides appealing to the PSI's desire to maintain unity within the trade union movement, Togliatti insisted on promoting détente, because "a resumption of the Cold War would [have made] it impossible to create a leftist coalition" in Italy.[114] For the PCI correspondent from New York Gianfranco Corsini another way to restore cooperation with the Socialists was to praise in 1963 a Soviet-dominated détente and a compliant Kennedy administration: this image fit the Socialists' (and Corsini's own) perceptions of a progressively milder but not smarter American leadership.[115] But the growing gap between Socialists and Communists had also led party leaders as diverse as Scoccimarro and Amendola to question a possible majority with the PSI, "standard bearer of revisionism."[116] The PCI became isolated in part also because of this self-segregating prejudice.

If political flexibility served Schlesinger's design well, so did diplomacy. Diplomatic maneuvering was extended beyond contacts with Britain's Labor Party. A reform-oriented Vatican, and the "warm, human, friendly, relaxed" Pope John XXIII, who represented that innovation, were key in projecting the image of reform capitalism, the same image the Kennedy administration assumed through its neo-Keynesian approaches. The Church, with its intensified concern for human misery, could undermine the connection the PCI had established between its internal appeal and its influence in the Third World. For that reason, in the spring of 1962, C. D. Jackson urged the Catholic president to "watch Italy" closely. A few months later Kennedy authorized Schlesinger to open a diplomatic channel with the Vatican to monitor the potential connection between the Church's new orientation and the Center-Left in Rome.[117]

Schlesinger not only used diplomacy for domestic purposes in Italy. He also understood the repercussions the Opening to the Left would have on shaping a consensual Europe around reform. As he explained to National Security Adviser McGeorge Bundy, "the success of the Italian experiment ha[d] a larger significance. If a CD-Socialist coalition [could] work in Italy, it [could] very likely provide an important model for France after de Gaulle, Germany after Adenauer, and Spain after Franco." In making these predictions, Schlesinger benefited from feedback from Italian and French leaders. Fanfani had told Harriman that the British Labor Party and also the French Socialists led by Mollet were "anxious to see Nenni's Socialists detach themselves from the Communists." Writing to Charles Bohlen, Assistant Secretary for European Affairs William Tyler reiterated that other European Socialist Parties, or the success of the *apertura* in Italy, could help reverse the trend toward a PCF-SFIO cooperation.[118] The whole Western Left was indeed following a transformation that gradually marginalized the neutralists and favored not only the social democratic factions within the PSI but also the

Sozialdemokratische Partei Deutschland (SPD) in Germany and the Labor Party in Britain.[119]

In fact, an opening to the Left in France seemed likely to turn into an "opening *within* the Left," a Popular Front against de Gaulle. The Parti Socialiste Unifié (PSU) was founded in 1960 to press the SFIO from the left for joint action with the PCF against the presidential regime and the Algerian war. With the March 1962 Evian Accords granting independence to Algeria, de Gaulle declared a referendum for direct presidential suffrage in October. The victory of the *oui* against the opposition of most parties led him to dissolve the National Assembly, and allowed him to win popular endorsement in the ensuing parliamentary elections, which penalized the Left. But the PCF gained considerable ground compared to 1958, while the Socialists retained many of their parliamentary seats only in the runoff ballot, after they decided to enter local arrangements with the Communists. This result pressed them harder to consider cooperation among the Left parties. As late as the fall of 1963, U.S. diplomats described left-wing SFIO leader François Mitterrand as "proud of that [Popular Front] name and of the 1936 experience."[120]

The contentious Fifth Republic, however, could also spur growing pro-Americanism among French public opinion, since the centrist parties, including many Socialists, often distinguished themselves from de Gaulle by posing as true friends of America. That was what Mollet did after the Italian *apertura* was completed, reassuring U.S. diplomats that his cooperation with the PCF in local elections was purely tactical. The PCF's role as the loyal Western guardian of Soviet interests, and Moscow's need to retain that fidelity in the Sino-Soviet split, also relieved the French Socialists: "If Moscow had let the PCF develop more in the image of the [PCI]," Mollet reminded the American officials, the pressure on the SFIO to cooperate could become "intolerable."[121] The SFIO secretary and Mitterrand, as the socialist presidential candidate also backed by the Communists in 1965, kept basing their assessment of a possible center-left coalition on developments in the Italian Left. But Washington rarely questioned the French Socialists' Atlanticism again.

Despite the disappointing results for the Center-Left in the Italian elections of April 1963—and the relative success of the PCI, rising to 25 percent of the vote—President Kennedy finally gave his endorsement to the Opening to the Left. By then Nenni had endorsed the MLF plan, further reassurance of his pro-NATO turn. On a visit to Italy in the summer of 1963, Kennedy met with the socialist leader. Italian politicians who had prided themselves in their pro-Americanism realized with astonishment that the U.S. president had come to terms with a Marxist who had commanded many anti-American campaigns.[122]

But ironically, both the economic miracle and the reformist thrust of the government slowed down beginning at the end of 1963. The main problem, as Schlesinger described it to President Kennedy, was that most DC leaders were keen on using the Opening to the Left to isolate the Communists, not to wage the necessary social reforms. This could reflect poorly on the progressive outlook of the new American administration, also because, Schlesinger wrote, "the hangover from the Luce period has convinced most Italians that we really favor the big business interests." Most DC leaders, for their part, were far more worried than leaders of other European nations about the potentially dire domestic consequences of a hasty détente, which might give too much credit to the Socialists, or even rekindle communist influence. These arguments did dampen the reformist fervor the Kennedy administration nurtured for Italy.[123] By catering to the groups that best would help split Marxist opposition in Italy, the United States gave them leeway to deviate not from NATO but from the reform agenda at home and détente abroad. What helped isolate the PCI temporarily could in fact constitute the prelude to its resurrection.

The importance of American diplomatic maneuvering and pressures for genuine social reform under a center-left Italian government cannot be overstated. Also important was the connection of this purpose to a reformist design for Europe, and even more, to a global design that envisioned similar developments under the Alliance for Progress in Latin America and other reform plans for politically fragile world regions. But the limits of this reformist impulse, the compromises the Kennedy administration was forced to make with local conservative elites, in Italy and elsewhere, must also be emphasized.[124] Those compromises stemmed partly from the usual ability of local elites to derail U.S. plans and partly from Washington's fading confidence that mild dissent could be channeled into Atlanticism. That confidence waned, as America's own sense of "world mission" and its application in Vietnam became globally questioned.

7 REDEFINING OPPRESSION

The 1960s, from Affluence to Youth Protest

Affluence?

Europe's economic miracles were not only about growth, prosperity, and full employment. With the arrival of mass consumption, the diffusion of visual media, and the shaping of a new social order that privileged the private sphere over communal life, the "miracle" also heralded a profound cultural transformation. Starting in the late 1950s, a consumer-oriented culture, in which advertising contributed to socializing the masses more successfully than old patterns of social solidarity, fulfilled the promise of the politics of productivity the United States had transmitted to Europe during the Marshall Plan years. Although the end of the dollar gap and rapid industrialization marked Europe's relative economic emancipation from the United States, the social transformation carried the American label more strongly than in the postwar period. In Italy, a wide, diffused prosperity confirmed patterns of consensus and Americanization, eroding the bases of left-wing support. The "ubiquity of American images," as Stephen Gundle explains, was partly a consequence of internal social imbalances: since Italy "lacked a genuine secular culture," rapid industrialization "created an enormous cultural gap that only ideas, themes, products, and norms of an American origin seemed able to fill." Furthermore, television, reaching remote rural areas, introduced "an ostensibly classless visual culture [that] clearly followed the American pattern." France, at a relatively more advanced stage of secularism and industrialization, experienced the socioeconomic change with fewer traumas. But even with all the confidence and inspiring force of the Gaullist leadership, the fear of cultural Americanization reached a peak during the early 1960s, as testified by the literary surge in defense of the French language (René Etiemble's *Parlez-vous franglais?* was published in 1964) or the widespread admission that the American model of mass consumerism had been finally adopted by French society.[1]

Fear of cultural submersion continued to match the fear of political subservience. In France, the "sociocultural critique gradually suffusing antiAmerican discourse," as Richard Kuisel noted, generated its own counterpoint. Even though French emulation of American mass consumption and mass culture "initially nourished anti-Americanism . . . in the long run

[it] also weakened it."[2] Debates within the French and Italian Communist Parties reveal this contrast between short- and long-term effects. Under further scrutiny, they also elucidate how this contrast, while becoming fully evident in the late 1960s, elicited the Communists' juxtaposition of ideological affirmation and awareness of neocapitalism's potential. This very contradiction, reflecting frictions within the extreme Left, made the Communists' worst fears about the demise of a proletarian outlook under the impact of modernization a self-fulfilling prophecy.

IDENTIFYING NEOCAPITALIST FLAWS

Between the late 1950s and early 1960s, until the escalation of the war in Vietnam, the Communists focused on the social menace of Americanism. French and Italian Communists were unhappy with the European settlement and continued to fight their countries' political and economic transatlantic bonds. But, as we have noted, they had moved toward partial acceptance of European integration. For a short time in the early 1960s, the PCF even acquiesced in France's continued membership in NATO, motivated by its need to form a political agreement with the Socialists. Long preceding the PCI's compromises with Atlanticism, this move was not matched by an adaptation to the new economic realities.

The PCF continued to exceed the PCI in economic orthodoxy, committing itself fully to the pauperization thesis. Despite evidence of improved living standards for the working class, Thorez in 1956 insisted that the workers were being exploited and impoverished (in absolute terms). At its onset in the mid-1950s, the campaign against pauperization was tied to anticolonial protests, which exposed the high cost of maintaining imperial ambitions. It was also combined with the already established cultural battle to defend small business against the monopolies. In this renewed context, that battle was in part an effort to regain popular support among the middle class, which tended to favor empire. This combination made the PCF the main representative of declining sectors in the economy, with strongholds "in cantons of industrial decay and demographic decline." At the intellectual level, the tradition of individualism, a component of French identity that the Left saw threatened mainly by U.S. modernization, favored the party's continuing attachment to the rural life and a precapitalist world. If this attitude contradicted the promise of socialist progress, it served the immediate purpose of resisting American cultural hegemony.[3]

While more flexible toward modernization, the PCI's response was marred by a "prejudicial hostility" toward neocapitalism. Furthermore, Italy remained more permeable than France to Americanization. The externally induced process compelled the party to excoriate the government's collusion and cultural subservience before an already harmful foreign import (since the Christian Democrat establishment adapted the U.S. model to archaic privileges). As Victoria de Grazia has illustrated, the introduction of supermarkets from the late 1950s, most successful in Italy notwithstanding the backwardness of its consumer indicators and its long tradition of small shopkeeping, was the "story of a purposeful, consumer-oriented globalizing capitalism." This transformation worked because the income gaps were higher there than in most of Western Europe, favoring the prospects for chain stores with lower food prices. The process was further assisted by Italy's favorable foreign investment legislation. One major consequence was that by the early 1960s, many of Italy's shopkeepers, "previously labeled as archetypal petit bourgeoisie" and even as supporters of fascism, began "to look to the Communist Party for protection."[4] The PCI welcomed the new struggling peon class. One of the main reasons for the party's initial opposition to the European Economic Community (EEC) was that in an integrated system, in the words of Arturo Colombi, "Italy's small businesses would not be able to compete with the organized foreign monopolies." Communist mayors in the leftist agricultural region of Emilia launched cooperative movements patterned along practices of the nineteenth century.[5]

Both the *ouvriériste* (workerist) tradition and the "petit bourgeois" turns of the two parties were reinforced by their doctrinal pessimism about modern capitalism. Unbridled competition, in this view, had produced a neocapitalism characterized by obsolescence, inefficiency, and superfluity. Reviewing two popular books, Claude Alphandéry's *L'Amérique est-elle trop riche?* (1960) and Claude Julien's *Le nouveau Nouveau monde* (1961), the PCF's journal of international affairs *Démocratie nouvelle* gave a strictly Marxist interpretation of two texts which argued that the main risks of a society based on abundance and consumerism were waste, conformity, unfulfillable desires, and consequent alienation. In fact, the reviewers pointed out, the majority of Americans were impoverished, the country's infrastructure was decrepit, and the disadvantaged groups (the workers, the ethnic minorities, the elderly) received inadequate assistance. Even in its own terms—the myth of rewards for individual initiative—American capitalism was failing: the "monopoly phase," shown by the high number of U.S. mergers, superseded the previous stage of capitalism based on individual entrepreneurship and "genius." Consumerism could be maintained only through wasteful expense on advertising, which surpassed the allocation of resources devoted to education. Neocapitalism also meant a growing tertiary sector, with consequent "hypertrophy of numerous unproductive services." Manufacturing, according to this "workerist" assumption, had to be preserved in France against the American transmission of such a "huge dissipation of human energy." The other danger was that America was clearly imposing a "catégorielle" (sectorial) view of trade unionism.[6]

Both French and Italian Communists highlighted the phony and insidious nature of neocapitalism. Intellectuals from both parties attacked the human relations management method, then being established in U.S. industry. This innovation perfected Fordist techniques by advancing mutual comprehension between management and labor. It included not only "fatter paychecks" but also a whole series of improvements in the working environment intended to narrow social gaps. Informality pervaded the social intercourse, workers and employers had lunch together, psychologists helped workers improve their satisfaction and performance, a whole team spirit—with intramural sports, for example—was encouraged for the same purposes. The theory was emblematic of the "myth of a prosperous and happy America," as the Italian communist reporter Elsa Bergamaschi argued in 1956. It was a fraudulent practice, she added, for the higher salaries of the specialized workforce resulted in higher productivity and higher profits, while also concealing the lower wages paid to the average worker.[7] The fact that in some industries workers became stockholders was not new, as the PCF's economic expert Henri Claude noted in a *Nouvelle critique* article in 1957: it had been tried in the 1920s, and it had collapsed with, and perhaps contributed to, the 1929 crash.[8] Furthermore, American capitalism could afford to preserve social peace at home thanks to its repressive tactics abroad, as in Guatemala or Iran. The very *in-group* solidarity encouraged by the theory, Bergamaschi pointed out, needed to evoke a competitive strain with the *other-group*: "The more the tension is directed on the outside against the stranger—the *enemy*, as in wartime—the stronger the solidity of the group is." The human relations approach thus not only perpetuated the "reduction of the worker to a tamed gorilla," according to the Gramscian definition; it also reflected the persistence of cutthroat competition at home and aggression abroad.[9]

Reiterating that monopoly capitalism was dependent on imperialism also helped highlight the United States' increasing vulnerability. America "appeared" rich, according to Jacqueline Vernes, because its imperialism enabled it to extract resources from developing countries. But while "America [was] rich, all the Americans [were] not." As Bergamaschi had argued, the American monopolies could concede a marginal increase in living standards to their most qualified workers only by exploiting workers in developing countries.[10] In any case, both parties optimistically concluded, imperialism, even in its neocolonial phase, was on the decline. The United States, facing growing resistance abroad, further shortchanged itself by overspending in the military sector and contradicting the requirements of its consumer economy.

This analysis was paralleled with a renewed faith in Soviet progress, inspired by the dream of plenty revived by Nikita Khrushchev. Although Lenin and Stalin had made mistakes, they "rarely allowed their emotions to determine their revolutionary priorities." Khrushchev's greatest mistake was to challenge the United States on its own terms: in the late 1950s he launched the slogan "'catch up and surpass America' as the cornerstone of the construction of Communism over the next twenty years." His predecessors had never allowed communism to be judged other than by its own criteria. Now the Russians began to compare their standards of living with those of the Americans.[11] Khrushchev's revolutionary romanticism may not have affected the French and Italian Communists when the Soviet leader bragged about nuclear weapons, given the two parties' continued reliance on pacifism to extend their popular appeal. But when he talked about competition with capitalism, he did catch their imagination. French and Italian communist press kept repeating like a mantra that, as Pierre Lefranc put it, "we are approaching the moment of truth, when the first socialist country is going to catch up and overtake the first capitalist country." New discoveries in the field of automation also revived the contrast between the job-killing machines in the capitalist West and technology at the workers' service in the Soviet dreamland. In a system not subordinate to the law of profit, the two parties' economic experts argued, unemployment was virtually impossible, and automated factories brought material *and* cultural improvement to the masses: Soviet workers benefited from higher productivity, growing salaries, and opportunities in technical education. Even the Vatican's 1961 encyclical *Mater et Magistra*, calling for greater social welfare, deploring the arms race and economic disparities among nations, appeared to both parties a serendipitous admission of capitalism's shortcomings, and an implied concession to the superiority of the Soviet system.[12]

These Soviet idealizations now seemed rhetorical or artificial to many Italian and French workers, while the benefits of Western consumerism were tangible. The prospect of individual, not collective, improvement captivated their imagination. The working class, including communist activists in both countries, craved higher individual living standards. Lotteries were becoming the "new opium of the poor." Small FIATS, Citröen 2CVs ("Deux Chevaux"), or Lambretta scooters may not have matched what American workers could afford, but they were luxuries worth many months of the average Italian or French worker's paycheck. Nevertheless, their number rose by the millions. By 1962 Giorgio Amendola, who distinguished himself for his economic expertise and political moderation, and Luciano Romagnoli, who directed the PCI's propaganda section, were among the first to recognize that "higher standards of living" were "genuine developments toward a more democratic society"; they also felt more compelled than ever to rouse the "workers' class consciousness." The PCI, as one of the rising leaders in the directorate, Enrico Berlinguer, exhorted, would not allow "American ideology" and "modernity" to weaken "the sort of political and moral tension, the sort of human spirit without which there cannot be revolutionary action."[13]

For the PCF it was easier to find a culprit outside the mechanisms of neocapitalism: Gaullist charisma. The party's political bureau recognized that the "grand illusions [of welfare inspired by the president] are the greatest obstacle to the unity of the working class." The PCF's persistent *ouvriérisme* not only alienated potential new social strata; it also weakened the very countersociety the party was striving to maintain among workers. There, too, increasingly affluent workers did not resist the lure of consumerism. As has been widely recognized, "the traditional, closed world of the worker, which reinforced an identification with the PCF, . . . slowly dissolved." The new urban landscape, with its anonymous high-rises, privileging "family, personal space, and 'modern' communications (principally television)—in a word 'individualism'—usurped the place of the locality and the party." As in America, people gradually began to shed their identity as workers as they aspired to middle-class status and comforts.[14]

All this communist anachronism seemed to reinvigorate the validity of economic determinism. Nelson A. Rockefeller, head of the International Basic Economy Corporation, which exported the main capital and management for Europe's supermarkets, offered the simple dictum "It is hard to be a Communist with a full belly."[15] But the impact of the periods of economic growth later labeled the Trente Glorieuses in France and the Anni del Miracolo in Italy was not so simple and straightforward.

FIGHTING DOMESTIC DISTORTIONS OF THE AMERICAN MODEL

Whatever went wrong with the pace of modernization in both countries could easily be blamed on the American model, or better, on the regime's distortions of that model. De Gaulle, in the PCF's denunciations, used his self-portrayal as a technocrat to justify his authoritarianism. A "managerial approach" to politics meant "mere demagogy" by a leader who "in fact continued to serve *le grand capital*."[16] Industrial interests, still steeped in old traditions, had little to do with Fordism in both countries. Bergamaschi's comments about Italy could have been applied to the French situation as well: "Unlike the successful American entrepreneur," she wrote, "who always follows the tradition of the pioneer, of the self-made man[,] . . . our successful entrepreneur, having reached a position that entitles him to dominate others, subconsciously is inspired by a model of superior caste that we inherited from centuries of feudalism." The middle-rank managers in both France and Italy would always compensate for the humiliation they suffered in "zealously serving [the *patron*] with a special effort to distinguish themselves from the manual workers." Under these conditions, the cordial, personable atmosphere of the "human relations" approach would at best be translated into conceited and paternalist concessions exacerbating instead of alleviating social hierarchies.[17] In general, Amendola wrote in June 1960, the economic boom was illusory, for "the truth in Italy is that economic development is not translated into a general improvement of the living and working conditions of the laboring masses." Consumerism was a palliative, he concluded, and the gap between the rich and the poor was widening. The PCF began to lump together American imperialism, a German-dominated EEC, and the "imported neocapitalism of the monopolies" as a global system aggravating the pauperization of the French masses.[18]

The PCI kept emphasizing that the country would further suffer from a poor adaptation of the already menacing American model of development. Under Mario Alicata, the party's cultural commission since 1956 had recognized its inadequate job in winning over technicians and mid-level scientific experts. In its effort to reform vocational and scientific schools, the party had urged members not to imitate blindly "positivist Olivettism" (the technocratic movement that took its name from the industry of the Olivetti family, then specializing in typewriters and subsequently in computers), and advocated a mixed system leaving ample room for the humanities.[19] In preparation for the first major economic conference organized by Rome's Gramsci Institute in 1962, the PCI's political bureau concurred that "it was impossible to talk of Italian neocapitalism, because the system is unable to resolve its new contradictions." These contradictions above all exhibited the premature arrival of a consumer culture in a society that did not have the necessary affluence, thus giving rise to unrealistic expectations among the working class. It would have been better to focus on production of necessary goods. The masses may have been captivated by the myths of neocapitalism, but under the paternalist, corporatist rule of the Christian Democrats—commented the PCI's economist Luciano Barca at the first sign of economic slowdown in 1964— this "leap toward advanced capitalism" had been mismanaged. "Sacrificing structural reform for the sake of investments in consumer goods" had made the Italian economy less competitive, and still suffering from low salaries.

The Gramsci Institute's seminars on public industry and U.S. investments in Italy led economist Eugenio Peggio to found the Centro Studi di Politica Economica (CESPE) as part of the Central Committee. Accepting some technocratic elements of neocapitalism, the institute however kept advocating nationalization of several industrial sectors.[20]

At a more deeply cultural level, filmmaker Pier Paolo Pasolini, one of the most anticonformist intellectuals in the PCI, best expressed the conjoined fears from the country's Catholic and communist worlds. In a 1963 television documentary titled *Anger* he commented: "When the classical world has finally been worn out, when all the artisans and peasants have died out, when industry has set up an unstoppable cycle of production and consumption, then history will have ended for us."[21]

Modernization was less traumatic for France, but, contrary to popular expectations that the Gaullist regime would follow an independent course for the nation's economy, instances of American dominance abounded. The partial takeover of automaker Simca by Chrysler Corporation in 1963 caught even the government by surprise. American multinationals had few qualms about laying off French workers without prior notice, as did the company of Remington-Rand France and Frigidaire in 1962. A joint venture negotiated between General Electric and the French computer manufacturer Machines Bull emphasized the ailing French company's technological dependence on the United States. The American presence was condemned in the instant bestseller by Jean-Jacques Servan-Schreiber titled *Le défi américain* (*The American Challenge*) (1967). The book argued that U.S. multinationals took advantage of Europe's integration process to wipe out competition from the continent's smaller businesses. In this premise, if not in its conclusions (that Europe should have responded with the creation of its own multinational conglomerates), it echoed communist denunciations of the EEC's vulnerability to U.S. interests. De Gaulle's main frustrations stemmed from his own earlier actions: on coming to power in 1958, he had tied his own hands by accepting a limited economic sovereignty through the EEC and, even more, by inviting American investments to boost his Fifth Republic. Despite his challenge to the dollar and his restrictive policies against "outside takeovers" in the mid-1960s, by 1967 he finally had to succumb to the need for modernization through American investments. His move was actually subtle, for in welcoming American investors, he helped "close the economic and technological gap with France's competitors in order, one day, to possess the capacity to behave independently." A degree of Americanization as an antidote to American predominance was the cure Servan-Schreiber was charting for Europe at that same time.[22]

Leading the Fédération de la Gauche, François Mitterrand joined the Communists in pursuing the goal of a truly independent Europe not by imitating the U.S. system but by nationalizing several sectors.[23] There was no doubt in the PCF that the Gaullist regime showed its true colors in its continuous merging of French monopolist interests with American ones. De Gaulle's own pursuit of a Paris-Bonn axis, the emerging PCF leader Waldeck Rochet reported to the Central Committee in February 1961, revealed his Atlantic subservience behind a veneer of nationalist rhetoric. His veto of Great Britain's adherence to the EEC in 1963 exposed intra-imperialist rivalries, but it also accentuated France's economic subordination to Germany and the United States. Even through the trade and currency battles inaugurated by de Gaulle himself, the United States used its influence over the EEC to assert its role as "gendarme du monde capitaliste." As I have noted, Casanova and Servin were expelled from the party for arguing that de Gaulle's nationalism showed signs of genuine emancipation from the United States.[24] After Servan-Schreiber's book, it appeared manifest to the party economists that European unity was necessary against U.S. predominance, but clearly had to come under the auspices of socialist cohesion—therefore, as a memo drafted for Rochet explained, polycentrism was still unadvisable.[25]

As the French Left found no redeeming qualities in Fordism until the mid-1960s, the American model continued to be studied, more intensely than in Italy, through the prism of its most incisive American critics. Although Sartre had broken with the Communist Party, his *Les Temps modernes* continued to denounce *américanisme*, emphasizing the dangers of conformity, passivity, and alienation. The journal published excerpts from William Whyte's *Organization Man* and David Riesman's *The Lonely Crowd* to prove the point.[26] As in Italy, Christian leftist philosophers such as Jean-Marie Domenach again converged with the Marxists in warning against hollow American efficiency, which revealed a state of human relations between the anxious and the vapid.[27] Jacques Tati's films *Mon oncle* (1958) and *Playtime* (1967) showed how technophobia, as in the 1920s, pervaded important sections of the French intellectual world.

The rapid loss of communal life in both countries did not exclude continuous longing for it. Both France and Italy revived humanism in the throes of a rising technical and consumerist mentality. What distinguished France and Italy was, in the most optimistic self-portraits, the ability to preserve the "art of living" amid mass consumerism and standardization. The *douceur de vivre* or *la dolce vita*, the ideal of a gentle, languid pace of life with all its aesthetic pleasures would coexist with the reckless pace of modernization. This longing extended the odd mixture of fascination with and repulsion toward America, as Federico Fellini's *La dolce vita* illustrated. The contrast is best exemplified both at the intellectual and popular levels by movies such as Jean-Luc Godard's *A bout de souffle* (*Breathless*, 1959) and Dino Risi's *Il sorpasso* (*The Easy Life*, 1962). Both films were about speed, mobility, and prosperity identified with possession of the automobile. They were about freedom *on the road*, in a radical interpretation of the American lifestyle. For Michel Poicard in *A bout de souffle* it is, even more tangibly, the fascination with the American cars he steals, the American actors he imitates, and the American woman he tries to seduce. The lure of absolute freedom and euphoria becomes maximum transgression for the two films' protagonists, who, by breaking all rules in pursuit of their American temptation, find their deaths.[28]

Communist leaders and intellectuals did not indulge in the pursuit of comforts and the hedonism of *la dolce vita*. They still exalted sacrifice and heroic duty over individualism. They nevertheless could profit politically from the new forms of alienation arising in consumerist society. Modern life introduced the relentless rhythms of "stressful America." Writer Luciano Bianciardi was one of Italy's most poignant critics of the economic boom. Gradually shifting to the communist ranks, he explained in 1960, through a character in one of his novels, "Here, we have Americanism without America's advantages. . . . [Stress] in America is multiplied by one thousand times, but at least there, next to tension and fatigue, the individual can have genuine rewards, if nothing else that of feeling part of an enormous world power."[29]

COMMUNIST ADAPTATIONS TO MODERNIZATION

But there were adaptations, too. The PCF modified its pauperist theses in an effort to enlist new social categories emerging from the advanced sectors of industry. Engineers and technicians, party leaders agreed at a summit in November 1961, should be subtracted from the influence of the bourgeoisie. The PCF leaders denounced the *patronat*'s efforts to persuade highly skilled workers that, with their expertise, they, instead of the capital owners, would soon rule the economy. Such capitalist tactics "inspired by the American methods of 'human relations'" had to be refuted with evidence that these workers' "living conditions [were] threatened by the politics of the monopolies favored by the Gaullist regime." "Only by siding with the proletariat," the party directive continued, "would the technicians be able to protect their living standards." This alliance would advance not only individual but also national opportunities. The PCF claimed to be the real steward of progress, for the bourgeoisie, with its "Malthusian" assumptions, "refuse[d] to train a number of engineers sufficient to a modern production system," thus placing "obstacles to the development of the [French] economy's national interest." Rehashing Moscow's rhetoric, the party concluded that the Soviet example proved that socialism would best guarantee the harmonious development of science, economic affluence, and national greatness. For that purpose, the CGT focused on retaining these skilled cadres through control of the newly formed Union des Ingénieurs et Techniciens (UNITEC) and its campaign "to defend national interests against the economic Malthusianism of the monopolies."[30]

Likewise, in Italy, the CGIL's Bruno Trentin urged "undertaking political initiative toward the technicians, given their [growing] weight and influence" in social life. The "corporatist" outlook of the Christian Democratic Left still loomed large. Its leader, Amintore Fanfani, began pursuing control over the state energy industry in 1958. The PCI then mobilized its intellectuals and economists to stress the risks of a technocracy developed under the auspices of a "confessionalist" school system. Reform in scientific research, Alicata noted in 1958, could only be advanced through a secular, democratic turn catering to the public school system.

When university students in both France and Italy began to voice their discontent in 1960–61, the two Communist Parties immediately conjoined their ideological arguments on secularism and democracy with technical issues, such as the need for more vocational schools for the proletariat, or the limits of education controlled by the monopolies. They paid much less attention to emerging existential questions.[31]

The Communists were quick to denounce backwardness, and to adapt the technocratic dream to the socialist one. But, as I have noted, the permanence of traditions also allowed the survival of a sense of community against pressures toward individualism. A certain resistance to change immunized the two countries from thorough Americanization. Small shopkeepers coexisted with supermarket chains; the American accent on method and organization would always be countered by a humanistic identity. The influence of the Church in Italy limited the public's full exposure to the most commercial aspects of consumerism (even television commercials were filtered through comical sketches, or storytelling akin to Italy's theater traditions, in the popular TV program *Carosello*). And the Fordist model was adapted, as in the case of FIAT, to the tradition of the paternalist, family-owned business. Since this cultural filter was more evident in Italy than in France, opinion polls in the two countries showed a divergence on Americanization: by 1962 only 38 percent of French public opinion viewed the U.S. model of capitalism favorably, whereas in Italy 56 percent expressed such admiration.[32]

American diplomats confirmed that consumerism and modernization did not always proceed in lockstep in France and Italy. In both U.S. embassies the consensus was that the poor results of redistributive reform should be blamed for the continued electoral strength of the two Communist Parties. Consumerism was credited for dampening protest and weakening the class consciousness that Communists assiduously tried to reinvigorate. According to the first secretary of the embassy in Rome, John Auchincloss, in late 1961, the PCI's membership had declined mainly because of growing "indifference to participation in political movements." In contrast, Ambassador Reinhardt noted several months later, under the communist banners converged all groups that felt excluded from the economic boom, with demographically declining groups such as sharecroppers and artisans joining the ranks of still dissatisfied workers. "With aid of hindsight," Reinhardt wrote, "it now seems that many people felt sharper desire to protest because they had not shared, at least sufficiently in their view, in economic progress." This discontent reflected "rising expectations" rather than revolutionary fervor. The main communist gains, the American experts pointed out, were not in Italy's industrial triangle of the North, but in their traditional strongholds of central Italy, the "triangle of protest" of Tuscany and Emilia-Romagna, and in the South, where "poverty [was] still extreme." Richard W. Boogaart, the Kansas entrepreneur who first probed Italy for the introduction of chain stores, addressed the problem even more bluntly: "We asked the Italians to push a Cadillac when they are unable to even buy a FIAT."[33]

The situation was more intriguing in France. Each American embassy's semiannual review, from de Gaulle's rise to power through the early 1960s, stressed that the PCF, despite its parliamentary weakness, was still able to mobilize vast "unitary" demonstrations of the Left, especially against the "anachronistic war" in Algeria. But on economic and institutional issues, protest was quite muffled. While, out of fear of being outlawed, the party remained cautious in proclaiming its total opposition to the new regime, it also failed to "convince" even the working class "that de Gaulle was a fascist." In August 1958 the embassy noted that communist sympathizers considered the party's "systematic opposition to a new constitution . . . illogical" and that the working class seemed "more interested in the coming summer vacation." The fact that the right-wing populist movement of former shopkeeper Pierre Poujade had in the late 1950s led the attack against modernization also confused the PCF's rank and file.[34]

But the "aberrations and excesses" of Gaullism could favor an atmosphere of anti-American and antimodernist retrenchment in France. What worried

Washington, as a memorandum from the Policy Planning Council put it in April 1964, was not so much de Gaulle's "disintegrative policy toward NATO" or "his effort to distort the EEC to a Gaullist pattern," for these policies would "fall of their own weight." It was rather the milieu of anachronism, of a grandeur "spirit . . . akin to that voiced in the old crusading slogan of medieval French kings, *Gesta dei per Francos*," that could cause trouble, for it fostered a "popular sentimental tide" that unrealistically equated France's glorious past and its current potential. This analysis exaggerated the old-fashioned nature of the president's nationalism and his "detachment from reality"; but it correctly pointed out that all this emphasis on Frenchness, while helping the country to take pride in its economic progress, could turn America into the scapegoat for all the shortcomings of modernization, feeding a rather indiscriminate, folksy anti-Americanism from which the extreme Left could profit.[35]

What continued to escape U.S. officials and the two Communist Parties alike was that the main source of worker discontent was not "unrealistic" but "rising" expectations. The ideal "revolution of rising expectations" first proffered by the Marshall planners had finally caught hold of them. Beyond the material expectations of the working class, this transformation affected all aspects of life and molded a new cultural dimension that both French and Italian Communists failed to comprehend fully.

Besides the setbacks in the modernization process, the political dimension of anti-Americanism during the Vietnam War helped the PCI and PCF stall the ideological onslaught of consumerism. During this phase the two parties followed a parallel path: they managed to both "internationalize" and "domesticate" issues of anti-Americanism. They used Vietnam to regain their own international prominence and to attack their domestic opponents. But they also failed to see other political and cultural ramifications of the global protest against the Vietnam War.

Vietnam and the Campaign against Imperialism

IN SEARCH OF GLOBAL ANTI-AMERICANISM

The Stockholm movement of the Peace Partisans rapidly lost steam in the late 1950s. Following the first détente under Eisenhower and Khrushchev, and the first Cold War agreements to limit nuclear testing and prevent nuclear proliferation in 1963–64, disarmament per se could no longer command global anti-Americanism. This unsettled the French and Italian Communists at the domestic level. On foreign policy issues, Gian Carlo Pajetta noted at the party's political bureau in early 1960, the "contradictions of the center-left coalition are most intense, but so is our feebleness." "In the country," he added, "we find a vacuum" in response to the peace appeals. That vacuum in France was filled with Gaullist pride—hence the PCF's emphasis on the president's warmongering attitude during the Berlin crisis of 1959–61, and subsequently its denunciation of his plan for a nuclear *force de frappe*.[36]

The effort to revitalize the peace campaign and the unity of the communist movement culminated at the Moscow meeting of eighty-one Communist Parties in November and December 1961. Both the French and the Italian parties sought to reinvigorate their international credentials by trying to cushion the impact of the Sino-Soviet split. The PCF was the more determined of the two partly because, with its parliamentary strength radically reduced between 1958 and 1962, it could not effectively tackle domestic issues, and partly because it struggled to preserve an identity that was revolutionary without the Chinese type of "adventurism" and orthodox without the heavy Soviet bureaucracy. With the PCF insisting on closing ranks against the imperialist offensive, and the PCI purveying the advantages of polycentrism, the Moscow meeting also underlined the two parties' intensified competition for ideological and political prominence in the West.[37] But the international experience of the French and Italian Communists in the 1960s occurred in the context of domestic pressures against Cold War bipolarism, ultimately favoring "polycentrist" options for both parties in the following decade.

Campaigning for disarmament, as Pajetta had suggested, inadequately served the propaganda for all sorts of national independence, in no small measure because the two superpowers had now seized control of the discourse on disarmament,[38] which they retained until the détente of the 1970s. But the struggle against American neocolonialism, as already proven by the PCI's and PCF's attempts at mediation in North Africa during the Suez and Algerian crises, left more room for maneuver. The French Communists in particular claimed credit for France's political transformation on colonial issues that began to take shape in the Arab world. At the birth of the Fifth Republic, the country had launched its own soft approach to the Middle East outside Algeria, an approach which, like Italy's, centered on access to oil, commercial relations, and a mediation role. By the early 1960s, de Gaulle was already shifting from a pro-Israel to a pro-Arab policy. By association, this turn fostered an anti-American posture during the Arab-Israeli war of 1967.[39]

The escalation of the war in Vietnam, however, offered an even better chance to reconcile the themes of peace, communist unity (at least in the West), and anti-Americanism. Togliatti followed his own revolutionary romanticism, conveying to the party leaders in November 1960 that Western communism could find renewed strength by maintaining its contacts with the vibrant Marxist movements "in Africa, Asia, Indonesia, and Japan [*sic*]." Amendola noted that on the issue of peace in Vietnam the PCI and PCF "could find reconciliation."[40] The PCF spearheaded diplomatic and commercial contacts with Vietnam's Party of Workers, sending delegations to Hanoi beginning as early as 1960. The secretary of the Central Committee, Léo Figuères, had already started a close relationship with a trip to Hanoi in 1950. After publishing his report, he was forced to hide from French authorities until the country's withdrawal from Indochina.[41] The first official mission to Vietnam by the Italian Communists occurred only in the spring of 1965. But the PCI, according to Pajetta, who headed that delegation, was the Western party that Ho Chi Minh held in highest regard, thanks to the doctrine of "unity within diversity," which helped Hanoi fend off pressure from Moscow and Beijing. It was by emphasizing the theme of peace, more than that of independence—Pajetta reported to his comrades—that the Western Communists would best serve Hanoi's cause, and extend the appeal to political forces that did "not identify with North Vietnam." The PCF had by then become more belligerent than its Italian counterpart, stressing the need to "fight back" against U.S. imperialism. Confirming the party's unflinching pro-Sovietism, Figuères noted in *Cahiers du communisme* the need to reiterate that it was "not the U.S.S.R. that made war here and there," and that it was "in the nature of the American imperialists to wage such wars."[42]

North Vietnam became an investment in every sense for both parties. The financial assistance they sent to Hanoi and to the National Liberation Front quickly soared. The range of material included medical supplies, clothing, farm equipment, and bicycles. Through imaginative fund-raising campaigns, such as the 1966 "Opération milliard," and, in 1968, "Un bateau pour le Vietnam," the French Communists collected money from party members and from small businesses. This aid also aimed at building a solid base for France's trade with Asia's communist regimes. In various meetings with Le Duc Tho in the summer of 1965, Waldeck Rochet proposed that these economic contacts should be formalized through trade agreements with the French government. This, he added, would help redirect de Gaulle's opposition to the war toward "mutually advantageous commercial, scientific, and cultural relations."[43] By early 1968 the PCF had also institutionalized its assistance to Vietnam with "National Action Committees for the Support of Victory of the Vietnamese People." The party thus not only stepped up aid but also embraced Moscow's hardened position, which called more for victory than a peace settlement.[44]

More important than the material investment in North Vietnam's success was the investment in "credibility," which, for French and Italian Communists mirrored the credibility issue that had induced the United States to intervene in Indochina. Seeking status within the international communist movement, both parties summoned a "united action against imperialism," blaming internal divisions on China's "adventurism."[45] Mediation efforts sometimes included the enemy camp. Confirming the renewed prestige accorded to the PCI, in 1966 Pope Paul VI established an informal diplomatic contact with North Vietnam through Berlinguer and other party leaders. In Berlinguer's case, as in Georges Marchais's, it also became a matter of personal prestige: by assuming an international profile through their struggle against Western imperialism, the two men surged to the leadership of their parties.[46]

Communist unity against American imperialism and containment of the pro-Chinese positions were paramount for the two parties' self-promotion in another important respect. Third World nationalism, best represented by the Vietnam War, may have rekindled revolutionary hopes among Western radicals, but it also presented a series of problems for the historical Left. Various fringe groups, from Trotskyists to Maoists, captivated important sections of the New Left in academic circles, and quickly pointed out the complacency and increasing irrelevance of the Soviet Union as well as of the traditional European proletariat, the main constituency for both the PCI and the PCF.

Another problem was that violent upheaval in the Third World undermined the pacifist designs of the Western communist establishment. While relishing his role as diplomatic agent serving the cause of peace, Berlinguer also, was the first to express concern, in 1965, that the Vietnam War was likely to arrest the process of détente. Behind Vietnam, there was also China, which used its own record of past suffering at the hands of *all* Western imperialism. Being "the most oppressed" among the non-Western nations, China claimed to be the most authentically revolutionary. To be sure, it was exhilarating and inspiring for a relatively powerless country like Italy that Vietnam, a "Third World David," had taken on the "Yankee Goliath."[47] But that satisfaction too was self-serving, nourishing the hope that Vietnam would bring down the whole NATO edifice in Europe by 1969, the date of the treaty's expected renewal, and open the path for an independent Europe, comprising East and West under true "collective security." At the end of 1966, the PCI directorate split: Ingrao and the leaders of the party's youth federation (Federazione Giovanile Comunista Italiana [FGCI]), Claudio Petruccioli and Achille Occhetto, emphasized the need for a world communist conference that would show the interplay of Third World and European affairs; the moderate Giorgio Napolitano and Gerardo Chiaromonte preferred a meeting of the European parties only, to reiterate the "unity within diversity" principle against China's hegemonic designs over Vietnam using its extremist anti-American position.[48]

Protesting the Vietnam War did not divert the French or Italian Communists from their Eurocentric priorities, which it actually served. The path to a genuine European third force had to be preceded by the achievement of full national independence. Furthermore, nationalism and renewed pacifism needed to be reconnected. Warning of the Vietnam War's possible escalation into nuclear warfare and a global conflict helped the Western Communists establish that connection. They believed that America's ill-concealed weakness and its recklessness were two sides of the same coin. By early 1965 the PCI already perceived a declining United States entering a quagmire and dragging the rest of the Western world, at least economically, into the Vietnamese "swamps." Supporting national independence for Vietnam meant supporting world peace, according to PCF reporter Georges Girard, and defending French sovereignty, too. In the aftermath of France's withdrawal from the North Atlantic Organization in 1966, it was essential that the PCF insist on withdrawal from the Western alliance altogether. Peace and nationalism became indistinguishable from each other in the equation of Vietnamese and French independence.[49]

Escalation and threat to national independence could come only as a consequence of U.S. actions and designs. Starting from the Johnson administration's actions against the newly established radical regime in the Dominican Republic in 1965, communist propaganda obsessively referred to the "aggressive Atlantic-American imperialism." The PCI modified the initiative for a European conference, finally summoning a meeting of all leftist parties in the Mediterranean region in the aftermath of Israel's victory over the Arab nations in the war of June 1967. Participants in the meeting, which took place in Rome the following April, warned that U.S. assistance to Israel and increasing involvement in the Middle East might transform the Mediterranean "into a potentially explosive new front" of possible confrontation between the U.S. Sixth Fleet and the newly introduced Soviet naval units.[50]

Once most liberals made pacifism part of their renewed attention to the developing world and its anti-imperialist surge, Western Communists could also reclaim the lead in the "peace offensive." Pacifism became more and more integral to their identity, mainly because it extended their appeal beyond their ranks. Significantly, the PCI used its increasing autonomy from Moscow to rekindle its anti-Americanism as well, and invoke a genuine European third force. That stance became more evident in 1968, when both the French and Italian Communists initially condemned the Soviet repression of the Prague Spring movement in Czechoslovakia.[51]

De Gaulle himself had turned peace into an instrument of grandeur. His criticism of Vietnam, his ability to redeem France from previous American criticism and to retort that Washington now failed to understand Third World nationalism, became his greatest challenge to U.S. dominance of the alliance.[52] This obviously preempted the French Communists' own anti-American appeal. But the PCF strove to take credit for this political turn in the same way that, with the PCI, it claimed credit for the Vatican's endorsement of welfare and pacifism. The party's political bureau, however, conscious of de Gaulle's strong Catholic following, made an important distinction between established Church and Catholic masses. In May 1966 it therefore reprimanded Garaudy for calling for dialogue with the Church instead of just with Catholic workers. As for de Gaulle's decision to withdraw from NATO, the party insisted on viewing it through a Leninist prism: it was to be appreciated but also explained and exploited as a sign of the mounting inter-imperialist conflict; for the president's move was mainly "intended to protect French monopolies."[53]

Pacifism and polycentrism had thus received a boost from this solidarity with Third World struggles. This turn, Berlinguer argued from 1964 on, marked the next stage in Europe's "emancipation from American imperialism," and even a "new diplomatic style" reflecting Europe's retreat from the use of military means.[54] For the first time, pacifism seemed to have an actual effect on international policies, so much that the PCI leadership gave it a large share of the credit for stymieing U.S. military might.[55] The distinction between Europe's "soft power" (in today's terms) and the American military-industrial complex reflected national pride. Better still, that pride gave renewed weight in world affairs to those opposition forces presumably representing the true national will in each European country.[56]

VIETNAM AND THE EEC

By the late 1960s the PCI had begun to refer to the conjunction between its fight against "imperialism" in support of North Vietnam and its European policy as "new internationalism," connecting with the Social Democrats of Sweden and West Germany. Through a reevaluation of Western European integration, most PCI leaders insisted, the Western Communist Parties could get recognition and win more control in their parliaments. For the PCI especially, this "Europeanism" reflected its own effort to transform détente into a vehicle for European emancipation from *both* superpowers. According to the party's main champion of rapprochement with the European Economic

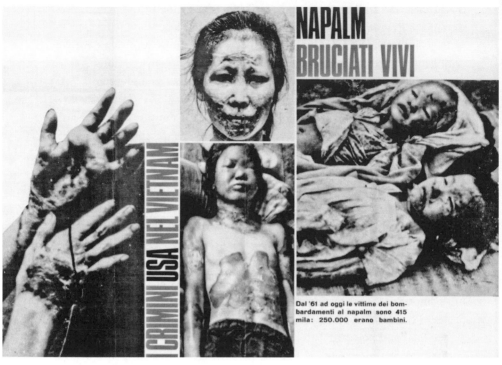

"American crimes in Vietnam. Napalm. Burnt alive. Since 1961 there have been 415,000 victims of napalm. 250,000 of them were children." The PCI's campaign against the Vietnam War. Courtesy Fondazione Istituto Gramsci Emilia Romagna, Bologna.

Community, Giorgio Amendola, Western integration would proceed anyway without a substantial leftist presence. To subvert the process from within, he suggested from as early as 1962, the party needed to propose the "democratic alternative" (state planning) to the industrial choices of the EEC, which favored monopolies. The party's chief economic expert, Eugenio Peggio, was also persuaded that the Common Market would help Italy accelerate its own modernization, provided it remained independent from American multinational corporations. By the end of the decade, Amendola became convinced that the Soviet repression of the Prague Spring movement in August 1968 had further improved the chances for a genuine European third force between the two superpowers. Thanks to its support of emancipation movements worldwide, Gerardo Chiaromonte had earlier emphasized, the Western European Left could secure a leading role in this third force.[57]

In 1969 the inflation induced by the Vietnam War had become the main factor in the global capitalist crisis. Amendola, aided by Peggio's analyses, reiterated the need to focus on the EEC. If truly integrated and extended to countries that coveted membership—Britain, Sweden, but also Yugoslavia and Hungary—the Common Market could actually better divorce itself from the discredited Bretton Woods system.[58] That same year, the PCI was the first among Europe's Communist Parties to have its deputies appointed at the Strasbourg parliament.

While not sold on the importance of the European Community per se, the PCF was in fact no less Eurocentric than its Italian counterpart. Much of the U.S. imperialist thrust, Waldeck Rochet argued at the end of 1965, was aimed not mainly at the Caribbean or Southeast Asia but at "reinforcing the Washington-Bonn axis." Two years later, the party directorate, skeptical about the steps toward recognition of the Eastern regimes by German Chancellor Kurt Kiesinger, insisted that Bonn, aided by the Americans, was pursuing the "liquidation" of the East German republic and the possession of nuclear weapons. But, like their Italian comrades, the French Communists concluded that, with the United States isolated in Western public opinion, it was time to turn the European tide against NATO and in favor of true détente and true continental integration.[59] The PCF, while far from endorsing the "third force" that Amendola or Chiaromonte began to accept, for the first time took some distance from Moscow. Shortly before the Soviets crushed the Prague Spring, the French Communists were the first to suggest a meeting of all European Communist Parties to avert the Soviet action.[60] While this confirmed the party's self-assigned mediation role within the communist movement, it also reasserted the main initiative of that movement in the West and took a critical stance against both blocs. For the PCF, however, this first squabble with Moscow remained tempered as well as temporary. The party rather reiterated the need to emancipate France from its exclusive relationship with Germany (the lynchpin of the Gaullist European policy) and to erase French subjugation, through the EEC, to U.S. industrial "monopolies."[61]

Despite the emphasis on a common Europe built around a collective security system, Communists on both sides of the Alps concurred with the Gaullist vision of a Europe of nations, for the movement toward supranationality could have hindered each member state's ability to conduct economic planning, and to break up NATO. For this last reason, too, it was crucial, Luigi Longo and Waldeck Rochet asserted during their summits in 1965 and 1966, to forge a new European unity around public opposition to the Vietnam War.[62]

INTERPLAY WITH DOMESTIC POLITICS

For all the energy devoted to their international profile, the main targets of both the PCI and the PCF remained primarily domestic. Their antiwar campaigns, in this sense, centered on the deleterious interplay between domestic and international affairs under U.S. dominance.

Solidarity with North Vietnam became an absolute necessity for the PCF from a domestic point of view. It was both a complement and a counterpoint to de Gaulle's anti-Vietnam policy. Trying to merge both intentions, and to expose inter-imperialist contradictions, the PCF contradicted itself: de Gaulle did end up taking the main credit for an independent position vis-à-vis the United States. The Communists' major hope lay in full cooperation with the Socialists on these issues. The SFIO did not associate itself with the antiwar demonstrations, and it was even more lukewarm on the threat of a rising American role in the Middle East. But at least it concurred with the PCF that the United States must halt its bombing of North Vietnam as a precondition for negotiations.[63] This position at first seemed closer to that of the French president. But the student movement's strident anti-Americanism in 1968 pressed de Gaulle to change direction and mend fences with Washington.[64] That was also why the PCF continued to make anti-Americanism its main raison d'être: anti-Americanism corroborated the party's orthodoxy and served its tactics to harness the youth movement, and it finally drove a wedge between the Socialists and the increasingly Atlanticist de Gaulle.

The head of the PCI's propaganda section in the late 1960s, Achille Occhetto, made no mystery of the goals of the anti–Vietnam War campaign as the 1968 general elections approached: through it, the PCI sought to "nail the Christian Democrats to their coresponsibility." The DC's silence on that issue revealed its "strongest complicity with the warmongering forces." Moreover, the Christian Democrats' support of American aggression was manifest in their support of NATO bases and of the crumbling Bretton Woods system pegged on an inflationary dollar. For Occhetto it was crucial to refute the Christian Democratic Party's "interclassist" appeal, pointing out that its cooperation with the United States, particularly through secret services from both sides, showed its "recurrent authoritarian vein." The Italian democracy was mortgaged on the same type of collusion Washington might use with Third World countries—hence, the young communist leader concluded, the importance of relating solidarity with Vietnam with the campaign against American interference in Italian affairs.[65]

The attack on the Christian Democrats was also instrumental in dividing the center-left coalition. From as early as 1965, Longo had recognized that the DC-PSI coalition "must not be attacked frontally" on domestic issues; rather, the Socialists' opposition to the Vietnam War and their need for more autonomy on international affairs could be exploited, showing that their "socialdemocratization [sic] was not yet completed." Two years later,

Amendola and Pajetta insisted on dropping the characterization of the DC as a "partito americano" from PCI propaganda, because there was still the possibility of a "common front not only with neutralist forces within the PSI, but also with Catholic pacifism." The Christian Democrats were especially dumbfounded by the increased U.S. support of Israel. The pro-Arab agenda of the government's "Mediterranean vocation," and the pacifist orientation of Catholic leaders such as Giorgio La Pira, could help the PCI soften at least the DC's pro-NATO position.[66]

The interplay between domestic and foreign policies favored the PCI for economic reasons as well. Industrial growth in France—the *Trente Glorieuses*—reached a peak in 1965–67, while the Italian economic miracle started fading in those same years. This difference allowed the already strong de Gaulle to garner consensus and take an increasingly autonomous stance in foreign policy far more easily than the Italian center-left coalition. Only with the 1968 events at home and in Czechoslovakia would the Gaullist grandeur policy be undermined.

The campaign against the Vietnam War brought the PCI and PCF back into the establishment, broadening their appeal on the center-left with their accent on a European third force, nationalism, and pacifism. Protesting the war also gave them control of the streets. Vietnam was the theme, the rallying point that apparently allowed them to bridge establishment and anti-establishment forces. In fact, the two parties straddled the two positions and contradicted themselves. They remained too radical for mainstream Italian and French societies and turned out to be too stifled, ingrained, and old-fashioned for the new radicals.

On Vietnam, the leader of the FGCI, Claudio Petruccioli, emphasized in April 1968, the whole Left and all generations "would find unity."[67] In fact, the traditional Left, trying to reach out to Catholic pacifism, often found itself outflanked by the more vocally anti-imperialist groups of the extra-parliamentary Left. When Party Secretary Longo met with student rebels that same week, the young militant leaders Luigi Moretti and Oreste Scalzone expressed their disappointment with an older generation that failed to understand "decisive revolutionary developments." These included the war in Vietnam, which needed to be interpreted "not merely within a pacifist endeavor."[68]

The PCF kept calling for victory in Vietnam. After a visit to Hanoi led by Waldeck Rochet, the party secretariat endorsed the militant "base committees," which increased French activism in favor of Ho Chi Minh. But this was also in part a response to students' expectations that the party would step beyond its "tamed" solidarity with Third World struggles.[69] Like their Italian cohorts, the French students idolized Ho Chi Minh and Che Guevara in a revival of revolutionary romanticism.

Pacifism nevertheless still seemed to hold a particular advantage: that of corroborating street protest with intellectual credentials. Just as in the 1950s, opposing war and imperialism offered the French and Italian Communist Parties the opportunity to strengthen ties with intellectuals. Icons who remained outside the two parties, such as Jean-Paul Sartre and Alberto Moravia, posed as spokesmen for the international youth protest against the war. Moravia joined other intellectuals from communist and liberal ranks, such as Alberto Asor Rosa, Goffredo Parise, and Paolo Spriano, in reportage trips to China and Cuba. They particularly contributed to the surging of the Castroist myth among the Italian youth.[70] The PCF more actively pursued intellectual support for the North Vietnamese cause. This in part was a reaction to the intellectuals' increasing sympathy for de Gaulle, as witnessed by the conversion of the self-named Groupe de 29 from opposition to endorsement of his critical stance on NATO. In May 1966 the party helped the Paris intelligentsia organize six public debates titled *Six heures pour le Vietnam*. The creation of the network of "Comités Vietnam de base" also owed much to the efforts of communist intellectuals. In 1967, Sartre added luster to the movement by chairing the Russell Tribunal on Vietnam, which found the United States guilty of genocide. The intellectual mobilization reached its apogee the following March, with the "Journée des intellectuels pour le Vietnam," which featured, among others, Sartre, de Beauvoir, Mauriac, Aragon, Vercors, and Picasso.[71]

For many of these intellectuals Third World revolutionary romanticism was as captivating as it was for students. Sartre since 1956 had veered away from the bureaucratized, inert, repressive Soviet system and had lent his powerful voice to anticolonial causes, starting with the Algerian independence movement. His preface to FLN advocate Frantz Fanon's *The Wretched of the Earth* called for "revolutionary violence" against the "violence of colonialism." His new revolutionary heroes were Castro, Ho Chi Minh, and, within the Soviet Union, the writers and artists who became known as "oppositionists" fighting the Stalinist heritage. By the late 1960s, Sartre conceived a new role for the intellectual, who, following the Chinese model more than the Gramscian one, worked closely with those in the struggle rather than just lending his stage presence. Régis Debray, after his days at the Ecole Normale Supérieure, actively participated in pro-Cuban Third World revolutionary politics. As many writers have acknowledged, this fascination with Third World socialist experiments came to an end by the early 1970s, with the increasing Sovietization of Castroist regimes, including in Cuba itself.[72] Before this happened, the convergence of bohemian and extremist attitudes of prominent intellectuals had already backfired on the French and Italian Communist Parties at the peak of the students' drive against the establishment.

U.S. Reactions: Understanding the Limits of the Antiwar Protest

Recent accounts of Lyndon Johnson suggest that, being a master of Senate rules and tactics, the president was in the best position to understand the interplay between domestic and international policies in the United States *and* elsewhere. But this adeptness was counterbalanced by his feeble grasp of foreign policy and his provincial approach to the world. We are reminded that LBJ "disliked meeting with foreign diplomats" and that National Security Advisor McGeorge Bundy "had to plead with the president to spend an hour a week doing so."[73] Johnson's understanding of diplomacy's ability to influence domestic politics in Europe thus suffered from his intermittent interest in those affairs. But this detachment was in turn compensated in France and Italy by the ambassadorship of two influential diplomats — Charles Bohlen in Paris and G. Frederick Reinhardt in Rome — who frequently drew the attention of the national security establishment to the two still fragile political situations.

Never trusting the parliamentary wrangling of Italian politics, or even the more stabilized situation in the French National Assembly, American diplomats tended to exaggerate the potential appeal of the Communists to left of center groups. Italy's socialist factions led by Nenni and Lombardi were never entirely trustworthy on pro-NATO politics. "The new, different, democratic Italian Communism is a myth," a memorandum from the U.S. embassy commented in late 1964, "but it will continue to impede the slow course of non-Communist left-wing Italian political thought toward democracy." A year later, the special assistant to President Johnson, Jack Valenti, recognized that "Viet Nam [was] the one issue that threaten[ed]" the relationship between Nenni and DC leader Aldo Moro, on which the center-left experiment depended.[74] In France even the stern anticommunist Guy Mollet, late in 1966, had to reassure the American ambassador that his Socialists were "not going to succumb to the PCF's superior organizational capacity"; he underlined that he was "no French Kerensky."[75] As to Catholic pacifism, most top officials in the Johnson administration remained convinced that it could only provide "unconscious assistance" to the Communists, given the presence of "dupes such as Christian Democrat Giorgio La Pira." McGeorge Bundy described the Florence mayor as "a rather fuzzy-minded non-Communist leftist who has been critical of our position in Vietnam." La Pira's trip to Hanoi in 1965 paralleled Berlinguer's efforts toward a peace settlement. Once the Pope himself endorsed these diplomatic moves, the administration became alarmed about a contagious anti-American pacifism in Italy, and among Roman Catholics worldwide.[76]

Just as fuzzy, and far more deleterious, were de Gaulle's own détente moves. At first Washington regarded his "ostensible rapprochement with the Soviet Union" as useful to siphon some votes from the PCF.[77] But when the French president matched the Communists' rhetoric on Vietnam, and, in a speech in Phnom Penh on 1 September 1966, condemned the U.S. strategy as imperialist, Charles Bohlen minced no words about the "anti-American obsession" at the Elysée, the poor taste of such pronouncements, and even the president's "senile" symptoms that might have caused them. By catering too much to anti-American sentiments, it seemed that even the chief guarantor of French stability might ironically destabilize his own regime in favor of the Left. Fortunately for the U.S. government, after a few years of this posturing, and also because of fear of student radicalism, the French public prompted de Gaulle "to ease off on his anti-American[ism]." Mainstream France had become "increasingly worried about [a] policy of going it alone in a world which [had] suddenly become more dangerous."[78] In October 1968, a report from the U.S. Embassy explained that "with [the] Soviets on [the] warpath this is no time to be feuding with [the] U.S.," and that the French government took the role as host to Vietnam negotiations "in part due to the evident unpopularity of 'way out' anti-U.S. rhetoric."[79] The upheaval of 1968 was particularly acute in France, but its ultimate effects on French foreign policy were welcome in Washington.

While a certain alarm persisted about the possible spread of anti-Americanism across the political spectrum, Washington remained reassured that feuds within the Left in both France and Italy would be sufficient to blunt their anti-Vietnam campaigns. The PCF was further limited by Moscow's preference of de Gaulle over Mitterrand, the party's political ally. Even Beijing, frustrated at the PCF's loyalty to Moscow, and with the hope of winning de Gaulle's favor, in 1965 labeled the socialist leader as the "American candidate." For its part, the PCF attacked the Chinese not only out of orthodoxy but also because of the French Communists' desire for a dominant influence in Hanoi.[80]

U.S. officials rather focused on the increasing diplomatic role of the PCI, noting that the Soviet Union would keep using the party "for subversive purposes outside Italy where it may not be convenient or practical for a direct CPSU hand to be taken." The PCI showed greater vulnerability than its

French counterpart in its internal conundrum between proestablishment acceptance and endorsement of the extreme leftist groups. In May 1965, the U.S. embassy noticed the awkward proposal by orthodox party leaders to send volunteers to Vietnam in order to improve their relationship with the "angry young men of [the] PCI left-wing." The emergence of a "New Left" within the party, a radical faction attuned to the Third World revolutionary moment but also opposing the rule of "democratic centralism," led to the "formal appearance of factions," the U.S. embassy concluded, at the party's Twelfth Congress in 1969.[81] The Vietnam issue did create divisions along ideological and generational lines.

These divisions seemed offset by the left-wing Socialists' growing sympathy for Third World causes, as witnessed by Nenni's trip to China in 1969 and by "recurrences of communist seductions" of factions in the PSI and among the Christian Democrats, who hoped for PCI external support of the government. La Pira continued to be the main culprit in U.S. eyes: "To the integralist," a 1966 memo from the embassy read, "the believer in absolute Catholic hegemony, as typified in its most extreme and irresponsible form by Giorgio La Pira, a dialogue with the Communists is no worse than one with the Socialists. To La Pira being a little atheist and anti-clerical is like being a little bit pregnant."[82] Domestic politics then seemed more favorable to the Italian than to the French Communists.

While perturbed by this potential Catholic-communist rapprochement on Third World issues, the national security establishment opted for minimum interference in Italian domestic politics. Conversely, it took a more active role in muffling anti-American sentiments in France. The Italian case fit a general tendency to reduce the U.S. investment in the European allies, shown at the cultural level by the shrinking funds for USIS libraries on the continent.[83] The Italian government had received lavish U.S. assistance until the Opening to the Left. But by the summer of 1965, Bundy admitted that "having begun with a sympathetic view that money might beat the Communists," he had now become "entirely converted" to the view of the late President Kennedy. The United States, the president had concluded shortly before his death, simply had not been "getting [its] full money's worth" due to lack of "energetic administrative leadership" in Italy. In August 1967 the CIA established that "the continuation of a large-scale covert action program in Italy . . . no longer had pertinence." Besides, an intelligence memo added, "the amount of covert assistance the U.S. is prepared to offer in light of other more pressing commitments no longer equates with the amounts needed to have other than peripheral impact on the Italian political scene." The solution to the administrative "feebleness" of the Italian government was, predictably, the continued catering to Rome's concern for appearances. "The Italians are quite sensitive about their position in the European structure," Jack Valenti had earlier reminded Johnson. It was natural for a "nation that once tasted great glory and then settled into decline" to crave such recognition. Therefore the president needed to "underscore the fact that the U.S. consider[ed] Italy to be part of a rectangle of London, Paris, Bonn, Rome." At the same time, any Italian "strong support of the U.S. Vietnam policy" had to be downplayed, lest the Communists make "some hay" from that convergence. As in the 1950s, Washington strove to accommodate the Christian Democrats' pacifist orientation and their hope to be at least acknowledged on Mediterranean affairs.[84]

Gaullist France needed no additional recognition. U.S. officials in Paris rather hoped they could help divide or moderate the Left opposition, ultimately even resorting to tactful dialogue with the Communists themselves. These officials realized that even among French Communist leaders, Italian doctrines and tactics—namely, polycentrism and a gradual acceptance of Western integration—were gaining credence. For this reason above all, the U.S. embassy in 1965 began to propose "discreet contacts" with such leaders, for this might "help break the orthodoxy [of the] PCF." Carefully screened meetings with PCI members had been taking place at the embassy in Rome since the late 1950s. Ambassador Bohlen was confident that contacts with selected French communist leaders would not further harm Washington's fragile entente with de Gaulle and would provide additional knowledge of the Communist Party organization, which, in his description, resembled that of an "American party machine." Embassy contacts with some reporters from L'Humanité began as early as December 1965, during the electoral battle between Mitterrand and de Gaulle.[85] By the summer of 1968, Ambassador Robert Sargent Shriver thought that extending contacts to prominent PCF leaders would further help soften their position on the student unrest and on Moscow's squelching of the Czech liberal movement. The chairman of the communist group at the National Assembly, Robert Ballanger, became an occasional visitor at the embassy. Shriver also reached out to Roger Garaudy, by then, in the ambassador's words, a "Politbureau maverick" who had just visited the United States "in connection with his work in [the] area of a Marxist-Christian dialogue."[86] In France more than in Italy, such dialogue was propitious to U.S. interests, as it drove a deep cleavage among PCF leaders.

Johnson's provincialism was in the final analysis an asset, as it gave ample discretion to U.S. diplomats who insisted on curbing the effects of anti-Vietnam protest in Europe with subtle diplomatic maneuvers rather than propaganda or covert support. But no diplomatic efforts affected the Western Communists as much as the American culture of dissent.

New Rebels and Ambivalent Anti-Americanism

U.S. ICONS AND THE ESTABLISHMENT

During the Vietnam War, an uncertain, subtle, contradictory and no longer naively optimistic America brought ambivalence back to left-wing anti-Americanism in Europe. The Communists' assessments of the United States now echoed and refined their equivocations of the immediate postwar period. The centrality of themes of dissent was manifest, and so was the renewed magnetism for the European Left of characters such as Walt Whitman, William Faulkner, and Ernest Hemingway. The lure of new cultural icons of rebel America, from Bob Dylan to Tom Hayden, was also strong for intellectuals, leaders, and the young from both parties.

Even more tellingly, from the early 1960s, the Communists became captivated by the icons of American mass culture who displayed the core contradictions of American society. The myth of John F. Kennedy was revisited posthumously. Earlier on, that of Marilyn Monroe seemed even more cogent. Most Communists in both France and Italy loved Marilyn Monroe. They especially loved her dead, for they valued her tragic contradictions. After her death, *Rinascita*'s correspondent Gianfranco Corsini commented that her life had been "enlightened by her efforts to be accepted for what she was, and not for a product of a consumerist society." The actress represented the fundamental contradiction of a "society that knows how to unleash the vitality of its components, only to engage them in a violent struggle which leads to its own destruction." Monroe epitomized the isolation and sense of alienation that Paul Goodman detected in a society in which, as Corsini paraphrased, "human nature could not fully develop or even exist." According to some French communist critics, Marilyn the icon was also an iconoclast. There was a beautiful inconsistency in her sexual rebellion against a puritanical and conformist society, because it made eroticism familiar and carefree for conformists as well. But in her "spontaneous defiance" she finally "devoured herself." Such comments met resistance within the two parties' leadership, and there was an intense polemic between new and old intellectuals, new and old guard. The younger group accused the older generation of "intellectual snobbery" toward the cultural ferment in the United States.[87]

Most of those who celebrated the Monroe myth eventually sympathized with the antiestablishment forces, in the East as in the West; most of those who did not understand "the message" preferred an establishment approach, through parliamentary means at home and through controlled reform in the Soviet East. Both groups concurred that mass culture, especially in its American manifestations, confirmed the prospect of an atomized humanity, an easy prey for the most "fascist" aspects of capitalism. The "old guard," however, kept viewing mass culture's potential to forge a "socialized being," in contrast to its commercialized version in the United States, whereas younger intellectuals became increasingly fascinated with subjective and transcending qualities of certain philosophies, such as existentialism or situationism, and with the novel elements of the American high and "pop" culture of dissent.

It was more difficult to hold unorthodox views regarding American culture in the PCF than in the Italian extreme Left. And yet the French party, mourning the death of one of its historic leaders, Pierre Courtade, in 1963, significantly noted that one of Courtade's foremost distinctions was his acumen in evaluating the American enemy. A few years earlier he had opposed the publication of a satirical booklet titled "Americaneries," arguing boldly that it was essential "to distinguish the American masses from those who waged the American empire." Within "the civilization that generated Lincoln, Whitman, and Franklin Roosevelt," he contended, the people were now simply "unfortunate" in their government.[88]

By the mid-1960s, this had also become the main difficulty faced by Soviet anti-Americanism. Once the American people could be seen as victims of their government's choices, it became increasingly difficult for Moscow to confront the enemy as a civilizational one.[89] At the same time, strategic and economic considerations gradually induced the Soviet Union to strike compromises, or a détente with the very U.S. regime that it officially loathed. As has been amply proven, détente helped the leaders of both superpowers protect their authority, deflecting attention from domestic difficulties or defusing the forces of protest—from Berkeley to Prague—by seizing control of the international peace process and domestic stabilization. Both sides of the Cold War, including China in the midst of its Cultural Revolution, aimed to reintegrate or isolate the antiestablishment pressure from students or dissidents.[90]

For the French and Italian Communists this issue was more complicated, as they continued to straddle their revolutionary and parliamentary traditions and wavered between support of radical protest in the West and East alike and détente at home and abroad. While facing these tactical dilemmas, they were also confronted with deeper questions concerning their own identity and the nature of oppression, which was redefined by the forces of modernization at home and by the protest in the United States.

This redefinition was largely inspired by the youth movement worldwide. The outbreak of unrest in France and Italy, as in most of the advanced industrialized world in the years 1967–69, has been amply analyzed. Several studies have also drawn attention to the long-term causes, both international and domestic, of that explosion. My intention here is rather to highlight, comparatively, the revealing trajectory of promises, hopes, and contradictions expressed by the established Marxist Left in connection with the international, transatlantic dimension of the new protest movements.

Most works have emphasized that the greatest protest mobilization in the Western world challenged the basic assumptions of the postwar order, the West's established institutions, traditional social hierarchies, and even lifestyles. The established Communist Parties were not exempt from criticism. The French and Italian Communists' response was inadequate and retrograde. But several accounts give the PCI partial credit for absorbing significant elements of the new cultural and political ferment. An almost equally strong consensus has shown that, after all, the youth movements, in France especially, were in fact limited, Marxist in tone, but deeply libertarian in aspirations, and that they were relatively soon reabsorbed in the ranks of the consumerist bourgeoisie. As one critic of this thesis put it, these works concluded that "today's capitalist society, far from representing the derailment or failure of [this movement's] aspirations, instead represents the accomplishment of its deepest desires."[91]

What needs to be clarified is the deep correlation between the two spheres, that the Communists' self-perception in response to the youth movement and the transatlantic discourse on oppression proved the extent of American influence.[92] This is not to reduce the complexity of the 1960s protest movements to the issue of Americanization. Nor do I mean to reiterate the argument in its well-known cultural terms: that a "transatlantic counterculture," drawing together the young, the intellectuals, and the new feminists from Europe and America against the previous age of conformity, fully emerged in those years; and that America provided these groups with the main values and metaphors to wage their cultural struggle against the traditionalist and Atlanticist political elite. Following my main thread, I seek to expose the complex interconnections between leadership and pressures from below, between the political, cultural, and diplomatic dimensions, even of developments that might seem to elude those links.

As in the United States, most radical students in Europe attributed to the university, the central institution for organizing, evaluating, and transmitting knowledge, a crucial role in bringing about change. But, whereas in the United States a predominantly affluent student body demanded political participation per se (the free speech movement), in Italy and France discontent was deeply rooted in material need as well. The two countries' university systems were ill-suited to the demands of their now advanced capitalist economies—educated unemployment and underemployment was common. In the mid-1960s, both Italy's center-left government and the Gaullist regime launched ambitious plans to modernize higher education institutions, consolidating the relationship between university and industry. The militant Left immediately contested these plans for their selective, "rationalizing," and socially elitist aspects. The funding for structures and scholarships remained woefully inadequate. Moreover, these top-down reforms clashed with both traditional humanist elitism and the students' desire for a more democratic higher education. In an age of large corporations and sagging government action the young felt increasingly frustrated with the emphasis on making money and the postponement of pleasures for the sake of a safe career.[93]

The suburban landscape, where several university campuses, such as the one in Nanterre, were located, was far more bleak than American suburbia. It is no wonder that the young generations of France and Italy thought these campuses reflected the mediocrity of an environment that predestined them to the stultifying national bureaucratic system.[94] Moviemakers of the economic miracle era, from Jean-Luc Godard to Federico Fellini and Michelangelo Antonioni, abandoned the neorealist nostalgic view of old city life, focusing instead on the cold and sterile new urban environment, with its outcasts and its disquieted bourgeoisie.

As in the United States, the young's first defiance was of sexual constraints. For the young generations, social justice became coterminous with personal liberation. In addition to their militancy in the civil rights movement, American students revolted against the strict monitoring of their private behavior. At the University of Florida in 1964, students inaugurated the battle proudly announcing with a banner headline on their newspaper that "no restriction may be placed on student drinking, gambling, sexual activity, or any such private moral decision." In Italy the open student revolt was ignited in 1966 by the authorities' attempt to muzzle a debate at an elite Milan high school over premarital sex and contraception. In Nanterre in 1967 student activist Daniel Cohn-Bendit rose to fame by confronting Gaullist minister François Missoffe over sexual repression and strict campus rules.[95]

All these issues exposed the problem as generational before it became political. Like the American youth that clashed with the generation that had come out of the Great Depression with an accentuated need for career and security, the young French and Italians diverged from the generation that had emerged from the war and the Resistance. Within communist ranks, the leaders who had been groomed by the Resistance faced accusations from the younger members and intellectuals of having adhered to a populist canon that ultimately adapted Marxism to a conformist, bourgeois national culture. The Communists often countered that in fact the new movements were the ones harboring social privilege, in spite of and also because of their cultural experimentalism.

If the Vietnam War, identified with the Cold War establishment, became the main political issue bonding many American students in vocal opposition, a more generalized rejection of colonialism sparked students' political militancy in France and Italy. The Union Nationale des Etudiants de France (UNEF) first challenged the Communist Party line by calling for immediate negotiations with the Algerian FLN in the late 1950s, and eventually adopting the liberation rhetoric of Third World Marxism. Many members of the Union des Etudiants Communistes (UEC) were expelled from the party and went on to form various Trotskyist and Maoist groups, including the prominent Jeunesse Communiste Révolutionnaire (JCR) and the Union des Jeunesses Communistes Marxistes-Léninistes (UJCLM). In their view, the PCF was no more than a new member of "His Gaullist Majesty's opposition."[96]

The rift over Algeria foreshadowed the protest against the Vietnam War as a generational as well as an ideological conflict. Also, through Vietnam, much of the French and Italian youth found inspiration in Maoism and came to idolize Che Guevara. While the PCI focused on issues like Vietnam to restore its initiative in Europe's integration, the youth's anticapitalism often morphed into a generalized hostility to "Westernism." Their utopia became so "Maoist" or "Castroist" that it challenged the agenda of the French and Italian Communists, who still placed Europe, not the Third World, at the center of the anti-imperialist/anti-American campaign. This was as contradictory as America's own domestic dissidence and Third Worldism, in which fascination with China's Cultural Revolution was often mistakenly correlated with demands for "participatory democracy." But it is an exaggeration to argue that a "self-deprecating" process for the West started in the United States and directly inspired Europe's youth. It is more correct to say, as Cesare Pavese did in 1946, that the United States had again turned into "an immense theater where our common drama was played out with greater frankness than elsewhere."[97] A hybrid of Third World myths and American cultural markers in Europe indeed characterized the new radical spirit, which defied the stale politics and bureaucracies at home more decisively than it opposed American imperialism.

What distinguished French and Italian upheavals from the American example was the apparent student-worker juncture. Students' and workers' actions most intensely converged and intersected in the Paris May 1968 protest.
This temporary alliance generated, as Kristin Ross has pointed out, the
"only general insurrection the overdeveloped world has known since World
War II." In Italy, as the movement actually escalated to its own largest wave
of strikes, known as the "Hot Autumn of 1969," the fusion proved perhaps
less immediately intense but more enduring. That endurance confirmed that
in Italy the upheaval was graver than in France, because in the abrupt transition from agrarian to advanced industrial economy "the disruptions of first
generation industrialization overlapped and collided with the discontents of
modernity."[98] It was key for the two Communist Parties to maintain the unrest of this "New Left" within the boundaries of traditional Marxism, and to
prod the youth movement's "workerist" inclination.

By 1968 youth culture had been a major focus of the two parties' attention and concerns for almost a decade. Much of the early discontent of the
European youth found expression in pop culture, and many of its "signifiers"
originated in American culture: from blue jeans to rock 'n' roll, from Hollywood icons such as James Dean to beatnik writers, who reached the top of
best-seller lists in Europe in the early 1960s. Of course, these cultural imports were adapted and blended with national and local pop icons, on radio
programs such as Italy's *Bandiera gialla* and France's *Salut les copains*, in
the films of the *Commedia all'italiana* and the *Nouvelle vague*, both appealing to young audiences.[99] It is hardly surprising that the Communists at first
identified the young generation's "malaise" with the empty ideals, with the
symbolic "rebels without a cause," or even simply with apolitical hedonism.

Optimistically, in 1960 Pajetta asserted that the Italian youth, while dissatisfied with the paternalism of old party politics, was still far more committed politically than the British "teddy boys," the Scandinavian *raggares*,
or the French *blousons noirs*, gangs of escapists who nurtured no significant
ideals and postponed adult life. Inquiring about the fashionable youth of the
various *blousons* groups in early 1960s Paris, the Italian magazine *Vie Nuove*
chastised their "abysmal ignorance," which seemed directly proportional to
their extreme care in attire and was to a large extent induced by their greater
familiarity with American habits and slang than with French spelling. But in
Italy, too, many PCI leaders grew exasperated with the "depoliticization" of a
youth culture so strongly defined by consumerism and banal, mostly "Americanized" music. The young seemingly developed feelings of independence
and irreverence through new musical styles that, in fact, were yet another example of marketed phenomena. According to *Démocratie nouvelle*, the new

musical trends were far from revolutionary, and were in fact "the most comfortable distraction" from politics.[100] But for the PCF, the orchestration was more straightforwardly political: echoing Soviet conspiracy theories on subversive rock 'n' roll, the political bureau insisted that the bourgeoisie deliberately "attempted to bridle the youth and to separate it from older generations, with the intention of weakening the workers movement." By contrast, the party needed "to popularize Soviet successes especially in [the] scientific field, compared to our decline in education, to rally more youth to our side." Pop art received the same criticism as pop music. With unbending faith in the canon of realist art, party critics from both countries sneered at the various "avant-garde" movements, rebellious "only in appearance," according to *Rinascita*, for they "left neocapitalism unscathed." Pop art was "transient, leaving social problems unresolved."[101]

Through the first half of the 1960s, Italian communist leaders recognized that the rejection of discipline, even among communist youth ranks, reflected a healthy rebellion against the "conformist mortification" caused by bourgeois society, and that individual emancipation would occur by eliminating the alienation in everyday life and in personal relations; but they also spurned early attempts of young militants to discuss officially issues relating to personal and sexual relations.[102] The revival of leftist pacifism during the Cuban missile crisis seemed to instill motivation, a cause to defend for progressive young French and Italians, helping the two parties "to get closer to them," as Roland Leroy reported to the PCF's political bureau in 1963. In fact the two Communist Parties distinguished themselves more for their attempts to "inculcate" such commitment in their youth, revealing their own fear that pacifism per se might further "narcotize" the younger generations. As in the times of the Stockholm appeal, those vocal protests needed to be channeled and regimented "at the service of the party," as FGCI leader Occhetto admitted years later.[103]

The youth culture had roots in intellectual debate as much as in popular culture. The origins of this intellectual "heresy" are normally traced back to the beginning of dissidence after the 1956 events. In the years immediately following the Hungarian revolt, the founding of journals with significant titles such as *Nuova Generazione*, *Salut les copains*, and *Giovane critica* expressed the dissatisfaction with the increasingly bureaucratized nature of the two Communist Parties and the consequently stifled artistic and intellectual expressions under their watch. Their outlook was often labeled Trotskyist, but, in their majority, intellectuals fought against standardization and determinism of any sort. Many of them took the cue for this battle liberally from the writings of C. Wright Mills, Paul Goodman, and the theories of the

Frankfurt School. One of the most significant Italian journals representing this dissent, *Quaderni piacentini*, founded in 1962, has been described as a rebellion of "angry young men" against the "mystifying effects of neocapitalism." They attacked reformed capitalism because they were afraid the PCI would be integrated in it. The Gruppo '63, another group of young leftist intellectuals (including Alberto Arbasino, Umberto Eco, and Edoardo Sanguineti), while nominally Marxist, rejected strict ideological guidance. They actually believed that neocapitalism, and even the economic boom, fostered their experimental, "modernist" literature. To them neorealism was obsolete and populist to the extent of actually distorting scientific Marxism.[104] At the same time, some Italian journals, most notably *Quaderni rossi* and *Classe operaia*, attempted to restore authority to the working class and its militancy, and inspired many young radicals to pursue an extraparliamentarian path to the dictatorship of the proletariat.[105]

In France, the origins of a "libertarian" streak, often inconsistently merged with Trotskyist doctrines, can be traced even further back to the "critical communism" of an intellectual like Jean-Pierre Vernant, who flourished in the 1930s and 1940s, or to the systematic critique of the journal *Socialisme ou barbarie*, founded in 1949 by Greek émigré Cornelius Castoriadis. Fervently opposed to the Soviet experience, and considering it no more than another form of class domination by an entrenched bureaucracy, Castoriadis was among those who spawned the next generation's *gauchiste* revolt. Vernant, whose Marxism was balanced by a "tradition of anticolonial enlightenment and socialist republicanism," inaugurated the debate among intellectuals and students, in the throes of the controversy on Algeria in the Communist Left, issuing in October 1958 a document from the self-declared "cellule Sorbonne-Lettres." The document denounced the authoritarian bureaucratization of the PCF, demanding true democratic participation in party decisions and more freedom of expression for the intellectual cadres. Two years earlier, the PCF had created the Union des Etudiants Communistes, with the aim of increasing its influence over intellectuals.[106]

Many of the young Italian intellectuals proclaimed their right to experiment also on the basis of Togliatti's final testimony. The party leader, in his *Yalta Memorandum*, pledged to advance "freedom in intellectual life, . . . free artistic expression, and . . . scientific progress." Among French communist intellectuals the debate also became more open by the mid-1960s. The journals that best reflected this intellectual surge, *La Nouvelle critique* and *Les Lettres françaises*, began to include articles on linguistics, psychoanalysis, aesthetics, the philosophy of structuralism, and the *Annales* school's approach to history. Roger Garaudy's invitation for an opening to progressive

Catholics came in the midst of this eclecticism and against the rigid scientific Marxism, as interpreted by the other most influential thinker in the PCF, Louis Althusser. Similar to Garaudy's appeal was Aragon's call for an official recognition of "creative freedom" for party intellectuals and artists at the Central Committee of Argenteuil in 1966.[107]

Facing a declining membership in the youth communist federations, on the eve of the student revolts of 1967–69, both parties reflected on their "unsatisfactory relationship with the new generations," as a FGCI memorandum of March 1967 put it. The document also commented on the new groups' "vice of extremism and their temptation toward global solutions."[108] Splintering into an archipelago of groups, the various Trotskyist, extremist groups generated more and more militant *groupuscules*, such as Lotta Continua, Avanguardia Operaia, Potere Operaio, the Comité de Liaison des Etudiants Révolutionnaires, and the Liaison des Etudiants Anarchistes. This last one, dominated by Daniel Cohn-Bendit, also gave birth to the Tendence Syndicale Révolutionnaire Fédéraliste. These groups' demand for *autogestion* mixed a libertarian revival with revolutionary discipline. At first, it was not the American cultural identifiers—the New Left in its multiple aspects—but rather the danger of factionalism that worried the communist leadership. The Cultural Revolution in China and this cultural turmoil in Western Europe, Pietro Ingrao explained to the PCI's political bureau in January 1966, brought the same result: a divided Socialist world in the struggle against Western imperialism.[109]

Fascination with Maoism or Third Worldism then needed to be harnessed, and the protest against the Vietnam War needed to be channeled toward demonization of the common enemy, the United States. In 1967 U.S. interference was exposed not only by the revelation of CIA funding of the Congress for Cultural Freedom, but also by the discovery of deals between the Italian secret service SIFAR and the CIA, involving neofascist military circles. Once the enemy was exhibited in its monolithic terms—Occhetto explained to the party's propaganda section in January 1968—once it was shown to have "control over our army, our secret services, our economic, political, and military life," then the party would rediscover its united front. Displaying typical political alchemy, Occhetto recommended that the PCI commemorate Che Guevara, to appeal to the student groups and reiterate its doctrine of "unity within diversity." The French Communists were first to recognize that the media could be used to muster support for the anti-imperialist campaign.[110] If, Occhetto also acknowledged in 1967, the PCI stimulated a less provincial outlook in television broadcasts, it would not only shed its image as a populist party tied to the establishment but also contrast its internationalist cultural approach with the parochial and "synthetic" one of the center-left parties. A concerted propaganda on Vietnam appeared auspicious because it exposed America's flaws, and, the FGCI's Petruccioli insisted, because it would help the youth "acquire a political conscience." Most important perhaps, it could restore, through mobilization of students, the primacy of revolution in the Western world.[111]

It was in this vein that the PCI analyzed the French revolt of May 1968. Once again, France represented one of the most socially and economically advanced Western experiences, Pajetta mused, and thus the threat of a one-dimensional humanity found there its foremost challenge. Furthermore, French centralization, according to Amendola, made the "class enemy more solidly entrenched" there than in Italy, against an equally concentrated industrial and intellectual force. From the standpoint of political tactics, Berlinguer had already argued, the revolt was more logical in France because of an already existing alternative for a coalition of the Left. These views reflected less the PCI's faith in parliamentary tactics than its hopes that revolution would be restored in the countries where neocapitalism was in its final throes. The campus sit-ins in Italy actually preceded the burst of protest at Nanterre in 1967 and were at once strictly coordinated with industrial strikes. The relative delay of neocapitalism in Italy notwithstanding, the PCI's adaptive guidance of the movement, in its leaders' view, would help accelerate revolution, and make Italy's Left as ready to rule as the French Left.[112]

These reflections attested that checking the anticapitalist thrust of the youth rebellion was as crucial as driving its anti-imperialist force. The "radicalization of the movement" according to PCI senator Paolo Bufalini, had to be "guided toward tangible reforms and a broader alliance with the working class." In France, the CGT took a strong role in directing the general strike, especially in the transportation sector, that paralyzed the country during the May events. The party deliberated that, "no matter how romanticized," the students' connection with the workers was the only way to "effectively refute the *gauchistes*' ideas."[113] For all their antihierarchical outlook, students accepted the authority of the working class. The *gauchistes*, as Michael Seidman has recently observed, were "overwhelmingly *ouvrièriste*, trusting that the workers—and no one else—must and would make the revolution." The Italian youth's alliance with the working class, lasting beyond the "Hot Autumn" of 1969, also had a deeper significance: an enduring Gramscian notion of the organic intellectual coexisted with the experimentalism of Gruppo '63 and similar initiatives. This led a minority of students to seek atonement for their bourgeois upbringing by working in factories. But even in Italy's enduring student/worker symbiosis, it soon became clear that the student groups aimed to radicalize industrial conflict and overturn the PCI's dominance of the trade union movement.[114] Moreover, though Marxist in tone, the rebellion harbored anarchist goals. And where the rebellion had its most disruptive potential, in Paris, it was also short-lived and ultimately moderate in its "Marxist" demands: for better conditions in the university and the workplace. It was quite radical, however, in calling for an end to moral censorship and any other limitations in lifestyle.

Perceptive contemporary analysts, such as Alain Touraine, immediately recognized that this was the birth of a "new social movement" in which new class struggles were "emerging and being organized in areas . . . outside the sphere of 'productive' activities: urban life, the management of needs and resources, education." Spontaneous and libertarian, most students were often too hedonistic, or, in one definition, "utopian individualists" to remain wedded to Marxism. In their anticonformist, antihierarchical opposition to consumer society, they challenged both the old regime and the socialist tradition, contributing, according to a widely shared thesis, to "France's final flirtation with socialism."[115]

Intellectuals and students, according to theories stressing their role as a "new working class," were those who now instigated the revolution, in the West as in Czechoslovakia. Higher education no longer created a privileged intellectual elite but instead produced another "subordinate, although highly skilled, proletarian workforce." Blue-collar workers, diminishing in number, also continued to restrict their vision to material improvement. The new class was more inclined to demand qualitative improvements in social life. Western Communists, in Italy especially, seemingly infused a welcome dynamic in class struggle by prizing the role of the intellectual. Sir Isaiah Berlin was closer to the truth when he described the 1960s movements as "the rebellion of the repentant bourgeoisie against the complacent and oppressive proletariat." Castoriadis pointed out that this revolt was about "resocialization"—founded on dreams of revolution, justice, and the search for deep truths—rather than about individualism.[116] But the real subversive motives of the revolt remained the antihierarchical and antirepressive ones. Next to the neo-Marxist tendencies, strong demands for personal and sexual freedoms continued to characterize the student movement in both countries. The May graffiti in Paris echoed Barry Rubin's call to "be realistic, demand the impossible," to "enjoy without obstacles," and to "take your desires for reality." Even the Italian students, conventionally dressed and austere in lifestyle through the first part of the decade, by 1968–69 adopted modes of transgression and anticonformism: long hair, beards, beads, exotic clothing, and, not least, the fight for sexual liberation against the Catholic establishment.[117]

At the peak of the May revolt in Paris, Georges Marchais could not contain his frustration with such distortions of the old socialist tradition. In a *L'Humanité* article he lambasted Cohn-Bendit as a German anarchist from a privileged background and the movement as a bourgeois development with pseudo-revolutionary claims, a psychedelic charade made of "disrupted lectures," "jazz shows, theatrical events," and "walls littered with graffiti." At the following Central Committee held in Nanterre, Rochet insisted that the student movement derived from the workers' class struggle but was not its new guide.[118] The rift between PCF and students thus deepened.

It was no accident that Giorgio Amendola, who led the moderate wing of the PCI, publicly lamented the "resurgence of extremist infantilism" and an anarchic tendency that equated criticism of the Soviet Union with that of American imperialism. In the secret debate within the party's political bureau in June, Amendola urged leaders not to "repeat . . . the same errors as the PCF." He also worried that the students, rather than advancing Maoist sectarianism, might instead, with their defiance "against all intellectual heritage," feed theories about "the end of ideologies." Pier Paolo Pasolini expressed similar concerns in much harsher tones. In a poem addressed to the young rebels that same month, he announced that, unlike "all the journalists in the world," he would not "lick the asses" of these "spoiled brats." In their clash with the authorities, he sympathized with the police, "because the cops are the sons of the poor." The poet moviemaker warned that "the Americans . . . with their stupid flowers, are inventing a 'new' revolutionary language, for their own! . . . But you cannot do it because in Europe we already have one: can you ignore it? Yes you want to ignore it. You ignore it by 'going more to the left' . . . you set aside the only instrument that truly threatens your parents: communism."[119]

This rebuke was too stern even for the most traditional party leaders. But it stirred their fear of losing the patriotic credentials they had so tirelessly earned. One had to be "careful not to accuse the *carabinieri* [the police force of the army] of being fascist," Pajetta had argued at the party bureau in May 1967, in the aftermath of the military coup in Greece. The Communists could "not afford to deprecate the military institutions" and repeat the errors of the Left of the 1920s. The fear of a fascist backlash suffused the party debate through the following years. After the election of Richard Nixon, that fear included the prospect of an increased interaction between U.S. secret services and Italy's right-wing military circles. In May 1969 PCI foreign policy ex-

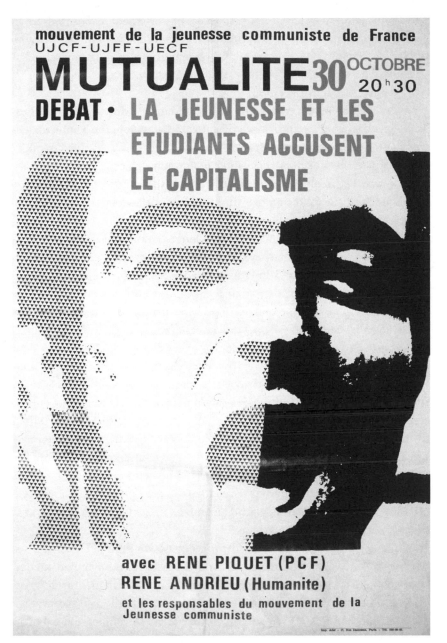

Youth Federation of the French Communist Party poster, 1968. Courtesy
Collection du PCF/Archives départementales de la Seine-Saint-Denis.

pert Carlo Galluzzi underlined that the student movement had caused "NATO circles to plot for an authoritarian state coup."[120] If not from military circles, the backlash could take the shape of terrorist groups from the extreme left or neofascist fringes. The "strategy of tension" started with fascist terrorist bombings in Milan in December 1969.[121]

In France, the reaction from the right could be less drastic but more tangible. Sectarianism, adventurism, and elitism, Rochet told the Nanterre Central Committee, could only serve de Gaulle's right-wing establishment.[122] They justified the president's decisions to summon a massive counterdemonstration waving tricolor flags on the Champs-Elysées on 29 May, to dissolve the parliament the following day, and to call for new elections. In June the PCF was penalized at the polls.

A factionalized Left was bound to challenge the rules of democratic centralism; echoes of American-style participatory democracy mixed with reverberations from events in Prague. PCI Party Secretary Longo recognized that the youth movement was "a struggle against authoritarianism . . . for greater participation of the masses in decision-making . . . both in capitalist and in socialist countries [where] the bureaucratic structure of power tends to suffocate and exclude the individual as well as the group."[123] The student movement, especially in Italy, saw this change as the precursor of true socialism. But by calling for the party to play a mere role of "coordinator" of factory and student councils, it was in fact undermining its Marxist-Leninist essence. Giorgio Napolitano, another leader of the moderates, insisted that, in the students' lexicon, participatory democracy meant "extraparliamentarianism."[124] Democratic centralism in the end could not be given up, because, with a genuine internal debate, the PCI and PCF would have become as factionalized as the other parties. Even the FGCI gave priority to the struggle for unity with the proletariat, gaining members in the following years, but at the price of its ideological cohesion.

While keeping a critical eye on the movements on their left, both parties tried to co-opt them, embracing some of their antiestablishment tactics. Ironically, this was especially true for the more "parliamentarian" PCI. Longo's meeting with the students in May seemingly reinforced the strategy of "attention." In an interview with *Rinascita* in December 1968, Longo showed his Leninist colors, arguing that insurrection was an option, particularly if youth and labor demonstrations continued to be met with violent repression.[125] But both the PCI and the PCF mainly intended to harness the antiestablishment forces. Longo prepared the May meeting to prevent student abstention in the forthcoming elections. The PCF proposed a government of popular democratic unity following the May 1968 events not to endorse the revolutionary tide but to channel it toward the narrow goal of unseating de Gaulle.[126]

Fear that antiestablishment pressures in the West might conjoin with those in the East was also a major reason for the French and Italian Communists' muddled response to the Prague Spring. The revolt in Czechoslovakia was inspired by the highly educated and began with protests by students who wished to improve democratic participation. But for intellectuals there, this meant pluralist democracy. Soon it became clear that "in the East the message of the Sixties was that you could no longer work within the 'system'; in the West there appeared no better choice."[127] This was certainly not what both French and Italian Communists expected when they first condemned the repression. Both parties, and especially the PCF, soon reconsidered, muffling their challenge to the Soviet "establishment"; they also suggested that students' demands for participatory democracy helped feed the mounting Anti-Sovietism in the West.[128]

Intensified Cultural Debate, Intensified Anti-American Ambivalence

The intellectual diaspora was more consequential for both the PCI and the PCF in 1968 than in 1956, *because* of the combined effects of the youth rebellion, the increasing gap between intellectuals and a "complacent proletariat," and events in Prague. Characteristic of left-wing intellectual autonomy in both countries was an amalgam of efforts to "create a more direct and unmediated contact with the people," using such dated instruments as the wall newspaper or the improved *Festival de "L'Unità"* (the annual fund-raising fair of the PCI). Also instrumental was the emergence of the media intellectual, distilling the debate but also highly "mediating" it for the masses. The two parties raised their cultural profile by establishing a dialogue with the new forms of protest that criticized Western models of development and by seemingly coming to terms with an increasingly individualized Western culture that was repelled by totalitarianism.

EXPERIMENTALISM, COUNTERCULTURE, AND AMERICA'S RENEWED CULTURAL APPEAL

In fact, French and Italian Communists faced two far more insidious, and for that reason insurmountable, challenges: from consumerism, and, conversely, from the theories of alienation against the consumerist society that turned upside down the conventional socioeconomic Marxist understanding of revolution. The mid-1960s saw the "exhumation" of the young Marx, the one who accented psychological more than social repression. The new generations took that philosophical turn to justify their emphasis on private desires over collective struggles. Adding fuel to this interpretation was the phenomenal popularity of German philosopher Herbert Marcuse, who, in his book *One-Dimensional Man* (1964), had faulted consumer societies for displacing people's real needs: civic, sexual, and aesthetic pleasures, and the environment. This was too bohemian for the old Left. Both the neo-Marxist and Marcusian challenges reflected the "individualist sensibilities of the age" they failed to comprehend.[129] In a 1966 study provided for the Centre d'Etudes et des Recherches Marxistes, Léo Figuères claimed that intellectuals, dissatisfied with their own "demotion at the service of monopoly capitalism" under de Gaulle, could still be co-opted into the new "technocratic" proletariat. But he also admitted that the "old" proletariat mistrusted intellectuals—a sort of "hard-hat" phenomenon French style, with most rank and file still loyal to the cult of personality and most party intellectuals hopelessly alienated from it.[130]

That alienation rekindled the intellectuals' tendency to compare dissidence in the West with the graver cases of the East. Attention to dissent had started earlier in France than in Italy, with communist intellectual Pierre Daix prefacing the first French edition of Aleksandr Solzhenitsyn's *One Day in the Life of Ivan Denisovich* in 1963. The journal *Les Lettres françaises* accepted dissident contributors from 1965, and its director Louis Aragon shed all his remnant orthodoxy and called the Soviet intervention in Czechoslovakia a "Biafra of the spirit." At the end of 1970 Marchais led the party's censure of the "ecumenical" Roger Garaudy, who had just published *Le grand tournant du socialisme*. The book had added fuel to the polemics within the Left for its denunciation of totalitarian excesses of all kinds, including some of the Latin America's Marxist movements, which, in Marchais's words, were "so bravely fighting their own bourgeoisie and American imperialism." Garaudy's book was also excoriated for its acceptance of the "Marcusian" argument that since the working class had been "integrated" into the "consumer society," it had lost its role as the guide to revolution, now waged by the still "excluded" students and other "social or intellectual outcasts." Garaudy was finally expelled from the PCF after he gave a critical speech at the Nineteenth Party Congress in 1970.[131]

From the ranks of the French New Left, Jean-Paul Sartre actually used his own induction into the student movement and his emphasis on a renewed, more activist role for the intellectual to refine his existentialist outlook. Though inspired by the Chinese, he ended up encouraging the individualist implications of the youth rebellion. Sartre's condemnation of the PCF's handling of the student movement matched his condemnation of Prague:

"Today the Soviet model," he declared, "smothered as it is by a bureaucracy, is no longer viable."[132]

Under the combined effect of existentialism and advanced economic conditions, the countercultural aspects of the youth rebellion held a broader appeal for the Left in France than in Italy. This was also because, with its individualist pathos, the French cultural scene fielded many intellectuals— including, on the left, André Glucksmann, Claude Lefort, Jean-Marie Domenach, Charles Tillon, André Gorz, Julia Kristeva, and Roger Garaudy— who, between the late 1960s and the mid-1970s, passionately embraced the human rights campaigns against the Soviet Union.

The PCI had better absorbed intellectual dissent starting in the mid-1960s. In 1962 the party's cultural commission had been reorganized under the more liberalized Gramsci Institute.[133] This transfer initially secured Togliatti's own reiteration of the Gramscian national popular concept of culture. But the party secretary already felt embattled by not only the intellectuals of Gruppo '63, but even by old rivals, such as Elio Vittorini, Italo Calvino, and Vittorio Sereni, who, with their new literary journal *Menabò*, departed from the neorealist and populist canon. Togliatti tried to blame the new *Age of Malaise* (from the title of a 1962 novel by young writer Dacia Maraini) on the existential problems in "capitalist democracies." Only "in a socialist society," he wrote that year, "is man no longer lonely, estranged, and does humanity become a living unity." But if the intellectual vanguards, Romano Ledda contended, now expressed their "alienation" rather than their role in mediating consensus, then everything in their vision was "split: theory and practice, science and craft, life and culture." Specialization and technocracy would define the new intellectual, who, unlike the "political intellectual" seeking integration "with the productive forces," would be "enslaved to the consumer society."[134] As in France, the Marxist Left in Italy ventured into the new social sciences. It also renewed its fascination with Sartre, who, Mario Alicata wrote in 1964, was a boon to a less "dogmatic, crystallized Marxism."[135]

With Togliatti's death in 1964, much of this feeble connection between orthodoxy and cultural experimentalism began to dissipate. In his *Yalta Memorandum*, as I have noted, the PCI's historic leader seemingly had begun liberalizing intellectual approaches. Under the new cultural chief Rossana Rossanda, the Gramsci Institute advocated experimental directions in the arts, seeking cooperation with Vittorini, Eco, Calvino, and other "anticonformists." At the Eleventh Party Congress in 1966 Rossanda was labeled a "modernist." That meeting also favored Amendola's moderate wing, open to political reform but rigid on cultural standards, against the radical one led by Ingrao, politically orthodox but more receptive to Rossanda's "cultural" experimentalism. This development eventually spawned a New Left group, which, under the initiative of Rossanda, Aldo Natoli, and Lucio Magri, founded the journal *Il manifesto* in 1969, with its peculiar mixture of libertarian and Maoist positions. This group became the first faction to be collectively expelled from the party. Their conviction that the West was ready for revolution and that Russia was also ready for an overhaul could only disturb the diplomatically and politically cautious PCI leadership. "They break everything," Pajetta blurted out at the meeting deciding the expulsion in October. "Then what? They break our balls, that's what they do!"[136]

On mass culture the communist approach also favored tradition. All communist efforts to reform the television and radio broadcasting system in France and Italy catered to populist notions—for example, broadcasting as much neorealism as possible on Italian channels, leveraging the Socialists from within the center-left government coalition.[137] The PCF had first to reckon with an influential literary figure, André Malraux, as de Gaulle's minister of culture. Known for his contempt for American mass culture, Malraux upheld traditional views of high culture. But this only confirmed the PCF's determination to advocate, next to its own elitist defense of national culture, a greater access to the media for the working class.[138] The party press, still agonizing from declines in sales in both countries, continued to veer toward more alluring formats for a mass audience: "The cultural sections of our paper," Alicata told the PCI's directorate in 1965, "are still too difficult and esoteric for the wide public; we need to incorporate more trivia with the serious message of our press."[139] In this case also, the "alienation" the two parties tried to remedy was that between intellectuals and the working class. They wanted to rein in both sides toward Marxist orthodoxy.

More "attuned" to the countercultural trends was radio broadcasting. The PCI's Oggi in Italia station relied on transmitters from Hungary until 1968. Budapest's decision to rescind the contract allowed the Italian stations to detach themselves, according to a party directive, from the "reasons of state in the East," and drove the PCI to adopt the French Communists' solution of using "private radio networks," soon crowding the FM dial, with an increasing youth audience. Just as diversified was the response of the PCI's Associazione Ricreativa Culturale Italiana (ARCI), providing working-class, "intelligent" leisure. ARCI's activities comprised television discussion groups, film screenings, and seminars on subjects ranging from avant-garde literature to Chinese medicine. The organization also sponsored Dario Fo's experimental Nuova Scena theater starting in 1968. But Fo's break with ARCI in 1970 showed the limits of party tolerance for such experiments.[140] In cinema as well the two parties barely tolerated the "self-indulgence" of directors such as Jean-Luc Godard, Alain Resnais, Marco Bellocchio, and Michelangelo Antonioni. Also, although Hollywood experienced a decline in European viewership during the 1960s, the conventions of U.S. cinema were absorbed into French and Italian movies, often with notable adaptations, whether in the *Nouvelle vague* or the spaghetti Westerns. The internationalization of the industry made domestic cinema still dependent on coproductions, with prevalent U.S. financing. This led the communist press to lament the increased dilution of national culture.[141]

Whatever the extent to which the cultural and political unrest was attributed to U.S. influence, the revelation of a multifaceted United States reinforced Western European Communists' fascination with, if not faith in, American pluralism. America's own ambivalence furthered the ambivalence of communist anti-Americanism. In March 1966 *Rinascita*'s correspondent to the United States, Gianfranco Corsini, in an article opening an issue of *Il Contemporaneo* dedicated to the "America of dissent," argued that there was "an America that does not dwell in complacency, and that prefers to pose the most daring questions, rather than remaining bound to an immutable belief system." Because of the "tight cultural interdependence of our time," Corsini concluded, "these [American] debates can help us understand ourselves better in a moment in which we try to interpret and correctly evaluate (without any prejudice) other peoples' troubles." Much of the rebellious youth in the United States may have "rejected . . . the discipline, the centralization" required by Marxist militancy, Louis Safir, another *Rinascita* correspondent, noticed; the New Left there was made of "ephemeral moralists" who would probably be reabsorbed in the system. But, reviving the distinction between rulers and ruled, Safir added that violent repression "from the Pentagon and the State Department [would] finally cause these young radicals, these American *narodniki* [socially conscious bourgeois] to embrace a consistent [Marxist] ideology." In 1966 Carl Oglesby, a leader of Students for a Democratic Society (SDS), triumphantly toured French and Italian communist youth gatherings, promising the advancement of the "other America." Following President Johnson's announcement on 31 March 1968 that he would not seek reelection, Amendola, never sympathetic to the youth movement, admitted that "mass movements, the students, and the peace forces [in the United States] were stronger than the forces of war." Longo, reporting to the party directorate after the assassination of Robert Kennedy, expressed as much disillusion with the institutional United States as hope for a socialist revival in American society.[142]

In France, Roger Garaudy was already controversial when he accepted an invitation to lecture at Harvard and St. Louis Universities in 1967. His report to Rochet on his return stirred further debate within the party. While Garaudy recognized that the student movement recoiled against a long tradition of anti-intellectualism in the United States, he also marveled at the particular sensitivity of the U.S. government to such moral condemnation, a sure sign of a resilient democracy. Even Rochet was ready to admit that in the United States the forces from below posed the most serious challenge to the warmongers at the top. Garaudy's contention, based on his reading of Marcuse and his experience overseas, that socialism should be emancipated from strict economic determinism, however, was one of the main causes of his expulsion from the party. Less prone than its Italian counterpart to laud the merits of American pluralism, the PCF leadership continued to see the protest in the United States as proof that "class consciousness was finally awakened" there.[143] Most French and Italian Communists never abandoned the hope that the American New Left would naturally join forces with and rejuvenate the Old Left there, and simply be reabsorbed in it at home.

This could happen without necessarily inviting party membership. Borrowing from the rather unorthodox writings of Theodor Adorno on the "authoritarian personality," even loyal intellectuals from both parties drew parallel conclusions on the American and European new social movements. By unveiling how even in democratic systems a tendency toward repression and conformity undermines individual freedoms, Adorno stressed the limits of the democratic revolution under neocapitalism. He also encouraged intellectual inquiry freed of any institutionalized constraint. It was comforting to conclude that, in France and Italy, as in the United States, the young generations would compensate for their lack of party affiliation with increased social and political commitment.[144]

The same theoretical references—from Herbert Marcuse to Max Horkheimer and Theodor Adorno—also viewed in mass culture the main instrument of manipulation of the younger generation. Only in the next decade would a commodified, commercialized mass culture morph into an instrument of emancipation. In the late 1960s the counterculture contained both potentials of the "unleashed American energies": for genuine anticonformity or for a lifestyle co-opted by marketing. Neither France nor Italy had beatniks or hippies on a large scale. Escape into "some artificial paradise" was from the start possible in the United States, because, according to functionalist sociology, it was a self-contained society that had almost no internal contradictions, and could only be "abandoned." In Italy, as in Germany, even countercultural exponents continued to stress the contradictions of the capitalist system and aimed at subverting more than evading it. Many extraparliamentarian activists ended up in clandestinity and terrorism. In France, dissent remained highly intellectual, antagonistic, but also closer to the individualistic aspects of the American counterculture. The possibility of an "alternative" rather than antagonistic lifestyle grew more alluring as the youth movement in France and Italy failed to reach all its goals.[145]

In part, the counterculture reignited the exoticism and openness of America as the pioneering land of experimentation, and in part it showed America's commercialized nature, with culture and counterculture fused together. In a series of articles published by *Les Lettres françaises* in the fall of 1969 under the title "Un patchwork américain," Jean Bouret analyzed the hippie culture, celebrating San Francisco as "one of the world's most beautiful cities" characterized by "an extreme gentleness" comparable to certain European urban areas. It was also, "more than New York[,] . . . the city of infinite possibilities," displaying a myriad of cultural experiences. "The tasteless American," he added, "is but a slogan, just as flawed as that of the uncultured American who chews gum." The hippie culture, however, generated as much intellectual speculation as "business speculation," as much sexual liberation as induction into "pornographic commerce."[146]

The PCF's writers union took a little longer to fathom the value of American counterculture. In 1971 it drafted a memorandum questioning whether this counterculture was an ephemeral phenomenon or the beginning of a genuine cultural revolution in the West spearheaded by the U.S. "underground" movement. "Would you pay considerable interest," the union asked the party leaders, "to what in the United States they now call the 'hip culture,' or do you dismiss it as a passing phenomenon, maybe even a backward one? What significance do you attribute to developments such as pop music, the new shows inspired by the 'happening,' the wall literature, the scriptless theater, the underground papers or films—in short, to all this movement that we should call 'cultural' and that is developing outside the traditional circles, in opposition to them?"[147] The party apparatus remained impermeable to these pressures. But the counterculture enticed the French youth of the 1970s as jazz had drawn the youth of the interwar period.

The most paradoxical aspect of all this ambivalence was that communist anti-Americanism found in the loss of U.S. exceptionalism the very reason for a renewed attractiveness of their Cold War enemy. In 1946 Cesare Pavese had lamented the U.S. "process of European spiritualization." Now, Safir commented in October 1966, the "New World where no religious wars, political assassinations, dark conspiracies and state coups" were ever supposed to happen, ended up resembling its "elder sibling nations" overseas. But since exceptionalism throughout the Cold War had been usurped by an establishment that fulfilled its "world mission" with proselytizing fervor, whether with ugly or good intentions, the emergence of a flawed, more self-conscious, more cynical, more human, more "European" America was actually an auspicious prospect for Western European Marxists. Moreover, communist commentators rejoiced that the "solemn words" of U.S. officials were contradicted by conscientious representatives, such as William Fulbright or Robert Kennedy, or by a cultural dissidence that spanned from the investigative reporting of *The Nation* to the voices of the Black Panthers and the writings of Noam Chomsky.[148] These conclusions, however, inferred that U.S. exceptionalism was not defunct at all. It had just been restored to its intellectual and popular dimension.

Exceptionalism also applied to the other American upheavals marking this era: the feminist and civil rights movements. Modern feminism did not receive full attention in French and Italian societies, including the communist establishment, until the early 1970s. Suffice it here to point out that, for both the PCF and the PCI, sexual liberation was, like the youth movement's own issues of personal fulfillment, an expression of individual discomfort in capitalist societies, prone to individualist excesses in the United States, and solvable only in a "workerist" framework.

BLACK AMERICA

The radicalization of civil rights by the mid-1960s was a different matter, for it finally exposed the conjunction of racial and social injustice. The civil rights movement engaged critically with the American liberal tradition, which upheld a meliorist view of society. For most American liberals of the Cold War, a bright future was almost automatic, and progress—technological, educational, and cultural—would bring greater freedom and equality for all. For all its liberal-progressive content, the civil rights movement, especially in the mid- to late 1960s, questioned the liberals' optimism, rejected many myths of progress, of "inevitable" improvement, and fought with increasing militancy against economic, more than legal, oppression. Those in power, as black activist John Lewis admonished in 1964 using the words of Frederick Douglass, were "not going to hand over [their interest]. Without agitation there can be no progress."[149]

This militant turn was appealing to French and Italian Communists not so much for its sophistic adherence to Marxism as for its refutation of entrenched arguments about America's "permanent revolution" (the progressive dream of thorough emancipation), and for its call for direct action. The assassinations of Malcolm X in February 1965 and Martin Luther King Jr. in April 1968 confirmed, in communist opinion, that "individual violence was a decisive component of American society," exposing its primordial sense of justice. For all its liberating force, ultimate individualism, this view suggested, might also mean pursuing one's own notion of justice through crime.[150] Racism was now proven to be "an essential instrument of the American economic and social system, aggravating its exploitative nature." Johnson's "War on Poverty," was, in the words of Galvano della Volpe, no more than "state charity," failing to solve structural problems. In an attempt to trace the youth rebellion in America to tangible socioeconomic causes, observers from both Communist Parties emphasized that the New Left "was born on 1 February 1960," when black and white students staged a sit-in at a segregated Woolworth's diner in Greensboro, North Carolina. At the cultural level, from this viewpoint, the new literature of black America appeared tied to the Beatnik movement more than inherited from the Harlem Renaissance. Even when not openly Marxist, it approximated a socialist outlook more than it expressed a new kind of black nationalism.[151] But contrary to communist expectations, even when King addressed issues of poverty, and the Black Panthers adopted a proletarian outlook, Marxism informed only a fringe of the civil rights movement.

AMERICANIZATION

Ultimately, more than actual solidarity with the embattled radicals in the United States, Europe's radical Left, whether new or old, "needed a divided, conflicted America which could simultaneously comprehend, and therefore sanction [its own] revolutionary ambitions and [its own] deep-seated Americanization." As Alessandro Portelli reminisced, "America was to us both the disease and the antidote: racism and civil rights, napalm and pacifism, the Hays codes and Marilyn Monroe, and so on. There was no need to go beyond America to find alternatives to America."[152]

Ten years after the Paris upheaval, French intellectual and student activist Régis Debray quipped, "The French path to America passed through May '68." This statement evoked the young rebels' ambivalence between opposition to the U.S. way of life and their redefinition of oppression based on the ethical, individualistic modes of American radicalism rather than the Marxist script or the "French-style revolutionary sensibility."[153] Earlier on, intellectual journalist Jean-François Revel had polemically disputed all forms of European anti-Americanism, particularly exposing the rigidity of the communist Left. In his in his best-selling *Ni Marx, ni Jésus* (*Without Marx or Jesus*, 1971), Revel contended that the United States was the new land of revolution. Next to the concern for the poor, black emancipation, and care for the environment, the New World had fully learned, through its counterculture, how to put human beings before the laws of competition and profit. While in Europe, according to Revel, Marxism suffocated revolution, and while the Soviet Union was gradually losing its appeal, the United States mastered change and genuine democracy again.[154]

Many of these predictions about the United States may have been flawed, while communist anti-Americanism may have entertained wishful thinking about the Marxist future of the New Left. But by reflecting the United States' own ambivalence and pluralism, these perceptions also proved its cultural dominion and confirmed its role as harbinger of Europe's future.

The U.S. Establishment and the Growing Value of Dissent

This appeal was beyond the direction of the U.S. political establishment. In fact, at first Washington felt it was losing control of the antiestablishment forces, confirming its fears that domestic and foreign anti-Americanism would be mutually nurturing.

Pessimism pervaded the intellectual and political leadership of the West by the late 1960s, not because of the ideological cohesion of the youth movement, but because of its chaotic nature. The movement, according to Raymond Aron, was illogical, irrational, and the expression of a "malaise of the entire Western Civilization"; it demonstrated "the fragility of the modern order." Years after May 1968, Malraux, again minister of culture under President Georges Pompidou, brooded that "the unprecedented abdication of the world's young people from Mexico to Japan unveiled one of the deepest crises our civilization has known."[155] Even if this would not benefit the Marxists, most U.S. officials thought, it would still foster a hedonistic, self-indulgent, and, in the conservative view, self-destructive tendency in Western culture. As U.S. Deputy Assistant Secretary of State for European Affairs George Springsteen observed to French conservative leader Raymond Barre, the generation gap in Eastern Europe meant that the youth was no longer interested in ideology. In the West, the two concurred, all the revolutionary romanticism *sounded* like a triumph of ideology and like a "virus" spreading from France to the rest of Europe. In fact, if "no system of spiritual, political and social values [was] immune," then the post–World War II generations had no reference at all, and their "real problems [could] spread into other areas and provide the foundation for frivolity." George Kennan, still a very influential intellectual, felt like many entrenched academics who did not embrace the New Left. He abhorred the student rebellion the same way he had disdained the student conformity of the 1950s. Even among the most open-minded U.S. officials, a desire for order prevailed over their favor of diversity.[156]

Ideally, in Washington's predominant view, the 1960s would have quickly fulfilled Daniel Bell's prediction that modern liberal capitalism was producing a classless society, making all ideologies irrelevant. This argument seemed compelling during the years of economic growth in the United States, but even more so in Europe. Class conflict could become obsolete and Marxism debunked. This confidence in economic performance matched the intellectual optimism, often intellectual swank, of the Kennedy years. For all the attention the Eisenhower administration had devoted to psychological warfare, its conservative mindset had stymied intellectual initiative and a progressive approach to anticommunism. Ostensibly, the Kennedy administration encouraged such intellectual initiative and nuance. But, at the same time, it also emphasized the record, in Kennedy's words at his inaugural speech, of "a new generation, tempered by war" and by the fight against Nazi and fascist totalitarianism. Its confrontation with "global communism" was therefore as unambiguous and self-righteous as its previous crusade. Kennedy's "proud sense of being on the side of the righteous," it has been noted, was continuous with that of the late 1940s, and also "with the equivalent sense that had emerged in the late 1930s and early 1940s." Even the intellectuals, rather self-congratulatory in their theories of modernization and counterinsurgency, "knew that when the crunch came, America was right and its enemies wrong."[157]

But America was proven wrong in many respects. Its economic affluence had already started a relative decline. Its "empire of production," as Charles Maier has specified in his most recent account, reached its "summer solstice" in 1958, with the freer flow of dollar funds made possible by the achievement of monetary convertibility in Europe and the end of investment restrictions in the United States. That turning point marked the beginning of a relative slowdown that, although it became visible only at the end of the following decade, spurred social unrest, especially in Europe. Core liberal ideas that inspired the optimism of the Kennedy years also were put to the test in foreign policy: President Johnson's decision to wage war in Vietnam was based on his commitment to New Deal principles and the perceived need to expand them. Historians of the New Left, following the lead of William Appleman Williams, through the late 1960s and early 1970s produced popular accounts showing that American liberalism was not exempt from a national tradition of classic imperialism, driven by self-serving economic interests.[158] The Cold War national consensus had reached its end.

But the apparent revival of ideological politics was indeed transient. The keenest U.S. officials' predictions about the youth movement were correct, while pessimistic about its chaotic nature. In hindsight, the youth rebellion was, in only a slight exaggeration, that of "rambunctious students, ungrateful for the white-collar future assured to them."[159] Their ideas remained those of the young Marx more than those of the older Mao. They revived the "alienation" theories of Gramsci's vision of Fordism more than those of Lenin's conflicting imperialisms.

The Vietnam years also gave way to more sober, yet more enlightened official U.S. self-perceptions. American officials wished for order, but many also realized that diversity did "humanize" the U.S. image in the world. In the final analysis, the United States' newly found weakness also highlighted its pluralistic and multifaceted character. William Fulbright, as chair of the Senate Foreign Relations Committee, eloquently explained his dissent from the administration on the Vietnam War in terms of genuine patriotism. There existed, he wrote, two Americas: "One is generous and humane, the other narrowly egotistical; one is self-critical, the other self-righteous; one is sensible, the other romantic; one good-humored, the other solemn; one is inquiring, the other pontificating; one is moderate, the other filled with passionate intensity; one is judicious and the other arrogant in the use of great power. Both are characterized by a kind of moralism, but one is the morality of decent instincts tempered by the knowledge of human imperfection and the other is the morality of absolute self-assurance fired by the crusading spirit." Fulbright, George Ball, Robert Kennedy, Walter Cronkite, and other members of the political and media establishment proved that dissent could be integral to foreign policy making and testimony to a "Higher Patriotism."[160] For many Vietnam veterans the definition of "Americanism" coincided with "the protection of civil liberties, especially the right to dissent."[161]

On the right, "higher patriotism" entailed the striving for "spiritual fulfillment" above material abundance. That was how William F. Buckley Jr.'s *National Review* had explained its repudiation of candidate Nixon in 1960. While finding in anticommunism their main "spiritual campaign," organizations such as Young Americans for Freedom expressed a dissent that resembled the New Left at least in its search for deeper meanings and missions in life.[162]

While soul-searching characterized a wide range of U.S. public opinion in the 1960s, as with many historical examples of such deep social transformations, most American intellectuals nurtured a renewed pride in *all* national culture. They regained confidence not in spite of but thanks to mass culture. As Louis Menand has best explained, in the 1940s and 1950s, Americans were a culturally insecure people: "Even well-educated Americans were extremely wary of being caught slumming in the realms of mass culture— of enjoying things that they were supposed to be too cultured to enjoy. But when Europeans took the mass culture the United States exported in the 1940s and 1950s and returned it in the 1960s in the form of a hip and sophisticated pop art, Americans began to feel comfortable with their own culture. It was a form of validation." Therefore, American writers came to represent the "modernist canon." American movies were reevaluated through the French *Nouvelle vague*. In pop music "the Beatles made rock and roll seem stylish, witty, and even deep," starting less a "British invasion" than a transatlantic dialogue celebrating its American roots.[163]

In this mixture of high political insecurity and cultural reassertion, most U.S. diplomats, beginning in the late 1960s, followed an approach that evoked Fulbright's emphasis on pluralism. Since the worst prospect in European affairs was that of a symbiosis between Communist Parties and anti-establishment groups, U.S. officials did the little they could to keep the two forces separate. Without compromising with the Communists, they maintained informal contacts with them. This was not only, as I have noted, to fathom the Communists' approach to international issues but also to suggest that détente served their domestic interests, too.

Recognizing that "May [1968] was not [the] PCF's best month," Ambassador Shriver believed it was actually in the U.S. best interest that, under these circumstances, the PCF had remained "the principal channel for working class protest" against what party members called "irresponsible anarcho-syndicalists." The embassy thus conveyed to the Communists that they should continue to cultivate an image of "republic [*sic*] responsibility and moderation." The embassy in Rome had for even a longer time nurtured the hope that radical events would induce the PCI to adopt "an honestly democratic program which would have to be based on the junking of the authoritarian Leninist concept of democratic centralism."[164] This was not to encourage communist inclusion in any area of government. In fact, it was essential to avoid "furnish[ing] grist to the Communist popular front mill," as the Rome embassy's William Fraleigh put it. Giving the Communists a certain respectability, most U.S. officials expected, would actually diminish their popularity, and perhaps their anti-Americanism, too. This became a particularly compelling argument during the summer of 1968, after the two Communist Parties denounced the Soviet crushing of the Prague movement.[165] Whether expedient for domestic purposes or sincerely concerned about the prospects of polycentrism, any anti-Soviet critique at the top level was destined to cause confusion among the two parties' working-class electorate. Naturally, Washington's main goal was to isolate them. A few U.S. officials — in Italy at least — did sincerely hope for a possible government "cohabitation" with a moderated Communist Party. But they remained a minority and in the lower diplomatic ranks.[166]

It seemed counterintuitive to maintain contacts with the Communists in order to isolate them. In most respects, this tactic resembled previous ones aimed at taming certain nationalist manifestations of anti-Americanism in order to outcast radical ones. Further testifying to a pluralistic approach, Washington's diplomacy did not side unwaveringly with French or Italian conservative reaction to the radical movements. President de Gaulle was perhaps effective in the short term against the May movement, rallying the people around the tricolor flag as opposed to the students' red ones. But the State Department and intelligence establishments thought his reverting to "powerful, challenging" autocracy caused a "simplistic division of France" and placed that country "on the knife edge of disaster." Shriver saw the danger of "the Gaullists . . . courting the extreme right . . . to compensate for the strong adverse vote they expect[ed] from the labor sector." After the powerful Gaullist counterdemonstration on the Champs-Elysées on 29 May and the subsequent conservative success in the June elections, Washington reevaluated the embattled French president. The Nixon administration, and Kissinger in particular, felt a double affinity with de Gaulle: for his charismatic role and for his realpolitik approach to a European integration still relying on nation-states and a balance of power. Old-fashioned nationalism had its merits during overwhelming antiestablishment opposition. But Shriver continued to warn that the PCF, still the leading party on the left with one-fifth of the electorate, might have "lost some battles but not the war." Above all, Gaullist and communist voters were antithetical in everything but their anti-Americanism.[167] Italy's Christian Democrats caused similar alarm, heightened however by their factionalization between groups determined to use force against the protestors and groups willing to open a dialogue with the PCI. Both tendencies corroborated Washington's decision to reduce CIA funding of the Christian Democrats' electoral and intelligence apparatus.[168]

While reducing their interaction with the ruling parties, the two embassies opened a dialogue with the new parties that sympathized with the youth movement. As with the Communists, they did not intend to compromise with these groups but rather to harness the Left coalition taking shape in France and foment more divisions within the Italian Left. As Ambassador Bohlen observed, the Parti Socialiste Unifié (PSU), which had been formed in 1960 as a "conscience of the Left" advocating Algerian independence, and

had gathered various splinter groups of the extreme Left, had little electoral weight but mattered for its "influence on intellectuals" and drew advantage from "its association with [former Radical Party leader] Pierre Mendès-
France." Its cooperation with the Communists and with the Federation of the
Left, the socialist group formed by François Mitterrand, was surely worrisome. Also, the PSU, under the growing clout of its secretary, Michel Rocard,
banked on its anti-American rhetoric, particularly on the Vietnam War. But
its most consequential impact was that of enlisting defectors from the communist ranks. Although the Left seemed to coalesce, factions were actually
corroding Marxist unity and causing a quick hemorrhage from the PCF.[169]

The same could be said about the equivalent Italian group, the Partito
Socialista Italiano di Unità Proletaria (PSIUP), founded in 1964. Though not
as popular with the students as the PSU, and more inclined to cooperate with
the Communists, it too held sway among intellectuals and caused divisions
within the PCI.[170] In both countries, the emergence of these new groups reflected a growing public aversion to established parties. U.S. officials' concern that for some of these leaders this meant the liquidation of any political
value was decisively offset by another consideration: the informality adopted
by these groups subverted the very notion of democratic centralism that both
French and Italian Communists tenaciously upheld.

In some cases, dissident leaders, such as those of the Manifesto group, or
Michel Rocard, drew the two embassies' attention for their efforts to harmonize modernity and Marxism. In September 1968 Rocard clarified to a U.S.
official that his party fought the "retrograde" forces of Gaullism and traditional communism. The Gaullists, he noted, combined "in one movement all
that is archaic and tradition-minded in France with the young French technocrats who wish to modernize the country," and the former group seemed
likely to prevail after the 1968 "scare." The Communists, he added, were
"stagnating," too, failing to "revise their own bureaucratic structure." Only
the PSU, he declared, intended to "take a crack at" the problem of how to
"highlight Socialism in a developed country." Despite his unwavering anti-
Americanism, Rocard also compared the lukewarm PCF defense of "free expression" in Czechoslovakia to the open criticism of the Vietnam War by
the U.S. media. These points were sufficient to keep the embassy interested
in this dialogue.[171] Both Rocard's tentative understanding of modernization
and his emphasis on freedom of debate in the West were clear signs that the
Communist Parties, after suffering from a dwindling working class, might
also lose their clout over intellectuals and technocrats.

It is plausible to argue that in the postwar era the United States had
exerted attraction through its productive capability, wealth, and social har-

mony. But by the late 1960s, it was through its disharmonious elements that it generated social groups, cultural references, and symbolic signifiers for each section of political opinion in Europe. In 1968 the communist world was divided as never before, and the renewed ambiguity of communist anti-Americanism in the West reflected the heightened pluralism of U.S. society. But the U.S. diplomatic maneuver aimed at nurturing that ambiguity and isolating the Communists had unwanted effects. Without Washington's unwavering support, the conservative forces in both France and Italy lost some confidence. The international and domestic stability attained in the United States through détente also fostered the internal détente in France and Italy, with possible Left coalitions including the PCF and a dialogue between Christian Democrats and the PCI.

Pluralism and dissent also caused a conservative backlash. American liberals' partial disowning of nationalism in favor of multiculturalism was for a while an asset for the U.S. reputation abroad. But it damaged their political fortunes at home, leaving to conservative Republicans the task of restoring national pride and revamping the image of the nation as a firm and militant cold warrior. By the early 1970s, this political turn revived left-wing anti-Americanism in Europe.

Furthermore, most U.S. diplomats' worst predictions about de Gaulle's or the Italian Christian Democrats' unpopularity turned out to be correct. The Gaullist victory in 1968 was a pyrrhic one. The following April, the president was forced to resign after the public repudiated his second institutional referendum. Heightened individualism brought about a secularization process that attacked normative Catholic culture—and in Italy the Christian Democrats who represented it—more than, in the immediate, it hurt communist orthodoxy. In both countries it was allegedly easier for the Communists than for the old regime to claim that the movements simply accelerated cultural and social transformations that their two parties had first set in motion. Their rising membership and vote totals in the following decade was in fact rather deceptive, a reflection of their temporary induction into the establishment more than of their capacity to absorb antiestablishment forces. Electorally, both parties did profit from the movements, however, by becoming receptacles of the voices of protest. Through the mid-1970s many members of the extraparliamentary Left converged into them, attracted by their power, organization, and effectiveness. The membership in their youth federations began to grow again.[172] Their intellectual magnetism was partially renewed thanks to their conditional loyalty to the Soviet Union and their critique of its human rights record. This outlook helped restore the PCF's cooperation with Mitterrand's Socialists (after a brief break in 1968–69), and it led the

PCI to reach its own "Historic Compromise," a tactical cooperation with the ruling Christian Democrats. But while both parties seemed more integrated, their understanding of modernization remained at best partial (for most PCI leaders), or obstinately "workerist" (especially in the PCF's case). Combined, these shortcomings would start taking their toll by the late 1970s.

8 REDEFINING INTERDEPENDENCE

The Eurocommunism of the 1970s and the U.S. Response

Prague and the Origins of the Communist "Third Force"

Affluence and protest in the 1960s, under an apparent revival of collectivist ideologies, marked in fact the beginning of an era mostly defined by individualist sensibilities and desire for personal fulfillment. At the same time, the Prague Spring contributed to the dismantling of ideological certainties. And yet the convergence of the protest movements in the East and the West rekindled hopes among Western Marxists that Western Europe could become again the center of revolutionary change, since the idea of a "socialism with a human face," as the Czech reformers called their agenda, had originated in the West, and in Italy especially. Furthermore, the twin attack on the establishment in the East and West encouraged the French and Italian Communists to pursue a European identity outside the two superpowers.

But the "Eurocommunist" experiment was made impossible, and not only by strategic and economic realities. The mass movements from both sides, and their stress on participatory democracy, exposed the most basic contradictions in Western European Communism. They made it impossible for the two parties to repudiate completely core Soviet doctrines, such as democratic centralism and the dictatorship of the proletariat, or the Soviet Union itself. Mounting anti-Sovietism in the West compelled them to amplify their anti-Americanism, if only to preserve their credibility and identity. The protest movements' accent on democratic participation ultimately revealed that Western radicalism was unable to break loose from the influence of U.S. politics and mass culture, while the majority of those radicals gradually departed from the extraparliamentarian Left that had apparently commanded the rebellions of the late 1960s.

In addition to this persistent American influence, the other reason for a diminished radicalism in the 1970s was mere necessity. After a period of relative prosperity, inflation and stagnation forced most of the radicals of the Western world to abandon many ideals and cling to their jobs. The economic downturn did increase the power of the Left opposition. With an embattled welfare state and a growing inability to "govern" in Paris and especially in Rome, the middle classes suffered above all, and lent growing support to the two Communist Parties. But this was not a solid constituency. Also, communist gains were in any case offset by a tendency of this discontent to turn inward rather than to champion profound social transformation. Even more, the convergence of some of the middle class with the traditional Left was counterbalanced in France by a socialist takeover of the Left, and in Italy by a violent upsurge of die-hard radicals, who, waging terrorism and wreaking havoc in the country's politics and society, also exposed how illusory any revolutionary goal was.

The social and cultural dimensions of this turn truly constituted the epilogue of communist power in Western Europe, and I will analyze them in the epilogue of this book. These aspects cannot be fully understood outside the political context that led both the Western Communists and the United States to reevaluate the politics and strategies of interdependence in the Western world. The anti-American implications of Italian-inspired Eurocommunism were more subtle than those of previous choices. The American response was also increasingly refined and self-reflective.

CONDEMNING MOSCOW

The more belated was the official repudiation of Stalinism, the more resolute was its reach for reformed communism. This was how Czechoslovakia, after experiencing the slowest transition in the East from the Stalinist years to reform, allowed its intellectuals to advance basic freedoms in the country. The Czech leaders even accepted the prospect of multiparty rule. As long as the country remained in the Warsaw Pact, the reform leader Alexander Dubček thought, Moscow would not react in the same way as it had against Hungary in 1956. But ideological cohesion was as crucial as strategic unity, as Leonid Brezhnev proved by authorizing armed intervention.[1]

The Prague Spring meant greater autonomy for Western Communists as well. It made it possible for them to imagine genuine emancipation from Moscow and even a rejuvenated revolutionary spirit in the West. Furthermore, the Czech version of socialism with a human face at first appeared to be the fulfillment of the Gramscian dream of cultural hegemony, of the organic intellectual truly integrated with the forces of the proletariat and bringing about the classless society. It could also be a special validation of the correctness of the Italian vision of (not just a path to) socialism, restoring the credibility of Western communism and its mixture of parliamentary and insurrectionary tactics.

Each time there had been a crisis in the East the two parties—the PCI especially—tried to relaunch their own initiatives in the West. Togliatti had done so in 1956, with his doctrine of polycentrism right after the publication of Khrushchev's report on Stalin in June. Resuming that doctrine's assertion that the path to socialism could occur without the Communist Parties' being the leading ones in a coalition, the PCI of Luigi Longo and Enrico Berlinguer kept envisioning a reformed socialism that incorporated some social democratic forms. At the international level, this vision produced an effort to reestablish relations with the European Left. The PCI endorsed German Chancellor Willy Brandt's *Ostpolitik*, his gradual diplomatic opening to the East. In domestic politics, this translated into a greater effort to be included in the parliamentary system.

Indeed, a major reason for both French and Italian Communists to promote a sharp break with Moscow in 1968 was their pursuit of domestic legitimacy. They both had to demonstrate that their brand of communism was compatible with the democratic process, and not just a short-term tactic. The electoral situation had favored this moderation for the PCI more than the PCF. In Italian national elections in May 1968, the PCI gained votes, proving it had in part channeled the radicalism of students and workers. In the French elections the following month, the PCF lost one-tenth of its electorate, revealing the party's double failure to harness the youth movement and to project a convincing image of democratic reliability.

The PCF's support of Alexander Dubček's reforms in Prague was very "tempéré." In July, Waldeck Rochet so strongly warned the Czech leader of the dangers of counterrevolution that Dubček wondered whether the warning came from the PCF or the U.S.S.R. A scandal erupted in France in 1970 after the press revealed that the French communist leadership had given the "normalized" Czech government documents from the exchange between Rochet and Dubček, which resulted in trials of several members of the dissident group Club 231. Worse still, the revelation coincided with the success of the movie *L'aveu* (*The Confession*) in French theaters. The movie was directed by Costa-Gavras and starred Yves Montand and Simone Signoret, who had all been close to the PCF. But the story was drawn from the book by Czech writer Arthur London, who recounted his experience in the Prague trials of the early Cold War.[2]

The PCI was more sympathetic to the winds of change in Prague. Carlo Galluzzi was adamant about giving Dubček unconditional support; so were the influential Berlinguer and Umberto Terracini. Initially, they were fully endorsed by Luigi Longo. But in July the party secretary asked the political bureau to alert Dubček that there were "dangerous positions within the movement (of the Prague Spring) . . . that threaten[ed] the very basis of socialism" and against which it was "necessary to fight."[3]

Both the PCI and the PCF condemned the joint intervention of the Warsaw Pact powers in August. Notable dissidents from the condemnation included Jeannette Thorez-Vermeersch, Emilio Colombi, and Pietro Secchia on the "orthodox" side, and Roger Garaudy, Terracini, and the PCI's Manifesto group on the radical/reformer side.[4] Even such minority disagreements were hard to tolerate.

A way out of the impasse both with the internal dissidents and with Moscow seemed to be the reiteration of the slogan "neither orthodoxy nor dogmatism," first expounded by the PCI and, by the mid-1960s, also adopted by the PCF. Both parties intended to clarify—or maybe to obscure—the meaning of their "peaceful way to socialism."[5] The slogan originated in the criticism of the flaws in the Soviet and Chinese versions of Marxism. But, in the view prevailing in Rome, it also offered a prospect of socialism "outside" the politics of the two blocs, and thus a way to emancipate Western Europe simultaneously from NATO (which was to be renewed in 1969) and from now tightening Soviet imperialism.[6] Aware of this trend, Moscow, until its decision to invade, had tried to co-opt the international ambitions of both French and Italian communist leaders by insisting on their possible mediation. While the PCF seriously pondered the option, an Italian delegation sent to Moscow in July turned down the suggestion. The PCI also tried to turn a French proposal for a meeting of the Western Communist Parties into an occasion for greater autonomy and sterner criticism of the Soviet position.[7]

Concerned about a consolidated international bipolarism, and worried about a renewed American imperialist thrust, several PCI leaders, including Berlinguer and Giorgio Amendola, argued that if Moscow's interference in the East was not rejected, the West could justify countercoups against socialism in the West.[8] This was how the PCI saw the events in Chile five years later, or the "strategy of tension" at home, which started with fascist terrorist bombings in December 1969, and which the PCI interpreted to be part of rightist plots against the Italian regime. The risk of an escalating aggression in Europe from both superpowers was first highlighted at the Rome Mediterranean Conference of Western Communist Parties in April 1968— the first one organized independently of Moscow. The PCI used the gathering to stake its independent position from Moscow. While it blamed primarily the United States for the growing tension, it also for the first time mentioned the possibility of "confrontation" originating from either side.[9] The conference marked the beginning of the PCI's slow separation from Moscow. Even more significant, the Mediterranean meeting for the first time showed that, for the Western Communists, true independence and a genuine continental third force required matching a resolute anti-Americanism with at least a moderate critique of the Soviet bloc, if not one that cast the United States and the Soviet Union as moral equivalents. French and Italian Communists welcomed the dialogue between the two superpowers, soon evident in the developing détente, but only if that helped their internal prospects, and if it did not confirm the division of Europe into spheres of influence.

When Warsaw Pact tanks rolled into Prague in August, fears of an aborted détente reached a peak. The invasion was traumatic for the leadership of both Western parties. This impact was, perhaps, best exemplified by the similarly passionate reactions of the two party secretaries, Rochet and Longo, both of whom fell ill soon after the invasion. Their deteriorating health let their top lieutenants, Georges Marchais and Enrico Berlinguer, take command years before their formal nominations as party secretaries. The simultaneous deaths of Togliatti and Thorez in 1964 had not led to significant transformations in the two parties. Instead, the new leadership emerging in the late 1960s further increased the divergence between the PCI and the PCF. Marchais was, in most respects, more orthodox than Rochet, while Berlinguer was considerably more flexible than Longo. The Italian leader stated immediately after the invasion of Czechoslovakia that the "U.S.S.R. suffer[ed] from an ideological retrenchment"; therefore, the Western Communists were likely to "engage in a political confrontation with the Soviet comrades."[10] Officials from the U.S. embassy in Rome even foresaw as early as September 1968 that the Prague events could induce the PCI to begin reevaluating its denial of Soviet expansionism and to seek shelter in the Western alliance for its own brand of socialism. That is what Berlinguer began to do, first by balking at the campaign to prevent the renewal of the NATO treaty in 1969.[11]

MAINTAINING DÉTENTE

Several factors, however, dictated a moderate response by the two parties to the Soviet repression of the Prague movement. They can be ascribed to their leaders' concerns about various possible domino effects should they express their criticism fully.

There was first the fear of a domino effect in the East. French and Italian communist leaders upheld the connection between détente and "controlled" socialist reform: the radical forces from below could be upsetting in the West, but they could be devastating in the East. For both parties, the choice to muffle antiestablishment pressures (from any direction) reflected their modified slogan, "Neither orthodoxy nor heresy."[12] An ideological domino originating from the discredited East was likely to affect the Western Communists as well. A full condemnation of Moscow could have meant a loss of credibility for socialism altogether, argued the most orthodox members in both parties.[13]

A domino effect could play out strictly domestically, too. The PCI in part hesitated because of the position of the Manifesto faction and of other extra-parliamentarian groups that favored China over the Soviet Union. Pressures from radicalism thus reinforced a tactical orthodoxy.[14] But an additional domino effect could have taken the form of loss of leverage, or even identity, in the balance with the moderate Left. Drawing a moral equivalence between the United States and the Soviet Union might force the PCI and especially the PCF to compromise at home with the Socialists and to surrender their practice of "democratic centralism." Concerns about grassroots connections also haunted the leadership of both parties. Steeped in Soviet myths, the parties' rank and file, much like in 1956, had more trouble than their leaders with estrangement from Moscow.

But above all, the political advantages of the emerging détente seemed to command a moderate response to the Soviet Union. Even the PCI in the end informally recognized normalization, in part out of fear that the forces of radicalism in Eastern Europe or Chinese intransigence would undermine détente in Europe and leave no room for the party's possible rapprochement with social democratic forces in the West. Aiming at this détente within the West, the PCI and PCF needed to maintain close relations with Moscow.[15]

Concerned about their possible loss of credibility and identity, both parties stressed the danger of establishing a moral equivalence between socialism and the "imperialist" United States. The net effect of the events in Prague for French and Italian Communists, even for those who, like Berlinguer, began to see a greater danger to security coming from the East, was a reinvigorated anti-Americanism. A break with the Soviet Union, PCF leaders admonished Garaudy after his sharp criticism of the invasion of Prague, would only serve the cause of Western imperialism. This reprimand was the first step leading to the party's censoring of Garaudy at the end of 1969, following the publication of his book *Le grand tournant du socialisme*.[16] Reacting with instinct than calculation, the two parties countered mounting anti-Sovietism with intensified remonstrations against the Vietnam War and NATO, keeping an eye on the interplay with domestic politics. They reproached the ruling coalitions, arguing that, given their enslavement to the United States through NATO and the EEC, they could not "afford to lecture" the two Western Communist Parties or the Soviet Union.[17] This view also reflected a belief system. The older generation of World War II communist resisters still upheld the Soviet myth, while remaining convinced that capitalism was steadily declining. That myth, still powerfully transmitted to the rank and file, also ascribed to the Soviet Union a sincere desire for détente, comparing it to a relentless imperialist drive from the United States.[18]

Ironically, some of the most rancorous PCI pronouncements against Moscow painted the Brezhnev-Kosygin leadership as "American agents" leading "the Soviet Union on the road to Nazism."[19] The two superpowers had just signed a Treaty of Nuclear Non-Proliferation, and Brezhnev gave no sign of worrying about a possible U.S. reaction to the Prague events. Implied in the PCI's anti-American rhetoric was the notion that a bipolar logic could hijack détente toward a consolidation of each sphere of influence, thus foiling the PCI's pursuit of internal legitimacy.

For the PCF, anti-Americanism remained essential, not only because of its orthodoxy, or its tactics to harness the youth movement, but also because de Gaulle himself had shifted direction, getting closer to Washington.[20] De Gaulle's successors would confirm this new orientation. "Even more now," the PCF's political bureau deliberated on 14 August, "given the bourgeois campaign against Socialism, because of Czechoslovakia, we must highlight the struggle for freedom in Vietnam." The media's constant parallel between Vietnam and Czechoslovakia, under the rubric of "freedom and independence," as the PCF's Roland Leroy, then heading the party's cultural section, told Roland Favaro, leader of the Mouvement de la Jeunesse Communiste Française, supplanted France's anti-American tradition with anti-Soviet animosity.[21]

Reconciliation for the PCF with the U.S.S.R. came as early as 3 November 1968. The French party accepted normalization in Czechoslovakia. Although it also endorsed the summoning of a conference of Communist Parties in Moscow the next June, the PCF made clear that it would have rejected the establishment of any formal international agency along the lines of the previous Cominform. The PCI refused to sign the common declaration; it approved only the document condemning imperialism. Also, the Italian Communists denounced normalization and upheld the notion of "pluralism," though only within a socialist framework. The party leadership also continued to express solidarity with the world of socialism and the Soviet Union in particular.[22] In part, the Italian Communists' caution was due to the PCF's full reconciliation with Moscow and the Italians' consequent fear of remaining isolated in the Western communist movement.[23]

This persistent allegiance, however, did not preclude a certain detachment from the Soviet Union. It was ironically Moscow's drive to consolidate its sphere of influence in Europe and expand it in the Third World that gave the French and Italian Communists some room for maneuver in international politics. By 1968 Moscow's diminished interest in the PCF and PCI was clear from the reduced financing it sent them. Soviet money now primarily went to Vietnam, Cuba, and the Arab countries. The two parties' protest against repression in Czechoslovakia lost them further subsidies, but it temporarily increased their autonomy. Massive financing from Moscow resumed in the early 1970s, primarily due to the Kremlin's fear that the autonomy of the Western Communists would be contagious in the East.[24] This renewed funding reflected the Soviets' own redefinition of national security. In 1956 Hungary had tried to defect, and Soviet intervention could be justified simply in terms of security. Without attempting defection, the Prague movement had questioned the model and application of Soviet communism. A more fluid international context than in 1956 made this "heresy" even worse for Moscow. Therefore, the Soviet Union, through the Brezhnev Doctrine, confirmed that ideological cohesion was an integral part of its national security. Furthermore, this had to be ideological cohesion *anywhere*, among Western Communists, too, because of the increasing ideological permeability of Moscow's Eastern satellites. In 1971 the PCI's Amendola first suggested the end of Soviet funding as a means for the PCI to regain more autonomy in international politics. But both the PCI and the PCF, facing increasing deficits, could not turn down aid that, after some cuts, still amounted to about $2 million per year for each of them during the following decade.[25]

Soviet subsidies were not the only barometer of the parties' relative autonomy. The crisis of 1956, together with other events, had moved the main international focus to the emerging Third World. The year 1968 was a different story: it restored hopes among Western European Communists that Europe (East and West) was undergoing a major—if not revolutionary—change.

The Meanings of Eurocommunism and "Historic Compromises"

By giving priority to foreign policy issues, the French and Italian Communists had for years aimed at getting more exposure and domestic recognition. From the early 1960s, they had sought to revive their international credentials by trying to mitigate the impact of the Sino-Soviet split. The PCF had been more active on this issue, starting from the Moscow meeting of the eighty-one parties in 1961. But the Italian comrades finally emphasized the need to balance détente with Sino-Soviet reconciliation. This was the main theme, in addition to the Prague events, of the meeting Gian Carlo Pajetta and Carlo Galluzzi held in Moscow with Andrej Kirilenko and Mikhail Suslov in July 1968.[26]

By the end of the decade though, it was primarily by reevaluating Western European integration that the French and Italian Communists obtained greater domestic leverage. While highly instrumental for national politics, their diplomacy had an international goal as well. For the PCI especially, this "Europeanism" reflected its effort to transform détente into a vehicle for European emancipation from both superpowers.

EUROCOMMUNISM AND THE THIRD FORCE

Indeed, the Soviet intervention in Czechoslovakia gave the two parties the pretext to further their attempt to overcome the "politics of the two blocs." The PCF, while wavering on this issue, in July was the first to propose a meeting of the Western European Communist Parties aimed at averting Soviet action—an initiative pursuing more room for maneuver in the West, besides the usual mediation role. Moscow caused that proposal to founder. For the pro-EEC Amendola, the Prague events would help stimulate a campaign for the "withdrawal of [both] imperialist forces from occupied Europe . . . and the achievement of a real 'European unity.'"[27] This position, prevalent in the PCI, favored full condemnation of Moscow, initially setting the tone against those who feared that the party's reprobation of Soviet conduct would set off an ideological domino effect. Denouncing Moscow, this argument went, could in fact give the party more leadership within the international socialist movement.[28]

It is now widely accepted that for the PCF and especially for the PCI, the decline of the Soviet model began in 1968, and that both parties fully acknowledged that decline only by the mid-1970s. In the late 1970s, the PCF reverted to orthodoxy, but this brought deep internal divisions. Until the mid-1970s, both parties still analyzed world politics through Soviet lenses: the United States was in decline and power was shifting to the Soviet side.[29] What the PCI seriously questioned from the late 1960s onward was the bipolarity implied in the détente process. Through that process, Moscow confirmed a mixture of official compromises with the United States and demonizing propaganda against it. The PCI questioned this contradictory Soviet policy as well as the internal practices of the Soviet camp.

After meeting with a Soviet delegation in Budapest in November 1968, Berlinguer rejected his counterparts' suggestion that he intensify anti-NATO propaganda, which the PCF had resumed after its own meetings with the CPSU a few weeks earlier. This pressure for tactical anti-Americanism, Berlinguer told Boris Ponomariov, was unacceptable.[30] It was the first time that the Italian Communists diverged from the Kremlin on the issue of anti-American propaganda.

By the mid-1970s, realizing that communism was no longer expanding, that its spread to Angola, and later, Afghanistan, was illusory, the Berlinguer leadership redefined the Soviet model from the geopolitical standpoint as well. In positioning itself as the middle path between social democracy and Soviet communism and in favor of European interdependence, the movement that Berlinguer initiated and that became known as Eurocommunism strove to deny both blocs. In January 1973 at a party meeting, Berlinguer defined a policy that would be "neither anti-Soviet nor anti-American."[31]

The Soviet model may have been a fading star, but that did not mean that the PCI was becoming fully Westernized either. In fact, although the party now rejected the most regimented forms of anti-Americanism, it continued to define its very identity in stark opposition to the United States. With its anti-U.S. accents and its anticonsumerist ethic, it continued to favor a catastrophic vision of capitalism. The corollary of this vision was that the PCI could revive "socialism with a human face" in all of Europe, including the East. Faith in this capacity was essential; otherwise, Western communism would have been just another social democracy. The PCI's call for a "third way" between Soviet communism and social democracy—not a real program but a hazy, even contradictory slogan—became the trademark of Berlinguer's leadership between the late 1970s and the early 1980s.[32]

The paradox was that by 1974 Berlinguer thought Western communism could only advance true socialism with a human face under the Atlantic umbrella.[33] Otherwise, a socialist Italy would suffer the same fate as Czechoslovakia. The PCI increasingly saw NATO as an instrument to secure peace and détente in the short or medium term. Once détente was achieved, emancipation from NATO would be possible. This view revealed a contrast between practice and rhetoric, and an increasingly schizophrenic identity. The acceptance of European integration *substantially* marked the Italian Communists' emancipation from Moscow, but *rhetorically* the party presented it as anti-Americanism first. This remained true even after Berlinguer, in 1976, officially consented to NATO protection.

To be sure, the renewed anti-Americanism was rooted in sincere concerns and persistent convictions about the fallibility of neocapitalism. Party economic expert Luciano Barca endorsed Amendola's European choice first on the basis of the repeated dollar and oil crises of the early 1970s. Particularly, Richard Nixon's decision to devalue the dollar in 1971 confirmed, in the opinion of both Barca and Giorgio Napolitano, the vulnerability of an export-dependent country such as Italy within such a pro-Atlantic continental integration. Europe, Barca concluded at the party's political bureau meeting of 8 September 1971, must expand its economic integration to the East. Interdependence remained intertwined with nationalism. Amendola added that this extension to the East was the only way "to make Italy count more."[34]

Berlinguer's own adherence to NATO was heavily qualified. By December 1974, at a meeting of the party directorate, he justified it only as an "instrument to preserve and *complete* détente." It was simply, he added, "unrealistic to have defections of single countries from one or the other alliance." That was "in essence the meaning of the slogan 'neither anti-American nor anti-Soviet.'" But, regardless of all these qualifications, leaders of the party's Left—Umberto Terracini, Gian Carlo Pajetta, Emilio Colombi, and Pietro Ingrao—objected to this implied "moral equivalence," if not even indictment of the Soviets for being less "pacifist" than the NATO alliance. This line of reasoning, Ingrao and Terracini pointed out, could backfire, helping to consolidate the Cold War bipolarism. Some leaders, like Claudio Imbeni, also warned the party that the remnants of the 1968 rebellions, now feeding the ranks of the Red Brigades and other Leftist terrorist organizations, could be further alienated by this "compromise with the imperialist enemy." Even the party rank and file, he added, would have trouble understanding it. Berlinguer swayed the majority of the directorate, however, by arguing that temporary support of NATO would help "diminish U.S. concerns and interference in Italy's domestic affairs." At that point, the party did think that U.S. meddling was behind domestic terrorism of fringe groups on the left and the right.[35] In his ultimate goal—emancipation from NATO and the United States—the PCI leader did not differ from the comrades who upheld a consistent, thorough anti-Americanism.

But Berlinguer's tactical compromise became so convincing that it appeared more and more like an actual choice of the Atlanticist camp. After the leader gave his official endorsement to the Atlantic Pact in an interview with *Corriere della Sera* published on 15 June 1976, *Le Monde*'s correspondent in Rome, Jacques Nobécourt, redefined Italian Eurocommunism as "NATO-Communism."[36]

Eurocommunism enjoyed a brief season of popularity and hope. For the scope of this work, it is sufficient to trace its milestones, achievements, and shortcomings in order to assess its inherent contradictions. The project was first addressed at a meeting between Marchais and Berlinguer in May 1973. That encounter paved the way for the conference of the Western Communist Parties held in Brussels the following year. Eurocommunism became the main banner of the ensuing meetings between Marchais and Berlinguer in November 1975, the PCF summit of a few days later with the Spanish Communists (Partido Comunista de España [PCE]), renewed encounters between the French and Italian leaders in Paris in June 1976, and, finally, the summit of the three leaders, hosted by the PCE's secretary, Santiago Carrillo, in Madrid in March 1977. Meanwhile, the plenary conference of all European

Communist Parties, held in Berlin in June 1976, had given the three parties the chance to present their autonomous views within the communist movement. Besides upholding their open cooperation with the Socialist and Social Democratic Parties, the Western Communists abided by the declaration signed by Marchais and Berlinguer at their 1975 meeting, which supported the promotion of basic rights and freedom in socialist societies.[37]

While it accepted the vision of a Europe as genuine third force between the two superpowers, Eurocommunism never truly coalesced with the forces of social democracy. The PCI's contacts with German Chancellor Willy Brandt and Swedish Prime Minister Olav Palme—which intensified only in the early 1980s, after the end of the Eurocommunist experiment—remained confined to issues of nuclear proliferation and aid policies for the Southern Hemisphere. Berlinguer's strategy consisted of finding a legitimate means to induct the PCI into the Western democratic system, while keeping to the party's role as an ideological bridge between East and West. It was a tough balancing act that would have required truly overcoming the Cold War. The "Europeanization" of the PCI, Silvio Pons has recently noted, was "never a choice of civilization." It was a "Westpolitik," as party foreign policy expert Sergio Segre put it in 1974, evoking Brandt's *Ostpolitik*. It was focused on détente rather than pluralism and democracy. The PCI chose this international focus only in part to deflect U.S. interference in Italy's domestic affairs. The choice also stemmed from fear of alienating the Soviet Union with a radical departure from democratic centralism. This last reason was of course inconsistent with the attempt to avoid a U.S. say in the country's domestic affairs. Berlinguer waged tactical Westpolitik rather than accepting Westernization also because he intended to keep the more orthodox PCF and the more radical PCE tied to the project. Carrillo had gone so far as to be flexible on American bases in Spain, and he underlined that flexibility by accepting an invitation to visit the United States in 1977 and meet with State Department officials. The French Communists, for their part, still made no distinction between the interests of the United States and those of the social democratic Left in Europe. For the PCF, Amendola reminded the party's political bureau in 1975, Brandt was a mere "traveling salesman for American imperialism."[38] It would take special efforts to persuade the French comrades to compromise on Western European integration.

Marchais's stubborn opposition to the EEC arose from his mistrust of the Western Socialist Parties, "still servants of U.S. imperialism." From the relaunching of Europe in 1972, and its expansion to include Great Britain, the PCF opposed the extension of a "Europe of the big trusts." Rehashing the Gaullist arguments of the previous decade, the party's international experts insisted that a British presence would foil any attempt to create a real third force: "The nine nations of the EEC," the author of a 1974 article in *Cahiers du communisme* wrote, "under the pretense of speaking with one voice, would in fact speak the voice of America." Worse still, the most "reformist" social democratic forces (namely, Willy Brandt) in fact served "le grand capital," according to Léo Figuères, even asking the communist opposition to dampen the workers' protest and to invite them to accept austerity measures "decided by governments following the directives from the monopolies." These monopolies in their turn capitulated to American economic diktats, which sacrificed the interests of France and other countries dependent on oil imports.[39]

Mitigating this anti-EEC posture was the party's decision to nominate its first candidates for deputies to the European parliament in 1974. Behind this choice was the forceful inspiration of Jean Kanapa, the party's foremost foreign affairs expert, who also pressed for intensified contacts with the Italian comrades.[40] While pro-Soviet, Kanapa was also a consummate tactician, pursuing a prominent role for the PCF in European affairs. Even after entering the European parliament, Marchais insisted on the expansion of the EEC to include countries not ruled by "state monopoly capitalism."[41] For the PCF, this expansion should have been the main purpose of détente and the main topic on the Eurocommunist agenda. By 1975, with the Helsinki conference confirming the division of Europe into spheres of influence, détente, according to Etienne Fajon, had in fact aggravated class conflict in Western Europe.[42] The French Communists continued to oppose détente as the validation of the status quo in the West, resenting its mitigating effect on their anti-U.S. campaigns.[43]

In this context, the party finally denounced "Stalinism"—for the first time at the Central Committee meeting of May 1975. Party historian Jean Elleinstein was a sort of maverick when, in two of his books on the Soviet experience, he said the socialism of the East had been "deformed" by Stalinist practices. But the Marchais leadership took this debate as an occasion to show the PCF's distance from Soviet "aberrations." In a 1978 collection of essays titled *L'URSS et nous*, party authors went as far as admitting that Stalinism was not an aberration but an expression of "inherent contradictions" within Soviet socialism.[44] But the necessities of political tactics (the unity pact with the Socialists) more than conviction informed these public pronouncements.

This criticism of the Soviet Union was too restrained for some of the least orthodox party members; it not only led notable intellectuals to leave the PCF (as I will discuss in the epilogue) but also aggravated the party's tension with some of its prominent groups, most notably with the Paris Federation

led by Henri Fiszbin. Relying on educated members from the liberal professions, those groups resented both the party's renewed neglect of the middle
classes and its lukewarm support of Eurocommunism. Intellectuals such as
Elleinstein, Jean Rony, Antoine Spire, and Maurice Goldring also demanded
a stronger adherence by the party to the reform principles of Eurocommunism.[45] By 1978 the party leadership reinforced the need for cohesion over
a pluralist debate. In the final analysis, Eurocommunism for the top PCF
leaders was a temporary expedient and even less of a choice of civilization
than for the PCI. The publication of *L'URSS et nous* was only the climax of this
internal debate. By the time the book came out, the party leaders had already
opted to break the alliance with the Socialists. The following year, they reiterated their loyalty to Moscow.

The Eurocommunist idea for the PCF remained anchored to the concept
of "unity within diversity," while for the PCI it was linked to an evolving policy
bridging East and West, and to finding a middle path between social democracy and communism. The only true meeting point between the two parties
was the need to intensify Europe's attention to the emancipation of the Third
World. But for the PCI this attention was meant first to be a sign of a further
break with Moscow, of a search for alternative socialist models to its bureaucratized and repressive rule, while for the PCF it continued to have exclusively anti-American, anti-imperialist connotations.[46]

Another reason for the Italian Communists' compromising attitude was
economic: simply, the recession of 1974–75 affected Italy much more deeply
than France, and the PCI saw the best possibility of resolution through the
EEC. This also led Sergio Segre to recommend, in a letter to Berlinguer on
10 October 1975, closer cooperation with the secretary general of the Italian
foreign ministry, Raimondo Manzini, who negotiated Italy's induction into
the financial summits of the main industrialized nations, thus extending the
original G-5.[47]

A thaw between the two Communist Parties seemed possible by 1977,
when an extended debate began in view of holding the first elections of the
European parliament by universal suffrage in 1979. This, in the PCI's view,
would be a chance to extend the parliament's powers and also to adjust the
common agricultural policies, which tended to favor the Central European
countries. In attempting a coalition of the Left, the Italian Communists
began to balk at the PCF's unrelenting anti-German attitude. Worse still,
the PCF press insisted, this new Europe granted to Bonn a "dominant position" in the new parliament, and it accepted the new German monetarist
economics in cooperation with Washington. It thus ultimately became "a
German Europe under American tutelage." All this, according to Pajetta,

justified soft-pedaling on issues of supranationality. To get the PCF on board, he told the PCI's political bureau, it was better to talk of a Europe of nations, just like the time when "we argued that there are national paths to socialism." Amendola, as the main PCI representative in the European assembly, agreed that the process of "Europeanization" had been taken too far; but he still believed in a third force offsetting the continent's "Americanization."[48] To underscore the importance of the third force, the PCF finally expressed its favor of "an independent French nuclear deterrent." The report by Jean Kanapa at the Central Committee meeting in May 1977 marked this breakthrough from the party's traditional opposition to "the bomb." But the change was qualified by a request that the decision to use the bomb be removed from the president to a "special committee," and by its emphasis on *national* deterrents separate from those of the United States, not tied to a common European defense.[49] Still, even if under the national banner, the endorsement of a nuclear force decoupled from NATO marked the party's progress toward a European pole independent of both superpowers.

The French and Italian Communists, however, diverged on the geopolitical distinction of this third force. While the Italians supported the EEC candidacies of Greece, Spain, and Portugal, the French comrades agreed with their government's decision to veto that extension.[50] Further complicating this contrast, the new Portugal under the socialist Mario Soares appealed to the Berlinguer leadership, whereas Marchais still supported the ambitions of Alvaro Cunhal, the pro-Soviet communist leader who had led the "Carnation Revolution" in 1974 against the former fascist regime. The Portuguese Communist Party's refusal to cooperate with the Soares Socialists became a major obstacle to the party's inclusion in the Eurocommunist project. In PCI circles, Cunhal was referred to as the "anti-Berlinguer."[51] From Spain, Carrillo warned about repercussions the Portuguese Communists' actions could have on his desired collaboration with the Socialists. The PCI for its part feared that the Portuguese Communists' actions would discredit the whole Eurocommunist project. With the Chilean lesson in mind, Berlinguer also emphasized that the United States, after backing the counterrevolution in Portugal, could see further justification for interference elsewhere in Europe.[52]

EUROCOMMUNISM AND ANTI-AMERICANISM

These fears were warranted, but they also revealed a persistent ambivalence toward the United States and the Western alliance. Eurocommunism, while compromising with NATO, continued to nurture anti-Americanism, fiercely attacking U.S. policies. The PCF continued to identify the Gaullist legacy with phony anti-Americanism and compromises with the United States. Spanish anti-Americanism had been strong since the Spanish-American War of 1898, but it was made more furious among democratic forces by U.S. strategic compromises with Francisco Franco's regime. The PCE simply rekindled the popular belief that the United States had made life easier for Franco.[53]

But all Eurocommunists, and the PCI especially, recognized that the U.S. political system now showed a mixture of increased pluralism and executive retrenchment. That pluralism may have suffered from the decline of the 1960s ideals, but it affected the U.S. establishment more extensively than in those radical years.

During the 1960s, communist protest against the Vietnam War frequently alluded to arguments resembling those of Graham Greene's novel *The Quiet American*, whose protagonist is the classic well-intentioned fanatic idealist who brings havoc to the people he intends to rescue. The Johnson administration's believers in modernization theories and counterinsurgency, the communist press insisted, certainly shared some of that character's bookish traits.[54] But Nixon's war appeared to have none of this idealism. His deescalation hardly muffled protest at home, and even less among European critics. Brutal air warfare, combined with stealth diplomacy involving China and the Soviet Union, hardened the European Left's conviction that the president and his national security adviser, Henry Kissinger, followed a realist approach to foreign policy that would also confirm America's hegemonic role in Europe. That policy best displayed what recently has been defined as the "Faustian" trait in modern U.S. foreign policy: the tendency to "cut deals with the devil," whether the "devil" came in the form of unsavory regimes with anticommunist credentials or that of the main communist adversaries themselves.[55] When dealing exclusively with the U.S.S.R. or China, the Nixon administration curbed Europe's initiative; its détente was the antithesis of the European-made détente the French and Italian Communists dreamed of; it was rather the consolidation of the Yalta covenant.

In opposing what was "Faustian" about U.S. foreign policy, the Eurocommunists also stressed the inherent contradictions of the whole American identity, which, with equal arrogance, matched claims to exceptionalism with frequent cynical compromises—and did so at a time when Americans were forced to debate their own evolving identity, conflicted between equality and freedom. This view of a cynical American establishment intensified the Communists' fear of international conspiracies. Supporting notions that domestic terrorism received U.S. support or instigation, Berlinguer argued as late as April 1976 that these "foreign groups [were] interested in creating a situation of economic and political chaos in Italy, because they oppose (in France and Italy) communist participation in a government majority."[56] Since Euro-communism envisioned closer cooperation with progressive and radical nations in the Third World, it remained axiomatic to target U.S. imperialism in that respect, too. Even though Soviet violations of détente in Third World areas were also egregious, the PCI castigated Washington and capitalist globalization for causing serious economic imbalances. Imperialism, as a *Rinascita* essay had put it in June 1973, now "killed even without bombs."[57]

But while denouncing the U.S. leadership, the Communists continued to acknowledge the multifaceted nature of U.S. society, and now, even of its inner-circle politics. The distinction between America's rulers and ruled was now extended to a perceived contrast between an unscrupulous executive and a relatively liberal Congress. That was how, for example, Berlinguer portrayed the bribery scandal involving the Lockheed aircraft industry and its contracts with the Italian government. Like other forms of covert operations, he told the party directorate, this one also led to a series of congressional investigations. Of course, the PCI welcomed this widened rift between the presidency and the Pentagon, on the one hand, and Congress, on the other, for an obvious reason: it seemingly foretold an institutional collapse that befit the imperialist power reckoning with its social and foreign policy crises. But just as strongly, Berlinguer suggested that American politics had lost its monolithic nature, and that American democracy was still open to the liberal pressures that had erupted during the Vietnam debacle.[58]

According to the Soviet script, anti-Americanism should not have enjoyed any qualification. Especially after President Jimmy Carter encouraged dissent in Eastern Europe through his accent on human rights, the position of the PCI became questionable from Moscow's point of view. Berlinguer's vision of a Europe that was "neither anti-American nor anti-Soviet" was unacceptable to Brezhnev, who, in a meeting with the Italian leader in November 1977, insisted that the PCI's role was to "unmask NATO" and the "aggressive policies of that bloc." By that time, however, Berlinguer had further loosened his party's ties with Moscow.[59]

Even in France, in a post-1968 atmosphere, anti-Americanism continued to be qualified and modulated. Under the increasing dominance of François Mitterrand, the Left battled U.S. influence in the economic and cultural sectors. But the Socialists challenged America's imperialism in the Third World much more than its command over NATO, underlining their own virtual acceptance of the Western alliance. As has been noted, the Parti Socialiste (PS) (formerly the Section Française de l'Internationale Ouvrière [SFIO]) was "Jacobin (read: nationalist) . . . on cultural issues" above all. So was the Gaullist Right, with authors such as Jacques Thibau denouncing the "colonization of the French soul."[60] In these interpretations, "individualism" and "cosmopolitanism" had more cultural than economic significance: the United States, under its appealing pluralism and improved egalitarianism, still threatened historic traditions and the organic cohesion of French society.

By comparison, the PCF was now less nationalist on cultural matters, while still vehemently against U.S. imperialism and the right-wing resurgence in American politics. The U.S. government, under Nixon, had not relented from its imperial practices. In fact, a 1971 memorandum from the party's economic secretariat contended, the U.S. government's use of French subsidiaries, IBM-France especially, helped American industries — courtesy of President Georges Pompidou — "invade the markets of the francophone countries," thus further supplanting "what used to be the preserve of French colonialism."[61] According to a series of articles published in *L'Humanité* in 1972, U.S. society and working conditions had improved, and its pluralism, while heavily monitored through the media, party politics, and the capitalist substructure, showed real prospects for individual freedoms and opportunities. America was no longer utterly demonized, but it was still the main enemy, dangerous, dominant over Europe, bent on dismantling Europe's welfare systems, and ready to wreck détente as the opportunity arose.[62]

While the Socialists began to dissent from strong cultural anti-American posturing, the Communists did not cease sounding the alarm that freedom, though apparently more widespread now, was still illusory in America. For that reason, the United States was even more dangerous than before. *L'Humanité*'s articles coincided with the climax of a relentless party campaign to "liberate Angela Davis." That campaign, coordinated with Moscow, was, according to the PCF's political bureau, intended "to recapture the solid support from all [French] radical students."[63] Being black and communist and, as a philosopher and UCLA professor, a campus activist, Davis became for over a year a symbolic rallying point for the PCF's — and to a lesser extent, the PCI's — propaganda. Her incarceration confirmed what both French and Italian Communists had claimed all along: neither civil rights nor university transformations had truly changed the social and intellectual world of that "limited" democracy. But at least, within American society, in Congress, and, by the late 1970s, even inside the White House, there were strong progressive currents that the Western Communists acknowledged and encouraged.

In the end, Eurocommunism had minimal impact on politics in the West; it did not result in the lifting of the U.S. veto on a communist sharing of power. But it did have a subversive effect in the East, for it drew the attention of East Germans, Romanians, Poles, and Yugoslavs. The Soviet Union

"Set Angela Davis free."
PCF poster, 1971. Courtesy
Collection du PCF/Archives
départementales de la
Seine-Saint-Denis.

became hostile largely because of this "magnetism" and because of its own
fear that Eurocommunism, with its increasing acceptance of NATO, would
ultimately favor the militarization of Western Europe.[64]

INTERPLAY WITH DOMESTIC POLITICS

These were not the only reasons for concern in Moscow. Although, during
this Eurocommunist phase, the French and Italian Communists ostensibly
waged their main actions internationally, they both claimed their independence from the Soviet Union first in their internal affairs.[65] Years after the
Prague events, both parties continued to define the defense of national autonomy as the main achievement of the reform movement in Czechoslo-

vakia. They shared a total rejection of a restored Cominform under any disguise.[66] With a higher international profile, both parties for a while seemed to lay claim to a real independent option of national unity governments, and, leaders in both Washington and Moscow feared, even for a national path to reformed socialism. This came, but not without deep contrasts and contradictions.

Again, traditions of nationalism and the nation-state, and even the nationalist belief that revolution had its roots in France, aggravated the PCF's imperviousness to any transnational option.[67] The PCI, too, naturally used nationalist appeals against U.S. interference. But, even more, as the ruling Italian parties had already done, it now saw Europe as an instrument for the country's emancipation from the heaviest political constraints of the Cold War.

The emancipation from the blocs was also inherent in the PCF's domestic choice of siding with the establishment represented by François Mitterrand. Internal and external détente clashed in France, where the Soviet Union favored the seemingly anti-Atlantic de Gaulle and his successors Georges Pompidou and Valéry Giscard d'Estaing to a presumably Atlanticist Mitterrand. It became essential for the Communists to have electable candidates.[68] After Mitterrand's loss in the presidential elections of 1974, narrower than any predictions, the PCF had to become the suitor in the relationship and part of the system. Moscow continued to bet on the Gaullist forces against the imponderable prospects of a Left dominated by the Socialists. Soviet influence may have thus been a factor in the PCF's decision to break the unity pact with the Socialists in 1977. But there is no conclusive evidence of pressures from the Kremlin except the PCF leaders' realization of their financial dependence on the Soviet Union.[69] The French Communists rather gave priority to their choice of "identity." They preferred to detach themselves from a reform movement that, under the common denominator of Eurocommunism, made them subordinate to an increasingly pro-Western Mitterrand. Their emphasis, through the last two years of the "common program," on nationalization of industry and on militant trade unionism was more than a pretext for divorce from the PS; it signaled their reiteration of a working-class, revolutionary, and thoroughly anti-American outlook. When the common program with the French Socialists foundered in 1978, the Communists reverted to orthodoxy not only on Soviet policies but also on matters of détente and European integration.[70]

A basic misunderstanding had also marred socialist-communist cooperation in France. For the PCF, that cooperation was a long-term process that it intended to dominate, aiming at the transition to a "socialism with the colors of France," whereas for Mitterrand it was only a tactic to rebalance the Left in his favor, weaning away communist supporters to the Socialists and himself. This motive, obvious to the PCF leaders by the late 1970s, was, with Kanapa's death in September 1978, a principal factor in the party's acceptance of renewed dependence on Soviet favor and financing, at a time that the PCI was loosening that tie. The Soviet invasion of Afghanistan offered the PCF another pretext to confirm its orthodoxy in defense of the Soviet actions. The main international issue still favoring cooperation with the PS was European integration and the promotion of the European parliament by universal suffrage. But it was clear that this was a search for common ground in extremis, while the PCF continued to follow the Soviet line on this matter, considering *Western* European integration a U.S.-German trap.[71]

For the PCI, Eurocommunism also had a crucial internal corollary. It meant the beginning of the "Historic Compromise" with the Christian Democrats, an external support for the main ruling party first proposed by Berlinguer in three *Rinascita* articles from October through December 1973. The leader aimed at eventually entering and transforming the government coalition. This was more of an anti-U.S. than an anti-Soviet move. Following the September coup in Chile that overthrew Salvador Allende, the Historic Compromise proposal was, in part, designed to prevent a similar scenario from occurring in Italy, invoking the common struggle against fascism, as in the postwar coalition of all democratic parties. Where Allende had failed, according to Berlinguer, was in his relative neglect of Chile's middle classes and of the Christian Democratic Party. Orthodox party leaders, such as Colombi, simply pointed out that in Chile the United States had orchestrated a "strategy of tension" similar to the one behind the first terrorist attacks in Italy.[72] While most public debate focused on the Chilean precedent, the party was also disquieted by rumors of a KGB attempt on Berlinguer's life during his visit to Sofia in October.[73]

At first, the Historic Compromise only relied on exploiting divisions within the Christian Democratic Party, and it counted on that party's relative flexibility—especially from the faction led by Aldo Moro, who had also headed the center-left governments—toward a broad coalition.[74] By late 1974 the PCI's program had become more ambitious, setting the goal of gradually replacing reformed capitalism with socialist or planning elements. Berlinguer elaborated on the notion that NATO would shelter this experimentalism from Soviet interference. In 1977, at the celebrations for the sixtieth anniversary of the Bolshevik revolution, he claimed polemically that only under a democracy which had a "universal historical value" could a socialist society be truly built.[75]

The Historic Compromise also meant that the utopian elements were muted by everyday administrative responsibilities, and the need to deal with an economic downturn that required not a massive redistribution of wealth but sacrifices from all in the short term. With its emphasis on moral issues, the party's campaign for austerity strove to fit these basic needs and responsibilities.

Austerity had a moral dimension that was presumed to redefine class warfare itself. For the main party "ascetics," the communist Catholics Franco Rodano and Antonio Tatò, the purifying drive of "austerity" should have not only reduced income gaps but also and above all transformed a consumerist society into a society founded on solidarity. In some respects, this was a return to the early Cold War criticism of the "civilization of abundance," with added censure of the hedonism of the generation that came of age in the 1960s. Berlinguer was indeed known and praised for his high moral rigor and frugal habits.[76] These theories also inspired the Berlinguer inner circle to further expand its own notions of "socialism with a human face." NATO, in this case, would provide the framework for not only security from Soviet influence, but also for a gradual transformation in economic and social terms. According to Rodano, Italy could spearhead the transformation of Europe through the use and diversion of a consumerist economy, shifting its dimension gradually from private to "public" or "social consumption."[77] This reasoning matched in paradox the tactics of accepting NATO as a political and strategic umbrella: a more affluent Europe, made possible by its permanence in NATO, would ultimately emancipate Europe socially and geopolitically from U.S. control.

No similar ascetic appeals came from the PCF. In its *ouvriériste* view, austerity was yet another imposition by the state-monopoly capitalist interests enmeshed in a world economy under the U.S. aegis. "When we fight the politics of the establishment, the austerity and the national abandonment," Jacques Denis wrote in April 1979, "we wage the struggle of the working class and of the French people, and thus contribute to the general struggle against imperialism."[78]

The difference between the two parties was also evident in the degree to which they appealed to the middle classes suffering from the economic downturn. The PCI of the mid-1970s, while doubling its membership in the blue-collar districts, further extended its reach to a discontented middle class, including many petit bourgeois and small entrepreneurs hard hit by the economic recession of middecade, or simply consternated by the numerous corruption scandals of the ruling parties. A growing number of intellectuals welcomed the party's departure from Soviet orthodoxy.[79] To a lesser extent, the PCF also continued to build its role as a refuge not only against capitalist exploitation (mostly affecting the working class) but also against the superstructure of oppressive values generated by capitalism (mostly affecting the middle classes). But while the latter appeal helped the party absorb intellectual and middle-class groups, overall the party's orthodoxy resulted in a steady decline of its strength through the late 1970s. Although formally united for the parliamentary elections of 1978, the PCF and PS had in every respect abandoned the common Left program. The PCF viciously attacked the Socialists for abandoning the working class and veering toward pro-Western policies. At the polls in March, the voters penalized the Communists and confirmed the electoral ascendancy of the PS. By breaking its alliance with the Socialists, the PCF thus further contributed to the demise of Eurocommunism. By 1981, when Mitterrand finally won the presidency, the PCF had lost more than half of its electorate (going to the PS) even in the "red belt" around Paris.[80]

In Italy, the PCI's newly assumed aura of government responsibility was compounded by its interpretation of left-wing terrorism. The PCI establishment downplayed the terrorists' ideological heritage and the roots of their ideas in the 1960s utopias; it instead highlighted their conspiratorial design aimed at halting the PCI's popular front operation. But this contributed to the lowering of the party's appeal to the youngest, most idealistic constituencies. While the party achieved its greatest electoral success in the administrative elections of 1975, with several major city and regional administrations falling under its rule, power at the national level remained precluded. This became apparent in its support of the one-party government of Giulio Andreotti in 1977, followed by the "national solidarity" government, still under Andreotti, in 1978. With the U.S. veto of communist participation in the government, terrorism at its high tide, and the fear of a right-wing backlash, the PCI could only provide external support to the Christian Democrat prime minister. This amounted to a great deal of responsibility without power. In most respects, the party's bureaucratic source of strength, so prominent in the immediate postwar era, in this new context became a liability.[81]

Terrorism struck with emblematic force when on 16 March 1978, while the Italian parliament cast its vote of confidence in the "solidarity government," the Red Brigades kidnapped the historic DC leader Aldo Moro. The former head of the center-left coalition had also worked hardest to integrate the PCI into the Italian democratic system. His assassination by his captors two months later further pressed the Communists to pose as guarantors of legal stability against leftist extremism. The party directorate even refrained from reiterating the hypothesis of a foreign plot.[82] With the priority given to law and order, the Andreotti cabinet failed to adopt any of the advanced reform proposals agreed under the solidarity pact. Berlinguer officially withdrew his support of the government majority the following January.[83] With this conclusion of the Historic Compromise, coinciding with the end of détente, the last chances for Eurocommunism to become a viable political force also passed the party by.

The PCI, the main force behind the movement, suffered from fundamental contradictions, due to its "political culture," which persistently identified with the Soviet legacy, regardless of the party's own discerning criticism of Soviet conduct. This problem of identity, or ideology, predated and even caused its political isolation in the 1980s. The PCI's failure to establish a workable relationship with Europe's social democratic forces and its "ambition to reform communism" in the East as well as the West were perhaps the "most influential and decisive" causes of its political defeat.[84] But these contradictions were also mutually nurturing with the external constraints on the PCI—namely, the DC's persistent exclusion of a full government role for the PCI, the evolution of Europe's Socialists toward Atlanticism, and the U.S. "veto" of Eurocommunism. But the U.S. role had not simply amounted to a veto of the whole experiment. Washington further refined its diplomatic handling of a situation that could have upset the very essence of its Cold War strategy in Western Europe.

U.S. Reactions to Eurocommunism

Détente did diminish the sense of communist threat worldwide. U.S. public opinion was no longer prone to consider its Communist Party a danger to domestic security. In fact, the House Un-American Activities Committee was abolished in 1975, while the Senate Select Committee to Study Government Operations (the "Church Committee") reduced the government's discretion in future covert actions.[85] The radical turns of the 1960s—prompted by the increased militancy among students, feminists, and civil rights activists—together with failures in Vietnam, had been answered by a conservative backlash in the national leadership. The election of Richard Nixon in 1968 reflected the public call for law and order and opened an age of conservative predominance in American politics that would persist until the end of the Cold War. This, however, also meant that the country's most acute fears about radicalism at home and communist expansion worldwide subsided.

But would this diminished alarm apply to the apparent advance of Eurocommunism? The now limited power of the executive and the CIA certainly explains how even Kissinger thought it counterproductive to fund operations and other forms of "black" psychological warfare to curb communist power in Western Europe.

FRANCE

Already at the start of his job as national security adviser in 1969, Kissinger had opposed a financing plan orchestrated by staff members of de Gaulle's presidential office and the State Department to launch an "Advertising Campaign in Support of U.S.-French Relations." Previous decisions to reduce funding of Italy's centrist parties had been based on the poor results of such operations. This time, NSC senior staff member Helmut Sonnenfeldt and Kissinger reflected primarily on other aspects of such U.S. financed projects. The "Advertising Campaign," they noted, would "raise hackles on Capitol Hill." Intensified diplomatic channels, they concluded, "cooperative private and government programs," and trade promotion would obtain the same political results in France without running that risk. The two advisers reiterated the importance of using diplomatic tools to gain clout in a country's internal affairs. This was in contrast to pressing invitations from Paris to use the more intrusive option of funding internal operations.[86]

In part, this detached attitude reflected a diminished alarm about communist power and propaganda in France. In July, the U.S. ambassador to Paris, Robert Sargent Shriver, showed a dispassionate view of the "alliance of the Left" reemerging between Mitterrand and the PCF. A share in power, he reflected, would erode the Communists' "tight alliance with Moscow" and their "doctrinaire positions." While this would not "make the Communists into non-Communists," it was clear that "the danger of a Communist takeover [was] not what it was in 1945." The ambassador therefore recommended a "U.S. policy . . . as sophisticated about the Communist danger as the Communist danger itself." Washington had to recognize that the popularity of the Left meant that social change was necessary in France, and thus the United States should never "take positions that [would] enable the Communists to claim a monopoly of demands for social change." Shriver concluded that the embassy's continuous contact with PCF members was "useful and not harmful," for it would allow it to have informative "and perhaps even influential contacts" with a party that now seemed more enmeshed with domestic politics than a tool of Moscow's international propaganda campaigns. Shriver's subtle and progressive approach reflected his own style at the embassy during his tenure from 1968 to 1970. The former Kennedy adviser brought to the office a new aura of cosmopolitanism and "panache" that drew the attention and admiration of the French public, regardless of political orientation.[87]

But the Nixon administration was rather removed from that style and approach. With a lowered profile on European integration, a conservative outlook, and an emphasis on international balance of power and strong leadership, the Nixon administration sympathized with de Gaulle and his successor Georges Pompidou. Kissinger mourned the General's fading star in the spring of 1969, because de Gaulle, from his position above party lines, "drawing support from right and left," was "particularly successful in confounding the Communists." He had achieved that result ironically thanks to his hard dealings with Washington. His successors might not be as able to keep the PCF in a "semi-neutral stance," and France, in the national security adviser's view, might "run the danger of moving in the direction of Italy, with a large, well-organized Communist Party on the far left, and a constantly shifting amalgam of left, center, and right parties governing through a narrow consensus." This turn could have consequences on the international stage, too. Kissinger worried that Gaullism, under the new leadership, could undermine détente. An exchange of visits between French cabinet officials and Chinese Foreign Minister Chou En-lai made Kissinger worried that Paris was "courting the Chinese by adopting a distinctly anti-American line." This bode ill for negotiations on Vietnam. Moreover, the French refusal to sign the Non-Proliferation Treaty hindered Washington's attempts to limit China's nuclear program.[88]

But the U.S. embassy soon contradicted Kissinger's views on French politics, pointing to the new star emerging on the Left. François Mitterrand confirmed Shriver's perception of a tamed communist group, because by 1971, as a memo from the State Department noted, the socialist leader had given "that battered group [the PS] and the non-Communist Left as a whole, a psychological shot in the arm they badly need[ed]." The "moribund non-Communist Left" was no longer riddled with petulant defeatism. U.S. officials saw Mitterrand as the "catalyst" who was provoking a lively debate, and forcing hard choices on Gaullists and Communists alike. In this view, Mitterrand's main merits were his shrewdness and his ability to be a tough bargainer with his communist allies. Finally, Mitterrand harbored no sympathy for the Chinese leadership. Even the PCF, in gaining credit with the North Vietnamese leadership, ended up colliding with the Chinese Communists.[89] The PCF's Eurocommunist turn a few years later, even when combined with Mitterrand's close defeat in the 1974 presidential elections, seemed only to confirm that a socialist-communist cohabitation would not cause any major change in French politics. The PCF appeared sufficiently weakened and tamed. Washington, while harboring no illusion that the PCF could be reformed, simply understood that the French Communists had diminished power. Furthermore, under socialist dominance, the French Left, as I have just noted, did not direct its anti-Americanism against U.S. international policies—the things that mattered most to the Nixon and Ford administrations—but rather focused on matters of cultural identity.

ITALY

All this could change if the real magnet of Eurocommunism, the PCI, was successful in its domestic design. Unlike the Socialists in France, the Italian Christian Democrats had actually increased their factionalism and quarreling. The two leaders of the center-left era, Fanfani and Moro, now disagreed on how to approach the Communists. Ever since the post-Prague events, their competition for the presidency, as Prime Minister Mariano Rumor admitted to Ambassador Graham Martin in July 1970, was "like a cancer . . . reinforc[ing] the PCI leverage" in the following elections. The Socialists, split between the Nenni, Lombardi, and Mancini groups, and also suffering from the unfulfilled promises of the center-left coalition, had allowed themselves, in the embassy's opinion, to become the Communists' "stalking horses." Their campaigns against the Vietnam War were just as animated as those of their comrades to the left.[90]

The temptation to combat communist influence from the right might have been strong. Kissinger was convinced that "one of Kennedy's worst mistakes was to force the opening to the Left" in Italy. Ambassador Martin and his successor, John Volpe, did not hesitate to establish connections with right-wing representatives such as the Italian Republican Party's deputy Pier Talenti, or even with an unsavory ultraconservative financial dealer, Michele Sindona, and with Paul Marcinkus, a Chicago bishop and corrupt administrator of the Vatican Bank. These dealings were discovered years later. But earlier revelations, by 1976, of further secret American financing of the Christian Democrats for the 1975 administrative elections, and of contacts between Martin and General Vito Miceli, the neofascist head of the Servizio Intelligenza Difesa (the Italian counterpart to the CIA), fueled the PCI's argument that the United States might have conspired with Italy's domestic terrorists in an effort to halt the Historic Compromise.[91]

Throughout his years as national security adviser and secretary of state, Kissinger maintained an adamant opposition to any form of communist participation, direct or indirect, in the Italian government. Early in 1970 Ambassador Hugh Gardner Ackley informed Kissinger that the PCI was managing to increase its power, if slowly.[92] Four years later, as secretary of state, Kissinger told a rather unalarmed Prime Minister Aldo Moro that he was "more worried about a responsible than an irresponsible Communist Party."

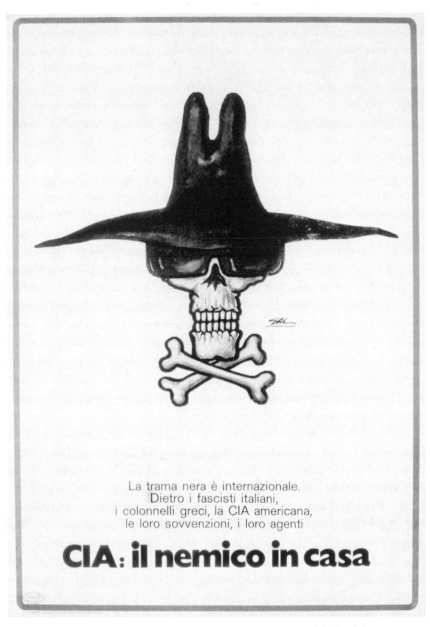

La trama nera è internazionale.
Dietro i fascisti italiani,
i colonnelli greci, la CIA americana,
le loro sovvenzioni, i loro agenti

CIA: il nemico in casa

"The CIA: The enemy within. The fascist conspiracy is international: behind the Italian fascists, the Greek colonels, is the American CIA, its funding, and its agents." PCI poster, 1973. Courtesy Fondazione Istituto Gramsci Emilia Romagna, Bologna.

Moro himself seemed persuaded by 1975 that "although the Italian Communists profess to support NATO, we know they won't." Kissinger's response was blunt: "We don't care if they sign onto NATO in blood"; a government with even external support by the PCI was simply "incompatible with continued membership in the alliance." Moro contended that it was hard to keep "rigid barriers" against the PCI "when you can see that the American president is talking to Soviet leaders." Public opinion, he reminded Kissinger, was "not very subtle."[93] But Kissinger was subtle, and one of his main fears was that the whole purpose of détente, which was to contain Soviet power, could be misunderstood as a form of appeasement in Europe, especially if NATO's Mediterranean powers allowed popular front governments to emerge as a consequence. Détente was designed also as a way to mitigate anti-American feelings and restore U.S. control over the alliance. Instead, Kissinger noted, while showing moderation in domestic politics, the Communist Parties of Europe had by 1975 "resumed [their] anti-Americanism for the first time in years." Eurocommunism could be even more destabilizing in the Soviet camp, perhaps inciting other revolts like the Prague Spring, a prospect Kissinger feared rather than welcomed.[94] While claiming to be neither anti-American nor anti-Soviet, the Eurocommunists were carrying out perhaps their most effective attack to date on the bipolar structure of power in Europe. Kissinger could not tolerate this challenge to a détente process which, in his view, could attain results only if both camps maintained the status quo with their allies.

The secretary of state had reasons to fear neutralist temptations in Europe. In 1973, in an awkward attempt to reevaluate transatlantic relations after years of focus on China, Vietnam, and the Soviet Union, Nixon and Kissinger had launched their project for a "Year of Europe." Suggesting a new "burden-sharing" agenda, by which the United States would remain responsible for global security and the Europeans for "regional" security, this proposal was received in Europe as hegemonic, insensitive to the allies' perception of their status as equals, and expecting their increased financial contributions. In July Italian Ambassador Egidio Ortona told Kissinger that the United States was losing "the weapon of European integration" against the appeals from the left in Europe.[95]

Adding these considerations to those on Italy's internal situation, Kissinger confirmed his hard line on Eurocommunism. While initially refraining from announcements to the Italian public, he recommended to President Ford as early as September 1974 a stern warning to Italian statesmen that "any Communists in the government would change our relationship." The pressure for such firm opposition came not only from the State Department but also from conservative Italian Christian Democrats Mariano Rumor and Giovanni Leone. Moro, and, later, Foreign Minister Arnaldo Forlani, another supporter of the Historic Compromise, thus received a repeated veto from the White House, which, as we will see, was reinforced by U.S. conditions on financial aid. By April 1976 Kissinger stepped up the warnings further, this time making his opposition to Eurocommunism public at a meeting of the American Society of Newspaper Editors, and even suggesting the expulsion of Italy from NATO in case of communist participation in the government.[96]

But more sober reflections from the U.S. embassy in Rome and the CIA mitigated Kissinger's blunt view. The CIA and National Security Adviser Brent Scowcroft, assessing the 1976 Italian postelectoral scenarios, took Berlinguer's acceptance of NATO rather seriously, though with a lingering fear that party hard-liners might prevent the PCI from becoming "overly social democratic." But the party's newfound responsibility given the prospect of achieving national power, according to the NSA study, could be useful to coax the trade unions to accept needed austerity measures—thus overall a boon to the Italian economy. The party's popularity could then decrease because of these very choices. Yet this might induce Berlinguer to compensate by blaming the problems on the ties with the U.S. economy and even the Western alliance.[97]

For all these reasons, after much deliberation, even so determined a hard liner as Ambassador Volpe decided to maintain low-level contacts with PCI spokesmen. Kissinger had originally opposed this tactic out of fear that it might come across as an endorsement of the Historic Compromise. But Volpe argued that talks with the PCI, besides working as sounding boards on the party's intentions, could also help Washington learn facts about communist local administrations and refute popular perceptions of their "proverbial efficiency." At the end of 1975, through these contacts, he had found out that Bologna, one of the "reddest" city administrations, had "the highest debt in the country." Furthermore, contacts through the embassy would defuse the Communists' suspicions that Washington might harbor a "Chilean" solution for Italy, thus muting their most vicious attacks on the administration.[98] The tenuous American links with PCI officials reflected the guarded ambivalence on both sides.

INFLUENCE THROUGH GRAND DIPLOMACY

In the final analysis, U.S. influence over Italian politics continued to work best when conducted through international initiatives, with only indirect reference to the country's internal politics. Grand diplomacy offered the opportunity to bolster the Italian government with international prestige. It was also effective because the initiative came from Rome. The Italian leaders' offer to the United States to play a special role in the Mediterranean persisted after the Arab-Israeli "Yom Kippur War" of 1973. The Italian government never criticized Kissinger's subsequent shuttle diplomacy as unilateral or hegemonic. In fact, even more than the old proponents of a Mediterranean vocation in the 1950s, the Italian leaders of the early 1970s pursued an ancillary role, offering Italy both as a secure base for U.S. military operations and as a possible mediator in various controversies in the area. As foreign minister, Aldo Moro conducted intense diplomacy in the aftermath of the Yom Kippur War. Perhaps to offset Washington's perception of mounting criticism, even among Christian Democrats, of U.S. foreign policy, Moro openly favored the Israeli government, going against the traditional Italian tendency to seek closer connections with the Arabs.[99] These diplomatic efforts were also meant to highlight Italy's reliability and stability in the midst of Mediterranean turmoil.

The comparison with the internal and external conflicts affecting the other southern members of NATO—Greece, Turkey, Portugal, and candidate Spain—seemed to favor Rome. President Nixon, meeting in 1970 with Fanfani, the first proponent of Italy's "Mediterranean vocation," recognized that Italy was "the greatest Mediterranean power" and that it should therefore play a role beside that of the United States. In 1974 the President Giovanni Leone reassured President Ford that Italy's apparent chronic government instability did not affect the country's "constant foreign policy." No pressure from the left, he added, would induce Rome to take a "French option" and leave NATO. Ambassador Volpe advocated the Italian renewed plea for a special relationship in the Mediterranean, arguing that, in that area, Italy was "the only sound democratic nation, who is an ally that will stay with us." Issues of prestige remained a powerful motive that Kissinger was willing to accommodate, in moderation, holding encounters with Italian leaders that he considered to be a facade.[100]

Self-promotion at the diplomatic level was counterbalanced by the usual contradictory appeals emphasizing internal weakness. In November 1975 Foreign Minister Mariano Rumor insisted with Volpe on the need for "greater attention from the United States . . . to help bolster the standing of the Christian Democrats." A year earlier Leone had been more ominous, arguing to Kissinger that if Italy fell to communism, all of the Mediterranean would go too.[101] The dominoes, Kissinger noted in a meeting with Pope Paul VI in June 1975, might in fact have already started to fall in Portugal, making orthodox communists acceptable there, then opening that possibility in Spain and finally in Italy. The Pope himself, while inviting détente between the superpowers, also warned against the advantages the PCI might draw from it. The Catholic Church in the United States had also sounded the alarm about Italy's next elections. Italian American members of Congress and business representatives joined forces in a fashion evoking the 1948 mobilization in favor of the Christian Democrats.[102] Funding operations for the DC resumed, only to be withdrawn when they were leaked to the press.

Kissinger focused on Italy's appeals based on weakness, rather than crediting Italy's diplomatic skills. "The problem with Italy," he told Ford in September 1974, "is that with the Communists in government, they would be competent—it would make them irresistible in France, isolate Germany, give [Greek socialist leader] Papandreou an opening in Greece. The Socialists never would have gained power in Germany if that nice idiot [Chancellor Kurt Georg Kiesinger in 1966] hadn't taken them into a coalition. That makes them respectable. The same would happen in Italy." Conservative European leaders concurred. The following day, the German Christian Democrat leader and foreign minister Hans-Dietrich Genscher reminded Kissinger that any form of communist government participation in Italy "would draw a cloud over other European countries." Then he added: "We don't want to see what NATO has prevented come about by the internal route."[103]

This domino effect could involve Third World areas as well. A rising trend of socialism in the developing world, and its implicit endorsement of the PCI's polycentrism gave Eurocommunism a potential command of neutralist tendencies worldwide. Kissinger and his staff feared that, in Europe, a combination of economic need for raw materials, the recession, and rising discontent over the two superpowers' control of détente could lead to popular front coalitions with a "less pro-Western," and "more pro–Third World, more neutralist" set of priorities.[104]

While expressing those fears, the United States had already set in place, through the summit meetings of the group of industrialized nations, a strategy combining diplomacy and economic choices. Diplomatic maneuvering was combined with an economic turn that helped tame not only Europe's Communists but its Social Democrats as well.

THE NEW INTERDEPENDENCE

Italy found its way into the group of the five industrialized nations, which by 1975 thus became the G-6, partly for reasons of prestige. While the summits' economic choices mattered in redesigning interdependence in the Western alliance, considerations of prestige were paramount in restoring political credit for the Italian Christian Democrats. On the eve of the G-5 meeting at Rambouillet, Kissinger, in agreement with French President Valéry Giscard d'Estaing and German Chancellor Helmut Schmidt, decided to include Italy in the group of the industrialized nations "for political reasons, even though [the Italians] might make no particular contribution." At the summit, Prime Minister Moro himself admitted that while the Italian economy was weak, this recognition was crucial to further sway the country's public opinion in favor of the United States. It was largely the political success at Rambouillet that convinced France and Germany to make the Italian membership permanent.[105]

But the G-6 also tailored economic assistance and reform in Italy along monetarist lines. The politics of productivity that followed the Marshall Plan in the early 1950s had been the first step in defusing class conflict in Europe. Mass consumption by the following decade had further eroded the patterns of socialization on which the French and Italian Communist Parties had founded their vision of emancipation from capitalism and the United States. By the 1970s the recession, a laissez-faire approach in the West, and the politics of austerity threatened to undo this political, social, and cultural edifice. These economic conditions and choices contradicted the Fordist-Keynesian design of the Marshall Plan's anticlassist approach. The reduction of welfare in Europe could have rekindled class conflict and, since the maneuver was orchestrated from Washington, anti-Americanism, too. In fact, the emergence of neoliberism, as it has been recently demonstrated, was quite consensual.[106]

The United States found a receptive interlocutor in Europe's leading economy, Germany. Better still, it was a social democrat, Helmut Schmidt who, as chancellor, endorsed anti-inflationary measures, deregulation, and privatization. The prospect of popular fronts in the Mediterranean countries of Europe was still strong, thanks to Mitterrand's rising influence. But in the end the German Social Democrats held sway, because of their country's economic power and also because of their renewed connection with the United States. Nothing could better combat neutralist and anti-American feelings in Europe, Kissinger recognized repeatedly in 1974–75, than giving ample credit to the *new* Social Democrats in Germany. After Ford's first meeting with Schmidt, the secretary of state reassured the president: "With the two of you working together, the West, the alliance is going to be all right." "If we will work with [Schmidt] on the economy," Kissinger argued at a national security meeting in May 1975, "he will support us on everything else. *The trick in the world now is to use economics to build a world political structure.*" Furthermore, by supporting Schmidt, the international weight of the rather unreliable French government would be diminished; in Germany, Brandt's wing of the SPD would be discredited, and so would be any attempt by the socialist forces in Europe to establish a dialogue with the Eurocommunists.[107]

And the "trick" worked. At the G-6 summit at Rambouillet in November 1975, years of economic rivalry between Western Europe and the United States were resolved under the rubric of liberism and monetarism. The main thrust of this conference and of its G-7 followup in Puerto Rico in June 1976 was the reform of government regulations and the "removal of restrictions to private enterprise." Schmidt himself recognized that the purpose of this meeting was more political than economic: the trend toward popular front solutions in Europe had to be halted.[108]

The summit in Puerto Rico also finalized the terms of the loan to Italy. U.S. economic *and* political control over the country became manifest in two ways: U.S. guidance proved essential to the handling of the institutional arrangements by the International Monetary Fund, and the aid package was made conditional on avoiding increased PCI influence over the government. Better still, it was not Kissinger but Schmidt who announced that Italy would not receive financial aid if the Communists came to power. There was no immediate anti-American backlash. In fact, the PCI, until the early 1980s, refrained from inciting public opinion against the new economic policies. On its own, the party came to the conclusion that austerity was the main solution to Italy's economic problems. Even more than economic blackmail, it was the substantial dismantlement of Keynesian solutions that hurt the prospects of Eurocommunism.[109] After the 1960s had redesigned interdependence with a transatlantic counterculture that favored pluralism, the 1970s redesigned interdependence in favor of laissez-faire and American leadership over Western economic cooperation.

These developments hit the Italian Communists in two ways. First, Berlinguer further lost the connection with Europe's social democratic forces. In terms of international economics, that connection was essential to wed the notion of a European third force to closer cooperation with the developing nations. Countering the G-7 approach, a group of seventy-seven developing nations in the United Nations had attempted to create a New International Economic Order favoring economic planning.[110] The U.S. and German turn, under the aegis of the International Monetary Fund, foiled that design. All this made the PCI's search for a third way between Soviet Communism and Western Social Democracy far less credible.

Communist power in Italy also suffered, if not immediately, from its loss of "populist" aura, due to its association with an Italian government that subscribed to the G-7's anti-inflationary measures. The party's grassroots understood that Berlinguer's acceptance of NATO was less a tactical move than evidence that the party had forsaken radical change.

This is not to say that the PCI's prospects were quickly sealed. In the 1976 national elections, the party reached a new peak in terms of popular support with 34.4 percent of the vote, only four percentage points below the Christian Democrats. The smaller parties of the Center-Left suffered the heaviest losses, and the country thus appeared more and more polarized between the extreme Left and the conservative Right. A 1970 National Security Study Memorandum on Italy still held true. Bureaucratic stagnation still alienated much of the Italian public from the Christian Democrats' thirty years of rule. Prosperity had not guaranteed stability either, because the public's "aspirations [rose] faster than living standards and impatience with bureaucratic inadequacy [grew]." Furthermore, the DC leaders themselves continued to resist economic and political pressures from Washington, in part, as the CIA postelection assessment noted, because they needed to appease the PCI in order to earn its support in carrying out the austerity measures. Their resistance was also a protraction of a "tacit agreement" with the Communists to "avoid giving the U.S. an opportunity to mobilize American and West European public opinions" against the Historic Compromise.[111]

In France things did not bode well either, with Giscard losing ground to Mitterrand's Left coalition. Although the socialist leader was a rather safe asset on NATO matters, his continued advocacy of the inclusion of the PCF could only encourage the more ominous participation of the PCI in the Italian government. It was in part for this reason that the Ford administration refused to meet with Mitterrand, in order to avoid granting him increased "respectability" as opposition leader.[112]

HOPES OF A SOFT APPROACH

At the height of its political power, the PCI welcomed the prospect of a new U.S. administration that would show greater flexibility toward Italy's internal détente, and toward a more multilateral international détente. On the eve of the Italian elections, both Berlinguer and the future party secretary Alessandro Natta counted on a "complementing" victory of Jimmy Carter in November to weaken those in the U.S. leadership who opposed the Historic Compromise. The PCI also started referring frequently to the Kissinger record after hardly paying attention to his positions on Europe during the Nixon presidency. The focus was now justified perhaps by the intensity of his anti-PCI pronouncements. But it was also a way for the PCI to underline his "fading star" in U.S. politics. From the foreign ministry, Manzini, fully persuaded about extending the DC's cooperation with the PCI, also eagerly awaited Kissinger's departure. He reassured Segre that his contacts in the State Department saw a "realistic attitude" toward Italy emerging against Kissinger's obstinacy.[113]

This moderation lulled the PCI into a false sense of confidence that the Carter administration might welcome the party's "induction" into European politics mainly through cooperation with Germany's Social Democrats. In November, Segre reported to Berlinguer that the nominee for national security adviser, Zbigniew Brzezinski, was hoping the PCI would help "lift Germany from its political malaise."[114] Segre's own perceptions may have been distorted by the warm welcome the American academic community gave to the prospect of a Historic Compromise. Peter Lange in 1975 seemed to have foretold this attitude among Democrats, writing a favorable article on the PCI in *Foreign Policy* magazine. The even more prestigious journal *Foreign Affairs* gave Segre himself, as well as Jean Kanapa, a stage on which to explain their own visions of Eurocommunism. Both intellectuals professed their parties' acceptance of NATO, at least for the time being.[115] The PCI's tendency to overestimate the influence of intellectuals in the United States was rooted in its own experience of academic clout at home. But the election of Jimmy Carter occurred during a general resurgence of American conservatism. Intellectuals from the right, and even the emergence of neoconservative ideas, were coming to affect the political debate on U.S. internal and foreign policies even more than the academic Left did. In the summer of 1977 a conference organized by the American Enterprise Institute for Public Policy Research in Washington to discuss the PCI had a high resonance among political circles: it featured, besides Kissinger, old and new conservative opponents of the Eurocommunist project.[116]

The American conservative outlook was even more tangible in economic terms. The monetarist turn of the Ford years was not modified. In fact, Carter's choices veered even more in that direction, until, in 1979, the White House endorsed the Federal Reserve's decision to increase interest rates dramatically. During the previous years, the IMF loan to Italy remained contingent on structural changes to its economy according to the Puerto Rico guidelines.[117]

Worse still, anti-Sovietism, even more than anti-Americanism, now worked against the PCI agenda. While the party, Giorgio Napolitano mused in July 1977, had no nostalgia for the Kissinger-Ford policies, the Soviet Union did. Moscow's hostility to the new administration and its emphasis on human rights clashed with the PCI's initial approval of the U.S. liberal turn.[118]

If the Italian Communists had reasons for confidence during the first year of the Carter administration, this was not because of its progressive leaning, but rather because of its indifference or extreme cautiousness in interfering with its European allies' internal affairs. That is how the historiography has portrayed the rather standoffish attitude of the Carter cabinet, emphasizing either its confusion or its set of priorities that did not include Italian politics.[119] It is true that President Carter paid scant attention to Eurocommunism. But the archival evidence shows that the administration, and National Security Adviser Brzezinski in particular, reexamined the subject with even more emphasis on the interlocking use of diplomacy and economic means than the Nixon-Ford White Houses had.

FINE-TUNING INTERDEPENDENCE

Carter initially refrained from direct intervention in part because of the usual concern about a possible backlash from public opinion in Italy and Europe in general. The president combined this concern with the expectation that the main European allies would maintain their vision of détente as a serious means to modify the conduct and politics of the Eastern bloc. A greater respect for the allies, and their maturity in both foreign policy and internal affairs was paramount to this approach. After meeting with Giscard in February 1977, Brezinski warned President Carter about the "danger of another 'Year of Europe' mentality here [in reference to Kissinger's European policies], through a failure to think through the complexities of relations with Europe." Therefore consultations had to be "kept real." Despite the affinity with Europe on issues of détente, the Carter administration was also aware that the NATO allies were "uneasy" about its "ability to manage relations with the Soviet Union," as Brzezinski noted in a memorandum a few months later. In France and Germany especially, there was a growing tendency toward realism and "nonconfrontation" on human rights issues. In general, Brzezinski worried about the "European ambivalence about American leadership." Too much specific action from Washington, however, would have "elicited Europe's criticism of U.S. dominance." But, "unlike times in the past," the national security adviser concluded, "the relative economic and political weight of the United States is not enough on its own to carry the day— against the ambivalence of Europeans, but perhaps to their ultimate self-interest"; therefore the U.S. leadership, more than in the past, would have to rely on "proding, cajoling, consulting—and a lot of stroking." This would also mean "accepting European views of policy that are different from ours," such as in the Middle East.[120] The determination that diplomacy had to be the first weapon of influence thus came from the realization of America's relatively diminished power and stature vis-à-vis its allies.

Furthermore, if détente assumed a transformative character, Euro-communism could be considered beneficial for its democratizing effects on the Eastern bloc. This consideration influenced the intellectual circles around the Institute of European Studies at Harvard and the Research Institute of Social Change at Columbia University, and it remained prominent in Brezinski's own view of the human rights campaign. Secretary of State Cyrus Vance was also persuaded that the PCI could disrupt the Soviet bloc more than it could the West.[121]

For all these reasons, the president repeatedly asserted his respect for the sovereign nations of Europe and their right to determine their own politics. His only direct references to Eurocommunism through 1977 simply emphasized that the United States would prefer that "no totalitarian element become dominant or influential."[122]

But the administration also relied on the Italian government's promise that it would effectively reform its economy along the IMF agenda, and it hoped that this would tarnish the PCI record in the eyes of its core electorate. Prime Minister Giulio Andreotti seemed bound to do just that in 1977. As the secretary of Italy's ultraleftist Party of Proletarian Unity, Lucio Magri, predicted, "Rather than using the PCI to control the economic crisis, Andreotti uses the economic crisis to control the PCI." Andreotti went further, assuring Carter during his visit to Washington in July 1977 that the PCI's external support to the government would have, counterintuitively, reinforced Italy's Atlantic ties, while also weakening, through the Eurocommunist appeal, the Warsaw Pact. The DC veteran Andreotti, whose conservative credentials were beyond doubt, was seen in Washington as an able maneuverer of Italy's intricate politics. But Andreotti was no Mitterrand, who enjoyed increasing clout over the French Left. Brzezinski actually did not trust either the French or the Italian leaders. In a memorandum preceding Andreotti's visit, he wrote to Carter that "the French Socialists and the Italian Christian Democrats each believe[d] they [could] somehow derive strength from the more energetic Communists, without succumbing to them." Both groups, in his view, seemed to have "lost [their] spirit and courage."[123]

Scant faith in Italian politics was not new, but a diminished faith in French politics allowed the Carter administration to place the threat of Eurocommunism in broader perspective. Italy could become perhaps the catalyst of a domino effect in Europe, but France presented the real problem if there were to be a chain reaction. That was, in essence, the conclusion Brzezinski had drawn by mid-1977, based on the analyses of academic specialists, especially Pierre Hassner, of the Fondation Nationale de Sciences Politiques in Paris; George Urban, expert on Eastern European affairs and director of Radio Free Europe; Richard McCormack, assistant secretary of state for economic affairs; and Robert Hunter, national security director for Western European affairs.

Although Hassner recognized the Historic Compromise as "the only practicable . . . formula" for Italy in the immediate, he also warned against the dangers at the foreign policy level. For, as much as the PCI had made progress toward democracy on domestic issues and in its international outlook, it remained in essence "anti-American." Its "Third-Worldist view of North South relations," and its emphasis on the "struggle against imperialism" was still far more compatible with Soviet than Western interests. These observations found corroborating evidence also in the PCF's move toward acceptance of French nuclear weapons, provided that this would not lead to closer cooperation with NATO. Most likely, Hassner warned, Eurocommunism would foster the "Finlandization" of Italy and other Western European countries.[124]

Urban also exempted the PCI from many of the worst characterizations of it by the previous presidency. "The Italian Communists, when closely observed," he wrote, "do not strike terror in one's heart"; their participation in the government would not necessarily be "an irreversible disaster." Nevertheless, he concluded, "we should be clear that the psychological impact of such participation, especially in France, would be disastrous and might unhinge the whole Western alliance." Hunter suggested the creation of an "interagency working group" on France and Italy. He admitted that the "stakes in France are higher than they are in Italy." The union of the Left under Mitterrand was closer to victory. Furthermore, France was "more vital to the European Community and to European defense"; and the German reaction to a victory of the Left in France would be "more intense, very likely leading to a sharp move to the right, a polarization within the European Community, and an isolation of the U.S.-German connection within the Atlantic Community."

These advisers all concurred that careful interference in Italy would be not only appropriate but actually "expected" by the moderate Italian political parties. "What the Italians cannot live with," Urban wrote, "is a sense of abdication on the part of the U.S." It was important, however, as Hunter pointed out, that Italy not be made to feel like a "backward country" or another Chile. More needed to be done in terms of economic cooperation than economic blackmail. In France there was virtually no room for interference. Pressures from Washington would have been deeply resented. In March Mitterrand had also made it clear that any explicit statement would hinder his plan to dominate the left-wing coalition and thus neutralize the Communists. France, Hunter argued, was "far less amenable to U.S. action." In fact, much in line with the tradition of Gaullism, there was a "certain value in a politician's being seen to counter U.S. initiatives."[125] This tactic of ostensible noninterference and even encouragement of a mild, therapeutic anti-Americanism among the French conservative parties had been used since 1947, when the United States was far more restrained in countering the provisional unity government in France than it was toward PCI power in Italy.

Two more considerations justified closer monitoring of Italian politics. McCormack worried that the State Department, under Cyrus Vance, judging the Christian Democrats to be unreliable and corrupt, would make the administration vulnerable to attacks from the right for being soft on communism. Less restrained than the advisers of the previous administration, McCormack even recommended a public announcement from the president pledging to "respond favorably to any reasonable request by democratic forces for political or economic assistance in the coming campaigns." At the same time this intervention, unlike in the immediate postwar period, would not have been unilateral. It would instead foster a concerted action within Europe, since, as McCormack added, the democratic parties in Germany were already providing financial assistance to Christian Democratic and Socialist Parties in Europe.[126]

This targeted assistance was to be complemented with the continued action, through the G-7 and the IMF, in support of the Italian economy. Far from revealing a mere economic determinism, this accent on financial tools still followed the Rambouillet summit's broader purpose of reorienting Europe's center-left forces toward nonstatist solutions, thus away from popular front temptations.[127]

Furthermore, this political strategy entailed a sharper focus on cultural aspects. Under careful scrutiny, Italy in the 1970s no longer seemed one of Europe's most Americanized countries. The ambassador to Rome, Richard Gardner, also a former academic, stressed that Italy had "not developed the same kinds of cultural relations with the United States . . . as have most of the Northern European states." In particular, he noticed the "gradual erosion of confidence in Western institutions—and even values—on the part of Italian intellectuals, including many of the center-left who should know better." This was not entirely a new discovery: Kissinger himself, while maintaining his realist approach, had reflected on the cultural peculiarities that made the communist appeal in France and Italy still so strong. This was against the antiradical trends of the 1970s; but it was consistent with a general disillusion in Europe with American guidance due to the Vietnam War and the economic downturns of the 1970s. Brzezinski also noted that Italy, because of its relatively passive foreign policy, was more inclined than France and the other European allies toward neutralism.

A pro-Western reorientation was urgent both at the political and cultural levels. Therefore, Gardner and other State Department officials recommended an increased budget for the Department's cultural affairs section and for the USIS in Rome, accelerating educational exchanges under the Fulbright program. On his own, the ambassador also took the initiative of entertaining Italian intellectuals at Villa Taverna, regardless of their political orientation. Indeed, he brought to the embassy an eclectic group, ranging from conservative Franco Zeffirelli and Luigi Barzini to leftists Alberto Moravia, Renato Guttuso, and Federico Fellini. Maintaining this balancing act among the "shapers of opinion in contemporary Italy" and "exposing them to visiting Americans of comparable stature" was, in the ambassador's opinion, "an important part of public diplomacy."[128]

Brzezinski took all this advice to heart. In a memorandum to the president in March 1977 he already indicated that the PCI's access to the government was potentially the greatest problem in Europe. By July he emphasized the need to reevaluate the noninterference policy toward the Italian Historic Compromise, above all because of its effects on France and on Franco-German affinities within the European Community. Agreeing with his academic colleagues, the national security adviser had earlier expressed concern about giving the impression of heavy interference in support of Giscard, "because of French 'Gaullism' of both left and right." Also, improvement of cultural programs in Italy was one of the main topics on the agenda for discussion with Andreotti during Brzezinski's visit in Rome the next year.[129] But it took almost as long for the administration to come up with an official statement about the PCI's government participation. In part, this hesitation was due to the simple fact that Europe was not the main priority for President Carter. Moreover, the administration, and Brzezinski especially, still thought that the Eurocommunists' anti-Americanism might be trumped by their anti-Soviet choices. In Hassner's opinion, despite the Eurocommunists' general affinity with Moscow on "anti-imperialism," a government role for both the PCI and PCF would lead to their "socialdemocratization," thus giving legitimacy to the reformist forces in the Soviet bloc.[130]

It was also primarily on the State Department's recommendation that the embassy intensified contacts with PCI members. Urban argued that the willingness of PCI bureau members to talk with him on Radio Free Europe was perhaps puzzling, but it was rather effective against the Soviet Union. Ambassador Gardner, though strongly opposed to the PCI, intended to use these contacts, like his predecessor Volpe, for "fact-finding" purposes, and to expose the party's faults. At the beginning of his mandate he also persuaded the State Department to open a Washington bureau for *L'Unità* and to start a new policy of issuing visas for Communist Party members. Meeting with moderates such as Giorgio Napolitano, and hard-liners such as Emanuele Macaluso and Ugo Pecchioli, further persuaded Gardner that the PCI was "hopelessly divided" in its views of the United States and of the party's own Westernization in general. The ambassador also confirmed his opinion that the party, while open on foreign policy issues, remained "internally authoritarian." Indeed, the paradox of the PCI's Westernization lay in its "undemocratic" way of imposing its new line on the party's old guard. In order not to give the impression of a U.S. endorsement of the Historic Compromise, Gardner kept these meetings with PCI leaders secret. Furthermore, those meetings were counterbalanced by the first significant contacts with the new anticommunist leadership of the Socialist Party, and with its new secretary Bettino Craxi in particular.[131]

But the new visa policy was much more sensational. It led to official visits by leaders such as Pietro Ingrao, who met with Vice President Walter Mondale in February 1977. Even more significant was Napolitano's tour of several Ivy League universities a year later. This did not result in U.S. officials' scrutinizing the moderate communist leader. In fact, Napolitano was allowed to counter many of the academic community's prejudices against the PCI. Brzezinski had for some time been persuaded that contacts with PCI officials would actually be more productive than a frontal attack, which would have likely increased their popularity. President Carter also thought that these official contacts were designed to moderate the PCI further, not in order to make it a government force, but rather to decrease its remaining populist strength.[132]

Another way to affect the political scene in both France and Italy was to suggest, in indirect ways, the holding of early parliamentary elections in 1978, since the polls seemed to indicate that the Left, especially in France, would not hold, and Eurocommunism would subsequently decline. In Italy, an election at the peak of the Historic Compromise might help polarize politics between the DC and the PCI. But Washington did not expect Andreotti to go along with this. Resistance from the DC leadership might actually rekindle its traditional tendency to "contain containment," a line that opposed the most blatant and, in the party leaders' opinion, counterproductive U.S. attempts to neutralize communist power in Italy. Even Fanfani, by 1977, seemed persuaded to accelerate the compromise with the PCI. During his visit to Washington, Andreotti had also reiterated that economic aid (through the IMF project) rather than pressures and blackmail remained the main political weapon against communist influence. So even at this crucial juncture, the administration continued to worry that if it issued a statement, and then the DC went ahead and compromised with the PCI, the United States "would look silly."[133]

On 12 January 1978, the day after the Presidential Review Committee had reached this conclusion, the State Department issued the president's official statement on the Western Communists. Its key passage read: "We do not favor [Communist participation in West European governments], and would like to see Communist influence in any Western European country reduced. . . . The United States and Italy share profound democratic values and interests, and we do not believe that the Communists share those values and interests."[134]

The statement corrected previous announcements committing to the principle of noninterference or expressing opposition confined to the unlikely prospect of a government "dominated" by communist forces. This relative moderation had been in part the consequence of the attempt to straddle between the need to look uninvolved in French politics and the urgency of blocking communist advances in Italy.[135] But, as both Brzezinski and Gardner (the latter taking most credit for this turn) claimed in their respective memoirs, the necessity of blocking a neutralist domino process starting from Italy and the prospect of looking soft on communism trumped all other qualms about sparking an anti-American backlash.[136]

Fears of a political domino effect in Europe may have been exaggerated, and may have rather been determined by domestic concerns about Republican opposition. But a more tangible and immediate concern was about an economic domino effect in all of Western Europe, also starting from Italy. In December 1977 it had become clear that Italy would not be able to meet the IMF's conditions on the reduction of public spending and wage controls. With the Rambouillet and Puerto Rico targets thus eluded, investors were losing confidence in the Italian government. If the PCI entered the government, the 11 January Presidential Review Committee meeting concluded, the flight of capital would become a certainty. If this further encouraged models of nationalization, most likely in France and Spain, the chain reaction could undo all the efforts undertaken in the G-7 meetings. The United States' budget could also be affected, because, as McCormack had warned a few months earlier, a weaker European Community and "a weaker NATO would compel President Carter to devote many additional billions to strengthen the armed forces of the United States," and "this would not only compromise his inflation fighting campaign, but would increase his political difficulties with the left wing of the Democratic Party."[137] These matters of economic and political credibility were inextricably linked, with the now added issue of the administration's domestic credibility.

The January statement was also meant to squelch rumors in Italy that the Carter administration intended to endorse Eurocommunism in order to destabilize Eastern Europe. This impression compounded previous views from a range of communist and moderate leftist Italian newspapers that the administration had de facto revoked the Kissinger veto. Italian ambassador to Washington Roberto Gaja resembled his 1940s predecessor Tarchiani in his insistence on a firm American line against communism. Right-wing Christian Democrats repeatedly complained about the U.S. embassy's "communist liaisons." Indeed, one of the results of the Brzezinski-Gardner contacts with the PCI was to reinforce the invitation from Italy's centrist forces for a stronger American role in the country's politics.[138] Interference, it seemed now confirmed, was not going to provoke any Gaullist anti-American backlash among conservative groups in Italy. To the contrary, it responded to a rising sense of urgency among the Christian Democrats and the center-left parties, who did not want to lose either their cohesion or U.S. support.

Immediately, however, the declaration of 12 January seemed to yield counterproductive results. In February Aldo Moro negotiated an agreement for the PCI's external support of the government. The communist press resumed its strident anti-Americanism, blurring the lines between conservative and liberal America. Worse still, these attacks seemed to fit a general sense of malaise in Europe against the indecisiveness of the Carter administration. With the forthcoming French parliamentary elections, the PCF also seemed to have received the boost from U.S. interference that Giscard and Mitterrand had so much dreaded. Brzezinski, in his weekly report to the president of 9 February, portrayed the trends in Europe as "ominous" due to the parallel French and Italian situations. German politics, too, the national security adviser thought, were "manifesting neutralism and anti-U.S. symptoms." Meanwhile, Schmidt's economic policy, on which the G-7 had relied so much, seemed "not helpful to the West's overall political and economic strength." NATO force improvements, initiated by the administration, now increasingly looked like an attempt to "use military measures to prop up a politically weakening alliance."[139]

The observation about Schmidt seemed to hold true, especially in light of Italy's inability to fulfill the IMF conditions. In addition, Carter never nourished the same mutual understanding with the German chancellor that had formed the core of Kissinger's European strategy. But overall, the Carter administration's diplomatic approach, less strident than that of its predecessors, yielded results, in part thanks also to French and Italian domestic events.

Voters in both France and Italy penalized the two Communist Parties.

In March the PCF suffered a severe setback in the French parliamentary elections. Later that spring, a national security report to President Carter waxed confident enough that "the [European] scene play[ed] into Giscard's quiet claims to special status because his [was] the most solid government in Europe."[140] A year later the PCI, after breaking its alliance with the Christian Democrats, also declined four percentage points in the national elections. That break, as I have noted, was partly the consequence of the crisis that followed the kidnapping and assassination of Aldo Moro and partly the result of the PCI's unfulfilled expectations for economic reforms. Despite immediate concerns that the seizure of Moro might lead to an emergency government including the Communists, the overall American assessment matched Hunter's suggestion that terrorism showed evidence of the PCI's weakness, and that "the activities of the Red Brigades tar[red] the PCI among many middle class voters."[141] The party had also broken loose from some of its traditional working-class supporters before it broke loose from the government: the Andreotti cabinet's program of March 1978, with the PCI's external support, insisted on retaining a market economy against the pressures for nationalizations, and on maintaining a hard line against terrorism; it also reiterated its allegiance to NATO. Following Brzezinski's fondest expectations, the Christian Democrats and their centrist allies, after Italy was excluded from the four-power (U.S., Britain, France, Germany) summit in Guadeloupe in January 1979, offered persuasive arguments to demonstrate their NATO orthodoxy in order to be included among America's most reliable partners. The situation in Italy was far from stabilized. But, as one of Brzezinski's advisers recognized, that instability was mitigated by the PCI's setbacks at the polls, the election of Pope John Paul II, and "the continued ability of the Italian leadership to form a decent and respectable government."[142]

The danger of a European rift with the United States also seemed averted. Opinion polls by the end of 1978 indicated the opposite trend: in Western Europe, the Soviet Union suffered much more than the United States in the battle for the people's hearts and minds,[143] and the Western Communists, at the forefront of anti-Americanism again starting in 1979, had failed to resolve the ambiguities of the Eurocommunist promise. These political contradictions were compounded by the social and cultural ones the two parties suffered during these same years. While their political epilogue started in the 1980s—paradoxically for the PCF, while it participated in the union government with the Socialists—their cultural decline had begun as their political leverage was reaching its height in the years of Eurocommunism.

EPILOGUE Cultural and Political Decline

The Disconnection between Communists and the
New Radical Movements

In the face of sharp economic downturns, the radicalism and optimism of the 1960s gave way to anxiety. Most radicals, it has been widely recognized, "abandoned 'the Revolution' and worried instead about their job prospects." This retrenchment did not necessarily mean a loss for the Communists. They still profited from the general social and economic "malaise" of the 1970s. At the peak of the Eurocommunist experiment in 1977, Henry Kissinger reflected that "the spread of Marxism" in Western Europe "[could] be one of the profound problems of the modern period, namely the alienation of the population from the modern industrial state, that in the modern industrial state no matter how it is governed the people feel that they have no influence over the real decisions, and if you couple that with certain left wing traditions in Italy and France you can see why it spreads."[1]

What Kissinger and other intellectual observers failed to see was that, in the end, the combination of social retrenchment and the persistent orthodoxy of the Communist Parties toward the radical 1960s legacy eroded the influence and even the identity of both the French and Italian Communists. The moment of their greatest political influence—as has been noted about the PCI especially—"coincided with the beginning of [their] definitive decline as a cultural force."[2] Through the 1970s both parties remained unable to address the new problems of education, individual liberties, and sexual liberation. This was evident in the PCF's and PCI's dialogue with the new feminist movement, with the radical youth, and in their approach to high and mass culture.

FEMINISM

After the controversies over Simone de Beauvoir's work and over the "Malthusian" campaigns on birth-control policies,[3] feminism continued to have trouble introducing its agenda in the PCF. The role of women in the communist movement was also forced into gender clichés. According to Yvonne Dumont, a frequent contributor to *Cahiers du communisme*, in France, as in the United States, women best defined their political role through pacifist demonstrations. "Their maternal instinct," she wrote in 1967, "renders them more quickly empathetic to the suffering and anguish of the women in

Vietnam; their instinctive horror of war makes them apt to understanding that there's no true security for *any* people as long as war rages in *any* part of the world."[4]

By contrast, the PCF still ignored issues of personal liberation. In a 1970 essay describing the main problems affecting women, Mireille Bertrand included exploitation in the workplace, war, and even sexual violence. But she did not stress the "right to choose" on abortion. In fact, the article presented an extended argument in favor of the "protection of the mother and the child" through "higher state contributions to families with dependents." Concerns about welfare were prominent, but birth control did not figure among the party's priorities.[5]

The new women's liberation movement (Mouvement de Libération des Femmes) had an official debut in France a few months later, when *Le Nouvel Observateur* published a manifesto signed by 343 women who declared that, illegally, they had had abortions. To underline the urgency of this matter, and the issue of sexism, the signatories provokingly called themselves *salopes* ("sluts" or "bitches"). The document included the names of Simone de Beauvoir, Marguerite Duras, actresses Catherine Deneuve and Jeanne Moreau, and lawyers Yvette Roudy and Gisèle Halimi. The government chose not to prosecute them. Four years later the government, prompted by President Valéry Giscard d'Estaing and on the initiative of Minister of Health Simone Veil, finally passed laws legalizing abortion.[6]

Among the "salopes" only a handful, including de Beauvoir, believed that women's true emancipation was impossible outside a socialist world. But the PCF's position had by then only slightly evolved. In October 1973, at the meeting of the Paris Central Committee, Bertrand said that one of the main problems with feminism was that it reflected women's "inadequate consciousness, compared to men, about the global character of capitalist exploitation." For this reason, she proudly reported, the party had, through various factory assemblies in the textile and mechanical sectors, contributed to raising that consciousness and redirecting women's protest against the system of state monopoly capitalism.[7] A few months later, Madeleine Vincent admitted that the parties in power had dominated the debate on abortion and contraception, while the PCF saw its main task as correlating "women's liberation" to the economic structure and to an improvement of [women's] living standards.[8] The PCF, while still orthodox on matters of sexual liberation, thus managed to become "the most feminized" among the French parties. Even better, this feminization owed much to the increasing number of young women among its rank and file.[9]

But the party's diffidence toward feminist demands persisted. This was in no small part because those demands were to a large extent modeled on the American example. Radical feminism had reached such levels in the United States of denouncing "male imperialism" and equating gender discrimination with class conflict. In fact, according to an essay by Marie-José Chombart de Lauwe concluding a series of articles on feminism published by *La Nouvelle critique* in 1972, the U.S. society best exemplified women's suffering from the "double alienation" identified by Karl Marx, August Bebel, and Friedrich Engels: from the production system and from the patriarchal family, all made worse by relentless consumerist pressures. It was not surprising, Chombart de Lauwe argued, that, in this extreme case, frustration had led to the "infantile, provocative" style of the women's liberation movement "burning brassieres" and virtually declaring a war on gender. On abortion, according to the author, the American movement had reached the excessive stage of claiming the right to choose as if it were a means to "withhold production, and thus put pressure on society" for improvement of the female condition. By so doing, Chombart de Lauwe added, women committed the same injustice against which they were fighting: objectifying the infant much like they had been sexually objectified. The argument had a foregone conclusion: in a socialist society, under the new type of family, no longer patriarchal, much of this problem would be solved through sexual education and the superseding of any stereotype based on color, sex, and age.[10]

By the mid-1970s, the PCF had begun to address issues of women's liberation, and sexism as a new form of oppression. It supported the law legalizing abortion and most laws prohibiting gender discrimination. But, with unwavering confidence, it followed Marchais's postulate at the party's Twenty-Second Congress that the issue, being largely a by-product of consumer-driven societies, would be solved under socialism. Austerity, the counterpoint of consumerism, also hurt women in the PCF's interpretation, for they became subject, far more than men, to underemployment and the need to accept temporary jobs.[11]

In the intellectual debate, feminism also fought an uphill battle against increasingly hegemonic tendencies favoring male-dominated psychoanalysis, best represented in those years by the towering figure of Jacques Lacan. Feminism also paradoxically found itself overtaken by the assertion of gay rights, as many intellectuals decided to "come out" and confront Catholic condemnations of homosexuality. As has been noted, "the French intellectual climate [of the 1970s], even on the Left, has thus on the whole been more unfavourable to women (whatever their sexuality) than to homosexual men."[12]

The PCI, despite its tentacular reach into all new cultural developments, especially through its cultural recreation organization ARCI, also failed to fully grasp the redefinition of oppression by the women's movement. In its attempt to establish a Historic Compromise with the Christian Democrats, it restrained its leadership in the divorce and abortion referenda of the mid-1970s and early 1980s. Feminism was at first dismissed as an "heir to the youth movement and its errors" and as "more an expression of social unease than a social movement."[13] These causes, most party leaders insisted, mainly belonged to a secular, elitist, non-Marxist Left, and focused on superstructural manifestations, rather than the structural causes of gender oppression.

Besides the constraints from Catholic traditions, the modern feminist movement also suffered, ironically, from its political origins in the extraparliamentarian Left of the early 1970s. For the main such leftist organization, Lotta Femminista, it was more important to obtain equal pay for equal work, and even salaries for housework, than to wage a battle against sexism.[14]

For a while, postwar Italian feminism was inscribed in the politics of "partitocracy," with the Unione delle Donne Italiane (UDI, or Union of Italian Women) as a PCI offspring.[15] Neofeminist organizations not directly associated with the party system emerged beginning in the late 1960s. But political opportunities, in addition to the intense network of the Left, allowed a dialogue between the UDI and the new groups more than in other Western nations' experiences.[16] Indeed, the PCI remained confident that the new feminists would be naturally absorbed in the workers movement, with the same ease with which many youth rebels were being co-opted. But the experience of the UDI had been subordinate within the party structure. And although early on the PCI promoted equal rights for women, asking for protective legislation for working women, it never "identified in the family the main locus of the oppression of women." Furthermore, the party's mobilization of women, as in France, had been strictly associated with pacifism, based on the assumption of women's "pacifist nature."[17] Historic PCI leader Nilde Jotti argued in 1965 that through pacifist militancy, political participation, and the campaign for divorce legislation, the women's movement could supersede the bourgeois notions of emancipation based on "formal rights." But, in a *Rinascita* interview, she cautioned that divorce would be a right to be exercised "with responsibility"; no one in Italy would "want to follow the American model" on this issue.[18]

The new feminists turned out to be less amenable than the PCI had expected. Contrary to Amendola's earliest predictions, modernization and secularization eluded traditional party controls. Like the student movement, the new feminist groups challenged the representativeness of the parties. The

PCI itself was often labeled "paternalistic." Also like the student movement, feminist theorization complemented Marxism, but not without finding inspiration in the New Left and the American women's liberation movement. Luisa Passerini has for example reminded us that the first female organizations among the student movement carried Marxist names, such as The Political Bureau of the Female Comrades within the Revolutionary Communications Group of Turin (Collettivo delle Compagne del Gruppo Comunicazioni Rivoluzionarie di Torino). But these women defied communist orthodoxy by seeking recognition of the private sphere of oppression based on their readings of women's rights movements in the United States. The party's cultural guardians rebutted by invoking Gramsci's reflections on feminism from his essays on "Americanism and Fordism." His warning, based on the experience of the early American feminism, was that in a society based on mass consumerism, women's liberation "in the private sphere" could easily fall prey to "libertine" impulses and protract sexual exploitation.[19] The PCI's electoral success in the mid-1970s allowed a thorough reabsorption of the feminist collectives into the old feminist organizations, such as the UDI. But on the most radical demands of women's liberation the party remained rigid.[20]

While the PCI took much deserved credit in the final battle for the referendum on divorce held in May 1974, it continued to stand pat on the issue of abortion. Italy trailed France closely on these issues. The Movimento della Liberazione delle Donne Italiane began its campaign to legalize abortion in 1975. Its main political source of support was the newly formed Radical Party.[21]

When the national debate over abortion rights gained steam in 1975, Nilde Jotti and the younger Adriana Seroni still argued that the problem was mainly socioeconomic for working-class women who could not afford the expenses to travel abroad and obtain an abortion. Jotti told the party directorate that by "unloading the liberalization of abortion on women, we would entitle women to a political say solely on gender issues, thus forcing them to make a step backward." Berlinguer added that the party should oppose "the abortionist ideology as an actual 'liberation' for women, since abortion [was] a trauma." Rather, the question needed to be addressed "in its social causes," as this was "an issue of social relevance," on which "women should not have the absolute liberty to decide." Science, in Berlinguer's opinion, also had to concentrate on how to prevent birth defects, while the welfare system would assist in "integrating those born with abnormalities."[22]

Later that year, Seroni noted that the Socialist Party had fully absorbed the prochoice campaign, while the "PCI could not establish any dialogue [on the issue] with the Christian Democrats." She then complained that the Socialists' radical platform on abortion had undermined the PCI's "savoir-faire" in dealing with the DC. She concurred with Paolo Bufalini that the party should emphasize "reasons of physical or mental health" over "social conditions" to justify abortion. Otherwise, Bufalini suggested, it might seem that "poverty in itself allowed the killing of the embryo."[23] As Berlinguer had suggested, education and prevention for most working-class Italians still offered the main ground for compromise with the Christian Democrats.

Among the party group leading the debate on this issue, a consensus emerged against the "rising tendency in capitalist democracies to present abortion as just another form of birth control." Abortion, in Jotti's opinion, remained contrary to the "real emancipation of women."[24] More than the influence of the Catholic Church, it was this particular frame of the debate on the Left, and especially the communist Left's focus on a working-class approach to feminist causes, that delayed the introduction of abortion laws in Italy. The new family code legalizing abortion was passed on 29 May 1978, and the new laws were confirmed by a national referendum in May 1981, after prolife movements had fought them for two years. But this long battle still failed to persuade most communist women that feminism was not on the decline. Analyzing the movement at the end of 1978, Adriana Seroni and Marina Buttiglione, together with a group of female activists, concluded that without a closer connection to the struggle against socioeconomic repression, feminism would keep disintegrating. "Field trips" to feminist groups in the United States confirmed this impression. In 1979 Margherita Repetto witnessed there a "troubled" movement. The main problem was that instead of militant organizations, American feminists privileged "individual action—according to cultural traditions rooted in Protestantism." Lobbying and the use of courts actually allowed, in Repetto's opinion, the backlash from the better organized conservative groups, including the evangelical "moral majority."[25] Only in the early 1980s would Berlinguer acknowledge that the problems raised by the women's movements held a value of their own, of which the party should take stock.[26] At that point the party was already undergoing a transformation that would actually erode its Marxist identity.

The American example, for French and Italian Communists, had a deleterious effect on their countries, because it was now following a modernization model too closely identified with personal fulfillment. Furthermore, that example carried a universal message implying that gender and other forms of discrimination were above the conflict between capital and labor.

**GIORNATA NAZIONALE
DI LOTTA DEGLI STUDENTI**

8 MARZO

**GIORNATA DI LOTTA
PER L'EMANCIPAZIONE
DELLA DONNA**

Senza emancipazione della donna
non è possibile
l'emancipazione del proletariato

Senza emancipazione
del proletariato non è possibile
l'emancipazione della donna

**DALLE SCUOLE
DALLE FABBRICHE
DALLE PIAZZE
CON IL VOTO SUL REFERENDUM
NO ALLA DC**

Comitato nazionale di coordinamento del movimento degli studenti
Collettivi politici studenteschi / Comitati unitari di base / Collettivi politici unitari

The Italian Student Communist Movement in solidarity with the women's emancipation movement announcing a demonstration on Women's Day, 8 March, 1970s. Courtesy Fondazione Istituto Gramsci Emilia Romagna, Bologna.

Regarding the problems of youth, unemployment, and the accent on personal fulfillment, the PCI was not as keen on attributing its diminished leverage to an "Americanized" socialization. By the early 1970s, the party recognized that vast sections of the Italian youth were "alienated from the country's democratic life." Even the campaign for the vote at age eighteen, Sereni warned, would likely reward the extreme "Manifesto" type of groups.[27] After the parliament passed the vote for eighteen-year-olds in 1975, Claudio Imbeni of the FGCI (the Communist youth organization) told the party directorate that it was insufficient to defend young Italians' right to vote; one needed to also defend "full youth employment and . . . advanced education opportunities for the masses." Drug trafficking and juvenile delinquency were also intensifying. To address them, the party, in this view, needed to engage the very young (age ten to eleven) in scout activities to help them in their formative years. Most antidrug legislation began at the local level, but, as FGCI leader Massimo D'Alema reminded the party in the spring of 1977, only two communist district administrations in Emilia and Lazio had kept up with that issue. According to Nilde Jotti, the party needed to promote law and order with a revived "popular frontism," combined with the radical spirit of the 1960s; neofascist terrorism might actually have the positive effect of reigniting the antifascist fervor of the 1968–69 movement.[28]

This persistent problem with youth and its discontents erupted in the campus protests of 1977–78. In part this movement was the offspring of the 1969 "Hot Autumn," which, while displaying "workerist" attitudes, had adhered more to anarchism.[29] One of the most militant student groups, Lotta Continua, was founded in 1969. In the opinion of most PCI leaders, this university movement, while based in the extreme Left, was even more critical and subversive of the party strategies than its 1968–69 predecessors. It was reminiscent of the petit bourgeois nihilism of the prefascist era. This movement, in Achille Occhetto's words, was a "direct offspring of welfarism, that is, of the [inadequate] response that the center-left coalition had given to the 1968 movement." It was more of a "degenerated" rebellion of young intellectuals against their marginalization, stressing their difficulty finding jobs commensurate to their education.[30] The shortage of jobs requiring high levels of training made this generation also impervious to the party's campaign for austerity. Berlinguer's sober appeals to frugality, manual work for unemployed intellectuals, and law and order against "deviant" social behavior had the effect of making the 1977 movement openly hostile to the Historic Compromise. Highly educated young Italians were now caught between countercultural disaffection toward the old political system and a long-term exposure to the culture of consumerism that raised their expectations of better jobs and compensation. The working class rapidly lost its appeal and its role as romantic referent for Italy's postindustrial educated youth. In the final analysis, according to D'Alema, less than a decade after the "Hot Autumn," Italy's jaded youth felt more "alienation" than a desire to participate and lead a new society.[31]

Worse still, the more the PCI attempted to engage with the new extremists in order to harness them, the greater the danger was that red terrorism would be strictly identified with the party's revolutionary origins. In the end, the party of the Historic Compromise stood firmly for law and order. But its insistence on fighting terrorists could not entirely refute the ideological matrix that public opinion still ascribed to the party. This matrix, it has recently been argued, could undeniably be appropriated by the extraparliamentarian Left. Not only Lotta Continua but also terrorist groups such as the Red Brigades forcefully argued that the PCI was now contradicting its own historic record as an insurrectionary party, and that the extraparliamentarian groups were the true heirs of Marx and Lenin. Another handicap for the PCI was the social composition of those who joined the red terrorists: most of them came from the educated middle class (and many, indeed, had belonged to PCI youth groups), over which the party did not have firm control.[32] Pasolini's quip about siding with the real proletarians, the cops, against the extremist elite, held even more true one decade later. The Red Brigades and other terrorist groups saw all their attempts to paralyze the nation and its political system frustrated within a few years, for all the parliamentary groups clustered together on the safe middle ground.

No matter how ostracized and confined to the fringe they were, the young radicals who toyed with or joined terrorist groups were a symptom of a greater problem: an individual alienation that eluded party controls. In a *Rinascita* essay of June 1979, Franco Cassano tackled the problem of the "new individualism" adopted by young Italians. The party's reduced influence could not be attributed simply to the problems of the economy, youth unemployment, and other "strictly national factors." It was also true that ending the Vietnam War was no longer the symbolic partisan struggle against the "American colossus" but rather a fight for independence and identity against the rival communist regimes of Cambodia and China. Meanwhile, the Soviet Union was now universally cited most for its human rights violations. In this context, Cassano admitted, the "new individualism acquires a new vitality not only in liberal thought, but also among Catholic circles [that] uphold traditional communal values together with a renewed emphasis on the *persona*."

The PCI, Cassano warned, could not simply dismiss this new individualism "with the exorcising formula of *americanismo* [or American influence]." The party instead should have adapted, aiming at "building socialism in complex societies with a fully articulated social and institutional pluralism." It should have worked as a "selective filter of *americanismo*, becoming able to read the potential liberties of the most developed society," in which emancipation has become a "complex notion" mostly hostile to "strict statism, and the restrictive practices revolving around the rule by the parties." Taking such action was urgent, lest the PCI lose the initiative to groups, such as the new Radical Party, that "denied the existence of class conflict."[33] While "Americanization" was not the main root of the problem, it could nevertheless become the end result of an "individualized" youth once its most radical dreams had faded.

Through the early 1970s, the French Communist youth continued to find inspiration and unity in the campaign against the Vietnam War. The problem with that campaign, as Roland Leroy noted in a conversation with youth leader Favaro following the events in Prague, was that it now conflated the slogans of "freedom and independence," thus inviting a parallel between U.S. and Soviet repression. To prevent the danger of "stirring anti-Sovietism," Favaro recommended organizing no fewer than forty debates that year to "restore the understanding of Marxist ideology" among the French youth. The party's insistence on an expanded military service and its rejection of civil service alternatives further clashed with the pacifist mindset the anti-Vietnam movement had helped instill among the French youth. In 1970 Favaro identified this contrast, along with the young radicals' "individualist" inclinations, to explain the membership decline in the Mouvement de la Jeunesse Communiste Française.[34]

But anti-Sovietism continued mounting in the early 1970s for complex reasons. The discourses of anticapitalism and anti-imperialism were no longer "woven together in an intricate mesh" as in 1968. In both leftist and conservative circles, there was a growing sense, more acute in France than in Italy, that the two superpowers, through their controlled détente, were ganging up on Europe. Finally, a "new discourse of ethical morality surrounding human rights" compounded an intellectual repudiation—mostly by ex-*gauchistes*—of the May 1968 movement, placing the helplessness of Eastern Europe rather than that of the Southern hemisphere at the center of media attention, even from the extreme left.[35] Domestically, *gauchisme* by the mid-1970s had itself become mere lobbying for radical reforms, more and more resuming the personal emancipatory elements of the counterculture rather than combined protest by intellectuals and workers.[36]

More vehemently than their Italian comrades, the French Communists also assumed the role of moral judges railing against the corrupt aspects of modern bourgeois society. The French youth, according to Favaro in 1972, was constantly disillusioned by the hypocrisy of a society that "pretended to fight . . . violence, drugs, pornography." Those vices, being "sources of profit" were the "object of publicity and commercialization without equal." The bourgeoisie was especially responsible now for "reorienting [the 1968 movement] toward dead-end goals," for reducing "gauchiste adventurism" to a mere "gesticulation without echo in public opinion," for leading the young "toward false solutions, toward dramatic impasses provoking drug consumption or disorderly individual behavior."[37]

But, admittedly for Secretary Marchais, *gauchisme* and its libertarian offspring had an increasing influence in the universities. Worse still, universities increasingly followed the American model of "autonomous intellectual institution[s] combining teaching and research in order to match the needs of an advanced industrial society," one that responded solely to the "profit of the military-industrial complex." Meanwhile, new causes, such as environmentalism or the spread of mysticism and communitarianism, were seen as backward evasion into the myth of the "bon sauvage," a return to nature that, according to Jacques Pesenti, also brought risks of a "return to social Darwinism." In other words, most students fell into either the technocratic or the libertarian mold—both types betraying what the PCF now recognized as the most noble and revolutionary aspirations of 1968.[38]

In both France and Italy, the youth movements had mutated from their 1960s precedents in a fundamental way: they now identified more with an alternative utopia than an antagonistic political environment that challenged the status quo directly. Their emphasis was "more on generation and gender than on class." In their most radical manifestations, they resembled the American movements that preceded them, seeking their potential "in marginal and outcast groups rather than in collective subjects centrally involved with the system, such as workers." Even their symbolic referents were found in America. For example, certain groups in the 1977 Italian movement called themselves "metropolitan Indians"; the typical intellectual newspaper of the young leftists in France, *Libération*, was often labeled for expressing itself in franglais; the success, in the late 1970s, of *Re Nudo*, a student Italian magazine emulating the American hippie culture, was even more indicative of this trend. As has been widely recognized, youth in Italy and France came to represent a distinct category for the first time in the mid-1970s. Most of their inspiration came from the Anglo-American rock and pop culture, and, in general, from American counterculture.[39]

Furthermore, and not without the full contradictions of postindustrial societies, the hippie "freak" aspects of the movement often coincided with the consumerist ones. What Jean-Marie Domenach had realized in the early 1960s from his observations of America was now true of the French and Italian youth, too: they had "transformed revolt itself into a social function." Anticonformism itself was reabsorbed by capitalism, which subverted images of rebellion and counterculture into consumerist symbols of liberation: youth icons, from Elvis Presley to Jim Morrison, from Che Guevara to Mao, entered mass culture under the aegis of consumption. Consumption itself replaced production as the new "arena of freedom."[40] Even the escapist trends in music that appealed to the majority of youth in the late 1970s could not be dismissed as mere signs of mass alienation. In a review of the movie *Saturday Night Fever*, Gianni Borgna—one of the rising young members in the PCI's cultural and propaganda sections—defined disco music as a "homologation [or harmonization from above] of popular taste," an "unwitting apology of the 'Lonely Crowd.'"[41] But this "harmonization" was none other than the evolution of the 1960s youth hedonism into a different form, expressing self-fulfillment without idealism.

MASS AND HIGH CULTURE

The PCI, despite its pervasive—and increasingly popular—fund-raising festivals for *L'Unità*, and its intense cultural activity through the recreational Case del Popolo, still failed to fully discern the importance of popular entertainment and mass communications. It did keep encouraging party intellectuals to assume an educational role, abandon elitist traditions, and collaborate more with schools and popular organizations. Among their tasks was to turn the various Case del Popolo into public structures no longer just meant for class mobilization but also intended to affect the leisure and habits of the common people from both the working and the middle class.[42] The reform of the Italian broadcast system (RAI) in 1970 gave the PCI and its ARCI considerable leverage, which they used to enhance the educational aspects of broadcasting while reducing advertising. But even at the peak of its political power, the party did not exert an equivalent influence in the most important medium, television, still largely controlled by the center-left parties. Much of this failure can be ascribed to a simple view of culture that, from a Marxist standpoint, excluded mass commercial entertainment. As party intellectual Enzo Forcella realized in 1976, "no Marxist theory of mass communications had ever been formulated."[43] Even color television did not go unquestioned in the party leadership. It was introduced in Italy belatedly in 1975, partly because of the PCI's opposition to the high start-up costs for national broadcast, and partly because of a natural aversion from defenders of cultural orthodoxy, such as Amendola, who, at a party meeting contemptuously defined color TV as "porcheria" (rubbish).[44]

During the years of the Union of the Left, the PCF ostensibly adopted a broader media approach. In 1974 it abandoned its hostility toward the noncommunist press and, in its foremost attempt at public relations, opened a *bureau de presse* of its own. The party also adapted to television and founded its own production house that same year. But while recognizing the impact of television and radio, the PCF would only admit that these media had slightly reduced the more important impact of propaganda through posters, newspapers, and assemblies. Modern media, a report at a June 1971 meeting of the Central Committee of Rosny-sous-Bois had concluded, could not replace the importance of "public debate," in which the "participant is not just a passive recipient but an active party in the exchange of ideas."[45]

Even when the media offered the Left crucial leverage on international issues, the French and Italian Communists gave it little credit. In evaluating the American debacle in Vietnam, for instance, the French communist press lauded the role of the United Nations and NGOs; it emphasized the impact of the student movement;[46] but it failed to understand the critical role of the media, especially television, in undermining the efforts and world reputation of the United States.

But this was not how Washington saw things. One of the factors feeding communist success and anti-Americanism generally, according to Secretary of Defense Donald Rumsfeld in 1975, was the grip that the Marxists had "over the universities and the media." European TV, he noted, was inundated with coverage of Vietnam, multinational corporations, and alleged CIA wrongdoings. In August 1976 a delegation of Italian American congressional leaders stressed how the press in Italy had shifted to the left, giving "poor treatment of America." It was true that dailies such as the newly founded popular *La Repubblica*, and even the conservative *Corriere della Sera*, included PCI representatives among their "privileged interlocutors." Several new publications in both France and Italy also inherited the *gauchiste* irreverence toward the establishment. But rather than a sign of increasing anti-Americanism or unquestioned procommunism, this trend denoted an effort to moderate—or, from the *gauchiste* side, challenge—the two Communist Parties.[47]

The two parties' misunderstanding of this apparent success, and their disconnection with the modern means of mass communication also evinced a rather unfocused, if not resigned, attack on the renewed U.S. dominance of mass media. By the mid-1970s, the European Left—including the moderate voices left of center—again complained about American cultural imperialism. For the next decade their focus was less the protection of indigenous cultures in Third World countries than European culture itself. During this time prominent French intellectuals, and Minister of Culture Jack Lang, called for the protection, as in the immediate postwar period, of French cinema, and now even of the French language against franglais.[48] The largest technologically advanced media companies were American. Television, the new VCR industry, and even European bookstores now seemed to suffer from an unprecedented American "invasion."[49]

Besides being unable to counter this appeal by popular taste, the Communists in both France and Italy continued to display ambivalence toward, if not fascination with, this renewed American media domination.[50] At least the new films, books, and TV programs confirmed the notion, which first reemerged in the 1960s, that the United States, in its diversity, was still the country that displayed most candidly the contradictions of the Western world. By the 1970s, this was also a consequence of Europe's feedback to America. As I have noted, the United States shifted from a sense of cultural inferiority to self-confidence, thanks in no small part to the success of French film noir mimicking the American gangster movies, Europe's celebration and imitation of American novelists, and the transformation of rock 'n' roll by the "British invasion." This feedback, rather than subjecting American mass culture to "spiritual Europeanization," restored the United States to its image as the country of constant experimentation, of introspective social analysis, with the now-added benefit of a strong transatlantic connection. Even "the transformation of Hollywood movies in the 1970s can be traced back to the French reception of American film in the 1940s."[51] One can add that also the Italian *film d'autore*, from neorealism to Fellini, Antonioni, and Zeffirelli, finally had a sophisticating impact on American moviemakers.

So the Communists, in all their evaluation of American pluralism as yet another sign of neocapitalist decline, missed one crucial point. Ironically, pluralism, whether at the intellectual level, where it reiterated a common Western heritage, or, at the mass level, where it came along with a plethora of perhaps more sophisticated yet superfluous products and vacuous homogeneous entertainment, did in fact confirm close transatlantic cultural ties. The Communists' ambivalence toward the Cold War enemy did not have the same self-empowering effect as in the past, because now the resistance to American influence and even its ambivalence came from a broader spectrum outside Marxism that, while addressing issues of modernization and globalization, did not frame them strictly in terms of the Cold War ideological confrontation. Simply put, the PCI and PCF no longer informed and influenced anti-Americanism as much as they had done in the previous three decades.

It was undeniable, however, that a renewed interest in Marxism in the mainstream French and Italian press—in large part stimulated by Euro-communism—reflected a resurgent intellectual clout for the two parties. But in the world of ideas, the two parties also lowered their guard, lulled into self-confidence by their apparent regained leverage among intellectuals. In the final analysis, the Italian Communists paradoxically obtained that influence and derived their confidence from their own emerging doubts about the Soviet experience, or even Marxism-Leninism; their French comrades instead drew similar attention because of their stalwart faith in the same experience and ideology. But neither party was still committed in a do-or-die struggle with Western integration and Americanization.

The PCF's self-confidence bordered on intolerance of leftist intellectuals who accepted positivist and structuralist variations of Marxism. By 1972 the editors of the party's experimental *La Nouvelle critique* admitted that many intellectuals refrained from publishing in the journal because they feared being ostracized by the party for their heterogeneous ideas. That same year, *Les Lettres françaises*, the most experimental of the party's newspapers, was also shut down due to lack of financial support from Eastern European countries. The last straw for the communist regimes was *Les Lettres*' defense, three years earlier, of Czech writer Arthur London and of other intellectuals who had inspired the Prague Spring. The PCF did nothing to rescue the journal.[52]

But the Soviet myth was rapidly losing its aura, notwithstanding the PCF's profession of loyalty. Détente and the Soviet repression of dissent contributed to mitigating intellectual anti-Americanism. Indeed, the French Communists supported, earlier than the PCI, the campaign for human rights in the East. A series of articles in the party's newspaper *L'Humanité* in October 1975 condemned the incarceration of high profile dissenters, the mathematician Leonid Plyoushch above all. But this criticism was still based on the belief that Soviet repression was merely a remnant of Stalinist distortions of socialism and national security. This is why a crucial exception was the more thoroughly dissenting Aleksandr Solzhenitsyn: the PCF mounted a virulent campaign against his most important anti-Soviet work, *The Gulag Archipelago*. But Solzhenitsyn was one of the key figures among Soviet dissidents; his work "allowed French intellectuals to identify their antitotalitarian politics with the universal." This identification was especially significant given France's domestic politics, because it also expressed fears by many intellectuals about the prospect—made likely by the Common Program of the Left—

of a PCF government condominium with the Socialists.[53] It is not surprising that the French Communists deflected the antitotalitarian attacks at the peak of their conflict with the Socialists in 1978, by calling public attention to the West's waging a human rights campaign against the allegedly "honorable" communist experience in Vietnam. According to an article in *L'Humanité dimanche*, the appeal in favor of Vietnamese émigrés was mainly a CIA plot using former "French ultras of the Indochina war," including Mitterrand, who "had supported all colonial ventures." Nonetheless, the PCF's anti-American fervor had become notably more nuanced than in previous years. Party foreign policy experts, such as Gaston Plissonnier and René Andrieu, meeting with a delegation from the Vietnamese government, added that the Chinese were behind the campaign with the goal of "eliminating an ideological competitor [Vietnam]."[54] In 1978, as I have noted, the collective work by party intellectuals, *L'URSS et nous*, admitted that Stalinism was more a reflection of the Soviet contradictions than an aberration. But a few weeks after the book came out, the party reconsidered its strict adherence to the union with Mitterrand's Socialists and realigned itself with Moscow.

The PCF's return to orthodoxy further alienated it from the leftist intellectual community. In the late 1970s, the attacks on the Soviets' shabby human rights record and totalitarianism of all colors came not only from the New Philosophers, led by Bernard-Henri Lévy and the reviews *Les nouvelles littéraires* and *Le Nouvel Observateur*. Jean-Marie Domenach and former Communists Pierre Daix and Vercors echoed those voices and denounced orthodox Marxism as scholastic. Even Louis Althusser, the main French theoretician of Marxism, by 1978 had admitted that several mistakes in the Soviet experience could be attributed to contradictions and shortcomings in Marxist theory itself. Many intellectuals left the PCF between 1978 and 1980 for three main reasons: first, they blamed the party's electoral defeat in 1978, and all the subsequent elections, on its sectarianism; second, the party, by fusing the CERM and the Institut Maurice Thorez into the Institut de Recherches Marxistes, and also by replacing *La Nouvelle critique* and *France nouvelle* with the more "orthodox" journal *Révolution*, deprived many intellectuals of their most experimental tribunes; and, third, the PCF virtually ceased its criticism of the Soviet Union's human rights record and endorsed its invasion of Afghanistan in December 1979. The party's inner circle had also lost what remained of its intellectual aura with the death of Jean Kanapa a year earlier.[55]

Still, this did not mean that leftist intellectuals now unquestionably embraced Atlanticism. In France the intelligentsia found only a few channels of communication with its American counterpart: a country steeped in revolutionary traditions could never attune its cultural paradigms to those of a country whose very revolution had shaped consensual politics.[56] Most former "68ers" still claimed they belonged to the May movement, but in fact they now endorsed only its most libertarian aspects. Former Maoists, such as André Glucksman and Julia Kristeva, or Trotskyists, such as Claude Lefort, broke with the Soviet Union, the country of the Gulag and democratic centralism. Some joined the New Philosophers, opening a brief but intense season that reevaluated Cold War patterns and the role of the intellectual in it. They now condemned totalitarianism, that of the Left especially, while they found themselves at ease in American universities. Pluralist democracy was their new keystone. Increasingly specialized, increasingly supplanted or co-opted by mass media, they also no longer held such a crucial control over the cultural debate.[57] The classic, universal, engagé intellectual, best personified by Jean-Paul Sartre and Raymond Aron, now gave way to the "specific intellectual," as defined by deconstructionist philosopher Michel Foucault. More pragmatic and cynical, if not less abstract, postmodernist and structuralist thinkers went back to enlightening and demystifying, rather than preaching. They preferred discussing specific problems, such as racism or human rights, rather than promoting revolutionary utopia.[58]

Postmodernism superseded even Gramsci or Marcuse in exposing society's impersonal structures and the unconscious assumptions underlying modern capitalism and consumerism. It showed how words and symbols, even more than economic structures, reinforced the existing social order and the power elite. The world as it existed was the creation, or "social construction," of those dominant groups, who used that construction to "hold sway over everybody else," thus hindering most forms of genuine popular emancipation. But the step from showing how the transmission of knowledge was manipulated to subverting all certainties was a short one. In an era of skepticism and individual introspection, these philosophers, psychologists, and literary critics, from Jacques Lacan to Jacques Derrida, questioned all rational social argument. Even those with a Marxist intellectual matrix, such as Foucault, no longer aimed at a social revolution but rather looked to individual liberation from the "constructed truths" of the dominating groups. No wonder that, with their emphasis on cultural "superstructures," their trendy skepticism, their unflinching individualism, and their esoteric claims, they became instant stars in academic circles, above all on U.S. campuses.[59]

While acknowledging the importance of "human rights," and a more liberalized intellectual environment in the East, the French Communists naturally clashed with the new intellectual trends at home. There was no distinction, in their view, between the esoteric postmodernists and the *gauchistes*.

The latter had cultivated a spirit of "spontanéisme," according to a 1976 essay by Michel Dion in *Cahiers du communisme*, a spirit that was, however, "impotent toward a monopolist bourgeoisie that since 1968 . . . had conceded only what was inevitable to concede to them"; giving voice to the base instead of to union organizations, and using assemblies and ephemeral publications, amounted to "pseudo-revolutionary verbalism." Finally, the *gauchistes'* anti-Sovietism and anticommunism did not differ from those of the bourgeoisie.[60] Likewise, postmodernism, in the PCF's opinion, failed to see the correlation between a "productivist" view of society and "real liberties for man." Changes in the forces of production or the structure of the government, most party leaders were forced to acknowledge by the late 1970s, would not suffice; the party also fought against "mentalities, habits, culture," arguing that this would liberate the individual more than the deconstructionists claimed to do.[61] Ostensibly, the PCF's battle against bourgeois domination became more comprehensive under the pressure of these new currents of thought. In fact, French Communism revealed its paralysis as it was caught between economic determinism and new concepts of individual alienation.

For all their strictures on mass culture, the Italian Communists experienced a season of intellectual revival, matching their political magnetism in the mid-1970s. Not only were intellectuals flocking to the opportunities offered by the still strong editorial and cultural industry connected to the party. The party also showed considerable flexibility toward the new currents of thought. After the first shocking impact of the new movements and their multifaceted Marxism in the 1960s, the party absorbed much of the dissent, welcoming insights ranging from Trotskyist to structuralist Marxist. It switched from mere tolerance to actual acceptance of Marxist dissent. The world of the natural sciences was also included in the party cultural apparatus through the party secretary's brother, Giovanni Berlinguer, a physiologist at the University of Rome.[62]

While drawn to some of the French esoteric philosophies or to the new American insights in the social sciences, Italy's communist intellectuals felt they came closer to fulfilling a popular role and reaching political power by confirming their public role in restructuring education and entertainment. This task followed their Gramscian expectations of attaining cultural hegemony. But that same cultural hegemony was challenged by the loss of coherence in socialist societies and the rising appeal of libertarian ideas.

In assessing the Soviet Union's human rights record, the Italian Communists remained more ambivalent than their French comrades. Since the party was far more critical of Moscow's international actions, until the early 1980s it refrained from launching a radical critique of Soviet domestic repression. This was not merely a political tactic. The party was troubled by the social and cultural contradictions of Soviet society, for its own identity and vision of Marxism had been based on Gramsci's certainties about the merits of communist social and cultural hegemony, best attained in the Soviet Union. In analyzing the case of Solzhenitsyn in 1974, Giorgio Napolitano insisted that despite its contradictions and errors, the "peculiar" Soviet experience remained the "grandiose" template within which the PCI experience would strive to carry on its diversity. The party would continue to resist the "cult of formal freedom" by fighting the "economic and cultural obstacles to the full application [of Italy's] constitutional liberties." Most communist intellectuals, without repudiating Gramsci, faulted the party for this caution. Soviet experts and historians such as Paolo Spriano complained that the party's criticism of the Eastern regimes was too "indirect and political, rather than going to the root of [those regimes'] economic, social, and cultural dynamics."[63] This incoherence was the first reason that the PCI lost the intellectual hegemony it had apparently attained in the early 1970s.

The second reason was that the party's opening to neo-Marxist ideas backfired on its still rigorously humanistic and populist tendencies. Dissent within the party was not limited to embracing neo-Marxist currents of thought. The interest of many leftist intellectuals in the social sciences as presented by Anglo-American theorists grew. In addition, the attention of several prominent intellectuals shifted to new currents, such as that of "weak thought." Best expounded by philosopher Massimo Cacciari, the concept of weak thought challenged communist historicism and questioned rationality based on class or science. Rather than pursuing ideological certainties, this intellectual movement, like postmodernism, pursued the infinite possibilities for the Left in a pluralistic society. Cacciari's ecumenical legitimation of thinkers such as Friedrich Nietzsche, Martin Heidegger, Karl Jaspers, Oswald Spengler, and Julien Benda stirred polemics within the PCI during the late 1970s, but it was accepted a decade later by a party that was losing its ideological certainties and was about to become extinct.[64]

By the late 1970s it had become clear that the theories of the Frankfurt School, weak thought, and the philosophy of Foucault seemed to fit Italy's complex evolution from historicism to cultural relativism: in the words of Biagio de Giovanni (writing in 1979), "The neoradicalism of the last ten years is an important part of the history of the Italian conscience, it is an essential, inseparable part of it. . . . No structural subject can any longer dominate the scene as hegemon and project its own image and worldview. . . . The forms, the particularities dominate reality as never before (beyond appearances)."[65]

But the party leadership, while accepting political pluralism, was still certain that culturally it could exert its hegemony. Burdened, however, with administrative responsibilities and its association with the government since 1976, it lost not only some popular support but also the esteem of many intellectuals. Berlinguer and the leaders who monitored the party's cultural apparatus—Franco Rodano, Giorgio Napolitano, and Aldo Tortorella—abandoned all traces of dogmatism, but they saw as valid their project of promoting a collective, anticonsumerist direction to Italian society—and of doing so through the appeal of austerity. Most intellectuals who subscribed to the idea with enthusiasm were quickly disillusioned by the poor results and saw their dream of achieving political power fading. Those, such as Lucio Colletti and Norberto Bobbio, who had criticized that same idea had their expectations confirmed: Berlinguer's austere rigor did not correspond to either Marx's emphasis on the satisfaction of needs or the resilience of neocapitalism and the resurgence of laissez-faire policies in the West.[66]

A few years after the end of the Historic Compromise, party intellectuals reconsidered the whole attempt at squaring the circle by trying to become a force of government under the Atlantic alliance. This was the product of a constant "miscommunication," Alberto Asor Rosa wrote in 1982, "between the Communist culture, unifying, centralizing, striving for rationalism [and] the pluralistic, discordant cultures generated by the capitalist social universe." It seemed, as Colletti had commented in reference to an article by Berlinguer four years earlier, in which the communist leader had evoked the nation's entire modern intellectual heritage, from Machiavelli to Vico and Togliatti, that the PCI had become "a sort of UPIM of ideologies."[67] (UPIM is Italy's main discount department store.) Meanwhile, the party began to mourn the many intellectuals who drifted into the reformed and procapitalist Socialist Party or the new libertarian Radical Party.

By the late 1970s most intellectuals in both France and Italy were—more or less explicitly, more or less steadfastly—assuming a mindset exemplified by a manifesto published in *Le Monde* in January 1978. The document announced the creation of the Committee of Intellectuals for a Europe of Freedoms; its subtitle added that culture itself was at war with totalitarianism and that freedom was "nonnegotiable."[68] The "End of the Ideological Age," as Raymond Aron had proposed prematurely twenty years earlier, seemed now fulfilled, at least in the sense that Western European intellectuals no longer strictly adhered to doctrinal programs. Their very anti-Sovietism, now trumping most of their anti-American feelings, was based as much on anti-doctrinal grounds as on Soviet misconduct.

The 1980s, the End of Communism, and
the Taming of Anti-Americanism

President Ronald Reagan had just been sworn in, and the PCI unflinchingly linked his inauguration to the pro-American turns of the Socialists in France and Italy. The party's anti-American prejudice marred its own perception of the interplay between domestic and foreign politics. The pro-Atlantic credentials of the new PSI leader Bettino Craxi were undisputed. His efforts to isolate the Communists were also unquestionable. But, like his French counterpart, François Mitterrand, by 1981 he did not rule out a left-wing alternative government supported by the Communists, if not directly involving them.[69] Berlinguer, however, doubted the sincerity of the offer and consistently mistrusted the moderate socialist leader, a mere "spokesman of Atlanticism," in his opinion, "on behalf of the Reagan administration." For the party ranks more attuned to a possible cooperation with social democracy at home and in the rest of Europe—especially the German group led by Willy Brandt, still seeking a revived *Ostpolitik*—such invective would not benefit the "democratic alternative" (as the party now called its opposition agenda) but rather would bring further isolation.[70] At a meeting of the directorate in February 1979, Pajetta insisted on "preserving our contacts with Europe's social democratic countries, even though Craxi sent a letter to those parties urging them not to attend our congress." There were indeed only a few European delegations at the 1979 Congress. Pajetta could solidly count on the friendship only of Olav Palme, with whom he shared concerns about the "nuclearization" of Europe. For most PCI leaders, however, Craxi became the party's nemesis, because, as Antonio Tatò expressed in a 1978 letter to Berlinguer, the new socialist leader exhibited "an ancestral, organic, visceral anticommunism and anti-Sovietism." Craxi, in this view, was no more than a "right-wing social democrat with a penchant for fascism."[71] This matter was no longer about the PSI's defection to Americanism but about its betrayal of socialism altogether.

The PCI's anti-Americanism was "prejudicial," but Berlinguer initially did show more openness than the other party leaders toward President-Elect Reagan. He was correct in his assessment of Craxi's intentions, and even under the auspices of a Left coalition, he would not accept a subordinate position for the PCI similar to that of the PCF; nor would the electoral strength of the party make this a realistic choice for the pro-Atlantic Italian Left. Toward Washington, Berlinguer rather revealed his full awareness of Cold War constraints and displayed the desperation of his attempts to overcome them. Immediately after Reagan's election, he had conveyed to U.S.

diplomats that the party's bid to enter the government would probably be opposed only by France's Giscard, since the PCI's participation in the government would have also "legitimize[d] the French Communist Party." Even more optimistically, he added that "the Reagan administration would realize that the PCI is ideologically an ally in real terms, since it pursues a line that is clearly distinct from the U.S.S.R." Berlinguer "predicted that the Reagan administration would be more pragmatic [than the Carter administration in its last years] and would seek a true basis for understanding with Moscow."[72]

This appeal to realpolitik ("the ally in real terms") and détente evinced both the PCI's innovative restraint in ideology, and its profound misunderstanding of Reagan's outlook. Berlinguer had taken further distance from Moscow. It was only after the Soviet invasion of Afghanistan that the PCI truly ceased to consider the Soviet Union a force of peace, more determined than the United States to pursue détente. At the end of 1981, after a Soviet-orchestrated coup in Poland repressed the Solidarity movement of trade union leader Lech Walesa, Berlinguer announced in a television interview that the PCI considered the "propulsive force" of the Bolshevik revolution and of the Eastern regimes "terminated."[73] Of course, even after the leader's tactically positive assessment of NATO, this was no prelude to any pro-American turn. It was rather evidence of the isolation the PCI felt in the aftermath of the failed Historic Compromise.

Berlinguer's futile appeal to American realism in 1980 was a last resort, in the hope that a Republican president, no matter how idealist (or ideological), might resume some of the pragmatism of the Nixon-Kissinger diplomacy, yet devoid of Kissinger's keen opposition to Eurocommunism. In the context of the renewed Cold War this reevaluation of Nixon's realpolitik helped several PCI leaders mitigate their criticism of the Soviet Union, justifying its conduct partly as a result of capitalist encirclement—an argument that further weakened the party's credibility. In hindsight, for Pajetta, Kissinger seemed a lesser evil than Brzezinski. At the February 1979 meeting, the veteran PCI leader attributed the emerging "idealism"—for both Democrats and Republicans—in American foreign policy to the "wrong lessons they learned from Vietnam." Brzezinski's "crusade" against communism justified support of repressive regimes in countries like Nicaragua or Iran. Carter's foreign policy was, Pajetta added, "dangerous because of its unpredictability," and because of a Wilsonian drive that matched "an expansionist and imperialist logic" in the name of "spreading democracy."[74] Observing the emergence of neoconservatism in the United States, PCI leaders worried about how many American liberal idealists had morphed into conservative proponents of the spread of democracy worldwide. Italian and French Communists—the latter more so in light of similar conservative turns by many former *gauchistes*—saw this phenomenon also as a logical offspring of the Vital Center Democrats' anti-communist principles.

Reagan turned out to be more "Wilsonian" than the PCI had predicted. His idealism reached the level of self-righteousness: "The era of self-doubt," he famously announced, "is over." That doubt had marred the liberal Democrats' international actions. Reagan restored national pride, and, even more, faith in a national identity that found nourishment in the spread of the American mission against its twentieth-century nemesis: communism. The president "cured" the moral relativism that, most Republicans now agreed, had misguided American conservatives' foreign policy. He thus finalized the transfer of an initially liberal principle, the spread of democracy worldwide, to the conservative sphere of American values.

Where he showed realism toward Italian politics was actually in compromising with the Left of Bettino Craxi, who, as prime minister from 1983 to 1986, adopted a staunch pro-NATO line, but also disagreed with Washington on issues such as the Arab-Israeli conflict or U.S. relations with right-wing Latin American regimes.[75]

In France, American realism took a similar turn. When Vice President George H. W. Bush tried to dissuade Mitterrand from including the PCF in his coalition, the French president-elect reassured him that having the Communists in the government was a better way to diminish their power.[76] In the French context, with a Communist Party still clinging to its subversive identity, co-option into government responsibility in a coalition dominated by the Socialists helped lose the extreme Left even more of its rapidly fading popular appeal. The Reagan administration had no other choice but to accept that counterintuitive strategy. Soon, it found its most optimistic hopes fulfilled, for Mitterrand, wary of Soviet repression in the East, and disillusioned with the effects of regulation on the French economy, quickly became an assertive Atlanticist and a proponent of market economics. The Socialist Party never became entirely pro-Reagan, but it did admire America's revived entrepreneurship, optimism, and the adaptability of its high-tech industry in the Reagan years. Mitterrand paid homage to Silicon Valley and Pittsburgh, new models for industrial innovation and preservation. Scholars of American studies also found that Reaganism elicited admiration from unexpected sources, such as *Le Monde*, *L'Express*, *Le Nouvel Observateur*, and many socialist intellectuals. By the mid-1980s, their articles extolled the president's virtues of leadership, enthusiasm, candor, even his economic vision and pioneering spirit as the quintessential traits of the "man of the West." This Reaganomania was ironic also in suggesting that the stereotypical, simple-hearted, corny new president was more reassuring than an indecisive Carter or a shady Nixon. Former *gauchistes*, paralleling the neoconservative evolution in the United States, became the most Americanophile intellectuals; they repudiated the *engagé* intelligentsia and marginalized the anti-American opinion makers.[77]

While Berlinguer stressed the Italian government's subservience to Washington, particularly during the Craxi years, he also quickly realized that no "realist" overture was forthcoming from Reagan, whose staunch anticommunism and rearmament policies surpassed the worst of the PCI's and PCF's expectations. No such overture came even after Mikhail Gorbachev rose to power in the Soviet Union in 1985, opening a new phase of internal reform and détente with Washington. Reagan's harnessing of NATO also marked an era of internal social, economic, and cultural processes reinforcing neocapitalist and conservative trends in Europe, leaving Western European Marxists little or no room to maneuver.

According to the now blossoming reevaluation of the Reagan presidency, the United States wielded "soft power" effectively, while also opting for rearmament and economic blackmail against the Soviet Union. The president prophesied in May 1981 that "the West won't contain communism, it will transcend communism. . . . it won't bother to . . . denounce it, it will dismiss it as some bizarre chapter in human history whose last pages are even now being written." Perhaps communism, in its Eastern and Western forms, was not as bizarre as Reagan made it out to be. But its implosion, its leader Gorbachev's inability to reform it using, by his own admission, much of the Eurocommunist model, seemed to prove that transcendence was indeed the way the West prevailed. In the last year of his presidency, Reagan lectured in Moscow itself about the advantages of capitalism "evoking computer chips, rock stars, movies, and the irresistible power of unarmed truth."[78] Again, the speech may have exaggerated its praise for the spontaneous forces of culture, and omitted how much the United States actually manipulated these factors throughout the Cold War. But it was true that the combination of postindustrial capitalism and the cultural—or even countercultural—allure of the West undermined the communist political and cultural cold war. In Western Europe that gradual erosion became visible, in the late 1960s, before it did in the East. Just as notably, when "truth" *was* armed, whether through actual rearmament or through psychological warfare, the Western Communists actually gained influence: pacifism and moral-nationalist campaigns against corruption and foreign interference remained their major strengths, in addition to their natural appeal to the economically oppressed or the intellectually ambitious.

The PCI especially maintained electoral strength through Berlinguer's renewed attacks on corruption in the ruling parties, and nationalism against an equally nationalist and preponderant Republican administration in Washington. But the party's greatest electoral success, in 1984, when the vote for the European parliament placed it for the first and only time at the top of the country's political forces, was mainly the public's emotional response to Berlinguer's dramatic death during a public speech one month earlier. The parliamentary elections of the following years confirmed the PCI's steady decline, falling back to the percentages of the 1960s. Under the leadership of an "old guard," Alessandro Natta, and, subsequently, of a member of the younger group, Achille Occhetto, the party completed its emancipation from Leninist principles, including the rule of democratic centralism; it also accepted most of the market-economy principles. Predictably, it quickly became the most enthusiastic supporter among Western Communist Parties of Mikhail Gorbachev's perestroika. Moreover, the party's new cadres were no longer instructed in party schools but emerged from autonomous mass movements and a highly educated background. They found their main references in the new social sciences, much less in the party's humanist traditions and antifascist experience. While still rejecting capitalist individualism, the PCI also completed its repudiation of bureaucratic collectivism. Environmentalism, feminism, and pacifism became as central to the party's concerns as the protection of the working class, even assuming priority after its majority's post–Cold War final repudiation of communism and official transmutation into the Partito Democratico della Sinistra (PDS, or Democratic Party of the Left).[79]

Rather than a decline, the PCF experienced a veritable political death. Its electoral setback in 1978 was followed by Georges Marchais's resounding defeat in the following presidential elections, which inaugurated the long era of Mitterrand's reformed socialism. In the legislative elections of the following month, the parliamentary presence of the Communists was decimated, whereas the Socialists carried a strong relative majority. The PCF's participation in the government until 1984 was no replica of its ascendancy, either national or institutional, of the immediate postwar period. Holding minor cabinet positions, the party was rather forced into this participation to avoid remaining marginalized. But, as Mitterrand had expected, the Communists' involvement in government politics satisfied neither the party militants, who were bitterly anti-Socialist, nor the general public, which penalized the PCF for its role as internal dissenter and for its unwavering pro-Sovietism. No longer able to reconcile its "socialism with the colors of France" with its allegiance to an increasingly reviled Soviet myth, the party lost most of its

Diamo
un volto nuovo
all'Europa.

Vota donna.
Vota Pci.

"Let's give a new face to Europe. Vote woman. Vote PCI." PCI poster, 1984. By the 1980s, the PCI had embraced European integration and combined it with its adaptation to the new emancipation movements. Courtesy Fondazione Istituto Gramsci Emilia Romagna, Bologna.

national credentials. Its only nationalist trait was its "chauvinist" appeal to "make French products," which corroborated its anachronistic opposition to European integration. In some key immigrant areas, such as Ivry, the Communists' battle to protect "French" products also took on a xenophobic turn, contradicting their tendency to romanticize Third World causes against Western imperialism. Furthermore, unlike the PCI, the French Communists approved of the Soviet-led repression of Poland's Solidarity movement and kept justifying the war in Afghanistan. Instead of approaching the media as it had done in the 1970s, the PCF chose to make it the scapegoat for its growing unpopularity. Marchais accused the main TV networks of colluding with the bourgeoisie and the Socialists in a relentless anticommunist campaign.[80]

Similar to the PCI, which by 1983 had abandoned its appeals for austerity in favor of militant syndicalism, the PCF led a head-on struggle against the economic programs of Prime Minister Pierre Mauroy. And much like the internal debate on the Euromissiles had further antagonized the PCI against the Craxi Socialists, Mitterrand's support of the NATO program contributed to the PCF's decision to leave the government in June 1984. Once in the opposition, the PCF continued to uphold its revolutionary credentials, relying on the CGT, and hoping that the "inevitable" crisis of the trusts would return power to the working class. Its "divorce from society" was completed by the late 1980s, with an electoral force reduced to less than 10 percent.[81] The extreme Right of Jean-Marie Le Pen's National Front became more appealing to many social outcasts than the obsoletely orthodox Communists.

Domestic isolation made the French and Italian Communists keener on seeking exposure through international politics. For a short time in the early 1980s, the PCI cultivated some of the high Vatican representatives (presumably Cardinal Casaroli himself) in order to offer a possible mediation with Moscow on the issues of Afghanistan and the Church in Poland. Significantly, Berlinguer hoped that, by resuming this diplomatic role, he would not only help Moscow redeem its record but also put all responsibility for the end of détente squarely on the United States. In its orthodox vein, the PCF pursued a more intimate connection with the Kremlin in order to organize its anti-American propaganda. Until the mid-1980s, this pressure was also founded on the party's conviction that the United States' warmongering policies would precipitate the decline of the capitalist world.[82]

Pacifism seemed to allow a brief revival of the PCF's appeal against the American nuclear buildup of the early 1980s.[83] But with France outside NATO, and Mitterrand's approval of the alliance's decision to install Pershing and Cruise missiles in Europe, communist protest echoed faintly in domestic public opinion. There was a brief moment of illusion that, through an appeal signed by one hundred personalities from the political and intellectual world, the PCF could resume the scope of the Stockholm peace movement of the early 1950s. Once Moscow had lost all its attractiveness to most French public opinion, however, such unilateral manifestations in its support no longer held sway.[84]

In Italy, pacifism, while drawing large crowds against the deployment of Cruise nuclear missiles in Sicily, never regained the strength it had in the early 1950s. The first setback in antinuclear demonstrations took place in 1959, when Italy allowed the installation of Jupiter missiles without much public outcry. The Italian acceptance of the NATO offer in 1983, however, had a much higher public profile. It also brought more antinuclear demonstrations into the streets. But this was more the result of an increasingly open democracy than of heightened anti-Americanism or powerful leverage by

"France must really say NO to the Star Wars program." PCF poster, 1985. Courtesy Collection du PCF/Archives départementales de la Seine-Saint-Denis.

la France doit dire vraiment **NON** à la guerre des étoiles

PCF

the PCI. Moreover, while at first critical of the Soviet decision to install SS-20 missiles against Europe, the PCI soon reverted to unilateral denunciation of the American moves. The installation of the weapons at the Comiso base began in 1984, with the enthusiastic support of Bettino Craxi, who had assumed the premiership a year earlier, and against a jaded communist opposition. "When in our parliament, we debated the installation of the missiles in Comiso," Father Ernesto Balducci wrote in *Critica marxista*, "the Montecitorio assembly was almost deserted. That vacuum was to me a sign that cynicism is now pervading our ruling class. The gravest of our parliament's decisions was taken amid bureaucratic squalor, without giving the Italian people evidence that its legislators know anything about this, know the great problems, the problems that affect our conscience."[85] Balducci was among the few Catholic thinkers to remain wedded to left-wing pacifism. During the previous decade, acrimony over issues of sexual liberation and the new divorce laws had eroded much of the entente the Communists had found with the charismatic La Pira on peace and support of Third World nations.

In their reactions to the Gorbachev leadership, the French and Italian Communists also differed. The PCF was at first enthusiastic about the new leader, hoping he would restore credit to the Soviet Union and to world revolution. Gorbachev's diplomatic initiatives helped deflect international anti-communism, while they underlined America's rigid militarism. Soviet internal reforms also legitimized, in Marchais's view, communism as the genuine expression of all social forces and true "universal democracy." But once one-party rule was challenged in the Soviet Union, and Gorbachev made amends with Europe's Social Democrats and with the European Common Market, the PCF reevaluated its earlier pronouncements on perestroika. At the end of 1988, Marchais declared that the Soviet Union had "ceased to be a model for the other Communist Parties."[86] Compared to Berlinguer's earlier reaction to the events in Poland, this announcement rather confirmed the PCF's orthodoxy, and even its renewed claim that revolution had its primacy in France, and was more truthfully applied in nations as Cuba or Vietnam than in the now reformed Soviet Union. On this issue, a few dissidents, who had formed a *refondateur* current led by Charles Fiterman within the party, asked for a whole reconsideration of the communist experience on the basis of Gorbachev's "pluralism."[87]

In Italy, conservative and socialist acclaim for Gorbachev's leadership made the PCI more cautious than the French comrades at first. Still claiming credit for most of the reformed communism in the West, the Italian Communists felt their record might be eclipsed by the Soviet leader's "Westpolitik." Starting in 1987 the PCI reestablished cordial relations with the Kremlin, to the point of finally showing enthusiastic support for Gorbachev's foreign and domestic policies. The leader of the PCI's reform wing, Giorgio Napolitano, expected those changes to be even more radical. Anti-Americanism took a back seat to this focus on reforms in the East. It became also instrumental for the PCI to reclaim its role in representing reformed communism, from Dubček to Gorbachev. But, in so doing, it further tied its own fate to that of the new Soviet leadership.[88] The PCI's choice to change its name in 1991 was compelled by the Soviet collapse.

Political collapse was compounded by further cultural decline for both the French and Italian Communists. High culture had a deceptive rebalancing between Europe and the United States. Ostensibly, postmodernism, the fascination with linguistics, and deconstruction signaled a European dominance. Starting in the late 1970s, American academia worshipped literary theorists such as Jacques Derrida and Paul de Man, cultural critics such as Michel Foucault, Jean Baudrillard, and Umberto Eco, and, among the heirs of the Frankfurt School, philosophers such as Jürgen Habermas. But the end result of this transatlantic connection was to reiterate the importance of a leftist dialogue that gave priority to causes identified with the new social revolutions outside the domain of European Marxism: multiculturalism, feminism, gay rights, and, only last, the empowerment of the working class. American intellectuals simply borrowed the new European developments because they best fit the new notions of social oppression that their country had best mastered at the expense of rather than in conjunction with Marxism. The formerly militantly anti-American Umberto Eco summed up the situation for many Western European intellectuals, recognizing that "Americanization might be simply a process which occurred wherever mental imagery and the decision to consume met each other." This phenomenon was negative only if Americanization was absorbed in its most vulgarized forms. In fact, prominent intellectuals, from Calvino to Moravia, reminisced how America had been the crucial rite of passage for them, helping them to shed the provincialism of Italian culture. After a period of perceived political decline (the United States as a "flawed giant" in the 1970s) America was "rediscovered," in Eco's words, as a myth, perhaps a haunting one, but in any case a cultural model that refuted most of the irrational forms of anti-Americanism.[89]

At first, most Italian Marxists, and some of their French counterparts as well, also began to share with American liberals a relative acceptance of multiculturalism. In the United States, this development stemmed from most liberals' lost "connection to war" after the trauma of Vietnam. By coming closer to the causes of oppressed minorities at home, these liberals also began to see in nationalism "the thrust toward the domination of weaker countries." But the American liberals' repudiation of nationalism, once confronted with the Republicans' appeal to national pride, soon gave way to a search for a better liberal articulation of their own brand of nationalism. Thus, from the late 1980s, popular writers and media producers such as James McPherson, Stephen Ambrose, Ken Burns, Stephen Spielberg, Ted Turner, and Tom Brokaw began to commemorate the liberal nationalism associated with the Civil War, World War II, and the early Cold War.[90] By the end of the Cold War, the American liberals' connection with European Marxists or neo-Marxists on themes of multiculturalism became tenuous at best.

Renewed liberal nationalism also nourished the Republican ranks with neoconservatives. Many of those who formed this new U.S. intellectual and foreign policy establishment were former Democrats. Several of them had held posts in the Reagan administration: notable ones—including Jeane Kirkpatrick, Richard Perle, Carl Greshman, Max Kampelman, and Richard Pipes—received appointments in the State and Defense departments and in national security. In 1987 *The New Republic* quipped about the "Trotskyist takeover" of the Reagan administration. While most neoconservatives maintained a certain openness toward social causes—they were not antiabortion or for religion in school, and, at least until the early years of the Reagan administration, they kept their liberal ideas on domestic issues—they just as strongly rejected adversary culture, or anything that might even hint at domestic anti-Americanism. Government, for them, was to remain a "mammoth" presence, especially in foreign affairs, reinforcing the globalist legacy of Wilson and Roosevelt, and promoting global democracy.[91]

Meanwhile, communist anti-Americanism in France and Italy lost further determination and influence. During the early 1980s, for many intellectuals in both countries, "the old evil"—U.S. imperialism—coexisted with the new one—Soviet imperialism. But, in reacting to Gorbachev's policies, Italy's main leftist thinkers differed from their French counterparts. As the PCI committed to the new Soviet reform, so did its intellectuals. Having already reflected, in the early 1980s, that some of Marx's key ideas were no longer applicable, many Italian thinkers found in the new Soviet leadership a confirmation of their own intellectual eclecticism. Gramsci's work remained a crucial reference for their political identity. But the PCI founder was now rediscovered for his now "presumed" post-Leninist theories, and, after the collapse of the Eastern European regimes, even for his allegedly postcommunist qualities.[92] In their enthusiasm about Gorbachev, some of these liberalized intellectuals polemically revamped the debate on past Soviet crimes. Most notably, in 1986, Federigo Argentieri invited the party to recant its position on the Hungarian events of 1956. Secretary Natta's unwillingness to do so was soon reconsidered by his reformist successor, Achille Occhetto. Two years later, a PCI delegation, led by the young Piero Fassino, paid homage in Paris to Imre Nagy during the fiftieth anniversary commemoration of his execution.[93]

As the debate on totalitarianism continued in France with more polemical tones than in Italy, leftist French intellectuals showed little appreciation of Gorbachev's reforms. By 1987 most of them concurred with the PCF that the new Kremlin leader was, with his own self-critique, bringing the Soviet system down.[94] But, in holding this position, most of these intellectuals did not share the PCF's fears about the fate of their country's revolutionary tradition, for they had already abjured their engagement with communism. The denunciations of radical utopianism by intellectuals like André Glucksmann and Bernard-Henri Lévy in their works of the late 1970s had a lasting influence. Alain Touraine and André Gorz, also widely acclaimed a few years later, further contributed to undermining the centrality of Marxist doctrines, emphasizing new approaches to the questions of production and consumption that no longer underwrote the distinction between productive and nonproductive classes.[95] Even more debilitating for the PCF's much vaunted connection of the French with the Bolshevik Revolutions were the analyses by an ex-communist, historian François Furet. His works, starting with *Penser la Révolution française* in 1978, dismantled many myths and established Marxist visions of radical social transformation, and were instrumental in discrediting communism altogether. In light of the Soviet experience, no more rationalizations could ignore, as Furet put it, that "today the gulag is leading to a rethinking of the Terror by virtue of identity in their projects." No matter how Furet tried to rebuke conservatives' efforts to use his work to "stigmatize the entire revolution with its supposed totalitarian descendants," particularly on occasion of the revolution's bicentennial in 1989, there was no doubt in the public's mind that, as a political project, Marxism was dead together with its archaic representative, the PCF.[96]

In general, as postindustrial societies, France and Italy came to accentuate social mobility. The notion that the working class was the decisive protagonist of social and political life lost its centrality. Highly educated, individualist, competitive tertiary-sector employees still sought unionization in France, but no longer opting for the CGT as in the past. In Italy, employees from these same sectors focused more on social advancement and status than on class conscience. Consumerism and upward mobility, no matter how unequally it was still distributed, now seemed to extend beyond the middle class to include the whole society. The progressive youth in both countries made its political choices less based on ideology than on specific causes. Most of the young French and Italians in the late 1980s became indifferent to the fate of communism.[97]

In this context, mass culture and consumerism were no longer strictly correlated to Americanization, or to the preservation of the social status quo. After the transition from production to consumption as the main "arena of freedom" in the 1970s, there was, by the 1980s, an increasing tendency among the young to perceive mass culture "no longer as an obstacle or an alternative to opposition and liberation, but as itself the arena of liberation largely realized." Subverting its own rebellion and counterculture into mass culture icons (for example the rock stars marketed by Music Television [MTV] or the independent film industry), the United States—and the Western world in general—absorbed their subversive nature, while eradicating most of their utopian traits. In the final analysis, America remained the "main theater" in which contradictions were played "more openly;" it "provid[ed] both the disease and the cure," but "we no longer know which is which."[98]

To be sure, the "Americanization" of television programs by Italian tycoon and future prime minister Silvio Berlusconi elicited horrified commentaries by Communists and Catholics alike. But, regardless of how inane and manipulative Berlusconi's programs were, the public's reaction was not unanimous. Many reacted either indifferently or selectively; the audience thus did not consistently fall prey to that manipulation as many had feared. Even the PCI, while consistently criticizing the Berlusconi network, came to accept private broadcasting as a complement to public radio and television. Whatever the reactions, mass media in the 1980s undermined the PCI's conventions on culture.

Within the increasingly ecumenical, less pedagogical PCI, new cultural leaders such as Ferdinando Adornato, Walter Veltroni, and Gianni Borgna, liberally engaged with commercial media, celebrated TV shows the party had previously spurned—such as the San Remo music festival—and even catered to the public's taste for icons of the American entertainment establishment—such as Rocky, Clint Eastwood, and the soap opera *Dallas*.[99] In sum, the shift of freedom from the world of production to that of consumption ran against the main principles and strengths of the Communist Parties, whether they kept appealing for the transformation of private into social consumption, as did the PCI, or continued to rely on the proletarian worldview, as did the PCF.

The difficult ideological transition for the PCI from pro-Sovietism to the acceptance of "liberal capitalist" values was more than a contradiction. By the early 1980s, it was often compared to an endless tunnel, or, as Napolitano once put it, to the crossing of a "swamp." That is what the party ultimately did at the end of the Cold War, when, through a process of self-annihilation, it reconstituted itself as the Democratic Party of the Left, causing orthodox factions to break away and form splinter communist groups. Its position in favor of European integration made fewer and fewer references to a "common European home" that would include Russia. The reference for its identity was no longer the East but Western Europe and, to a certain extent, liberal America. In 1996, one of the PDS's prominent leaders, Walter Veltroni, as vice–prime minister of a center-left coalition government, reflected the party's majority when he placed Bill Clinton at the top of his most admired international leaders. He also confirmed the party's faith in NATO at the moment of its first significant expansion to include the former Soviet satellite countries.[100]

The PCF was crossing the ideological "swamp" from a mere institutional point of view. Its participation in the first Left coalition under President Mitterrand had no effect on its own ideological tenets. While this participation at first seemed to pull the party out of isolation more effectively than the PCI's call for a "democratic alternative," it in fact confirmed its minority, contradictory position within an increasingly promarket, PS-dominated government, proving correct Mitterrand's predictions about the Communists' obsolescence. At the moment the PCF took on a self-assigned function as the government's "tribune" of the modern proletariat—to borrow Georges Lavau's expression—it virtually renounced its revolutionary outlook. Rather, the party confirmed its ambiguity between adherence and opposition to the system, underlining its political culture as that of a "countersociety."[101] The PCF's critique of the United States continued, if in a somewhat abated form. But it had little or no consequence, not even when, in 1992, the establishment of Euro Disneyland on the outskirts of Paris raised public concerns about the "Americanization" of France's leisure industry. Jack Lang, the socialist minister of culture, did not hide his own misgivings in that sense; but overall, he expressed admiration for most of the American entertainment industry, and even more for the "bold and inventive ideas" in American culture and society.[102] Polls showed that a large majority of French citizens agreed with him; and French intellectuals virtually agreed with Eco's rediscovery of a constantly self-renewing, experimental America.

Political anti-Americanism would still lend ammunition to the Marxist Left in France and in Italy as well, particularly in the years of the ambivalently pro-NATO President Jacques Chirac and the unabashedly pro-American conservative leader Silvio Berlusconi. But the Communists, reformed or not, no longer had the capacity or the will to resist "Americanism" in all its aspects. While criticism of political and cultural choices of the sole superpower, or, as it became known in post–Cold War language, "hyperpower," continued to abound,[103] the very notion of Americanization or cultural imperialism had by then been diluted into more accurate perceptions of the realities of multiculturalism.

CONCLUSION

Communist strength in France and Italy was a pivotal threat to U.S. interests for most of the Cold War. In itself, it warranted attention and carefully crafted strategies in Washington. But, seen in the context of European anti-Americanism, the threat transcended the confines of French and Italian politics. From the point of view of the French and Italian Communists, the challenge of a modernization process largely influenced by the United States signified also a confrontation with the inequities of capitalism. For all their failures, we must keep in mind an important aspect of the French and Italian Communists' political presence throughout the Cold War: in many respects, the two parties, with their staying power, became vehicles of social justice for the lower classes and disadvantaged groups. While the PCI and PCF aspired to a much more profound social transformation and to the promotion of a Soviet agenda, they did crucially increase the pressure on the ruling parties in both countries to reform the capitalist system—often in cooperation with the United States—through welfare provisions, social policies, and cultural adaptations.[1] Their failures, mostly determined by their inability to adapt or finally, in the PCI's case, by its decision to conform to most modernizing trends at the expense of its ideological identity, also has a deeper significance than the internal mechanisms of the two nations' politics and society. They testify to the broader issue of Marxism's confrontation with the forces of modernization and the ethical individualism, values, and sensibilities that characterized these trends in the Western world. Those forces, together, undermined the collective identities so strenuously championed by the Communists.

For the United States, this confrontation was not only about French and Italian politics. The appeal of communism in Western Europe compelled U.S. policy and opinion makers to address more general issues about the management of the Western alliance, the American image abroad (not only in Western Europe), and even the value of its "exceptionalist" assumptions. Confronting anti-Americanism in its most articulated form in the Western world, American officials and intellectuals were further encouraged to ask soul-searching questions about America's identity and world leadership. While overall the record for the United States and its image was successful, it also contained a considerable share of mistakes and shortcomings. It was not simply that militant anticommunism often backfired because of the strong pressures—economic, political, and cultural—that the United States brought to bear on France and Italy. At crucial times, even measures that seemed to obtain lasting results, such as the superseding of traditional class conflict under Marshall Plan designs, caused problems with the rising expectations of large social groups in France and Italy and their consequent feeling of exclusion when those expectations were delayed or went unfulfilled. Even masterly diplomatic moves, such as the white propaganda initiatives of the Truman and Eisenhower administrations, often fed charges of American arrogance and exceptionalism by Europe's public opinion.

The power of the anti-American appeal by Marxists in France and Italy has been widely recognized but not sufficiently analyzed. Being directly exposed to the American political and cultural presence, French and Italian Communists began to articulate a full range of anti-American themes before being directed to do so by Moscow and the Cominform. Turning America into a metaphor for all the worst vices that could beset Western civilization, they conjured an image of a new superpower that was both tough and stupid, a combination of greed, aggressiveness, naiveté, and irresponsibility. American dominion, in their view, posed a twin threat to Europe's independence and intelligence. In waging their opposition in these terms, they benefited from a vast repertoire of cultural constructs and specific denunciations of American policies or social landscape that other groups in Europe had presented before or were presenting simultaneously.

The Communists, at crucial times in the early Cold War, managed to establish a firm connection between economic justice, moral issues, patriotism, and even cultural representation of national thought. For at least the full first decade of the Cold War, both the PCI and the PCF could easily equate capitalist oppression with American "domination," combining a promise of material improvement with the defense of national independence. The Soviet-dominated world remained at safe distance, and only after the Prague Spring did national independence for the Western Communists (especially the PCI and the PCE) appear more secure within a European integration driven by Western social democracy, or even within NATO.

From the early 1950s, Washington's main worry was not about the Cominform-inspired communist propaganda per se in France and Italy but rather about the cultural and political connection these anti-American manifestations found with the moderate, neutralist groups (reviews such as *Esprit* and *Nuovi Argomenti* or prominent representatives of Catholic and socialist thought). The PCI and the PCF even found a common intent, if not an alliance, with groups they generally opposed, based on a similar goal of limiting America's presence or expansion worldwide. For example, the PCI established a dialogue with the influential Catholic leader Giorgio La Pira, and the PCF matched the Gaullists in a resolute fight against the European Defense Community project. Italy's Christian Democrats nurtured a truculent anticommunism, but the PCI gave credit to its own peace campaign for pressing the DC rulers toward a more conditional loyalty to the United States, for example over issues of trade with the East, or Vietnam, or, in general, over the U.S. emphasis on military preparation and burden-sharing within NATO. Similarly, the PCF took partial credit for de Gaulle's vision of a Europe from the Atlantic to the Urals.

With an anti-Americanism that was almost always thorough, visceral, and distorting, the French and Italian Communists were nevertheless able to feed public fears, more or less justified, about the American presence in Europe. Their protest against U.S. foreign policies stressed humanitarian aspects, too. The most powerful condemnations of America by the two Communist Parties portrayed a subjugated Europe where cultural devastation would be interlaced with the physical destruction that the powerful and foolish American empire would bring along. At the start of the thermonuclear age, prospects of apocalypse captured Europe's popular imagination. The communist peace campaigns of the early 1950s owed their success in large part to this collective fear, which blended with the recent memories of war devastation. At the end of the Vietnam War, the Italian communist press could claim that American capitalism had "killed" both with its bombs and with the economic imbalances caused by its globalizing trends. During the American nuclear rearmament of the late 1970s and early 1980s, the French and Italian Communists could easily point to hypocrisy in the "idealist" Carter and Reagan administrations, and to their ill-concealed intentions of wrecking détente.

The two Communist Parties were naturally quick and effective in condemning U.S. social imbalances, as well as the inequities and inanities of a hedonistic consumer society. They emphasized McCarthyist tendencies in U.S. society long after the anticommunist witch hunt in the United States had ended. The battle for civil rights by African Americans, other ethnic minorities, and women was of course an occasion to stress the limits and dysfunction not only of American society but of capitalism in its most modernized version.

Communist anti-Americanism retained its cultural clout best when it was discerning and nuanced. The Communists' lingering fascination with the "other Americas"—of the "lost" New Deal opportunities, of social and intellectual critics, of racial minorities, of protest movements, finally, by the 1970s, even of dissenters within the political establishment—gave depth and keenness to their denunciations of American influence. This ambiguity was to a large extent inspired by all the leftist intellectuals, within the party or fellow travelers, who found themselves particularly attracted to the "theater" where the contradictions of the Western world were played with "greatest frankness." Most communist intellectual analyses cast the Cold War enemy as both insidious and fascinating. When they made room for such analyses, this perceptiveness increased the intellectual appeal of the French and Italian Communist Parties.

Sometimes the ambivalence expressed by party leaders was simply tactical, as when both parties compromised with Grand Alliance politics in the immediate postwar period, or when the PCI endorsed NATO in the early 1970s. In the case of Berlinguer, acceptance of the Western alliance stemmed from a sincere belief that NATO could shelter national paths to socialism in the West against Soviet interference. The ambiguity of that view lay not just in its contradictions and profound irony but also in the persistence, throughout these tactical compromises, of an instinctive, relentless, and virulent philosophical anti-Americanism by even the most moderate PCI leaders.

Communist anti-Americanism also gained strength through its international appeal. Long after the communist threat had lost its urgency in France and Italy, both the PCI and the PCF continued to present insidious dangers to U.S. Cold War strategy. Their propaganda retained contagious effects on French and Italian government forces, whether those forces adapted their arguments, used them to obtain more concessions from the United States, or used them in a nationalist posture to inoculate the European governments against accusations of servility to Washington. From the late 1950s, communist anti-Americanism also had contagious effects on Third World emancipation movements. By the late 1960s, as the transatlantic consensus was marred with rifts in the NATO alliance and with social unrest in the Western world, left-wing anti-Americanism in Europe became mutually nurturing with dissent and protest movements in the United States.[2] More than Marxist influence, most U.S. officials feared that especially the youth movement on both sides of the Atlantic would turn any radical mode of thought into a deeper expression of a malaise in Western societies, bordering on nihilism, which of course would also seriously weaken Western resolve and cohesion in the Cold War.

Communist anti-American propaganda was to a great deal orchestrated, often distorting, and at times wrongheaded; but this should not lead us to conclude that it was easily dismissed. It mattered a great deal to leaders in Washington, Paris, and Rome, for all the reasons I have just mentioned. Moreover, orchestration from Moscow did not diminish the popular appeal of certain communist causes. The Stockholm peace movement is a case in point. Also, the notion that all of the two parties' anti-American campaigns were almost exclusively orchestrated from above with the goal of misleading the public should be laid to rest. Ideological conviction mattered more. Communist leaders in France and Italy developed their views of America based only in part on a script, from the Cominform or from their own directives.[3] Most archival evidence shows that the leaders' deep-seated prejudice against America also stemmed from a combination of ideology, domestic factors attributed to U.S. influence, and a plethora of conceptions, images, and tropes of America absorbed and recycled from other currents of European thought stretching back to the nineteenth century.

Another argument against the relevance of communist propaganda is that wisdom or common sense generally prevailed in French and Italian public opinion. For all the ideological and political drive of communist leaders, the argument goes, the large majority of the French and Italian working class always proved pragmatic, shunning extremism.[4] Yet this belief overlooks the fact that the PCF's and PCI's rank and file was often more "orthodox" than the party leaders. Many workers may have balked at the politicized nature of the insurrectionary strikes against the Marshall Plan; but they were also ready to take up arms after the assassination attempt against Togliatti in 1948, or to turn violent during the "peace" demonstrations against General Ridgway in France. Their anti-Americanism surpassed that of their leaders during the Italian "Hot Autumn" of 1969; so did—within or outside the working class—the students' hatred of the American "imperialists" in Vietnam. Indeed, on several occasions, U.S. officials worried that party leaders might lose control of the forces they had unleashed. The embassies in Paris and Rome opened diplomatic channels with PCF and PCI representatives in the 1960s partly to encourage their leadership's self-restraint and to enable them to better control the student movement or, later in Italy, to confront "red" terrorism.

For all its strengths and appeal, communist anti-Americanism contained even more contradictions and weaknesses. Despite all the ideological conviction, the large degree of regimentation, internal or through the Cominform, was certainly evident. The Communists' belief system based on collective identities ran counter to the privatization trends, mass consumerism, and individualism gaining strength in Western societies. The same postwar developments that gave prominence to mass parties, which, in the case of the Communists, strove to create cohesion by comprising all aspects of social and political life, also generated pressures against their practice of and faith in democratic centralism. By the 1960s, even leftist extremists sought new causes and modes of expression—socially and individually more permissive—in alternative groups. The working class also lost its centrality as an agent of social change. By clinging to labor as main referent, the PCF lost numbers and political relevance. By adapting to social democratic trends, the PCI lost its class-centered identity together with its Marxist character.

Private consumption in modernized Europe was mutually fed with mass media and entertainment. The American input in the development of mass media was especially strong in Italy. In an effort to counter the "cosmopolitan" influences from the American model, and to disparage the reductive or hedonistic aspects of modern media, the Communists in France and Italy also fought a rearguard battle against popular taste and aspirations. Their adaptations of folk traditions and popular taste produced a thriving "countersociety," but one that either remained relatively isolated from the political system or was diluted into mass-marketing techniques that defied the two parties' ideological purity (the modified content and format of the two parties' main dailies are a case in point). In most cases also, the two parties' approach to mass culture remained dogmatic and, with its preference for realist canons until the late 1960s, excessively populist as well.

Even the counterculture, stemming from unfulfilled expectations in capitalist societies and challenging many of their norms, did not ultimately benefit the French and Italian Communists. The accent in the 1960s movements on personal self-fulfillment, individual expression, and cultural experimentation, along with the economic and political mistakes of the "flawed giant" United States, may have stalled neocapitalism and American hegemony; but even more it eroded Marxist social and cultural assumptions. It also further undermined both the proletarian outlook of the two parties and their practice of democratic centralism. At the peak of the anti–Vietnam War movements, the protest was an occasion for both the PCI and the PCF to rally all the anti-American groups of the Left. But instead of an anti-American consensus, protest created a cacophony. The main problem, as PCI's Pietro Ingrao put it in 1966, was that the Left was messy, nerve-racking, and divided against American imperialism. In their attraction—temporary for the PCF— to the antiestablishment forces in Eastern Europe following the Prague Spring, the French and Italian Communists also unwittingly favored an antiestablishment critique in the West that defied the role of mass parties. It is only partially correct to state the limits of Americanization as its "export[ing of] not only consumer goods and mass culture, but also a confused groping for values and standards."[5] In fact, this "confusion" during the 1960s and 1970s signaled America's continued role as the first place where developments occurred in the neocapitalist world; it also powerfully restored the pluralistic nature of U.S. democracy. While protest movements happened simultaneously on both sides of the Atlantic, the main direction for the flow of political inspiration and cultural references was from the United States to Europe. Finally, the consumerist turn in the counterculture and youth "pop" cultures by the mid-1970s further rewarded neocapitalist trends.

Communist influence in the intellectual world also suffered from these developments. While the intellectual appeal of French and Italian Communism remained strong throughout the Cold War, a problem persisted when it came to orchestrating anti-American campaigns in the intelligentsia. Many French and especially Italian intellectuals felt disenchanted with America, not prejudicially opposed to its civilization. The Soviet myth for a while captured the imagination of perceptive intellectuals such as Jean-Paul Sartre and Italo Calvino. But their confidence in the Soviet Union as model for their countries was rarely strong. The very ambivalence of many communist leaders and intellectuals toward certain American social and cultural developments contained the most blatant contradiction of all. Cold War America committed many sins, but the greatest of all for most Marxist intellectuals were losing its originality vis-à-vis Europe, compromising with the oppressive groups in their own nations, and thus undertaking a process, in Cesare Pavese's words, of "European spiritualization." Implicit in this judgment was these thinkers' and leaders' acceptance or, for some of them, conversion to the American social and cultural appeal, even to the notion of its exceptionalism.

The many intellectuals who left the two Communist Parties did so for many reasons — not the least of which was the quick fading of Soviet myths — but this ambiguity toward America's "permanent revolution" (with all the limits in its fulfillment) was a paramount one, even when they did not announce it explicitly as their main motive. In the intellectual debate, too, as in the patterns of mass socialization, that "revolution," addressing existential questions and issues of individual expression, subverted most Marxist doctrines, above all the historicism and the economic determinism that underlay them. Postmodernism itself, frequently under neo-Marxist guise, shifted the attention of many leftist intellectuals from social revolution to individual liberation from the "constructed truths" of not only capitalism but any ideology whatsoever. Yet in their skepticism and emphasis on the manipulation of knowledge, they turned out to be much more subversive of the ideologies, such as communism, that claimed the strongest certainties. These intellectual developments, in sum, announced the final collapse of Marxism.

There was also a double paradox in the French and Italian Communists' demise. Even when they shed a great deal of their planning and collectivist goals, the two parties retained their natural identity as defenders of the oppressed and the excluded. The first paradox was that, with the sense of social community disappearing in a postindustrial, consumerist society, protecting labor rights gradually lost its effectiveness in forging communal solidarity; by the late 1970s that protection appeared instead to favor entitlements. Thomas Friedman, a shrewd observer of the social and economic effects of globalization, has aptly used the "flat world" definition to explain the growing permeability of national borders and the diminished competitiveness of Western societies. His argument can be also applied to the communist decline in France and Italy. In the developing world, Friedman reminds us, including China, or West Bengal, which has the oldest elected communist government left in the world today, the advantages of global technology and outsourcing has informed *adaptive* political decisions, making information technology an "essential service." These "proletarian" regimes can thus restrict workers' rights against the interference of outsourcing Western firms. This adaptation, while repressing human rights, also reveals the pressure on these regimes to keep their economies competitive without bankrupting the state.[6]

In modernized, democratic, welfare-oriented France and Italy, the trend of the past fifty years has gone the opposite way. By the 1970s, the Communists had turned from assisting the workers' pursuit of social justice to defending their entitlements, as well as the entitlements of the lower middle class and of the increasing ranks of pensioners. Berlinguer's appeal to commit to austerity and modify individualist consumerist patterns into social consumption founded on solidarity stood against that trend, but it drew few cheers from the party's grassroots. The party then set that campaign aside in the early 1980s, when the government rolled back much of the inflation-indexed salary system introduced in 1970. The Italian and French workers had become "too modern" in that sense, and not as *adaptive* as in current Marxist regimes of countries needing rapid development. In other words, French and Italian workers embraced the same complacency that, in the globalized economy, would lower the competitiveness of many Western economies.

But cheerleading for globalization has been heavily contradicted, too, showing the second paradox of the communist defeat in Western Europe. Victory for the West in the Cold War was swift but not sweet, not only because of the resulting complacency Friedman talks about but also because the Western advanced economies—and the United States especially—have been striving to retain control over the developing nations by forcing them to conform to textbook economics that does not make much sense for these countries' particular economic conditions. That is how Joseph Stiglitz, a

Nobel Prize–winning economist and former advisor to the Clinton administration, has described the inherent flaws and arrogance of IMF policies, particularly during the 1997 collapse of Southeast Asian economies. Because of old rules set by the West, globalization has, in general, hindered instead of encouraged these countries' development. The "invisible hand" of market economics, Stiglitz asserts, is not workable in developing countries that naturally lack key information or markets required for important kinds of transactions. Worse still, globalization, as in 1997, has accelerated the worldwide chain reaction of regional crises, striking the Western economies as well. Similarly, for former socialist economies, Stiglitz has been favoring a "gradualist" transition to market economies, rather than the widely applied "shock therapy," which has produced some disastrous effects.[7] So, some of the worst fears the French and Italian Communists held in the 1970s and 1980s about the effects of triumphant neocapitalism have come true: globalization has increasingly favored financial elites at the expense of working-class people and the poor everywhere; it also tends to transmit bad turns in the economy faster than good ones.

In dealing with the strength of the French and Italian Communist Parties, the United States considered not only the workings and consequences of the two countries' domestic politics but also the repercussions of Western communist propaganda internationally. From Washington's standpoint, until the early 1960s, the PCF's anti-Americanism seemed more alarming than the anti-American currents of the Italian Left, because of France's international position, and because the impact of the party's propaganda, more than that of the PCI, was strengthened by widespread anti-Americanism across the nation's political spectrum. The combination of these two realities could heavily affect the neutralist debate internationally. By the late 1960s, with the relative autonomy the PCI claimed from Moscow, and Berlinguer's diplomatic action aimed at coalescing with Europe's social democratic forces, the neutralist "domino" effect seemed more likely to originate from Rome. It had by then become clear that, as Emilio Sereni had predicted to his comrades early in 1947, the United States had to reckon with the PCI for at least one reason that was opposite to the PCF's situation: Italy's relatively low international prominence gave the party a chance to become an international force of consequence.

American reactions to communist power and propaganda in France and Italy to a great extent relied on the policies of foreign aid and covert actions. But every time the United States surrendered to the temptation of foreign aid for short-term political objectives, it obtained meager results, with perhaps the exception of the 1948 Italian elections. That successful instance also showed how economic development needed to be a long-term project, closely coordinated with, to use Charles Maier's expression, "the politics of productivity." But for all the importance attributed to the effects of the Marshall Plan and its follow-ups, time and again, U.S. officials realized the limits of economic determinism. The conclusion of a 1952 intelligence study on France, that "only a rough correlation exist[ed] between poverty and adherence to the . . . Communist Party," held true for both countries through the rest of the Cold War. Even realists came to this conclusion. Twenty-five years later, Henry Kissinger, in a vein similar to George Kennan's early Cold War analyses, acknowledged that communism in the West to a large extent originated in the "alienation of the population from the modern industrial state," a sense of exclusion from power or social status, and "left-wing traditions" in countries like France and Italy. Not even the rise of technocratic elites starting in the 1950s, or the growth of the middle class and the consumerist revolution affecting the working class in both countries from the early 1960s managed to curb the communist appeal substantially—at least, not quickly. The "politics of productivity" and the subsequent "empire of consumption" did not account for the large numbers of people whose gratification was delayed, because of economic dislocation or simply as a result of the "revolution of rising expectations" that the United States itself represented and helped advance in Europe. These masses of discontented among the working and middle classes, or among intellectuals and the frustrated youth of the 1960s, remained unfulfilled, sullen, and distrustful of America or their own country's rulers who followed America without question. Even the Communists' nationalist calls for grandeur against capitalist and American oppression included the economic and status aspirations of sectors outside the working class, for these appeals concentrated public attention on the combined effects of social dislocations and American influences.

In addition to recognizing these social trends and national traditions, immediately at the start of the Cold War, the United States realized the importance of the PCI's and PCF's bureaucratic strength. That presence in the countries' civil service, which both parties retained after their expulsion from government in 1947, contributed not only to their staying power but also to their influence over public opinion. How this influence reinforced the two parties' propaganda was obvious: for example, through control of the majority of the trade union movement in the early 1950s and, for the PCI, the early 1980s, the Communists turned their labor representatives into the best spokespeople of a well-orchestrated anti-American propaganda effort (against rearmament) and a strong economic appeal (against the corporate collusion with such rearmament and its consequent costs for the labor force). But the indirect influence of the communist occupation of various mid-level and local bureaucratic positions caused even greater concern in Washington. For instance, during the efforts to restructure and rearm its NATO allies, the United States feared that communist presence in the French bureaucracy could discourage foreign investments in the French economy, increasing the country's "chronic economic difficulties" and inability to "support a greater defense effort." In an already "war-weary" country as France was in the early 1950s, this situation seemed to lead to apathy against the Soviet threat, and to neutralism. It certainly seemed to heighten the country's desire for greater autonomy from NATO.[8] In both France and Italy communist bureaucratic strength, particularly through their trade unions, the CGIL and the CGT, facilitated trade arrangements with the Eastern European regimes, thus encouraging an *Ostpolitik* of sorts by the two governments. These developments often seemed to foster neutralist sentiment in noncommunist public opinion, if not all-out resentment of American presence and conditions for the alliance. In turn, these feelings occasionally made it difficult for the U.S. government to commit Congress and American public opinion to these allies.

American solutions to this problem ranged from the overt aspects of the productivity drives and the G-7 coordination of free-market economics to covert operations by the Psychological Strategy Board, or by CIA funding programs aimed at neutralizing the Communists' bureaucratic presence. Contradictions persisted. Since Washington gave priority to overcoming any isolationist temptation at home, or any accusations of being soft on communism—for example, during the Carter administration—it also accepted options involving heavy meddling in others' domestic affairs, provoking some anti-American backlash.

Propaganda and cultural diplomacy also had advantages as well as drawbacks. Projecting images of prosperity and social mobility was quite effective in recumbent nations as France and Italy. Through these models, promises, and through literature, music, and Hollywood entertainment the United States conveyed its fulfillment of the masses' expectations. But, as American intellectuals and diplomats soon realized, this inordinate faith in mass consumerist culture also confirmed many stereotypes of a culturally debased, tasteless, superficial, and conformist U.S. society. The other risk was that of assuming an excessively unilateralist approach to this cultural "projection." Even William Fulbright's gospel of cultural tolerance contained an assumption of Western superiority, and to a great extent followed the credo of American exceptionalism.

Government initiatives such as the Foreign Leader Program, or heavily orchestrated intellectual sponsorships such as the Congress for Cultural Freedom (CCF), in part remedied the problem of self-stereotyping and unilateralism. They mitigated the "be like us" appeals of postwar American propaganda; they also emphasized the cultural vitality of the *common* Western heritage. This "transatlantic" cultural approach was also instrumental in debunking Marxist ideology as obsolete and utopian, celebrating instead empirical realism. By enticing the European Non-Communist Left, it also conducted the most daring and flexible American campaign against communist and fellow-traveler intellectuals. This erosion of the Communists' intellectual prestige was limited, however, by evidence of orchestration of the CCF initiatives, even before the CIA hand in the initiatives was revealed in 1967. Furthermore, the "end of ideology" argument still implied "exceptionalist" tones that were bound to grate on European intellectuals. As it turned out, it was the American disdain of authority, which became most manifest in the 1960s and was only implicitly suggested in the double debate over the "end of ideology" and American exceptionalism, that inspired many intellectual defections from the Marxist camp. To really entice the intellectual Left in countries such as France and Italy, the United States had to demonstrate that, as Seymour Martin Lipset put it, "the American revolutionary libertarian tradition does not encourage obedience to the State and law."[9] This rebellious spirit counterbalanced the Americans' high degree of patriotism and sense of national identity based on their constitutional values. It also found a strong correlation with the French and Italian traditions of individualism and, in recent decades, with their evolution toward cultural relativism.

The economic, covert, cultural, and propaganda aspects of American anticommunism in Western Europe thus combined with mixed results. But American diplomacy, previously overlooked, was also crucial. It constituted the most indirect form of U.S. intervention in French and Italian internal affairs. The United States' evolution toward a diplomatic approach, to be sure, was not linear or consistent. Even after diplomats at the Rome and Paris embassies, or within the psychological warfare apparatus, realized that economic measures were insufficient and that covert operations often backfired, the urgency of the communist threat, perceived or real, prompted heavy U.S. meddling in French and especially Italian affairs—with the "Civic Action" program, for example, or through blackmailing of both governments on Off-Shore Procurement (OSP) contracts. But diplomatic maneuvering, using the interconnection between domestic and foreign policies in France and Italy, became dominant by the late 1950s. During this time Washington's diplomacy in the Middle East, for example, and its calculated effects on Gaullist choices in France or Christian Democratic ones in Italy, isolated the

Communists far more than did the specific political and cultural programs sponsored by the Operations Coordinating Board and the Congress for Cultural Freedom. In the early 1970s Nixon and Kissinger's détente, harnessing Europe into a subordinate role, for a while gave the Communists ammunition against both NATO and a European integration subject to U.S. policies. The specter of the U.S. "monolith," in the view of most European leaders, was back. But Washington's turn toward a more multilateral approach through the diplomacy of the G-7 group was instrumental in isolating the Communists both internationally (hindering the Eurocommunist project) and socially (forging a consensus in favor of free markets and against the Eurocommunists' advanced reform agenda).

U.S. public diplomacy, beginning at least in the Eisenhower years, also helped defuse the communist appeal. But it was not an easy maneuver, for it had to attune its rhetoric to the distinct political and cultural realities of each ally. In France it had to make room for national pride more than in Italy, whereas in Italy it had to emphasize pacifism more than in France. Eisenhower's public diplomacy initiatives, from Atoms for Peace to Open Skies, tried to meet both these needs, also calibrating them with the need to inspire public mobilization and a level of reassurance. Neither initiative directly targeted the Western European Communists. But this subtlety was what made them such effective forms of intervention in French and Italian affairs.

Above all, U.S. diplomatic maneuvers throughout most of the Cold War favored Europe's increasing propensity for mastering interdependence, instead of resorting to a traditional balance of power. Economic assistance itself was contextualized in this broader goal. The Marshall Plan, as George Kennan had envisioned it, had to be complemented with political targeting (helping America's political allies), Keynesian reform to undermine the radical communist appeal, and international coordination—which would reveal to Europe's governments the advantages of interdependence over those of economic and political nationalism. While never leading to a genuine European third force between the two superpowers, this accent on *Western* interdependence at least helped reinforce transatlantic ties without compromising Europe's emancipation from U.S. control. The strength and appeal of the European Community thus greatly weakened the two Communist Parties' anti-NATO propaganda. Mastery of interdependence also tamed old style nationalism, which contributed to the strength of the Communists' anti-American campaigns.

Nationalist sensitivities in Europe, however, needed to be acknowledged. Leftist orientations needed to be tamed. The United States showed its highest diplomatic acumen by becoming flexible toward manageable anti-

American trends and personalities in French and Italian politics and culture in order to isolate the unmanageable ones. The Congress for Cultural Freedom followed this intent deliberately when it co-opted the Non-Communist Left. This co-optation also restored the respectability of American culture among left-wing thinkers in Europe—a respect best earned by highlighting critical thinking independent from any ideological affiliation, thus permitting a great deal of criticism of the United States itself.

But American tolerance of "dangerous opinions" became even more feasible in the diplomatic sphere. Diplomats, including those with a clear sense of "anticommunist" mission, such as Jefferson Caffery, David Bruce, Robert Komer, Sargent Shriver, and Richard Gardner, avoided the subtext of exceptionalism, and the crusading impulse of many American "cultural" cold warriors. Engaging leaders who strongly asserted themselves against U.S. diktats helped Washington overcome its own fears that these leaders might veer toward neutralism. The first consistent diplomatic initiative to foster strong independent nationalist posturing in France was during the debate for the European Defense Community in the early 1950s. Subsequently, Washington welcomed Charles de Gaulle's return to power as an acceptable antidote to both the insecure nationalism of the Fourth Republic and the Communists' appeal for popular frontism. In Italy, the United States encouraged the sometimes sharp criticism by left-wing Christian Democrats in order to isolate not only the Communists but also those DC leaders who had an even more disapproving view of U.S. culture and policies. The American endorsement of the "Opening to the Left" had a similar purpose, now making room for Italy's Socialists, who certainly did not mince criticism of the United States. The Opening to the Left offered the additional advantage, as Arthur Schlesinger predicted, of fostering reform-oriented coalitions in the rest of Europe. This "social democratic" domino effect for a while bore upon the orientations of social democratic forces, especially in Germany, and in general the balance of power within the Socialist International. But it had little consequence for the emerging cooperation between Communists and Socialists in France.

The United States' flexible approach toward anti-Americanism connoted a capacity for self-inquiry, too. Informed largely by the liberal principles that in the immediate post–Cold War embraced exceptionalism, this approach found its deepest meaning in admitting America's own fallibility. As Peter Beinart has observed in reference to the "Cold War liberals" of the Vital Center, "Knowing that democracy is something we pursue, rather than something we embody, we advance it not merely by exhorting others but by battling the evil in ourselves."[10] Recognizing the corrupting effects of power, the

United States thus exerted its most effective influence ironically not when it waged its own power without restraint but when it recognized its own limits and fallibility. America's examination of its own weaknesses and contradictions, showing its pluralism, its experimentalism even, inspired others, ultimately including many Western European Marxists.

The end of communism in Europe has not marked the end of a leftist anti-Americanism that still borrows from many of the Marxist themes against a modernization model largely inspired by the United States. Jean-François Revel, in his "indictment" of anti-Americanism in 2003, saw the antiglobalization movement almost entirely as a refurbished Marxist campaign ascribing most inequality and poverty in the world to American liberal capitalism. This analogy is quite misleading, not only because it ignores other sources of criticism, such as the one by Stiglitz I mentioned above, but also because most opponents of globalization have brought spontaneous and libertarian elements to their campaigns on issues inside and outside the sphere of productive activities—such as the environment, urban life, education, and gender—restructuring, as Alain Touraine observed in the late 1960s, class struggles into new social movements.[11] Much less insidious against most aspects of American culture and civilization, these movements further confirm the disappearance of the communist vision, even in France and Italy. Nevertheless, American and capitalist imperfections continue to be highlighted with fervor and effectiveness in both countries.

The Communist Party is now marginal in France. According to conservative President Nicolas Sarkozy, the whole French Left is now anachronistic. As interior minister and presidential hopeful in 2006, he snidely remarked in a television interview that "the Left has nothing to propose, nothing to say, nothing to defend; it can only feed off the Right's mistakes."[12] Aside from the pre-electoral polemical exaggeration of this political "death," the mistakes from the right apparently abound, and Sarkozy rather seemed to express frustration at persistent and vocal forms of social discontent in France. The degree to which that discontent is also addressed against the United States depends in part on the amount of Franco-American feuding, which has been more notable over political than over cultural issues.

The Left in Italy has also continued to express its grievances against American foreign policy (most notably during the presidency of George W. Bush), especially when it has resonated domestically through the pro-American choices of Prime Minister Silvio Berlusconi. But the Left's cultural alignment with the United States is also notable. Having shed their communist identity, the Italian Democrats of the Left became a government force, dominating the center-left coalitions that came to power in the first post–Cold

War decade. The historic leader of the reform wing of the PCI, Giorgio Napolitano, is currently the president of the Italian Republic. While the office carries no policy-making powers, it is nevertheless one of the most revered institutional positions, the arbitrating function of which is further enhanced by a high public esteem. The socialist leader Sandro Pertini, in particular, marked his tenure as president from the late 1970s to the mid-1980s with charisma and populism. Those who followed have thus also informally used their mostly ceremonial role as constitutional guarantors to affect and inspire public sentiment, particularly in contrast to the frequent squabbles and heavy partisanship of chronically unstable government coalitions. This did not escape the attention of U.S. President Barack Obama, who, meeting with Napolitano in July 2009, praised his qualities of "integrity" and "great leadership."

Considering the universalistic tones of the confrontation between Western European Marxists and America during the Cold War, the Napolitano-Obama encounter testifies to the power of adaptation—including an improved mastery of the media—by former Communists in Italy. In the United States tones of exceptionalism have not abated. But the confrontation with a world much more multifaceted and unpredictable than that of the Cold War era—and a world where, in the words of Roger Cohen, "anti-Americanism [is] perhaps the fastest growing force"[13]—may warrant less triumphalism than a guarded diplomacy calibrating national security with careful attention to issues of image.

Notes

Abbreviations The following abbreviations are used throughout the notes.

AHMAE Archives Historiques du Ministère des Affaires Etrangères, Paris

AHR *American Historical Review*

AN Archives Nationales

APCF Archives du Parti Communiste Français, Paris, Archives Départementales de la Seine-Saint-Denis

APCI Archivio del Partito Comunista Italiano, Istituto Gramsci, Rome

APP Archives de la Préfecture de Paris

APS Arthur Schlesinger Jr. Papers

AS Administration Series

ASMAE Archivio Storico del Ministero degli Affari Esteri Italiano, Rome

AW Ann Whitman Files

b. Box

BP Bureau Politique

CBLP Clare Boothe Luce Papers

CC Comité Central/Comitato Centrale

CO Country Files

Conv. Conversation

Country Files Presidential Country Files for Europe and Canada

CS Carte della Scrivania (Togliatti)

Cult. Comm. Cultural Commission (PCI)

DDEL Dwight D. Eisenhower Library, Abilene, Kans.

DDRS Declassified Documents Reference System

Dec. Decisions

DGAP Direzione Generale Affari Politici

Emb. Embassy

f. Folder

FC Fondo Cassaforte

FP J. William Fulbright Papers

FRC Federal Records Center

FRUS U.S. Department of State, *Foreign Relations of the United States* (Washington, D.C.: U.S. Government Printing Office, various vols.)

GFKP George F. Kennan Papers

GFL Gerald R. Ford Library, Ann Arbor, Mich.

GMF George C. Marshall Foundation, Lexington, Va.

GP Fonds Gaston Plissonnier

HAK Henry A. Kissinger Office Files

HSTL Harry S. Truman Library, Independence, Mo.

IISTP Harry S. Truman Papers

INR Bureau of Intelligence and Research

JCL Jimmy Carter Library, Atlanta, Ga.

JFDP John Foster Dulles Papers

JFKL John F. Kennedy Library, Boston, Mass.

LC Library of Congress, Manuscript Division, Washington, D.C.

LF Fonds Léo Figuères

M Archivio Mosca (PCI)

MAE Ministère des Affaires Etrangères/Ministero degli Affari Esteri

mf. Microfilm

MP	Motion Pictures	PSB	Psychological Strategy Board
Mtg.	Meeting		
Mtg. Direz.	Meeting Direzione	PSF	President's Secretary Files
NA	National Archives and Records Administration, College Park, Maryland	Recs.	Records
		RG	Record Group
		RL	Fonds Roland Leroy
NAC	National Advisory Council	SMOF	Staff Members and Office Files
n.d.	No date		
NP	Nixon Presidential Material Staff	SSP	Sezione Stampa e Propaganda
NSSM	National Security Studies and Memoranda	Subj.	Subject
		Tel./Tels.	Telegram/s
OEA	Office of European Affairs	TelCons	Telephone Conversations
OIR	Office of Intelligence and Research	TP	Thorez Papers
		VD	Verbali Direzione
ORE	Office of Reports and Estimates	VS	Verbali Segreteria
		WEA	Records of the Office of Western European Affairs
OSR	Office of the Special Representative	WH	White House
POF	President's Office Files	WHCF	White House Central Files
POL 12-FR	Political Affairs—France	WHO	White House Office
POL 12-IT	Political Affairs—Italy	WR	Weekly Reports
PPS	Policy Planning Staff	WRP	Waldeck Rochet Papers
PPS Recs.	Records of the Policy Planning Staff		

Introduction

1. Names of parties and their adherents are capitalized throughout when they refer to specific national groups, even when collectively identified (e.g., "the two Communist Parties," "the sixty-eight Communist Parties," "Communists in France and Italy," or "the Western European Communists"). Those terms are not capitalized when used in adjective form (e.g., "the Italian communist press"), or when, as nouns, they refer to a philosophy or ideology (e.g., "communism," "socialism"). In quotations, capitalization or lowercasing of these terms is left unvaried from the original source. The term "Fascism" is capitalized only when specifically referring to the regime of Benito Mussolini.

2. "Ma come sono cretini!," *L'Unità*, 20 May 1947. See also letter Togliatti to De Gasperi, 27 May 1947, M, mf. 246, APCI. Four years later the French Communist journal *La Nouvelle critique* similarly spelled out the twin danger of political enslavement and cultural degradation that America would bring about: "The French do not want to become robots, nor intellectuals the trusts' mercenaries"; America's influence over France represented "obscurantism . . . censorship, moral perversion," and even "painters' transformation into manual workers, and the death of literature"; editorial, *La Nouvelle critique*, 27 June 1951, 3–4.

3. See esp. Stephanson, *Kennan*, chaps. 7 and 8; Hixson, *George F. Kennan*; and Botts, "'Nothing to Seek . . . Nothing to Defend.'" On Kennan's political influence, see esp. Miscamble, *George F. Kennan*.

4. Kennan to Hooker, 17 Oct. 1949, GFKP, b. 23.

5. On this, see also George F. Kennan, "Fair Day Adieu!," pt. 2, chap. 1, GFKP, b. 25; and Kennan's lecture "Where Do We Stand?," National War College, 21 Dec. 1949, GFKP, b. 17.

6. Stephanson, *Kennan*, 228; Kennan to Hooker, 17 Oct. 1949, GFKP, b. 23.

7. Stephanson, *Kennan*, 237.

8. Joseph S. Nye coined the term and has explained this distinction; see esp. Nye, *Soft Power*.

9. See esp. Pons, *L'impossibile egemonia*; Pons, *Berlinguer*; Gori and Pons, *Dagli archivi*; Aga-Rossi and Zaslavski, *Togliatti e Stalin*; Riva, *Oro*; Donno, *La Gladio*; Gualtieri, *Il PCI*; various essays on both parties in Aga-Rossi and Quagliarello, *L'altra faccia*; Courtois, *Du passé*; Courtois and Lazar, *Histoire*; Courtois et al., *Le livre noir*; Wolton, *La France*; Kotek, *La jeune garde*; and Bartošek, *Les aveux*. Among older influential accounts that did not benefit from the archival sources from the Soviet Union, see Spriano, *Stalin*; Wall, *French Communism*; Urban, *Moscow*; and Rieber, *Stalin*.

10. In this sense, the most notable works are Kuisel, *Seducing the French*, chaps. 1–3; and Gundle, *Between Hollywood and Moscow*. Cf. the previous and broader Italian edition: Gundle, *I comunisti*.

11. Each chapter will develop this definition. In this introduction, I intend to highlight common notions and misconceptions about the character and relevance of communist anti-Americanism in Western Europe.

12. See esp. essays in Lacorne, Rupnik, and Toinet, *The Rise*; Roger, *The American Enemy*; and Katzenstein and Keohane, *Anti-Americanisms*. Cf. Chiarenza and Vance, *Immaginari a confronto*; Craveri and Quagliarello, *L'antiamericanismo*; Ajami, "The Falseness of Anti-Americanism."

13. Gitlin, "A View from the Patriotic Left."

14. As examples of recent contentious treatments of anti-Americanism, see works by Paul Hollander, esp. *Anti-Americanism* and *The End of Commitment*. See also Hollander, *Understanding Anti-Americanism*; Revel, *Anti-Americanism*; Vidal, *Perpetual War*; Ross and Ross, *Anti-Americanism*; Berman, *Anti-Americanism*; Ceaser, "A Genealogy"; Teodori, *Maledetti americani*; Teodori, *Benedetti americani*; and Hodge, "Old Wine and Old Bottles." More balanced accounts are in Katzenstein and Keohane, *Anti-Americanisms*; Berghahn, "The Debate on 'Americanization'"; Lacorne, Rupnik, and Toinet, *The Rise*; Craveri and Quagliarello, *L'anti-americanismo*; Gienow-Hecht, "Always Blame the Americans" (see also other articles in this *AHR* Forum titled "Historical Perspectives on Anti-Americanism"); Friedman, "Anti-Americanism"; van Elteren, "Rethinking Americanization Abroad"; Sweig, *Friendly Fire*; Roger, *The American Enemy*; Kroes, Rydell, and Bosscher, *Cultural Transmissions* (esp. David W. Ellwood, "Anti-Americanism in Western Europe, A Comparative Perspective," in ibid.); Ellwood, "The American Challenge Renewed"; D'Attorre, *Nemici*; Fehrenbach and Poiger, *Transactions*; Spiro, "Anti-Americanism"; and Federico Romero, "Americanization and National Identity: The Case of Postwar Italy," in Tosi, *Europe*.

15. Before settling the New World, Europeans had begun to perceive it as the receptacle of their foremost fears and hopes; cf. Kroes, *If You've Seen One*, 1–13; quotations from 1, 8.

16. On these aspects and "Americanism," see esp. Lipset, *American Exceptionalism*, 31–33; Huntington, *Who Are We?*; and Marie-France Toinet, "Does Anti-Americanism Exist?," in Lacorne, Rupnik, and Toinet, *The Rise*, 219–23.

17. On predominance of leftist anti-Americanism during the Cold War, see esp. Kuisel,

Seducing the French, chaps. 2–3; Chebel d'Appollonia, *Le Temps*, 11–53; Judt, *Past Imperfect*; and Gundle, *Between Hollywood and Moscow*.

18. On orchestrated anti-Americanism in the U.S.S.R., see esp. Shiraev and Zubok, *Anti-Americanism*.

19. Most previous works on anti-Americanism in Europe have focused on cultural and ideological aspects, while those on the United States's handling of its Western allies have followed primarily a diplomatic history approach. Very few scholars have established a full dialogue between the two areas. Among them, those working on themes closest to my subject are Kuisel, *Seducing the French*; Pells, *Not Like Us*; Duggan and Wagstaff, *Italy*; Ellwood, *Rebuilding Europe*; Ventresca, *From Fascism to Democracy*; and McKenzie, *Remaking France*. See also remarks on Europe in Friedman, "Anti-Americanism." Studies rich in insights on cultural matters, though not as thorough in establishing the interplay between culture and diplomacy, include Wall, *The United States*; Costigliola, *France*; and Domenico, "'For the Cause of Christ.'" Frank Ninkovich and Michael H. Hunt have provided remarkable contributions from the standpoint of U.S. foreign relations by intersecting cultural and diplomatic aspects; see esp. Ninkovich, *The United States* and *The Wilsonian Century*; and Hunt, *American Ascendancy*. Cf. essays on U.S.-European relations in Hogan, *The Ambiguous Legacy*; and Costigliola, "Tropes of Gender."

20. Primarily I refer to Lazar, *Maisons*; Flores, *L'immagine dell'URSS*; Flores, *1956*; various essays in Aga-Rossi and Quagliarello, *L'altra faccia*; Spriano, *Stalin*; Blackmer and Tarrow, *Communism*; and, for a more focused series of case studies at the local level, Guiat, *The French and Italian Communist Parties*.

21. Gundle, *Between Hollywood and Moscow*. On impact of American consumer culture in Europe, see esp. de Grazia, *Irresistible Empire*.

22. See, e.g., McPherson, *Yankee No!* See also Nye, *Soft Power*. Kuisel's *Seducing the French* and Pells's *Not Like Us* use a mixed record of statistical and intellectual evidence.

Chapter 1

1. Togliatti returned after eighteen years, and Thorez, who had been condemned for desertion in 1939, was now pardoned by General de Gaulle. On Togliatti's "Salerno turn," see n. 7 (this chapter). On Thorez, see esp. Robrieux, *Histoire intérieure*, 19–30; Buton, "Le Parti communiste français à la Libération"; cf. Georges-Henri Soutou, "General de Gaulle and the Soviet Union, 1943–45: Ideology or European Equilibrium," in Gori and Pons, *The Soviet Union*.

2. Lazar, *Maisons*, esp. 18–27, 329–40. See also Marc Lazar, "La strategia del PCF e del PCI dal 1944 al 1947: Acquisizioni della ricerca e problemi irrisolti," in Aga-Rossi and Quagliarello, *L'altra faccia*. Lazar stresses the similarities more than the differences. See also Gaetano Quagliarello, "La transizione alla democrazia in Italia e Francia," in Aga-Rossi and Quagliarello, *L'altra faccia*, 51–78. For more traditional accounts emphasizing differences, and highlighting the PCI's moderation and flexibility, see esp. Greene, "The Communist Parties of Italy and France"; Urban, *Moscow*, esp. 179–83, 209–15; and Blackmer and Tarrow, *Communism*, esp. the essay by Sidney Tarrow, "Communism in Italy and France: Adaptation and Change," 575–640. See also McInnes, *The Communist Parties*; and Guiat, *The French and Italian Communist Parties*.

3. On how the war experience worsened the Italians' already poor "state vocation," the

best source is Galli della Loggia, *L'identità italiana*, 59–84. See also John Agnew, "The Myth of Backward Italy," in Allen and Russo, *Revisioning Italy*, 36–37.

4. On how the sense of statehood enhanced the sense of nationhood in France, see esp. Pierre Nora, introduction to Nora, *Realms of Memory*, vol. 3; Gildea, *The Past*, 112–65; Brubaker, *Citizenship*, 1–8; Brian Jenkins and Nigel Copsey, "Nation, Nationalism and National Identity in France," in Jenkins and Sofos, *Nation*, 105–14; and Michael Kelly, *The Cultural and Intellectual Rebuilding*.

5. Marc Lazar describes the tendency to follow the Soviet script as *allegro vivace* for the PCF and *allegro moderato* for the PCI; Lazar, *Maisons*, 73. For accounts highlighting the PCI's subordination to Moscow, see essays in Aga-Rossi and Quagliarello, *L'altra faccia*; Riva, *Oro*; Donno, *La Gladio*; and Aga-Rossi and Zaslavsky, *Togliatti e Stalin*. For slightly differing views on this issue, see esp. Silvio Pons, "L'URSS e il PCI nel sistema della guerra fredda," in Gualtieri, *Il PCI*; and Flores and Gallerano, *Sul PCI*, 68–82.

6. Lazar, *Maisons*, 56–57, 74. On meanings of *partito nuovo*, see also Togliatti, *Opere*, 5:80–108; and Urban, *Moscow*, 16–17. On the PCF, cf. Ronald Thiersky, "Alliance Politics and Revolutionary Pretensions," in Blackmer and Tarrow, *Communism*, 421–27; Tarrow, "Communism," 581–84; Browder, *The New Jacobins*.

7. Both quotations from Urban, *Moscow*, 180, 213. See also Tarrow, "Communism," 597–600; cf. speeches by Togliatti in Togliatti, *La politica di Salerno*. On the still heated debate over the Svolta and new documentation, cf. Aga-Rossi and Zaslavsky, *Togliatti e Stalin*, 80–87; and Ennio Di Nolfo, "I vincoli internazionali di una diplomazia incompiuta," in Giovagnoli, *Interpretazioni*, 123. See also Di Nolfo, "La svolta di Salerno"; and Gualtieri, *Togliatti*, 24–27.

8. Lazar, *Maisons*, 333–34; cf. Molinari, *Les ouvriers*; Marcello Flores, "Il PCI, il PCF, gli intellettuali: 1943–1950," in Aga-Rossi and Quagliarello, *L'altra faccia*, 101–17.

9. Cf. Wall, *French Communism*, 21–22; Lecoeur, *Le PCF*. Both authors show that the spontaneous acts of resistance—and of indiscipline—by French Communists during 1940 and 1941 "saved their party's honor" (Wall, *French Communism*, 21) as did their lonely opposition to Vichy. On reasons for communist preeminence in the Resistance, see Mortimer, *The Rise*, 310–13; and Spriano, *La Resistenza*. On the PCI and the purges, see esp. Dundovich, *Tra esilio e castigo*; Giusti, *I prigionieri*; and Gori, *Italiani*. Cf. Aga-Rossi and Zaslavsky, *Togliatti e Stalin*, 157–78. On ambivalence during the fascist years, see also docs. cited in Spriano, *I fronti popolari*, 171–73.

10. Qtd. in René Girault, "La sinistra europea di fronte alla crisi del dopoguerra," in Petricioli, *La sinistra*; quotation from Maurice Thorez, "Au service de la France 30 juin 1945," in Thorez, *Une politique de grandeur*, 373; see also Robrieux, *Histoire intérieure*, 151–57. Bidault in Elgey, *Histoire*, 156. On PCF from "communard" to "national," see Jenkins, *Nationalism*, 149–50; and Kriegel, *Ce que j'ai cru comprendre*, 317.

11. Togliatti, *Opere*, 5:14 (see also 5:79) and 4:145–46; *L'Unità*, 19 Sept. 1945; cf. William Brierley and Luca Giacometti, "Italian National Identity and the Failure of Regionalism," in Jenkins and Sofos, *Nation*, 175–76.

12. Letter Togliatti to Scoccimarro, 9 June 1944, Togliatti Papers, CS, APCI; also highlighted, with a different interpretation, in Aga-Rossi and Zaslavsky, *Togliatti e Stalin*, 105.

13. Togliatti, *Opere*, 4:320; second quote in Dominique Colas, "Logique et symbolique de la nation chez de Gaulle et les communistes," in Courtois and Lazar, *50 ans*, 156. See also Marcel Cachin, "Anti-communisme anti-France," *L'Humanité*, 8 Dec. 1944.

14. Rioux, *The Fourth Republic*, 54–55. See also Thorez, "Une politique française: Renaissance, démocratie, unité," in Thorez, *Une politique de grandeur*, 348–49; Bosworth, *Italy*, 56; Rusconi, *Se cessiamo*, 52–53, 74–75; and Spriano, *La Resistenza*.

15. See Letter Pratolongo (Trieste) to Togliatti, 17 July 1946, Meeting "Segreteria," 26 July 1946, M, mf. 271, APCI. The most updated accounts on this issue are Gualtieri, *Togliatti*, 104–5, 117–19; and Aga-Rossi and Zaslavsky, *Togliatti e Stalin*, 138–56. Cf. Leonid Gibjanskij, "Mosca, il PCI e la questione di Trieste (1943–1948)," in Gori and Pons, *Dagli archivi*; Marco Galeazzi, "Togliatti fra Tito e Stalin," in Galeazzi, *Roma Belgrado*; Emma Pietrafesa, "La ferita in alto Adriatico: Togliatti e la questione di Trieste fra Roma e Mosca," in Pizzigallo, *Amicizie*. Quotation from Palmiro Togliatti, "Imperialismo di vassalli," *L'Unità*, 13 Sept. 1945.

16. Quotation from Maurice Thorez, "La lutte pour l'indépendance nationale et le paix," *Cahiers du communisme*, May 1950, 51; Serge Bernstein, "Le Parti communiste français et de Gaulle sous la IVe République: Confrontations et convergences," in Courtois and Lazar, *50 ans*, 82; Rice-Maximin, *Accommodation*, 26–39. Cf. Caffery to Sec. State, 8 Apr. 1946, *FRUS*, 1946, V: 422–25.

17. See esp. Maurice Thorez, "Un grand Français vous parle," in Thorez, *Oeuvres choisies*, 2:277–78; M. Magnien, "La France grande puissance," *L'Humanité*, 14 Nov. 1944; cf. Furet, *The Passing*. On Joan of Arc myth, see Colas, "Logique et symbolique," 159. Cf. Winock, *Parlez-moi*, 154–61; Wall, *French Communism*, 102 (also stressing the importance of the *fils du peuple* myth). Patriotic symbols began to emerge in the Popular Front years; see esp. Browder, *The New Jacobins*. The political legacy of the French Revolution also meant that nationhood in France was strictly identified with the struggle of the "oppressed" against the social elites, thus benefitting the communist discourse; cf. Jenkins, *Nationalism*, 11–12. Also comparing "Soviet passion" and "French passion," see Lazar, *Le communisme*, esp. 27–98.

18. Togliatti quotation from Togliatti, *Opere*, 4:375. See also ibid., 5:14 and 76; Mario Montagnana, "Nell'interesse della Nazione," *Rinascita*, July 1946; and Girolamo Li Causi, "La classe operaia alla testa della lotta di liberazione nazionale," *Rinascita*, Aug.–Sept. 1944 (emphasizing the bourgeois "betrayal" of the nation). Cf. Gentile, *La grande Italia*, 43–44 and 328–35; Galli della Loggia, *Morte della patria*, 63.

19. See Eisenhower, *Crusade in Europe*, 297–98; Caffery to State Dept., 23 June 1945, 851.41, RG59, NA; Mtg. Badoglio-Donovan, 28 Jan. 1944, FC, Italia-USA, "Missione Pazzi," ASMAE; and Badoglio to Roosevelt, 3 Apr. 1944, *FRUS*, 1944, III: 1087–88. On "'empire' by invitation," see Lundestad, *The American "Empire."*

20. De Gaulle, *Unity*, 574; De Gasperi to Byrnes, 22 Aug. 1945, *FRUS*, 1945, IV: 1024–29. On the public's awareness, see Caffery to State Dept., 23 June 1945, 851.41, NA. For a discussion of "borrowed" grandeur, see Brogi, *A Question*, 14–35.

21. Percy Allum, "The Changing Face of Christian Democracy," in Duggan and Wagstaff, *Italy*, 121–22.

22. Del Pero, *L'alleato*; Del Pero, "Containing Containment"; Domenico, "'For the Cause of Christ'"; Formigoni, *L'Italia dei cattolici*, 135–49; Angelo Ventrone, "L'avventura americana nella classe dirigente cattolica," in D'Attorre, *Nemici*, 142–47.

23. Gentile, *La grande Italia*, quotation on 342 (see also Croce letter to Albert Einstein of 28 July 1944, qtd. in ibid., 83). On national identity and the DC, see also Formigoni, *L'Italia dei cattolici*; and Giovagnoli, *Il partito*.

24. Pierre Nora, "Gaullists and Communists," in Nora, *Realms of Memory*, 1:207–8.

25. First quotation from Nora, "Gaullists and Communists," 219. See also de Gaulle, *The Call*, 1; Brogi, *A Question*, 14–19; Hoffmann, *Decline or Renewal?*, 95; and Gordon, *A Certain Idea of France*, 5–6. "The collective memory of defeat," Robert Gildea has written, "has itself served as a crucible of national solidarity and national revival." Gildea, *The Past*, 133–34.

26. Thorez, "Au service de la France," 372; de Beauvoir, *Force of Circumstance*, 4.

27. Nora "Gaullists and Communists," 234; Winock, *Parlez-moi*, 152–53.

28. See Colas, "Logique et symbolique," 161–63.

29. Serge Bernstein, "Le Parti communiste français," 92; Stéphane Courtois, "Gaullisme et le communisme: La double réponse à la crise d'identité française," in Courtois and Lazar, *50 ans*, 330–31.

30. On Moscow's influence, see esp. Aga-Rossi and Zaslavsky, *Togliatti e Stalin*; Michail Narinski, "La politica estera sovietica verso l'Europa occidentale (1941–1945)," and Stéphane Courtois, "Il PCF e la lotta per il potere durante la resistenza e la liberazione" (both in Aga-Rossi and Quagliariello, *L'altra faccia*); Lazar, "La strategia del PCF e del PCI," 85–89; Lévêque, "La place de la France," 28–33. For more nuanced views, see Pons, *L'impossibile egemonia*, 72–77; and Vacca, *Togliatti*.

31. See, e.g., Tel. 3551, Caffery to Sec. State, 24 June 1945, 851.00; Tels. 620, 784, 806, Caffery to Sec. State, 21 Nov., 3 and 5 Dec. 1944, 851.01; Tel. A-468, Kirk to Sec. State, 13 July 1945, 865.00; cf. Taylor to Truman and Stettinius, 20 Apr. 1945, 865.00B, all in RG59, NA; Hull, *The Memoirs*, 2:1554–59.

32. First quotation in Colas, "Logique et symbolique," 158; second one in Elgey, *Histoire*, 52. Nora, "Gaullists and Communists," 227; third quote in Thorez, "'Français, unissez-vous!,' Rapport à la session du Comité centrale, Ivry, 19 May 1939," in Thorez, *Une politique de grandeur*, 224–25. See also Roger Martelli, *Le rouge et le bleu*.

33. First quotation from Mafai, *Botteghe Oscure, addio*, 105–7. Cf. Marcello Flores, "Il mito dell'URSS nel secondo dopoguerra," in D'Attorre, *Nemici*, 493; Giolitti, *Lettere*, 29. Second quote from Togliatti's report to Central Committee, in CC, 18 Oct. 1946, APCI. On "doppiezza," see esp. Giovanni Gozzini, "Il PCI nel sistema politico della repubblica," in Gualtieri, *Il PCI*, 103–6; and Di Loreto, *Togliatti*. On the U.S.S.R. seen by the PCI as sole hope in the 1930s, see Galli, *Storia del PCI*, 70–71.

34. On Stalin myth affecting Togliatti, see esp. Donald Sassoon, "Italian Images of Russia, 1945–1956," in Duggan and Wagstaff, *Italy*, 190. On charisma as derived for Thorez (as opposed to de Gaulle), see esp. Colas, "Logique et symbolique," 158; and Courtois, "Gaullisme et le communisme," 328. See also Spriano, *Stalin*, chap. 18. Quotation from Flores and Gallerano, *Sul PCI*, 69.

35. On first conclusion, see Pons, *L'impossibile egemonia*; Di Loreto, *Togliatti*. On second conclusion, see esp. Aga-Rossi and Zaslavsky, *Togliatti e Stalin*; and Michail Narinski, "Stalin, Togliatti e Thorez (1944–1948)," in Gori and Pons, *Dagli archivi*.

36. The best sources on this theme remain Novick, *The Resistance versus Vichy*; Werth, *France*, 239–41 and chap. 13; and Rousso, "L'Epuration." For a good synthesis, see Julian Jackson, *France*, 577–92. On Italy, see Claudio Pavone, "La continuità dello Stato: Istituzioni e uomini," in Piscitelli et al., *Italia*; Quazza, *Resistenza*; Ginsborg, *A History*, 39–112; Christopher Duggan, "Italy in the Cold War and the Legacy of Fascism," in Duggan and Wagstaff, *Italy*, 1–8; and Franzinelli, *L'amnistia*.

37. Quotations from *L'Humanité*, 17 Jan. 1946; and Thorez in Mtg. CC, 21–23 Jan. 1945, APCF, 10. On PCF's "battles of production," see Maurice Thorez, "S'unir, combattre, tra-

vailler," in *Oeuvres de Maurice Thorez*, vol. 5, tome 20; Adereth, *The French Communist Party*, 141–42; and Elgey, *Histoire*, 57–60 (stressing PCF compromises). On opposition to Mendès-France's program, see Wall, *French Communism*, 35. On this period, see esp. Buton, *Les lendemains*, 107–94; Annie Kriegel, "Le Parti communiste français, la Résistance, la Libération et l'établissement de la IVe République (1944–1947)," in Kriegel, *Communismes*.

38. Phillippe Buton, "Il PCF e la partecipazione governativa (1945–1947)," in Aga-Rossi and Quagliarello, *L'altra faccia*, 166–70; Billoux, *Quand nous étions ministres*, chap. 2; Rieber, *Stalin*, 229–37; for a synthesis on these developments, see Courtois and Lazar, *Histoire*, 221–39.

39. Elgey, *Histoire*, 202–4. On the PCF and the CGT, see Courtois and Lazar, *Histoire*, 212–13. Quotations from Maurice Thorez, "Union française et démocratique," interview with *Temps présent*, in Thorez, *Oeuvres choisies*, 2:302–7; and Garaudy, *L'Eglise*. Dec. BP, 3 Jan. 1946, APCF. For precedents of the *main tendue*, see Rice-Maximin, "The *Main Tendue*."

40. Sassoon, *The Strategies*, 50–52; Harper, *America*, 19–20; Di Nolfo, *Le paure*, 164–65, 232–33. On fears of repeating the post-WWI experience, see Togliatti, *Lezioni sul fascismo*. Cf. Severino Galante, "The Genesis of Political Impotence: Italy's Mass Political Parties in the Years between the Great Alliance and the Cold War," in Becker and Knipping, *Power in Europe?*, 189–90; McCarthy, "I comunisti italiani."

41. Togliatti in Mtg. Direz., 29 July 1945; Togliatti in CC, 18 Sept. 1946, M, APCI.

42. Quagliarello, "La transizione alla democrazia," 72–74.

43. Gramsci, qtd. in Donald L. M. Blackmer, "Continuity and Change in Postwar Italian Communism," in Blackmer and Tarrow, *Communism*, 30. Pajetta in Mtg. Direz., 24 Aug. 1945, VD, APCI. See also Eugenio Reale, "Comunisti e cattolici," *Rinascita*, June 1944. On Christian Left, see Sergio Bertelli, "Sinistri cristiani o reazionari d'avanguardia?," in Aga-Rossi and Quagliarello, *L'altra faccia*; and Landolfi, *Il Gladio rosso di Dio*.

44. On this point, see esp. Buton, "Il PCF e la partecipazione governativa," 161–62 and 171; and Spriano, *Stalin*, chap. 19.

45. Eric Johnston Evidence to the House Committee on Un-American Activities (1947), http://www.terramedia.co.uk/documents/index.html; accessed 22 June 2005; Cafagna, *C'era una volta*, 44; Palmiro Togliatti, "Discorso su Gramsci nei giorni della Liberazione," in Togliatti, *Gramsci*. See also Palmiro Togliatti, "Gli intellettuali e il Fronte nazionale (5 luglio 1943)," in Togliatti, *Da Radio Milano Libertà*.

46. Julian Jackson, *The Popular Front*, 114–15; Sapiro, *La guerre des écrivains*; Sirinelli, "Les normaliens."

47. Antonio Gramsci, "The Formation of Intellectuals," in Gramsci, *The Modern Prince*, 121–22; Gundle, *Between Hollywood and Moscow*, 12. On these aspects, see also Stephen Gundle, "The Legacy of *The Prison Notebooks*: Gramsci, the PCI and Italian Culture in the Cold War Period," in Duggan and Wagstaff, *Italy*, 136–39; Flores, "Il PCI," 108–9; Fiori, *Gramsci, Togliatti, Stalin*; Ajello, *Intellettuali*; Wall, *French Communism*, 116–17; Caute, *Communism*, chap. 6 and 237–58 (reexamining the cases of André Gide, André Malraux, and Jean-Paul Sartre); Ory and Sirinelli, *Les intellectuels*; Lottman, *The Left Bank*; and Verdès-Leroux, *Au service du parti*, chaps. 2–3. On working class finding emancipation through high culture, see esp. Desanti, *Les staliniens*, 128–29.

48. On this point, see esp. Hazareesingh, *Intellectuals*, 25–43; and Nicolet, *L'idée républicaine*.

49. Winock, *Parlez-moi*, 154; Jeremy Jennings, "Introduction—Mandarins and Samurais: The Intellectual in Modern France," in Jennings, *Intellectuals*, 18–19. Gide's first indictment was in *Retour de l'URSS* (1936). On intellectuals' rejection of Vichy and the Third Republic, see esp. Judt, *Past Imperfect*, 33–74; and Chebel d'Appollonia, *Des lendemains*, 69–97. On the relative autonomy and varieties of the French intellectual *engagé*, see Chebel d'Appollonia, *Des lendemains*, 11–33; and Lottman, *The Left Bank*. In Italy the Action Party, which during the Resistance was the strongest non-Marxist alternative for several intellectuals, never managed to forge a genuine program and soon fell into oblivion.

50. Quotation from Caute, *Communism*, 175. Judt, *Past Imperfect*, 87, 169, 264.

51. See esp. David Drake, *Intellectuals*, 23–33, 51–62; Winock, *Le siècle*; Poster, *Existential Marxism*; and Birchall, *Sartre against Stalinism*.

52. Quotation from Gavi, Sartre, and Victor, *On a raison*, 26. See also Contat and Rybalka, *The Writings*; and David Drake, *Sartre*, 65–69.

53. De Beauvoir and Mounier, qtd. in David Drake, *Intellectuals*, 9; on Italy, quotation from Di Nolfo, *Le paure*, 13. On long-term revolutionary traditions and rejection of bourgeois past, see Judt, *Marxism*, 107–9; and Judt, *Past Imperfect* (quotations on Sartre, p. 40). Saba, quoted in Ajello, *Intellettuali*, 90. On the Manichean worldview, also see Judt, *Postwar*, 198–99.

54. Sartre, qtd. in Chebel d'Appollonia, *Des lendemains*, 25; see also Jean-Paul Sartre, 'Qu'est-ce que la littérature?," reprinted in Sartre, *Situations II*. "Picasso comunista," *Rinascita*, Oct.–Nov.–Dec. 1944; the article reported an interview the artist had given to the American left-wing journal *New Masses*. Quotations from Roger Garaudy, "Le communisme et la liberté," *Cahiers du communisme*, Apr. 1946, 720; and Louis Aragon, "La cultura francese contro il nemico," *Rinascita*, I, no. 4, Oct.–Nov. 1944, 31. On search for certitudes, see esp. Jean-François Sirinelli, "Les intellectuals français au temps de la Guerre froide: Entre communisme et gaullisme?," in Lazar and Courtois, *50 ans*, 259–60. On the PCF's intellectual ascendancy in the 1930s, see esp. Ritaine, *Les stratèges*, 42–69. On communism as a secular religion, see Monnerot, *Sociologie*.

55. See esp. Palmiro Togliatti, "Croce e il comunismo," in Cecchi, Leone, and Vacca, *I corsivi*; and Ajello, *Intellettuali*, 99–101. Ajello also highlights the desire of many Italian intellectuals to rid themselves of the *trasformismo* that had characterized much of the liberal-bourgeois parliamentary tradition.

56. Alicata, in "Tutto il popolo espresso nel partito nuovo," *L'Unità*, 4 Jan. 1946. On professional advantages, see David Drake, *Intellectuals*, 40–43. On PCF's thesis regarding capitalism, see Roger Garaudy, "Impuissance et malfaisance du spiritualisme politique," and Laurent Casanova, "Responsabilités de l'intellectuel communiste," *Cahiers du communisme*, Mar. 1946 and Apr. 1949, respectively.

57. Judt, *Postwar*, 209–10.

58. Gramsci, *Quaderni del carcere*, 3:1988–99.

59. See esp. Strauss, *Menace*; Roger, *The American Enemy*; and David W. Ellwood, "A Brief History of European Anti-Americanism," unpublished manuscript, delivered at the 2003 convention of the Organization of American Historians, Memphis, 6 Apr. 2003.

60. See esp. Kuisel, *Seducing the French*, 16–36; Costigliola, *France*; essays in Lacorne, Rupnik, and Toinet, *The Rise*; and Winock, "'US Go Home,'" 7–20.

61. Rossi, *The Image of America*; Prezzolini, *Diario*; Ojetti, *L'America*. See observations in D'Attorre, "Sogno americano e mito sovietico," in D'Attorre, *Nemici*, 16–25.

62. D'Attorre, "Sogno americano," 27–28; Ventrone, "L'avventura americana," and

Bruno Wanroij, *"Pro Ara et Focis*: Morale cattolica e identità nazionale in Italia, 1945–1960," in D'Attorre, *Nemici*; David Ellwood, "Italy, Europe and the Cold War: The Politics and Economics of Limited Sovereignty," in Duggan and Wagstaff, *Italy*; sources cited in n. 22.

63. Roger, *The American Enemy*, 316–17.

64. Duhamel, *America*; cf. Tardieu, *Devant l'obstacle*. On struggle against plutocracy, see esp. Nacci, *L'antiamericanismo*, 46–70. "Mechanical hell" in D'Attorre, 'Sogno americano," 22. Cf. Michele Abbate, "Il sogno americano di Mussolini: La continua ricerca di un'intesa politico-diplomatica con Washington, 1922–1932," in Abbate, *L'Italia fascista*; Renzo de Felice, "Aspetti politico-diplomatici delle relazioni culturali tra Italia e Stati Uniti," in Barnes, *Italia-USA*, 185–203; and Gentile, "Impending Modernity." For a brief survey of postwar French anti-Americanism, see Winock, *Nationalism*, chap. 3.

65. Siegfried, qtd. in Roger, *The American Enemy*, 286; Nacci, *L'antiamericanismo*, chap. 1.

66. Siegfried, *America Comes of Age*; see also Ferrero, *Amérique*; Michela Nacci, "Contro la civiltà dell'abbondanza: L'antiamericanismo del PCI," in Aga-Rossi and Quagliarello, *L'altra faccia*; Strauss, *Menace*, 33–80.

67. Aron and Dandieu, *Le Cancer*. Cf. Roger, *The American Enemy*, 297–98; Loubet del Bayle, *Les non-conformistes*; Armus, *French Anti-Americanism*, 19–47.

68. Kroes, *If You've Seen One*, 21–32; Nacci, *L'antiamericanismo*, 93–119.

69. Duhamel, *America*, 34.

70. Kuisel, *Seducing the French*, 16–18; Wall, *The United States*, 20–34; D'Attorre, "Sogno americano," 26–27; Cavallo, "America sognata"; Aga-Rossi, *A Nation Collapses*, chap. 3. Quotation from Pells, *Not Like Us*, 156.

71. Reinhold Niebuhr, "The Perils of American Power," *Atlantic Monthly*, June 1932; Beuve-Méry, qtd. in Winock, *Nationalism*, 46.

72. On France, see Strauss, *Menace*, 263. Quotation from Pier Paolo D'Attorre, "Americanism and Anti-Americanism in Italy," in Stirk and Willis, *Shaping Postwar Europe*, 49.

73. See Mauro Scoccimarro, editorial, *L'Unità*, 3 Nov. 1943. On Seventh Comintern Congress (1935) speech, see Dimitrov, *Selected Works*, 86–119. On discrediting Anglo-American liberators, see esp. Flores, "Il PCI," 111; and Aga-Rossi and Zaslavsky, *Togliatti e Stalin*, 106–8.

74. Longo, Sereni, in Mtg. Direz., 26 June 1945, VD, and Mtg. Milan Committee, 29 June 1945, "Materiale attività culturale," folder 1945, Commissione Cultura, APCI; "La FIAT e gli americani," *L'Unità*, 8 Sept. 1945.

75. "Le Général Eisenhower salue Paris vainqueur," *L'Humanité*, 9 Sept. 1944; Marcel Cachin, "Le Traité d'assistance mutuelle franco-soviétique, gage de la sécurité et de la grandeur de la France," *Cahiers du communisme*, no. 3, Jan. 1945, 21; Hervé, *La Libération*.

76. Marty in CC, 15–16 June 1946, APCF. Lacroix-Riz, "Négociation"; Portes, "Les origines."

77. Qtd. in Camus, *Carnets*, 186; also highlighted in David Drake, *Intellectuals*, 65.

78. Togliatti in Mtg. Direz., 30 June 1945, VD, APCI; Gualtieri, *Togliatti*, 32–33. On Thorez's interview with the *Times*, see comments by Kriegel, *Ce que j'ai cru comprendre*, 365. Thorez's conclusion at CC, 20–21 Apr. 1946, APCF; cf. Lévêque, "La place de la France," 28–33.

79. Cf. R. C. "TVA, vittoria democratica," and A. A., "US, la classe operaia entra nella lotta politica," *Il Politecnico*, 13 and 27 Oct. 1945. Cf. Patrick McCarthy, "America: L'altro

mito della cultura comunista," in D'Attorre, *Nemici*, 224–26; McCarthy, "I comunisti italiani"; Pierre Courtade, "La controverse Byrnes-Wallace," *Cahiers du communisme*, Oct. 1946.

80. Nenni, *Tempo*, 301; Thorez in CC, 20–21 Apr. 1946, APCF. Thorez had far more success than Nenni in obtaining a public relations success for the PCF and the U.S.S.R. See Wall, *The United States*, 53; and Di Nolfo, *Le paure*, 182.

81. Notably, the PCI continued to nurture the hope for unconditional U.S. aid as late as April 1947, at the eve of its expulsion from the government. See Terracini and Colombi in Mtg. Direz., 17 Apr. 1947, VD, APCI. Cf. Marty in CC, 15–16 June 1946, and Duclos in CC, 1 Sept. 1945, esp. p. 34, APCF. Cf. McCarthy, "I comunisti italiani"; and Margairaz, "Autour des accords Blum-Byrnes."

82. Italy's Futurist movement in the arts and its offsprings in Russia had since World War I symbolized such ambivalent fascination. It was used for opposite political ends, fostering the Fascist and the Bolshevik revolutions.

83. See Ilya Ehrenburg, "Non potete capirci niente se dimenticate che è un paese giovane," *L'Unità*, 18 Aug. 1946. Italo Calvino, in "Petrov e Ilf in America," *L'Unità*, 23 Mar. 1946, wrote that "two young civilizations, competing and opposed but tend in the last instance to identify with each other, in an inevitable reciprocal evolution of technical experiences on the one side, social on the other." See also Elena Aga-Rossi and Giovanni Orsina, "L'immagine dell'America nelle stampe comuniste italiana, 1945–1953," in Craveri and Quagliarello, *L'antiamericanismo*; and Flores, *L'immagine dell'URSS*, 343–48.

84. Antonio Gramsci, "Americanism and Fordism," in Gramsci, *Selections*, 281, 303, 310; see also Gramsci, *Note sul Machiavelli*, 329–40. In general, see also the essay collection Jeannet and Barnett, *New World Journeys*.

85. Much of my interpretation here relies on the work of Patrick McCarthy and Alberto Asor Rosa. See esp. McCarthy, "America"; and Asor Rosa, *Intellettuali*, 580–87. See also Franco de Felice, introduction to Gramsci, *Americanismo e fordismo*.

86. Gramsci, "Americanism and Fordism," 305, 307.

87. Ball, *Imagining America*; Bailes, "Alexei Gastev."

88. Pavese, quoted in McCarthy, "America," 222; Pavese, *La letteratura*, 194.

89. Italo Calvino, "Hemingway e noi," *Il Contemporaneo*, 13 Nov. 1954.

90. Pavese, *La letteratura*, 194; Vittorini, *Diario*, 234. See also Michele Bottalico, "A Place for All: Old and New Myths in the Italian Appreciation of American Literature," in Gutman, *As Others Read Us*.

91. Ingrao, qtd. in McCarthy, "America," 223. On cinema, see the work by Americanist Giaime Pintor, who died as a partisan fighter in 1943, esp. "The Struggle against Idols," in Pintor, *Il sangue d'Europa*. Cf. Brunetta, "The Long March of American Cinema in Italy: From Fascism to the Cold War," in Ellwood and Kroes, *Hollywood in Europe*.

92. McCarthy, "America," 217.

93. Roger, *The American Enemy*, 385. Cf. Judt, *Past Imperfect*, 191–96.

94. On these aspects, see Brogi, *A Question*, chap. 1; and Cogan, *Oldest Allies*, chaps. 1–2. On Wilson and Italy, see esp. Rossini, *Woodrow Wilson*.

95. Jean-Paul Sartre, "American Novelists in French Eyes," *Atlantic Monthly*, no. 178 (August 1946). See also Peyre, "American Literature"; Pells, *Not Like Us*, 248; and de Beauvoir, *Force of Circumstance*, 3–4. On the impact of American literature, see also Lottman, *The Left Bank*. On French intellectual fascination with jazz, see also Jeffrey Jackson, *Making Jazz French*. Cf. Ludovic Tournès, "La reinterpretation du jazz: Un phénomène

de contre-américanisation dans la France d'après-guerre (1945–1960)," in Mathé, *L'Anti-américanisme.*

96. Jean-Paul Sartre, "Individualism and Conformism in the United States" (1945), in Sartre, *Literary and Philosophical Essays*, 110–11. Also instructive are Sartre's descriptions of New York. To the existentialist philosopher New York became attractive because, unlike most European cities, it neither protected individuals nor held them down. It was a "light, ephemeral city," whose simple "juxtaposition of rectangular parallelepipeds" never seemed oppressing or depressing. In an ode to freedom that also contained the fear of the undetermined, Sartre concluded, "You can experience the anguish of solitude here but never that of oppression." See Sartre, "New York, the Colonial City" (from *Town and Country*, 1946), in *Literary and Philosophical Essays*, 126–32.

97. Writer Maurice Sachs, qtd. in Jeffrey Jackson, *Making Jazz French*, 119 (see also 116–22). This fascination with jazz continued in the postwar era; *Les Lettres françaises*, for example, between the summer and fall of 1946, published an extensive biography of Louis Armstrong, "king of Jazz."

98. Quotation from Magny, *The Age of the American Novel*, 38; cf. Pells, *Not Like Us*, 248–52.

99. "Le Général Eisenhower salue Paris vainqueur," *L'Humanité*, 9 Sept. 1944; Courtade highlighted in Caute, *Communism*, 173.

100. On this invitation, see also Strauss, *Menace*, 253–54.

101. Claude Roy, "Le ciel est ma frontière," *Les Lettres françaises*, 1 Nov. 1946.

102. Pavese, *La letteratura*, 196; Calvino, "Hemingway e noi"; Mario Alicata, "La corrente *Politecnico*," *Rinascita*, May–June 1946. Cf. Heiney, *America*, 85 and 247; Firmus, "Vita e morte del jazz," *Il Politecnico*, no. 22, 23 Feb. 1946.

103. This crucial turning point in the PCI's cultural policy has been amply examined. Here I highlight the elements of the controversy that most directly affected the party's perception of the emerging Cold War. I also believe these elements are essential in understanding the party's evolving anti-Americanism. The account that comes closest to these conclusions is Gundle, *Between Hollywood and Moscow*, 27–30. For the most accurate accounts of the episode, see also Ajello, *Intellettuali*, 113–37; Lucia, *Intellettuali*, 81–92; Asor Rosa, *Scrittori*; and Luperini, *Gli intellettuali*. See also in general Misler, *La via.*

104. Alicata, "La corrente *Politecnico*."

105. Quotation from Banfi, *Scritti*, 255; also highlighted, with different emphasis, in Ajello, *Intellettuali*, 134; editorial, "Relazione sui *Quaderni del carcere*: Per una storia degli intellettuali italiani," *Rinascita*, 3 Mar. 1946; and Elio Vittorini, "Politica e cultura: Lettera a Togliatti," *Il Politecnico*, no. 35 (Jan.–Mar. 1947).

106. Palmiro Togliatti, "Politica e cultura: Una lettera di Palmiro Togliatti," *Il Politecnico*, no. 2, 33–34 (Oct. 1946), 3–4; Felice Platone, "La politica comunista e i problemi della cultura," *Rinascita*, July 1947, 187–90.

107. Quotation from Gundle, *Between Hollywood and Moscow*, 30. Gundle's conclusion about the party's inflexibility is correct, but also a bit strong, hence the minor exception I am taking in this following paragraph.

108. Michel Gordey, "L'Amérique n'est pas le Nouveau monde," *Les Lettres françaises*, 10 Jan. 1947.

109. Lazar, *Maisons*, 61. The previous paragraph also follows Lazar's argument and evidence closely; see also editorial, "Informazione sopra una polemica," *Rinascita*, IV, May

1947. On the PCF's strictly following the Zhdanovian line, see also McInnes, *The Communist Parties*, 79.

110. Sartre, "Qu'est-ce que la littérature?," in *Situations II*, 2:280; Garaudy, *Literature*, 9, emphasis in the original. See also David Drake, *Intellectuals*, 30 (also last quotation from p. 28).

111. G. Gak, "Un courant à la mode de la philosophie bourgeoise," *Cahiers du communisme*, May 1947; Garaudy, *Literature*; Alicata, "La corrente *Politecnico*"; Platone, "La politica comunista."

112. Cf. remarks in Judt, *Past Imperfect*, chaps. 9–10. Flores, "Il PCI," 111–12.

113. Pavese, *La letteratura*, 196. Similar feelings were routinely expressed between 1946 and 1947 in *Il Politecnico*, but occasionally also in *Rinascita* and *Les Cahiers du communisme*.

Chapter 2

1. This was the title of a best-selling book published in 1951 under the auspices of *Fortune* magazine; Russell Wheeler Davenport, *USA: The Permanent Revolution* (originally published as a special issue of *Fortune* in Feb. 1940).

2. Qtd. in Lipset, *American Exceptionalism*, 18.

3. Jean-Paul Sartre, "La fin de la guerre," *Les Temps modernes*, Oct. 1945; cf. Chebel d'Appollonia, *Des lendemains*; Judt, *Past Imperfect*.

4. Jean-Paul Sartre and Maurice Merleau-Ponty, "Les jours de notre vie," *Les Temps modernes*, Jan. 1950.

5. Calvino, *Hermit*, 194; Flores, *L'immagine dell'URSS*, 345–48.

6. Flores, *L'immagine dell'URSS*, 345–48; on Garaudy, see chap. 1. Quotation from P. Longo Jr., in *Vie Nuove*, no. 32 (1948). On celebrations of Stalin's seventieth birthday in France, see Goulemot, *Pour l'amour de Staline*.

7. Zeldin, *The French*, 34.

8. For a similar argument on harnessing the forces of interdependence, see Ninkovich, *The Wilsonian Century*. For an argument on the difference between Hamiltonian and Jacksonian America, see esp. Mead, *Power*.

9. Acheson, *Present at the Creation*, 375; Kennan, qtd. in Gaddis, *Strategies*, 52.

10. Cf. comments in Costigliola, "Tropes of Gender." For a general account on the depiction of the communist threat as "monolithic" by U.S. and British officials, see Selverstone, *Constructing the Monolith*.

11. Reinhold Niebuhr, "The Foreign Policy of American Conservatism and Liberalism," in Niebuhr, *Christian Realism*, 66.

12. Quotations from Reinhold Niebuhr, "Why Is Communism So Evil?," *New Leader*, 8 June 1953; Neibuhr, "Christianity and Crisis," 8 July 1946, 2; and Neibuhr, "Ideology and the Scientific Method" (1953); all rpt. in Brown, *The Essential Reinhold Neibuhr*, 208. See also Reinhold Niebuhr, "The Children of Light and the Children of Darkness," in ibid., 176–77.

13. For similar observations on the link with McCarthyism, but ones that do not link the elite's pedagogic and demagogic styles, see Brands, *The Devil We Knew*, 34–35. For a general argument, see Alpers, *Dictators*. For a different opinion on Niebuhr and McCarthyism, see Ronald Brownstein, "Pragmatic Path to an Ideal World," *Financial Times*, 27 Mar.

2005. For an overview of the importance of religion in the making of U.S. foreign policy, see Preston, "Bridging the Gap."

14. To be sure, a conflation of pedagogy and demagogy could be found in many modern national experiences. In Cold War Europe Charles de Gaulle was the most apparent example of that combination. But in the United States the hybrid between the two attitudes was more pronounced than anywhere else because of the nation's renewed discovery that its dream of perpetual security was constantly challenged by global threats—strategic, economic, or ideological—and because of the nation's contradiction between isolationist temptation and full awareness of global interdependence, and between provincialism and maximum mobilization.

15. First quotations in Peter Beinart, "The Rehabilitation of the Cold War Liberal," *New York Times*, 30 Apr. 2006; cf. Beinart, *The Good Fight*. Graham qtd. in Whitfield, *The Culture of the Cold War*, 80–81. On Burnham, see Daniel Kelly, *James Burnham*.

16. See chap. 1.

17. On this point, see esp. Fukuyama, *State-Building*, 99–100; and Tony Smith, *America's Mission*.

18. See the seminal Schlesinger, *The Vital Center*, esp. chap. 4.

19. The expression is used by Kuisel in "American Historians," 308; cf. Costigliola, "Tropes of Gender," 165–66. Several diplomats at the time referred to the situations in both nations as anomalous; Caffery to Sec. State, 3 Jan. 1945, *FRUS*, 1945, IV:665 (France as "neurotic"); Tel. 2298, Harrison (Bern) to Sec. State, 13 Apr. 1945, 865.01, RG59, NA (Italians as "despondent"); and, later, an exchange between George Kennan and Charles Bohlen on the "hysterical French," in Kennan to Bohlen and Bohlen to Kennan, 12 and 29 Oct. 1949, Bohlen Records., Gen. Correspondence 1946–49, b. 1, RG59, NA.

20. Tel. 2402, Kirk (Rome) to Byrnes, 21 Aug. 1945; Tel. 1417, Byrnes to Kirk, 22 Aug. 1945; Tel. 1528, Acheson to Kirk, 6 Sept. 1945, 865.00, RG59, NA; Kirk to Byrnes, 25 Aug. 1945, *FRUS*, 1945, IV:983–84. On de Gaulle, see Caffery to Sec. State, 5 May 1945, *FRUS*, 1945, IV:686; Stanley Hoffmann, "Paradoxes of the French Political Community," in Hoffmann, *In Search of France*, 58; Cogan, *Oldest Allies*, 5. On promotion of U.S. hegemony, see Lundestad, *The American "Empire."*

21. Sforza in Murphy (Salerno) to Sec. State, 10 Apr. 1944, *FRUS*, 1944, III:1090–91; Tarchiani in Memo by W. Phillips, 30 May 1945, *FRUS*, 1945, IV:1260–61; Truman to Acting Sec. State, 2 July 1945, ibid., 1265–66. Quotation from Ad Hoc State-War-Navy Coordinating Committee, 6 Sept. 1945, *FRUS*, 1945, IV:1038. See also Ennio Di Nolfo, "The United States and the PCI: The Years of Policy Formation, 1942–1946," in Serfaty and Gray, *The Italian Communist Party*, 38.

22. De Gaulle in Caffery to Sec. State, 5 May 1945, *FRUS*, 1945, IV:686; Eisenhower in Caffery to Sec. State, 20 Oct. 1944, *FRUS* 1944, III:743. On similar statements by Fourth Republic leaders, see, e.g., comments on Foreign Minister Georges Bidault in Tel. 2061, Bonnet to MAE, 19 June 1947, in Série Amérique 1944–52, Etats-Unis, vol. 124, AHMAE; cf. Young, *France*, 39–40.

23. De Gasperi to Sec. State, 22 Aug. 1945, *FRUS*, 1945, IV:1024–25; Tardini in Tel. A-8, Franklin C. Gowen to Sec. State, 20 Mar. 1947, 865.00, RG59, NA. On U.S.-Vatican relations in this period, see also Di Nolfo, *Vaticano*.

24. The best account of the domino theory remains Ninkovich, *Modernity*.

25. Churchill to Roosevelt, 13 Mar. 1944, and Cordell Hull to Chapin (forwarding mes-

sage of Roosevelt to Churchill), 15 Mar. 1944, *FRUS*, 1944, III:1043–44 and 1053–55; cf. Gat, *Britain and Italy*, 38–40.

26. See docs. in *FRUS*, Conference of Berlin, vol. 2, 1078–87. Cf. Gat, *Britain and Italy*, 91–95 (for Churchill quotation); Ellwood, *Italy*, 110–19; and Miller, *The United States*, 111–21.

27. Alexander in Kirk to Sec. State, 30 May 1945, *FRUS*, 1945, IV:1008. Cf. Miller, *The United States*, 156–57. Churchill's successor from July 1945, the Labor Prime Minister Clement Attlee, confirmed that his alignment with the U.S. thesis on Italian rehabilitation was an anti-Soviet move.

28. Churchill to Roosevelt, 16 Nov. 1944, and Mtg. Roosevelt-Stalin, 4 Feb. 1945, *FRUS*, Malta and Yalta: 284–86, 570–73.

29. Briefing Book (Paper of the Executive Secretariat of the Department of State), *FRUS*, Malta and Yalta: 300–304 (quotation on 302); Stettinius to Roosevelt, 4 Jan. 1945, ibid., 293–94; Statement by President Truman, 18 May 1945, *FRUS*, 1945, IV:690–91.

30. Caffery to Sec. State, 27 Jan. 1946, *FRUS*, 1946, V:407. On Caffery in general, see Dur, *Jefferson Caffery*.

31. See esp. Caffery to Sec. State, 3 Jan. 1945, *FRUS*, 1945, IV:661–65 (also arguing that German and Vichy propaganda against U.S. imperialism had left a trace); cf. Wall, *The United States*, 11–12.

32. Memo top secret Caffery to Byrnes, 30 July 1945, 851.00B, RG59, NA; quotation from Caffery to Sec. State, 19 Feb. 1947, *FRUS*, 1947, III:690–92. On PCF and Soviet vs. Anglo-American obstructionism, see Caffery to Sec. State, 8 Apr., 12 July 1946, *FRUS*, 1946, V:422–25, 465–66.

33. Kirk to Sec. State, 30 May 1945, 3 Aug. 1945, *FRUS*, 1945, IV:1008–9, 1015–16; cf. Harper, *America*, 3–5. On the peace treaty the best treatments are in Poggiolini, *Diplomazia*; and Miller, *The United States*. On James Dunn's role starting from the fall of 1946, see esp. Mistry, "The Case," 304–5.

34. Grew to Sec. War Stimson, 15 June 1945, and Grew to Truman, 30 June 1945, *FRUS*, 1945, V:1008–10. Cf. Conv. Charles F. Bohlen (Spec. Asst. to Sec. State) James Byrnes (Sec. State), 14 Sept. 1945, *FRUS* II:163–66.

35. Eisenhower in Report by an Ad Hoc Committee of the State-War-Navy Coordinating Committee, 10 Oct. 1945, *FRUS*, 1945, IV:1037; Acting Sec. State to Kennan (Chargé to Soviet Union), 10 Jan 1946, and Kennan to Sec. State, 25 Jan 1946, *FRUS*, 1946, V:825–27; Alexander qtd. in Kirk to Sec. State, 3 Aug. 1945, *FRUS*, 1945, IV:1015–16.

36. The argument was first forcefully presented in such terms in Parri (President of Italian Council of Ministers) to Truman, 22 Aug. 1945, *FRUS*, 1945, IV:1022–24; and De Gasperi to Sec. State, 22 Aug. 1945, *FRUS*, 1945, IV:1024–25.

37. Caffery qtd. in Young, *France*, 39. See also Grew to Caffery, 6 June 1945, *FRUS*, 1945, IV:734–35; Irwin Wall, "Harry S. Truman and Charles de Gaulle," in Paxton and Wahl, *De Gaulle*. Even after de Gaulle left power, Caffery argued, the PCF feared the general much more than it feared his successors; Tel. 3050, Caffery to Sec. State, 22 June 1946, 851.00, RG59, NA. For a followup, see Michael H. Harrison, "French Anti-Americanism under the Fourth Republic and the Gaullist Solution," in Lacorne, Rupnik, and Toinet, *The Rise*.

38. E.g., Kirk to Sec. State, 28 Dec. 1945, *FRUS*, 1945, IV:1101–2; Tel. 428, Dunn to Sec. State, 28 Feb. 1947, 851.00, RG59, NA; cf. Christopher Duggan, "Italy in the Cold War and the Legacy of Fascism," in Duggan and Wagstaff, *Italy*.

39. Quotation from "Seduta del 23 maggio 1944," in Archivio Centrale dello Stato, *22 aprile 1944–18 giugno 1944*, 110–11; cf. Memo by Walter C. Dowling, 17 Sept. 1946, WEA, Italy, 1943–51, b. 1, RG59, NA.

40. The CIO's Arthur Goldberg, the ILGWU's David Dubinski, the AFL's president William Green, its vice president Matthew Wall, and the ILGWU's vice-president and AFL delegate Luigi Antonini all had contacts with moderate labor leaders in France and Italy during the immediate postwar period. Many of the State Department's labor attachés were drawn from the AFL. See esp. Romero, *The United States*, 3–17, 31–52; Filippelli, *American Labor*, 20–32; and Wall, *The United States*, 48–49.

41. Caffery to Sec. State, 27 Jan. 1946, *FRUS*, 1946, V:407. the new approach of Caffery and the State Department is also noted in Rice-Maximin, "The United States," 730–33; cf. Maier, "The Two Postwar Eras," 446–47.

42. Caffery to Sec. State, 9 Feb., 8 Apr. 1946, *FRUS*, 1946, V:412–13, 422–23; Caffery to Sec. State, 23 May 1946, 851.00, RG59, NA; Lacroix-Riz, "Négociation," 423–24. On Blum's ties with America and other characteristics, see Tel. 780, Lacoste to Bidault, 9 Apr. 1946, Amérique, E-U, vol. 246, AHMAE; Colton, *Léon Blum*, 459–60.

43. On possible support of the PSIUP, see Faenza and Fini, *Gli americani*, 86–88. On Nenni's "blinders," see Miller, *The United States*, 216.

44. Dunn to State Dept., 11 Feb., 11 June 1947, 865.00, RG59, NA; Caridi, *La scissione*, 293–94; Romero, *The United States*, 74.

45. First two quotations from Gaddis, *The Long Peace*, 154–55; following ones from Gaddis, *Strategies*, 43.

46. Tel. 2895, Caffery to Sec. State, 23 May 1945, 851.00, RG59, NA; Caffery to Sec. State, 19 Feb. 1947, *FRUS*, 1947, III:690–92. On PCI's contradictions regarding Trieste, see Marco Galeazzi, "Togliatti fra Tito e Stalin," in Galeazzi, *Roma Belgrado*; and Aga-Rossi and Zaslavsky, *Togliatti e Stalin*, 144–56.

47. Memo Conv. Dowling–Armand Bérard (Counselor French Embassy), *FRUS*, 1946, II:37–38; Caffery to Sec. State, 27 Jan. 1946, *FRUS*, 1946, V:407; Tels. 2221, 4507, Caffery to Sec. State, 8 May, 10 Sept. 1946, 851.00, RG59, NA.

48. On "Third War," see Caffery to Sec. State, 8 May 1946, 851.00, RG59, NA; Togliatti's decisions in Mtg. Segreteria, 28 June 1945, M, VS, mf. 271, APCI. See also Letter Togliatti to Pratolongo, 17 July 1946, in ibid. Report by Jacques Duclos and Maurice Thorez at CC, 20–21 Apr. 1946, Gentilly, pp. 55–60, APCF (Duclos also reiterated the need to maintain the closest solidarity with German comrades). Nenni's article, qtd. in Tel. 2344, Key (Rome) to State Dept., 8 May 1946, 865.00, RG59, NA.

49. Togliatti in Mtg. Direz., 30 June 1945, VD, APCI. On Stalin's demanding caution, cf. Narinski, "La politica estera," 37–45; Pons, "Stalin," 3–11; and Pons, *L'impossibile egemonia*, 145–62.

50. Tel. 3551, Caffery to Sec. State, 14 June 1945, 851.00, RG59, NA; Intelligence Report no. 141 signed "n.b.c." transmitted in Caffery to Byrnes, 30 July 1945, 851.00B, RG59, NA.

51. Togliatti in Mtg. Direz., 26 June 1945, M, VD, mf. 231, APCI. On origins of Italy's initiative that prompted Soviet recognition, see esp. Memo Prunas (special envoy to Moscow), 10 Jan. 1944, in Ministero degli Affari Esteri, *Renato Prunas*, 51–52. Toscano, *Designs*, 271–75, 284–94, Bruno Arcidiacono, "L'Italia fra sovietici e angloamericani: La missione di Pietro Quaroni a Mosca (1944–1946)," in Di Nolfo, Rainero, and Vigezzi, *L'Italia*, 100–102; cf. Morozzo della Rocca, *La politica estera*.

52. Tel. 2895, Caffery to Sec. State, 23 May 1945, 851.00, RG59; Serge Bernstein, "French

Power Seen by the Political Parties after WWII," in Becker and Knipping, *Power in Europe?*, 169. Tel. 2344, Key (Rome) to State Dept., 8 May 1946, 865.00, RG59, NA; Nenni, *Tempo*, 133–41.

53. On these developments, see a thorough argument in Brogi, *A Question*, 48–69.

54. Harper, *America*, 64–68; Young, *France*, 98–99; Hill, "American Efforts," 509–17. On the emerging planning consensus in France, see Hitchcock, *France Restored*, 29–40; and Lynch, "Resolving the Paradox," 229–43.

55. Quotations from intelligence report in Desp. 4352, Key (Rome) to Sec. State, 22 Nov. 1946, 865.00, RG59, NA; see also Memo Norris Chipman, 23 Nov. 1946, *FRUS*, 1946: 471–77.

56. Tel. 6754, Caffery to Sec. State, 13 Nov. 1946, 851.00B, RG59, NA; Memo Chipman, 23 Nov. 1946, *FRUS*, 1946: 471–77; Rice-Maximin, "The United States," 732–34; Wall, *The United States*, 44–48; Key to Sec. State, 6 and 11 Dec. 1946, 865.00B, RG59, NA; Desp. 4352, David McKey to State Dept., 22 Nov. 1946, 865.00B, RG59, NA; Miller, *The United States*, 191–93.

57. Tel. 158, Caffery to State Dept., 10 Jan. 1946, 851.00 and Tel. 36, Key to State Dept., 7 Jan. 1947, 865.00 RG59, NA.

58. Quotations from Tel. 2919, Gallman (London) to Sec. State, 12 Mar. 1946; and Tel. 2688, Caffery to State Dept., 31 May 1946, 851.00, RG59, NA. CIG Memo 26 Nov. 1946, Memo Series, 1945–49, PSF, Intelligence File, b. 249, HSTL. On Washington's preparation for intervention, in case of insurrection, see Memo Hickerson, Bonbright, Acheson, 3 May 1946, *FRUS*, 1946, V:435–38. On "doppiezza," see chap. 1. On PCI's and PCF's self-restraint regarding early chances of insurrection, see esp. Sassoon, *The Strategies*, 31–33; Robrieux, *Histoire intérieure*, 170–75; and Pons, "Togliatti, il PCI e il Cominform," in Aga-Rossi and Quagliarello, *L'altra faccia*, 275–66.

59. Clay qtd. in Miller, *The United States*, 183; Sturzo in Ellwood, *Italy*, 92.

60. E.g., PPS/1, 23 May 1947, *FRUS*, 1947, III:227; PPS/13, 6 Nov. 1947, *FRUS*, 1947, I:771. For a full analysis of this argument, see chap. 3.

61. On all aspects, see esp. Maier, "The Politics of Productivity"; Harper, *America*; Hill, "American Efforts"; David W. Ellwood, "The American Challenge and the Origins of the Politics of Growth," in Smith and Stirk, *Making the New Europe*, 183–94; Hogan, *The Marshall Plan*, 1–53; Milward, *The Reconstruction*.

62. Maier, "The Politics of Productivity," 625.

63. Quotation from Caffery to Sec. State, 9 Feb. 1946, *FRUS*, 1946, V:412–13. Clayton in Minutes NAC Mtgs., 25 Apr. 1946, 6 May 1946, *FRUS*, 1946, V:431–34, 440–46. Cf. Hill, "American Efforts," 508–9. For a detailed narrative on this and the next paragraphs, see Brogi, *A Question*, 79–84.

64. Minutes NAC mtgs., 4 Mar. 1946, 19 Apr. 1946, *FRUS*, 1946, V:894–97, 902–6; Memo by Hickerson, 6 Jan. 1947, *FRUS*, 1947, III:837–38; cf. esp. Miller, *The United States*, 215–19.

65. Tarchiani in Ortona, *La ricostruzione*, 1:184; Pesenti in Miller, *The United States*, 219; Lacouture, *Léon Blum*, 487–89. On formation of bipartisan consensus, cf. Mtg. De Gasperi–Clayton, 14 Jan. 1947, 033.6511, RG59, NA; Martel, *Lend-Lease*, chaps. 6–7.

66. See esp. Kuisel, *Capitalism*, 219–25; Margairaz, "Autour des accords Blum-Byrnes." On Italy, see Key to Sec. State, 5 Sept. 1946, *FRUS*, 1946, V:930–32; and Harper, *America*, 67–69, 101–3.

67. Cf. texts (with conditions but also additional concessions from the United States):

FRUS, 1946, V:461–64; and FRUS, 1947, III:859–61; Tel. 3356–7, Bidault to Bonnet, 28 May 1946, Amérique, 1944–52, vol. 246, AHMAE.

68. Byrnes to Emb. Paris, 18 Jan. 1946, 951.4061, MP; Caffery to Sec. State, 23 Oct. 1946, 851.4061 MP; Tel. 2966, Kirk to Sec. State, 5 Oct. 1945, and Memo Gene Caprio, 3 Nov. 1945, 865.4061 MP, RG59, NA; cf. Costigliola, France, 56; Ellwood and Brunetta, Hollywood in Europa, chap. 1.

69. Dunn to Sec. State, 3 and 7 May, 1947, FRUS, 1947, III:889–92, 895–97; second quotation also in Mistry, "The Case," 307; Dowling to H. Freeman Matthews, 21 Nov. 1946, 865.00, RG59, NA, also highlighted in Harper, America, 109–10; Caffery to Sec. State, 9 Feb. 1946, FRUS, 1946: 471–77 (my emphasis); Kennan (1 Apr. 1946), qtd. in Wall, The United States, 59; Truman, qtd. in Gaddis, The Cold War, 95.

70. Surveying the literature on American Communism is beyond my scope, but the following works have helped me frame this argument: Diggins, The Rise and Fall of the American Left (quotation on 22–23); Klehr, Haynes, and Anderson, The Soviet World of American Communism; Gornick, The Romance of American Communism; Levy, The Cause That Failed; Shannon, The Decline of American Communism; Brown et al., New Studies in the Politics and Culture of U.S. Communism; and Heale, McCarthy's Americans.

71. Within a few years, however, Hollywood reigned supreme in Germany's Western zones. See de Grazia, Irresistible Empire, 333–35 (quoting Billy Wilder); and Schivelbusch, In a Cold War Crater, 137–53.

72. On this communist campaign, see chap. 5. Quotation from Tel. 3478, Caffery to Sec. State, 23 Oct. 1946, 851.4061 MP, RG59, NA; cf. Portes, "Les origines."

73. Letter John Murphy to W. Benton (Asst. Sec. State), 6 Nov. 1945; cf. Kirk to Sec. State, 5 Oct. 1945 (after the Italian Parliament passed legislation favoring Italian cinema), both in 865.4061 MP, RG59, NA.

74. See chap. 5. On the immediate postwar impact of neorealism, see Gundle, Between Hollywood and Moscow, 26–27. Yet another irony of neorealism was that it was more successful abroad than at home, where the Italian masses continued to prefer Hollywood escapism to the art films that portrayed their everyday lives.

75. Cf. Costigliola, Awkward Dominion; Rosenberg, Spreading the American Dream; Whitfield, Culture of the Cold War; de Grazia, Irresistible Empire, chaps. 1–5.

76. Qtd. in Michael Kelly, "The Nationalization," 19; on the invitation, see Strauss, Menace, chap. 16.

77. Hearings before the Subcommittee of the Committee on Appropriations, U.S. Senate, 79th Congress, 1st Session, H.R. 2603, June 1946, p. 53, FP. Previous quotations from ibid., 51–52; J. William Fulbright, foreword to Johnson and Colligan, The Fulbright Program, viii; Pells, Not Like Us, 59; and Randall Woods, Fulbright, 131–36. On the program's focus on Europe, cf. essays on Europe in Arndt and Rubin, The Fulbright Difference; cf. Cull, The Cold War, 24–43 (also highlighting the roles of William B. Benton and George V. Allen as assistant secretaries of state for public relations-affairs).

78. See esp. Berghahn, America; Oliver Schmidt, "Small Atlantic World: U.S. Philanthropy and the Expanding International Exchange of Scholars after 1945," in Gienow-Hecht and Schumacher, Culture; Bremner, American Philanthropy; Iriye, "A Century of NGOs."

79. Ninkovich, The Diplomacy, 67. Cf. Wieck, Ignorance Abroad; Rosenberg, Spreading the American Dream, 217–28; Oliver Schmidt, "No Innocents Abroad: The Salzburg Im-

petus and American Studies in Europe," in May and Wagnleitner, *Here, There, and Everywhere.*

80. Harper, *America*, 118; Wall, *The United States*, 71. On Italy, the most definitive account is Formigoni, "De Gasperi," 361–88. A similar broad coalition ended simultaneously in Belgium.

81. Dunn to Marshall, 3 May 1946, *FRUS*, 1947, III:889–92; see also Dunn to Sec. State, 12 Apr. 1947, ibid., 880. Much of the pressure for a tougher U.S. stance against the PCI had come from Italian authorities. On Tarchiani and De Gasperi, see esp. Acheson to Sec. State, 9 Apr. 1947, Memo Conv. by Matthews, 20 May 1947, *FRUS*, 1947, III:536–37, 508–9; Dowling to Matthews, 2 May 1947, 865.01, RG59, NA; Memo Tarchiani-Matthews, 8 May 1947, 865.00, RG59, NA; Tarchiani, *Dieci anni*, 133–36. On covert funding in immediate postwar period, see esp. Timothy Naftali, "ARTIFICE: James Angleton and X-2 Operations in Italy," in Chalon, *The Secrets War.*

82. Caffery to Sec. State, 6 May 1947, 851.00, RG59, NA; for invitations coming from the French side, see also Tels. 5463, 1493, and 1745, Caffery to Sec. State, 31 Oct. 1946, 14 and 27 Apr. 1947, 851.00, RG59, NA.

83. Memo Chipman, 23 Nov. 1946, *FRUS*, 1946: 471–77; Key to Sec. State, 6 Dec. 1946, *FRUS*, 1946, V:948–50; Togliatti and Basso in Dunn to Sec. State, 1 Apr. 1947, 865.00, RG59, NA; Tel. 308, Caffery to Sec. State, 23 Jan. 1947, 851.00 RG59, NA. On fears of bureaucratic influence, see Caffery to Sec. State, 31 Mar. 1947, *FRUS*, 1947, III:695–96; MacArthur II to Woodruff Wallner, Top Sec., 26 Mar. 1947, 851.00B, RG59, NA; on De Gasperi, see Formigoni, *La Democrazia cristiana*, 128–42.

84. On problems within the SFIO, see Tel. 1883, Caffery to Sec. State, 8 May 1947; Memo Matthews to Acheson, 11 July 1947, WEA 1941–51, Records of the French Desk, b. 2, RG59, NA; on Italy, see Tels. 1500 and 1534, Dunn to Sec. State, 11 and 13 June 1947, 865.00, RG59, NA.

85. Cf. Dunn to Sec. State, 9 Apr. 1947, 865.00, and Caffery to Sec. State, 30 Apr. 1947, 851.00, RG59, NA.

86. Etienne Fajon on communist isolation because of Indochina in CC, 18 Jan. 1947 (Paris) (p. 86), APCF. Victor Michaut and Gaston Monmousseau on trusts and Renault and Joanny Berlioz on SFIO in CC, 3 May 1947, p. 140, APCF. On PCF's hesitation to enter the Ramadier cabinet, see Caffery to Sec. State, 4 Jan. 1947, 851.00, RG59 NA. Cf. Rice-Maximin, *Accommodation*, 48–53. In general, cf. Philippe Buton, "L'éviction des ministres communistes," in Bernstein and Mitra, *L'année 1947*; and Ruscio, *Les communistes français.*

87. See interventions by Longo, Sereni (qtd.), Terracini, and Togliatti in Mtg. Direz., 16–19 Apr. 1947, VD, mf. 272, APCI; For Togliatti's quoted statement on Saragat, see Mtg. Direz., 19 Jan. 1947, ibid. For different interpretations, see Di Loreto, *Togliatti*, 161–64; and Galante, *La fine.*

88. Thorez in CC, 3 May 1947, pp. 141–45, APCF. On Soviet reactions, see Spriano, *Stalin*, 185–86.

89. On Togliatti's *L'Unità* article "Ma come sono cretini!," see introduction. Terracini in Mtg. Direz., 16–19 Apr. 1947, pp. 21–22; Dec. BP, 13 Mar. 1947, APCF; see also Pierre Courtade, "Les dollars ont une odeur," *L'Humanité*, 20 May 1947.

Chapter 3

1. Davenport, *USA: The Permanent Revolution.*

2. Cleveland's statement is recalled several times by David Ellwood, most recently in Ellwood, "The Propaganda," 226. Ellwood highlights the economic-material aspects conveyed by the statement; the pursuit of prosperity it underlined included, however, a broader notion of individual fulfillment, a sense of self-mastery that had also informed the practices of Fordism.

3. The leading revisionist account that minimizes the economic impact of the Marshall Plan is Milward, *The Reconstruction*; see also Milward, *The European Rescue.* Michael Hogan, while stressing U.S. influence, concludes that "participating countries were not clay in the hands of American potters"; Hogan, *The Marshall Plan*, 445. For recent syntheses, cf. Killick, *The United States*, and William I. Hitchcock, "The Marshall Plan and the Creation of the West," in Leffler and Westad, *The Cambridge History*, vol. 1.

4. See esp. Esposito, *America's Feeble Weapon*; and Hogan, *The Marshall Plan*, 427–51.

5. Quotation from S. A. Shucker, in Maier, "The Two Postwar Eras," 357; cf. esp. Wexler, *The Marshall Plan*, 249–55.

6. Kennan in Gaddis, *Strategies*, 45. The best work on psychological effects is Ellwood, *Rebuilding Europe*, 226–36. For an updated version, see David W. Ellwood, "Italian Modernisation and the Propaganda of the Marshall Plan," in Cheles and Sponza, *The Art of Persuasion*. For a thesis that U.S. maneuvers prevented a Soviet acceptance of the plan, see Cox and Pipe-Kennedy, "The Tragedy of American Diplomacy?"

7. See esp. de Grazia, *Irresistible Empire*; and Maier, *Among Empires*, chaps. 5–6. Maier instead defines the postwar period to the 1960s as an "Empire of Production," while he relates the "Empire of Consumption" to the globalizing effects of America's "voracious desire for imports" and the need of other economies for modernization from the 1960s on. Tracing this phenomenon further back is Hoganson, *Consumers' Imperium.*

8. Quotations from David W. Ellwood, "'You Too Can Be Like Us,'" 39; and Kennan, in Paper PPS, "Aid to Western Europe," 23 May 1947, *FRUS*, 1947, III:223–30 (quotation 225).

9. Bohlen to Kennan, 2 Oct. 1947, Bohlen Recs., b. 6, RG59, NA; NSC 1/1, 14 Nov. 1947, *FRUS*, 1947, III:724; Hoffman, *Peace.* See also Ellwood, "Italian Modernisation," 28.

10. ORE 6–48, "Consequences of Communist Accession to Power in Italy by Legal Means," 5 Mar. 1948, HSTP, PSF, CIA reports, b. 214, HSTL; Marshall to Emb. Rome, 25 Mar. 1948, 865.00, RG59, NA; Tel. 2503, Caffery to Sec. State, FW851.00, RG59, NA.

11. David W. Ellwood, "The Impact of the Marshall Plan on Italy, the Impact of Italy on the Marshall Plan," in Kroes, Rydell, and Bosscher, *Cultural Transmissions*, 100. On the impact of Marshall Plan propaganda, see esp. Ellwood, "Italian Modernisation"; and (also for definition of public diplomacy) McKenzie, *Remaking France.*

12. On these uncertainties and orders from Cominform, see the memoirs of Eugenio Reale, *Nascita del Cominform*, esp. 31–33, 116–22, 147. Cf. esp. Pons, *L'impossibile egemonia*, 189–227; Gori and Pons, *Dagli archivi*, 135–68; Procacci et al., *The Cominform*, 37–503; Anna Di Biagio, "The Marshall Plan and the Founding of the Cominform, June–September 1947," in Gori and Pons, *The Soviet Union*, 208–21; Aga-Rossi and Zaslavsky, *Togliatti e Stalin*, 205–9; Martinelli, *Il "Partito nuovo"*; and Narinski, "L'entretien."

13. Wall, *French Communism*, 58–64; Sassoon, *The Strategies*, 62–70.

14. Terracini and Negarville in Mtg. Direz., 16–19 Apr. 1947, VD, APCI. On public sector, see conclusion of transcript; cf. Mtg. Direz., 1–4 July 1947, VD, APCI; Togliatti, *Discorsi parlamentari*, 1:144–69. Cf. Gori and Pons, *Dagli archivi*, doc. 17; Pierre Courtade, "L'offensive de l'impérialisme américain," *Cahiers du communisme*, June 1947; Maurice Thorez, "Guide idéologique de la classe ouvrière et du peuple," *Cahiers du communisme*, July 1947, esp. 588–92.

15. Quotation from Georgi Dimitrov's Diary in Pons, *L'impossibile egemonia*, 198. Cf. Dec. BP, 24 July 1947 (urging a campaign to uphold the Potsdam agreements).

16. Terracini in Allegato no. 4 (letter of 6 Nov.) to Mtg. CC, 11 Nov. 1947, APCI. Cf. Terracini and Togliatti in Mtg. Direz., 16–19 Apr. 1947.

17. Cf. Togliatti in Direz., 16–19 Apr. 1947, 1–4 July 1947; Dec. BP, 28 Aug., 4 Sept. 1947, APCF.

18. Zhdanov in Spriano, *Stalin*, 298; Thorez in CC, 29–30 Oct. 1947, Paris, p. 13, APCF; Franco Rodano, qtd. in Sassoon, *The Strategies*, 69–70. On how the PCF planned its anti-American arguments, see Magnien to Thorez, 18 July 1947, TP, 626 AP b. 127, AN; Gualtieri, *Togliatti*, 168; Bocca, *Togliatti*, 504–17; and "Il Piano Marshall," *Rinascita*, June 1947.

19. Georges Soria, qtd. in Roger, *The American Enemy*, 322.

20. Dec. BP, 3 and 24 July 1947, APCF; Togliatti in Mtg. Direz., 1–4 July 1947, VD, APCI, and CC, 11 Nov. 1947 (for quotation); cf. "Mediterraneo e Stati Uniti," *Rinascita*, Mar. 1947.

21. Pierre Courtade, "On peut crever de faim avec le téléphone," *L'Humanité*, 16 Feb. 1948. See Courtade's articles in the issues of 15, 19, and 21 Feb. and 6 Mar. For similar PCI perceptions, see Michela Nacci, "Contro la civiltà dell'abbondanza: L'antiamericanismo del PCI," in Aga-Rossi and Quagliarello, *L'altra faccia*, 241–42.

22. "Con chi siete intellettuali americani?," *Rinascita*, Sept. 1947; Thorez, "Guide idéologique," 588–89; Maurice Thorez, "Non, pas de nouveau Munich!," *Cahiers du communisme*, Oct. 1947; Courtade, qtd. in Roger, *Rêves et cauchemars*, 247–48; Thorez, CC, 29–30 Oct. 1947, APCF, pp. 9–15.

23. On Togliatti's May 1947 *L'Unitá* article, see introduction; and Mtg. Direz., 1–4 July 1947, APCI.

24. "Dio e il dollaro," *Rinascita*, Aug. 1947.

25. Reale-Molotov in Pons, *L'impossibile egemonia*, 194; Zhdanov in *Cominform*, 453–56.

26. On "American parties," see esp. Soria, *La France*, 48; for second quotation, see *L'Humanité*, 19 Nov. 1947. Cf. Maurice Thorez, "Le combat pour la République et pour l'indépendance nationale," *Cahiers du communisme*, Nov. 1947.

27. Courtois and Lazar, *Histoire*, 283.

28. For similar opinions, see Courtois and Lazar, *Histoire*, 282–84; Pons, *L'impossibile egemonia*, 220–27; and Spriano, *Stalin*.

29. Mtg. Direz., 7–10 Oct. (see also interventions by Longo and Novella), 10 Nov. 1947, VD, APCI; CC, 11 Nov. 1947, vol. 2, APCI. Party hard-liners especially clung to the myth of the Resistance, claiming, as Luigi Longo did, that the PCI would break the "corrupting influence of the dollar," much as it had fought Nazi oppression; Luigi Longo, "I servi sono rimasti," *L'Unità*, 16 Dec. 1947.

30. Kriegel, qtd. in Courtois and Lazar, *Histoire*, 257; see also 281. At the December Central Committee meeting Jacques Duclos commented that, in order to fend off charges of having politicized the strikes, the party needed to clarify the danger of the American presence. The masses "suffer a sort of crisis of conscience," he said, "feeling, albeit confus-

edly, that our country is threatened by American imperialism"; CC, 22–23 Dec. 1947, Ivry, APCF.

31. Pajetta in Mtg. Direz., 7–10 Oct. 1947, VD, APCI; Longo in Mtg. Direz., 24–25 May 1948, VD, APCI; see also Galante, *L'autonomia possibile*, 47–48; Galeazzi, "Luigi Longo," 120–21. Aron, qtd. in Marc Lazar, "The Cold War Culture of the French and Italian Communist Parties," in Scott-Smith and Krabbendam, *The Cultural Cold War*, 215.

32. Dunn to Sec. State, 28 Nov. 1947, 865.00B, RG59, NA; ORE-47 "The Current Situation in Italy," HSTP, PSF, CIA reports, b. 214, HSTL.

33. Caffery to Sec. State, 26 July 1947, 851.00; cf. Caffery to Sec. State, 16 Sept. 1947, *FRUS*, 1947, III:750–51; Caffery to Sec. State, 9 Dec. 1947, 851.00, RG59, NA.

34. Norris B. Chipman, "Report to the Third European Intelligence Conference," Frankfurt, 2–7 June 1948, in Caffery to State Dept., 10 June 1948, 851.00B, RG59, NA; also in Rice-Maximin, "The United States," 739. On elections, see also Lovett to Emb. Paris, 25 Oct. 1947, *FRUS*, 1947, III:790–92.

35. Caffery to Sec. State, 9 Jan. 1948, 851.00; Dunn to Sec. State, 12 Jan. 1948, 865.00, RG59, NA, Caffery to State Dept., 5 Oct. 1948, *FRUS*, 1948, III:662–64; "Italy: ERP Program for April–June 1948," 30 Apr. 1948, "S10b Country Submissions," FRC accession 53A441, RG286, NA.

36. Caffery to Sec. State, 6 Feb. 1948, 851.00B, Director OEA to Under Sec. State, 11 July 1947, French Desk Files, 1941–51, b. 2, f. "France, 1947–48," RG59, NA; Memo Conv. by Acting Sec. State, 16 Sept. 1947, *FRUS*, 1947, III:969–70; Kennan to Lovett (on both parties), 6 Oct. 1947, PPS Recs., Chron. Series, b. 33, RG59, NA; Dunn to Sec. State, 16 Dec. 1947, *FRUS*, 1948, III:752.

37. Pons, *L'impossibile egemonia*, 116 211–20; Gori and Pons, *Dagli archivi*, doc. 20; Bocca, *Palmiro Togliatti*, 486–89; Report "Organisation militaire du PCF," 21 Mar. 1948, b. BA 2248, APP.

38. Memo PPS, 24 Sept. 1947, *FRUS*, 1947, III:969–70, 976–81; NSC 1 and NSC 1/2, *FRUS*, 1948, III:724–26, 765–69; Bevin in Bohlen to Lovett, 16 Apr. 1948, Bohlen Recs., Memo Series, b. 4, RG59, NA. See also exchange between Dunn and Eugenio Reale in Dunn to Sec. State, 16 Dec. 1947, 865.00, RG59, NA. On this phase, cf. Miller, *The United States*, 236–39.

39. Memo Berger to Bohlen, 16 Dec. 1947, Bohlen Recs., Subj. Files, b. 6; see also Memo André Boulloche–James C. H. Bonbright, 30 Sept. 1947, both in 851.00, RG59, NA.

40. Memo Marshall, "Possible Developments of Prospective French Political Crisis," 28 June 1947, Bohlen Recs., Memo Series, b. 5, RG59, NA; NSC 1/1 complete version in PSF, Subj. Files, NSC Mtgs., b. 176, HSTL.

41. Filippelli, *American Labor*, 90–154; Romero, *The United States*, 96–113, 138–74; Miller, *The United States*, 255–63; Wall, *The United States*, 96–113; Guasconi, *L'altra faccia*, 51–65.

42. Maier, "The Politics of Productivity," 626; Caffery to Sec. State, 20 Dec. 1947, *FRUS*, 1947, III:819–20.

43. Memo Conv. by Hickerson, 21 Jan. 1948; Kennan to Sec. State, *FRUS*, 1948, III:9–12, 7–8. Cf. Gaddis, *The Long Peace*, chap. 3; Harper, *American Visions*, 122–32.

44. Quotation from Caffery to Sec. State, 5 Oct. 1948, *FRUS*, 1948, III:663. Policy Statement Dept. of State, 20 Sept. 1948, ibid., 651–59. The U.S. embassy had previously expressed similar fears; see esp. Memo (unsigned) to W. Wallner, Acting Chief Division WEA, State Dept., 8 Dec. 1947, Paris Embassy Recs., Top Secret Files, 1944–49, RG84, NA.

45. Ellwood, *Rebuilding Europe*, 91. On Fulbright's early favor of European political integration, see Randall Woods, *Fulbright*, 137–53.

46. Pons, *L'impossibile egemonia*, 87; cf. Zubok and Pleshakov, *Inside the Kremlin's Cold War*, 111–13. On PCI's and PCF's initial rejection of European integration, see esp. Galante, *Il Partito comunista*; Marcou, *Le mouvement*; and Wall, *French Communism*.

47. Recent studies that best showed how America's development of political and psychological warfare began in Italy are Mistry, "The Case"; Mistry, "The Dynamics"; and Del Pero, "The United States."

48. Sinatra's offer discussed in Marshall to Dunn, 22 Mar. 1948; Dowling to Marshall, 24 Mar. 1948; Dunn to Sec. State, 24 Mar. 1948, all in 865.00, RG59, NA. On Radio Broadcasts' results, see Dunn to Sec. State, 15 Apr. 1948, *FRUS*, 1948, III:875–76 (qtd.); cf. M. J.[anowitz] and E. Marvick, "U.S. Propaganda Efforts and the 1948 Italian Elections," in Daugherty and Janowitz, *A Psychological Warfare Casebook*, 320–25.

49. Dunn to Sec. State, 13 Jan. 1948; Marshall to Dunn, 29 Jan. 1948; Dunn to Sec. State, 25 Feb. 1948, 865.00, RG59, NA; Dunn to Sec. State, 21 and 29 Jan., 21 Feb. 1948, *FRUS*, 1948, III:819–22, 824, 832–35; cf. Donno, *La Gladio*, 243–48; Zaslavsky, *Lo stalinismo*, 83–89.

50. Caffery to Sec. State, 29 Dec. 1947, and Bonbright (Paris) to Sec. State, 27 Feb. 1948, 865.00, RG59, NA; Letter Bidault to Marshall, 4 Mar. 1948, Papiers d'Agents (H. Bonnet), vol. 1, AHMAE.

51. Douglas (London) to Sec. State, 27 Feb. 1948, 865.00, RG59, NA; Varsori, "La Gran Bretagna"; Garret (Dublin) to Sec. State, 12 Apr. 1948, and Ehrardt (Vienna) to State Dept., 1 Mar. 1948, 865.00, RG59, NA.

52. Dunn to Sec. State, 7 Feb. 1948, *FRUS*, 1948, III:827–30; Mistry, "The Case"; Mistry, "The Dynamics." See also Ellwood, "The 1948 Elections," 19–34. On broader implications for U.S. interests of the loss of Italy, see also memo by PPS, 24 Sept. 1947, *FRUS*, 1947, III:976–81, in ibid.; see also Kirby, "Divinely Sanctioned."

53. Luconi, "Anti-Communism," 285–302; Wendy L. Wall, "America's 'Best Propagandists:' Italian Americans and the 1948 'Letters to Italy' Campaign," in Appy, *Cold War Constructions*.

54. On importance of tying historical traditions to the Cold War debate, cf. esp. Ventresca, *From Fascism to Democracy*, chap. 6; and Novelli, *Le elezioni*.

55. Parsons (Vatican City) to Sec. State, 28 Jan., 21 Feb. 1948, 865.00; Parsons to Sec. State, 5 Mar. 1948, 865.00B, RG59, NA; Parsons to Sec. State, 11 Dec. 1947, *FRUS*, 1948, III:745–46.

56. Parsons to Sec. State, 5 Mar. 1948, 865.00B, RG59, NA; on "letters to Italy," see *Il Progresso italo-americano*, 19 Jan. 1948; on Church campaigns and Gedda, cf. Ventresca, *From Fascism to Democracy*, chaps. 3 and 5; on taking over letter campaign, see Marshall to Dunn, 3 Mar. 1948, 811.911, RG59, NA; Luconi, "Anti-Communism," 289–90.

57. Dunn to Marshall, 10 Mar. 1948, *FRUS*, 1948, III:845–47; Dunn to Marshall, 26 Jan. 1948, 865.00, RG59, NA; Bosworth, *Italy*, 90; Formigoni, *La Democrazia cristiana*, 168–70; Galante, *L'autonomia possibile*, 177–89. James Miller stresses that the Vatican became more attuned to Italy's nascent democracy thanks to the anticommunist campaign; Miller, "Taking Off the Gloves," 44.

58. Pietro Secchia, "Il Partito comunista e gli intellettuali," *L'Unità*, 5 Feb. 1948. On the "Alleanza per la Difesa della Cultura," see esp. Vittoria, *Togliatti*, 12–13; and Ajello, *Intellettuali*, 155–77.

59. Togliatti to regional secretaries, urgent memorandum, 21 Apr. 1948 (also first quote), Archivio della Segreteria, Circolari e decisioni scritte, 1944–1951, APCI.

60. Ottavio Pastore, "I liberali del XX secolo," *L'Unità*, 31 Aug. 1948; Mario Alicata, "Una linea per l'unità degli intellettuali progressivi," *Rinascita*, Dec. 1948.

61. On Basso, Nenni, and their maximalist class rhetoric since 1945, see esp. Caffery to Sec. State, 29 Dec. 1947, 865.00, RG59, NA; Di Nolfo, *Le paure*, 173–78; Collotti, Negt, and Zannino, *Lelio Basso*. Nenni in Fedele, *Fronte Popolare*, 136; cf. Nenni, *Tempo*, 424.

62. Memo Bohlen (n.d., presumably Mar.), Bohlen Recs., Memo Series, b. 4, RG59, NA; Dunn to Sec. State (reporting conversation between Carey and Di Vittorio), 13 Mar. 1948, 840.50; Dunn to Sec. State, 17 and 20 Mar. 1948, 865.00, RG59, NA; cf. Harper, *America*, 153. A case of much more heavy-handed blackmail was the U.S. government threat to deny visa entries to communist cardholders, a move State Department officials correctly believed would have a significant impact on Southern Italians. This was, however, the prelude to the McCarran-Walter Immigration Act of 1952; cf. Dunn to Sec. State, 13 Mar. 1948, 865.00B and Dunn to Sec. State, 13 Apr. 1948, 711.65, RG59, NA.

63. Memo Conv. by Assistant Sec. State for Political Affairs (Armour) with Tarchiani, 8 Feb. 1948; Dunn to Sec. State, 12 Jan. 1948, *FRUS*, 1948, III:830–32, 816–19. On Soviet diplomatic support, cf. Morozzo della Rocca, *La politica estera*, 183–84. The Italian American community had already unleashed all its patriotic fervor, displaying an equally divided triple allegiance to America, the Church, and the Risorgimento.

64. The foreign minister specified he was "not doing this to obtain [the] return of Trieste, but simply to win the elections"; Dunn to Sec. State, 1 Mar. 1948, 865.00; Dunn to Sec. State, 4 and 18 Mar. 1948, *FRUS*, 1948, III:509–10, 515–16; Tel. 16523, Tarchiani to Sforza, 24 Apr. 1948, Fondo Cass., b. 7, ASMAE.

65. Memo Dept. of State to Embassy Soviet Union, 20 Mar. 1948, Dunn to Sec. State, 22 Mar. 1948, *FRUS*, 1948, III:517–18, 858–60; quotation from Miller, "Taking Off the Gloves," 52.

66. NSC 1/3; see full version in PSF, Subj. Files, NSC Mtgs., b. 176, HSTL; for authorization, see NSC 4 and 4/A, 9 and 17 Dec. 1947, *FRUS*, *Emergence of the Intelligence Establishment, 1945–1950* [Intell.]: 640–45; cf. Barnes, "The Secret Cold War," 405–10. Both the PPS and the NSC ruled out military intervention, then proposed by George Kennan under a scenario of provocation and outlawing of the PCI; Kennan to Sec. State, 15 Mar. 1948, *FRUS*, 1948, III:848–49.

67. Dunn to Sec. State, 16 Jan. 1948; Memo Director EA to Undersec. State, 3 Mar. 1948; Marshall (Tokyo) to Kennan, 5 Mar. 1948, 865.00, RG59, NA; Barnes, "The Secret Cold War," 408–13. On Soviet support, see Aga-Rossi and Zaslavsky, "L'URSS, il PCI e l'Italia," 953–54; Zaslavsky, *Lo stalinismo*, 123–26; Nina D. Smirnova, "Soviet-Italian Relations, 1945–48," in Gori and Pons, *The Soviet Union*, 377–78 (which shows the Soviets' cautious response to the PCI's repeated requests for financial aid); and Riva, *Oro*, 156–75.

68. Dunn to Sec. State, 1 and 10 Mar. 1948, *FRUS*, 1948, III:836–37, 845–47.

69. Miller, "Taking Off the Gloves," 46–47, 53; Cline, *Secrets*, 98–102; Thomas, *The Very Best Men*, 28–29; Corson, *The Armies*, 297–300. On thrust as well as limits of the CIA operation compared to the Vatican's mobilization, see esp. Ventresca, *From Fascism to Democracy*, 91–99, chap. 5; and Formigoni, *La Democrazia cristiana*, 178.

70. Dunn to State Dept., 1, 11, 17 Apr. 1948, 865.00, RG59, NA; Dunn to State Dept., 16 June 1948, *FRUS*, 1948, III:879–82.

71. On this development, see esp. Mistry, "The Case," 302, 317.

72. PPS Memo, "The Inauguration of Organized Political Warfare," 30 Apr. 1948, Lot File 64 D 563, B. 11A, RG59, NA; also highlighted in Mistry, "The Case," 302.

73. For similar observations, see esp. Anders Stephanson, "Fourteen Notes on the Very Concept of the Cold War," in Tuathail and Dalby, *Rethinking Geopolitics*, 62–85; and Del Pero, "The United States," 1304–5.

74. On this episode, see esp. Gozzini and Martinelli, *Dall'attentato*, 22–44.

75. PPS Memo, 30 Apr. 1948, Lot File 64 D 563, b. 11A, RG59, NA.

76. Mtg. Direz., 20–21 Jan. 1948, 28 June 1948, APCI; Pons, *L'impossibile egemonia*, 220–24.

77. Platt and Leonardi, "American Foreign Policy," 201–3; Filippelli, *American Labor*, 132–35; Varsori, "La Gran Bretagna."

78. CIA report qtd. in Corson, *The Armies*, 299; cf. CIA 5–48, "Review of the World Situation as It Relates to the Security of the United States," 12 May 1948, PSF, Subj. Files, NSC, b. 176, HSTL. The consequences for Italian democracy of the client-patron relationship established in 1948 are also stressed in Ventresca, *From Fascism to Democracy*; and Karabell, *Architects*, 42–49.

79. Togliatti Report at Mtg. Central Committee, 4 May 1948, APCI.

80. White in Ellwood, *Rebuilding Europe*, 209.

81. Kuisel, *Seducing the French*, 70–102; Ellwood, "Italian Modernisation," 29–33, 39–41; McKenzie, *Remaking France*, 3, 25, 45–49 (also on Smith-Mundt Committee's approving the financing for these initiatives); Pisani, *The CIA*, 91–92, 117–18.

82. Quotation from "A Review of the Activities and Performance of the Information Division of the Special Mission to Italy," June 1948–Dec. 1950, n.d. (1951), ECA Washington, Information Division, Office Director, International Country File, "Italy" subfile, RG286, NA. Cf. Ellwood, "Italian Modernisation," 33, 36 (Berding quotation); Hemsing, "The Marshall Plan's European Film Unit"; Whelan, "Marshall Plan Publicity."

83. McCarthy to Marshall, 26 Oct. 1947, Marshall Papers, b. 134, f. 40, GMF. See Guigueno, "L'écran," 117–24.

84. Quotation from Endy, *Cold War Holidays*, 34, 47. Cf. McKenzie, *Remaking France*, 111–40.

85. Cf. PPS, "Aid to Western Europe," 23 May 1947, *FRUS*, 1947, III:223–30.

86. Memo for the file, 16 Nov. 1948, *FRUS*, Intell:732–33; Ellwood, "The Propaganda," 227.

87. "US Information Policy with Regard to Anti-American Propaganda," 20 July 1948, 711.00, RG286, NA.

88. "Notes Dictated by Berding for Use in Congressional Presentation," 16 Jan. 1950, OSR Info. Div., Info. Subj. Files, "Previous Testimony," Subf., RG286, NA, also in Ellwood, "Italian Modernisation," 29–30.

89. Bloch-Lainé and Beauvier, *La France*; Bottiglieri, *La politica economica*, 107–17; Kuisel, *Capitalism*, 237–49; Esposito, *America's Feeble Weapon*, 104–19, 178–98.

90. See ECA Mission Chief to Costa, corresp. Nov. 1951, ECA-Italy, Office of Director, Subj. Files, 1948–57, "Productivity Drive" subfile, RG469, NA; Vera Zamagni, "American Influence on the Italian Economy (1948–1958)," and David W. Ellwood, "Italy, Europe and the Cold War: The Politics and Economics of Limited Sovereignty," both in Duggan and Wagstaff, *Italy*, 83–86, 36–37; Pier Paolo D'Attorre, "Il Piano Marshall: Politica, economia, relazioni internazionali nella ricostruzione italiana," in Di Nolfo, Rainero, and Vigezzi, *L'Italia*, 520–35; and Kuisel, *Seducing the French*, 95–102.

91. Milward, *The European Rescue*; Romero, "L'Europa"; Brunetau, "The Construction"; cf. Charles S. Maier, "Supranational Concepts and National Continuity in the Framework of the Marshall Plan," in Maier and Hoffmann, *The Marshall Plan*.

92. Memo qtd. in Hitchcock, "France," 612. Maurice Vaïsse and Pierre Melandri, "France: From Powerlessness to the Search for Influence," in Becker and Knipping, *Power in Europe?*, 469; Bossuat, *L'Europe*, 151–63.

93. Mtg. Bohlen-Bevin, 4 Oct. 1948, Bohlen Recs., b. 4, RG59, NA; Milward, *The Reconstruction*, chap. 5; Young, *Britain*, 122–24; Antonio Varsori, "L'Italia nel sistema internazionale post-bellico: Dalle illusioni di grande potenza alla realtà di una media potenza," in Varsori, *La politica estera*.

94. For an extended argument showing the vying of France and Italy for U.S. favor at this stage, see Brogi, *A Question*, chap. 3. Ramadier quoted in Pierre Guillen, "France and the Defense of Western Europe: From the Brussels Pact (March 1948) to the Pleven Plan (October 1950)," in Wiggershaus and Forster, *The Western Security Community*, 125–26.

95. Conv. with Beuve-Méry, 8 Feb. 1951, b. 35, RG84, NA; Jean-Paul Sartre, "Le RDR et le problème de la liberté," *La Pensée socialiste*, no. 19 (1948). The U.S. embassy also became alarmed about the growing collaboration between *Le Monde*, the radical newspaper *Combat*, and U.S. citizen Louis Dolivet, editor of *United Nations World*; Bohlen (Paris) to Sec. State, 9 Apr. 1951, 851.001, RG59, NA.

96. Memo Myers to H. G. Reed, 4 June 1949, ECA-France, Office Director, Subj. Files, 1948–56, b. 2, and Entry 1192, Memo Kenneth Douty (Chief, Labor Division, ECA-France), 7 Feb. 1950, "Is It 1929 in France?," ibid., b. 111, RG469, NA; McKenzie, *Remaking France*, 26, 38–49; Ellwood, "Italian Modernisation," 39–41.

97. Memo J. D. Neal to Williamson-WE, 7 July 1950, Recs. Office WEA, Italy 1943–51, RG59, NA; Dunn to Sec. State, 21 Jan. 1952, *FRUS*, 1952–54, VI:1565–69.

98. Quoted in Russel Brooks (Lyon) to State Dept., 12 June 1947; Caffery to Sec. State, 7 Sept. 1947; Memo Conv. Boulloche-Bonbright, 30 Sept. 1947, all in 851.00, RG59, NA. Cf. esp. Georges-Henri Soutou, "Georges Bidault et la construction européenne, 1944–1954," in Bernstein, Mayeur, and Milza, *Le MRP*; Ritsch, *The French Left*, 19–26.

99. Letter Dunn to Dowling, 1 Mar. 1949, 865.00, RG59, NA. Ventrone, "L'avventura americana"; Elisabetta Vezzosi, "La sinistra democristiana tra neutralismo e patto atlantico," in Di Nolfo, Rainero, and Vigezzi, *L'Italia*, 197–201; Pombeni, *Le "Cronache Sociali,"* esp. 46, 165, and chap. 4. See also Nacci, "La civiltà non cattolica"; cf. Giorgio Rumi, "Un anti-americanismo di 'la Civiltà Cattolica'?," and Vera Capperucci, "Le correnti della Democrazia cristiana di fronte all'America. Tra differenziazione culturale ed integrazione politica, 1944–1954," both in Craveri and Quagliarello, *L'anti-americanismo*.

100. D'Attorre, "Americanism and Anti-Americanism in Italy," 46–84; Formigoni, "La sinistra cattolica," 659–60; Capperucci, "Le correnti della DC," 270–89; Soutou, "Georges Bidault."

101. The above paragraph follows David Ellwood's arguments and quotations drawn, in this order, from Ellwood, "'You Too Can Be Like Us,'" 37; Ellwood, *Rebuilding Europe*, 180; and Ellwood, "The Propaganda," 232.

102. Memo Conv. Caffery, Queille, Marshall, 18 Nov. 1948, *FRUS*, 1948, III:677–82.

103. Intelligence Report no. 6140, "The French Communist Party: Its 1952 Record and Prospects for 1953," 30 Dec. 1952, OIR, RG59, NA.

104. Caffery to Sec. State, 5 Oct. 1948. On de Gaulle's economic ineptitude, see Hicker-

son to Labouisse, 12 Oct. 1948, *FRUS*, 1948, III:662–67. Memo L. M. Dayton to Ambassadors Draper, Bunker, et al., 7 June 1952, Recs. US For. Assistance Agencies, 1948–61, Mission to Italy, Office Director Subj. Files, 1948–57, b. 36, RG469, Entry 1259, NA; Ellwood, "Italy, Europe and the Cold War," 36.

105. Hogan, *The Marshall Plan*, 19; Maier, "The Politics of Productivity," 608–10.

106. Caffery to Sec. State, 22 Dec. 1948, 851.00, RG59, NA.

107. Policy Paper by the Foreign Assistance Correlation Committee, 7 Feb. 1949, Memo by Undersec. State, 2 June 1949, *FRUS*, 1949, I:250–57, 326; Douglas to Sec. State, 26 Mar. 1949, *FRUS*, 1949, IV:250–51; Hickerson to Williams, 27 Nov. 1948, PPS Recs. 1947–53, Lot 64 D563, b. 27, RG59, NA.

108. See esp. Pach, *Arming the Free World*, chaps. 5 and 7.

109. Bruce to Sec. State, 7 Oct. 1949, *FRUS*, 1949, IV:668–96.

110. Bruce to State Dept., 1 Sept. 1950, Byroade (German Affairs, Dept. State) to Marshall (Sec. Defense), 16 Oct. 1950, Bonsal (Chargé in Paris) to Sec. State, 16 Oct. 1950 (first quote), *FRUS*, 1950, III:1383–87, 1408–12, 1416–17.

111. For commentary on De Gasperi's advocacy of Art. 2, see Bohlen to Acheson, 21 Feb. 1949, Bohlen Recs., Corresp., b. 1, RG59, NA. On Italian arguments regarding the peace treaty, see Docs. in *FRUS*, 1951, IV:606–18. Cf. Timothy Smith, *The United States*.

112. Dunn to Sec. State, 21 Jan. 1952, *FRUS*, 1952–54, VI:1565–69; Acting U.S. Special Rep. in Europe (Porter) to Acting Administrator for Economic Cooperation (Bissel), 6 Sept. 1951, *FRUS*, 1951, III:265–67.

113. Memo by Dept. State for the President, 5 Jan. 1951, *FRUS*, 1951, III:396–400.

114. Bruce to State, 22 Sept. 1950, *FRUS*, 1950, III:311–14. On European unity's fostering security *and* solvency, see Memo Norrall to Drummond, 1 Aug. 1950, OSR Info. Div., Subj. File, "Mission Memoranda" subf., RG286, NA.

115. Bruce to Sec. State, 28 July 1950, *FRUS*, 1950, III:151–58. Nitze first expressed this opinion in early 1949 when he was assistant secretary of state for economic affairs; Memo Nitze, 31 Jan. 1949, *FRUS*, 1949, IV:54–60.

116. For a different opinion, see Hitchcock, *France Restored*; and Creswell, *A Question*.

Chapter 4

1. See esp. Yves Santamaria, "Intellectuals, Pacifism, and Communism: The Mandarins and the Struggle for Peace (1914–1953)," in Jennings, *Intellectuals*, 131. See also Santamaria, "D'Amsterdam à Stockholm"; Santamaria, *Le pacifisme*; and Santamaria, *Le parti de l'ennemi*, 49–74. On early PCI initiatives against the Atlantic Pact, see esp. Vecchio, *Pacifisti*, 49–61, 72–86; Guiso, *La colomba*, 5–143; and Mariuzzo, "Stalin."

2. Cf. Fisher, *Romain Rolland*, 148–77; and Jozef Laptos, "Le pacifisme apprivoisé: Le Congrès des intellectuels pour la défense de la paix en 1948," in Vaïsse, *Le pacifisme*. See also Wolton, *La France*, 110–11, which, however, exaggerates the instrumentality of Paris for Soviet designs.

3. Philippe Buton, "Le pacifisme communiste de la Seconde guerre mondiale à la Guerre froide," in Vaïsse, *Le pacifisme*, 318–22; Wall, *French Communism*, 97–98. On communist success in appropriating the word *peace*, see Caute, *The Fellow-Travellers*, 279.

4. Le Cour Grandmaison, "Le mouvement," 125; Giacomini, *I partigiani*, 63–126; Gozzini and Martinelli, *Dall'attentato*, 174.

5. At the end of 1950 Thorez boasted that it was the French-led campaign that dissuaded the United States from using the atomic bomb in Korea; Bohlen to Sec., 27 Dec. 1950, *FRUS*, 1950, III:1451–53; Nenni, in Giacomini, *I partigiani*, 54–55.

6. Riva, *Oro*, 156–57, 194–98, 223–32. On desire for peace among Italy's conservatives, see Lanaro, *Storia*, 117.

7. Dec. BP, 23 Sept. 1948, APCF.

8. "Vietnam proves that the Marshall Plan was from the onset a war pact," said Jacques Duclos at the political bureau; Duclos in BP, 17 Feb. 1950, APCF. See also Dec. BP, 21 July, 6 Oct. 1949, APCF.

9. The protest against rearmament started early; see "Direttive di lavoro della risoluzione del Comitato centrale," 4–6 May 1948, in Circolari e decisioni scritte, mf. 219, APCI. First quote from Memo Stanley Wolff (WEA) to Williams (Deputy Director WEA), 10 Oct. 1951, *FRUS*, 1951, IV:721–23; second quote from "Nota alla segreteria dalla sezione economica" (Scoccimarro), 17 Dec. 1953, VS, APCI.

10. Palmiro Togliatti, "L'Italia e la guerra," *Rinascita*, July 1950.

11. Dec. BP, 19 Aug. 1948, APCF; VD, 23 Sept. 1949, APCI; See also VD, 12 Apr. 1950 (Scoccimarro report); on "marshallization" bringing war and pauperization, see, e.g., Duclos in CC, 16–17 June 1953, APCF.

12. Report Duclos CC, 3 Sept. 1952 (Montreuil-sous-Bois), APCF; "Direttive di lavoro . . . ," 4–6 May 1948, 4–6 May 1948, in Circolari e decisioni scritte, mf. 219, APCI.

13. Nenni, qtd. in Vecchio, "Movimenti pacifisti," 7. See also Ruggero Grieco, "La guerra e la pace secondo il marxismo," *Rinascita*, July 1950; also qtd. in Vecchio, "Movimenti pacifisti," 2.

14. Lecoeur at CC, 18 June 1952 (Gennevilliers), APCF. Even when the peace movement was declining by 1953, the party leaders praised CGT action as its most effective feature; see Dec. BP, 3 Dec. 1953, APCF. On CGIL, see interventions of Sereni, Roveda, and Togliatti in Mtg. Direz., 24 Jan. 1950; and Scoccimarro in Mtg. Direz., 12 Apr. 1950, VD, APCI.

15. "Appunti per l'organizzazione della petizione per la pace," Mtg. Direz., 12 Apr. 1949, VD, APCI; for quotation about tactical extension of appeal, see Dec. BP, 24 Aug. 1950, APCF.

16. On the PCI and the prospect of nuclear armageddon, cf. Guiso, *La colomba*, 311–34; on PCF, see Santamaria, *Le parti de l'ennemi*, 111–38.

17. Yvonne Dumont, "Pour l'enfance, fleur de la vie, contre les semineurs de mort," *Cahiers du communisme*, June 1950; "Direttive di lavoro . . . ," 4–6 May 1948, in Circolari e decisioni scritte, mf. 219, APCI; Dec. BP, 20 Apr. 1950 and 3 Dec. 1953, APCF. Stil in CC, 3–4 Sept. 1952 (Montreuil), APCF. On similar campaigns denouncing Italy's occupants, see "É tornata l'aria di tombolo," and G. Arduini, "Gli americani a Trieste hanno trovato l'America," *Vie Nuove*, no. 27, 1951, no. 38, 1953.

18. Santamaria, *Le parti de l'ennemi*, 212–27; Pigenet, *Au coeur*; "Con un grande comizio Roma dirà il 'no' al gauleiter americano," and Gian Carlo Pajetta, "Protesta patriottica," both in *L'Unità*, 18 Jan. 1951 (also in Vecchio, "Movimenti pacifisti," 16).

19. Party directive qtd. in Le Cour Grandmaison, "Le mouvement," 128. Nenni in Vecchio, "Movimenti pacifisti," 12; see also Nenni, *Tempo*, 509–10. Lecoeur in CC, 4 Sept. 1952, APCF.

20. Mtg. Direz., 26 Sept. 1951, VD, APCI; see also Dec. BP, 20 Apr. 1950, APCF.

21. Lecoeur in CC, 13–14 Feb. 1952 (Aubervilliers), APCF.

22. "L'Italia portaerei americana," *Vie Nuove*, 9 Mar. 1952; Dec. BP, 6 Nov. 1947, and 30 June 1950, APCF; Tillon's letter qtd. in Roger, *The American Enemy*, 323; Thorez in Dec. BP, 1 Dec. 1949, APCF; cf. For PCI's analogies of Mussolini's vicarious imperialism to Nazi Germany, see Togliatti, "Verità e menzogna sulle armi atomiche," *Rinascita*, May 1950; and Togliatti, "L'Italia e la guerra," *Rinascita*, July 1950.

23. Luigi Astesano, "Come i comunisti lottano per la pace," *Rinascita*, Dec. 1948; Galeazzi, *Togliatti*, 101–35; Mtg. Direz., 18 Sept. 1953, 20 May 1954, VD, APCI. De Gasperi tried to convince Truman that if the peace campaign could be offset with allied concessions on Trieste, the PCI's nationalist appeal would be thwarted and "the remaining problem in Italy w[ould] be largely economic"; Mtg. de Gasperi–Truman, 25 Sept. 1951, *FRUS*, 1951, IV:701.

24. Gozzini and Martinelli, *Dall'attentato*, 199–210; Bianchini, "Le PCI et le cas Magnani"; Robrieux, *Histoire intérieure*, 309–32; Courtois and Lazar, *Histoire*, 273–75 (271 on competition between the PCI and the PCF). These events cost the peace movement external support; see Le Cour Grandmaison, "Le mouvement," 124–25.

25. Both qtd. in Lazar, *Maisons*, 67; cf. Vecchio, *Pacifisti*, 181–92.

26. Dec. BP, 3 Mar. 1949, 6 Apr. 1951, 28 Jan. 1954, 31 Dec. 1954, APCF.

27. Dec. BP, 6 and 21 Apr. 1951, APCF; Roger Garaudy, "Le piège des Etats-Unis d'Europe," and "Eisenhower sans légende," *Cahiers du communisme*, Feb. 1949, Feb. 1951; Mtg. Direz., 5 Nov. 1953, 8 Jan. 1954 (Sereni quotation on p. 3), VD, APCI.

28. In *L'Humanité*, 11 Sept. 1952; cited also in Le Cour Grandmaison, "Le mouvement," 135 (see also 130–36). On the PCF's troubles following strict Soviet directives and turnabouts on the German question, see Santamaria, *Le parti de l'ennemi*, 185–210; and Philippe Buton, "Le mouvement des Partisans de la paix," in Dockrill et al., *L'Europe*, 236–38. Cf. Vecchio, *Pacifisti*; and Gozzini and Martinelli, *Dall'attentato*, 149.

29. Pons, "Stalin," 25; Lazar, *Maisons*, 79–80.

30. The State Department defined the peace movement as "the most important political instrument in Soviet hands for furthering the campaign of neutralism in Europe"; Memo Perkins (Asst. Sec. State Eur. Affairs) to Sec. State, 22 Sept. 1950, and Background Paper Public Affairs Policy Adv. Staff, n.d., *FRUS*, 1950, V:329, 327.

31. Pajetta-Sereni in Mtg. Direz., 4 Feb. 1954, VD, APCI. On PCF and trade with East, see Bruce to State Dept., 1 Oct. 1951, 751.00, RG59, NA; and Joanny Berlioz, "Europe, nation, internationalisme," *Cahiers du communisme*, July 1949, quotations on 816–19.

32. Romero, "L'Europa"; Giuseppe Berti, "Le contraddizioni dell' imperialismo americano," *Rinascita*, Aug.–Sept. 1949; "Inchiesta sulla CED," *Vie Nuove*, no. 22 (1954). In 1947 the PCI set out to participate in the European Federalist Movement, based in Milan, in order to "oppose the policy of blocs," and to "defend our positions within that framework" (quotations from Tel. 2892 to Movimento Federalista Europeo, 4 Aug. 1947, and Mtg. Segr., 5 Aug. 1947, VS, APCI). The Cominform's two-camp strategy did not affect this choice.

33. Quotation from Dec. BP, 2 Apr. 1954; cf. Dec. BP, 28 Jan. 1954, APCF; Report Duclos at CC, 3 Sept. 1952, APCF.

34. Mtg. Direz., 15 June 1950, VD, p. 6; "Dio e il Patto atlantico," *Rinascita*; Mtg. Direz., 6 Apr. 1954 (p. 4), VD, APCI. On Giordani and La Pira, cf. Vecchio, *Pacifisti*, 21, 133–34, 315–24. On war psychosis in Italy favoring neutralist sentiments in the early 1950s, see Simona Colarizi, "La Seconda guerra mondiale e la Repubblica," in Galasso, *Storia*, 652–57.

35. Dec. BP, 9 June, 15 July 1949 (in 1949, the French Episcopate tried to excommu-

nicate Catholics who supported the Peace Partisans); Dec. BP, 24 Aug. 1950, 11 Jan. 1951, APCF; Victor Leduc, "Le Vatican et les princes de l'Eglise contre l'Union des partisans de la paix," *Cahiers du communisme*, Apr. 1952.

36. BP, 11 Jan. 1951, and Dec. BP, 26 Sept. 1952, 2 June 1953, APCF; "Appunti per l'organizzazione della petizione per la pace," Mtg. Direz., 12 Apr. 1949, VD, APCI.

37. Dec. BP, 6 Nov. 1948, APCF; Sereni in Mtg. Direz., 6 Dec. 1950, p. 10, VD, APCI; Paul Belmigère, "L'idéologie socialdémocrate au service de l'impérialisme," *Cahiers du communisme*, Mar. 1952.

38. Courtois and Lazar call the PCF's anti-EDC campaign "ingenious"; Courtois and Lazar, *Histoire*, 285. Memo "Le fasi della Missione De Gasperi negli Stati Uniti," 28 Sept. 1951, Documenti Riservati, M, mf. 196, APCI.

39. Dulles to Emb. Paris, 12 Aug. 1954, *FRUS*, 1952–54, V:1029–31; Soutou, "La France"; Sforza in J. H. F. Ferguson to Greene (WEA), 13 Apr. 1951, PPS Recs., b. 18, RG59, NA. PSB D-37 "Evaluations of the Psychological Impact of U.S. Foreign Economic Policies and Programs in France," 9 Feb. 1953, WHO, NSC Staff, PSB, b. 14, DDEL. Cf. Vardabasso, "La CED."

40. Quotations from Birchall, *Sartre against Stalinism*, 136; cf. Jean-Paul Sartre, "The Chances of Peace," *Nation*, 30 Dec. 1950.

41. Erenburg and Banfi, qtd. in Vecchio, "Movimenti pacifisti," 9–10.

42. Simone Téry, "La grande enquête," *L'Humanité*, 8 May 1951; Togliatti in Vecchio, "Movimenti pacifisti," 19.

43. PSB D-37, "Evaluations of the Psychological Impact of U.S. Foreign Economic Policies and Programs in France," 9 Feb. 1953, WHO, NSC Staff, PSB, b. 14, DDEL.

44. This is Santamaria's conclusion in *Le parti de l'ennemi*, 348–49.

45. For these arguments, see Aga-Rossi and Zaslavsky, *Togliatti e Stalin*, 268–80; and sources cited by authors.

46. Memo "French and Italian Elections," 6 July 1951, SMOF, PSB, b. 11, HSTL.

47. Eisenhower in Gaddis, *Strategies*, 152; PSB, "Notes on a Grand Strategy for Psychological Operations," 1 Oct. 1951, SMOF, PSB, HSTL; also in Del Pero, "The United States," 1305 (cf. remarks on 1304–6). Also on total conflict, see Osgood, *Total Cold War*.

48. Memo Office of Asst. Sec. State Public Affairs, Apr. 1950 (date unspecified), *FRUS*, 1950, V:296–302; Campaign of Truth in Editorial Note, ibid., 304; Memo A. E. Manell (USIE), 15 July 1952, 511.51, RG59, NA. Cf. Hixson, *Parting the Curtain*, 11–16; Lucas, "Campaigns."

49. C. Tyler Wood (ECA U.S. Special Rep. in Europe) to Howard Bruce, 5 Feb. 1951, C. T. Wood Papers, b. 4, GMF. See also Acheson in Harper, *American Visions*, 293.

50. Alphand in McCloy to Sec. State, 4 June 1951, *FRUS*, 1951, I:785–86; *Combat* in Harper, *American Visions*, 321.

51. Quotations from USIS Report on "VOA Broadcasting," Rome, Mar. 1950, 511.65, RG59, NA; cf. Draft Paper U.S. State Dept., 9 Dec. 1949, *FRUS*, 1949, V:847–48 (section titled "Long-Range Program to Explode the Soviet Myth"). On systematic campaign, see "Report on European Trip, Aug. 22–Sept. 8, 1952," by Charles Norberg, Major, U.S. Air Force, SMOF, PSB, b. 11, HSTL.

52. NSC 68 in http://www.fas.org/irp/offdocs/nsc-hst/nsc-68.html, accessed 21 Feb. 2007. Lucas, *Freedom's War*, 79; Scott-Smith, *The Politics*, 41.

53. Caffery to Sec. State, 18 Mar. 1949, 851.00B; Memo H. Freeman Matthews to Bruce,

18 July 1951, 751.001, RG59, NA; Progress Report on various Psychological Operations in France and Italy, by OCB, 23 Feb. 1954, WHO, NSC Staff, OCB Central Files, b. 82, DDEL; on beginning of funding of Sogno's organization, see Memo Conv. Clare B. Luce with Sogno, 1 Apr. 1954, 765.001, RG59, NA; cf. Guasconi, *L'altra faccia*, 136–47. On ACUE, see Scott-Smith, *The Politics*, 76–77; quotation from Aldrich, *The Hidden Hand*, 343.

54. On U.S. encouragement of French and Italian statesmanship as leaders of Europe, see Brogi, *A Question*, chaps. 3–4. The following paragraphs resume and expand some of the book's arguments (140–44).

55. Edward P. Lilly, "The Psychological Strategy Board and Its Predecessors: Foreign Policy Coordination, 1938–1953," in Vincitorio, *Studies*, 363–66; Hixson, *Parting the Curtain*, 16–19; DDRS, 1996, 2901D. On OPC reassignment, see Memo Davis, 24 Oct. 1951, SMOF, PSB, b. 31, HSTL. Truman, previously an infrequent participant in the NSC, now began to attend the meetings regularly in order to help carry out the offensive against Soviet propaganda; Rothkopf, *Running the World*, 49–60.

56. Dunn to Sec. State, 11 July 1952, and Bruce to Sec. State, 27 Dec. 1951, PSB, b. 1, RG59, NA. Bonbright to Webb, 19 Sept. 1951, 751.001, RG59, NA; Lenap Committee, 23 July 1952, SMOF, PSB, b. 23, HSTL.

57. Panel C, "Plan B," Draft, 13 Nov. 1951, SMOF, PSB, b. 24, HSTL; Memo Gray to Sec. State, "Reduction of Communist Power . . . in France and Italy," 5 Dec. 1951, 751.001, RG59, NA; cf. Del Pero, *L'alleato*, 151. Quotation from Public Affairs Officer Emb. France (Tyler) to Sec. State, 3 Feb. 1950, *FRUS*, III:1357–59; practice of indirect propaganda confirmed in PSB D-29, "Evaluation of the Psychological Effect of U.S. National Effort in Italy," 26 Feb. 1953, b. 1; USIS Semi-annual Eval., Paris, 15 July 1952, 511.51, RG59, NA.

58. PSB, Panel C [coordinating the two plans and eventually renamed LENAP Committee], Sub-Committee on Present Actions, "Reduction of Communist Strength and Influence in France and Italy," 26 Oct. 1951, SMOF, PSB, b. 24, HSTL; PSB D-14 "Psychological Operations for the Reduction of Communist Power in France—'Cloven,'" (best version 12 Dec. 1951), and PSB D-15, "Psychological Operations . . . in Italy—'Demagnetize,'" 21 Feb. 1951, ibid., b. 5 and 7; Mtg. Cloven-Demagnetize Coordinating C.ttee, 4 Apr. 1952, Mtg. Sub-Panel to Panel C, Sub-C.tee on Present Actions, 5 Nov. 1951, SMOF, PSB, b. 23 and 24, HSTL Cloven-Demagnetize C.ttee, 19 Mar. 1952, DDRS, 1991, 3398; PSB D-14-C (Midiron), 31 Jan. 1952, 751.001, and PSB D-15-C (Clydesdale), 765.001, RG59, NA.

59. III Mtg. PSB, 27 Sept. 1951, Bureau of European Affairs, Office of Eur. Regional Affairs, PSB, b. 1, RG59, NA; Del Pero, "The United States," 1314; Dunn to State Dept., Nov. 1950, 765.001, RG59, NA.

60. First quotation in Merchant to Dillon, 31 Dec. 1954, Lot Files 58D357, Subj. Files on Italy, 1944–56, b. 17, NA. Second quotation from PSB D-14, PSB D-14-C (Midiron), 31 Jan. 1952, 751.001 (p. 16), and Dunn (from Paris) to Sec. State, 8 May 1952, 751.001, RG59, NA.

61. Merchant to Dillon, Merchant to Dillon, 31 Dec. 1954, Lot Files 58D357, Subj. Files on Italy, 1944–56, b. 17, NA; Thompson to Sec. State, 3 Oct. 1951 (on link between PCI's campaigns for peace and for wages), 765.001, RG59; qtd. PSB D-29, "An Evaluation of the Psychological Effect of U.S. National Effort in Italy, 26 Feb. 1953 (p. 12), PSB, b. 4, RG59, NA; PSB D-14-C (Midiron) (pp. 16–17), 31 Jan. 1952, 751.001, and PSB D-15-C (Clydesdale) (p. 5 for argument that years of Italian dependence on the United States had also modified Italian attitudes toward America).

62. Cloven and Demagnetize Coordinating Committee, First Report to the Director of the PSB, 8 May 1952, PSB, b. 2, RG59, NA, cf. PSB D-14, and Merchant to Dillon, 31 Dec. 1954.

63. Hixson, *Parting the Curtain*, 19; Osgood, *Total Cold War*, 44–45; Lucas, *Freedom's War*, 128–54. For sources highlighting the PSB's importance, see Del Pero, "The United States"; Guasconi, *L'altra faccia*; and Wall, *The United States*, 213–18.

64. PSB D-14/a, p. 5; Del Pero, *L'alleato*, 102–3; Memo Cox to Sherman, "Economic Operations under LENAP," 30 June 1952, SMOF, PSB, b. 23, HSTL.

65. Memo Berger to Norberg, "French and Italian Projects—Priorities," 21 Oct. 1952, 751.001, RG59; second quote from Informational Guidance for 1952 to All MSA Information Officers, 16 Jan. 1952, Recs. U.S. Foreign Assist. Agencies, 1948–61, Mission France, Office of Director, Subj. Files, 1948–56, b. 3, Entry 1192, RG469, NA.

66. Panel qtd. in Dunn to Sec. State, 20 Aug. 1952, PSB, b. 1. On the "middle path," see L. E. Thompson to H. Freeman Matthews, 23 Aug. 1951, 765.001; Bonbright to Acting Sec. State, 20 Feb. 1952, PSB, b. 1, RG59, NA.

67. Memo (Berger), "French and Italian Elections," 6 July 1951, SMOF, PSB, 091.4 Europe, b. 11, HSTL.

68. Vecchio, "Movimenti pacifisti," 24–25; Lazar, "The Cold War Culture," 221; Kuisel, *Seducing the French*, 33; quotation from "Report on Foreign Public Op.—French Attitudes toward the U.S.," 11 Sept. 1953, USIA Recs., b. 2, RG306, NA.

69. Mtg. LENAP, 8 Oct. 1952, SMOF, PSB, b. 23, HSTL; Rep. Duclos at CC, 3 Sept. 1952, APCF; Dunn to State Dept., 21 Jan. 1952, *FRUS*, 1952–54, VI:1565–69; Dunn to State Dept., 26 Aug. 1952, 511.51, RG59, NA.

70. Dunn to State Dept., 25 July 1952, *FRUS*, 1952–54, VI:1234–35.

71. Miller, "Roughhouse Diplomacy," 298. Cf. Del Pero, *L'alleato*, 116–23; Guasconi, *L'altra faccia*, 65–92. The best source on State Dept. opposition is Lucas, *Freedom's War*, 143–54.

72. See esp. Osgood, *Total Cold War*, 55, 82–88.

73. Jackson Committee Report, *FRUS*, 1952–54, II:1838; for a different opinion, see Osgood, *Total War*, 99–103 (quotation from 99). Quotation from Ninkovich, *Modernity*, 212–14. On the administration's "white propaganda," see esp. Yarrow, "Selling," 28–40.

74. On rollback in Western Europe, see Del Pero, *L'alleato*, 178–84.

75. Dunn (Paris—LENAP) to Sec. State, 4 Dec. 1952, 751.001, RG59, NA; PSB Draft of Western European Plan, 17 Mar. 1953, cited in Osgood, *Total Cold War*, 110.

76. Osgood, *Total Cold War*, 88–93; Ninkovich, *The Diplomacy*, conclusions; Tobia, *Advertising America*, 106–19.

77. Dillon to State Dept., 4 Aug. 1953, *FRUS*, 1952–54, VI:1372–75; Dillon to Sec. State, 31 Mar. 1954, Paris Emb. Recs., EDC and Intl. Org. 1951–55, RG84, NA.

78. On inner circle, see Hixson, *Parting the Curtain*, 22–37; Cook, *The Declassified Eisenhower*, 123–27; and Martin, *Henry and Clare*, 301–3. One State Department official described Dulles as "obsessed with his God-ordained mission to reverse the tide of international communism"; Broadwater, *Anti-Communist Crusade*, 114.

79. Luce to Jackson, 18 June 1953, *FRUS*, 1952–54, VI:1612–13. Cf. Ortona, *La diplomazia*, 16–19, 57–76; Luce to Gen. Alfred Gruenther (Supreme Commander NATO), 11 Dec. 1953, PPS Recs. Lot File 64D563, b. 72e "Italy," RG59, NA; Gruenther to Luce, 18 Dec. 1953, Gruenther Papers, b. 1, DDEL.

80. Memo Berger, 6 July 1951, "French and Italian Elections," 6 July 1951, SMOF, PSB, 091.4 Europe, b. 11, HSTL; Dillon to State Dept. (LENAP), 28 Sept. 1953, 751.001, RG59, NA. NSC 5411/2 "U.S. Policy toward Italy," fully declass. version in Recs. State Dept. Particip. in NSC, 1947–63, Lot File 63D351, RG59, NA; Memo Conv. Eisenhower–J. F. Dulles, Hoover Jr.–Merchant, 30 Oct. 1954, JFDP, White House Memo Series, b. 1, DDEL. On Luce, see also Del Pero, "American Pressures," 421–25.

81. Galambos, *The Papers*; Winand, *Eisenhower*, 29–34; Dulles in Ninkovich, *Modernity*, 214. Cf. François David, "Du Traité de Versailles à Jean Monnet: John Foster Dulles est-il un père de l'Europe?," in Barjot and Réveillard, *L'américanisation*.

82. PSB Draft of Western European Plan, 17 Mar. 1953; NSC 5509, Status of USIA Program, 2 Mar. 1955, *FRUS*, 1955–57, IX:504–21; Dulles to Rome Emb. 27 Nov. 1953, Recs. State Dept. in OCB (Lot File 62D430), b. 33, RG59, NA; PSB D-38 "A National Psychological Strategy for Western Europe," 23 Feb. 1954, WHO, NSC Files, b. 82, DDEL.

83. Gaddis, *Strategies*, 127–34. On Ike and withdrawal from Europe, see Winand, *Eisenhower*, 36; Trachtenberg, *A Constructed Peace*, 147–56; and Ed. Note, *FRUS*, 1955–57, IV:349.

84. "Report on European Trip 1952, Aug. 22–Sept. 8, 1952," by Charles Norberg, Major, U.S. Air Force, SMOF, PSB, b. 11, HSTL (pp. 23–24). On Laniel, see Dillon to Sec. State, 7 Aug. 1953, Recs. U.S. Foreign Assist. Agencies, 1948–61, Mission France, Office Director, Subj. Files, 1948–56, b. 115, RG469, NA. Dillon to State Dept., 28 Sept. 1953, 751.001, RG59, NA.

85. Quotation from PSB D-29, PSB D-29, "An Evaluation of the Psychological Effect of U.S. National Effort in Italy," 26 Feb. 1953 (p. 9), PSB, b. 4, RG59, NA. Tasca to Merchant, 28 June 1955, WEA, Italian Desk, f. "Luce," RG59, NA., Tasca to State Dept., 3 Sept. 1954, *FRUS*, 1952–54, VI:1699–1700; Del Pero, "American Pressures," 414–21.

86. PSB D-15/a (p. 15), SMOF, PSB, b. 5, HSTL. Mtg. Luce– Vittorio Valletta (FIAT), 11 Mar. 1955, BEA, WEA, Recs., Austrian and Italian Desk Files, Italy, 1953–56, Lot File 58D71, RG59, NA; Del Pero, "American Pressures," 425–26; Sebesta, *L'Europa*, 218–30. On the patriotic PCI, see James Bonbright–II. Freeman Matthews, 11 July 1951, SMOF, PSB, b. 5, HSTL.

87. Luce to Henry Luce, 31 Oct. 1954, CBLP, b. X22, LC; Del Pero, "Containing Containment"; Del Pero, *L'alleato*, 207–95; cf. Ferraresi, *Threats*.

88. Thompson to Sec. State, 26 July 1951, 765.001, RG59, NA; Mtg. LENAP, 8 Oct. 1952, SMOF, PSB, b. 23, HSTL.

89. Dunn to State Dept., 17 Feb. 1953; Dulles to Emb. Paris, 26 Mar.; Dillon to Sec. State, 20 Sept. 1953, US Del. Tripartite For. Ministers Mtg. State Dept., 18 Oct. 1953, *FRUS*, 1952–54, V:732–33, 781–84, 808–12, 826–27.

90. Letter Mendès-France to Laniel, 21 May 1954, in JFD, Gen. Corresp. and Memo, b. 3, DDEL; cf. Mtg. Pinay-Dulles, 2 Oct. 1953, *FRUS*, 1952–54, VI:1389–91; Dillon to State Dept., Dulles to Emb. Paris, 12 Aug. 1954, *FRUS*, 1952–54, VI:1026–33; Serge Bernstein, "The Perception of French Power by the Political Forces," in Becker and Knipping, *Power in Europe?*

91. Quotation from Del Pero, "The United States," 1329. Cf. Luce to State Dept., 15 Dec. 1954, *FRUS*, 1952–54, VI:1714; J. F. Dulles to Luce, Apr. (n.d.), 1955, Subj. Files of the INR, 1945–60, Lot File 58 D 776, b. 12, RG59, NA; and Rossi, "Il governo Scelba."

92. De Gasperi had firmly established this point, in conjunction with his campaign for

the implementation of NATO's Article 2, during his visit to the United States in September 1951, and his successors never departed from it; Mtg. de Gasperi–Acheson, 24 Sept. 1951, *FRUS*, 1951, IV:681–87.

93. See chap. 6.

94. De Castro, *La questione*, 265–77, 822–23; Mtg. Eisenhower-Gronchi, 28 Feb. 1956, *FRUS*, 1955–57, XXVII:337–39; Ortona, *La diplomazia*, 151–76.

95. Rep. 283 Quaroni (Paris) to MAE, 27 Feb. 1954, DGAP, ASMAE; PSB D-37, "Evaluations of the Psychological Impact of U.S. Foreign Economic Policies and Programs in France," 9 Feb. 1953, WHO, NSC Staff, PSB, b. 14, DDEL; NSC 160/1, 17 Aug. 1953, AW, NSC Series, Policy Papers Subs.; Luce to Eisenhower, 11 Apr. 1955, AW, Intl. Series, b. 30, f. 7, DDEL; Dillon to Sec. State, 7 Oct. 1954, 751.001, RG59, NA.

Chapter 5

1. Comparative studies of U.S. and Soviet propaganda include, recently, Caute, *The Dancer*; and, on French and Italian Communists, the works of Marcello Flores, Marc Lazar, and Cyrille Guyat. Other authors cited in this book who deal extensively and noncomparatively with one of the two Communist Parties' or the United States' cultural cold war strategies are Volker Berghahn, Frances Stonor Saunders, Victoria de Grazia, Walter Hixson, Nicolas Cull, Giles Scott-Smith, Brian Angus McKenzie, Peter Coleman, Yves-Henri Nouailhat, Pierre Grémion, Luigi Bruti Liberati, Simona Tobia, Stephen Gundle, Albertina Vittoria, Nello Ajello, Patrick McCarthy, Richard Kuisel, Marie-Claire Lavabre, Yves Santamaria, Philippe Roger, David Drake, Gino Raymond, and Irwin Wall.

2. Lazar, *Maisons*, 69.

3. Salinari, "Promemoria sul lavoro culturale" to PCI Secretariat, in Mtg. Secretariat, 11 July 1951, VS, mf. 191, APCI.

4. Report Thorez at CC, 29–30 Oct. 1947, Paris (pp. 19–20), CC, print copies, APCF.

5. Kennan in Scott-Smith, *The Politics*, 43; Macdonald, qtd. in Wreszin, *A Rebel*, 254–55. On *The Seven Arts*, see esp. Kroes, *If You've Seen One*, 48–59.

6. Cf. Chappell, *A Stone*, 27; Suri, *Henry Kissinger*, 117.

7. Richard M. Bissell, "The Impact of Rearmament on the Free World Economy," *Foreign Affairs* 29 (Apr. 1951): 404–5; Luce (letter) to Eisenhower, 20 Aug. 1954, AW, AS, b. 25, DDEL.

8. PSB D-37, "Evaluations of the Psychological Impact of U.S. Foreign Economic Policies and Programs in France," 9 Feb. 1953, WHO, NSC Staff, PSB, b. 14, DDEL; on Sartre and individualism, see chap. 1.

9. Eisenhower, qtd. in Osgood, *Total Cold War*, 54 (quotation from author, 57).

10. Quotation from Caute, *The Dancer*, 6–8. Zubok, *A Failed Empire*, 103–4.

11. Caute, *The Dancer*, 7.

12. This was Roger Garaudy's statement in an article published by *Les Lettres françaises* in November 1946.

13. All these quotations, including de Beauvoir's statements, are from Roger, *The American Enemy*, 397–98. My conclusions are however slightly different; for an alternative view, see Caute, *The Dancer*, 11.

14. Report Sereni for Cultural Commission, Mtg. Cult. Comm. 15–16 June 1949, Cult. Comm., APCI. On reactions to Lysenkoism, see also Ajello, *Intellettuali*, 262–68. Cf. Vittoria, "La commissione."

15. Gundle, *Between Hollywood and Moscow*, 49–52; Stephen Gundle, "The Legacy of the *Prison Notebooks*: Gramsci, the PCI and Italian Culture in the Cold War Period," in Duggan and Wagstaff, *Italy*; Vittoria, *Togliatti*, 20–22. Brunetta, *Storia*.

16. Resolution "Contro l'oscurantismo imperialista e clericale," Aug. 1949, Cult. Comm, APCI; see comments in "Relazione sull'attività culturale del PCI dal VI al VII Congresso," n.d., 1950, esp. pp. 7–13, in ibid.; Mazzeri, "Comunisti"; cf. Gundle, *Between Hollywood and Moscow*, 55–57; Amendola and Ferrara, *É la festa*. On mass theater, see, most recently, Guiso, *La colomba*, 517–28. Similar theater initiatives were resumed in the early 1960s; see Guiat, *The French and Italian Communist Parties*, 131–39.

17. Giulio Trevisani, "La cultura popolare," *Rinascita*, Dec. 1952; Gundle, *Between Hollywood and Moscow*, 67–70; *Vie Nuove*, 2 July 1950 (also highlighted by Gundle).

18. Report Thorez at CC, 29–30 Oct. 1947, Paris (pp. 19–20), CC, print copies, APCF. Cf. Wall, *French Communism*, 69; Marie, *Le cinéma*, 67–86.

19. Gérôme and Tartakowsky, *La Fête*.

20. Lazar, *Maisons*, 209.

21. Lavabre, "La collection." In the 1930s, the *Almanach* changed its name from *Almanach ouvrier et paysan* to *Almanach de "L'Humanité."*

22. Gundle, *Between Hollywood and Moscow*, 55, 68; Kriegel, *The French Communists*, 357–64.

23. On this point, see Carlo Lizzani, "I film per il 'Partito nuovo,'" in Tranfaglia, *Il 1948*; Marcello Flores, "Il PCI, il PCF, gli intellettuali: 1943–1950," in Aga-Rossi and Quagliarello, *L'altra faccia*, 115–16.

24. Report Sascia Villari, in Mtg. Commissione Nazionale Stampa e Propaganda, 20 Oct. 1952, Cult. Comm., APCI. Mtg. Direz., 25 Sept. 1952, VD, mf. 261 and Mtg. Direz., 6 Dec. 1950, VD, mf. 190, APCI. On the evolution of Italian cinema in the 1950s, see Gundle, "Hollywood Glamour," esp. 104–12.

25. Ramette in CC, 26 Mar. 1952 (Saint-Denis), transcripts of CD no. 3, APCF; cf. report by Gaston Monmousseau, in ibid., CD no. 2. At the next CC meeting in Saint-Denis, in 1954, Etienne Fajon acknowledged that the content and style of *L'Humanité* was "ennuyeux" and recommended that its reporters stop mimicking the "grand masters of French journalism" and become more "accessible to the masses"; CC, Saint-Denis, 12 Nov. 1954, print copies, 261 J 2/30, APCF.; Dec. BP, 24 Nov., 29 Dec. 1955, APCF.

26. Dec. BP, 14 Oct. 1954, APCF; cf. Rep. Villari to Commissione Stampa e Propaganda, 20 Oct. 1952, Cult. Comm., APCI.

27. Report Salinari to Cultural Commission, 6 July 1951 (see also Report by Antonio Banfi to Cultural Commission, 30 Oct. 1951), Cult. Comm., APCI.

28. Salinari at Mtg. Commissione Nazionale Stampa and Propaganda, 20 Oct. 1952, Cult. Comm., APCI; Mtg. Direz., 18 Mar. 1955, no. 117, APCI. Two years earlier, Italo Calvino had said that "Italian cinema was a citadel against American colonization" then added, in reference to Rossellini's most famous postwar movie, "Must literature remain an 'open city?'"; Calvino, "Letteratura città aperta?," *Rinascita*, Apr. 1949. On greater attention to mass culture under Salinari, see also Flores and Gallerano, *Sul PCI*, 199.

29. Alicata in Mtg. Direz., 18 Mar. 1955, VD, APCI. On the PCI as a cultural world of its own, see esp. Shore, *Italian Communism*, 10–14. On Alicata, see Lucia, *Intellettuali*, 178–82.

30. Dec. BP, 2 Apr. 1954, APCF. On book sales, cf. Caute, *The Fellow-Travellers*, 12–13; Lazar, "Les 'batailles.'" Quotation from Lavabre, "La collection," 109.

31. Rep. Salinari at Mtg. Cult. Comm. Nov. 1953, pp. 33–42, APCI; cf. Carlo Salinari, "Per battere l'oscurantismo clericale occorre il legame con la classe operaia," *Rinascita*, July 1953.

32. "L'offensiva del maccartismo contro il cinema italiano," *Rinascita*, Aug.–Sept. 1954; see also Tommaso Chiaretti, "Contenuto e prospettive del neorealismo italiano," *Rinascita*, Dec. 1953.

33. Louis Aragon, "Victor Hugo," *Les Lettres françaises*, 28 June 1951.

34. Kuisel, *Seducing the French*, 41–46; cf. Chebel d'Appollonia, *Le Temps*, 121–41.

35. Sanzo, *L'officina*, 255–83.

36. Franco Minganti, "Rock 'n' Roll in Italy: Was It True Americanization?," in Kroes, Rydell, and Bosscher, *Cultural Transmissions*, 143, 145. On Italian adaptations of rock 'n' roll, see also Capussotti, *Gioventù perduta*, 215–68. On the impact of rock and jazz rebel culture in both West and East, see a good example in Poiger, *Jazz*.

37. Alfredo Orecchio, "I fianchi di Elvis," *Vie Nuove*, 12 Nov. 1956; cf. Gianni Toti, "Sesseuropa," *Vie Nuove*, 3 Jan. 1964 (on the commercialization of sex in Europe thanks to American and British pop music). On early impact of rock 'n' roll in Italy, see Capussotti, *Gioventù perduta*, 215–34.

38. Both cited in Marc Lazar, "The Cold War Culture of the French and Italian Communist Parties," in Scott-Smith and Krabbendam, *The Cultural Cold War*, 221–22; see also Montebello, "Joseph Staline."

39. Rodolfo Sabbatini, "Forse tra loro un nuovo Joe Di Maggio," *Vie Nuove*, no. 47 (1953).

40. Mtg. Secretariat, 22 Sept. 1952, APCF; Marie, *Le cinéma*, 97–98; Umberto Barbaro, "Come interpretare Charlot," *Rinascita*, Oct.–Nov. 1957; Mino Argentieri, "L'ultimo re di Hollywood," *Vie Nuove*, 1960, no. 46.

41. Wagnleitner, "The Empire," 506; McKenzie, *Remaking France*, 33; Ninkovich, *The Diplomacy*, 119.

42. USIE Semi-annual Evaluation for Period 31 May–1 Dec. 1951, 29 Dec. 1951; William Tyler (Public Affairs Officer) to State Dept., 8 Feb. 1950, and USIS Semi-annual Evaluation of Cultural Activities (by Leslie S. Brady), 31 May 1950, 511.51, RG59, NA; Reports on the decline of communist press circulation in France seemed to confirm that *L'Humanité* and other periodicals were "embattled." In 1953 Theodor Achilles noted that the PCF had reduced its provincial dailies from thirty-two to fourteen, and that more than twenty leftist weeklies had folded in 1952; Tel. 2173, Achilles to State Dept., 2 Dec. 1953, USIA Country Plans, b. 2, RG306, NA; cf. Tyler to State Dept., 16 Aug. 1950, 511.51, RG59, NA. On the impact of American libraries, see also Osgood, *Total Cold War*, 104. On early USIS activity in France, cf. Nouailhat, "Aspects."

43. Among the first officials to appeal for "common interest" vs. disseminating information was Public Affairs Officer William R. Tyler; Tyler Report to State Dept., 16 Aug. 1950, 511.51, RG59, NA.

44. David W. Ellwood, "Il cinema e la proiezione del modello americano," in Ellwood and Brunetta, *Hollywood in Europa*, 25–26. On the impact of Hollywood in Italy and France, see also Shaw, *Hollywood's Cold War*, 23–33.

45. "USIE Motion Pictures and Filmstrip Activities for the Six Months Ending November 30, 1951," attached to USIE Evaluation, 31 May–1 Dec. 1951, 29 Dec. 1951, 511.51, RG59, NA; Progress Report by Lloyd A. Free (Director USIS Italy) to State Dept, 24 Feb. 1953, 511.65, RG59, NA. For an example of a Disney production for USIS, see a version of the

1954 *Infant Care and Feeding*, on http://www.youtube.com/watch?v=xJW7BoB7NM, accessed 1 Mar. 2008.

46. USIS Desp. 107 (no author, n.d., Dec. 1952), 511.51, Memo Conv. John Howard (Ford Foundation) with S. B. Wolff (WE-State Dept.), 16 July 1951, 511.65, RG59, NA.

47. Semi-annual Evaluation of Cultural Activities (by Leslie S. Brady), 31 May 1950, 511.51, RG59, NA; USIE Semi-annual Evaluation Report (by Outerbridge Horsey, Counselor of Embassy, Rome), 30 Nov. 1950 (forwarding "Libraries" evaluation by D. A. Bullard), 511.65, RG59, NA.

48. For an example of the first signs of the VOA's declining ratings, see USIS Report File No. 811.20200(D) (by Joseph Ravetto), Mar. 1950, 511.65, RG59, NA; see also Report Lloyd A. Free, 24 Feb. 1953, 511.65, RG59, NA. On films, see Guback, *The International Film Industry*, 40–46.

49. E.g., Letter John N. La Corte to J. F. Dulles, 17 Feb. 1953, JFD, Gen. Corr. Series, b. 5, DDEL; Lloyd A. Free, 24 Feb. 1953, 511.65, RG59, NA; Tel. 22, Philip F. Dur (Consul Lyon), to State Dept., 10 Aug. 1950, 751.00, RG59, NA.

50. C. Burke Elbrick to William F. Clark (Asst. Director for Europe), 24 July 1956, 511.65, RG59, NA.

51. Dunn to State Dept., 15 Feb. 1949, 7 Dec. 1949, 865.00B; Dunn to State Dept., 19 Sept. 1950, 765.001, RG59, NA.

52. Semi-annual USIS Report, 15 July 1952; Semi-annual USIS Report 13 Jan. 1953, 511.51, RG59, NA; Memo Jack D. Neal to Williamson, 7 July 1950, Files ITALOT 600 (Italian Foreign Rels.), RG59, NA.

53. Esp. Hixson, *Parting the Curtain*, chaps. 5–6; de Grazia, *Irresistible Empire*, 446–57; Elizabeth Vihlen, "Jammin' on the Champs-Elysées: Jazz, France, and the 1950s," in May and Wagnleitner, *Here, There, and Everywhere*; and Yarrow, "Selling a New Vision," 40–44. On USIA's new initiatives in the mid- to late 1950s, see Cull, *The Cold War*, 104–61.

54. USIS Semi-annual Evaluation, 29 Dec. 1951, 511.51, RG59, NA; on Italy, cf. Bruti Liberati, *Words*.

55. See esp. Scott-Smith, *Networks*, 346–49; on Italy, see Combined (USIS/MSA) Information Services, Progress Report, 24 Feb. 1953, 511.65, RG59, NA.

56. USIS Semi-annual Evaluation for Period 1 Dec. 1951–31 May 1952, Paris, 15 July 1952, 511.51, RG59 USIS Semi-annual Evaluation, 29 Dec. 1951, 511.51, RG59, NA; Tobia, *Advertising America*, 268–80.

57. Scott-Smith, *Networks*.

58. Memo from Franco-American Commission (from Jambrun), Oct. 1973 (History of Commission), General Files, b. 111, CU.

59. Overseas Report of Dr. Walter Johnson, Member of U.S. Advisory Commission on International Education and Cultural Affairs, 1–28 Sept. 1962 (on both France [Duroselle qtd.] and Italy), General Files, b. 103, and Annual Report on the Educational Exchange Program, 1 July 1963–30 June 1964, 8 Oct. 1964, Group XVI, b. 317, CU. Cf. "Country Assessment Report for the Year 1960: France," 22 Mar. 1961, USIA Country Plans, West. Eur. (1955), 1958–1973, b. 4, RG306, NA. Cf. Tiziano Bonazzi, "The Beginnings of American History in Italy," in Arndt and Rubin, *The Fulbright Difference*; and Giorgio Spini, "America," in Jeannet and Barnett, *New World Journeys*, 105–6. On the Ford Foundation and Olivetti, see Berghahn, *America*, 171.

60. USIS Semi-annual Evaluation of Cultural Activities, 27 Dec. 1950, FP, Series 72, b. 19.

61. Robert P. Joyce to State Dept., 23 May 1955, 511.51, RG59, NA; see also Section F. 1 in D-33, in ibid.

62. Eisenhower, qtd. in Jean-Marie Domenach, "Le modèle américain," *Esprit*, July–Aug. 1960, 1364; Bohlen to State Dept., 24 Oct. 1950, 751.00, RG59, NA; Dunn to Sec. State, 21 Jan. 1952, *FRUS*, 1952–54, VI:567. On Bruce, see Lankford, *The Last American Aristocrat*; and Letter Luce to J. F. Dulles, 15 June 1956, JFD, Corr.-Memo Series, Strictly Confid., b. 2, DDEL.

63. Dunn to Sec. State, 9 Oct. 1950, 765.001, RG59, NA. Qtd. Pells, *Not Like Us*, 69.

64. Schlesinger, *The Vital Center*, 184; Scott-Smith, *The Politics*, 41–44; Wald, *The New York Intellectuals*, 267–71; Pells, *The Liberal Mind*, 84–97. On uses and misuses of *The God That Failed*, see esp. Saunders, *The Cultural Cold War*, 63–66; and Coleman, *The Liberal Conspiracy*, 24–27.

65. On this point I agree with and borrow from the argument in Scott-Smith, *The Politics*. I also highlight the contradiction of this political sponsorship, as, more polemically, Saunders has done in *The Cultural Cold War*.

66. Grémion, *Intelligence*, 24–25; quotation from Scott-Smith, *The Politics*, 104.

67. Grémion, *Intelligence*, 80–82; Caute, *The Dancer*, 395. For the French opinion within the CCF, see, e.g., Aron, *The Opium* (first pub. in 1955).

68. Scott-Smith, *The Politics*, 4–6, 94, 105; Coleman, *The Liberal Conspiracy*, 21–22.

69. Schlesinger, *The Vital Center*, 52; also, together with *Time* article qtd. in Cotkin, "French Existentialism," 333; cf. Louis Menand, "The Promise of Freedom, the Friend of Authority: American Culture in Postwar France," in Kazin and MacCartin, *Americanism*, 216–17; Raymond Aron, "Politics and the French Intellectuals," *Partisan Review* 17 (Sept.–Oct. 1950): 604; on Sartre's peak as a "fellow-traveler," see chap. 4.

70. Coleman, *The Liberal Conspiracy*, 9; Grémion, *Intelligence*, 101.

71. Coleman, *The Liberal Conspiracy*, 53–54; Grémion, *Intelligence*, 145. The CCF Vienna journal *Forum* addressed Austrian and Hungarian audiences; for the Spanish readership, Paris publishers provided *Cuadernos*. On the CCF in Italy, see also Eugenio Capozzi, "L'opposizione all'antiamericanismo: Il *Congress for Cultural Freedom* e l'Associazione italiana per la libertà e la cultura," in Craveri and Quagliarello, *L'anti-americanismo*.

72. Scott-Smith, *The Politics*, 76, 123; Grémion, *Intelligence*, 74. On the Ford Foundation role, see esp. Berghahn, *America*, chap. 8.

73. Coleman, *The Liberal Conspiracy*, 60–61, 220; Saunders, *The Cultural Cold War*, 71–72; Christopher Lasch, "The Cultural Cold War: A Short History of the Congress for Cultural Freedom," in Lasch, *The Agony*, 106.

74. Quotation from Warner, "Origins"; Grémion, "Regards," 61. Scott-Smith, *The Politics*, 66–86, 91–93; Coleman, *The Liberal Conspiracy*, 47–48, 220; Berghahn, *America*, 214–30; Saunders, *The Cultural Cold War*, 1, 152–53.

75. As Richard Pells has argued in *Not Like Us*, 72. On the demise of the CCF and its second life as the IACF, see esp. Coleman, *The Liberal Conspiracy*, 225–26, 240, 244–45; and Berghahn, *America*, 250–83.

76. On this point, see Powers, *Not without Honor*, 210–11; for Bondy quote, see Scott-Smith, *The Politics*, 126.

77. Tobia, *Advertising America*, 223–68.

78. Qtd. in Saunders, *The Cultural Cold War*, 3.

79. Bell, *The End of Ideology* (first pub. 1960), 16 (emphasis added); Lipset, *Political*

Man; Aron, *The Opium*. Cf. Scott-Smith, *The Politics*, 140–53; Grémion, *Intelligence*, 153–56.

80. This is Giles Scott-Smith's main thesis in *The Politics*, chap. 6.

81. Pietro Secchia, "Il partito comunista e gli intellettuali," *L'Unità*, 5 Feb. 1948.

82. French attendees at the congress included Frédéric Juliot-Curie, Pablo Picasso, Paul Eluard, Fernand Léger, and Julien Benda; Italians included Salvatore Quasimodo, Alberto Moravia, Renato Guttuso, and Elio Vittorini; and Americans included Arthur Miller, Aaron Copeland, Norman Mailer, Charlie Chaplin, Leonard Bernstein, and Albert Einstein.

83. De Beauvoir, *Force of Circumstance*, 241–43; Sartre in Contat and Rybalka, *The Writings*, 207–11; Kuisel, *Seducing the French*, 51; Birchall, *Sartre against Stalinism*, 137–42; "Come Sacco e Vanzetti," *Vie Nuove*, 28 Sept. 1953.

84. On this point, see esp. Kuisel, *Seducing the French*, 126–27; and Roger, *The American Enemy*, 424–45.

85. Cf. Ajello, *Intellettuali*, 143–51; Verdès-Leroux, *Au service du parti*, 87–91, 269–328.

86. See chap. 1.

87. On Kravchenko affair the best sources remain Wall, *French Communism*, 94–95; and Chebel d'Appollonia, *Le Temps*, 58–65. On Rousset, see Judt, *Past Imperfect*, 113–15.

88. Bianchini, "Le PCI"; Barbagallo, "Il PCI dal Comiform al '56."

89. Salinari in Mtg. Stampa and Propaganda of Cultural Section, 17 Mar. 1953, Cult. Comm.; and Mtg. Cult. Comm. (n.d.), Nov. 1953, Cult. Comm., APCI.

90. See, e.g., "Résolution du parti relative aux questions culturelles et artistiques," in Dec. BP, 20 Jan. 1951; Intervention Laurent Casanova, in Dec. BP, 2 Apr. 1954, APCF; Memo regarding the "cadre de l'Ecole centrale de quatre mois" (party school) on "Le travail du parti parmi les intellectuels," draft by Victor Michaut for period 7 Mar.–9 July 1955, in Fonds Victor Michaut, 271 J, b. 1, APCF; cf. Lazar, "Les partis communistes italien et français."

91. Lazar, *Maisons*, 71; Kotek and Kotek, *L'affaire Lyssenko*; the most vivid description of the controversy over Picasso's portrait of Stalin is in Caute, *The Dancer*, 582–84; see also Fougeron, "Une 'affaire'"; in general, see Marcel Servin, "L'activité du parti parmi les intellectuels," *Cahiers du communisme*, Apr. 1956.

92. Palmiro Togliatti, "Intervento alla commissione culturale, 3 aprile 1954," in Togliatti, *Opere*, 5:827–28. Aragon qtd. and compared to Togliatti also in Lazar, *Maisons*, 72–73. See also "Pour la défense de la culture française," *La Nouvelle critique*, no. 49, Nov. 1953. Quotation from Flores and Gallerano, *Sul PCI*, 198.

93. Ajello, *Intellettuali*, 245–53; Misler, *La via italiana*, 219–35. Guttuso in Mtg. Cult. Comm., 14–16 June 1949, Cult. Comm., APCI.

94. Norberto Bobbio, "Libertà e potere," *Nuovi Argomenti*, no. 14 (May–June 1955); Roderigo di Castiglia (Togliatti), "Ancora sul tema della libertà," *Rinascita*, July–Aug. 1955. See also Bobbio, "Democrazia e dittatura," and "Della libertà dei moderni comparata a quella dei posteri," *Nuovi Argomenti*, nos. 6 and 11 (Jan.–Feb. 1954 and Nov.–Dec. 1954); cf. Vacca, *Intellettuali*.

95. Calvino's 1954 article on *Civiltà operaia* and Alicata's reprimand both cited in Vittoria, *Togliatti*, 83, 95; Calvino and Corsini, qtd. in Mtg. Cult. Comm., 13–24 July 1956; see also response by Alicata in Mtg. Cult. Comm., 15–16 Nov. 1956. For similar critical views of the PCI's provincialism, see Roberto Guiducci, "Pamphlet sul disgelo e sulla cultura di sinistra," *Nuovi Argomenti*, no. 17–18 (Nov. 1955–Feb. 1956); Chiaretti, "Contenuto."

Corsini eventually wrote about the political crisis of post-Vietnam America and allegedly became President Nixon's "favorite communist"; see Alpert, *Fellini*, 59.

96. Pierre Hentges, "Walt Whitman poète d'un nouveau monde," *La Nouvelle critique*, no. 68 (Sept.–Oct. 1955); cf. Mario Alicata, "Note su Whitman," *Rinascita*, May 1951. Celebrating certain American writers also helped demythologize others; see, e.g., Rossel Hope Robbins, "Il mito di T. S. Eliot," *Rinascita*, Apr. 1950.

97. Gundle, *I comunisti*, 119; Aragon and CC Argenteuil in Verdès-Leroux, *Le réveil*, 118–19; cf. Belloin, "Le Comité."

98. Cf. Lazar, *Maisons*, 73; cf. Vittoria, *Togliatti*, xxii–xxvii.

99. See this point in Rosenberg, *Spreading the American Dream*, 36.

100. See, e.g., Robbins, "Il mito di T. S. Eliot," Gianfranco Corsini, "Gli intellettuali europei di fronte al fascismo americano," and "L'offensiva del maccartismo contro il cinema italiano," *Rinascita*, Apr. 1950, Oct. 1953, Apr. 1954; Paul Balmigère "L'idéologie socialdémocratique au service de l'impérialisme," *Cahiers du communisme*, Mar. 1952; Jean Poperen, "Le maccarthyisme en échec," *La Nouvelle critique*, no. 49 (Nov. 1953); and Barbaro, "Come interpretare Charlot."

101. Cotkin, "French Existentialism," 335; cf. Nora, "America," 327.

102. "Scienze sociali e azione politica in un libro di Wright Mills," *Rinascita*, 9 Feb. 1963. In 1953 Salinari lauded the initiative by *Nuovi Argomenti* to start publishing excerpts of America's social critics; Mtg. Cult. Comm., Nov. 1953, p. 30, Cult. Comm., APCI.

103. Percentages in Dudziak, *Cold War*, 141.

104. On this point, see esp. Jeff Woods, *Black Struggle*. Cf. Roland Weyl, "Fascistation aux U.S.A." *La Nouvelle critique*, no. 64 (Apr. 1955). The rise of the civil rights movement was extensively covered in *L'Unità* and *L'Humanité*, with greater attention by the early 1960s.

105. De Beauvoir, *America Day by Day*, 65.

106. On U.S. embarrassment, see esp. Dudziak, *Cold War*; on Sartre's play, see Caute, *The Dancer*, 307–8. Luce in Jeff Woods, *Black Struggle*, 69.

107. De Beauvoir, *America Day by Day*, 329–33.

108. Mike Fioravanti, "La signora Reverendo," *Vie Nuove*, 12 Mar. 1960; cf. Giuseppe Garritano, "Il bisturi in mano alle donne," in ibid., on the emancipation of Soviet women.

109. Confalonieri, "Parties," 128–29; Giorgio Amendola, "Il progresso dell'emancipazione," *Rinascita*, Mar. 1961.

110. On the PCF's charge that birth control was Malthusian, see adoption Resolution Vermeersch in Decisions BP, 13 Apr. 1956; at the time, this was also a diversion from the debate over de-Stalinization; see also Dec. BP, 30 Nov. 1961, APCF; cf. Yvonne Dumont, "Les femmes, leurs problèmes et leurs luttes," *Cahiers du communisme*, Jan. 1967, 75–84.

111. Cf. comments in David Drake, *Intellectuals*, 147.

112. Kuisel, *Seducing the French*, 103.

113. Domenach, "Le modèle," 1523–29; also in Kuisel, *Seducing the French*, 116.

114. Pier Paolo D'Attorre, "Sogno americano e mito sovietico," in D'Attorre, *Nemici*, 51.

115. Cf. Silvio Pons, "L'URSS e il PCI nel sistema della guerra fredda," in Gualtieri, *Il PCI*, 22–23; Martinelli, "Togliatti." Quotation from Aga-Rossi and Zaslavsky, *Togliatti e Stalin*, 290.

116. Roger Martelli, *1956*, 367, 394; Maurice Thorez, "Quelques questions capitales posées au 20e congrès du PCUS," *L'Humanité*, 27 Mar. 1956.

117. Aga-Rossi and Zaslavsky, *Togliatti e Stalin*, 291 (which exaggerates Togliatti's role in

Khrushchev's decision to intervene); Dec. BP, 10 Nov. 1956, APCF; Wall, *French Communism*, 103; cf. Klenjanszky, "L'impact." For a comparison, see esp. Lazar, *Maisons*, 95–98; and Marcou, *Le mouvement*.

118. Wall, *French Communism*, 102; cf. Thorez and Vermeersch at CC, of 9–10 May 1956 (Arcueil), in CC, 261 J 2/32, APCF. Franco Andreucci documents the cult of personality of Togliatti but without the same connection to Stalin as that of Thorez; Andreucci, *Falce e martello*, 182–83.

119. Jean-Paul Sartre, "Le réformisme et les fétiches" (Feb. 1956), in *Situations VII*, 110. Next quotations from Birchall, *Sartre against Stalinism*, 162–67; and Judt, *Past Imperfect*, 129. For the polemic against these positions, see Fejtö, *The French Communist Party*.

120. Caute, *Communism*, 228; cf. Hazareesingh, *Intellectuals*, 146; Verdès-Leroux, *Le réveil*, 50–62; Sirinelli, *Intellectuels*, 175–87.

121. Cf. Sereni in Mtg. Direz., 21 Nov. 1956, p. 5; Giolitti, *Lettere*, 99–102; Ajello, *Intellettuali*, 403–6; Vittoria, *Togliatti*, 109–25; Saunders, *The Cultural Cold War*, 215.

122. Meliadò, *Il fallimento*, 182; Sassoon, *The Strategies*, 107. On the membership decline and how the events of 1956 not only constituted the roots the social democratization of much of the Italian Marxist Left but also favored the rise of the extraparliamentarian Left, see Breschi, *Sognando la rivoluzione*, 21–46. Immediately after the Soviet invasion, Togliatti emphasized the danger of a "wave of anti-Sovietism and anti-communism" and said, "We must stay on our side, even when it makes mistakes"; Mtg. Direz., 30 Oct. 1956, VD, mf. 127, APCI.

123. All in Mtg. Direz., 12 Sept. 1957, VD, mf. 197, APCI.

124. Blackmer, *Unity*, 125; Mtg. Cult. Comm. 15–16 Nov. 1956, p. 5, and Alicata in Mtg. Direz., 26 Nov. 1957, VD, mf. 197, APCI.

125. Luce to Sec. State, 13 Nov. 1956; Dillon (Paris) to State Dept., 21 July 1956; Jernegan to State Dept., 2 Aug. 1956, Memo Niles Bond, 29 Jan. 1958, all in Rome Emb. Recs., 1956–58, Lot File 63 D 78, RG84, NA.

Chapter 6

1. Memo Lodge to Dulles, 22 Sept. 1954, PPS Recs., Lot 65 D 101, b. 87, RG59, NA; on Lodge's role in the administration, see Brands, *Cold Warriors*, 163–81.

2. PSB, "Notes on a Grand Strategy for Psychological Operations," 1 Oct. 1951, SMOF, PSB, HSTL; Memo (J. M. Jones), Status Report on the Work of Panel C of the PSB, 21 Nov. 1951, SMOF, PSB, b. 24, HSTL.

3. Eisenhower to Rockefeller, 5 Aug. 1955, AW, Eisenhower Diary Series, b. 11, Aug. 1955 (1), DDEL; also in Osgood, *Total Cold War*, 81. Osgood's otherwise admirable work on Eisenhower's propaganda does not sufficiently clarify this distinction between the administration's artful manipulation of public opinion and its sometimes agonizing reflections on the meanings of propaganda for the leading world's democracy. In 1952, even the Paris office of the USIS, an agency designed to orchestrate propaganda, presented its best case by arguing that "the efficacy and the strength of . . . propaganda depends, in the final analysis, on the basic validity of the decisions the U.S. government makes and the policies it adopts and executes"; USIS Semi-annual Evaluation Report, 15 July 1952, 511.51, RG59, NA.

4. Del Pero, "The United States," 1330.

5. Ferguson, *Empire*; cf. Osgood, *Total Cold War*, 149–50.

6. MSA-JCS Mtg. 28 Jan. 1953, *FRUS*, 1952–54, V:711–18. On Mattei, see Memo

John H. Ferguson, 29 May 1953, PPS Recs., Lot File 64 D 563, Chron. Files, b. 35, NA; National Intelligence Estimate (NIE), NIE-99, 23 Oct. 1953, *FRUS*, 1952–54, II:551–62; and Dillon to State Dept., 4 Oct. 1955, *FRUS*, 1955–57, XVIII:222–24.

7. Congressional report qtd. in Connelly, *A Diplomatic Revolution*, 37. On modernization, see comments in ibid. See also Latham, *Modernization*; and Black, *Comparative Modernization*.

8. On these contrasts, see Ross, *Fast Cars*; and Connelly, *A Diplomatic Revolution*.

9. 276th NSC Mtg., 9 Feb. 1956, *FRUS*, 1955–57, XXVII:331; 340th NSC Mtg. 17 Oct. 1957, AW, NSC Series, b. 9, DDEL; Letter Luce to J. F. Dulles, 15 June 1956, Corr.-Memo Series, Strictly Confid., b. 2, DDEL.

10. 157th NSC Mtg., 30 July 1953, AW, NSC Series, b. 4, DDEL; 164th NSC Mtg., 1 Oct. 1953, *FRUS*, 1952–54, I:545–48.

11. Memo Luce to Eisenhower, 20 Aug. 1954, AW, AS, b. 25, DDEL; Eisenhower in 136th NSC Mtg., 11 Mar. 1953, *FRUS*, 1952–54, VIII:1122; PSB D-47, "Operating Procedures and Staff Organization, Psychological Operations Coordinating Committee," 1 May 1952, PSB, b. 2, RG59, NA.

12. Qtd. Osgood, *Total Cold War*, 154. On public diplomacy and domestic opinion, see esp. Winkler, *Life*; Oakes, *The Imaginary War*; and Boyer, *By the Bomb's Early Light*, 289–351. On sincere apprehension among Soviet leaders and scientists, see Holloway, *Stalin*, 336–37. While Osgood comes closest to my conclusions, no study has adequately highlighted the gap between internal mobilization and public reassurance abroad, comparing U.S. public relations with reactions from Europe's opposition forces.

13. Sassoon, *The Strategies*, 90 (also highlighting Togliatti's speech); Dec. BP, 21 July 1954, APCF.

14. Osgood, *Total Cold War*, 65 (see also 153–80). See also Osgood, "Form before Substance"; Wenger, *Living with Peril*, 94–99. In general, cf. also Vaicbourdt, "L'administration Eisenhower."

15. Eisenhower's address before the American Society of Newspaper Editors, Apr. 16, 1953, in *Public Papers: Dwight D. Eisenhower, 1953*, 179–88; Robert L. Ivie, "Eisenhower as Cold Warrior," in Medhurst, *Eisenhower's War of Words*, 14 (also highlighted in Osgood, *Total Cold War*, 61–64); Washburn to Jackson, 6 Apr. 1953, Jackson Recs., b. 7, DDEL.

16. Young, *Winston Churchill's Last Campaign*; Holloway, *Stalin*; Mastny, *The Cold War*, 171; Zubok, *A Failed Empire*, 94–122. Cf. comments in Rockefeller to Eisenhower, 8 Aug. 1955, AW, AS, b. 30, N. Rockefeller, 1952–55 (3), DDEL.

17. Medhurst, "Eisenhower's 'Atoms for Peace'"; Osgood, *Total Cold War*, 159–61.

18. Memo by State Dept, 18 Aug. 1954, *FRUS*, 1952–54, II:1501–2; Eisenhower to Jackson, 31 Dec., 1953, AW, Eisenhower Diaries Series, b. 4, DDEL; Osgood, *Total Cold War*, 166–69; Bowie and Immerman, *Waging Peace*, 230–41. The main role in this public relations coup was handed to psy-war director C. D. Jackson; Brands, *Cold Warriors*, 128–29.

19. Qtd. in Osgood, *Total Cold War*, 176.

20. Prime Minister A. Eden to Eisenhower, 6 May 1955, J. F. Dulles (Paris) to State Dept., 9 May 1955, 249th NSC Mtg. 19 May 1955, *FRUS*, 1955–57, V:164–65, 174–75; Eisenhower, *Mandate for Change*, 506; Wittner, *Resisting the Bomb*, 10–14, 128–30.

21. Osgood, *Total Cold War*, 192–94; Hixson, *Parting the Curtain*, 99–100.

22. Renato Mieli, "La politica estera americana da Truman a Eisenhower," *Rinascita*, Apr. 1953; Renato Mieli, "I primi passi verso la fine della guerra fredda," and "Gli atomi per la pace," *Rinascita*, July–Aug. 1955; cf. Togliatti in Mtg. Direz., 17 Nov. 1955, VD, APCI.

23. Lazar, *Maisons*, 87; Palmiro Togliatti, "Per un accordo tra comunisti e cattolici per salvare la civiltà umana," in Togliatti, *Opere*, 5:832–46; Thorez in Williamson to State Dept., 23 Mar. 1955, 765.001, RG59, NA; qtd. Secchia in Mtg. Direz., 17 July 1953, VD, APCI. Secchia made his point on the U.S.S.R.'s shortcomings to defend Stalin's legacy against Beria's "warmongering" tendencies.

24. Dec. BP, 29 Mar., 18 Apr. 1956, APCF.

25. Pajetta and Togliatti in Mtg. Direz., 9 Dec. 1954, and Togliatti in Mtg. Direz., 17 Nov. 1955, VD, APCI. The exception was the replacement of the staunch anti-American Emilio Sereni in the party secretariat with the more moderate Celeste Negarville, who reorganized the peace movement seeking stronger connections with left-wing DC leaders such as Giorgio La Pira; see Williamson (Florence) to State Dept., 22 Nov. 1955, 765.001, RG, NA.

26. Qtd. Ingrao in Mtg. Direz., 25 May 1960; see also Togliatti in Mtg. Direz., 14 July 1961; cf. Negarville, Alicata, and Dozza in Mtg. Direz., 28 May 1957; and Pajetta in Mtg. Direz., 3 July 1958, all in VD, APCI; cf. Dec. BP, 12 Apr. 1960, APCF. On this period, cf. Santamaria, *Le parti de l'ennemi*, 315–45.

27. Dulles to Emb. Belgium, 24 May 1956, *FRUS*, 1955–57, IV:444; qtd. NIE, 29 July 1958, *FRUS*, 1958–60, VII, 1:63–64. Cf. Lundestad, *"Empire" by Integration*, 49–57.

28. Conv. de Gaulle–Eisenhower, 20 Apr. 1952, *FRUS*, 1952–54, VI:1200–1203; Dulles in U.S. Deleg. at Tripartite For. Mins. Mtg., 18 Oct. 1953, *FRUS*, 1952–54, V:827; Luce to State Dept., 1 July 1954, ibid., 992–94.

29. C. D. Jackson to Eisenhower, 29 Sept. 1953, AW, Dulles-Herter, b. 1, DDEL; Knight to Bonbright, 29 Oct. 1952, Recs. WEA 1941–54, Italy-Austria, Subj. files, b. 11, RG59, NA; Aimaq, *For Europe?*; De Leonardis, *La "diplomazia atlantica."*

30. Eisenhower in 138th NSC Mtg., 25 Mar. 1953. On nuclear share, see Trachtenberg, *A Constructed Peace*, 146–200; Luce to State Dept., 7 Aug. 1953, *FRUS*, 1952–54, VI:1624–30; Luce to Eisenhower, 20 Aug. 1954 (p. 36), and Luce to Eisenhower, 31 Aug. 1954 (qtd.), both in AW, AS, b. 25, DDEL.

31. Luce to Eisenhower, Dulles, et al., 6 June 1955, CBLP, b. 634, f. "Missions, Investigations, Heroine 1955," LC; cf. Del Pero, *L'alleato*, 265–66; 187th NSC Mtg., 4 Mar. 1954, *FRUS*, 1952–54, V:886–87.

32. Brogi, *A Question*; on this point applied to NATO's smaller nations, see Frank Costigliola, "Culture, Emotion, and the Creation of the Atlantic Identity, 1948–1952," in Lundestad, *No End*, 23–24.

33. Mtg. Direz., 23 Apr. 1958, VD, APCI, pp. 8–9.

34. Minutes BP, 8 Jan. 1957 (qtd.—also refuting charges of protectionism), see also Minutes BP, 15 Jan. 1957; Dec. BP, 18 Apr. 1956 (on EURATOM); intervention Pierre Villon at CC, 14 Feb. 1957, summary tape no. 153, cote d'archives 1AV 121/7026, all in APCF; qtd. Allegato a Verbale Direzione, 20–21 Mar. 1957, VD, and Scoccimarro qtd. in Mtg. Direz., 14 Feb. 1957, VD (p. 31), APCI; Celeste Negarville, "I trattati 'europeistici' nel quadro dell'attuale politica dell'imperialismo," *Rinascita*, Mar. 1957.

35. See esp. Maggiorani, *L'Europa*; and Gualtieri, "Giorgio Amendola."

36. Togliatti in Mtg. Direz., 2 Jan. 1959, VD (p. 8; also previous quote by Pajetta in ibid., p. 5), APCI.

37. Maggiorani, *L'Europa*, 112–13, 103–5. On EURATOM, see Mtg. Direz., 14 Feb. 1957, VD. On possible connections with national liberation movements, see Scoccimarro in Mtg. Direz., 16 July 1959, VD; cf. Romagnoli in Mtg. Direz., 25 May 1960, VD, APCI.

38. Maggiorani, *L'Europa*, 81–83.

39. On Peggio, see ibid., 134–35.

40. Qtd. in ibid., 138. Cf. Gualtieri, "Giorgio Amendola," 33–34.

41. Lazar, *Maisons*, 105; Dec. BP, 20 Sept. 1962, APCF. On PCF's distinction between "true" and "phony" Western European integration, see Maurice Goldring, "La Grande Bretagne et le Marché Commun," *La Nouvelle critique*, no. 143, Mar. 1963.

42. Maggiorani, *L'Europa*, 166.

43. Pajetta in Mtg. Direz., 2 Jan. 1959 (p. 5), VD, APCI; Palmiro Togliatti, "Per una sinistra europea," *Rinascita*, Mar. 1959; Dec. BP, 24 Feb. 1959, 10 May, 20 Sept. 1962, APCF.

44. Herz to State Dept., 12 Oct. 1952, Paris Emb., Recs. EDC and Intl. Org., b. 1, RG 84, NA; See also his observations in Mtg. LENAP C.ttee, 8 Oct. 1952, SMOF, PSB, b. 23, HSTL.

45. Eisenhower, qtd. in Ambrose, *Eisenhower*, 143–44; Eisenhower, *Mandate for Change*, 13–22; Dulles to Eisenhower, 6 Sept. 1953, *FRUS*, 1952–54, II:457–59; Luce to Eisenhower, 20 Aug. 1954 (quotation from p. 23), AW, AS, b. 25, DDEL; cf. Luce to State Dept., 7 Aug. 1953, *FRUS*, 1952–54, VI:1624–30.

46. Dunn to State Dept., 11 Oct. 1952, *FRUS*, 1952–54, VI:1256–59; Dunn to State Dept. (LENAP), 4 Dec. 1952, 751.001, RG59; Bruce to Sec. State, 1 Oct. 1953, Paris Emb., Recs EDC and Intl. Org., 1951–55, b. 1, RG 84, NA.

47. PSB D-37, 9 Feb. 1953 (pp. 16–17), WHO, NSC Staff, PSB, b. 14, DDEL; Memo Herz to State Dept., 16 Sept. 1954, *FRUS*, 1952–54, V:1113.

48. Letter Eisenhower to Gruenther, 22 June 1953, AW, AS, b. 16, DDEL.

49. Luce to Eisenhower, 20 Aug. 1954 (pp. 34–35 of memo; emphases in text), AW, AS, b. 25, DDEL.

50. Dulles referring from Luce in 247th NSC Mtg., 5 May 1955, AW, NSC Series, b. 6, DDEL; Luce to State Dept., 7 Aug. 1953, *FRUS*, 1952–54, VI:1624–30; Luce to Eisenhower, 20 Aug. 1954, AW, AS, b. 25, DDEL; Jernegan to State Dept., 2 Aug. 1956, and Luce to State Dept., 12 Sept. 1956, both in RG84, Rome Embassy, General Recs., 1956–58, Lot File 63D78, NA; on the development of Italian trade with the U.S.S.R., see Bagnato, *Prove*.

51. Pella and Fanfani quotes in Maria Rosaria Grieco, "Politica estera italiana e mondo cattolico: La parabola del neo-atlantismo negli anni '50," in Minolfi, *L'Italia*, 85, 89. For thorough analysis of neo-Atlanticism, see Brogi, "Ike and Italy."

52. Luce to C. D. Jackson, 29 Sept. 1954, Jackson Papers, b. 70, f. "Luce, Henry and Clare," DDEL; Luce to Dulles, 24 Aug. 1954, and Mtg. Luce-Segni (prime minister), 24 Aug. 1956, both in 765.00, RG59, NA. Cf. Intelligence Report no. 7641, "'Neo-Atlanticism' as an Element in Italy's Foreign Policy," 10 Jan. 1958, OIR files, NA.

53. Qtd. Luce to Dulles, 10 Oct. 1956, 611.65; Mtg. Luce-Segni, 24 Aug. 1956, 765.00, RG59, NA; Colby and Forbath, *Honorable Men*, 108–27; qtd. Tasca to Luce, 18 Feb. 1956, CBLP, b. X60, f. "Subject, Memos, Interoffice 1956," LC; Miller, "Roughhouse Diplomacy," 306–9; Dulles in 394th NSC Mtg., 22 Jan. 1959, AW, NSC Series, DDEL; see also 395th NSC Mtg., 29 Jan. 1959, in ibid.

54. Qtd. Roger, *The American Enemy*, 404; see also el-Machat, *Les Etats-Unis*; Thomas, "France's North African Crisis"; Wall, *France*, 85–86 (on JFK); Holmes to Dulles, 29 Sept. 1955, *FRUS*, 1955–57, XVIII:105–10.

55. On Italy and NATO in general, see Brogi, *L'Italia*. On such contrasts and convergence between France, Italy, and the United States, see Brogi, "Competing Missions."

56. Cf. Pinay to Couve de Murville, 26 May 1955, DDF, 1955, I, doc. 300; Houghton to State Dept., 28 May, 27 Nov. 1957, 751S.00; Yost to State Dept., 4 Apr. 1957, 611.51, RG59, NA.

57. Brogi, *L'Italia*, 280–92; Alessandro Brogi, "Fanfani e l'unilateralismo americano nel Mediterraneo," in Giovagnoli and Tosi, *Amintore Fanfani*.

58. Frankel, *Mattei*, 94–96; Ilaria Tremolada, "Mattei, Fanfani, l'ENI e le relazioni internazionali dell'Italia," in Giovagnoli and Tosi, *Amintore Fanfani*; J. W. Jones to Under Sec. State, 29 Aug. 1957 (enclosed Progress Report on 5411/2, section "Mattei's Threat"), Recs. State Dept. participation in OCB and NSC, b. 21, NA. On Gronchi, cf. esp. Memo OCB, 3 May 1955, OCB files, b. 111, DDEL; and Ortona, *La diplomazia*, 128–29.

59. Quotation from Wall, *French Communism*, 188. Cf. statements by Léon Feix at the Aubervilliers Central Committee meeting in Feb. 1952 in CC, 12–13 Feb. 1952, print copy, APCF. Cf. Moneta, *Le PCF*; Dazy, *La partie*; Cohen, "The Algerian War."

60. Dec. BP, 3 Mar. 1956 (qtd.), 8 Jan. 1957, 26 Nov. 1957, APCF.

61. Mollet and Thorez, qtd. in Wall, *French Communism*, 190–92; cf. Thorez in Mtg. BP, 21 Nov. 1957, APCF. Cf. Thorez in CC, 14–16 May 1957, summary tape no. 162, 1AV 121/7035, and Léon Feix at CC, 16 Sept. 1957, summary tape no. 184, 1AV 121/7057, APCF.

62. Quotation from Marty at CC, 13–14 Feb. 1952 (Aubervilliers) (pp. 12–13), APCF; cf. BP, 21 Nov. 1957, APCF.

63. Quotation from Courtois and Lazar, *Histoire*, 312. cf. Ulloa, *Francis Jeanson*, 142–43. The PCF also used its attack on American imperialism to denounce Yugoslavia's revisionism; e.g., Raymond Guyot at CC, 30 Apr. 1958, CD no. 56, 4AV11/165, APCF.

64. See Jernegan to Dept., 25 Jan. 1957 RG 84 Rome Emb., Gen. Recs., 1956–58, Lot File 63D78, RG59, NA; Amendola in Mtg. Direz., 3 July 1958, VD, APCI; Renato Mieli, "L'Italia nel Mediterraneo: Un'assenza ingiustificata," *Rinascita*, June 1957. On La Pira's conferences, see chap. 4. On Soviet financing from 1956, see Riva, *Oro*, 243–46. On the rising role of the PCI in Mediterranean diplomacy in general, see Riccardi, *Il "problema Israele*," 116–33.

65. Urban, *Moscow*, 232.

66. Togliatti in Mtg. Direz., 5 Dec. 1956, VD, APCI; Zellerbach to State Dept., 22 Oct. 1957, 765.001, RG59, NA. Togliatti in Mtg. Direz., 18 Sept. 1959, VD, APCI.

67. See chap. 5; cf. USIS Italy Country Assessment Report for 1960, 8 Feb. 1961, RG306, For. Service Despatches, b. 1, Europe, NA; Dulles to Emb. Paris, 30 Sept. 1957, 811.411, RG59, NA; Michele Salerno, "Mito e realtà dell' 'anticolonialismo' USA," *Rinascita*, Dec. 1958.

68. Dillon to State Dept., 29 Nov. 1956 751.00, RG59, NA; 151st Mtg. NSC (reporting CIA evidence of coup plans), 25 June 1953, AW, NSC, b. 4, DDEL; cf. de la Gorce, *Apogée et mort*, 516–17.

69. NSC 5721/1, 19 Oct. 1957, *FRUS*, 1955–57, XXVII:181–83; Dulles at 356th NSC Mtg., 27 Feb. 1958, AW, NSC, b. 9, DDEL; Dulles to Emb. Bonn, 2 Apr. 1958, *FRUS*, 1958–60, VII:4–5; cf. Wall, "The United States," 506–9.

70. Dulles at 299th NSC Mtg. 4 Oct. 1956, AW, NSC Series, b. 8, DDEL. Dillon to Dulles, 29 Nov. 1956, 751S.00, RG59, NA; For similar observations by Undersecretary of State Robert Murphy, see Murphy to Acting Sec. State, 3 Mar. 1956, AW, Intl. Series, b. 12, DDEL; and Murphy, *Diplomat among Warriors*, 382.

71. Dulles in NSC 356th Mtg., 27 Feb. 1958, Memo by Dept. of State (for Becker quotation), 2 Apr. 1958, *FRUS*, 1958–60, XIII:759, 838–40; NSC 5721/1, 19 Oct. 1957, *FRUS*, 1955–57, XXVII:181–93. On Morocco, see *FRUS*, 1955–57, XVIII:579–80.

72. See esp. Memo Wilkins to Rountree, 26 Oct. 1956; Memo Col. Doyle (SHAPE Liaison Officer) to Dept. Defense, 26 Mar. 1958, 751S.00, RG59, NA; and Wall, *France*, chaps. 3–5.

73. Houghton to State Dept., 15 May 1958, *FRUS*, 1958–60, VII:9–10; Houghton to State Dept., 29 May 1958, 751.00, NA.

74. Memo B. E. L. Timmons to Elbrick, 2 June 1958, Recs. WEA, Subj. Files France, 1944–60, b. 2, and Houghton to Dulles, 21 May 1958, 751.00, RG59, NA. On Republicans' predilection for de Gaulle, see Wall, *France*, esp. 151–54.

75. Bozo and Melandri, "La France," 203–6; Wall, "The United States," 510. On the economy, see Houghton to Dulles, 21 May 1958, cit; Vaïsse, *La grandeur*, 43; cf. Cerny, *The Politics.*

76. Mtg. Von Brentano–Dulles, 5 June 1958, 751.00, RG59, NA; Bozo and Melandri, "La France," 207–8. Qtd. Elbrick to Herter, 27 May 1958, *FRUS*, 1958–60, VII:17; Memo of Conference Dulles-Eisenhower, 3 July 1958, *FRUS*, 1958–60, VII:50–52.

77. Richard Kuisel talks of a Gaullist "exorcism"; Kuisel, *Seducing the French*, chap. 6. See also Michael M. Harrison, "French Anti-Americanism under the Fourth Republic and the Gaullist Solution," in Lacorne, Rupnik, and Toinet, *The Rise*; and Brogi, *A Question*, 233–37.

78. See esp. how Fanfani, with these arguments, managed to placate Ambassador Luce, who had previously antagonized him; Mtg. Luce, Manzini (Fanfani's Emissary), Getz, 31Oct. 1956, 665.00, RG59, NA. On Fanfani's foreign policy during this phase, see also Evelina Martelli, *L'altro atlantismo.*

79. Qtd. Jernegan to Dulles, 11 Sept. 1957, 665.80; qtd. Sohm to State Dept., 27 Aug. 1958, 765.13, RG59, NA; Brogi, "Ike and Italy," 28–29. This and the following paragraphs resume similar arguments from Brogi, *A Question*, 237–44.

80. Biographical Note Fanfani, by Asst. Sec. Jandrey, 27 July 1958, 765.13, Sohm to State Dept., 11 and 27 Aug. 1958, 765.13; Zellerbach to State Dept., 25 Nov. 1958, 765.00 RG59, NA; Interview Horace Torbert Jr., 2 Nov. 1965, Oral History, pp. 2–3, SGML.

81. A. Dulles at 381st NSC Mtg., 2 Oct. 1958, AW, NSC, b. 10, DDEL.

82. Ibid.; cf. OIR Report 7870, "The Outlook for Italy," 10 Dec. 1958, pp. 26–28, OIR files, NA.

83. Mtg. Eisenhower-Dulles, 5 Feb. 1957, DDRS, 1989, doc. 3426.

84. Mtg. Fanfani-Dulles and others, and Mtg. Fanfani-Eisenhower, 29–30 July 1958, *FRUS*, 1958–60, VII:466–73; Sohm to State Dept., 22 Sept. 1958, 665.00 and Mtg. Torbert-Fanfani, 3 Oct. 1958, 765.13, RG59, NA; Evelina Martelli, *L'altro atlantismo*, 53–56. On IRBMs, see references to Italy in Lauris Norstad Papers, b. 89, DDEL. The literature emphasizing a correlation between Italy's Mediterranean policies and its contribution to European integration is now conspicuous, but see most recently Varsori, *La Cenerentola*, esp. 121–56; Massimo De Leonardis, "L'atlantismo dell'Italia tra guerra fredda, interessi nazionali, e politica interna," in Ballini, Guerrieri, and Varsori, *Le istituzioni*, 253–56; and, for a strong emphasis on the DC's pro-Atlanticism even during Rome's pursuit of more room for maneuver, Gualtieri, *L'Italia*, 130–43; cf. Brogi, "Orizzonti," and Brogi, "Competing Missions." Cf. Archivio storico del Senato della Repubblica, Fondo Amintore Fanfani, b. 31, f. 2, Amintore Fanfani, "La crisi del comunismo e la Democrazia cristiana," speech at Nouvelles Equipes Internationales Conference, Arezzo, 24–27 Apr. 1957, cited in Evelina Martelli, *L'altro atlantismo*, 18.

85. Sohm to State Dept., 27 Aug. 1958, 765.13, RG59, NA; OIR Report 7870, 10 Dec. 1958, OIR files, NA; Zellerbach to Dulles, 9 Sept. 1958, 665.00, RG59, NA.

86. On these events, see the extended discussion in Brogi, *L'Italia*, 325–39.

87. See Resolution Central Committee of 9–10 June 1958, in CC, CD no. 66, 4AV11/175,

APCF; see also Courtois and Lazar, *Histoire*, 323; quotation from Dec. BP, 24 June 1958, APCF; Pierre Villon, "De Gaulle ce n'est pas l'indépendance nationale," *Cahiers du communisme*, Sept. 1958; Léon Merino, "Qu'est-ce que la grandeur française?," *Cahiers du communisme*, Oct. 1958; Claude, *Gaullisme*.

88. Dec. BP, 1 June, 7 Sept. 1961, APCF.

89. *L'Humanité*, 5 July 1960, Marcel Servin, *France nouvelle*, 28 Jan. 1960; Interventions by Casanova in CC, 13–15 Jan. 1961, CD 176–93, 4AV11/285, APCF; Kriegel, qtd. in Courtois and Lazar, *Histoire*, 322 (see also 327–31); cf. Dec. BP, 14 Feb. 1963, APCF; Bell and Criddle, *The French Communist Party*, 86–87.

90. Longo in Mtg. Direz., 18 Feb. 1959, VD, APCI; Togliatti in Mtg. Direz., 2 Jan. 1959 (quotation from p. 9), VD, APCI; Mario Alicata, "Perchè è caduto Fanfani," *Rinascita*, Feb. 1959; Provasi, *Borghesia industriale*, 135–36.

91. See esp. Amendola and Novella in Mtg. Direz., 27 Jan. 1959, VD, APCI.

92. Briefing on Fanfani's Conversations, 31 July 1958, 611.65, RG59, NA; Memo Conv. Dulles–de Gaulle, 5 July 1958, Mtg. Brosio-Eisenhower, 6 Oct. 1958, *FRUS*, 1958–60, VII, 2:64–67, 88–89.

93. Kissinger to Rockefeller, 21 Nov. 1956, Special Studies Project, b. 54, f. 596; and Kissinger to Berle, 3 Dec. 1956, Special Studies Project, b. 1, f. 3, Rockefeller Archives. (I wish to thank Thomas A. Schwartz for sharing these documents with me.)

94. Eisenhower's comments in Hughes, *The Ordeal*, 276, 280.

95. Memo Conv. Eisenhower-Dulles, 24 Mar. 1958, *FRUS*, 1958–60, III:567–72; Larson, *Anatomy*, 72–106; Osgood, *Total Cold War*, 199–210; Stephen J. Whitfield, "The Road to Rapprochement: Khrushchev's 1959 Visit to America," in Foreman, *The Other Fifties*.

96. PSB D-37 (p. 8); on Eisenhower's devoutness, see Caute, *The Dancer*, 177–78.

97. See esp. Kuklick, *Blind Oracles*, 66–71.

98. Gus Hall, "La 'peur' de la paix aux USA," *Démocratie nouvelle*, Dec. 1959; Gus Hall and Hyman Lumer, "Les Etats-Unis au crépuscule du 'siècle américain,'" *Démocratie nouvelle*, Mar. 1960.

99. Valentin Zorin, "Le brain trust Kennedy," *Démocratie nouvelle*, July 1963; Gianfranco Corsini, "L'elezione di Kennedy e l'inquietudine americana," *Rinascita*, Dec. 1960, and "Falchi e colombe alla Casa Bianca," *Rinascita*, 15 Dec. 1962; cf. Report Guyot at CC, Ivry, 27 Sept. 1961 (pp. 42–43 on Kennedy administration's massive rearmament), 261 J 2/37, APCF; Franco di Tondo, "La terza guerra si combatterà così," *Vie Nuove* 28 Mar. 1963; PS, "Il solito volto bestiale dell'America di Kennedy," *Nuova Generazione*, 18 and 19 May 1963; cf. Leo J. Wollemborg, "Italy and the New Frontier," *New Republic*, 12 June 1961.

100. Qtd. Interview Reinhardt with J. O'Connor, Nov. 1966, Oral History Reinhardt, 10, JFKL.

101. Kennedy's speech of 4 July 1962 in *Public Papers of the Presidents, John F. Kennedy, 1962*, 538–39; Letter Segni to Kennedy, 27 Oct. 1963, JFK Papers, Office Files, Countries File b. 119a; see also Memo Conv. Amb. Harriman-Gronchi, 11 Mar. 1961, NSC Files, Italy, b. 120, JFKL.

102. Memo Reinhardt forwarded to Bundy, 18 May 1962, NSC Files, Italy, b. 120, JFKL.

103. Cf. Thomas A. Schwartz, "Victories and Defeats in the Long Twilight Struggle: The United States and Western Europe in the 1960s," in Kunz, *The Diplomacy*, 122–36; Bozo, *Two Strategies*, 73–94; Winand, *Eisenhower*, 203–43.

104. For extensive narrative, see esp. Nuti, *Gli Stati Uniti*; Silveri, *L'Italia*; Alan A. Platt, "U.S. Policy toward the 'Opening to the Left' in Italy," Ph.D. diss., Columbia Univer-

sity, 1973. For general context, see also Ballini, Guerrieri, and Varsori, *Le istituzioni*; and Scirocco, *"Politique d'Abord."*

105. On this operation, known as "Gladio," see esp. Nuti, *Gli Stati Uniti*, 100–103. Cf. NSC 6014, 19 Jan. 1961, Arthur M. Schlesinger Jr. Papers [ASP], Subj. Files: Italy, b. WH 12, JFKL.

106. Jernegan to John Wesley Jones, 26 June 1956, 765.00, RG59, NA, also in Nuti, *Gli Stati Uniti*, 62–67; see also Nuti, "The United States," 42; cf. Mtg. Lister-Lombardi, 3 Feb. 1958, 765.00, RG59.

107. Nuti, "The United States," 45; see also Favetto, "La nascita."

108. "Policy Recommendations" drafted as part of dispatch 899 of 11 Apr. 1961 in DDRS 1978 281B; cf. Arthur M. Schlesinger Jr., "The Kennedy Administration and the Center-Left," in Di Scala, *Italian Socialism.*

109. Memo Schlesinger to Walt W. Rostow, 6 July 1961, NSC Files, Country: Italy, b. 120; cf. Memo Schlesinger to Bundy, 26 Apr. 1962, ASP, Subj. File: Italy, b. WH12a, JFKL. On crucial social reform, see Mtg. Harriman-Saragat, 11 Mar. 1961, NSC Files, b. 120, JFKL.

110. Rusk to Reinhardt, 18 Oct. 1961, NSC Files, Italy, b. 120, and Oral History Reinhardt, 3, JFKL; Rusk to Kennedy, 20 Feb. 1962, *FRUS*, 1961–63, XIII:826–29. Cf. Pietro Nenni, "Where the Italian Socialists Stand," *Foreign Affairs* 40 (2 Jan. 1962); Nenni, *Gli anni*, 288–89, 302. Cf. Fanfani to Kennedy, 6 Mar. 1963, *FRUS*, 1961–63, XIII:871–75; Nuti, *Gli Stati Uniti*, 645–46.

111. Komer to Bundy, 9 May 1962, and Komer to Schlesinger and Bundy, 12 Sept. 1962, ASP, b. WH12, JFKL.

112. Reinhardt to Undersec. State Ball and Amb. Tyler, 3 Jan. 1962, NSC, b. 120; Memo REU-28, 20 Feb. 1962 and Memo REU-44, 8 June 1962 (for quotation), both from INR–Roger Hilsman, ASP, WH Files, Italy, b. WH12, JFKL.

113. Togliatti qtd. in Bocca, *Togliatti*, 593; Memo Komer to Bundy, 24 Apr. 1962, and Mtg. Schlesinger–W. and V. Reuther, 28 May 1962, ASP, WH Files, Italy, b. WH12, JFKL; Mtg. Schlesinger, Komer, Tyler, Pieraccini, 2 Aug. 1962, Rome Emb. 1962–64, b. 8, f. PSI Memos, RG84, NA; cf. Nuti, *Gli Stati Uniti*, 465–500.

114. Di Vittorio in Mtg. Direz., 25 Jan. 1954 (p. 5), VD, APCI; Mtg. Direz., 28 Feb. 1962, "Preparazione alla conferenza economica dell'Istituto Gramsci," VD, APCI; Togliatti in Mtg. Direz., 25 May 1960, 31 Oct. 1962, VD, APCI. Cf. "Campagna per Italia neutrale e senza basi atomiche," *Propaganda*, 1963, no. 31 (17 Oct.) (with speech by Pajetta addressed to a PSI gathering).

115. Gianfranco Corsini, "Lo spirito di Mosca," *Rinascita*, 28 Sept. 1963.

116. Amendola and Scoccimarro (qtd.), in Mtg. Direz., 27 Jan. 1959, VD, APCI; Mtg. Direz., 28 Feb. 1962, VD, APCI; cf. Pajetta in Mtg. Direz., 20 Sept. 1962, VD, APCI.

117. Memo by C. D. Jackson, 7 Aug. 1962 Overseas Report, Confidential, forwarded to JFK by John D., JFK Papers, Office files, b. 119a, JFKL; Schlesinger to Bernabei, 8 Nov. 1962, ASP, Subj. File, 1961–64, b. 23, JFKL.

118. Memo Schlesinger to Bundy, 19 Oct. 1962, NSC, Italy, b. 120, JFKL; Mtg. Harriman-Fanfani, 11 Mar. 1961, NSC Files, Italy, b. 120, JFKL; William R. Tyler to Bohlen, 11 June 1963, POL12-FR, RG59, NA.

119. Cf. Sassoon, *One Hundred Years.*

120. See analysis by Bohlen to Sec. State, 21 Nov. 1962, NSC Files, France, b. 71A, JFKL: Research Memo by George C. Denney Jr. to Acting Sec. State: "Socialist-Communist Collaboration in France: A New 'Popular Front?,'" 6 Aug. 1963, POL 12-1 France, RG59, NA.

Mitterrand described in John A. Bovey Jr. to Dept., 19 Sept. 1963, POL 12-FR, RG59, NA. Allen Dulles thought that the Socialists' co-option in Italy might precipitate a schism within the SFIO, letting its left wing "go the way of the Nenni Socialists"; Dulles in 371st Mtg. NSC, 5 July 1958, AW, NSC, b. 10, DDEL.

121. Bovey to State Dept., 24 July 1964; Mtg. Mollet–Wells Stabler, 17 July 1964, POL 12-FR, NA.

122. Memo Conv., 1 July 1963 (in the Quirinale garden, Kennedy greeted Togliatti as well); Mtg. Colombo-Kennedy, 4 Oct. 1963, *FRUS*, 1961–63, XIII: 888–90; Mtg. Kennedy-Saragat, 15 Feb. 1963, ibid., 869–70.

123. Memo Schlesinger for President (visit Fanfani), 10 June 1961, POF, Countries Files, b. 119A, JFKL; cf. Schlesinger, "The Kennedy Administration," 189; Nuti, "Commitment to NATO."

124. On these points, see esp. Nuti, "Commitment to NATO"; Nuti, "The United States," 47–48; and Rabe, *The Most Dangerous Area*.

Chapter 7

1. Gundle, *Between Hollywood and Moscow*, 76, 75, 78; Strauss, *Menace*, 271–75; Jean-Marie Domenach, "Le modèle américain," *Esprit*, July–Aug. 1960, 1221.

2. Kuisel, *Seducing the French*, 103–4.

3. Qtd. Judt, *Marxism*, 293; Goguel, *Modernisation*. On the roots of the pauperist campaign, link with anticolonialism, and defense of small business, cf. Wall, *French Communism*, 81–82, 205; Bernard Jourd'hui, "L'offensive des monopoles contre le petit commerce et l'artisanat," *Cahiers du communisme*, Feb. 1960; Dec. BP, 12 Sept. 1957, APCF. On attachment to rural life, see Strauss, *Menace*, 263–64.

4. De Grazia, *Irresistible Empire*, 376–415 (qtd. 379, 389, 411).

5. Colombi in Mtg. Direz., 2 Jan. 1959, VD, APCI; see also Colombi in Mtg. Direz., 7 May 1958, and Pecchioli in Mtg. Direz., 13 Feb. 1963, VD, APCI. In 1964, Amendola, one of the PCI's leaders most open to modernization, also declared that the defense of the small industries and artisanal enterprises was one of the party's priorities; Mtg. Direz., 23 Jan. 1964, VD, APCI. On cooperatives, see Lanaro, *Storia*, 230.

6. Jacqueline Vernes, review of *L'Amérique est-elle trop riche?*, by Claude Alphandéry, *Démocratie nouvelle*, Sept. 1960; Pierre Lefranc, review of *Le nouveau Nouveau monde*, by Claude Julien, ibid., Mar. 1961 (quotations from both reviews).

7. Bergamaschi, "Dottrine sociologiche al servizio dei grandi monopoli industriali," *Rinascita*, Jan. 1956; Jean-François Le-Ny, "Le bon sourire du patron, ou les 'relations humaines,'" *La Nouvelle critique*, no. 48, Sept.–Oct. 1953; Giovanni Cesareo, "Ma è esistito davvero Henry Ford?," *Vie Nuove*, 8 Aug. 1963.

8. Henri Claude, "Le mythe du 'capitalisme populaire' américain," *La Nouvelle critique*, Jan. 1957, 41; cf. Nicola Sarzano, "Siamo tutti Rockefeller," *Vie Nuove*, 5 Mar. 1964.

9. Bergamaschi, "Dottrine," 7; Le-Ny, "Le bon sourire."

10. Vernes, review of *L'Amérique*, 71; Bergamaschi, "Dottrine," 8.

11. Qtd. Gaddis, *The Cold War*, 77; qtd. Shiraev and Zubok, *Anti-Americanism*, 13–14.

12. Lefranc, review of *Le nouveau Nouveau monde*, 74; Jacqueline Vernes, "Les USA face au défi économique de l'URSS," *Démocratie nouvelle*, July 1960, 54–61; Jean Bruteau, "Problèmes de l'automatisation," *La Nouvelle critique*, Sept.–Oct. 1957, 21–34; Philippe Cazelle, "Cybernétique et communisme," *Cahiers du communisme*, Jan.–Feb. 1963; Sarzano,

"Siamo tutti"; Carlo Marcucci, "Le quattro lezioni dei giochi," *Vie Nuove*, 17 Sept. 1960; Antoine Casanova, "La doctrine sociale de l'Eglise et le marxisme," *La Nouvelle critique*, no. 141, Dec. 1962. For attribution of a corporatist outlook to Catholic reformism, see Bruno Trentin in Mtg. Direz., 28 Feb. 1962, VD, APCI; see also Alfredo Reichlin a Segreterie, Federazioni e Comitati Regionali, 22 Aug. 1962, SSP, mf. 494, APCI.

13. Amendola and Romagnoli quotations in Mtg. Direz., 28 Feb. 1962, VD, APCI; other quotation from Gundle, *Between Hollywood and Moscow*, 90 (Berlinguer also qtd. on p. 90; see also p. 80).

14. Dec. BP, 24 May 1962, APCF. Quotation from Bell and Criddle, *The French Communist Party*, 220; cf. Lazar, "Le réalisme," 60–62; Roger Martelli, "De Gaulle et les communistes entre traditions et modernité," in Courtois and Lazar, *50 ans*; Kriegel, *The French Communists*, 92–97, 250–53.

15. Rockefeller, qtd. in de Grazia, *Irresistible Empire*, 378.

16. Dec. BP, 21 Jan. 1960, APCF.

17. Bergamaschi, "Dottrine," 11; cf. Kuisel, *Seducing the French*, 90–91.

18. Giorgio Amendola, "Lotte di massa e nuova maggioranza" (1960), in Amendola, *Classe*, 34; also cited in Gundle, *Between Hollywood and Moscow*, 89; Dec. BP, 10 May, 20 Sept. 1962, APCF; Claude, "Le mythe,'" 42–43.

19. Fulvio Jacchia in Mtg. Cult. Comm., 23–24 July 1956, Alessandro Natta quotation from Mtg. Cult. Comm., 15–16 Nov. 1956, Cult. Comm., APCI.

20. Quotation from Vitelli in Mtg. Direz., 28 Feb. 1962 (see also Trentin and Scoccimarro in ibid.); Barca in Mtg. Direz., 23 Jan. 1964, VD, APCI; cf. Togliatti, "Battere il partito della guerra e lottare per una decisiva svolta a sinistra," *L'Unità*, 6 Oct. 1961. On CESPE, see Vittoria, *Togliatti*, 161–62.

21. *La rabbia*, by Pier Paolo Pasolini and Giovanni Guareschi, cited in David W. Ellwood, "Italy: Containing Modernity, Domesticating America," in Stephan, *The Americanization*, 263; see also Pasolini, *Il caos*.

22. Quotation from Kuisel, *Seducing the French*, 183 (see also ibid., chap. 7 and 206–10 on all these aspects). On de Gaulle and modernization, cf. Michael H. Harrison, "French Anti-Americanism under the Fourth Republic and the Gaullist Solution," in Lacorne, Rupnik, and Toinet, *The Rise*, 173; and Vaïsse, *La grandeur*, 43, 52.

23. Charles Fiterman, "Pour une Europe indépendante, démocratique et pacifique," *Cahiers du communisme*, Apr. 1966 and Apr. 1968; Mitterrand in Kuisel, *Seducing the French*, 209.

24. See chap. 6. Rochet report at CC, Ivry, 23–24 Feb. 1961 (pp. 34–36), 261 J2/37, APCF. See also Dec. BP, 5 Aug. 1960 and 10 May 1962; qtd. Dec. BP, 20 Sept. 1962, APCF; cf. Waldeck Rochet, "Rapport d'activités au CC, du XVIe Congrès du PCF, 11–14 Mai 1961," *Cahiers du communisme*, June 1961; Claude, *Gaullisme*; Duclos, *Gaullisme*.

25. Jean Jerome to Rochet, "Quelques remarques sur les problèmes économiques de notre monde," 19 Dec. 1967, in WRP, b. 173, APCF.

26. Harold Rosenberg, "Fantaisie orgaméricaine," *Les Temps modernes*, no. 152 (1958); also in Kuisel, *Seducing the French*, 128–29. On Fordism, see Jane Jenson, "The French Left: A Tale of Three Beginnings," in Hollifield and Ross, *Searching*, 86.

27. Kuisel, *Seducing the French*, 122–23.

28. For different interpretations, cf. Ross, *Fast Cars*, 40; Gundle, *I comunisti*, 173.

29. Bianciardi, *L'integrazione*, 29–30.

30. Minutes of Mtg. Bureau Politique, 30 Nov. 1961, APCF. Cf. Maurice Loi, "Les monopoles et l'Université," *La Nouvelle critique*, 126, May 1961.

31. Mtg. Direz., 28 Feb. 1962 "Preparazione alla conferenza economica dell'Istituto Gramsci," VD, APCI; Mario Alicata, "Degradazione della cultura italiana in regime democristiano e clericale," *Rinascita*, Mar. 1958; Georges Cogniot, "Les moyennes de formation de la jeunesse," *Cahiers du communisme*, Feb. 1960; Loi, "Les monopoles"; Gian Carlo Pajetta, "Una svolta delle generazioni," *Rinascita*, special issue, Summer 1960.

32. Gundle, *I comunisti*, 151, 172–73; Kuisel, *Seducing the French*, 120; polls from Pierangelo Isernia, "Anti-Americanism in Europe during the Cold War," in Katzenstein and Keohane, *Anti-Americanisms*, 69.

33. Auchincloss to State Dept., 17 Nov. 1961, POL 12-IT, RG59, NA; Reinhardt to Sec. State, 13 May 1963, NSC Files, Italy, b. 120, JFKL. On "triangle of protest" and the South, see Letter Frederick G. Dutton (Asst. Sec. State) to Sen. Kenneth B. Keating, 3 Jan. 1962, 765.001, RG59, NA. Boogaart qtd. in de Grazia, *Irresistible Empire*, 395.

34. Quotation frm Randolph Kidder to State Dept., "Communism in France— Semi-annual Review (January–June 1958)," 6 Aug. 1958, 751.001, RG59, NA; see also the following semiannual reviews to 1962. Cf. Hoffmann, *Le mouvement*.

35. Memo L. W. Fuller to Rostow, 30 Apr. 1964, Recs. PPC 1963–64, b. 252, RG59, NA; Cf. Mtg. Harriman—Brodolini, Dep. Sec. PSI (on subject of PCI and PCF's strengths), 12 Aug. 1966, and McBride to State Dept., 23 July 1966, POL 12-FR, RG59, NA.

36. Pajetta in Mtg. Direz., 9 Dec. 1960, VD, mf. 024, APCI; Dec. BP, 10 Oct. 1959, and 12 Apr. 1960, APCF. In general on decline of pacifism during the first Cold War coexistence, see Santamaria, *Le parti de l'ennemi*, 237–63.

37. Cf. Fejtö, *The French Communist Party*, 225; "Résolution du CC, du PCF, 14 décembre 1962," *L'Humanité*, 15 Dec. On the PCF's continued dependence on Moscow, see esp. Letter Raymond Guyot to Thorez, 27 Mar. 1962, TP, 626 AP, AN. For a strong emphasis on the split between the PCI and PCF, see Lazar, *Maisons*, 102–6. On the PCI and the Sino-Soviet split, cf. Höbel, "Il PCI nella crisi."

38. Pajetta in Mtg. Direz., 9 Dec. 1960, VD, APCI; cf. Berlinguer in Mtg. Direz., 12 Feb. 1965, and Togliatti in Mtg. Direz., 19 Sept. 1961, VD, mf. 025, APCI.

39. See esp. Styan, *France*, 49–67.

40. Togliatti in Mtg. Direz., 7 Nov. 1960, Amendola in Mtg. Direz., 9 Nov. 1960, VD, mf. 024, APCI.

41. Dec. BP, 17 Nov. 1960; on Figuères, see his Note Biographique in Archives Personnelles Déposées aux Archives Départmentales, no. 93, pp. 104–6, APCF.

42. Pajetta in Mtg. Direz., 21 May 1965, VD, APCI; Pajetta, "Perchè andiamo ad Hanoi," *Rinascita*, 24 Apr. 1965; Léo Figuères, "Pour un vraie politique de paix et d'indépendance nationale," *Cahiers du communisme*, Apr. 1966, 5.

43. Report Mtg. Direz., 21 July 1966, VD, mf. 018; Berlinguer in Mtg. Direz., 25 Sept. 1969 (bicycles), VD, mf. 006, APCI; Enrico Berlinguer, "Al fianco del Vietnam," *Rinascita*, 12 Apr. 1968; Dec. BP, 15 Apr. 1965, Dec. BP, 22 Sept. 1966 (Operation Milliard), APCF; "Intervention de Waldeck Rochet au cours des entretiens avec la délégation des travailleurs du Vietnam," 25 Aug.–17 Sept. 65, GP, 264J, b. 7/8, APCF.

44. Tel. A-1564, Amembassy to State Dept., 1 Mar. 1968, and A-168, 18 Mar. 1968, POL12 FR, RG59, NA; "Le Parti communiste a versé 216 millions pour le bateau de la solidarité," *L'Humanité*, 21 Feb. 1968; "Des communistes français au Vietnam: Etienne Fajon raconte,"

L'Humanité dimanche, no. 160 (Mar. 1968); Alice Kahn, "Les communistes français et le combat des peuples d'Indochine," *Cahiers du communisme*, Sept. 1970.

45. Longo in Mtg. Direz., 4 Jan. 1966, Note on Mtg. Longo with Brezhnev and Ponomariov, 18 Aug. 1966, Report Berlinguer to Directorate, 27 Dec. 1966 (after mission to Vietnam and Moscow), all in VD, mf. 018, APCI; Dec. BP, 22 July 1965, and Waldeck Rochet reply to Billoux in Mtg. BP, 2 Dec. 1965, both in BP, 1965–72, APCF; "Dichiarazione comune del PCF e del PCI," *L'Unità*, 5 May 1966.

46. On Paul VI, see Enzo Roggi, "Una pagina di storia rivelata: 'Così Paolo VI scrisse a Ho Chi Minh,'" in http://www.dsrai.it, accessed Jan. 2008. Raymond, *The French Communist Party*, 58.

47. Berlinguer in Mtg. Direz., 12 Feb. 1965, VD, mf. 029, APCI; David-Goliath quote adapted from Kuisel, *Seducing the French*, 194.

48. "Dichiarazione comune del PCF e del PCI"; Mtgs. Direz., 14 and 27 Dec. 1966, VD, mf. 018, APCI; see also Rochet's response to Billoux in Mtg. BP, 2 Dec. 1965, APCF.

49. Silvia Ridolfi, "Gli americani nelle paludi," *Rinascita*, 20 Feb. 1965; Scoccimarro in Mtg. Direz., 4 Jan. 1966, VD, mf. 018, APCI. Georges Girard, "La juste cause du peuple vietnamien l'emportera," *Cahiers du communisme*, Dec. 1966, 81–91; "'Escalation': Come si arriva alla guerra nucleare" (publishing essay by Herman Kahn), *Rinascita*, 22 May 1965; on PCF turning anti-imperialism into anti-Americanism, cf. Jenkins, *Nationalism*, 164.

50. Dec. BP, 28 May 1965 (also comparing Johnson's base policies and aggression in the Caribbean with U.S. bases in France), APCF; on Mediterranean Conference, see Mtg. Direz., 20 Sept. 1967, VD, mf. 019, APCI; Special Report CIA, "Italian Communist Party Draws Further Away from Moscow," 25 Oct. 1968, *FRUS*, 1964–68, XII, doc. 144; cf. Riccardi, *Il "problema Israele*," 296–97.

51. Described in chap. 8.

52. Costigliola, *France*, 139; Vaïsse, *La grandeur*, 674; Pierre Melandri, "The Troubled Friendship: France and the United States, 1945–1989," in Lundestad, *No End*, 124–25.

53. Dec. BP, 31 May 1966 (on Garaudy); Rochet's reply to Billoux in Mtg. BP, 2 Dec. 1965, APCF, and Dec. BP, 24 Mar., 7 July 1966 (on de Gaulle and NATO), APCF.

54. Enrico Berlinguer, "Risposta al compagno Leroy sul promemoria di Yalta," *Rinascita*, 24 Oct. 1964; quotations from Gerardo Chiaromonte, "Rifare l'Europa," *Rinascita*, 2 June 1967.

55. The PCI was also more ecumenical than the PCF in embracing struggles for emancipation in the Arab world. Although the Middle East was a more vulnerable spot than Indochina for U.S. imperialism, Sereni noted, the French comrades were reluctant to endorse a movement that had very few socialist elements and very strong religious connotations; Mtg. Direz., 22 June 1967, VD, mf. 019, APCI; see also Occhetto in Mtg. Direz., 7–8 May 1969, VD, mf. 06, APCI.

56. Enrico Berlinguer, "A fianco del Vietnam," *Rinascita*, 12 Apr. 1968.

57. Eugenio Peggio, "Come uscire dalla crisi del MEC?," *Rinascita*, 28 Nov. 1964; Amendola intervention at Central Committee PCI, in *L'Unità*, 28 Aug. 1968. Cf. Giorgio Amendola, "Il nostro internazionalismo," *Rinascita*, 6 Sept. 1968; Chiaromonte, "Rifare l'Europa"; on Amendola's pro-EEC choices cf. Gualtieri, "Giorgio Amendola"; and Maggiorani, *L'Europa*, 133–34 (Peggio), 166–68, 254–55. Thorez had immediately disagreed with Peggio's analyses of the EEC: see esp. Note drafted by Jacques Denis for Thorez, "Sur la rédaction commune d'un article sur le Marché commun à Prague," 26 July 1961, in TP, 626 AP, b. 34, AN.

58. See Amendola and Galluzzi in Mtg. Direz., 7–8 May 1969, VD, mf. 06, APCI.

59. "Dichiarazione comune PCF-PCI"; Rochet to Billoux, Dec. BP, 16 Apr. 1967, APCF.

60. Dec. BP, 27 June 1968, APCF.

61. Memo Léo Figuères for BP, "Les contradictions de l'impérialisme et la politique des communistes," n.d. (1961), LF, 270J, b. 2, APCF. Pierre Villon, "Trois politiques étrangères," *Démocratie nouvelle*, May 1965; Jacques Kahn, "Monopoles, nations et Marché Commun," *Cahiers du communisme*, Apr. 1966; and Fiterman, "Pour une Europe." See also Belloin, "Le Comité."

62. Fiterman, "Pour une Europe"; Maggiorani, *L'Europa*, 245, 261–66; Report Mtg. Longo-Rochet, 24–25 May 1965 (p. 3), WRP, Secretariat, b. 5, APCF.

63. Cf. Thomas Gomart, "Le PCF au miroir des relations franco-soviétiques (1964–1968)," *Relations internationales*, no. 114 (Summer 2003): 249–66. On SFIO, see Dec. BP, 6 July 1967, and 14 Dec. 1967, APCF. For a recent account on the French Socialists and the United States, see Fuks, *L'anti-américanisme*.

64. See below on U.S. perceptions of such change.

65. Report Achille Occhetto to the "attivo nazionale di propaganda sulla campagna elettorale 1968," 26–27 Jan. 1968, SSP, P. 2248, mf. 547, pp. 3–4; Report Occhetto in Mtg. Direz., 29 May 1967, VD, mf. 019, APCI.

66. Report Longo in Mtg. Direz., 30 Mar. 1965, VD, mf. 029; Amendola in Mtg. Direz., 6 Sept. 1967 (see also comments by Longo on DC and Middle East in ibid.), VD, mf. 019, APCI.

67. Claudio Petruccioli, "Sul Vietnam ci si unisce," *Rinascita*, 28 Apr. 1968.

68. Mtg. Longo with comrades Jacoviello, Bandiera, Olivetti, Moretti, De Sanctis, D'Agostini, Scalzone (19 Apr. 1968), Archivio Longo, mf. 441, pp. 5099–131, APCI; Rossanda, *L'anno*, 116–17; Giovanni Berlinguer, "Studenti e partito: Un anno decisivo," *Critica marxista*, Nov. Dec. 1968; Gian Carlo Pajetta, "I giovani non sono 'una difficoltà' ma sono un problema," *Rinascita*, 10 Mar. 1967; Höbel, "Il PCI di Longo," 435–38; Tarrow, *Democracy and Disorder*, 161–63.

69. Letter Charles Fourniau to Secretariat, 4 Apr. 1968, GP 264 J, b. 2; cf. Dec. BP, 9 May 1968, APCF.

70. Ajello, *Il lungo addio*, 66–67; Hollander, *Pellegrini*, 654–57.

71. Cf. Sirinelli, *Intellectuels*, 241; David Drake, *Intellectuals*, 151. For a followup during the Nixon years, see "L'appel des Onze (onze personnalités contre la guerre au Vietnam)," *L'Humanité*, 5 Dec. 1973.

72. Christofferson, *French Intellectuals*, 39–46; Jean-Paul Sartre, "Idéologie et révolution," *Obliques*, no. 18–19 (1979); David Drake, *Intellectuals*, 136–37; and David Drake, *Sartre*, 114. For a recent update on these issues, see Wolin, *The Wind*.

73. See esp. Schwartz, *Lyndon Johnson*, 26–33 (quotation on 30); Randall Woods, *LBJ*, 701–5.

74. William N. Fraleigh (Counselor Emb.) to State Dept., 30 June 1968, and Letter Fraleigh to Givan Walker (Officer in Charge of Italian Affairs), 10 Mar. 1965, *FRUS*, 1964–68, XII, docs. 101 and 107; Fraleigh to Givan Walker, 8 Apr. 1965, Gen. Recs. BEA, Country Director, Italy, 1943–1968, Lot 68 D 436, RG59, NA; and Memo Special Assistant (Valenti) to President Johnson, *FRUS*, 1964–68, XII, doc. 109.

75. Bohlen to State Dept., 17 and 23 Dec. 1966, POL 12-FR, RG59, NA; cf. John A. Bovery Jr. to State Dept., 1 Oct. 1964, and Tel. 3066 Bohlen to State Dept., 3 Dec. 1965, in ibid.

76. On La Pira, see Guthrie (Rome) to State Dept., 22 Nov. 1965; Bundy to Johnson, 28 Nov. 1965 (for quotation), *FRUS*, 1964–68, XII, docs. 119, 120. For alarm about Catholics' connections with communist campaigns; see Reinhardt to State Dept., 9 Apr. 1965, ibid., doc. 108; and Memo Conv. Governor Harriman, Frazier Draper (Ital. Affairs)—Giacomo Brodolini (Vice Sec. Italian Socialist Party), 17 Aug. 1966, POL 12-IT, RG59, NA.

77. Bohlen to State Dept., 24 Apr. 1965, *FRUS*, 1964–68, XII, doc. 46.

78. Bohlen to State Dept., 1 Sept. 1966, and 27 July 1967, and Shriver to State Dept., 28 May 1968, *FRUS*, 1964–68, XII, docs. 66, 76, and 79; Cf. Institut Français d'Opinion Publique, *Les Français*, 88, 299. The U.S. embassy noted that Vietnam, for the Communists, remained a "pole of protest around which to rally the masses" (including Gaullists); but the Communists would rather "expect most of their votes to come to them on other issues"; Tel. A-498, Emb. Paris to State Dept. (unsigned), 29 Sept. 1966, POL12-FR, RG59, NA.

79. Tel. Emb. Paris to State Dept., 10 Oct. 1968, *FRUS*, 1964–68, XII, doc. 84.

80. Tel. 3066, Bohlen to State Dept., 3 Dec. 1965; Tel. 3325, Bohlen to State Dept., 13 Dec. 1965; Tel. 3202, McBride (Peking) to Emb. Paris and State Dept., 8 Dec. 1965, all in POL 12-FR, RG59, NA.

81. Quotations from Memo Fraleigh to State Dept., "The 11th Congress of the PCI," 4 Mar. 1966, Reinhardt to State Dept., 20 May 1965, and Ackley to State Dept., 18 Feb. 1969, all in POL 12-IT, RG59, NA.

82. Memo Thomas L. Hughes (INR) to Sec. State, "Italy: Communist 'Kindness' Embarrasses Government," 8 May 1969, and Memo Gammon to Ambassador, "Your Meeting with Nenni—China," 8 May 1969, POL 12-IT, RG59, NA; Tel. A-1439, Melloy to State Dept., 26 May 1966, POL 1-IT, RG59, NA.

83. Memo by Charles Frankel to Undersec. State Ball, 9 Dec. 1965; Letter Harry R. Most (Chairman Bureau of Education and Cultural Affairs—Fulbright Program) to Dean Rusk, 16 Dec. 1965, both in CU, Country Files, b. 239, CU. On cultural activities in this period, cf. Cull, *The Cold War*, chaps. 5 and 6.

84. Memo Bundy to Pres. Johnson, 4 Aug. 1965 and Memo for the Record by INR, "Italy—Covert Action Program for FY 1968," *FRUS*, 1964–68, vol. XII, docs. 116, 133; Memo Valenti to Johnson, 16 Apr. 1965, *FRUS*, 1964–68, XII, doc. 109.

85. John A. Bovey Jr. (Counselor Emb. Paris) to State Dept., 30 Apr. 1965; Bohlen to State Dept., 13 Dec. 1965; McBride to State Dept., 10 Dec. 1965, all in POL 12-FR, RG59, NA; Tel. 1184, Memo Conv. Earl Sohm with Eugenio Reale, 19 Mar. 1958, 765.00, RG59, NA.

86. Tel. A-2450, Shriver to State Dept., 24 July 1968 (on both Ballanger and Garaudy); Memo Conv. Shriver-Ballanger, 15 Oct. 1968, POL 12-FR, RG59, NA.

87. Gianfranco Corsini, "Marilyn tra mito e verità," *Rinascita*, 11 Aug. 1962; Jean-Marc Aucuy, "Hommage à Marilyn Monroe ou la décolonisation par l'érotisme," *La Nouvelle critique*, no. 140, Nov. 1962; Corsini, "Marilyn e gli intellettuali," *Rinascita*, 8 Sept. 1962; cf. "'Miller: Mia moglie è geniale; Marilyn: Mio marito è matto': Intervista," *Vie Nuove*, 23 Apr. 1960. Similar celebrations and disagreements marked the two parties' reactions to the deaths of other American icons, such as Clark Gable or Walt Disney. The latter was celebrated for seemingly giving mass culture a "poetic expression"; Mino Argentieri, "L'ultimo re di Hollywood," *Vie Nuove*, 19 Nov. 1960; Renato Nicolai, "L'altra faccia della cronaca: Disney" (for quotation), *Vie Nuove*, 22 Dec. 1966; G. S. "Walt Disney," *Les Lettres françaises*, no. 1162, 28 Dec. 1966. Icons often discussed or interviewed in both journals included

Marlon Brando, Truman Capote, Orson Wells, Buster Keaton, and Robert Oppenheimer. Some of the paragraphs here resume arguments presented in Alessandro Brogi, "France, Italy, the Communists, and the Prague Spring," in Bischof, Ruggenthaler, and Karner, *The Prague Spring*.

88. "Pierre Courtade nous a quittés," *Démocratie nouvelle*, June 1963, 83.

89. Cf. Shiraev and Zubok, *Anti-Americanism*, 14–15.

90. Suri, *Power and Protest*. For similar point about de Gaulle, see Georges-Henri Soutou, "Paris and the Prague Spring," in Bischof, Ruggenthaler, and Karner, *The Prague Spring*.

91. Ross, *May '68*, 6. There is no need here to reference the vast literature on the protest movements in France and Italy. Where pertinent to my argument, the most significant contributions are cited in this chapter. For a recent debate and continued polemics particularly regarding the Paris uprising, see Vigna, "Clio"; Ross, Hatzfeld, and Artous, "Mai '68"; Gildea, "1968 in 2008"; Seidman, introduction to *The Imaginary Revolution*; and Marino, *Biografia*.

92. Among sources highlighting connections between Americanization and the new protest movements, but lacking a comparative analysis comprising official and intellectual views from both sides of the Atlantic, see esp. Maria Malatesta, "Il rifiuto dell'americanizzazione nella cultura italiana degli anni '60," in D'Attorre, *Nemici*; Gundle, *Between Hollywood and Moscow*, chap. 4 (with further information in the Italian edition); Alessandro Portelli, "The Transatlantic Jeremiad: American Mass Culture, and Counterculture and Opposition Culture in Italy," in Kroes, Rydell, and Bosscher, *Cultural Transmissions*; Flores and De Bernardi, *Il sessantotto*; Roger, *The American Enemy*, 401–9; Kristin Ross, *May '68*; Seidman, *The Imaginary Revolution*; Fink, Gassert, and Junker, *1968*; and Marwick, *The Sixties*.

93. Tarrow, *Democracy and Disorder*, 155–57; Gundle, *I comunisti*, 277–80; Alberto De Bernardi, "Il Sessantotto in Italia," in Cherubini et al., *Il miracolo*, 317–19; Seidman, *The Imaginary Revolution*, 53–59; Joffrin, *Mai 68*, 42–55.

94. Cf. Lefebvre, *The Explosion*, 104; Dutucil, *Nanterre*.

95. Lumley, *States of Emergency*, 94–99; Cohn-Bendit in Reader (with Wadia), *The May 1968 Events*, 7.

96. Jean-Pierre Vernant, "Le PCF et la révolution algérienne," in Vernant, *Entre mythe et idéologie*, 543–44; David Drake, *Intellectuals*, 129–30; Singer, *Prelude*, 56–57.

97. For a thesis emphasizing the causation between American dissidence and Europe's anti-Americanism, see esp. Hollander, *Anti-Americanism*. On Pavese, see chap. 1.

98. Qtd. Kristin Ross, *May '68*, 4; see similar view in Singer, *Prelude*, xv, 152–85. Cf. Touraine, *The May Movement*, chap. 5. On Italy, quotation from Judt, *Postwar*, 413; cf. Lumley, *States of Emergency*, 3, 244–46; Ginsborg, *A History*, chap. 9.

99. Romero, "Indivisibilità," 935–50; Baglioni, *I giovani*; Franco Minganti, "Juke-Box Boys: Postwar Italian Music and the Culture of Covering," in Fehrenbach and Poiger, *The American Cultural Impact*; David Drake, *Intellectuals*, 128–29; Richard J. Golsan, "From French Anti-Americanism and Americanization to the 'American Enemy,'" in Stephan, *The Americanization*, 56–57.

100. Gian Carlo Pajetta, "Una rivolta delle generazioni," *Rinascita*, special issue, Summer 1960; Aldo Zerbi, "La noia dei topi d'oro: Giovani bene a Parigi," *Vie Nuove*, 27 June 1963; cf. Paul Morette, "La chanson subie," *Démocratie nouvelle*, May 1964.

101. Dec. BP, 15 Oct. 1959, 21 Nov. 1963, APCF; cf. Marcel Cornu, "Frank Lloyd Wright:

Dieu le père de l'architecture moderne ou grand sorcier?," *Les Lettres françaises*, 1 Dec. 1966; Mario Spinella, "Sviluppo capitalistico e cultura d'opposizione," *Rinascita*, 1 Dec. 1962; Antonio del Guercio, "La Pop Art passa ma i problemi rimangono," *Rinascita*, 11 July 1964.

102. Qtd. "Problemi dei giovani," *Rinascita*, 27 Oct. 1963; Claudio Pavolini, "I giovani non sono una difficoltà," *Rinascita*, 3 Mar. 1967; Alessandro Curzi, "Sessanta, sesso, sinistra," in Veltroni, *Il sogno*.

103. "Problemi dei giovani"; Paolo Spriano, "La cultura per la pace," *Rinascita*, 24 Nov. 1962; Leroy report to BP, in Dec. BP, 21 Nov. 1963, APCF; Occhetto, *A dieci anni*, 41–42.

104. Quotation from Malatesta, "Il rifiuto," 297; see also Giuseppe Vacca, "Politica e teoria del marxismo italiano negli anni sessanta," in Vacca, *Il marxismo*; and Ajello, *Il lungo addio*, 63–65. On the Gruppo '63, see Ferretti, *Il mercato*, 130–33.

105. Breschi, *Sognando la rivoluzione*, 99–140; Grandi, *La generazione*, 5–8; Richard Drake, "Vivere la rivoluzione."

106. On *Socialisme ou barbarie*, see Hirsch, *The French New Left*, 108–31; on Vernant, see Barbagallo, "L'intellettuale," quotation on 19; Vernant, "Lettre de la cellule Sorbonne-Lettres," in Vernant, *Entre mythe et idéologie*; on intellectuals and student movement "Débat: Sur l'ampleur et les conséquences de la révolte de l'intelligence," *Démocratie nouvelle*, Nov. 1965, 27–34; on UEC, see Dec. BP, 9 Aug. 1956, APCF.

107. Togliatti, *Memoriale di Yalta*, 10; Lazar, *Maisons*, 126; Verdès-Leroux, *Le réveil*, 190.

108. Memo on FGCI by G. F. Borghini to "Membri della Commissione Giovanile della Direzione Nazionale del PCI," 10 Mar. 1967, Istituti e organismi vari, mf. 544, APCI.

109. Mtg. Direz., 4 Jan. 1966, VD, mf. 018, APCI. For the French case, see Bourg, "The Red Guards."

110. Occhetto Report to "attivo nazionale di propaganda, di propaganda sulla campagna elettorale 1968," 26–27 Jan. 1968, SSP, P. 2248, mf. 547, pp. 16–19; see also Occhetto in Mtg. Direz., 29 May 1967, VD, mf. 019, APCI; Report Duclos to BP, in Dec. BP, 31 Oct. 1963, APCF; Henri Krasucki, "La culture, les intellectuels et la nation," *Cahiers du communisme*, May–June 1966.

111. Occhetto in Mtg. Direz., 29 May 1967; Petruccioli, "Sul Vietnam ci si unisce"; Claudio Petruccioli, "Per un modo nuovo di fare politica," *Rinascita*, 4 Oct. 1968.

112. Gian Carlo Pajetta, "Francia ancora combattente," *Rinascita*, 5 July 1968; Amendola and Berlinguer in Mtg. Direz., 6 June, 3 June 1968, VD, mf. 020, APCI.

113. PCI CC debate in *L'Unità*, 27–29 Mar. 1968; F. Di Giulio, "Lotta sindacale e svolta politica," *Rinascita*, 3 May 1968; Lumley, *States of Emergency*, 245. On the CGT, see George Ross, *Workers*, 179–206; and Kriegel, *The French Communists*, 346–49. Cf. Dec. BP, 9 May 1968, APCF. See also Caute, *The Year*, 232–36; and Gerd-Rainer Horn, "The Changing Nature of the European Working Class," in Fink, Gassert, and Junker, *1968*, 352–56.

114. Seidman, *The Imaginary Revolution*, 17; Lumley, *States of Emergency*, 109–16; Breschi, *Sognando la rivoluzione*, 185–209. On the challenge to the PCI's hegemony over unions, see Grisoni and Portelli, *Le lotte*, 108–11; and Tarrow, *Democracy and Disorder*, 178–86.

115. Quotations from Touraine, *The May Movement*, 23; Lipovetsky, "Changer la vie," 100; and Feenberg and Freedman, *When Poetry Ruled*, 68.

116. Quotation from Horn, "The Changing Nature," 361. Cf. Touraine, *The May Move-*

ment, 25–26; Rossanda, *L'anno*, 168–69. Quotation from Morin, Lefort, and Castoriadis, *Mai '68*, 185–86.

117. Qtd. in Seidman, *The Imaginary Revolution*, 7; Lumley, *States of Emergency*, 70–72.

118. Georges Marchais, "De faux révolutionnaires à démasquer," *L'Humanité*, 3 May 1968. Cf. "Mise en garde contre les manifestations decidées en dehors des organisations de la classe ouvrière," *L'Humanité*, 27 May 1968. Rochet report, "Les événements de mai–juin 1968," CC, 8–9 July 1968, Nanterre, cote 4AV10/128 CD 18, APCF.

119. Giorgio Amendola, "Necessità della lotta sui due fronti," *Rinascita*, 7 June 1968; Amendola in Mtg. Direz., 6 June 1968, VD, mf. 020, APCI; Pier Paolo Pasolini, "Il PCI ai giovani!" (first pub. in *Nuovi Argomenti*, no. 10, 17 Oct. 1968), in Pasolini, *Empirismo*, 151–59. Cf. Pasolini, *Il caos*, 139–41; and Francesco Ciafaloni and Carlo Donolo, "Contro la falsa coscienza del movimento studentesco," *Quaderni piacentini*, no. 39 (July 1969). Further contradicting himself, Pasolini later joined Lotta Continua.

120. Mtg. Direz., 29 May 1967, VD, mf. 019 and Mtg. Direz., 8 May 1969, VD, mf. 020, APCI.

121. Giovanni Berlinguer, "Studenti e partito: Un'anno decisivo," *Critica marxista*, Nov.–Dec. 1968, 39–40; Ferraresi, *Threats*, 90–114.

122. Rochet report, "Les événements."

123. Longo in Höbel, "Il PCI di Longo," 438. Cf. G. Borghini, "La crisi dei vecchi organismi rappresentativi," *Il Contemporaneo*, 23 Feb. 1968; and "Atti del convegno nazionale."

124. Occhetto, *A dieci anni*, 90–94; Napolitano in Ufficio Politico, 11 Dec. 1968, mf. 020, APCI.

125. *Rinascita*, 28 Dec. 1968; also Luigi Longo, "Il movimento studentesco nella lotta anticapitalistica," *Il Contemporaneo*, 3 May 1968; Luigi Longo, "L'agonia del centrosinistra non deve essere pagata dai lavoratori," *L'Unità*, 21 June 1968. Cf. Höbel, "Il PCI di Longo"; and Becker, *Le Parti communiste*.

126. Jean-Jacques Becker, "Communisme et gaullisme dans la crise de Mai 1968," in Courtois and Lazar, *50 ans*; cf. Roger Martelli, *Mai 1968*; Rochet report, "Les événements."

127. Judt, *Postwar*, 447.

128. Cf. Höbel, "Il PCI di Longo"; and Lafon, "Le PCF," 96. I analyze the other motives for the PCI and PCF's reactions in chap. 8.

129. Quotations from Gundle, *Between Hollywood and Moscow*, 130; and Raymond, *The French Communist Party*, 159. Cf. Judt, *Postwar*, 403; Philippe Fuchsmann, "Karl Marx, notre contemporain," *Cahiers du communisme*, Feb. 1969; Amendola in Direz., 6 June 1968, VD, mf. 020, APCI (asking for sharper criticism of Marcuse's book, which had sold 100,000 copies in Italy). In France, the book, which was translated in 1968, sold more than 350,000 copies in two months; see Combes, *La littérature*. Gramsci, Lukács, and Luxemburg, whom many interpreted as diverging from most Leninist practices, were also rediscovered in the 1960s.

130. Léo Figuères, "Les intellectuels sont une des couches sociales lesées par la politique du pouvoir," and Léo Figuères, "Les intellectuels et les classes sociales," both reports to BP (1966, no date specified), LF, 270J, b. 2, APCF.

131. Courtois and Lazar, *Histoire*, 355–56; cf. Grémion, *Paris-Prague*. "Communiqué du Bureau politique sur un livre de Roger Garaudy," *Cahiers du communisme*, Jan. 1970; cf. precedent in Letter Marchais to BP, 18 Dec. 1969, in Dec. BP, APCF.

132. Sartre, qtd. in David Drake, *Intellectuals*, 135; cf. Birchall, *Sartre against Stalinism*, 199–220; Brillant, "Intellectuels."

133. Vacca, "Politica e teoria"; Vittoria, *Togliatti*.

134. Palmiro Togliatti, "Il destino dell'uomo," *Rinascita*, 30 Mar. 1962; Romano Ledda, "La cultura e le masse," *Rinascita*, 2 Mar. 1963; also in Ajello, *Il lungo addio*, 31–34.

135. Alicata, "Sartre e i comunisti," *Rinascita*, 4 Apr. 1964; cf. Vittoria, *Togliatti*, chap. 4.

136. Qtd. in Mtg. Direz., 13 Oct. 1969, VD, mf. 006, APCI; cf. Ajello, *Il lungo addio*, 94–95; Rossanda, "Report to PCI Secretariat on Activities Cultural Section," 12 Oct. 1965, Sezione Culturale, pp. 5–7, APCI. On the Amendola-Ingrao clash leading to the Eleventh Party Congress, see Giorgio Amendola, "Il socialismo in Occidente," *Rinascita*, 7 Nov. 1964; and Pietro Ingrao, "Un nuovo programma per tutta la sinistra," *Rinascita*, 25 Dec. 1965. Cf. Amyot, *The Italian Communist Party*, chaps. 3, 10; Carlo Galluzzi, "I comunisti e il centro-sinistra," *Critica marxista*, 1972, no. 5.

137. Ivano Cipriani, "La RAI-TV dopo l'anno della grande crisi," *Rinascita*, 8 Jan. 1966; Lorenzo Gruppi, "Cultura di massa o unità culturale?," *Rinascita*, 24 Dec. 1966; Mtg. Cult. Comm., 24–25 May 1966, Sezione Culturale, APCI; cf. Malatesta, "Il rifiuto," 295–97.

138. See Memo by Léo Figuères, n.d. (but late 1964), p. 4, LF, 270J, b. 2, APCF.

139. Alicata in Mtg. Direz., 29 Jan. 1965, VD, mf. 029, APCI.

140. Memo Ilio Gioffredi on Radio-TV for Section Press and Propaganda, 13 Mar. 1968, SSP, mf. 547, APCI. On ARCI, see Gundle, *I comunisti*, 295–301.

141. See, e.g., Mino Argentieri, "Il Western casereccio," *Il Contemporaneo*, Jan. 1966; "Quattro domande agli uomini del cinema," *Rinascita*, 25 Aug. 1967; Memo by Léo Figuères, n.d. (late 1964), LF, 270J, b. 2, APCF; Jacques Ourévitch, "Bardot dans le cirque américain," *Les Lettres françaises*, 30 Dec. 1965; cf. Marie, *Le cinéma*, 221–63.

142. Gianfranco Corsini, "L'America del dissenso," *Il Contemporaneo*, Mar. 1966; Louis Safir, "'Presa della Bastiglia' degli studenti a Berkeley," *Rinascita*, 25 Dec. 1965; Oglesby tour described in *Bollettino: I comunisti* 2, no. 1, Apr. 1966, p. 11, SSP, mf. 0530, APCI; Giorgio Amendola, "Le ragioni della crisi americana," *Rinascita*, 5 Apr. 1968; Longo in Mtg. Direz., 17 June 1968, VD, mf. 020, APCI.

143. "Note de Roger Garaudy sur son voyage aux Etats-Unis," date unspecified (1967), WRP, Secretariat, b. 7; Closing speech by Rochet at sixth week of "Pensée Marxiste," 20 Nov. 1967, WRP, Secretariat, b. 8; Report by Marie-Claude Vaillant-Couturier, "Quelques aspects de la situation et des politiques actuelles des Etats-Unis," to members BP, 23 Feb. 1968, WRP, b. 8; Memo Jérôme to Rochet, "Quelques remarques sur les problèmes économiques de notre monde," 19 Dec. 1967, in WRP, b. 173, APCF. For the last quotation, see Report by PCF's Foreign Policy Section, "Les relations franco-américaines," 15 June 1970 (p. 3), WRP, b. 11; all in APCF.

144. Tullio Aymone and Mario Spinella, "La ricerca di nuovi valori nella gioventù italiana di oggi," *Rinascita*, 25 Feb. 1968, Paolo Spriano, "Studenti, professori, operai," *Rinascita*, 19 Apr. 1968; cf. Petruccioli in Mtg. Direz., 26 July 1968, VD, mf. 020, APCI; cf. Jean Colpin, "Les communistes et la jeunesse d'aujourd'hui," *Cahiers du communisme*, Dec. 1970.

145. Quotation from Singer, *Prelude*, 66. Cf. Le Goff, *Mai 68*, part 3; Lumley, *States of Emergency*, chap. 10. On the alternative-antagonistic distinction, see also Portelli, "The Transatlantic Jeremiad," 131–32.

146. Jean Bouret, "Un patchwork américain," parts 1–4, *Les Lettres françaises*, 27 Aug.–1 Oct. 1969; quotations from parts 2 and 4.

147. Memo by Union des Ecrivains (to Cultural Section BP), "A propos de la politique culturelle," 2 Feb. 1971, by Bernard Pingaud, RL, 263 J65, APCF.

148. On Pavese, see chap. 1. Louis Safir, "Un vendicatore per Kennedy," *Rinascita*, 1 Oct. 1966. Cf. Amendola, "Le ragioni"; Gisèle Halimi, "L'America e le sue febbri," *Rinascita*, 5 and 26 Apr. 1968; Jacques Roubaud, "Invitation à la lecture de Noam Chomsky," *Les Lettres françaises*, 24 Jan. 1968.

149. Qtd. in Chappell, *A Stone*, 76.

150. Luigi Pintor, "Assassinio di una donna"; qtd. Romano Ledda, "Fine dell'America dei 'liberals'"; and Louis Safir, "Le profonde radici della violenza americana," *Rinascita*, 3 and 12 Apr., 14 June 1968; Jean-Maurice Hermann, "Où va Mister Johnson?," *Démocratie nouvelle*, July–Aug. 1965.

151. Qtd. Ledda, "Fine dell'America"; qtd. Galvano della Volpe, "I negri d'America e le due democrazie," *Critica marxista*, May–June 1965, 328–30; qtd. Safir, "'Presa della Bastiglia'"; cf. Gianfranco Corsini, "La rivoluzione poetica dei giovani americani," *Il Contemporaneo*, Jan. 1965; Claude Lightfoot, "Le nationalisme noir aux U.S.A.," *Démocratie nouvelle*, Nov. 1962.

152. Quotations from Federico Romero, "The Meanderings of American Culture in Cold War Italy," paper delivered at annual mtg. of the American Historical Association, Jan. 1999, 5; and Portelli, "The Transatlantic Jeremiad," 131.

153. Debray, qtd. in Roger, *The American Enemy*, 405; Roger, *The American Enemy*, 405.

154. Revel, *Without Marx or Jesus*.

155. Aron and Malraux qtd. in Seidman, *The Imaginary Revolution*, 2–3.

156. Memo Conv. Raymond Barre (Vice Pres. Commission of Eur. Communities) with George S. Springsteen (Dep. Asst. Sec. for Eur. Affairs) and Abraham Katz (Director Office of OECD, Eur. Comm. and Atlantic Affairs), 5 June 1968, *FRUS*, 1964–68, XIII:699–705; USIS Report, "The Students' Movement: Facts and Prospects," in Klieforth (Rome) to USIA, 15 Jan. 1969, POL 12-IT, RG59, NA. Kennan in Anders Stephanson, "George F. Kennan," entry in Pons and Service, *Dictionary*.

157. On Bell, see Maier, *Among Empires*, 235–36; quotations from Kuklick, *Blind Oracles*, 13, 15.

158. Williams, *The Tragedy*, 59–89.

159. Maier, *Among Empires*, 228–37.

160. Fulbright, *The Arrogance*, 245–46, 20; also qtd. in Alan McPherson, "Americanism against American Empire," in Kazin and McCartin, *Americanism*, 178.

161. Quotation from McPherson, "Americanism," 177.

162. Suri, *Power and Protest*, 99–101.

163. Menand, "The Promise," 217–18.

164. Shriver to State Dept., 31 May, 12 June 1968, POL 12-FR, RG59, NA; Memo Intelligence, 31 May 1968, *FRUS*, 1964–68, XII, doc. 80; Fraleigh to State Dept., 30 June 1964, *FRUS*, 1964–68, XII, doc. 101.

165. Ibid. Cf. Tel. A-2450, Shriver to State Dept., 24 July 1968, POL 12-FR, RG59, NA; Memo Conv. Shriver-Ballanger (PCF), 15 Oct. 1968, and Ackley to State Dept., 13 Sept. 1968, both in POL 12-IT, RG59, NA.

166. Cf. Fraleigh to Walker Givan (the Chargé of Italian Affairs who saw the PCI's democratic potential), 10 Mar. 1965, and Special Report by CIA, 25 Oct. 1968, *FRUS*, 1964–68, XII, docs. 107, 144; Research Memo, REU-72, George C. Denney Jr. to Sec. State, "The Italian Communist Party: Wolf, Sheep or Both?," 31 Dec. 1969, POL 12-IT, RG59, NA.

167. Quotation from Intelligence Memo, 31 May 1968, *FRUS*, 1964–68, XII, doc. 80; Shriver to State Dept., 12 June 1968; Tel. 17742, Shriver to State Dept., 10 July 1968, POL 12-FR, RG59, NA. On Kissinger's admiration of de Gaulle, see esp. Suri, *Kissinger*, 37–38.

168. Reinhardt to State Dept., 9 Apr. 1965; USIS Memo, "The Students' Movement"; Tel. A-1738, Report, "The Student Movement," 30 Dec. 1968, POL 12-IT, RG59, NA; cf. Special Report by CIA, 25 Oct. 1968, *FRUS*, 1964–68, XII, doc. 144; and Bundy's evolution away from a belief in the value of covert operations in Italy, as described earlier in this chapter.

169. Tel. A-1177, Bohlen to State Dept., 27 Jan. 1967, POL 14-FR, and Tel. 15133, Shriver to State Dept., 29 May 1968, POL 12-FR, RG59, NA.

170. Tel. A-1738, Report, "The Student Movement."

171. Memo Conv. Michel Rocard–Peter Semler (Second Sec. Embassy), Paris, 4 Sept. 1968, POL 12-FR, RG59, NA; cf. Tel. 997, Ackley to State Dept., 10 Feb. 1969, POL 12-IT, RG59, NA.

172. Julian Jackson, "De Gaulle and May 1968," in Gough and Horne, *De Gaulle*; Lazar, *Maisons*, 133–34.

Chapter 8

1. The following paragraphs resume arguments in Alessandro Brogi, "France, Italy, the Communists, and the Prague Spring," in Bischof, Ruggenthaler, and Karner, *The Prague Spring*.

2. Courtois and Lazar, *Histoire*, 353; cf. Dec. BP, 27 Aug. 1968 and Letter Garaudy to Rochet, 2 Sept. 1968, in Dec. BP Files, APCF. For an analysis, based on documentation from the archives of Jacques Duclos, at the Musée de l'Histoire Vivante in Montreuil, of the PCF's ambiguous condemnation of the intervention from the start, see Lafon, "Le PCF." On the PCF scandal, see Watson to State Dept., 16 May 1970, POL 12-FR, RG59, NA.

3. Enrico Berlinguer, "Il Partito comunista italiano e il movimento operaio internazionale," *Rinascita*, 8 Mar. 1968. Cf. Giuseppe Boffa, "La crisi cecoslovacca," in Vacca, *Luigi Longo*, 113; Longo in Mtg. Direz., 17 July 1968, VD, mf. 020, APCI.

4. Garaudy to Rochet, 2 Sept. 1968; Courtois and Lazar, *Histoire*, 355; Colombi in Mtg. Direz., 23 Aug. 1968, VD mf. 020, APCI; Luigi Longo, "Sulla Cecoslovacchia: Rapporto alla sessione del Comitato Centrale del PCI del 27–28 agosto 1968," in *L'Unità*, 28 Aug. 1968; Rossanda (Il Manifesto), in *L'Unità*, 18 Oct. 1968; cf. G. Marini, "La repressione della primavera cecoslovacca: Dal 'grave dissenso' alla 'riprovazione,'" in Vacca, *Luigi Longo*, 120; Höbel, "Il PCI, il '68 cecoslovacco," 1149, 1164–65.

5. Qtd. George Cogniot, "Vingt ans après la déclaration de Maurice Thorez au 'Times,'" *Cahiers du communisme*, Nov. 1966, qtd. 80; cf. "Le PCF et la question en Tchécoslovaquie," *Cahiers du communisme*, Aug.–Sept. 1968.

6. Berlinguer, "Il Partito comunista"; Berlinguer in Mtg. Direz., 23 Aug. 1968, VD, mf. 020 (p. 894).

7. Dec. BP, 14 Aug. 1968, APCF; Pajetta, *Le crisi*, 123–27; cf. Höbel, "Il PCI, il '68 cecoslovacco," 1149.

8. Cf. Giorgio Amendola, "Il nostro internazionalismo," *Rinascita*, 6 Sept. 1968; cf. Colombi in Mtg. Direz., 18 Sept. 1968, VD, mf. 020, APCI.

9. Special Report CIA, "Italian Communist Party Draws Further Away from Moscow,"

25 Oct. 1968, *FRUS*, 1964–68, XII, doc. 144. Cf. Dec. BP, 25 Apr. 1968 (Billoux's report at the conference showing competition between the PCI and the PCF for leadership in both the anti-imperialist struggle and in the approach to Arab nationalism).

10. In Mtg. Direz., 18 Sept. 1968, mf. 020 (p. 939), APCI. See also Report Berlinguer to Political Bureau in Mtg. Direz., 16 Nov. 1968, ibid.

11. Ackley to State Dept., 13 Sept. 1968, POL12-IT, RG59, NA; Berlinguer in Mtg. Direz., 16 Nov., 5 Dec. 1968, VD, mf. 020, APCI.

12. Dec. BP, 14 Aug. 1968, APCF; Höbel, "Il PCI, il '68 cecoslovacco," 1150–51; Pons, *Berlinguer*, 11.

13. See, e.g., Colombi in Mtg. Direz., 23 Aug. 1968, mf. 020, APCI; cf. Boffa, "La crisi cecoslovacca," 114; Jeannette Vermeersch in CC, 20–21 Oct. 1968, Ivry-sur-Seine, transcripts of Audio CD nos. 41 and 42, cote AV: 4AV10/151, APCF.

14. Berlinguer in Mtg. Direz., 18 Sept. 1968 (p. 939). Dalmasso, *Il caso "Manifesto,"* 69–70.

15. E.g., Bufalini in Mtg. Direz., 18 Sept. 1968, VD, mf. 020, APCI; cf. Pons, *Berlinguer*, 9; Amendola, "Il nostro internazionalismo"; Napolitano in Mtg. Direz., 8 Nov. 1968, 1123, mf. 020, APCI; Report Billoux to Bureau Politique, in Dec. BP, 7 Aug. 1969, APCF.

16. Marini, "La repressione," 123–24; Dec. BP, 27 Aug. 1968; Letter Garaudy to Rochet, 2 Sept. 1968, in ibid., APCF; Dec. BP, 17 Jan. 1969, APCF. Full text of Garaudy's intervention at Nanterre CC, 8 July 1968, with Rochet's annotations; WRP, b. 4, APCF; Letter Marchais to BP, 18 Dec. 1969, in Dec. BP, APCF. For more analysis of Garaudy's expulsion, see chap. 7.

17. Dec. BP, 14 Aug. 1968, APCF; Luca Pavolini, "Autonomia e internazionalismo," *Rinascita*, 26 July 1968; Longo in Mtg. Direz., 23 Aug. 1968, VD, mf. 020, APCI; "Le PCF et la question."

18. Pons, *Berlinguer*, 13.

19. Quotations from Report CIA, "Italian Communist Party Draws Further Away from Moscow," 25 Oct. 1968, *FRUS*, 1964–68, XII, doc. 144. On U.S. fears of conflict with Moscow, see Günter Bischof, "No Action: The Johnson Administration and the Warsaw Pact Invasion of Czechoslovakia in August 1968," in Bischof, Ruggenthaler, and Karner, *The Prague Spring*.

20. Tel. Emb. Paris to State Dept., 10 Oct. 1968, *FRUS* 1964–68, XII, doc. 84. See also chap. 7.

21. Dec. BP, 14 August 1968, APCF (see background in Letter Charles Fourniau to Secretariat, 4 Apr. 68, GP, 264 J, b. 2, APCF); Memo Conv. Leroy-Favaro, 16 Sept. 1968, RL, 263 J 65, b. 37, APCF; cf. Amendola, "Il nostro internazionalismo," for similar points.

22. Mtg. Direz., 31 Oct. 1968, mf. 020 (pp. 1085–86), APCI. Berlinguer in VD, 20 June 1969, mf. 006 (pp. 1722–29), Fondo Berlinguer, f. 81, APCI; Galluzzi, *La svolta*, 211–14. Höbel, "Il PCI, il '68 cecoslovacco," 1168; Lazar, *Maisons*, 144–47; Marcou, *Le mouvement*, 81–88.

23. Amendola in Mtg. Direz., 7–8 May 1969, VD, mf. 06; cf. Ufficio Segreteria, 2 Sept. 1968 (p. 1488), mf. 020, APCI.

24. In general on this phase of Soviet financing, see Riva, *Oro*, chap. 20.

25. On redefinition of Soviet national security, see Ouimet, *The Rise*. Amendola in Mtg. Direz., 8 Jan. 1971, mf. 017, APCI. Cf. also, for further moves in the late 1970s toward more autonomy for the PCI, Cervetti, *L'oro*. Cf. Riva, *Oro*, 457–70; and Montaldo, *Les secrets*.

26. On Moscow Meeting of 1961, see chap. 7; *L'Unità*, 28 July 1968.

27. Dec. BP, 17 July 1968, APCF; Amendola intervention at Central Committee PCI, *L'Unità*, 28 Aug. 1968.

28. Cf. Amendola, "Il nostro internazionalismo." On PCF's persistent skepticism, see Charles Fiterman, "Pour une Europe indépendante, démocratique et pacifique," *Cahiers du communisme*, Apr. 1966 and Apr. 1968, 14–26.

29. See a fine example in Memo Plissonnier to BP, 3 May 1975, GP, 264 J, b. 10, APCF.

30. Berlinguer in Mtg. Direz., 16 Nov. 1968, VD, mf. 020, APCI.

31. Berlinguer in Mtg. Direz., 31 Jan.–1 Feb. 1973, VD, mf. 041, 420–23; cf. Nota Riservata Sergio Segre to Berlinguer, 12 Mar. 1976, VD, mf. 239; Pajetta in Mtg. Direz., 18 July 1977 (afternoon), VD, mf. 299; Amendola in Mtg. Direz., 20 Feb. 1979, VD, mf. 7906, APCI.

32. On the PCI's "third way" in general, see esp. Pons, *Berlinguer*.

33. The most significant archival record is Berlinguer in Mtg. Direz., 5 Dec. 1974, VD, mf. 073, APCI; cf. also Barbagallo, *Enrico Berlinguer*, 217.

34. All in Mtg. Direz., 8 and 29 Sept. 1971, VD, mf. 017, APCI; see also Antonio Pesenti, "L'Europa continua a pagare la crisi del dollaro," and "L'assemblea del dollaro arrogante," *Rinascita*, 14 May 1971, 27 Oct. 1972.

35. Mtg. Direz., 5 Dec. 1974, VD, mf. 073, APCI.

36. Giampaolo Pansa, "Berlinguer conta 'anche' sulla Nato per mantenere l'autonomia da Mosca," *Corriere della Sera*, 15 June 1976; Nobécourt qtd. in Enzo Forcella, "Il 'New Deal' comunista," *La Repubblica*, 20 June 1976.

37. Cf. Claudio Terzi, "The PCI, Eurocommunism, and the Soviet Union," in Serfaty and Gray, *The Italian Communist Party*; Hincker, *Le Parti communiste*, 166–69; Fabien, *La guerre*. For a recent general assessment, see Silvio Pons, "The Rise and Fall of Eurocommunism," in Leffler and Westad, *The Cambridge History*, vol. 3.

38. Pons, *Berlinguer*, qtd. xxi; see also 52–60 (Segre qtd. p. 55). Cf. Lussana, "Il confronto"; on these aspects, see also Silvio Pons, "L'Italia e l'Europa nella politica del PCI," in Romero and Varsori, *Nazione*, 1:320–29; Maggiorani and Ferrari, *L'Europa da Togliatti a Berlinguer*, 161–83; Amendola qtd. from Mtg. Direz., 23 Apr. 1975, VD, mf. 203; on Carrillo, see Berlinguer in Mtg. Direz., 11 Nov. 1977, VD, mf. 309, APCI.

39. Jacques Kahn, "Pourquoi la relance politique de l'Europe des trusts," Gérard Streiff, "Alliance atlantique, défense européenne et Marché commun: Les choix du pouvoir," and Léo Figuères, "Sur les contradictions et le compromis interimpérialistes," *Cahiers du communisme*, May 1972, Jan. 1974, and Jan. 1975.

40. Streiff, *Jean Kanapa*, 1:553; cf. Etienne Fajon, "Nous sommes les partisans d'une Europe véritable," *L'Humanité*, 15 Apr. 1972; and, in general, Boujout, *Le fanatique*.

41. Gérard Bordu, "Parlement européen: L'activité des députés communistes" (also citing the letter Marchais wrote to Pompidou on 26 Nov. 1973), *Cahiers du communisme*, Feb. 1974. In March 1972, Marchais told the Central Committee that "la petite Europe de Pompidou, à six ou à dix, n'est que la Sainte-Alliance du grand capital et de la réaction"; CC, 23 Mar. 1972, 261 J 2/48, paper copies (p. 9), APCF.

42. Marchais and Fajon, qtd. in Mtg. Direz., 26 Sept. 1975, mf. 208, APCI.

43. See, e.g., Kanapa in CC, 18–19 Jan. 1974, paper transcripts from CC-PCF, 1974, APCF.

44. Elleinstein, *Histoire de l'URSS*; Ellenstein, *Histoire du phénomène stalinien*; Adler et al., *L'URSS*; Courtois and Lazar, *Histoire*, 381–82; Hincker, "Le groupe dirigeant."

45. Fiszbin, *Les bouches*; Courtois and Lazar, *Histoire*, 400–403.

46. See esp. Ledda, *L'Europa fra Nord e Sud*. Cf. Streiff, "Alliance atlantique"; and Bordu, "Parlement européen."

47. Segre to Berlinguer, 10 Oct. 1975, in VD mf. 208, APCI.

48. Mtg. Direz., 26 Jan. 1977, VD, mf. 288, APCI; qtd. Alain Rouy and Claude Montagny, "Vers une Europe allemande sous tutelle américaine?," *Cahiers du communisme*, Nov. 1978; cf. Sylvain Dreyfus, "Les partis politiques face à l'élection à l'Assemblée européenne," *Cahiers du communisme*, Apr. 1979; for background, cf. Luigi Conte, "Cola a picco il Mezzogiorno d'Europa," *Rinascita*, 18 Jan. 1974.

49. Courtois and Lazar, *Histoire*, 383.

50. See comments by Amendola in Mtg. Direz., 13 Oct. 1977, VD, mf. 304, APCI; Dreyfus, "Les partis politiques."

51. Pajetta in Mtg. Direz., 24 July 1975, VD, mf. 203, APCI; cf. McLeod, *La révolution*.

52. Mtg. Berlinguer-Carrillo, 8 July 1975, Fondo Berlinguer, Movimento Operaio Internazionale, f. 125; Mtg. PCI delegation with Kirilenko and Zagladin, 24 Mar. 1975, Estero, mf. 204, 593–94, APCI. On these aspects, see Mario Del Pero, "Distensione, bipolarismo, e violenza: La politica estera americana nel Mediterraneo durante gli anni '70 — Il caso portoghese e le sue implicazioni per l'Italia," in Giovagnoli and Pons, *L'Italia*.

53. Victor Alba, "Spain's Entry into NATO," in Kaplan, Clawson, and Luraghi, *NATO*, 97–98.

54. Cf. Silvia Ridolfi, "Gli americani nelle paludi," Louis Safir, "Il vendicatore di Kennedy," and Giorgio Signorini, "Il Vietnam non è un errore," *Rinascita*, 20 Feb. 1965, 1 Oct. 1966, 3 Nov. 196; Jean-Maurice Hermann, "Où va Mister Johnson?," *Démocratie nouvelle*, July–Aug. 1965, 41–46. Cf. Napolitano in Mtg. Direz., 12 Feb. 1965, VD, mf. 029, APCI.

55. Hoff, *A Faustian Foreign Policy*, see esp. 1–5.

56. Mtg. Direz., 23 Apr. 1976, VD, mf. 227, APCI.

57. Goffredo Linder, "L'imperialismo uccide anche senza bombe," *Rinascita*, 21 June 1973.

58. Mtg. Direz., 23 Apr. 1976, VD, mf. 227, APCI.

59. Berlinguer in Mtg. Direz., 11 Nov. 1977, VD, mf. 0309, 61–74; cf. Silvio Pons, "L'Italia e il PCI nella politica estera dell'URSS di Breznev," in Giovagnoli and Pons, *L'Italia*, 947–51; cf. Riva, *Oro*.

60. Both quotations from Kuisel, *Seducing the French*, 216–17; cf. Denis Lacorne, "Modernists and Protectionists: The 1970s," in Lacorne, Rupnik, and Toinet, *The Rise*, 143–59; Fuks, *L'anti-américanisme*.

61. Memo, "L'imperialisme français," by Marie-France Lhériteau, Daniel Debatisse, Gérard Kebabdjan, Bernard Marx, in GP, 264 J, b. 20, APCF; quotation from pp. 13–14.

62. "Réalités américaines," *L'Humanité*, 18–20 and 25–28 Jan. 1972; cf. Kuisel, *Seducing the French*, 216.

63. Cf. Lacorne, "Modernists," 145; André Maine, "Angela Davis parle," *Cahiers du communisme*, Jan. 1972; Dec. BP, 7 July 1971 (on coordination with Moscow), Dec. BP, 9 Sept. 1971 (qtd.), APCF; cf. La Porta, "Introduzione al carteggio di Angela Davis" (with letters exchanged with Berlinguer, Lukács, Bloch); Louis Safir, "Il meccanismo della repressione," *Rinascita*, 22 Jan. 1971.

64. See Pons, *Berlinguer*, 37, 100, 104–15; Pons, "L'Italia," 941–43.

65. Cf. Tel. A-183, Report by Shriver (Paris Embassy), "The French Communist Party in Mid-1969," 29 July 1969, POL 12-FR, RG59, NA.

66. See Longo in Mtg. Direz., 7–8 May 1969, VD, mf. 006, APCI; Dec. BP, 15 July 1972, APCF.

67. Even at the Eurocommunist level cooperation was problematic: Carrillo requested that Spanish workers in France be granted minority status; but the PCF objected that France had to remain heavily centralized, lest the xenophobic forces make gains. See Report by Berlinguer in Mtg. Direz., 9 Feb. 1974, VD, mf. 073, APCI.

68. Dec. BP, 12 Nov. 1970, APCF; cf. Gomart, "Le PCF."

69. Cf. Robrieux, *Histoire intérieure*; Montaldo, *Les finances*.

70. Raymond, *The French Communist Party*, 60–63; Cole, *François Mitterrand*, 74; Lazar, *Maisons*, 137–38.

71. Kriegel, *Communismes*, 251; Lazar, *Maisons*, 149–50; cf. Report Jean Kanapa to CC, 25–26 May 1973, transcripts CD no. 7-8-9/12, APCF.

72. See interventions by Berlinguer, Pajetta, and Colombi in Mtgs. Direz., 12 Sept., 9 Oct. 1973, VD, mf. 041, APCI; Rubbi, *Il mondo*, 53–57; Giovagnoli, *Il caso Moro*, 9–13; Agostino Novella, "Il Cile, la DC e noi," *Rinascita*, 20 Sept. 1973; and special issues of *Il Contemporaneo*, "Riflessione sul Cile," Dec. 1973.

73. On KGB plot, see Fabien, *La guerre*; Fasanella and Incerti, *Sofia*.

74. See esp. Ginsborg, *A History*, 370–79; and Gualtieri, *L'Italia*, 165–203. Cf. Alberto Scandone, "Aspetti e significati della teologia cristiana di sinistra," *Il Contemporaneo*, Apr. 1972; and special issue of *Il Contemporaneo*, "La questione democristiana," May 1973.

75. Enrico Berlinguer, "Discorso di Mosca in occasione del 60mo anniversario della Rivoluzione d'Ottobre," *L'Unità*, 3 Nov. 1977; cf. Tatò, *Comunisti*.

76. Enzo Forcella, "Il progetto Berlinguer," *La Repubblica*, 19 Jan. 1977; Enrico Berlinguer, "L'austerità," (from speech delivered in Milan, 30 Jan. 1977), in *L'Unità*, 19 Sept. 1992. Cf. Ajello, *Il lungo addio*, 120–27; and Ginsborg, *A History*, 354–58.

77. Qtd. in Pons, *Berlinguer*, 43–44.

78. Jacques Denis, "La situation internationale et le rapport des forces dans le monde," *Cahiers du communisme*, Apr. 1979, 73; cf. Jean Magniadas, "L'austerité n'est pas fatale, mais l'action est nécessaire," *Cahiers du communisme*, Oct. 1976.

79. Marc Lazar emphasizes this new composition in *Maisons rouges*, 221; see also Luperini, *Marxismo*. Others note the party's renewed appeal to the working class and youth; see, e.g., Hellman, *Italian Communism*; and Revelli, *Lavorare*, chap. 5.

80. Raymond, *The French Communist Party*, 141, 70–72; Hazareesingh, *Intellectuals*, 286; Platone, "Les adhérents," 53.

81. Amyot, *The Italian Communist Party*; Golden, *Labor Divided*. On the Red Brigades' roots in and contrasts with the PCI, see Orsini, *Anatomia*.

82. Mtgs. Direz., 16 and 30 Mar. 1978, VD, mf. 7805, APCI; Giorgio Amendola, "L'Italia dopo il 16 marzo: Isolare il nemico," *Rinascita*, 24 Mar. 1978; and Gian Carlo Pajetta, "A difesa della repubblica," *Rinascita*, 21 Apr. 1978; Tranfaglia, "La strategia," 989–98. In general, see Richard Drake, *The Revolutionary Mystique*, 63–77; and Orsini, *Anatomia*.

83. Cf. Francesco Barbagallo, "Il PCI dal sequestro di Moro alla morte di Berlinguer," in Giovagnoli and Pons, *L'Italia*, 843–47.

84. This point is particularly emphasized in Pons, *Berlinguer*.

85. In November 1974 former CIA Director John McCone acknowledged to President Gerald Ford that the agency's image had been tarnished in Europe even more than at home, thus lowering the leverage and the morale of its officials abroad; Memo Conv. McCone, Scowcroft, Ford, 11 Nov. 1974, NSA Papers, Memo Convs., b. 7, GFL.

86. Memo Sonnenfeldt to Kissinger, 20 May 1969, NP, NSC files, Country Files: France, b. 674, vol. 2, NA.

87. Shriver to State Dept., 29 July 1969, POL 12-FR, RG59, NA; Tassel, *Sarge*.

88. Memo Kissinger for the President, 28 Apr. 1969, and Memo Sonnenfeldt to Kissinger, 24 Sept. 1970, NP, NSC, Country Files: France, b. 674, Vol. 2, and b. 677, Vol. 6, NA.

89. Note Bureau Intelligence and Research, 6 July 1971, Tels. Emb. to State Dept., 21 June and 13 July 1971, POL 12-FR, 1970–73, RG59, NA.

90. Memo Conv. Martin-Rumor, 10 July 1970, and Martin to State Dept., transmitting Memo Conv. Sen. Percy with Fanfani (Senate President) and Pertini (Chamber of Deputies President), 13 Nov. 1970, NP, NSC, Country Files: Italy, b. 695, NA.

91. Kissinger, qtd. in Memo Conv. Kissinger-Ford, 25 Sept. 1975, NSA, Memo Convs. GFL. Jimmy Carter's ambassador to Italy, Richard Gardner, in his recent memoirs, may have exaggerated the determination of his predecessors to maintain these ties with the Right; see Gardner, *Mission Italy*, 35–36.

92. Ackley to State Dept., 18 Feb. 1970, POL 12-IT, 1970–73, b. 2393, RG59, NA. Cf. Umberto Gentiloni Silveri, "Gli anni settanta nel giudizio degli Stati Uniti: 'Un ponte verso l'ignoto,'" in Giovagnoli and Pons, *L'Italia*.

93. Memo Conv. Ford, Kissinger, Leone, Moro, 25 Sept. 1974, and Memo Conv. Ford, Kissinger, Moro, Rumor, 1 Aug. 1975 NSA, Memo Convs., b. 6, and b. 13, GFL. On Kissinger's mistrust of Moro, see esp. Mario Del Pero, "L'Italia e gli Stati Uniti: Un legame rinnovato?," in Romero and Varsori, *Nazione*, 1:305–12.

94. Memo Conv. Ford, Kissinger, 18 Jan. 1975, NSA, Memo Convs., b. 8, GFL. For previous fears of PCI's threatening détente, see Memo Martin J. Hillenbrand to Kissinger, re: NSSM 88, 30 Mar. 1970, NP, NSC Institutional Files, NSSM, b. H-169, NA; Kissinger, *Years of Renewal*, 99; cf. Wall, "L'amministrazione Carter," 181–82.

95. Memos Convs. Kissinger, Sonnenfeldt, Gaja, Ducci, Ortona, 16–17 July 1973, and Memo Conv. Michel Jobert, Kissinger, 8 June 1973, in NP, NSC, HAK, Country Files: Europe, b. 65, b. 56, NA. On this theme, cf. Kahler and Link, *Europe*, 79–85.

96. Memo Conv. Ford Kissinger, 25 Sept. 1974, NSA, Memo Convs., b. 6, GFL; Memo Conv. Leone-Kissinger, 9 Apr. 1974, NP, NSC, HAK, Country Files: Europe, b. 65, NA; Memo Conv. Ford, Kissinger, Moro, Rumor, 1 Aug. 1975, and Memo Conv. Ford, Forlani, 29 Sept. 1976, NSA Memo Convs., b. 21, GFL; Wollenborg, *Stars*, 179–210.

97. Memo Scrowcroft to Ford, "CIA Interim Assessment of Italian Elections," n.d., June 1976, NSA, Country Files: Italy, b. 8, GFL.

98. Tel. 8205, Emb. Rome to Assistant Sec. State Hartman, 25 June 1975; Memo by George H. W. Bush, "The Electoral Outlook in Italy," 19 May 1976, both in NSA, Country Files: Italy, b. 8, GFL; Memo Conv. Ford-Volpe, 6 Nov. 1975, NSA, Memo Convs., b. 16, GFL; cf. Boffa, *Memorie*, 165–68.

99. See USIA, Office of Research and Assessment, "The Current Climate of Opinion in Italy toward the US and toward West European Countries," USIA Recs., b. 20, R 10, 73, 1972–73, 16 Apr. 1973; various docs. in POL 12-IT, b. 2393, all in RG59, NA. For background and context of these initiatives, cf. Pedaliu, "'A Sea'"; and Massimiliano Cricco, "La politica estera italiana in Medio Oriente: Dal fallimento della missione Jarring alla conclusione dello Yom Kippur (1972–73)," in Romero and Varsori, *Nazione*, vol. 2.

100. Memo Conv. Nixon-Fanfani, 7 July 1970, NP, NSC Files, Country Files: Europe, b. 695, NA; Memo Conv. Leone, Moro, Ford, Scowcroft, 25 Sept. 1974; Memo Volpe, Scowcroft, Ford, 25 Mar. 1975, NSA, all in Memos Convs., b. 6, GFL. Cf. Memo Conv. Ford, Scow-

croft, and Italian-American Leaders, 4 Aug. 1976, NSA, Memo Convs., b. 17, GFL; Memo Conv. Ford-Kissinger, 25 Sept. 1974, NSA, Memo Convs., b. 6, GFL. In August 1975 Rumor and Moro told Kissinger that "every time" Italy was excluded from summits, "it gives several percentage points to the Communists"; Memo Conv. Ford, Kissinger, Rumor, Moro, 1 Aug. 1975, NSA, Memo Convs., b. 13, GFL. Kissinger, *White House Years*, 101–2.

101. Mtg. Ford-Rumor, 23 Sept. 1975, NSA, Memo Convs., b. 15; Scowcroft to Ford, 6 Nov. 1975, NSA, Country Files: Italy, b. 8, GFL; Memo Conv. Leone-Kissinger, 9 Apr. 1974, NP, NSC, HAK, Country Files: Europe, b. 65, NA.

102. Mtg. Ford, Pope Paul VI, C. Casaroli, Kissinger, 3 June 1975, NSA, Memos, b. 12; see also Memo Conv. Kissinger, James L. Schlesinger (Sec. Defense), Scowcroft, 2 Apr. 1975, NSA, Memos, b. 10, both in GFL; Scowcroft to Ford (Mtg. with Cardinal Braum), 5 June 1976, DDRS, and Memo Conv. "Italian-American Leaders," 4 Aug. 1976, NSA, Memo Convs., b. 17, GFL. In general, cf. Del Pero, "Distensione," 123–44.

103. Memo Conv. Kissinger-Ford, 25 Sept. 1975; Memo Conv. Ford, Kissinger, Genscher, 26 Sept. 1974, NSA, Memos Convs., b. 6, GFL.

104. Memo Conv. Kissinger-Jorgensen (Danish Prime Minister), 20 Jan. 1976, NP, HAK Files, b. 16, NA. Cf. Simon and Seidman to Ford, Nov. 1975, William Seidman Files, 1974–77, Briefing Papers, b. 312, Memo 1, GFL.

105. Memo Kissinger to Ford, 27 Sept. 1975, NSA, Country Files: France, b. 3, GFL; Conv. Kissinger, Schmidt, Genscher, 27 July 1975, NSA, and Moro and Giscard in Fourth Session Rambouillet Summit, 17 Nov. 1975 (p. 7), Memo Convs., b. 13 and b. 16, GFL.

106. See Duccio Basosi and Giovanni Bernardini, "The Puerto Rico Summit and the End of Eurocommunism," and Fiorella Favino, "Washington's Economic Diplomacy and the Reconstruction of U.S. Leadership," in Nuti, *The Crisis*. I am borrowing part of the following argument on economic diplomacy from these two essays. See also Duccio Basosi, "Helsinki and Rambouillet: US Attitudes towards Trade and Security during the Early CSCE Process, 1972–75," in Wenger, Mastny, and Nuenlist, *Origins*.

107. Conv. Ford, Kissinger, Scowcroft, 6 Sept. 1974; Conv. Ford, Kissinger, Schmidt, 6 Dec. 1974; Conv. Ford-Kissinger, 18 Jan. 1975; Conv. Ford, Kissinger, Rumsfeld, Scowcroft, 24 May 1975 (for quotation; emphasis added); Conv. Kissinger, Schmidt, Genscher, 27 July 1975, all in NSA, Memo Convs., b. 5, b. 7, b. 8, b. 11, and b. 13, respectively, GFL.

108. First doc. qtd. in Basosi and Bernardini, "The Puerto Rico Summit," 261; Schmidt in Memo Conv. Kissinger, Schmidt, Genscher, 27 July 1975, NSA, Memo Convs., b. 13, GFL.

109. Basosi and Bernardini, "The Puerto Rico Summit," 262; Memo Conv. Ford, Kissinger, et al., 18 May 1976, DDRS.

110. Memo Conv. Kissinger-Jorgensen, 20 Jan. 1976, NP, HAK Files, b. 16, NA.

111. Memo Hillenbrand to Kissinger (NSSM 88), 30 Mar. 1970, NP, NSC Institutional Files, NSSM, b. H-169, NA; "CIA Interim Assessment of Italian Elections," June 1976, NSA, Country Files: Italy, b. 8, GFL.

112. Clift to Kissinger, 11 Aug. 1975; Kissinger to Ford, 5 Dec. 1975, NSA, Country Files: France, b. 3, GFL.

113. Mtgs. Direz., 5 May, 9 June 1976; on Kissinger, Mtg. Direz., 23 June (also enclosing Letter Segre to Berlinguer of 12 Mar. 1976, re: Manzini), both in VD, mf. 239, APCI; cf. Segre to Berlinguer, 24 Sept. 1976 (on Jimmy Carter's entourage), in mf. 243, APCI.

114. Letter Segre (Bonn at Trilateral Commission on Economic Affairs) to Berlinguer, 4 Nov. 1977, Sezione Esteri 1977, Protocollo 2592/S, APCI.

115. Peter Lange, "What Is to Be Done about Italian Communism?," *Foreign Policy* 21 (Winter 1975–76); Sergio Segre, "The 'Communist Question' in Italy," *Foreign Affairs*, July 1976; Jean Kanapa, "A 'New Policy' of the French Communists?," *Foreign Affairs*, Jan. 1977.

116. Ramney and Sartori, *Eurocommunism*; cf. Wall, "Les Etats-Unis," 376–77. For more on the neoconservative resurgence, see the epilogue.

117. Solomon to Bluementhal, "Summary of Major Treasury Activities," 24 Feb. 1977, DDRS; Basosi and Bernardini, "The Puerto Rico Summit," 263.

118. Mtg. Direz., 18 July 1977, VD, mf. 299, APCI.

119. See, respectively, Njølstad, "The Carter Administration"; and Wall, "L'amministrazione Carter."

120. Brzezinski to Carter, 26 Feb. 1977, Weekly Report no. 2, and Brezinski to Carter, "Western Europe: An Overview," 23 July 1977, NSA, Brzezinski Material, Subject File, WR, b. 41, JCL.

121. Wollenborg, *Stars*, 197–205; Cf. Memo Conv. Roberto Gaja (Italian Ambassador)–Brezinski, 31 Mar. 1977, NSA, Brezinski Material, Subject File, b. 33, JCL; on Vance, cf. George Urban to Brzezinski, 19 Mar. 1977, WHCF, Subj. File, Countries, CO-37, JCL. On Soviet anti-Eurocommunist activities, see also Andrew (with Mitrokhin), *The Sword*, 294–301.

122. Wollenborg, *Stars*, 231–34, 249–60; cf. Bourne, *Jimmy Carter*, 98; Wall, "Les Etats-Unis," 374–75.

123. Magri, qtd. in Memo Pierre Hassner to Brezinski, "For Ever Creeping?," 23 Feb. 1977, WHCF, Subj., CO-37; Brzezinski to Carter, "Visit of Italian Prime Minister Andreotti," 23 July 1977; Brzezinski to Carter, "Western Europe: An Overview," 23 July 1977, NSA, Brzezinski Material, VIP Visit File, b. 7, JCL.

124. Hassner to Brezinski, "For Ever Creeping?," 23 Feb. 1977; on the PCF and the *force de frappe*, see Situation Room to Brzezinski, 12 May 1977, NSA, Brezinski Material, President's Daily Reports File, b. 2, JCL.

125. Urban to Brzezinski, 19 Mar. 1977; Hunter to Brzezinski, 5 July 1977, NSA, Brzezinski Material, Country File, b. 38, JCL. Robert Hunter was also influenced by the opinion of Servan-Schreiber, now president of the French Radical Party; Hunter to Brzezinski, 9 Aug. 1977, WHCF, Subj. Files, CO-25, Folder CO 51, JCL.

126. Memo McCormack to Brzezinski, 23 June 1977, WHCF, Subj. Files, CO-37, JCL; cf. Wall, "L'amministrazione Carter," 189–90.

127. Hunter to Brzezinski, 5 July 1977, NSA, Brzezinski Material, Country Files, b. 38, JCL; Presidential Review C.ttee Mtg., 11 Jan. 1978, Remote Access Capture, NLC 33-9-31-1-1, JCL; Staff Offices, NSA, Special Projects, Summit—Tokyo, 15 June 1979 (folder 3), JCL.

128. Gardner in Hunter to Brzezinski, 5 July 1977; Brzezinski, *Power and Principle*, 311–13; quotation from Gardner, *Mission Italy*, 84. On Kissinger, see Henry A. Kissinger, "Communist Parties in Western Europe: Challenge to the West," in Ramney and Sartori, *Eurocommunism*, 183–96; Mtg. Kissinger with Reps. of Foreign Service Class, 6 Jan. 1977, NP, Kissinger TelCons, 1973–77, Staff Material, NA.

129. Brzezinski, *Power and Principle*, 312; Brzezinski to Carter, "Western Europe," 23 July 1977; Brzezinski to Carter, Weekly Rep. no. 2, 26 Feb. 1977; John E. Reinhardt (Director of International Communication Agency, Washington, D.C.) to Brzezinski, 10 May 1978, NSA, Brzezinski Material, Country File, b. 39, JCL.

130. Memo Gregory Treverton to Brzezinski, 15 Dec. 1977 (forwarding Hassner's memo), WHCF, Country Files, CO-51, France, JCL; also highlighted in Wall, "L'amministrazione Carter," 191, also emphasizing Carter's relative indifference.

131. Urban to Brzezinski, 19 Mar. 1977; Presidential Review C.ttee Mtg., 11 Jan. 1978, Remote Access Capture, NLC 33-9-31-1-1, JCL; Gardner, *Mission Italy*, 46, 184–85; on Craxi, see Hunter to Brzezinski, 5 July 1977.

132. Wall, "Les Etats-Unis," 371–73 (also on Brzezinski's opinion); Giorgio Napolitano, "Il PCI spiegato agli americani," *Rinascita*, May 1978; cf. Rubbi, *Il mondo*, 58–59. Carter in Njølstad, "The Carter Administration," 81.

133. Presidential Review Committee Mtg., 11 Jan. 1978; Notes on Andreotti, 27 July 1977, NSA, Brzezinski Material, VIP Visit File, b. 7, JCL.

134. Statement issued by the Department of State, 12 Jan. 1978, *American Foreign Policy*, 514–55.

135. This point is reiterated in Njølstad, "The Carter Administration."

136. Gardner, *Mission Italy*, 2; Brzezinski, *Power and Principle*, 311–13.

137. Brzezinski to Carter, Weekly Rep. no. 40, 16 Dec. 1977, NSA Brzezinski Material, Subj. Files, WR, b. 41, JCL; Presidential Review Committee Mtg., 11 Jan. 1978; McCormack to Brzezinski, 23 June 1977.

138. Wollenborg, *Stars*, 261–70; Gardner, *Mission Italy*, 77. On Gaja, see, e.g., Memo Conv. Gaja-Brzezinski, 31 Mar. 1977, NSA, Brezinski Material, Subject File, b. 33, JCL.

139. Brzezinski to Carter, Weekly Rep. no. 46, 9 Feb. 1978, Brzezinski Material, Subj. File, b. 41, JCL (see also Weekly Rep. no. 40, 16 Dec. 1977); Njølstad, "The Carter Administration," 86; Wall, "L'amministrazione Carter," 194–95.

140. Weekly Report no. 63, 16 June 1978, Brzezinski Material, Subj. Files, b. 41, JCL.

141. Situation Room to Brzezinski, 17 Mar. 1978, NSA, Brzezinski Material, President's Daily Reps. File, b. 5, and Hunter to Brzezinski, "Moro Kidnapping," no. 2, 16 Mar. 1978, NSA, Brzezinski, Country File, b. 38, JCL; cf. Giovagnoli, *Il caso Moro*, 161–65.

142. Weekly Rep. no. 92, 30 Mar. 1979, Brzezinski Material, Subj., WR, b. 42, H. Wayne Gillies (Houston) to Brzezinski, 19 Jan. 1979, WHCF, Subj. File, CO-37, JCL.

143. Weekly Rep. no. 83, 28 Dec. 1978, Brzezinski Material, Subj., WR, b. 41, JCL.

Epilogue

1. Judt, *Postwar*, 453; Kissinger with Reps. of Foreign Service Class, 6 Jan. 1977, NP, Kissinger TelCons, 1973–77, Staff Material, NA.

2. Gundle, *Between Hollywood and Moscow*, 154.

3. See chap. 5.

4. Yvonne Dumont, "Les femmes, leurs problèmes et leurs luttes," *Cahiers du communisme*, Jan. 1967, 76.

5. Mireille Bertrand, "La lutte des communistes français pour l'émancipation de la femme," *Cahiers du communisme*, Dec. 1970, 118–27; on PCF and feminism, cf. Rousseau, *Les femmes rouges*.

6. Reader, *Intellectuals*, 69–72.

7. De Beauvoir, *After "The Second Sex,"* 32; Bertrand qtd. in CC, 25 Oct. 1973, transcripts CD 4/13, track 3, APCF. On propaganda work among women, see also Colette Coulon, "Les femmes dans l'Union populaire pour le programme commun," and Yvonne Dumont, "La

femme et le travail: L'idéologie du pouvoir et du patronat," *Cahiers du communisme*, Oct. 1972, Feb. 1974.

8. Vincent in CC, 19 Jan. 1974, Paris, transcripts CD 1/10, track 2, APCF.

9. Courtois and Lazar, *Histoire*, 390.

10. Marie José Chombart de Lauwe, "Images d'une oppression, images d'une libération," *La Nouvelle critique* (n.s.), no. 53 (Apr. 1972), 35–36.

11. Guy Poussy, review of *Femmes, quelle libération?*, by Madeleine Vincent, and Jackie Hoffmann, "La lutte contre la pauvreté pour le changement au féminin," *Cahiers du communisme*, July–Aug. 1976, Dec. 1977.

12. Quotation from Reader, *Intellectuals*, 71 (see also 61–68 and 73–74 on Lacan). Cf. Bernard Muldwort, "Psychanalise et communistes," *La Nouvelle critique* n.s., no. 30 (Jan. 1970); Hirsch, *The French New Left*, 215–21; and essays in Marks and de Courtivron, *New French Feminism*.

13. Qtd. in Gundle, *Between Hollywood and Moscow*, 150.

14. Eletta Bertani, "Occupazione femminile e alleanze (tribuna congressuale)," *Rinascita*, 3 Mar. 1972.

15. See chap. 5.

16. Confalonieri, "Parties," 134; Joyce Gelb, "Feminism and Political Action," in Dalton and Kuelcher, *Challenging the Political Order*.

17. Cf. Zuffa, "Le doppie militanze," 21–22; qtd. Confalonieri, "Parties," 136.

18. Jotti in Mtg. Direz., 11 May 1965, VD, mf. 029, APCI; Intervista con Nilde Jotti, "Il duro cammino dell'emancipazione," *Rinascita*, 26 Apr. 1968.

19. Luisa Passerini, "Il movimento delle donne: Rien ne serait plus comme avant," in Agosti, Passerini, and Tranfaglia, *La cultura*; Bucci, "Proletariato."

20. Parts of the preceding paragraph are informed by the findings and arguments in Confalonieri, "Parties," esp. 136–46. Cf. Gramaglia, "Affinità e conflitto"; Sydney Tarrow, "The Phantom of the Opera: Political Parties and Social Movements of the 1960s and 1970s in Italy," in Dalton and Kuelcher, *Challenging the Political Order*, 251–73; and Mary Nolan, "Consuming America, Producing Gender," in Moore and Vaudagna, *The American Century*.

21. Despite later claims by the PCI's leading woman, Nilde Jotti, the party kept trailing the Socialists and the new Radical Party on this issue and even on the legalization of divorce; cf. "Abbiamo sempre detto 'no' all'indissolubilità (intervista a Nilde Jotti a cura di Marcella Ferrara)," *Rinascita*, 12 Apr. 1973, and "La posizione dei partiti sul diritto familiare (tre domande di *Rinascita* a Renato Ballardini del PSI, Franco Boiardi del PSIUP, Nilde Jotti del PCI, Eletta Martini della DC)," *Rinascita*, 18 June 1971.

22. Qtd. from Mtg. Direz., 8 Jan. 1975, VD, mf. 203; and Mtg. Direz., 25 Nov. 1975, VD, mf. 209, APCI.

23. Qtd. from Mtg. Direz., 25 Nov. 1975, VD, mf. 209; and Mtg. Direz., 26 Feb. 1976, VD, mf. 211, APCI.

24. Qtd. Natta and Jotti from Mtg. Direz., 29 July 1976, VD, mf. 243, APCI.

25. Collective interview, "Quale crisi del femminismo," *Rinascita*, 22 Dec. 1978; Margherita Repetto, "Viaggio fra le donne americane," *Rinascita*, 2 Feb. 1979; cf. Giovanna Carlo, "Viaggio nel femminismo americano," *Rinascita*, 18 May 1979.

26. Enrico Berlinguer, "Rinnovamento della politica e rinnovamento del PCI," *Rinascita*, 4 Dec. 1981.

27. Mtg. Direz., 26 Apr. 1972, VD, mf. 032, APCI.

28. Imbeni and Jotti in Mtg. Direz., 9 Oct. 1975, VD, mf. 208, D'Alema in Mtg. Direz., 5 Mar. 1977, VD, mf. 296, APCI. For a precedent for this debate, cf. Fiamma Lussana, "Politica e cultura: L'Istituto Gramsci, la Fondazione Basso, l'Istituto Sturzo," in Lussana and Maramao, *L'Italia*, 106–7.

29. See chap. 7.

30. Occhetto, *A dieci anni*, 109; Valentini, *Berlinguer*, 148–49. cf. Giuseppe Chiarante, "Per una Università di massa e qualificata," *Il Contemporaneo*, Mar. 1971.

31. Occhetto, *A dieci anni*, 109; cf. remarks by Alberto Reichlin in Mtg. Direz., 5 Mar. 1977, VD, mf. 296, APCI; Laura Lilli, "Compagno Amendola, le prediche non bastano," *La Repubblica*, 6 Feb. 1977; Massimo D'Alema, "Estranei o protagonisti?," *Il Contemporaneo*, 28 Jan. 1977.

32. For these arguments, see Orsini, *Anatomia*, esp. 180–232 (186–91 for social composition of the Red Brigades); and Breschi, *Sognando la rivoluzione*.

33. Franco Cassano, "I nostri problemi di fronte al nuovo individualismo," *Rinascita*, 29 June 1979. Cf. Vittoria Franco, "USA: Democrazia e partecipazione," *Critica marxista* 19, no. 4 (1981).

34. Memo Conv. Leroy-Favaro, 16 Sept. 1968; Memo Favaro for Bureau Politique, 23 Mar. 1970, both in RL, 263J65, b. 37, APCF.

35. Ross, *May '68*, 11–12.

36. David Drake, *Intellectuals*, 147; Ross, *May '68*, 12.

37. Roland Favaro, "Une autre vie pour la jeunesse," *Cahiers du communisme*, Feb. 1972.

38. Marchais and Fajon in CC, Paris, 10–11 June 1974, CD 10/15, plages 3–4, APCF; Norman Rudish and Jack Zipès, "L'université américaine: Autonomie et big-business," *La Nouvelle critique*, no. 48 (Dec. 1971); Jacques Pesenti, "Irrationalisme de la faillite ou faillite de irrationalisme" (II), *La Nouvelle critique*, no. 75 (June–July 1974).

39. Quotation from Portelli, "The Transatlantic Jeremiad," 133; Kuisel, *Seducing the French*, 219; Gundle, *Between Hollywood and Moscow*, 154–58; Borgna, *Il tempo della musica*.

40. On Domenach, see chap. 5; Portelli, "The Transatlantic Jeremiad," 134 (qtd. and adapted here).

41. Gianni Borgna, "Ma la colpa è solo dei giovani?," *Il Contemporaneo*, 14 July 1978.

42. Asor Rosa, *Intellettuali*; Giovanni Berlinguer, *Dieci anni dopo*, 202–7.

43. Qtd. from Gundle, *Between Hollywood and Moscow*, 153 (see also 141, 144–45, and 151–52); cf. Chiarenza, *Il cavallo*; and Dario Valori, "Come concepiamo la nuova RAI-TV," *Rinascita*, 26 Jan. 1973.

44. Valori and Amendola in Mtg. Direz., 10 Apr. 1975, VD, mf. 203, APCI; cf. Gerardo Chiaromonte, "Un tonico illusorio e pericoloso (TV a colori)," *Rinascita*, 22 Sept. 1972.

45. Report René Piquet at CC, Rosny-sous-Bois, 3–4 June 1971, 261 J 2/47 (paper records), APCF. Cf. Platone and Ranger, "Le Parti communiste."

46. Quotation from Roger Mayer, "Détente et coexistence pacifique: Le rôle de l'opinion publique," *Cahiers du communisme*, Dec. 1973, 56–71; cf. Mireille Nadaud, "L'impérialisme des États-Unis face au 'défi contemporain,'" *Cahiers du communisme*, July–Aug. 1975, 110–16.

47. Mtg. Ford, Kissinger, Rumsfeld, Scowcroft, 24 May 1975, NSA, Memo Convs., b. 12, GFL. Memo Conv. Ford, Scowcroft, and Italian American Leaders, 4 Aug. 1976, NSA, Memo Convs., b. 17, GFL; Ajello, *Il lungo addio*, quotation from 157.

48. Tomlinson, *Cultural Imperialism*; Pells, *Not Like Us*, 270–77.

49. See, e.g., Tunstall, *The Media*; Denis Lacorne and Jacques Rupnik, "Introduction: France Bewitched by America," in Lacorne, Rupnik, and Toinet, *The Rise*.

50. One only has to look at the various film reviews by Mino Argentieri's in *Rinascita* throughout the 1970s to understand this communist fascination with the anticonformist, anti-Hollywood trends in U.S. mass culture. See also, on television, Gino Frezza, "La traduzione televisiva dell'uomo ragno," *Rinascita*, 14 July 1978; and Giorgio Fabre, "La tecnologia americana alle prese con lo sceneggiato" (on the series *Roots*), *Rinascita*, 15 Sept. 1978.

51. See chapter 7; Louis Menand, "The Promise of Freedom, the Friend of Authority: American Culture in Postwar France," in Kazin and MacCartin, *Americanism*, 217.

52. Letter Francis Cohen (director of *La Nouvelle critique*) to PCF Secretariat, 11 July 1968, and Memo Cohen, Antoine Casanova, Jacques de Bonis, "Sur la situation et les perspectives de *La Nouvelle critique*," to Secretariat, 16 June 1972, RL, 263J58, b. 68, APCF; Courtois and Lazar, *Histoire*, 356.

53. René Andrieu, "De grâce, pas de leçons," *L'Humanité*, 25 Oct. 1975; David Drake, *Intellectuals*, 148–50; Elleinstein, *L'histoire du phénomène stalinien*; Christofferson, *French Intellectuals*, 89–106 (qtd. 91); Grémion, *Intelligence*, 602–3; Hazareesingh, *Intellectuals*, 275–85; Bernard Michaux, "Remarques sur l'idée du totalitarisme," *Cahiers du communisme*, May 1978.

54. "Avec le peuple vietnamien," *L'Humanitè dimanche*, 24 Nov. 1978; Memo Mtg. Plissonnier, René Andrieu, Théo Ronco with delegation from Vietnam, 25 Oct. 1978, GP, 264 J, b. 7/8, APCF.

55. Elliot, *Althusser*; David Drake, *Intellectuals*, 150–53; Raymond, *The French Communist Party*, 157–59; Khilnani, *Arguing Revolution*, 151–53.

56. Nora, "America."

57. Kuisel, *Seducing the French*, 220–23; Diana Pinto, "The French Intelligentsia Rediscovers America," in Lacorne, Rupnik, and Toinet, *The Rise*; Grémion, *Paris-Prague*.

58. Diana Pinto, "Where Have All the Sartres Gone? The French Intelligentsia Born Again," in Hollifield and Ross, *Searching*; David Drake, *Intellectuals*, 149–66; Jeremy Jennings, "Of Treason, Blindness and Silence: Dilemmas of the Intellectual in Modern France," in Jennings and Kamp-Welch, *Intellectuals*, 78.

59. Richard Bernstein, quoted in Lipset, *American Exceptionalism*, 184; Judt, *Postwar*, 478–81; for an incisive critique of postmodernist success in American universities (where intellectuals "matter not at all" and therefore can "continue to play with names and ideas whose time has gone"), see Judt, *Past Imperfect*, 298–301.

60. Michel Dion, "Le gauchisme et la politique," *Cahiers du communisme*, Jan. 1976; cf. François Hincker, "Quelques réflexions sur l'idéologie gauchiste aujourd'hui," *Cahiers du communisme*, Mar. 1972.

61. Quotation from Jacques Chambraz, "Les communistes et les intellectuels," *Cahiers du communisme*, June–July 1978, 26–31; cf. Claudin, "Some Reflections"; Hirsch, *The French New Left*, 190–204; Reader, *Intellectuals*, 37–60.

62. Gundle, *Between Hollywood and Moscow*, 142–43; see also Luigi Rosiello, "N. Chomsky, 'Aspetti della teoria della sintassi,'" and Massimo Modica, "Michel Foucault, 'Scritti letterari,'" *Rinascita*, 21 and 28 Aug. 1971; Biagio de Giovanni, "Intellettuali e potere," *Critica marxista* 15, no. 6 (June 1977); Massimo Stanzione, "Nuovi percorsi foucaultiani," *Critica marxista* 18, no. 1 (Jan. 1979).

63. Giorgio Napolitano, "Ancora sul caso Solgenitsyn," *Rinascita*, 22 Feb. 1974; Spriano,

"Le riflessioni." On Berlinguer's reassuring Brezhnev regarding human rights, see Report Berlinguer on Mtg. with Brezhnev, Ponomariov, Suslov, 19 Oct. 1978, VD, mf. 7812, APCI. Cf. Lazar, *Maisons*, 317–20; and Albertina Vittoria, "L'attività dell'Istituto Gramsci (1957–1979)," in Vittoria and Lussana, *Il "lavoro culturale"*; and Lomellini, *L'appuntamento mancato*.

64. Cacciari, *Krisis*; Vattimo and Rovatti, *Il pensiero debole*; Ajello, *Il lungo addio*, 129.

65. Biagio de Giovanni, "Da Adorno a Foucault," *Il Contemporaneo*, 20 July 1979.

66. Gabriele Giannantoni, "Politica e cultura negli anni Settanta—II," *Critica marxista* 16, no. 2 (1978): 60–61; Gundle, *Between Hollywood and Moscow*, 158–60.

67. Both qtd. in Ajello, *Il lungo addio*, 186.

68. Cited in David Drake, *Intellectuals*, 151.

69. Craveri, "L'ultimo Berlinguer"; Roberto Gualtieri, "Il PCI tra solidarietà nazionale e 'alternativa democratica' nelle lettere e nelle note di Antonio Tatò a Enrico Berlinguer," in De Rosa and Monina, *L'Italia*, 4:291–94.

70. Berlinguer in Mtg. 28 Jan. 1981 and Napolitano in Mtg. 5 Feb. 1981, VD, mf. 8107, APCI; also emphasized in Pons, *Berlinguer*, 198–200.

71. Tatò to Berlinguer, 18 July 1978, Fondo Berlinguer, politica interna, f. 526, APCI; also in Gualtieri, "Il PCI,'" 283. Cf. Gervasoni, "Un miroir abimé."

72. Pajetta in Mtg. Direz., 20 Feb. 1980 (p. 5), VD, APCI; Berlinguer in Situation Room to Brzezinski, 2 Dec. 1980, NSA, Brzezinski Material, President's Daily Report File, b. 17, JCL.

73. Silvio Pons emphasizes that, throughout the Polish crisis leading to the Soviet repression, the PCI never established contacts with Walesa and continued to hope for a reform from above; Pons, *Berlinguer*, 186–87.

74. Mtg. Direz., 20 Feb. 1979 (p. 2), VD, APCI. Communist historian Carlo Maria Santoro in 1980 argued that the Carter administration had been "Kissingerian without Kissinger," without, that is, the "baggage of experience and the ability to calculate interests" which helped the Nixon administration actually negotiate détente; Santoro, "Carter, un kissingeriano senza Kissinger," *Il Contemporaneo*, 28 Mar. 1980.

75. On U.S.-Italian relations during the Craxi years, see esp. Di Nolfo, *La politica estera*.

76. Lundestad, *The United States*, 214.

77. On these points, see esp. Denis Lacorne and Jacques Rupnik, "France Bewitched by America," in Lacorne, Rupnik, and Toinet, *The Rise*, 3–6.

78. Both quotations from Gaddis, *The Cold War*, 223 and 233; Lazar, *Maisons*, 172–73. On Gorbachev and Eurocommunism, see Gorbachev, *Le idee*; cf. Lévesque, *The Enigma*, 19–21, and English, *Russia*, 88–89.

79. Giovanni Gozzini, "Il PCI nel sistema politico della repubblica," in Gualtieri, *Il PCI*, 137–38. Cf. in Francesco Barbagallo, "Il PCI dal sequestro di Moro alla morte di Berlinguer," in Giovagnoli and Pons, *L'Italia*; Fabbrini, "Le strategie"; Ignazi, *Dal PCI al PDS*; and Kertzer, *Politics*, esp. 84–152.

80. Cf. (with slightly different interpretation) Courtois and Lazar, *Histoire*, 407–13.

81. Andolfatto, *PCF*, 61–75; Buton, "The Crisis," 32–33; Buton, "Le Parti communiste français depuis 1985"; Lazar, "Les partis communistes de l'Europe occidentale"; Hincker, "Le PCF divorce"; Lavabre and Platone, *Que reste-t-il?*

82. Tatò to Berlinguer, 22 July 1981, Fondo Berlinguer, pol. interna, f. 526; Rubbi to Berlinguer, 8 May 1984, Fondo Berlinguer, movimento operaio internazionale, f. 182, APCI; described also in Gualtieri, "Il PCI,'" 286–87; Fabien, *Les nouveaux secrets*, 23–62.

83. E.g., Jacques Denis, "Les missiles américaines contre la paix," Maxime Gremetz, "Paix et désarmement en Europe," and Jacques Denis, "Paix, désarmement: Par millions autour de l'Appel de Paris," *Cahiers du communisme*, Feb. 1980, June 1980, Dec. 1981.

84. Lazar, "De la crise."

85. Ernesto Balducci, "La libertà e i missili," *Critica marxista* 23, nos. 1–2 (Jan. 1984), 96; cf. Nicola Badaloni, "Per un pacifismo rinnovato," in ibid.; Lazar, "De la crise." For comparison of nuclear issues between the late 1950s and the 1980s, see Nuti, *La sfida*.

86. Francis Cohen, "La réform révolutionnaire du socialisme," *Cahiers du communisme*, Dec. 1986; Georges Marchais, "Une chance pour le socialisme," *L'Humanité*, 10 Feb. 1987; cf. Lazar, *Maisons*, 164.

87. Jacques Lévy, "Un espace communiste"; cf. Rey, "La gauche française."

88. Rubbi, *Incontri*, 89; Giorgio Napolitano, "Non basta dire 'comunismo reale,'" *L'Unità*, 29 Aug. 1989; "Il progetto Gorbaciov," supplement to *Rinascita*, 23 May 1987; Lazar, *Maisons*, 168–69, 320–21; Roberto Gualtieri, "L'ultimo decennio del PCI," in Borioni, *Revisionismo socialista*.

89. Eco, Ceserani, and Placido, *La riscoperta*; Rubeo, *Mal d'America*; quotation from David W. Ellwood, "Italy: Containing Modernity, Domesticating America," in Stephan, *The Americanization*, 265.

90. Quotation from Gary Gerstle, "In the Shadow of Vietnam: Liberal Nationalism and the Problem of War," in Kazin and McCartin, *Americanism*, 128–30.

91. Cf. Lipset, *American Exceptionalism*, 193–202 ("mammoth" quotation from critic Patrick Buchanan in ibid.).

92. See, e.g., Cesare Luporini, "Commemorazione del centenario di Carlo Marx," in "L'uomo, il politico, lo scienziato," supplement of *L'Unità*, 6 Mar. 1983; "Antonio Gramsci dopo la caduta di tutti i muri," supplement to *L'Unità*, 15 Jan. 1991, also in Gundle, *I comunisti*, 531.

93. Argentieri and Giannotti, *L'Ottobre*; Federigo Argentieri, "Il silenzio di Nagy," *L'Unità*, 18 June 1988.

94. Lacorne and Rupnik, "Introduction: France Bewitched," 20; Rey, "La gauche française."

95. Glucksmann, *La cuisinière*; Bernard-Henri Lévy, *La barbarie*. For a good discussion of Touraine's and Gorz's works, see Reader, *Intellectuals*, 117–21.

96. Furet, *Interpreting the French Revolution*, 12. For a balanced examination of Furet's work and political impact, see Christofferson, *French Intellectuals*, 229–58 (quotation from 255). The best-selling record, accompanied by controversies, continued after the end of the Cold War with Furet, *The Passing*; Bartošek, *Les aveux*; and Courtois et al., *Le livre noir*. For a counterargument to this last book, cf. Dreyfus et al., *Le siècle*.

97. Terrail, *Destins*; Giovannini, "Generazioni"; Ginsborg, *A History*, 424–25; Cavalli and De Lillo, *Giovani*; Lazar, *Maisons*, 160–61.

98. Portelli, "The Transatlantic Jeremiad," 134–35 (see also previous section).

99. Gundle, "From *Apocalittici* to *Integrati*," 15–17.

100. Ellwood, "Italy: Containing Modernity," 267–68; Lazar, *Maisons*, 325–26.

101. Lavau, *A quoi sert*, 342–46; Kriegel, *The French Communists*; Bernard, *Un monde défait*; Andolfatto, *PCF*; Roger Martelli, *L'archipel communiste*, 69–128 (both also for a followup to the post–Cold War period); and Lazar, *Le communisme*, introduction and conclusion. For a comparison, cf. Marantzidis, "Les stratégies."

102. Kuisel, *Seducing the French*, 228–29.

103. Cf. Stam and Shohat, "Variations," 152–55. Cf. in general Teodori, *Maledetti ameri-cani.*

Conclusion

1. See a similar conclusion about the PCI in Gundle, *Between Hollywood and Moscow,* 211.

2. Actually exaggerating the effects of the 1960s domestic anti-Americanism on public opinion abroad is Hollander, *Anti-Americanism.*

3. The works by Elena Aga-Rossi and Victor Zaslavsky as well as Valerio Riva have shown the extent of Moscow's control over the PCI. While, in light of this new evidence, that subservience of even the "moderate" PCI appears much stronger than once thought, I have also shown how, once applied to the national context, the PCI's propaganda operated with considerable leeway, combining the Soviet script with a rather eclectic plethora of anti-American themes drawn from the nation's historical experience and current modernization problems. While more sedulously applying the Kremlin's agenda, the PCF also utilized a repertoire of anti-Americanism that was even more ingrained in France's political and intellectual world than in the Italian one.

4. This notion is implied in Cogan, *Oldest Allies;* Kuisel, *Seducing the French;* Gundle, *Between Hollywood and Moscow;* and Teodori, *Maledetti americani;* as well as in most works by David Ellwood.

5. Hollander, *Anti-Americanism,* 404.

6. Friedman, *The World.*

7. Stiglitz, *Globalization;* see also Stiglitz, *Freefall.*

8. See PSB D-14/a, and Memo Berger to Norberg, "French and Italian Projects—Priorities," 21 Oct. 1952, 751.001, RG59, NA.

9. Lipset, *American Exceptionalism,* 21.

10. Peter Beinart, "The Rehabilitation of the Cold War Liberal," *New York Times,* 30 Apr. 2006.

11. Revel, *Anti-Americanism;* Touraine, *The May Movement.*

12. Qtd. in Elaine Sciolino, "Chirac Will Rescind Labor Laws That Caused Wide French Riots," *New York Times,* 11 Apr. 2006.

13. Roger Cohen, "As U.S. Image Free-Falls, Spin Wobbles into Ditch," *International Herald Tribune,* 17 May 2006.

Bibliography

Archival Sources

France
    Archives de la Préfecture de Paris
        Memoranda by Paris Police on PCF activities
    Archives du Parti Communiste Français, Paris, Archives Départementales de la
        Seine-Saint-Denis
        Comité Central—Paper copies and transcripts of Compact Disc Recordings
        Décisions Bureau Politique
        Décisions Secrétariat
        Fonds Etienne Fajon
        Fonds Gaston Plissonnier
        Fonds Léo Figuères
        Fonds Marius Magnien
        Fonds Roland Leroy
        Fonds Victor Michaut
        Fonds Waldeck Rochet
        Meetings Bureau Politique
    Archives Historiques du Ministère des Affaires Etrangères, Paris
        Série B—Amérique, Sous-Série: Etats-Unis
        Série Papiers d'Agents, 217—Henri Bonnet
        Série Z—Europe
    Archives Nationales, Paris
        Papiers Maurice Thorez
Italy
    Archivio Centrale dello Stato, Rome
        Verbali del Consiglio dei Ministri
    Archivio del Partito Comunista Italiano, Istituto Gramsci, Rome
        Archivio Togliatti
        Circolari e Decisioni Scritte
        Comitato Centrale
        Commissione Culturale
        Documenti Riservati
        Fondo Berlinguer
        Movimento Studentesco (Rome)
        Segreteria
        Sezione Culturale
        Sezione Esteri
        Sezione Stampa e Propaganda
        Togliatti—Carte della Scrivania
        Ufficio Segreteria
        Verbali Direzione

Archivio Storico del Ministero degli Affari Esteri Italiano, Rome
   Ambasciata Parigi
   Direzione Generale Affari Politici
   Fondo Cassaforte
   Segreteria di Gabinetto
   Telegrammi Ordinari
Archivio Storico del Senato della Repubblica
   Fondo Amintore Fanfani
United States
   David W. Mullins Library, University of Arkansas, Fayetteville
      Bureau of Education and Cultural Affairs Historical Collection
      J. William Fulbright Papers
   Dwight D. Eisenhower Library, Abilene, Kansas
      Dwight D. Eisenhower Papers
         White House, National Security Council Staff
         White House Central Files, 1953–61
         Ann Whitman File (Papers as President of the United States, 1953–61),
            various series
      John Foster Dulles Papers, 1951–59, various series
      C. D. Jackson Papers
      White House Office, National Security Council Staff
         OCB Central Files
         PSB Central Files
   George C. Marshall Foundation, Lexington, Virginia
      George C. Marshall Papers
   Gerald R. Ford Library, Ann Arbor, Michigan
      Briefing Papers
      Robert T. Hartmann Files
      National Security Advisor Papers—Country Files
      National Security Advisor Papers—Memoranda of Conversations
      Office of Economic Affairs (L. William Seidman)
   Harry S. Truman Library, Independence, Missouri
      B-File—Student File
      Intelligence Files, Central Intelligence Reports (in President's Secretary Files)
      President's Secretary Files
      Staff Members and Office Files, Psychological Strategy Board Files
   Jimmy Carter Library, Atlanta, Georgia
      National Security Advisor—Brzezinski Material
      National Security Advisor—Staff Offices, Special Projects
      National Security Advisor—Weekly Reports
      Presidential Review Memoranda
      White House Central Files
   John F. Kennedy Library, Boston, Massachusetts
      National Security Files—Country Files
      National Security Files—Robert W. Komer
      Oral History—G. Frederick Reinhardt
      President's Office Files

Arthur Schlesinger Jr. Papers—White House Files
White House Central Files
Library of Congress, Manuscript Division, Washington, D.C.
Papers of Clare Boothe Luce
National Archives and Records Administration, College Park, Maryland
Lot Files
Intelligence Bureau, Office of the Director, 1950–59
Records of Charles E. Bohlen, 1942–52
Records of the Office of Assistant Secretary and Under Secretary of State Dean
Acheson, 1941–48, 1950
Records of the Office of Western European Affairs (various French and Italian
Files)
Records of the Officer in Charge of Northern African Affairs, 1945–56
Records Relating to State Department Participation in the Operation
Coordinating Board and the National Security Council
Subject Files of the Bureau of Intelligence and Research, 1945–60
Nixon Records
Kissinger Telephone Conversations, 1973–77
National Security Files—Country Files
National Security Files—Henry A. Kissinger Country Files
National Security Institutional Files (National Security Studies and
Memoranda)
Office of Intelligence Research Files
Office of Research and Estimates Files
Policy Planning Staff Records
Psychological Strategy Board Records
Record Group 59: General Records of the Department of State, Decimal File
Record Group 84: Paris Embassy Records, Rome Embassy Records
Record Group 218: Joint Chiefs of Staff
Record Group 273: Records of the National Security Council
Record Group 286: Records of the Agency for International Development
Record Group 306: Records of the United States Information Agency
Record Group 469: Records of U.S. Foreign Assistance Agencies, 1948–61
Entry 1192—Office of the Director, Mission to France
Entry 1259—Office of the Director, Mission to Italy
Seeley G. Mudd Library, Princeton University, Princeton, New Jersey
John Foster Dulles Papers
George F. Kennan Papers

Newspapers and Periodicals

Atlantic Monthly	*Esprit*
Cahiers du communisme	*Financial Times*
Critica marxista	*Foreign Affairs*
Il Contemporaneo	*Foreign Policy*
Corriere della Sera	*International Herald Tribune*
Démocratie nouvelle	*L'Humanité*

L'Humanité dimanche   La Pensée socialiste
Les Lettres françaises   Partisan Review
Nation   Il Politecnico
La Nouvelle critique   Il Progresso italo-americano
Le Nouvel Observateur   Quaderni piacentini
New Republic   La Repubblica
New York Times   Rinascita
Noi Donne   Socialist Review
Nuova Generazione   Les Temps modernes
Nuovi Argomenti   L'Unità
Obliques   Vie Nuove

Published Primary Documents

American Foreign Policy: Basic Documents. Washington, D.C.: Department of State, 1983.

Archivio Centrale dello Stato. *22 aprile 1944–18 giugno 1944.* Vol. 2 of *Verbali del Consiglio dei Ministri.* Rome: Presidenza del Consiglio dei Ministri, Dipartimento per l'Informazione e l'Editoria, 1996.

"Atti del convegno nazionale degli studenti universitari comunisti: Firenze, Palagio di Parte Guelfa, 17–18–19 marzo 1968." *Nuova Generazione,* 6 July 1968.

Cecchi, Ottavio, Giovanni Leone, and Giovanni Vacca, eds. *I corsivi di Roderigo: Interventi politico-culturali dal 1944 al 1964.* Bari: De Donato, 1976.

Declassified Documents Reference System. Various vols. Woodbridge, Conn.: Research Publications International, 1982–.

Galambos, Louis, ed. *The Papers of Dwight D. Eisenhower: NATO and the Campaign of 1952.* Vol. 12. Baltimore: Johns Hopkins University Press, 1989.

Institut Français d'Opinion Publique. *Les Français et de Gaulle.* Edited by Jean Charlot. Paris: IFOP, 1970.

Ministero degli Affari Esteri. *Renato Prunas.* Collana di testi diplomatici, no. 2. Rome: Tipografia del Ministero degli Affari Esteri, 1974.

Procacci, Giuliano, et al., eds. *The Cominform: Minutes of the Three Conferences, 1947/1948/1949.* Milan: Feltrinelli, 1994.

Togliatti, Palmiro. *Discorsi parlamentari.* 2 vols. Rome: Camera dei Deputati, 1984.

———. *Memoriale di Yalta.* Rome: Riuniti, 1970.

U.S. Department of State. *Foreign Relations of the United States.* Washington, D.C.: U.S. Government Printing Office (various vols.).

Books

Abbate, Michele, ed. *L'Italia fascista tra Europa e Stati Uniti d'America.* Roma: Centro Falisco di Studi Storici, 2002.

Acheson, Dean. *Present at the Creation: My Years in the State Department.* New York: W. W. Norton, 1969.

Adereth, Maxwell. *The French Communist Party: A Critical History (1920–1984)—From Comintern to the Colours of France.* Manchester, U.K.: Manchester University Press, 1984.

Adler, Alexander, et al. *L'URSS et nous*. Paris: Editions Sociales, 1978.

Aga-Rossi, Elena. *A Nation Collapses: The Italian Surrender of September 1943*. Translated by Harvey Fergusson II. Cambridge: Cambridge University Press, 2000.

Aga-Rossi, Elena, and Gaetano Quagliarello, eds. *L'altra faccia della luna: I rapporti tra PCI, PCF e Unione sovietica*. Bologna: Il Mulino, 1997.

Aga-Rossi, Elena, and Victor Zaslavsky. *Togliatti e Stalin. Il PCI e la politica estera staliniana negli archivi di Mosca*. 2nd ed. Bologna: Il Mulino, 2007.

Agosti, Aldo, Luisa Passerini, and Nicola Tranfaglia, eds. *La cultura e i luoghi del '68*. Milan: Franco Angeli, 1991.

Aimaq, Jasmine. *For Europe or Empire? French Colonial Ambitions and the European Army Plan*. Lund, Sweden: Lund University Press, 1996.

Ajello, Nello. *Il lungo addio. Intellettuali e PCI dal 1958 al 1991*. Bari: Laterza, 1997.

———. *Intellettuali e PCI, 1944–1958*. Bari: Laterza, 1979.

Aldrich, Richard J. *The Hidden Hand: Britain, America, and the Cold War Secret Intelligence*. New York: Overlook, 2001.

Allen, Beverly, and Mary J. Russo, eds. *Revisioning Italy: National Identity and Global Culture*. Minneapolis: University of Minnesota Press, 1997.

Alpers, Benjamin L. *Dictators, Democracy, and American Public Culture: Envisioning the Totalitarian Enemy, 1920s–1950s*. Chapel Hill: University of North Carolina Press, 2003.

Alpert, Hollis. *Fellini: A Life*. New York: Simon and Schuster, 2000.

Ambrose, Stephen E. *Eisenhower: The President*. New York: Simon and Schuster, 1984.

Amendola, Eva Paola, and Marcella Ferrara. *É la festa: Quarant'anni con "L'Unità"*. Rome: Riuniti, 1984.

Amendola, Giorgio. *Classe operaia e programmazione democratica*. Rome: Riuniti, 1966.

Amyot, Grant. *The Italian Communist Party: The Crisis of the Popular Front Strategy*. New York: St. Martin's, 1981.

Andolfatto, Dominique. *PCF: De la mutation à la liquidation*. Monaco: Rocher, 2005.

Andreucci, Franco. *Falce e martello: Identità e linguaggi dei comunisti italiani fra stalinismo e guerra fredda*. Bologna: Bononia University Press, 2005.

Andrew, Christopher (with Vasili Mitrokhin). *The Sword and the Shield: The Mitrokhin Archive and the Secret History of the KGB*. New York: Basic Books, 1999.

Appy, Christian G., ed. *Cold War Constructions: The Political Culture of United States Imperialism, 1945–1966*. Amherst: University of Massachusetts Press, 2000.

Argentieri, Federigo, and Lorenzo Giannotti. *L'Ottobre ungherese*. Rome: Valerio Levi, 1986.

Armus, Seth D. *French Anti-Americanism, 1930–1948: Critical Moments in a Complex History*. Plymouth, U.K.: Lexington, 2007.

Arndt, Richard, and David Rubin, eds. *The Fulbright Difference, 1948–1992*. New Brunswick, N.J.: Transaction, 1993.

Aron, Raymond. *The Opium of the Intellectuals*. New York: Norton, 1962 [1955].

Aron, Robert, and Arnaud Dandieu. *Le cancer américain*. Paris: Rioder, 1931.

Asor Rosa, Alberto. *Intellettuali e classe operaia*. Florence: La Nuova Italia, 1973.

———. *Scrittori e popolo*. Rome: Samonà e Sapelli, 1972.

Baglioni, Guido. *I giovani nella società industriale*. Milan: Vita e Pensiero, 1962.

Bagnato, Bruna. *Prove di Ostpolitik. Politica ed economia nella strategia italiana verso l'Unione Sovietica, 1958–1963*. Florence: Leo S. Olschki, 2003.

Ball, Alan M. *Imagining America: Influence and Images in Twentieth-Century Russia.* Lanham, Md.: Rowman and Littlefield, 2003.

Ballini, Pier Luigi, Sandro Guerrieri, and Antonio Varsori, eds. *Le istituzioni repubblicane dal centrismo al centrosinistra (1953–1968).* Rome: Carocci, 2006.

Banfi, Antonio. *Scritti letterari.* Rome: Riuniti, 1970.

Barbagallo, Francesco. *Enrico Berlinguer.* Rome: Carocci, 2006.

Barjot, Dominique, and Christophe Réveillard, eds. *L'américanisation de l'Europe occidentale au XXe siècle.* Paris: PUPS, 2002.

Barnes, S., et al., eds. *Italia-USA: Giudizi incrociati.* Turin: Feltrinelli, 1979.

Bartosek, Karel. *Les aveux des archives: Prague-Paris-Prague.* Paris: Seuil, 1996.

Becker, Jean-Jacques. *Le Parti communiste veut-il prendre le pouvoir?* Paris: Seuil, 1981.

Becker, Josef, and Franz Knipping, eds. *Power in Europe? Great Britain, France, Italy and Germany in a Postwar World, 1945–1950.* Berlin: Walter de Gruyter, 1986.

Bell, Daniel. *The End of Ideology: On the Exhaustion of Political Ideas in the Fifties.* Cambridge: Harvard University Press, 1988 [1960].

Bell, David Scott, and Byron Criddle. *The French Communist Party in the Fifth Republic.* Oxford: Oxford University Press, 1994.

Berghahn, Volker R. *America and the Intellectual Cold Wars in Europe: Shepard Stone between Philanthropy, Academy, and Diplomacy.* Princeton, N.J.: Princeton University Press, 2001.

Berlinguer, Giovanni. *Dieci anni dopo. Cronache culturali, 1968–1978.* Bari: De Donato, 1978.

Berman, Russell A. *Anti-Americanism in Europe: A Cultural Problem.* Stanford, Calif.: Hoover Institution Press, 2004.

Beinart, Peter. *The Good Fight: Why Liberals—and Only Liberals—Can Win the War on Terror and Make America Great Again.* New York: Harper and Collins, 2006.

Bernstein, Serge, Jean-Marie Mayeur, and Pierre Milza, eds. *Le MRP et la construction européenne.* Brussels: Complexe, 1993.

Bernstein, Serge, and Pierre Mitra, eds. *L'année 1947.* Paris: Presses de Science Po, 2000.

Bianciardi, Luciano. *L'integrazione.* Milan: Bompiani, 1960.

Billoux, François. *Quand nous étions ministres.* Paris: Editions Sociales, 1972.

Birchall, Ian H. *Sartre against Stalinism.* New York, Oxford: Berghahn, 2004.

Bischof, Günter, Peter Ruggenthaler, and Stefan Karner, eds. *The Prague Spring and the Warsaw Pact Invasion of Czechoslovukia in 1968.* Lanham, Md.: Lexington, 2010.

Black, Cyril E. *Comparative Modernization: A Reader.* New York: Free Press, 1976.

Blackmer, Donald L. M. *Unity in Diversity: Italian Communism and the Communist World.* Cambridge: MIT Press, 1968.

Blackmer, Donald L. M., and Sidney Tarrow. *Communism in Italy and France.* Princeton, N.J.: Princeton University Press, 1975.

Bloch-Lainé, François, and Jean Beauvier. *La France restaurée, 1944–1954: Dialogue sur le choix d'une modernisation.* Paris: Fayard, 1986.

Bocca, Giorgio. *Palmiro Togliatti.* Bari: Laterza, 1973.

Boffa, Giuseppe. *Memorie dal comunismo. Storia confidenziale di quarant'anni che hanno cambiato volto all'Europa.* Florence: Ponte alle Grazie, 1998.

Borgna, Gianni. *Il tempo della musica. I giovani da Elvis Presley a Sophie Marceau.* Bari: Laterza, 1983.

Borioni, Paolo, ed. *Revisionismo socialista e rinnovamento liberale. Il riformismo nell'Europa degli anni ottanta*. Rome: Carocci, 2001.

Bossuat, Gérard. *L'Europe des Français, 1943–1959: La IVe République aux sources de l'Europe communautaire*. Paris: Publications de la Sorbonne, 1996.

Bosworth, Richard J. B. *Italy and the Wider World, 1860–1960*. London: Routledge, 1996.

Bottiglieri, Bruno. *La politica economica dell'Italia centrista (1948–1958)*. Milan: Comunità, 1984.

Boujout, Michel. *Le fanatique qu'il faut être: L'énigma Jean Kanapa*. Paris: Flammarion, 2004.

Bourne, Peter G. *Jimmy Carter: A Comprehensive Biography from Plains to Postpresidency*. New York: Scribner, 1997.

Bowie, Robert R., and Richard H. Immerman. *Waging Peace: How Eisenhower Shaped an Enduring Cold War Strategy*. New York: Oxford University Press, 1998.

Boyer, Paul. *By the Bomb's Early Light: American Thought and Culture at the Dawn of the Atomic Age*. Chapel Hill: University of North Carolina Press, 1985.

Bozo, Frédéric. *Two Strategies for Europe: De Gaulle, the United States, and the Atlantic Alliance*. Translated by Susan Emanuel. London: Rowman and Littlefield, 2001.

Brands, H. W. *Cold Warriors: Eisenhower's Generation of American Foreign Policy*. New York: Columbia University Press, 1988.

———. *The Devil We Knew: Americans and the Cold War*. New York: Oxford University Press, 1993.

Bremner, Roebert H. *American Philanthropy*. Chicago: University of Chicago Press, 1988.

Breschi, Danilo. *Sognando la rivoluzione. La sinistra italiana e le origini del '68*. Florence: Mauro Pagliai, 2008.

Broadwater, Jeff. *Eisenhower and the Anti-Communist Crusade*. Chapel Hill: University of North Carolina Press, 1992.

Brogi, Alessandro. *L'Italia e l'egemonia americana nel Mediterraneo*. Florence: La Nuova Italia, 1996.

———. *A Question of Self-Esteem: The United States and the Cold War Choices in France and Italy, 1944–1958*. Westport, Conn.: Praeger, 2002.

Browder, Daniel R. *The New Jacobins: The French Communists and the Popular Front*. Ithaca, N.Y.: Cornell University Press, 1968.

Brown, Michael E., et al., eds. *New Studies in the Politics and Culture of U.S. Communism*. New York: Monthly Review Press, 1993.

Brown, Robert, ed. *The Essential Reinhold Neibuhr: Selected Essays and Addresses*. New Haven, Conn.: Yale University Press, 1986.

Brubaker, Rogers. *Citizenship and Nationhood in France and Germany*. Cambridge: Harvard University Press, 1992.

Brunetta, Gian Piero. *Storia del cinema italiano dal neorealismo al miracolo economico, 1945–1959*. Rome: Riuniti, 1982.

Bruti Liberati, Luigi. *Words, Words, Words. La Guerra fredda dell'USIS in Italia, 1945–1956*. Milan: CUEM, 2004.

Brzezinski, Zbigniew. *Power and Principle: Memoirs of the National Security Adviser, 1977–1981*. New York: Ferrar Straus Geroux, 1983.

Buton, Philippe. *Les lendemains qui déchantent: Le Parti communiste français à la Libération*. Paris: Presses de la FNSP, 1993.

Cacciari, Massimo. *Krisis: Il pensiero negativo da Nietzsche a Wittgenstein*. Milan: Feltrinelli, 1976.

Cafagna, Luciano. *C'era una volta*. Venice: Marsilio, 1991.

Calvino, Italo. *Hermit in Paris: Autobiographical Writings*. New York: Pantheon, 2003.

Camus, Albert. *Carnets: Janvier 1942–mars 1951*. Paris: Gallimard, 1964.

Capussotti, Enrica. *Gioventù perduta. Gli anni cinquanta dei giovani e del cinema in Italia*. Florence: Giunti, 2004.

Caridi, Paola. *La scissione di Palazzo Barberini*. Naples: ESI, 1990.

Caute, David. *Communism and the French Intellectuals, 1914–1960*. New York: Macmillan, 1964.

———. *The Dancer Defects: The Stuggle for Cultural Supremacy during the Cold War*. Oxford: Oxford University Press, 2003.

———. *The Fellow-Travellers: A Postscript to the Enlightenment*. London: Weidenfeld and Nicolson, 1973.

———. *The Year of the Barricades: A Journey through 1968*. New York: Harper Collins, 1988.

Cavalli, Alessandro, and Antonio De Lillo. *Giovani anni 80*. Bologna: Il Mulino, 1986.

Cerny, Philippe G. *The Politics of Grandeur: Ideological Aspects of de Gaulle's Foreign Policy*. Cambridge: Cambridge University Press, 1980.

Cervetti, Gianni. *L'oro di Mosca*. 2nd ed. Milan: Baldini & Castoldi, 1999.

Chalon, George C., ed. *The Secrets War: The Office of Strategic Services in World War II*. Washington, D.C.: NARA, 1992.

Chappell, David L. *A Stone of Hope: Prophetic Religion and the Death of Jim Crow*. Chapel Hill: University of North Carolina Press, 2004.

Chebel d'Appollonia, Ariane. *Des lendemains qui déchantent*. Vol. 1 of *Histoire politique des intellectuels en France, 1944–1954*. Brussels: Complexe, 1991.

———. *Le Temps de l'engagement*. Vol. 2 of *Histoire politique des intellectuels en France, 1944–1954*. Brussels: Complexe, 1991.

Cheles, Luciano, and Lucio Sponza, eds. *The Art of Persuasion: Political Communication in Italy from 1945 to the 1990s*. Manchester, U.K.: Manchester University Press, 2001.

Cherubini, Giovanni, et al. *Il miracolo economico e il centro sinistra*. Vol. 24 of *Storia della società italiana*. Milan: Teti, 1990.

Chiarenza, Carlo, and William L. Vance, eds. *Immaginari a confronto: I rapporti culturali tra Italia e Stati Uniti—La percezione della realtà fra stereotipo e mito*. Venice: Marsilio, 1993.

Chiarenza, Franco. *Il cavallo morente. Trent'anni di radiotelevisione italiana*. Milan: Bompiani, 1978.

Christofferson, Michael Scott. *French Intellectuals against the Left: The Antitotalitarian Movement of the 1970s*. New York: Berghahn, 2004.

Claude, Henri. *Gaullisme et grand capital*. Paris: Editions Sociales, 1960.

Cline, Ray S. *Secrets, Spies and Scholars: Blueprint of the Essential CIA*. Washington, D.C.: Acropolis, 1976.

Cogan, Charles G. *Oldest Allies, Guarded Friends: The United States and France since 1940*. Westport, Conn.: Praeger, 1994.

Colby, William, and Peter Forbath. *Honorable Men: My Life in the CIA*. New York: Simon and Schuster, 1978.

Cole, Alistair. *François Mitterrand: A Study in Political Leadership*. London: Routledge, 1994.

Coleman, Peter. *The Liberal Conspiracy: The Congress for Cultural Freedom and the Struggle for the Mind of Postwar Europe*. New York: Free Press, 1989.

Collotti, Enzo, Oskar Negt, and Franco Zannino, eds. *Lelio Basso. Teorico marxista e militante politico*. Milan: Angeli, 1979.

Colton, Joel. *Léon Blum: Humanist in Politics*. New York: A. A. Knopf, 1966.

Combes, Patrick. *La littérature et le mouvement de mai 1968: Ecriture, mythes critiques et écrivains, 1968-1981*. Paris: Seghers, 1984.

Connelly, Matthew. *A Diplomatic Revolution: Algeria's Fight for Independence and the Origins of the Post-Cold War Era*. Oxford: Oxford University Press, 2002.

Contat, Michel, and Michel Rybalka, eds. *The Writings of Jean-Paul Sartre*. Vol. 2, *Selected Prose*. Translated by Richard McCleary. Chicago: Northwestern University Press, 1985.

Cook, Blanche Wiesen. *The Declassified Eisenhower: A Startling Reappraisal of the Eisenhower Presidency*. New York: Penguin, 1984.

Corson, William R. *The Armies of Ignorance: The Rise of the American Intelligence Empire*. New York: The Dial Press, 1977.

Costigliola, Frank. *Awkward Dominion: American Political Economic, and Cultural Relations with Europe, 1919-1933*. Ithaca, N.Y.: Cornell University Press, 1984.

———. *France and the United States: The Cold Alliance since World War II*. New York: Twayne, 1992.

Courtois, Stéphane, ed. *Du passé faisons table rase! Histoire et mémoire du communisme en Europe*. Paris: Laffont, 2002.

Courtois, Stéphane, and Marc Lazar. *Histoire du Parti communiste français*. Paris: Presses Universitaires de France, 2000.

Courtois, Stéphane, and Marc Lazar, eds. *50 ans d'une passion française: De Gaulle et les communistes*. Paris: Balland, 1991.

Courtois, Stéphane, et al. *Le livre noir du communisme: Crimes, terreur et répression*. Paris: Laffont, 1997.

Craveri, Piero, and Gaetano Quagliarello, eds. *L'antiamericanismo in Italia e in Europa nel secondo dopoguerra*. Soveria Mannelli: Rubbettino, 2004.

Creswell, Michael. *A Question of Balance: How France and the United States Created Cold War Europe*. Cambridge: Harvard University Press, 2006.

Cull, Nicholas J. *The Cold War and the United States Information Agency: American Propaganda and Public Diplomacy, 1945-1989*. Cambridge: Cambridge University Press, 2008.

Dalmasso, Sergio. *Il caso "Manifesto," e il PCI degli anni '60*. Turin: Cric, 1989.

Dalton, Russell J., and Manfred Kuechler, eds. *Challenging the Political Order: New Social and Political Movements in Western Democracies*. Cambridge: Cambridge University Press, 1990.

D'Attorre, Pier Paolo, ed. *Nemici per la pelle: Sogno americano e mito sovietico nell'Italia contemporanea*. Milan: Franco Angeli, 1991.

Daugherty, William E., and Morris Janowitz, eds. *A Psychological Warfare Casebook*. Baltimore: Operations Research Office, Johns Hopkins University Press, 1958.

Davenport, Russell Wheeler. *USA: The Permanent Revolution*. New York: Prentice-Hall, 1951.

Dazy, René. *La partie et le tout: Le PCF et la guerre franco-algérienne*. Paris: Syllepse, 1990.

de Beauvoir, Simone. *After "The Second Sex."* New York: Pantheon, 1984.

———. *America Day by Day* (1954). Translated by Carol Cosman. Berkeley: University of California Press, 1999.

———. *Force of Circumstance*. New York: Putnam's Sons, 1965.

De Castro, Diego. *La questione di Trieste: L'azione politica e diplomatica italiana dal 1943 al 1954*. Trieste: LINT, 1981.

de Gaulle, Charles. *The Call to Honor*. Vol. 1 of *War Memoirs*. New York: Simon and Schuster, 1955.

———. *Unity*. Vol. 2 of *War Memoirs*. New York: Simon and Schuster, 1959.

de Grazia, Victoria. *Irresistible Empire: America's Advance through Twentieth-Century Europe*. Cambridge: Belknap/Harvard University Press, 2005.

de la Gorce, Paul-Marie. *Apogée et mort de la IVe République, 1952–1958*. Paris: Grasset, 1979.

De Leonardis, Massimo. *La "diplomazia atlantica" e la soluzione del problema di Trieste (1952–1954)*. Naples: ESI, 1992.

Del Pero, Mario. *L'alleato scomodo: Gli USA e la DC negli anni del centrismo (1948–1955)*. Rome: Carocci, 2001.

De Rosa, Gabriele, and Giancarlo Monina, eds. *L'Italia repubblicana nella crisi degli anni settanta*. Vol. 4. Soveria Mannelli: Rubbettino, 2003.

Desanti, Dominique. *Les staliniens, 1944–1956: Une experience politique*. Paris: Fayard, 1975.

Diggins, John P. *The Rise and Fall of the American Left*. Rev. ed. New York: Norton, 1992.

Di Loreto, Pietro. *Togliatti e la "doppiezza": Il PCI tra democrazia e insurrezione, 1944–1949*. Bologna: Il Mulino, 1991.

Dimitrov, Georgi. *Selected Works*. Vol. 2. Sofia: Sofia Press, 1972.

Di Nolfo, Ennio. *Le paure e le speranze degli italiani, 1943–1953*. Milan: Mondadori, 1986.

———. *Vaticano e Stati Uniti (1939–1952): Dalle carte di Myron C. Taylor*. Milan: Franco Angeli, 1978.

———, ed. *La politica estera italiana negli anni ottanta*. Manduria: Piero Lacaita, 2003.

Di Nolfo, Ennio, Romain H. Rainero, and Brunello Vigezzi, eds. *L'Italia e la politica di potenza in Europa (1945–1950)*. Florence: Marzorati, 1986.

Di Scala, Spencer M., ed. *Italian Socialism between Politics and History*. Amherst: University of Massachusetts Press, 1996.

Dockrill, Saki, Robert Frank, Georges-Henri Soutou, and Antonio Varsori, eds. *L'Europe de l'Est et de l'Ouest dans la guerre froide, 1948–1952*. Paris: Presses de l'Université de Paris Sorbonne, 2002.

Donno, Gianni. *La Gladio rossa del PCI (1945–1967)*. Soveria Mannelli: Rubbettino, 2001.

Drake, David. *Intellectuals and Politics in Postwar France*. London: Palgrave, 2002.

———. *Sartre*. London: Haus, 2005.

Drake, Richard. *The Revolutionary Mystique and Terrorism in Contemporary Italy*. Bloomington: Indiana University Press, 1989.

Dreyfus, Michel, et al. *Le siècle des communismes*. Paris: L'Atelier, 2000.

Duclos, Jacques. *Gaullisme, technocratisme, corporatisme*. Paris: Editions Sociales, 1963.

Dudziak, Mary L. *Cold War Civil Rights: Race and Image of American Democracy*. Princeton, N.J.: Princeton University Press, 2000.

Duggan, Christopher, and Christopher Wagstaff, eds. *Italy in the Cold War: Politics, Culture and Society, 1948–1958*. Oxford: Berg, 1995.

Duhamel, Georges. *America the Menace: Scenes from the Life of the Future*. Translated by Charles Miner Thompson. Boston: Houghton Mifflin, 1931.

Dundovich, Elena. *Tra esilio e castigo. La repressione degli antifascisti italiani in Unione sovietica (1936–1938)*. Rome: Carocci, 1998.

Dur, Philip E. *Jefferson Caffery of Louisiana, Ambassador of Revolutions*. Lafayette, La.: University Libraries, 1982.

Dutueil, Jean-Pierre. *Nanterre, 1965–1968: Vers le mouvement du 22 mars*. Paris, 1988.

Eco, Umberto, Gian Piero Ceserani, and Beniamino Placido. *La riscoperta dell'America*. Bari: Laterza, 1984.

Eisenhower, Dwight D. *Crusade in Europe*. Garden City, N.Y.: Doubleday, 1948.

———. *Mandate for Change, 1953–1956: The White House Years*. Garden City, N.Y.: Doubleday, 1963.

Elgey, Georgette. *Histoire de la IVe République: La République des illusions, 1945–1951*. Rev. ed. Paris: Fayard, 1993.

Elleinstein, Jean. *Histoire de l'URSS*. Paris: Editions Sociales, 1972–75.

———. *Histoire du phénomène stalinien*. Paris: Grasset, 1975.

Elliot, Gregory. *Althusser: The Detour of Theory*. New York: Verso, 1987.

Ellwood, David W. *Italy, 1943–1945*. New York: Holmes and Meier, 1985.

———. *Rebuilding Europe: Western Europe, America, and Postwar Reconstruction*. London: Longman, 1992.

Ellwood, David W., and Gian Piero Brunetta, eds. *Hollywood in Europa: Industria, politica, pubblico del cinema, 1945–1960*. Florence: Ponte alle Grazie, 1991.

Ellwood, David W., and Rob Kroes, eds. *Hollywood in Europe: Experiences of a Cultural Hegemony*. Amsterdam: VU University Press, 1994.

el-Machat, Samya. *Les Etats-Unis et l'Algérie: De la méconnaissance à la reconnaissance, 1945–1962*. Paris: L'Harmattan, 1996.

Endy, Christopher. *Cold War Holidays: American Tourism in France*. Chapel Hill: University of North Carolina Press, 2004.

English, Robert. *Russia and the Idea of the West: Gorbachev, Intellectuals, and the End of the Cold War*. New York: Columbia University Press, 2000.

Esposito, Chiarella. *America's Feeble Weapon: Funding the Marshall Plan in France and Italy, 1948–50*. Westport, Conn.: Greenwood, 1994.

Fabien, Jean. *La guerre des camarades*. Paris: Olivier Orban, 1985.

———. *Les nouveaux secrets des communistes*. Paris: Albin Michel, 1990.

Faenza, Roberto, and Marco Fini. *Gli americani in Italia*. Milan: Feltrinelli, 1976.

Fasanella, Giovanni, and Corrado Incerti. *Sofia 1973: Quando Berlinguer doveva morire*. Rome: Nuova Iniziativa, 2006.

Fedele, Santi. *Fronte Popolare. La sinistra e le elezioni del 18 aprile 1948*. Milan: Bompiani, 1978.

Feenberg, Andrew, and Jim Freedman. *When Poetry Ruled the Streets: The French May Events of 1968*. Albany: State University of New York Press, 2001.

Fehrenbach, Heide, and Uta G. Poiger, eds. *Transactions, Transgressions, Transformations: American Culture in Western Europe and Japan.* New York: Berghahn, 2000.

Fejtö, François. *The French Communist Party and the Crisis of International Communism.* Cambridge: MIT Press, 1967.

Ferguson, Niall. *Empire: The Rise and Demise of the British World Order and the Lessons for Global Power.* New York: Basic Books, 2004.

Ferraresi, Franco. *Threats to Democracy: The Radical Right in Italy after the War.* Princeton, N.J.: Princeton University Press, 1996.

Ferrero, Léo. *Amérique: Miroir grossissant de l'Europe.* Paris: Rieder, 1939.

Ferretti, Gian Carlo. *Il mercato delle lettere.* Milan: Il Saggiatore, 1994.

Filippelli, Ronald L. *American Labor and Postwar Italy, 1943–1954.* Stanford, Calif.: Stanford University Press, 1989.

Fink, Carole, Philipp Gassert, and Detlef Junker, eds. *1968: The World Transformed.* Cambridge: Cambridge University Press, 1998.

Fiori, Giuseppe. *Gramsci, Togliatti, Stalin.* Bari: Laterza, 1991.

Fisher, David James. *Romain Rolland and the Politics of Intellectual Engagement.* Berkeley: University of California Press, 1988.

Fiszbin, Henri. *Les bouches s'ouvrent.* Paris: Grasset, 1980.

Flores, Marcello. *L'immagine dell'URSS. L'Occidente e la Russia di Stalin (1927–1956).* Milan: Il Saggiatore, 1990.

———. *1956.* Bologna: Il Mulino, 1996.

Flores, Marcello, and Alberto de Bernardi. *Il sessantotto.* Bologna: Il Mulino, 1998.

Flores, Marcello, and Nicola Gallerano. *Sul PCI: Un'interpretazione storica.* Bologna: Il Mulino, 1992.

Foreman, Joel, ed. *The Other Fifties: Interrogating Midcentury American Icons.* Urbana: University of Illinois Press, 1997.

Formigoni, Guido. *La Democrazia cristiana e l'alleanza occidentale (1943–1953).* Bologna: Il Mulino, 1996.

———. *L'Italia dei cattolici: Fede e nazione dal Risorgimento alla Repubblica.* Bologna: Il Mulino, 1998.

Frankel, Paul. *Mattei: Oil and Power Politics.* New York: Praeger, 1966.

Franzinelli, Mimmo. *L'amnistia Togliatti.* Milan: Mondadori, 2006.

Friedman, Thomas L. *The World Is Flat: A Brief History of the Twenty-First Century.* New York: Farrar, Straus and Giroux, 2006.

Fuks, Jennifer. *L'anti-américanisme au sein de la gauche socialiste française: De la libération aux années 2000.* Paris: Harmattan, 2010.

Fukuyama, Francis. *State-Building: Governance and World Order in the Twenty-First Century.* Ithaca, N.Y.: Cornell University Press, 2004.

Fulbright, J. William. *The Arrogance of Power.* New York: Random House, 1966.

Furet, François. *Interpreting the French Revolution.* Translated by Elborg Forster. New York: Cambridge University Press, 1981.

———. *The Passing of an Illusion: The Idea of Communism in the Twentieth Century.* Translated by Deborah Furet. Chicago: University of Chicago Press, 1999.

Gaddis, John L. *The Cold War: A New History.* Oxford: Oxford University Press, 2005.

———. *The Long Peace: Inquiries into the History of the Cold War.* New York: Oxford University Press, 1987.

————. *Strategies of Containment: A Critical Appraisal of Postwar American National Security Policy*. 2nd ed. New York: Oxford University Press, 2005.

————. *We Now Know: Rethinking Cold War History*. Oxford, U.K.: Clarendon, 1997.

Galante, Severino. *L'autonomia possibile. Il PCI del dopoguerra tra politica estera e politica interna*. Florence: Ponte alle Grazie, 1991.

————. *La fine di un compromesso storico: DC e PCI nella crisi del 1947*. Milan: Franco Angeli, 1980.

————. *Il Partito comunista e l'integrazione europea: Il decennio del rifiuto, 1947-1957*. Padova: Liviana, 1988.

Galasso, Giuseppe, ed. *Storia dell'Italia dall'unità alla fine della prima repubblica*. Milan: Tea, 1996.

Galeazzi, Marco. *Togliatti e Tito: Tra identità nazionale e internazionalismo*. Rome: Carocci, 2006.

————, ed. *Roma Belgrado: Gli anni della Guerra fredda*. Ravenna: Longo, 1995.

Galli, Giorgio. *Storia del PCI. Il Partito comunista italiano (Livorno 1921–Rimini 1991)*. Milan: Kaos, 1993.

Galli della Loggia, Ernesto. *L'identità italiana*. Bologna: Il Mulino, 1998.

————. *Morte della patria*. Bari: Laterza, 1996.

Galluzzi, Carlo. *La svolta. Gli anni cruciali del Partito comunista italiano*. Milan: Sperling & Kupfer, 1983.

Garaudy, Roger. *L'Eglise, le communisme et les chrétiens*. Paris: Sociales, 1949.

————. *Literature of the Graveyard*. New York: International, 1948.

Gardner, Richard N. *Mission Italy: On the Front Lines of the Cold War*. Lanham, Md.: Rowman and Littlefield, 2005.

Gat, Moshe. *Britain and Italy, 1943–1949: The Decline of British Influence*. Brighton, U.K.: Sussex Academic, 1996.

Gavi, Philippe, Jean-Paul Sartre, and Pierre Victor. *On a raison de se révolter*. Paris: Gallimard, 1974.

Gentile, Emilio. *La grande Italia. Ascesa e declino del mito della nazione nel ventesimo secolo*. Milan: Mondadori, 1997.

Gentiloni Silveri, Umberto. *L'Italia e la nuova frontiera: Stati Uniti e centrosinistra, 1958-1965*. Bologna: Il Mulino, 1998.

Gérôme, Noëlle, and Danielle Tartakowsky. *La Fête de "L'Humanité": Culture communiste, culture populaire*. Paris: Messidor, 1988.

Giacomini, Ruggero. *I partigiani della pace. Il movimento pacifista in Italia negli anni della prima Guerra fredda*. Milan: Vangelista, 1984.

Gide, André. *Retour de l'URSS*. Paris: Gallimard, 1936.

Gienow-Hecht, Jessica C. E., and Frank Schumacher, eds. *Culture and International History*. New York: Berghahn, 2003.

Gildea, Robert. *The Past in French History*. New Haven, Conn.: Yale University Press, 1994.

Ginsborg, Paul. *A History of Contemporary Italy: Society and Politics, 1943–1988*. London: Penguin, 1990.

Giolitti, Antonio. *Lettere a Marta. Ricordi e riflessioni*. Bologna: Il Mulino, 1992.

Giovagnoli, Agostino. *Il caso Moro. Una tragedia repubblicana*. Bologna: Il Mulino, 2005.

————. *Il partito italiano. La Democrazia cristiana dal 1942 al 1994*. Rome: Bonacci, 1996.

————, ed. *Interpretazioni della Repubblica*. Bologna: Il Mulino, 1998.

Giovagnoli, Agostino, and Silvio Pons, eds. *L'Italia repubblicana nella crisi degli anni settanta*. Vol. 1. Soveria Mannelli: Rubbettino, 2003.

Giovagnoli, Agostino, and Luciano Tosi, eds. *Amintore Fanfani e la politica estera italiana*. Venice: Marsilio, 2010.

Giusti, Maria Teresa. *I prigionieri italiani in Russia*. Bologna: Il Mulino, 2003.

Glucksmann, André. *La cuisinière et le mangeur d'hommes: Essai sur les rapports entre l'Etat, le marxisme et les camps de concentration*. Paris: Grasset, 1975.

Goguel, François. *Modernisation économique et comportement politique*. Paris: FNSP, 1969.

Golden, Miriam. *Labor Divided: Austerity and Working Class in Contemporary Italy*. Ithaca, N.Y.: Cornell University Press, 1988.

Gorbachev, Michail. *Le idee di Berlinguer ci servono ancora*. Rome: Sisifo, 1994.

Gordon, Philip H. *A Certain Idea of France: French Security Policy and the Gaullist Legacy*. Princeton, N.J.: Princeton University Press, 1993.

Gori, Francesca. *Italiani nei lager di Stalin*. Bari: Laterza, 2006.

Gori, Francesca, and Silvio Pons, eds. *Dagli archivi di Mosca: L'URSS, il Cominform, e il PCI (1943-1951)*. Rome: Carocci, 1998.

————, eds. *The Soviet Union and Europe in the Cold War, 1943-53*. London: Macmillan; New York: St. Martin's, 1996.

Gornick, Vivian. *The Romance of American Communism*. New York: Basic Books, 1978.

Gough, Hugh, and John Horne, eds. *De Gaulle and Twentieth-Century France*. London: Hodder Arnold, 1995.

Goulemot, Jean Marie. *Pour l'amour de Staline: La face oubliée du communisme français*. Paris: CNRS, 2009.

Gozzini, Giovanni, and Renzo Martinelli. *Dall'attentato a Togliatti all'VIII congresso*. Vol. 7 of *Storia del Partito comunista italiano*. Turin: Einaudi, 1998.

Gramsci, Antonio. *Americanismo e fordismo. Quaderno 22*. Turin: Einaudi, 1978.

————. *The Modern Prince and Other Writings*. London: Lawrence and Wishart, 1957.

————. *Note sul Machiavelli, sulla politica e sullo stato moderno*. Turin: Einaudi, 1955.

————. *Quaderni del carcere (The Prison Notebooks)*. Vol. 3. Edited by Valentino Gerretana. Turin: Einaudi, 1975.

————. *Selections from "The Prison Notebooks"*. Edited and translated by Quintin Hoare and Geoffrey Nowell Smith. London: Lawrence and Wishart, 1971.

Grandi, Aldo. *La generazione degli anni perduti. Storie di potere operaio*. Turin: Einaudi, 2003.

Grémion, Pierre. *Intelligence de l'anticommunisme: Le Congrès pour la Libertè de la Culture à Paris, 1950-1975*. Paris: Fayard, 1995.

————. *Paris-Prague: La gauche française face au renouveau et à la régression tchéchoslovaques, 1968-1978*. Paris: Julliard, 1985.

Grisoni, Dominique, and Hugues Portelli. *Le lotte operaie in Italia dal 1960 al 1976*. Milan: Rizzoli, 1977.

Gualtieri, Roberto. *L'Italia dal 1943 al 1992. DC e PCI nella storia della Repubblica*. Rome: Carocci, 2006.

————. *Togliatti e la politica estera italiana. Dalla Resistenza al trattato di pace, 1943-1947*. Roma: Riuniti, 1995.

————, ed. *Il PCI nell'Italia repubblicana, 1943-1991*. Rome: Carocci, 2001.

Guasconi, Maria Eleonora. *L'altra faccia della medaglia. Guerra psicologica e diplomazia sindacale nelle relazioni Italia-Stati Uniti durante la prima fase della guerra fredda (1947–1955)*. Soveria Mannelli: Rubbettino, 1999.

Guback, Thomas. *The International Film Industry: Western Europe and America since 1945*. Bloomington: Indiana University Press, 1969.

Guiat, Cyrille. *The French and Italian Communist Parties: Comrades and Culture*. London: Frank Cass, 2003.

Guiso, Andrea. *La colomba e la spada. "Lotta per la pace" e antiamericanismo nella politica del Partito comunista italiano (1949–1954)*. Soveria Mannelli: Rubbettino, 2006.

Gundle, Stephen. *Between Hollywood and Moscow: The Italian Communists and the Challenge of Mass Culture, 1943–1991*. Durham, N.C.: Duke University Press, 2000.

———. *I comunisti italiani tra Hollywood e Mosca*. Milan: Giunti, 1995.

Gutman, Huck, ed. *As Others Read Us: International Perspectives on American Literature*. Amherst: University of Massachusetts Press, 1991.

Harper, John L. *America and the Reconstruction of Italy, 1945–1948*. Cambridge: Cambridge University Press, 1986.

———. *American Visions of Europe: Franklin D. Roosevelt, George Kennan, and Dean G. Acheson*. Cambridge: Cambridge University Press, 1994.

Hazareesingh, Sudhir. *Intellectuals and the French Communist Party: Disillusion and Decline*. Oxford, U.K.: Clarendon, 1991.

Heale, Michael J. *McCarthy's Americans: Red Scare Politics in State and Nation, 1935–1965*. Basingstoke, U.K.: Macmillan, 1998.

Heiney, Donald. *America in Modern Italian Literature*. Newark, N.J.: Rutgers University Press, 1964.

Hellman, Stephen. *Italian Communism in Transition: The Historic Compromise in Turin, 1975–80*. New York: Oxford University Press, 1988.

Hervé, Pierre. *La Libération trahie*. Paris: Grasset, 1945.

Hincker, François. *Le Parti communiste au carrefour*. Paris: Albin Michel, 1981.

Hirsch, Arthur. *The French New Left: An Intellectual History from Sartre to Gorz*. Boston: South End, 1981.

Hitchcock, William I. *France Restored: Cold War Diplomacy and the Quest for Leadership in Europe, 1944–1954*. Chapel Hill: University of North Carolina Press, 1998.

Hixson, Walter L. *George F. Kennan: Cold War Iconoclast*. New York: Columbia University Press, 1989.

———. *Parting the Curtain: Propaganda, Culture and the Cold War, 1945–1961*. New York: St. Martin's, 1997.

Hoff, Joan. *A Faustian Foreign Policy: From Woodrow Wilson to George W. Bush*. New York: Cambridge University Press, 2008.

Hoffman, Paul G. *Peace Can Be Won*. London: Michael Joseph, 1951.

Hoffmann, Stanley. *Decline or Renewal? France since the 1930s*. New York: Viking, 1974.

———. *Le mouvement Poujade*. Paris: A. Collin, 1956.

———, ed. *In Search of France*. Cambridge: Harvard University Press, 1963.

Hofstadter, Richard. *Anti-Intellectualism in American Life*. New York: Alfred A. Knopf, 1966.

Hogan, Michael J. *The Marshall Plan: America, Britain and the Reconstruction of Western Europe*. New York: Cambridge University Press, 1987.

———, ed. *The Ambiguous Legacy: U.S. Foreign Relations in the "American Century."* Cambridge: Cambridge University Press, 1999.

Hoganson, Kristin. *Consumers' Imperium: The Global Production of American Domesticity, 1865–1920.* Chapel Hill: University of North Carolina Press, 2007.

Hollander, Paul. *Anti-Americanism: Critics at Home and Abroad, 1965–1990.* New York: Oxford University Press, 1991.

———. *The End of Commitment: Intellectuals, Revolutionaries, and Political Morality in the Twentieth Century.* Chicago: Ivan R. Dee, 2006.

———. *Pellegrini politici.* Bologna: Mulino, 1981.

———, ed. *Understanding Anti-Americanism: Its Origins and Impact at Home and Abroad.* Chicago: Ivan R. Dee, 2004.

Hollifield, James F., and George Ross. *Searching for the New France.* New York: Routledge, 1991.

Holloway, David. *Stalin and the Bomb: The Soviet Union and Atomic Energy, 1939–1956.* New Haven, Conn.: Yale University Press, 1994.

Hughes, Emmet J. *The Ordeal of Power: A Political Memoir of the Eisenhower Years.* New York: Atheneum, 1963.

Hull, Cordell. *The Memoirs of Cordell Hull.* Vol. 2. New York: Macmillan, 1948.

Hunt, Michael H. *The American Ascendancy: How the United States Gained and Wielded Global Dominance.* Chapel Hill: University of North Carolina Press, 2008.

Huntington, Samuel P. *Who Are We? The Challenges to American National Identity.* New York: Simon and Schuster, 2004.

Ignazi, Piero. *Dal PCI al PDS.* Bologna: Il Mulino, 1992.

Jackson, Jeffrey H. *Making Jazz French: Music and Modern Life in Interwar Paris.* Durham, N.C.: Duke University Press, 2003.

Jackson, Julian. *France: The Dark Years, 1940–1944.* New York: Oxford University Press, 2001.

———. *The Popular Front in France: Defending Democracy, 1934–1938.* Cambridge: Cambridge University Press, 1988.

Jeannet, Angela M., and Louise K. Barnett, eds. *New World Journeys: Contemporary Italian Writers and the Experience of America.* Westport, Conn.: Greenwood, 1977.

Jenkins, Brian. *Nationalism in France: Class and Nation since 1789.* New York: Routledge, 1990.

Jenkins, Brian, and Spyros A. Sofos, eds. *Nation and Identity in Contemporary Europe.* London: Routledge, 1996

Jennings, Jeremy, ed. *Intellectuals in Twentieth-Century France: Mandarins and Samurais.* London: Palgrave, Macmillan, 1992.

Jennings, Jeremy, and A. Kamp-Welch, eds. *Intellectuals in Politics: From the Dreyfus Affair to Salman Rushdie.* New York: Routledge, 1997.

Joffrin, Laurent. *Mai 68: Histoire des événements.* Paris: Seuil, 1988.

Johnson, Walter, and Francis Colligan. *The Fulbright Program: A History.* Chicago: University of Chicago Press, 1965.

Judt, Tony. *Marxism and the French Left.* Oxford: Oxford University Press, 1986.

———. *Past Imperfect: French Intellectuals, 1944–1956.* Berkeley: University of California Press, 1992.

———. *Postwar: A History of Europe since 1945.* New York: Penguin, 2005.

Kahler, Miles, and Warner Link. *Europe and America: A Return to History*. New York: Council on Foreign Relations Press, 1996.

Kaplan, Lawrence S., Robert W. Clawson, and Raimondo Luraghi, eds. *NATO and the Mediterranean*. Wilmington, Del.: Scholarly Resources, 1990.

Karabell, Zachary. *Architects of Intervention: The United States, the Third World, and the Cold War, 1946–1962*. Baton Rouge: Louisiana State University Press, 1999.

Katzenstein, Peter G., and Robert O. Keohane, eds. *Anti-Americanisms in World Politics*. Ithaca, N.Y.: Cornell University Press, 2006.

Kazin, Michel, and Joseph A. MacCartin, eds. *Americanism: New Perspectives on the History of an Ideal*. Chapel Hill: University of North Carolina Press, 2006.

Kelly, Daniel. *James Burnham and the Struggle for the World: A Life*. Wilmington, Del.: ISI Books, 2002.

Kelly, Michael. *The Cultural and Intellectual Rebuilding of France after the Second World War (1944–1947)*. New York: Palgrave, Macmillan, 2005.

Kertzer, David I. *Politics and Symbols: The Italian Communist Party and the Fall of Communism*. New Haven, Conn.: Yale University Press, 1996.

Khilnani, Sunil. *Arguing Revolution: The Intellectual Left in Postwar France*. New Haven, Conn.: Yale University Press, 1993.

Killick, John. *The United States and European Reconstruction, 1945–1960*. Edinburgh: Keele University Press, 1997.

Kissinger, Henry. *White House Years*. Boston: Little, Brown, 1979.

———. *Years of Renewal*. New York: Simon and Schuster, 1999.

Klehr, Harvey, John Earl Haynes, and Kirill M. Anderson. *The Soviet World of American Communism*. New Haven, Conn.: Yale University Press, 1998.

Kotek, Joël. *La jeune garde: La jeunesse entre KGB et CIA, 1917–1989*. Paris: Seuil, 1998.

Kotek, Joël, and Dan Kotek. *L'affaire Lyssenko*. Brussels: Complexe, 1986

Kriegel, Annie. *Ce que j'ai cru comprendre*. Paris: Laffont, 1991.

———. *Communismes au miroir français*. Paris: Gallimard, 1974.

———. *The French Communists: Profile of a People*. Translated by E. Halperin. Chicago: University of Chicago Press, 1972.

Kroes, Rob. *If You've Seen One You've Seen the Mall: Europeans and American Mass Culture*. Urbana: University of Illinois Press, 1996.

Kroes, Rob, Robert W. Rydell, and D. F. J. Bosscher, eds. *Cultural Transmissions and Receptions: American Mass Culture in Europe*. Amsterdam: VU University Press, 1993.

Kuisel, Richard F. *Capitalism and the State in Modern France: Renovation and Economic Management in the Twentieth Century*. Cambridge: Cambridge University Press, 1981.

———. *Seducing the French: The Dilemma of Americanization*. Berkeley: University of California Press, 1993.

Kuklick, Bruce. *Blind Oracles: Intellectuals and War from Kennan to Kissinger*. Princeton, N.J.: Princeton University Press, 2006.

Kunz, Diane B., ed. *The Diplomacy of the Crucial Decade: American Foreign Relations during the 1960s*. New York: Columbia University Press, 1994.

Lacorne, Denis, Jacques Rupnik, and Marie-France Toinet, eds. *The Rise and Fall of Anti-Americanism: A Century of French Perception*. Translated by G. Turner. New York: St. Martin's, 1990.

Lacouture, Jean. *Léon Blum*. Translated by G. Holoch. New York: Holmes and Meier, 1982.

Lanaro, Silvio. *Storia dell'Italia repubblicana. Dalla fine della guerra agli anni novanta*. Venice: Marsilio 1992.

Landolfi, Antonio. *Il Gladio rosso di Dio. Storia dei cattolici comunisti*. Rome: SEAM, 1998.

Lankford, Nelson D. *The Last American Aristocrat: The Biography of David K. E. Bruce, 1898–1977*. Boston: Little, Brown, 1996.

Larson, Deborah Welch. *Anatomy of Mistrust: U.S.-Soviet Relations during the Cold War*. Ithaca, N.Y.: Cornell University Press, 1997.

Lasch, Christopher. *The Agony of the American Left*. New York: Alfred Knopf, 1969.

Latham, Michael E. *Modernization as Ideology: American Social Science and Nation-Building in the Kennedy Era*. Chapel Hill: University of North Carolina Press, 2000.

Lavabre, Marie-Claire, and François Platone. *Que reste-t-il du PCF?* Paris: Autrement, 2003.

Lavau, Georges. *A quoi sert le Parti communiste français?* Paris: Fayard, 1981.

Lazar, Marc. *Le communisme: Une passion française*. Paris: Perrin, 2002.

———. *Maisons rouges: Les partis communistes français et italien de la Libération à nos jours*. Paris: Aubier, 1992.

Lecoeur, Auguste. *Le PCF et la Résistance, août 1939–juin 1941*. Paris: Plon, 1968.

Ledda, Romano. *L'Europa fra Nord e Sud: Trent'anni di politica internazionale*. Rome: Riuniti, 1989.

Lefebvre, Henri. *The Explosion: Marxism and the French Revolution*. Translated by Alfred Ehrenferd. New York: Monthly Review Press, 1969.

Leffler, Melvyn P., and Odd Arne Westad, eds. *The Cambridge History of the Cold War*. 3 vols. New York: Cambridge University Press, 2009.

Le Goff, Jean-Pierre. *Mai 68: L'"héritage impossible."* Paris: La Découverte, 1998.

Lévesque, Jacques. *The Enigma of 1989: The USSR and the Liberation of Eastern Europe*. Berkeley: University of California Press, 1997.

Lévy, Bernard-Henri. *La barbarie à visage humain*. Paris: Grasset, 1977.

Levy, Guenter. *The Cause That Failed: Communism in American Political Life*. New York: Oxford University Press, 1990.

Lipset, Seymour Martin. *American Exceptionalism: A Double-Edged Sword*. New York: W. W. Norton, 1996.

———. *Political Man: The Social Basis of Politics*. New York: Doubleday, 1960.

Lomellini, Valentine. *L'appuntamento mancato. La sinistra italiana e il dissenso nei regimi comunisti (1968–1989)*. Florence: Le Monnier, 2010.

Lottman, Herbert. *The Left Bank: Writers, Artists, and Politics from the Popular Front to the Cold War*. Chicago: University of Chicago Press, 1998.

Loubet del Bayle, Jean-Louis. *Les non-conformistes des années 30: Une tentative de renouvellement de la pensée politique française*. Paris: Seuil, 2001 [1969].

Lucas, Scott. *Freedom's War: The American Crusade against the Soviet Union*. New York: New York University Press, 1999.

Lucia, Piero. *Intellettuali italiani del secondo dopoguerra: Impegno, crisi, speranza*. Naples: Guida, 2003.

Lumley, Robert. *States of Emergency: Cultures of Revolt in Italy from 1968 to 1978*. New York: W. W. Norton, 1990.

Lundestad, Geir. *The American "Empire" and Other Studies of US Foreign Policy in a Comparative Perspective*. London: Oxford University Press, 1990.

———. *"Empire" by Integration: The United States and European Integration, 1945-1997*. Oxford: Oxford University Press, 1998.

———. *The United States and Western Europe since 1945: From "Empire" by Invitation to Transatlantic Drift*. Oxford: Oxford University Press, 2003.

———, ed. *No End to Alliance: The United States and Western Europe: Past, Present and Future*. London: Macmillan, 1998.

Luperini, Romano. *Gli intellettuali di sinistra e l'ideologia della ricostruzione nel dopoguerra*. Rome: "Ideologie," 1971.

———. *Marxismo e gli intellettuali*. Venice: Marsilio, 1974.

Lussana, Fiamma, and Giacomo Maramao. *L'Italia repubblicana nella crisi degli anni settanta*. Vol. 2. Soveria Mannelli: Rubbettino, 2003.

Mafai, Miriam. *Botteghe Oscure, addio. Com'eravamo comunisti*. Milan: Mondadori, 1996.

Maggiorani, Mauro. *L'Europa degli altri. Comunisti italiani e integrazione europea (1957-1969)*. Rome: Carocci, 1998.

Maggiorani, Mauro, and Paolo Ferrari, eds. *L'Europa da Togliatti a Berlinguer, 1945-1984*. Bologna: Il Mulino, 2005.

Magny, Claude-Edmonde. *The Age of the American Novel: The Film Aesthetic of Fiction between the Two Wars*. Translated by Eleanor Hochman. New York: Ungar, 1972.

Maier, Charles S. *Among Empires: American Ascendancy and Its Predecessors*. Cambridge: Harvard University Press, 2006.

Maier, Charles S., and Stanley Hoffmann. *The Marshall Plan: A Retrospective*. Boulder, Colo.: Westview, 1984.

Marcou, Lilly. *Le mouvement communiste international depuis 1945*. Paris: Presses Universitaires de France, 1980.

Marks, Elaine, and Isabelle de Courtivron, eds. *New French Feminism*. Brighton, U.K.: Harvester, 1980.

Marie, Laurent. *Le cinéma est à nous: Le PCF et le cinéma français de la Libération à nos jours*. Paris: L'Harmattan, 2005.

Marino, Gian Carlo. *Biografia del sessantotto: Utopie, conquiste, sbandamenti*. Milan: Bompiani, 2004.

Martel, Leon. *Lend-Lease, Loans, and the Coming of the Cold War*. Boulder, Colo.: Westview, 1979.

Martelli, Evelina. *L'altro atlantismo: Fanfani e la politica estera italiana, 1958-1963*. Milan: Guerini, 2008.

Martelli, Roger. *L'archipel communiste: Une histoire électorale du PCF*. Paris: Editions Sociales, 2008.

———. *Mai 1968*. Paris: Messidor/Sociales, 1988.

———. *Le rouge et le bleu: Essai sur le communisme dans l'histoire française*. Paris: L'Atelier, 1995.

———. *1956: Le choc du 20e Congrès*. Paris: Editions Sociales, 1982.

Martin, Ralph G. *Henry and Clare: An Intimate Portrait of the Luces*. New York: G. P. Putnam and Sons, 1991.

Martinelli, Renzo. *Il "Partito nuovo" dalla Liberazione al 18 aprile*. Vol. 6 of *Storia del Partito comunista italiano*. Turin: Einaudi, 1995.

Marwick, Arthur. *The Sixties: Cultural Revolution in Britain, France, Italy, and the United States, 1958–1974*. New York: Oxford University Press, 1998.

Mastny, Vojtech. *The Cold War and Soviet Insecurity: The Stalin Years*. New York: Oxford University Press, 1996.

Mathé, Sylvie (Groupe de Recherche et d'Etudes Nord-Américaines), ed. *L'Antiaméricanism: Anti-Americanism at Home and Abroad*. Aix-en-Provence: PU Provence, 2000.

May, Elaine Tyler, and Reinhold Wagnleitner, eds. *Here, There, and Everywhere: The Foreign Politics of American Popular Culture*. Hanover, N.H.: University Press of New England, 2000.

McInnes, Neil. *The Communist Parties of Western Europe*. Oxford: Oxford University Press, 1975.

McKenzie, Brian Angus. *Remaking France: American Public Diplomacy and the Marshall Plan*. New York: Berghahn, 2005.

McLeod, Alexander. *La révolution inopportune: Les partis communistes français et italien face à la révolution portugaise, 1973–1975*. Montreal: Nouvelle Optique, 1994.

McPherson, Alan. *Yankee No! Anti-Americanism in U.S.–Latin American Relations*. Cambridge: Harvard University Press, 2003.

Mead, Walter Russell. *Power, Terror, Peace and War: America's Grand Strategy in a World at Risk*. New York: Alfred Knopf, 2004.

Medhurst, Martin J., ed. *Eisenhower's War of Words: Rhetoric and Leadership*. East Lansing: Michigan State University Press, 1994.

Meliadò, Valentina. *Il fallimento dei "101": Il PCI, l'Ungheria e gli intellettuali italiani*. Rome: Liberal, 2006.

Miller, James E. *The United States and Italy, 1940–1950: The Politics and Diplomacy of Stabilization*. Chapel Hill: University of North Carolina Press, 1986.

Milward, Alan S. *The European Rescue of the Nation State*. London: Routledge, 1992.

———. *The Reconstruction of Western Europe, 1945–1951*. Berkeley: University of California Press, 1984.

Minolfi, Salvatore, ed. *L'Italia e la NATO. Una politica estera nelle maglie dell'alleanza*. Naples: CUEN, 1993.

Miscamble, Wilson D. *George F. Kennan and the Making of American Foreign Policy, 1947–1950*. Princeton, N.J.: Princeton University Press, 1993.

Misler, Nicoletta. *La via italiana al realismo. La politica culturale e artistica del PCI dal 1944 al 1956*. Milan: Mazzotta, 1975.

Molinari, Jean-Paul. *Les ouvriers communistes: Sociologie de l'adhésion ouvrière au communisme*. Thonon-les-Bains: L'Albaron, 1991.

Moneta, Jacob. *Le PCF et la question algérienne, 1920–1965*. Paris: Maspero, 1971.

Monnerot, Jules. *Sociologie du communisme: Echec d'une tentative religieuse au XXe siècle*. Paris: Hallier, 1979.

Montaldo, Jean. *Les finances du PCF*. Paris: Albin Michel, 1977.

———. *Les secrets de la banque soviétique en France*. Paris: Albin Michel, 1979.

Moore, Robert L., and Maurizio Vaudagna, eds. *The American Century in Europe*. Ithaca, N.Y.: Cornell University Press, 2003.

Morin, Edgar, Claude Lefort, and Cornelius Castoriadis. *Mai '68: La brèche*. Paris: Fayard, 1988.

Morozzo della Rocca, Roberto. *La politica estera italiana e l'Unione Sovietica (1944–1948)*. Rome: Goliardica, 1985.

Mortimer, Edward. *The Rise of the French Communist Party, 1920–1947*. London: Faber and Faber, 1984.

Murphy, Robert. *Diplomat among Warriors*. London: Collins, 1964.

Nacci, Michela. *L'antiamericanismo in Italia negli anni Trenta*. Turin: Bollati Boringhieri, 1989.

Nenni, Pietro. *Gli anni del centro-sinistra: Diari, 1957–1966*. Milan: Sugarco, 1982.

———. *Tempo di guerra fredda: Diari, 1943–1956*. Milan: Sugarco, 1981.

Nicolet, Claude. *L'idée républicaine en France*. Paris: Gallimard, 1982.

Niebuhr, Reinhold. *Christian Realism and Political Problems*. New York: Charles Scribner's Sons, 1953.

Ninkovich, Frank. *The Diplomacy of Ideas: U.S. Foreign Policy and Cultural Relations, 1938–1950*. Cambridge: Cambridge University Press, 1981.

———. *Modernity and Power: A History of the Domino Theory in the Twentieth Century*. Chicago: University of Chicago Press, 1994.

———. *The United States and Imperialism*. New York: Blackwell, 2001.

———. *The Wilsonian Century: U.S. Foreign Policy since 1900*. Chicago: University of Chicago Press, 2001.

Nora, Pierre, ed. *Realms of Memory: Rethinking the French Past*. Vol. 3. New York: Columbia University Press, 1998.

Novelli, Edoardo. *Le elezioni del Quarantotto. Storia, strategie e immagini della prima campagna elettorale repubblicana*. Rome: Donzelli, 2008.

Novick, Peter. *The Resistance versus Vichy: The Purge of Collaborators in Liberated France*. New York: Columbia University Press, 1968.

Nuti, Leopoldo. *La sfida nucleare: La politica estera italiana e le armi atomiche, 1945–1991*. Bologna: Il Mulino, 2007.

———. *Gli Stati Uniti e l'apertura a sinistra: Importanza e limiti della presenza americana in Italia*. Rome: Laterza, 1999.

———, ed. *The Crisis of Détente in Europe: From Helsinki to Gorbachev, 1975–1985*. London: Taylor and Francis, 2008.

Nye, Joseph S. *Soft Power: The Means to Success in World Politics*. New York: Public Affairs, 2004.

Oakes, Guy. *The Imaginary War: Civil Defense and American Cold War Culture*. Oxford: Oxford University Press, 1994.

Occhetto, Achille. *A dieci anni dal '68*. Edited by Walter Veltroni. Rome: Riuniti, 1978.

Ojetti, Ugo. *L'America e l'avvenire*. Milan: Fratelli Treves, 1905.

Orsini, Alessandro. *Anatomia delle Brigate rosse: Le radici del terrorismo rivoluzionario*. Soveria Mannelli: Rubbettino, 2009.

Ortona, Egidio. *La diplomazia, 1953–1961*. Vol. 2 of *Anni d'America*. Bologna: Il Mulino, 1986.

———. *La ricostruzione, 1943–1953*. Vol. 1 of *Anni d'America*. Bologna: Il Mulino, 1984.

Ory, Pascal, and Jean-François Sirinelli. *Les intellectuels en France: De l'affaire Dreyfus à nos jours*. 3rd ed. Paris: Armand Colin, 2002.

Osgood, Kenneth. *Total Cold War: Eisenhower's Secret Propaganda Battle at Home and Abroad*. Lawrence: University Press of Kansas, 2006.

Ouimet, Matthew J. *The Rise and Fall of the Brezhnev Doctrine in Soviet Foreign Policy.* Chapel Hill: University of North Carolina Press, 2003.

Pach, Chester J., Jr. *Arming the Free World: The Origins of the United States Military Assistance Program, 1945–1950.* Chapel Hill: University of North Carolina Press, 1991.

Pajetta, Gian Carlo. *Le crisi che ho vissuto: Budapest, Praga, Varsavia.* Rome: Riuniti, 1982.

Pasolini, Pier Paolo. *Empirismo eretico.* Milan: Garzanti, 1981.

———. *Il caos: L'orrendo universo del consumo al potere.* Edited by Gian Carlo Ferretti. Rome: Riuniti, 1995.

Pavese, Cesare. *La letteratura americana e altri saggi.* 3rd. ed. Turin: Einaudi, 1959.

Paxton, Robert O., and Nicholas Wahl, eds. *De Gaulle and the United States: A Centennial Reappraisal.* Oxford, U.K.: Berg, 1994.

Pells, Richard. *The Liberal Mind in a Conservative Age: American Intellectuals in the 1940s and 1950s.* Hanover, N.H.: Wesleyan University Press, 1989.

———. *Not Like Us: How Europeans Have Loved, Hated, and Transformed American Culture since World War II.* New York: Basic Books, 1997.

Petricioli, Marta, ed. *La sinistra europea nel secondo dopoguerra, 1943–1949.* Florence: Sansoni, 1981.

Pigenet, Michel. *Au coeur de l'activisme communiste de Guerre froide: La manifestation Ridgway.* Paris: L'Harmattan, 1992.

Pintor, Giaime. *Il sangue d'Europa.* Turin: Einaudi, 1950.

Pisani, Sallie. *The CIA and the Marshall Plan.* Lawrence: University Press of Kansas, 1991.

Piscitelli, Enzo, et al., eds. *Italia, 1945–1948: Le origini della Repubblica.* Turin: Gappichelli, 1974.

Pizzigallo, Matteo, ed. *Amicizie mediterranee e interesse nazionale, 1946–1954.* Milan: Franco Angeli, 2006.

Poggiolini, Ilaria. *Diplomazia della transizione. Gli alleati e il problema del trattato di pace italiano (1945–1947).* Florence: Ponte alle Grazie, 1990.

Poiger, Uta G. *Jazz, Rock and Rebels: Cold War Politics and American Culture in a Divided Germany.* Berkeley: University of California Press, 2000.

Pombeni, Paolo. *Le "Cronache Sociali" di Dossetti, 1947–1951: Geografia di un movimento di opinione.* Florence: Vallecchi, 1976.

Pons, Silvio. *Berlinguer e la fine del comunismo.* Turin: Einaudi, 2006.

———. *L'impossibile egemonia: L'URSS, il PCI e le origini della guerra fredda (1943–1948).* Rome: Carocci, 1999.

Pons, Silvio, and Robert Service, eds. *A Dictionary of 20th Century Communism.* Princeton: Princeton University Press, 2010.

Poster, Mark. *Existential Marxism in Postwar France: From Sartre to Althusser.* Princeton, N.J.: Princeton University Press, 1976.

Powers, R. Gid. *Not without Honor: The History of American Anti-Communism.* New York: Free Press, 1995.

Prezzolini, Giuseppe. *Diario, 1900–1941.* Milan: Rusconi, 1978.

Provasi, Giancarlo. *Borghesia industriale e Democrazia cristiana: Sviluppo economico e mediazione politica dalla Ricostruzione agli anni settanta.* Bari: De Donato, 1976.

Pudal, Bernard. *Un monde défait: Les communistes français de 1956 à nos jours.* Bellecombe-en-Bauges: Croquant, 2009.

Quazza, Guido. *Resistenza e storia d'Italia*. Milan: Feltrinelli, 1976.

Rabe, Stephen G. *The Most Dangerous Area in the World: John F. Kennedy Confronts Communist Revolution in Latin America*. Chapel Hill: University of North Carolina Press, 1999.

Ramney, Austin, and Giovanni Sartori. *Eurocommunism: The Italian Case*. Washington, D.C.: American Enterprise Institute for Public Policy Research, 1978.

Raymond, Gino G. *The French Communist Party during the Fifth Republic: A Crisis of Leadership and Ideology*. London: Palgrave Macmillan, 2006.

Reader, Keith A. *Intellectuals and the Left in France since 1968*. New York: St. Martin's, 1987.

——— (with Khursheed Wadia). *The May 1968 Events in France: Reproductions and Interpretations*. London: St. Martin's, 1993.

Reale, Eugenio. *Nascita del Cominform*. Milan: Mondadori, 1958.

Revel, Jean-François. *Anti-Americanism*. New York: Encounter, 2004.

———. *Without Marx or Jesus: The New American Revolution Has Begun*. Translated by J. F. Bernard. Garden City, N.Y.: Doubleday, 1971.

Revelli, Marco. *Lavorare in Fiat: Da Valletta ad Agnelli a Romiti—Operai sindacati robot*. Milan: Garzanti, 1989.

Riccardi, Luca. *Il "problema Israele." Diplomazia italiana e PCI di fronte allo stato ebraico (1948–1973)*. Milan: Guerini, 2006.

Rice-Maximin, Edward. *Accommodation and Resistance: The French Left, Indochina, and the Cold War, 1944–1954*. Westport, Conn.: Greenwood, 1986.

Rieber, Alfred J. *Stalin and the French Communist Party, 1941–1947*. New York: Columbia University Press, 1962.

Rioux, Jean-Pierre. *The Fourth Republic, 1944–1958*. New York: Cambridge University Press, 1987.

Ritaine, Evelyne. *Les stratèges de la culture*. Paris: Presses de la Fondation Nationale des Sciences Politiques, 1983.

Ritsch, Frederick F. *The French Left and the European Idea, 1947–1949*. New York: Pageant, 1966.

Riva, Valerio. *Oro di Mosca. I finanziamenti sovietici al PCI dalla Rivoluzione d'Ottobre al crollo dell'URSS*. Milan: Mondadori, 1999.

Robrieux, Philippe. *Histoire intérieure du Parti communiste (1945–1972). De la Libération à l'avènement de Georges Marchais*. Paris: Fayard, 1981.

Roger, Philippe. *The American Enemy: The History of French Anti-Americanism*. Translated by Sharon Bowman. Chicago: University of Chicago Press, 2005.

———. *Rêves et cauchemars américains: Les Etats-Unis au miroir de l'opinion publique française, 1945–1953*. Lille: Presses Universitaires du Septentrion, 1996.

Romero, Federico. *The United States and the European Trade Union Movement, 1944–1948*. Translated by Harvey Fergusson II. Chapel Hill: University of North Carolina Press, 1992.

Romero, Federico, and Antonio Varsori, eds. *Nazione, interdipendenza, integrazione. Le relazioni internazionali dell'Italia (1917–1989)*. 2 vols. Rome: Carocci, 2005.

Rosenberg, Emily. *Spreading the American Dream: American Economic and Cultural Expansion, 1890–1945*. New York: Hill and Wang, 1982.

Ross, Andrew, and Kristin Ross, eds. *Anti-Americanism*. New York: New York University Press, 2004.

Ross, George. *Workers and Communists in France: From Popular Front to Eurocommunism.* Berkeley: University of California Press, 1982.

Ross, Kristin. *Fast Cars, Clean Bodies: Decolonization and the Reordering of French Culture.* Cambridge: MIT Press, 1995.

———. *May '68 and Its Afterlives.* Chicago: University of Chicago Press, 2002.

Rossanda, Rossana. *L'anno degli studenti.* Bari: De Donato, 1968.

Rossi, Joseph. *The Image of America in Mazzini's Writings.* Madison: University of Wisconsin Press, 1954.

Rossini, Daniela. *Woodrow Wilson and the American Myth in Italy.* Cambridge: Harvard University Press, 2008.

Rothkopf, David J. *Running the World: The Inside Story of the National Security Council and the Architects of American Power.* New York: Public Affairs, 2005.

Rousseau, Renée. *Les femmes rouges: Cronique des années Vermeersch.* Paris: Albin Michel, 1983.

Rubbi, Antonio. *Incontri con Gorbachev.* Rome: Riuniti, 1989.

———. *Il mondo di Berlinguer.* Rome: Roberto Napoleone, 1994.

Rubeo, Ugo. *Mal d'America.* Rome: Riuniti, 1987.

Ruscio, Alain. *Les communistes français et la guerre d'Indochine, 1944–1954.* Paris: L'Harmattan, 1985.

Rusconi, Gian Enrico. *Se cessiamo di essere una nazione: Tra etnodemocrazie regionali e cittadinanza europea.* Bologna: Il Mulino, 1993.

Santamaria, Yves. *Le pacifisme: Une passion française.* Paris: Armand Colin, 2005.

———. *Le Parti de l'ennemi: Le Parti communiste français dans la lutte pour la paix, 1947–1958.* Paris: Armand Colin, 2006.

Sanzo, Alessandro. *L'officina comunista: Enrico Berlinguer e l'educazione dell'uomo, 1945–1956.* Rome: Aracne, 2003.

Sapiro, Gisèle. *La guerre des écrivains (1940–1953).* Paris: Fayard, 1999.

Sartre, Jean-Paul. *Literary and Philosophical Essays.* Translated by Annette Michelson. London: Rider, 1955.

———. *Situations, II: qu'est-ce que la littérature?* Paris: Gallimard, 1948.

———. *Situations, VII: problèmes du marxisme, II.* Paris: Gallimard, 1965.

Sassoon, Donald. *One Hundred Years of Socialism: The West European Left in the Twentieth Century.* New York: New Press, 1996.

———. *The Strategies of the Italian Communist Party, from the Resistance to the Historic Compromise.* New York: St. Martin's, 1981.

Saunders, Frances Stonor. *The Cultural Cold War: The CIA and the World of Arts and Letters.* New York: The New Press, 2001.

Schivelbusch, Wolfgang. *In a Cold War Crater: Cultural and Intellectual Life in Berlin, 1945–1948.* Berkeley: University of California Press, 1998.

Schlesinger, Arthur M. Jr. *The Vital Center: The Politics of Freedom.* New York: Riverside, 1949.

Schwartz, Thomas A. *Lyndon Johnson and Europe: In the Shadow of Vietnam.* Cambridge: Harvard University Press, 2003.

Scirocco, Giovanni. *"Politique d'Abord." Il PSI, la guerra fredda, e la politica internazionale (1948–1957).* Milan: Unicopli, 2010.

Scott-Smith, Giles. *Networks of Empire: The U.S. State Department's Foreign Leader*

Program in the Netherlands, France, and Britain, 1950–70. Brussels: P. I. E. Peter
   Lang, 2008.

———. *The Politics of Apolitical Culture: The Congress for Cultural Freedom, the CIA,
   and Post-war American Hegemony*. New York: Routledge, 2002.

Scott-Smith, Giles, and Hans Krabbendam, eds. *The Cultural Cold War in Western
   Europe, 1945–1960*. New York: Routledge, 2003.

Sebesta, Lorenza. *L'Europa indifesa. Sistema di sicurezza atlantico e caso italiano*.
   Florence: Ponte alle Grazie, 1991.

Seidman, Michael. *The Imaginary Revolution: Parisian Students and Workers in 1968*.
   New York: Berghahn, 2004.

Selverstone, Marc. *Constructing the Monolith: The United States, Great Britain, and
   International Communism, 1945–1950*. Cambridge: Harvard University Press, 2009.

Serfaty, Simon, and Lawrence Gray, eds. *The Italian Communist Party: Yesterday, Today
   and Tomorrow*. Westport, Conn.: Greenwood, 1980.

Shannon, David A. *The Decline of American Communism*. Chatman, N.J.: Chatman, 1959.

Shaw, Tony. *Hollywood's Cold War*. Amherst: University of Massachusetts Press, 2007.

Shiraev, Eric, and Vladislav Zubok. *Anti-Americanism in Russia: From Stalin to Putin*.
   New York: Palgrave, 2000.

Shore, Cris. *Italian Communism: The Escape from Leninism*. London: Pluto, 1990.

Siegfried, André. *America Comes of Age: A French Analysis*. Translated by H. H.
   Hemming and Doris Hemming. New York: Harcourt, Brace, 1927.

Singer, Daniel. *Prelude to Revolution: France in May 1968*. 2nd ed. Cambridge, Mass.:
   South End, 2002.

Sirinelli, Jean-François. *Intellectuels et passions françaises: Manifestes et pétitions au
   XXe siècle*. Paris: Fayard, 1990.

Smith, Peter M., and M. L. Stirk, eds. *Making the New Europe: European Unity and the
   Second World War*. London: Pinter, 1993.

Smith, Timothy. *The United States, Italy, and NATO: 1947–52*. London: Macmillan, 1991.

Smith, Tony. *America's Mission: The United States and the Worldwide Struggle for
   Democracy in the Twentieth Century*. Princeton, N.J.: Princeton University Press,
   1994.

Soria, Georges. *La France deviendra-t-elle une colonie américaine?* Paris: Pavillon, 1948.

Spriano, Paolo. *I fronti popolari, Stalin, la guerra*. Vol. 3 of *Storia del Partito comunista
   Italiano*. Turin: Einaudi, 1967.

———. *La Resistenza: Togliatti e il Partito nuovo*. Vol. 5 of *Storia del PCI*. Turin:
   Einaudi, 1975.

———. *Stalin and the European Communists*. London: Verso, 1985.

Stephan, Alexander, ed. *The Americanization of Europe: Culture, Diplomacy, and Anti-
   Americanism after 1945*. New York: Berghahn, 2007.

Stephanson, Anders. *Kennan and the Art of Foreign Policy*. Cambridge: Harvard
   University Press, 1989.

Stiglitz, Joseph. *Freefall: America, Free Markets, and the Sinking of the World Economy*.
   New York: W. W. Norton, 2010.

———. *Globalization and Its Discontents*. New York: W. W. Norton, 2002.

Stirk, Peter M. R., and David Willis, eds. *Shaping Postwar Europe: European Unity and
   Disunity, 1945–1957*. New York: St. Martin's, 1991.

Strauss, David. *Menace in the West: The Rise of French Anti-Americanism in Modern Times*. Westport, Conn.: Greenwood, 1978.

Streiff, Gérard. *Jean Kanapa, 1921–1978: Une singulière histoire du PCF*. Paris: L'Harmattan, 2001.

Styan, David. *France and Iraq: Oil, Arms and French Policy Making in the Middle East*. London: I. B. Tauris, 2006.

Suri, Jeremy. *Henry Kissinger and the American Century*. Cambridge: Harvard University Press, 2007.

———. *Power and Protest: Global Revolution and the Rise of Détente*. Cambridge: Harvard University Press, 2003.

Sweig, Julia A. *Friendly Fire: Losing Friends and Making Enemies in the Anti-American Century*. Washington, D.C.: Public Affairs, 2005.

Tarchiani, Alberto. *Dieci anni tra Roma e Washington*. Milan: Mondadori, 1955.

Tardieu, André. *Devant l'obstacle: L'Amérique et nous*. Paris: Emile Paul Frères, 1927.

Tarrow, Sidney. *Democracy and Disorder: Protest and Politics in Italy, 1965–1975*. New York: Oxford University Press, 1989.

Tassel, Scott. *Sarge: The Life and Times of Sargent Shriver*. Washington, D.C.: Smithsonian Books, 2004.

Tatò, Antonio, ed. *Comunisti e mondo cattolico oggi*. Rome: Riuniti, 1977.

Teodori, Massimo. *Benedetti americani: Dall'Alleanza atlantica all guerra al terrorismo*. Milan: Mondadori, 2003.

———. *Maledetti americani: Destra, sinistra e cattolici. Storia del pregiudizio americano*. Milan: Mondadori, 2002.

Terrail, Jean-Pierre. *Destins ouvriers: La fin d'une classe?* Paris: Presses Universitaires de France, 1990.

Teugels, Patrick. *PCF: L'écartèlement idéologique*. Brussels: Editions Tribord, 2009.

Thomas, Evan. *The Very Best Men: Four Who Dared—The Early Years of the CIA*. New York: Simon and Schuster, 1995.

Thorez, Maurice. *Oeuvres choisies*. Vol. 2. Paris: Editions Sociales, 1966.

———. *Oeuvres de Maurice Thorez*. 5 vols. Paris: Editions Sociales, 1950.

———. *Une politique de grandeur française*. Paris: Editions Sociales, 1945.

Tobia, Simona. *Advertising America: The United States Information Service in Italy (1945–1956)*. Milan: LED, 2008.

Togliatti, Palmiro. *Da Radio Milano Libertà*. Rome: Editori Riuniti, 1974.

———. *Gramsci*. Rome: Riuniti, 1972.

———. *Lezioni sul fascismo*. Rome: Riuniti, 1970.

———. *Opere, 1944–1955*. Vols. 4, 5. Rome: Riuniti, 1981–1984.

———. *La politica di Salerno: Aprile–dicembre 1944*. Rome: Riuniti, 1969.

Tomlinson, John. *Cultural Imperialism: A Critical Introduction*. Baltimore, Md.: Johns Hopkins University Press, 1991.

Toscano, Mario. *Designs in Diplomacy*. Baltimore: Johns Hopkins University Press, 1970.

Tosi, Luciano, ed. *Europe, Its Borders and the Others*. Naples: ESI, 2000.

Touraine, Alain. *The May Movement: Revolt and Reform*. Translated by Leonard F. X. Mayhew. New York: Random House, 1979.

Trachtenberg, Marc. *A Constructed Peace: The Making of the European Settlement, 1945–1963*. Princeton, N.J.: Princeton University Press, 1999.

Tranfaglia, Nicola, ed. *Il 1948 in Italia: La storia e i film*. Florence: La Nuova Italia, 1991.

Tuathail, Gearóid Ó, and Simon Dalby, eds. *Rethinking Geopolitics*. New York: Routledge, 1998.

Tunstall, Jeremy. *The Media Are American*. New York: Columbia University Press, 1977.

Ulloa, Marie-Pierre. *Francis Jeanson: A Dissident Intellectual from the French Resistance to the Algerian War*. Translated by J. Todd. Stanford, Calif.: Stanford University Press, 2008.

Urban, Joan. *Moscow and the Italian Communist Party: From Togliatti to Berlinguer*. Ithaca, N.Y.: Cornell University Press, 1986.

Vacca, Giuseppe. *Il marxismo italiano degli anni sessanta e la formazione teorico-politica delle nuove generazioni*. Rome: Riuniti, 1972.

——. *Togliatti sconosciuto*. Rome: Carocci, 1994.

——, ed. *Intellettuali di sinistra e la crisi del 1956*. Rome: Riuniti, 1978.

——, ed. *Luigi Longo: La politica e l'azione*. Rome: Riuniti, 1992.

Vaïsse, Maurice. *La grandeur: Politique étrangère du Général de Gaulle, 1958–1969*. Paris: Fayard, 1998.

——, ed. *Le pacifisme en Europe des années 1920 aux années 1950*. Brussels: Bruylant, 1993.

Valentini, Chiara. *Berlinguer il segretario*. Milan: Mondadori, 1997.

Varsori, Antonio. *La Cenerentola d'Europa? L'Italia e l'integrazione europea dal 1947 a oggi*. Soveria Mannelli: Rubbettino, 2010.

Varsori, Antonio, ed. *La politica estera italiana nel secondo dopoguerra (1943–1957)*. Milan: LED, 1993.

Vattimo, Gianni, and Pier Aldo Rovatti. *Il pensiero debole*. Milan: Feltrinelli, 1983.

Vecchio, Giorgio. *Pacifisti e obiettori nell'Italia di De Gasperi (1948–53)*. Rome: Studium, 1993.

Veltroni, Walter. ed. *Il sogno degli anni '60*. Rome: Savelli, 1981.

Ventresca, Robert A. *From Fascism to Democracy: Culture and Politics in the Italian Election of 1948*. Toronto: University of Toronto Press, 2004.

Ventrone, Angelo. *Il nemico interno: Immagini e simboli della lotta politica nell'Italia del Novecento*. Rome: Donzelli, 2005.

Verdès-Leroux, Jeannine. *Au service du parti: Le Parti communiste, les intellectuels et la culture (1944–1956)*. Paris: Fayard/Minuit, 1983.

——. *Le réveil des somnambules: Le Parti communiste, les intellectuels et la culture (1956–1985)*. Paris: Fayard/Minuit, 1987.

Vernant, Jean-Pierre. *Entre mythe et idéologie*. Paris: Seuil, 1996.

Vidal, Gore. *Perpetual War for Perpetual Peace: How We Got to Be So Hated*. New York: Nation, 2002.

Vincitorio, Gaetano L. *Studies in Modern History*. New York: St. John's University Press, 1968.

Vittoria, Albertina. *Togliatti e gli intellettuali. Storia dell'Istituto Gramsci negli anni cinquanta e sessanta*. Rome: Riuniti, 1992.

Vittoria, Albertina, and Fiamma Lussana, eds. *Il "lavoro culturale": Franco Ferri direttore della Biblioteca Feltrinelli e dell'Istituto Gramsci*. Rome: Carocci, 2000.

Vittorini, Elio. *Diario in pubblico*. 2nd ed. Milan: Mondadori, 1957.

Wald, Alan. *The New York Intellectuals: The Rise and Decline of the Anti-Stalinist Left*. Chapel Hill: University of North Carolina Press, 1987.

Wall, Irwin M. *France, the United States, and the Algerian War*. Berkeley: University of
California Press, 2001.

———. *French Communism in the Era of Stalin: The Quest for Unity and Integration,
1945–1962*. Westport, Conn.: Greenwood, 1983.

———. *The United States and the Making of Postwar France, 1944–1954*. Cambridge:
Cambridge University Press, 1991.

Wenger, Andreas. *Living with Peril: Eisenhower, Kennedy, and Nuclear Weapons*.
Lantham, Md.: Rowman and Littlefield, 1997.

Wenger, Andreas, Vojtech Mastny, and Christian Nuenlist, eds. *Origins of the European
Security System: The Helsinki Process Revisted, 1965–1975*. London: Routledge, 2008.

Werth, Alexander. *France, 1940–1955*. New York: Holt, 1956.

Wexler, Immanuel. *The Marshall Plan Revisited: The European Reconstruction Program
in Economic Perspective*. Westport, Conn.: Greenwood, 1983.

Whitfield, Stephen J. *The Culture of the Cold War*. Baltimore: Johns Hopkins University
Press, 1991.

Wieck, Randolph. *Ignorance Abroad: American Educational and Cultural Foreign Policy
and the Office of Assistant Secretary of State*. Westport, Conn.: Praeger, 1992.

Wiggershaus, Norbert, and Roland G. Forster. *The Western Security Community:
Common Problems and Conflicting National Interests during the Foundation Phase of
the North Atlantic Alliance*. Oxford: Berg, 1993.

Williams, William Appleman. *The Tragedy of American Diplomacy*. New York: World,
1959.

Winand, Pascaline. *Eisenhower, Kennedy and the United States of Europe*. New York:
St. Martin's, 1993.

Winkler, Allan M. *Life under a Cloud: American Anxiety about the Atom*. Oxford: Oxford
University Press, 1993.

Winock, Michel. *Le siècle des intellectuels*. Paris: Seuil, 1997.

———. *Nationalism, Anti-Semitism, and Fascism in France*. Translated by Jane Marie
Todd. Stanford, Calif.: Stanford University Press, 1998.

———. *Parlez-moi de la France*. Paris: Plon, 1995.

Wittner, Lawrence S. *Resisting the Bomb: A History of the World Nuclear Disarmament
Movement, 1954–1970*. Stanford, Calif.: Stanford University Press, 1997.

Wolin, Richard. *The Wind from the East: French Intellectuals, the Cultural Revolution,
and the Legucy of the 1960s*. Princeton, N.J.: Princeton University Press, 2010.

Wollenborg, Leo J. *Stars, Stripes, and the Italian Tricolor: The United States and Italy,
1946–1989*. New York: Praeger, 1990.

Wolton, Thierry. *La France sous influence: Paris-Moscou, trente ans de relations secretes*.
Paris: Grasset, 1997.

Woods, Jeff. *Black Struggle, Red Scare: Segregation and Anti-Communism in the South*.
Baton Rouge: Louisiana State University Press, 2004.

Woods, Randall B. *Fulbright: A Biography*. Cambridge: Cambridge University Press, 1995.

———. *LBJ: Architect of American Ambition*. New York: Free Press, 2006.

Wreszin, Michael. *A Rebel in Defense of Tradition: The Life and Politics of Dwight
Macdonald*. New York: Basic Books, 1994.

Young, John W. *Britain, France, and the Unity of Europe, 1945–1951*. Leicester, U.K.:
Leicester University Press, 1984.

———. *France, the Cold War, and the Western Alliance, 1944–49: French Foreign Policy and Post-War Europe*. New York: St. Martin's, 1990.

———. *Winston Churchill's Last Campaign: Britain and the Cold War, 1951–5*. Oxford, U.K.: Clarendon, 1996.

Zaslavsky, Victor. *Lo stalinismo e la sinistra italiana. Dal mito dell'URSS alla fine del comunismo, 1945–1991*. Milan: Mondadori, 2004.

Zeldin, Theodore. *The French*. New York: Vintage, 1984.

Zubok, Vladislav M. *A Failed Empire: The Soviet Union in the Cold War, from Stalin to Gorbachev*. Chapel Hill: University of North Carolina Press, 2007.

Zubok, Vladislav M., and Constantine Pleshakov. *Inside the Kremlin's Cold War: From Stalin to Khrushchev*. Cambridge: Harvard University Press, 1996.

Journal Articles

Ajami, Fouad. "The Falseness of Anti-Americanism." *Foreign Policy* (September–October 2003).

Bailes, Kendall E. "Alexei Gastev and the Soviet Controversy over Taylorism, 1918–24." *Soviet Studies* 29, no. 3 (July 1977).

Barbagallo, Francesco. "L'intellettuale comunista e libertario." *Studi storici* 41, no. 1 (January 2000).

———. "Il PCI dal Cominform al '56: I 'casi' Terracini, Magnani, Giolitti." *Studi Storici* 31, no. 1 (January 1990).

Barnes, Trevor. "The Secret Cold War: The CIA and American Foreign Policy in Europe, 1945–1956." Part 1. *Historical Journal* 24 (1981).

Belloin, Gérard. "Le Comité central d'Argenteuil de 1966." *Communisme* 76–77 (2003–4).

Berghahn, Volker R. "The Debate on 'Americanization' among Economic and Cultural Historians." *Cold War History* 10, no. 1 (February 2010).

Bianchini, Stefano. "Le PCI et le cas Magnani." *Communisme* 29–31 (1991).

Botts, Joshua. "'Nothing to Seek . . . Nothing to Defend': George F. Kennan's Core Values and American Foreign Policy, 1938–1993." *Diplomatic History* 30, no. 5 (November 2006).

Bourg, Julian. "The Red Guards of Paris: French Student Maoism of the 1960s." *History of European Ideas* 31, no. 4 (2005).

Bozo, Frédéric, and Pierre Melandri. "La France devant l'opinion américaine: Le retour de de Gaulle, début 1958- printemps 1959." *Relations internationales*, no. 58 (Summer 1989).

Brillant, Bernard. "Intellectuels: Les ombres changeantes de mai 68." *Vingtième siècle: Revue d'histoire*, no. 98 (2008).

Brogi, Alessandro. "Competing Missions: France, Italy, and the Rise of American Hegemony in the Mediterranean." *Diplomatic History*, 30, no. 4 (September 2006).

———. "Ike and Italy: The Eisenhower Administration and Italy's 'Neo-Atlanticist' Agenda." *Journal of Cold War Studies* 4, no. 3 (Summer 2002).

———. "Orizzonti della politica estera italiana: Stati Uniti, Europa e Mediterraneo (1945–1960)." *Passato e presente* 22 (2004), no. 62.

Brunetau, Bernard. "The Construction of Europe and the Concept of the Nation-State." *Contemporary European History* 9, no. 2 (July 2000).

Bucci, Tonino. "Proletariato, Freud e femminismo: Gramsci, ma quale rivoluzione oggi?" *Liberazione* 11 (2007).

Buton, Philippe. "The Crisis of Communism and Trade Unionism in Western Europe since 1968." *Journal of Communist Studies* 6, no. 4 (December 1990).

———. "Le Parti communiste français à la Libération: Stratégie et implantation." *L'information historique* 51, no. 3 (1989).

———. "Le Parti communiste français depuis 1985: une organisation en crise." *Communisme* 18/19 (1988).

Cavallo, Pietro. "America sognata, America desiderata: Mito e immagine USA in Italia dallo sbarco alla fine della guerra (1943–1945)." *Storia contemporanea* 4 (August 1985).

Ceaser, James. "A Genealogy of Anti-Americanism." *Public Interest*, Summer 2003.

Claudin, Fernando. "Some Reflections on the Crisis of Marxism." *Socialist Review* 45 (May–June 1979).

Cohen, William B. "The Algerian War and French Memory." *Contemporary European History* 9, no. 3 (Fall 2000).

Confalonieri, Maria Antonietta. "Parties and Movements in Italy: The Case of Feminism and the PCI." *Il politico* 60, no. 1 (1995).

Costigliola, Frank. "Tropes of Gender and Pathology in the Western Alliance." *Diplomatic History* 21, no. 2 (Spring 1997).

———. "'Unceasing Urge for Penetration': Gender, Pathology, and Emotion in George Kennan's Formation of the Cold War." *Journal of American History* 83 (March 1997).

Cotkin, George. "French Existentialism and American Popular Culture, 1945–1948." *Historian* 61, no. 2 (Winter 1999).

Cox, Michael, and Caroline Pipe-Kennedy. "The Tragedy of American Diplomacy? Rethinking the Marshall Plan." *Journal of Cold War Studies* 7, no. 1 (Winter 2005).

Craveri, Piero. "L'ultimo Berlinguer e la 'questione socialista." *Ventunesimo secolo* 1, no. 1 (March 2002).

Del Pero, Mario. "American Pressures and Their Containment in Italy during the Ambassadorship of Clare Boothe Luce, 1953–56." *Diplomatic History* 28, no. 3 (June 2004).

———. "Containing Containment: Rethinking Italy's Experience during the Cold War." *Journal of Modern Italian Studies* 8, no. 4 (December 2003).

———. "The United States and Psychological Warfare in Italy, 1948–1955." *Journal of American History*, March 2001.

Di Nolfo, Ennio. "La svolta di Salerno come problema internazionale." *Storia delle relazioni internazionali* 1, no. 1 (1985).

Domenico, Roy. "'For the Cause of Christ Here in Italy': America's Protestant Challenge in Italy and the Cultural Ambiguity of the Cold War." *Diplomatic History* 29, no. 4 (September 2005).

Drake, Richard. "Vivere la rivoluzione: Raniero Panzieri, *Quaderni rossi* e la sinistra extraparlamentare." *Nuova storia contemporanea* 7, no. 6 (November–December 2003).

Ellwood, David W. "The American Challenge Renewed: U.S. Cultural Power and Europe's Identity Debates." *Brown Journal of World Affairs* (Winter/Spring 1997).

———. "The 1948 Elections in Italy: A Cold War Propaganda Battle." *Historical Journal of Film, Radio and Television* 13 (1993).

———. "The Propaganda of the Marshall Plan in Italy in a Cold War Context." *Intelligence and National Security* 18 (2003).

———. "'You Too Can Be Like Us': Selling the Marshall Plan." *History Today* 48, no. 10 (October 1998).

Fabbrini, Sergio. "Le strategie istituzionali del PCI." *Il mulino* 39, no. 5 (September–October 1990).

Favetto, Ilaria. "La nascita del centro-sinistra e la Gran Bretagna: Partito socialista, laburisti, Foreign Office." *Italia contemporanea* 202 (March 1996).

Formigoni, Guido. "De Gasperi e la crisi politica italiana del maggio 1947: Documenti e reinterpretazioni." *Ricerche di storia politica* 6, no. 3 (October 2003).

———. "La sinistra cattolica e il Patto atlantico." *Il politico* 50, no. 4 (December 1985).

Fougeron, Lucie. "Une 'affaire' politique: Le portrait de Staline par Picasso." *Communisme* 53–54 (1998).

Friedman, Max Paul. "Anti-Americanism and U.S. Foreign Relations." *Diplomatic History* 32, no. 4 (September 2008).

Galeazzi, Marco. "Luigi Longo e la politica internazionale: Gli anni della Guerra fredda." *Studi storici* 31, no. 1 (January 1990).

Gentile, Emilio. "Impending Modernity: Fascism and the Ambivalent Image of the United States." *Journal of Contemporary History* 28, no. 1 (January 1993).

Gervasoni, Marco. "Un miroir abimé: L'anticommunisme dans le socialisme italien, 1917–1997." *Communisme* 62–63 (2000).

Gienow-Hecht, Jessica C. E. "Always Blame the Americans: Anti-Americanism in Europe in the Twentieth Century." *American Historical Review* 3, no. 4 (October 2006).

Gildea, Robert. "1968 in 2008." *History Today* 58, no. 5 (May 2008).

Giovannini, Paolo. "Generazioni e mutamento politico in Italia." *Rivista italiana di scienza politica* 18, no. 3 (December 1988).

Gitlin, Todd. "A View from the Patriotic Left: Gore Vidal and Other America Haters." *Granta* 77 (Spring 2002).

Gomart, Thomas. "Le PCF au miroir des relations franco-soviétiques (1964–1968)." *Relations internationales* 114 (Summer 2003).

Gramaglia, Mariella. "Affinità e conflitto con la nuova sinistra." *Memoria* 1–2, no. 19–20 (January–April 1987).

Greene, Thomas H. "The Communist Parties of Italy and France: A Study in Comparative Communism." *World Politics* 26, no. 4 (October 1968).

Grémion, Pierre. "Regards sur la diplomatie américaine des idées pendant la Guerre froide." *Communisme* 62–63 (2000).

Gualtieri, Roberto. "Giorgio Amendola dirigente del PCI." *Passato e presente* 24, no. 67 (2006).

Guigueno, Vincent. "L'écran de la productivité: 'Jour de fête' et l'américanisation de la société française." *Vingtième siècle: Revue d'histoire* 46 (1995).

Gundle, Stephen. "From *Apocalittici* to *Integrati*: The PCI and the Culture Industry in the 1970s and 1980s." *Newsletter of the Association for the Study of Modern Italy* 11 (1987).

———. "Hollywood Glamour and Mass Consumption in Postwar Italy." *Journal of Cold War Studies* 4, no. 3 (Summer 2002).

Hemsing, Albert. "The Marshall Plan's European Film Unit, 1948–1955: A Memoir and Filmography." *Historical Journal of Film, Radio and Television* 14, no. 3 (September 1994).

Hill, John S. E. "American Efforts to Aid French Reconstruction between Lend-Lease and the Marshall Plan." *Journal of Modern History* 64, no. 3 (September 1992).

Hincker, François. "Le groupe dirigeant du PCF dans les années 70." *Communisme* 10 (1986).

———. "Le PCF divorce de la société." *Communisme* 11/12 (1986).

Hitchcock, William I. "France, the Western Alliance, and the Origins of the Schuman Plan." *Diplomatic History* 21, no. 4 (Fall 1997).

Höbel, Alexander. "Il PCI di Longo e il '68 studentesco." *Studi storici* 45, no. 2 (April 2004).

———. "Il PCI, il '68 cecoslovacco e il rapporto col PCUS." *Studi storici* 42, no. 4 (October 2001).

———. "Il PCI nella crisi del movimento comunista internazionale tra PCUS e PCC (1960–1964)." *Studi storici* 46, no. 2 (April 2005).

Hodge, Carl Cavanagh. "Old Wine and Old Bottles: Anti-Americanism in Britain, France, and Germany." *Journal of Transatlantic Studies* 7, no. 2 (June 2009).

Iriye, Akira. "A Century of NGOs." *Diplomatic History* 23, no. 3 (Summer 1999).

Kelly, Michael. "The Nationalization of French Intellectuals in 1945." *South Central Review* 17, no. 4 (Winter 2000).

Kirby, Dianne. "Divinely Sanctioned: The Anglo-American Cold War Alliance and the Defence of Western Civilization and Christianity, 1945–48." *Journal of Contemporary History* 35, no. 3 (July 2000).

Klenjanszky, Sarolta. "L'impact de la révolution hongroise de 1956 sur le mouvement communiste en France." *Communisme* 88–89 (2006–7).

Kuisel, Richard. "American Historians in Search of France: Perceptions and Misperceptions." *French Historical Studies* 19, no. 2 (Fall 1995).

Lacroix-Riz, Annie. "Négociation et signature des accords Blum-Byrnes (octobre 1945–mai 1946) d'après les archives du Ministère des affaires étrangères." *Revue d'histoire moderne et contemporaine* 31, no. 3 (July–September 1984).

Lafon, François. "Le PCF e l'intervention soviétique à Prague." *Communisme* 97–98 (2009).

La Porta, Lelio. "Introduzione al carteggio di Angela Davis." *Critica marxista*, May 1988.

Lavabre, Marie-Claire. "La collection des *Almanachs* par le Parti communiste français: Un example de tradition." *Pouvoirs* 42 (1987).

Lazar, Marc. "De la crise des Euromissiles à la détente gorbatchevienne: PCF, PCI, Euromissiles et lutte pour la paix, 1979–1987." *Communisme* 18–19 (1988).

———. "Le réalisme socialiste aux couleurs de la France." *L'histoire* 45 (March 1982).

———. "Les 'batailles du livre' du Parti communiste français (1950–1952)." *Vingtième siècle: Revue d'histoire* 10 (1986).

———. "Les partis communistes de l'Europe occidentale face aux mutations de la classe ouvrière." *Communisme* 17 (1988).

———. "Les partis communistes italien et français et l'après-Staline." *Vingtième siècle: Revue d'histoire* 28 (1990).

Le Cour Grandmaison, Olivier. "Le Mouvement de la Paix pendant la Guerre froide: Le cas français (1948–52)." *Communisme* 18–19 (1988).

Lévêque, François. "La place de la France dans la stratégie soviétique de la fin de la guerre en Europe (fin 1942–fin 1945)." *Matériaux pour l'histoire de notre temps* 36 (October–December 1994).

Lévy, Jacques. "Un espace communiste: Géographie de la crise du PCF." *Communisme* 22–23 (1990).

Lipovetsky, Gilles. "Changer la vie, ou L'irruption de l'individualisme transpolitique." *Pouvoirs* 39 (1986).

Lucas, Scott. "Campaigns of Truth: The Psychological Strategy Board and the American Ideology, 1951–1953." *International History Review* 18, no. 2 (May 1996).

Luconi, Stefano. "Anti-Communism, Americanization and Ethnic Identity: Italian Americans and the 1948 Parliamentary Elections in Italy." *Historian* 62, no. 2 (Winter 2000).

Lussana, Fiamma. "Il confronto con le socialdemocrazie e la ricerca di un nuovo socialismo nell'ultimo Berlinguer." *Studi storici* 45, no. 2 (April 2004).

Lynch, Frances M. B. "Resolving the Paradox of the Monnet Plan: National and International Planning in French Reconstruction." *Economic History Review* 37, no. 2 (May 1984).

Maier, Charles S. "The Politics of Productivity: Foundations of American International Economic Policy after World War II." *International Organization* 31, no. 4 (Fall 1977).

———. "The Two Postwar Eras and the Conditions for Stability in Twentieth-Century Europe." *American Historical Review* 86, no. 2 (April 1981).

Marantzidis, Nikolaos. "Les stratégies des partis communistes ouest-européens après 1989." *Communisme* no. 76–77 (2003–4).

Margairaz, Michel. "Autour des accords Blum-Byrnes: Jean Monnet entre le consensus national et le consensus atlantique." *Histoire, économie et société* 82, no. 3 (Summer 1982).

Mariuzzo, Andrea. "Stalin and the Dove: Left Pacifist Language and Choices of Expression between the Popular Front and the Korean War (1948–1953)." *Modern Italy* 15, no. 1 (February 2010).

Martinelli, Renzo. "Togliatti, lo stalinismo e il XXII Congresso del PCUS: Un discorso ritrovato." *Italia contemporanea* 219 (June 2000).

Mazzeri, Catia. "Comunisti e cultura a Modena negli anni della ricostruzione (1945–54)." *Rassegna di storia dell'Istituto storico della resistenza in Modena e provincia*, n.s., 1, no. 1 (January 1981).

McCarthy, Patrick. "I comunisti italiani, il "New Deal" e il difficile problema del riformismo." *Studi storici* 33, 2–3 (April–September 1992).

Medhurst, Martin J. "Eisenhower's 'Atoms for Peace' Speech: A Case Study in the Strategic Use of Language." *Communication Monographs* 54, no. 2 (June 1987).

Miller, James E. "Roughhouse Diplomacy: The United States Confronts Italian Communism, 1945–1958." *Storia delle relazioni internazionali* 5, no. 2 (1989).

———. "Taking Off the Gloves: The United States and the Italian Elections of 1948." *Diplomatic History* 9, no. 1 (Winter 1983).

Mistry, Kaeten. "The Case for Political Warfare: Strategy, Organization and U.S. Involvement in the 1948 Italian Election." *Cold War History* 6, no. 3 (August 2006).

———. "The Dynamics of U.S.-Italian Relations: American Interventionism and the Role of James C. Dunn." *Ricerche di storia politica* 12, no. 2 (August 2009).

Montebello, Fabrice. "Joseph Staline et Humphrey Bogart: L'hommage des ouvriers." *Politix* 24, no. 6 (December 1993).

Nacci, Michela. "La civiltà non cattolica: Una certa immagine dell'America." *Il mulino* 340, no. 2 (March–April 1992).

Narinski, Michail. "L'entretien entre Maurice Thorez et Joseph Staline du 18 novembre 1947." *Communisme* 45–46 (1996).

Njølstad, Olav. "The Carter Administration and Italy: Keeping the Communists Out of Power without Interfering." *Journal of Cold War Studies* 4, no. 3 (Summer 2002).

Nora, Pierre. "America and the French Intellectuals." *Daedalus* 107 (Winter 1978).

Nouailhat, Yves-Henri. "Aspects de la politique culturelle des Etats-Unis à l'égard de la France de 1945 à 1950." *Relations internationales* 25 (Spring 1981).

Nuti, Leopoldo. "Commitment to NATO and Domestic Politics: The Italian Case and Some Comparative Remarks." *Contemporary European History* 7, no. 3 (November 1998).

———. "The United States, Italy, and the Opening to the Left, 1953–1963." *Journal of Cold War Studies* 4, no. 3 (Summer 2002).

Osgood, Kenneth A. "Form before Substance: Eisenhower's Commitment to Psychological Warfare and Negotiations with the Enemy." *Diplomatic History* 24, no. 3 (Summer 2000).

Pedaliu, Effie G. H. "'A Sea of Confusion': The Mediterranean and Détente, 1969–1974." *Diplomatic History* 33, no. 4 (September 2009).

Peyre, Henri. "American Literature through French Eyes." *Virginia Quarterly Review* 23, no. 3 (1947).

Platone, François. "Les adhérents de l'apogée." *Communisme* 7 (1985).

Platone, François, and Jean Ranger. "Le Parti communiste français et l'audiovisuel." *Revue française de sciences politiques* 29, no. 2 (April 1979).

Platt, Alan A., and Robert Leonardi. "American Foreign Policy and the Postwar Italian Left." *Political Science Quarterly* 93, no. 2 (Summer 1978).

Pons, Silvio. "Stalin, Togliatti, and the Origins of the Cold War in Europe." *Journal of Cold War Studies* 3, no. 2 (Spring 2001).

Portes, Jacques. "Les origines de la légende noire des accords Blum-Byrnes sur le cinéma." *Revue d'histoire moderne et contemporaine* 33, no. 2 (April 1986).

Preston, Andrew. "Bridging the Gap between the Sacred and the Secular in the History of American Foreign Relations." *Diplomatic History* 30, no. 5 (November 2006).

Rey, Marie-Pierre. "La gauche française face à la perestroïka." *Communisme* 76–77 (2003–4).

Rice-Maximin, Edward. "The *Main Tendue*: Catholics and Communists during the Popular Front in France." *Contemporary French Civilization* 4, no. 2 (Winter 1980).

———. "The United States and the French Left, 1945–1949: The View from the State Department." *Journal of Contemporary History* 19, no. 4 (October 1984).

Romero, Federico. "Indivisibilità della guerra fredda: La guerra totale simbolica." *Studi storici* 38, no. 4 (October 1997).

———. "L'Europa come strumento di nation-building: Storia e storici dell'Italia repubblicana." *Passato e presente* 13, no. 36 (1995).

Ross, Kristin, Nicolas Hatzfeld, and Antoine Artous. "Mai '68: Le débat continue." *RILI* 6 (July–August 2008).

Rossi, Mario G. "Il governo Scelba tra crisi del centrismo e ritorno anticomunista." *Italia contemporanea*, no. 197 (Fall 1994).

Rousso, Henry. "L'Epuration en France: Une histoire inachevée." *Vingtième siècle: Revue d'histoire* 33 (January–March 1992).

Santamaria, Yves. "D'Amsterdam à Stockholm, 1932–1952: Deux générations de lutte pour la paix." *Communisme* 78–79 (2004).

Sirinelli, Jean-François. "Les normaliens de la rue d'Ulm après 1945: Une génération communiste?" *Revue d'histoire moderne et contemporaine* 33, no. 4 (October–December 1986).

Soutou, Georges-Henri. "La France et les notes soviétiques de 1952 sur l'Allemagne." *Revue de l'Allemagne* 20, no. 3 (Summer 1988).

Spiro, Herbert J. "Anti-Americanism in Western Europe." *Annals of the American Academy of Political and Social Science* (May 1988).

Spriano, Paolo. "Le riflessioni dei comunisti italiani sulle società dell'Est e il 'socialismo reale.'" *Studi storici* 82, 1 (January–March 1982).

Stam, Robert, and Ella Shohat. "Variations on an Anti-American Theme." *CR: The New Centennial Review* 5, no. 1 (Spring 2005).

Thomas, Martin. "France's North African Crisis, 1945–1955: Cold War and Colonial Imperatives." *History* 92, no. 306 (April 2007).

Tranfaglia, Nicola. "La strategia della tensione e i due terrorismi." *Studi storici* 39, no. 4 (October 1998).

Vaicbourdt, Nicolas. "L'administration Eisenhower et la diplomatie de l'anticommunisme." *Communisme* 80–82 (2004–5).

van Elteren, Mel. "Rethinking Americanization Abroad: Toward a Critical Alternative to Prevailing Paradigms." *Journal of American Culture* 29, no. 3 (September 2006).

Vardabasso, Valentina. "La CED était-elle déjà morte en 1953? Le poids du facteur italien dans son échec (janvier–mars 1953)." *Relations internationales* 129 (Spring 2007).

Varsori, Antonio. "La Gran Bretagna e le elezioni politiche italiane del 18 aprile 1948." *Storia contemporanea* 13, no. 1 (January 1982).

Vecchio, Giorgio. "Movimenti pacifisti e anti-americanismo in Italia (1948–53)." Florence: European University Institute, Working Paper no. 7, 1986.

Vigna, Xavier. "Cho contre Carvalho: L'historiographie de '68." *RILI* 5 (May–June 2008).

Vittoria, Albertina. "La commissione culturale del PCI dal 1948 al 1956." *Studi storici* 31, no. 1 (January–March 1990).

Wagnleitner, Reinhold. "The Empire of the Fun, or Talkin' Soviet Union Blues: The Sound of Freedom and Cultural Hegemony in Europe." *Diplomatic History* 23, no. 3 (Summer 1999).

Wall, Irwin M. "L'amministrazione Carter e l'eurocomunismo." *Ricerche di storia politica* 9, no. 2 (August 2006).

———. "Les Etats-Unis et l'eurocommunisme." *Relations internationales* 119 (Fall 2004).

———. "The United States, Algeria, and the Fall of the Fourth Republic." *Diplomatic History* 18, no. 4 (Fall 1994).

Warner, Michael. "Origins of the Congress for Cultural Freedom." *Studies in Intelligence* 38, no. 5 (Summer 1995).

Whelan, Bernadette. "Marshall Plan Publicity and Propaganda in Italy and Ireland, 1947–1951." *Historical Journal of Film, Radio and Television* 23 (October 2003).

Winock, Michel. "'US Go Home': L'antiaméricanisme français." *L'histoire* 50 (November 1982).

Yarrow, Andrew L. "Selling a New Vision of America to the World: Changing Messages in Early Cold War Print Propaganda." *Journal of Cold War Studies* 11, no. 4 (Fall 2009).

Zuffa, Grazia. "Le doppie militanze: Donna comunista, donna femminista." *Memoria*, nos. 19–20 (1987–88).

Index

Berlinguer, Giovanni, 364
Berlusconi, Silvio, 379, 381, 396
Bernanos, Georges, 16
Bernstein, Leonard, 437 (n. 82)
Bertrand, Mireille, 348
Beuve-Méry, Hubert, 36, 114
Bevin, Ernest, 99
Bianciardi, Luciano, 253
Bidault, Georges, 17, 69, 70, 102–3, 128, 154, 156, 213
Billoux, François, 25, 157
Bissel, Richard, 159
Black Panthers, 292, 293
Blum, Léon, 38, 68, 69, 75. *See also* Blum-Byrnes agreements
Blum-Byrnes agreements, 38, 40, 46, 76–77, 79, 93
Bobbio, Norberto, 186, 189–90, 366
Bogart, Humphrey, 172
Bohlen, Charles, 88–89, 99, 105, 180, 241, 267, 268, 270, 298
Bolshevism, 22, 23
Bondy, François, 184, 185
Boogaart, Richard W., 255
Book centers/traveling libraries: PCI, 163–64, 168; and "Battle for the Book," 164; in France, 169
Borgna, Gianni, 358, 379
Bosworth, Richard, 104
Bouret, Jean, 291
Bourguiba, Habib, 228
Bradley, Omar, 203
Brando, Marlon, 172, 453 (n. 87)
Brandt, Willy, 313, 314, 335; and *Ost-politik*, 304, 313, 367
Brezhnev, Leonid, 303, 308, 318; Brezhnev Doctrine, 309
Brokaw, Tom, 376
Brown, Irving, 100, 184
Bruce, David K. E., 118, 120, 180, 220, 395
Brzezinski, Zbigniew: and Eurocommunism, 337–38; and Historic Compromise, 339, 341, 344, 345, 346; and NATO, 338, 344; PCI's view of, 368
Buckley, William F., Jr., 57, 296
Bufalini, Paolo, 280, 352
Bulgaria, 72

Bullit, William, 68
Bundy, McGeorge, 241, 267, 269
Burke, Edmund, 2
Burnham, James, 57, 59, 181
Burns, Ken, 376
Bush, George H. W., 369
Bush, George W., 396
Buttiglione, Marina, 352
Byrnes, Jimmy, 20. *See also* Blum-Byrnes agreements

Cacciari, Massimo, 365
Cachin, Marcel, 38
Cafagna, Luciano, 28, 199
Caffery, Jefferson, 64–79 passim, 184, 395; and de Gaulle, 117, 413 (n. 37); and expulsion of PCF from government, 83–84; and French public opinion, 100; and interim aid to France, 98; and Marshall Plan, 89, 97, 116; and trade unions in France, 100
Cahiers du communisme, 95, 167, 258, 314, 347, 364, 411 (n. 113)
Caldwell, Erskine, 44
Calendario del popolo, Il, 164
Calvino, Italo, 55, 189–90, 287, 388; and anti-Americanism, 55, 433 (n. 28); leaves PCI, 188, 199; and U.S. culture, 42, 376, 409 (n. 83)
Cambodia, 355
Campaign of Truth, 137, 173, 201
Camus, Albert, 30, 122
Capote, Truman, 172, 453 (n. 87)
Capra, Frank, 101
Carey, James B., 105–6
"Carnation Revolution." *See* Portugal
Carnegie Foundation, 184
Carosello, 254
Carrillo, Santiago, 312, 313, 316, 462 (n. 67)
Carter, Jimmy, 318, 336, 370; administration, 337–38, 384, 392; and budget, 344; and Eurocommunism, 337–38, 343–45. *See also* Human rights
Casanova, Laurent, 49, 157, 188, 233
Casaroli (Cardinal), 373
Case del Popolo (PCI), 163, 164, 358

142, 156, 188; end of, 200; founding of, 91; and Marshall Plan, 95–96; and pacifist campaign, 122, 126; and realism in culture, 162

Comitato Amministrativo Soccorsi ai Senzatetto, 110

Comitato di Liberazione Nazionale, 17

Comité de Liaison des Etudiants Révolutionnaires, 179

Committee of Intellectuals for a Europe of Freedoms, 366

Common Council of American Unity, 174

Communism: in Eastern Europe, 4, 27, 91, 93, 302, 308–9, 371, 375, 377; in Western Europe, 4, 217, 305, 312–13, 371, 379. *See also* Communist International Conferences; Eurocommunism; PCF; PCI

Communist International Conferences: Berlin (1976), 313; Brussels (1974), 312; of eighty-one parties, 257, 309; of Europe of Six, 217; of Mediterranean parties, 260; Moscow (1969), 308; of sixty-eight parties, 212; of Western parties, 305

Communist Party of Germany, 69

Communist Party of Poland, 69

Communist youth/youth federations: in France, 22, 277, 283, 300, 308, 356; in Italy, 259–60, 265, 277, 279, 284, 300, 354

Confédération générale du Patronat Français, 91

Confederazione Italiana Femminile, 110

Congresses for Peace and Christian Civilization, 133

Constitutional Assembly (Italy), 26–27

Consumerism: in France, 244, 248–49, 255, 285, 378, 387–88; in Italy, 244, 246, 248–49, 250, 254, 255, 285, 355, 358, 378–79, 387–88; in U.S., 40, 41, 193, 246–47; in Western Europe, 5, 8, 11, 244, 334, 358, 386–87

Contemporaneo, Il, 289

Cooper, Gary, 172

Copeland, Aaron, 437 (n. 82)

Coppi, Fausto, 172

Corbino, Epicarmo, 84

Corriere della Sera, 312, 359

Corsini, Gianfranco, 190, 241, 271, 289, 438 (n. 97)

Costa-Gavras, Constantin, 304

Counterculture: in France, 290–91, 356–58, 387; in Germany, 290–91; in Italy, 288, 290–91, 354, 357–58, 387; "transatlantic," 273, 357–58, 378–79, 387–88; in U.S., 281–82, 290–91, 293–94

Courtade, Pierre, 46, 93–94, 272

CPUSA (Communist Party of the United States), 28, 78, 94, 325

Craxi, Bettino, 343, 367, 369, 374

Critica marxista, 374

Croce, Benedetto, 21, 24, 31–32, 48, 55, 181, 183

Croizat, Ambroise, 25

Cronache Sociali, 115

Cronkite, Walter, 296

Cuadernos, 436 (n. 71)

Cuba, 193, 266, 308, 375; missile crisis in, 238, 277

Cucchi, Aldo, 130, 187

Czechoslovakia, 311; and Marshall Plan, 91; 1948 coup in, 83, 107. *See also* Prague Spring

Daix, Pierre, 286, 362

Daladier, Edouard, 128

D'Alema, Massimo, 354, 355

Dallas, 379

Dandieu, Arnaud: *Le cancer américain,* 35

D'Attorre, Pier Paolo, 196

Davis, Angela, 319–20

DC (Democrazia Cristiana), 20, 21, 393; anti-American groups in, 20, 115; cooperation with PCI, 298, 343; and economic/social reform, 233–34, 243, 250, 254, 352; and Eurocommunism, 315, 343, 345; and European integration, 132; factionalism in, 328, 339; left-wing factions of, 155, 221, 343; and mass culture, 165–66; and NATO summits, 346; and 1948 elections, 103–10; and 1953 elections, 149–51, 152; and 1958 elections, 222; and 1975 elections, 328; and

passim; and expulsion of PCI from government, 83–84; and interim aid to Italy, 98; and Marshall Plan, 97, 115; in Paris, 219–20; and psy-war, 77, 141, 142, 145
Durante, Jimmy, 101
Duras, Marguerite, 348
Duroselle, Jean-Baptiste, 178
Dylan, Bob, 271

Eastman, Max, 59
Eastwood, Clint, 379
Eccles, Marriner, 75, 76
Eco, Umberto, 278, 287, 376, 381
Economic Cooperation Administration. *See* Marshall Plan
EDC (European Defense Community), 10, 120–21, 128, 131, 132, 134, 139, 152, 154, 212, 213–14, 218–19, 384, 395
Egypt, 197, 223, 231–32. *See also* Suez crisis
Ehrenburg, Ilya, 135
Einaudi, Luigi, 98, 106
Einstein, Albert, 135, 437 (n. 82)
Eisenhower, Dwight D., 160; and "Atoms for Peace," 208, 209–10; and "Chance for Peace," 208–9; and cultural cold war, 161, 180; and decolonization, 223; and de Gaulle, 62, 213, 395; and domino fears, 203; Eisenhower Doctrine, 224, 226, 235; and European integration, 149, 151–52, 213–14, 219, 234; and exceptionalism, 235–36; as general in World War II, 19, 20, 46, 130; and Italian diplomacy, 230–31; and Italy (postwar), 66; and McCarthyism, 148, 206; and New Look, 151–52; and "Open Skies," 208, 210; and psy-war, 137, 146–47; and psy-war diplomatic measures, 201–2, 207–10, 235–36, 394, 439 (n. 3); as Supreme Commander of NATO, 119, 126, 149
Eisenhower administration: assistance to France, 154; and French 1958 crisis, 229; and propaganda, 208–10; and psy-war, 146–56 passim, 160, 176–77, 295
Elbrick, C. Burke, 176
Eliot, T. S., 191

Ellenstein, Jean, 314, 315
Ellwood, David W., 89, 418 (n. 2)
Eluard, Paul, 437 (n. 82)
Emerson, Ralph, 42
Encounter, 183, 184
Enlightenment, 29, 48, 57
Environmentalism, 371
Esprit, 29, 30, 31, 114, 170, 183, 383
Eurocommunism, 10, 302, 338; and anti-Americanism, 303, 311, 316–20; and Berlinguer, 311, 312–13, 316, 317, 325; and Eastern Europe, 319–20, 330, 339, 345, 346, 370; explained to U.S. public, 337, 343; and intellectuals, 315, 361, 366; and PCE, 312–13, 316; and PCF, 312–16, 321, 462 (n. 67); summits of, 312–13; and Third World, 315, 318. *See also* Historic Compromise; United States
Euro Disneyland, 381
European Atomic Energy Community, 213, 216, 217
European Community Movement, 179
European Economic Community, 213
European integration, 64, 113–14, 139. *See also* EDC; France; Italy; Marshall Plan; PCF; PCI; United States
European Recovery Plan (ERP). *See* Marshall Plan
European Youth Campaign, 139
Exceptionalism (U.S.), 4, 7, 53, 58, 81, 86, 152, 184, 185–86, 234, 235, 236, 237, 291, 317, 382–83, 392–93, 395, 397
Existentialism, 29–30, 50; and counterculture, 287; and Marxism, 30; and PCF, 54, 186; and Soviet Union, 54; and U.S. intellectuals, 50, 183, 199. *See also* Sartre, Jean-Paul
Express, L', 369

Fajon, Etienne, 314, 433 (n. 25)
Fanfani, Amintore, 115, 221–22, 230–32, 254; and Opening to the Left, 233, 240, 241; and PCI, 233, 328, 343; and U.S. hegemony, 231, 234, 332
Fanon, Frantz: *The Wretched of the Earth*, 266

Farrel, James T., 181

Fascism: and anti-Americanism, 34, 35, 41, 42, 43; in Italy, 15, 17, 24, 26, 32

Fassino, Piero, 377

Fast, Howard, 95, 135

Faulkner, William, 42, 44, 135, 271

Favaro, Roland, 308, 356, 357

Fellini, Federico, 274, 342, 360; *La dolce vita*, 253

Feminism: and abortion laws, 348, 351–52; in Europe, 376; in France, 194, 292, 347–48; in Italy, 195, 292, 350–52; and pacifism, 347–48, 350; and PCF, 194–95, 292, 347–49, 350; and PCI, 194–95, 292, 350–53, 371; in U.S., 11, 325, 347, 349–50, 352

Feste de L'Unità, 164, 165, 285, 358

Fête de L'Humanité, 164, 169

FIAT, 37, 76, 84, 153, 155, 254

Figaro, Le, 177

Figuères, Léo, 258, 286, 314

Fioravanti, Mike, 194

Fiszbin, Henri, 315

Fiterman, Charles, 375

Fitzgerald, F. Scott, 45

FLN (Front de Libération Nationale), 225, 275

Flores, Marcello, 55

Fo, Dario, 288

Forcella, Enzo, 358

Force Ouvrière, 96, 100, 144

Ford, Gerald, 330, 332, 334, 335, 462 (n. 85); administration, 328, 336

Ford, Henry, 40–41, 45; and Fordism, 43, 247, 249, 252. *See also* Gramsci, Antonio

Ford Foundation, 175, 179, 184

Foreign Affairs, 337

Foreign Assistance Coordinating Committee, 117

Foreign Leader Program, 177, 178, 392–93

Foreign Policy, 337

Forrestal, James, 108

Fortini, Franco, 199

Forum, 436 (n. 71)

Foster, William Z., 95

Foucault, Michel, 363, 365, 376

Fraleigh, William, 297

France, 2, 19, 21; bourgeoisie in, 17–19; and China, 327; and decolonization, 205, 223–24; and economic downturn in 1970s, 302, 315, 334, 347; economic growth in, 249, 265; and European integration, 114, 118, 120–21, 134, 213, 218–19, 238, 394; exceptionalism in, 32, 55; Fourth Republic of, 143, 220, 227–29, 395; and Franco-Soviet Treaty of 1944, 38, 39, 62, 70, 71, 72; and German rearmament, 121, 131; and G-7, 334; and Historic Compromise in Italy, 333–34, 339–41, 343; and insurrection in, 98; and Italian elections, 102, 107; Marshall Plan in, 87–101 passim, 110–17; national identity of, 14–15, 36; nationalism in, 131–33, 144, 153, 154, 176, 212, 394–95; and NATO, 212, 214–15, 223–24, 260, 373; neutralism in, 114, 119, 131–32, 133, 134–36, 143, 145, 148, 170, 201, 202, 203, 204, 219, 227, 340, 344, 383, 392; 1946 elections in, 25; 1947 elections in, 91, 97; 1951 elections in, 130, 132; 1958 crisis in, 227–29; 1958 elections in, 232; 1968 elections in, 284, 298; 1978 elections in, 324, 346; 1981 elections in, 324; and Opening to the Left in Italy, 241–42; partitocracy in, 73, 143; postwar reconstruction of, 13, 75, 76; prestige and, 63, 64, 214, 218–19; psychological impact of World War II in, 44, 53, 59; Soviet myth in, 53, 54, 388; Third Republic of, 31, 61; U.S. myth in, 53; U.S. pressures resisted by, 134, 152, 154–55, 236. *See also* Algerian War; Americanization; Anti-Americanism; Catholicism; French Revolution; May 1968 movement; Modernization; PCF; United States; Vichy regime; Youth movements

France nouvelle, 167, 362

Franco, Francisco, 317

Frankfurt School, 278, 365, 376

Free Trade Union Committee, 184

French Revolution: legacy of, 14, 19, 22, 29, 36, 37, 44, 55, 180, 363, 378, 404 (n. 17)

Friedman, Georges, 43

Friedman, Thomas, 389
Frost, Robert, 45
Fulbright, William J., 80–81, 86, 292, 296–97, 392
Furet, François: *Penser la Revolution française*, 378
Futurism, 409 (n. 82)

Gable, Clark, 172, 452 (n. 87)
Gaja, Roberto, 345
Galbraith, John Kenneth: *American Capitalism*, 192
Galluzzi, Carlo, 284, 304, 309
Garaudy, Roger, 26, 33, 49–50, 270; and anti-Americanism, 130; and Catholics, 261, 278–79; *Le grand tournant du socialisme*, 286, 307; and Marxism, 31, 55, 290; and Soviet Union, 187, 199, 287, 305, 307, 432 (n. 12); in U.S., 289–90
García Lorca, Federico, 190
Gardner, Richard, 341–43, 344, 345, 395, 463 (n. 91)
Garibaldi, Giuseppe, 106
Garibaldi Brigades, 19, 27
Gauchisme, 278, 280, 357, 364; ex-, 356, 369, 370
Gay rights: in France and Italy, 349, 376, 380
Gedda, Luigi: and civic committees, 104, 176
General Electric, 251
Geneva Summit (1955), 210
Genscher, Hans-Dietrich, 333
Gentile, Emilio, 21
Germany: during World War II, 15, 16
Germany, East, 131, 133, 263; and Berlin crisis, 257
Germany, West, 240, 241; and Berlin crisis, 257; and European integration, 114, 133, 213, 252; and Historic Compromise in Italy, 333–35, 340–41, 345; and Marshall Plan, 93, 94, 100; in NATO, 209, 210; postwar, 10, 61, 68, 72, 74, 76, 79, 82, 416 (n. 71); and rearmament, 121, 123, 128, 131, 215, 218–19, 220, 238; Social Democratic Party in, 242, 333, 334–35, 395. *See also* Eurocommunism

Geymonant, Ludovico, 190
Gide, André, 29, 406 (n. 47), 407 (n. 49)
Gingembre, Léon, 113
Ginsberg, Allen, 190
Giolitti, Antonio, 23, 199
Giordani, Igino, 133
Giovane critica, 277
Giscard d'Estaing, Valéry, 321, 334, 336, 338, 345, 346, 348, 368
Gitlin, Todd, 6
Globalization, 360, 388–90, 396
Glucksmann, André, 287, 363, 377–78
Godard, Jean-Luc, 274, 289; *A bout de souffle*, 253
God That Failed, The, 181
Goldberg, Arthur, 414 (n. 40)
Goldring, Maurice, 315
Goodman, Paul, 271, 277
Gorbachev, Mikhail, 370, 377; and perestroika, 371, 375
Gorz, André, 287, 378
Graham, Billy, 59
Gramsci, Antonio, 15, 55, 163, 189, 363, 455 (n. 129); and cultural hegemony, 29, 32–33, 157, 303, 364–65; and feminism, 351; and Fordism, 10–12, 247, 296; and organic intellectuals, 37, 48, 280; and theory of bureaucracy, 24, 27
Gramsci Institute, 191, 250, 251, 287
Grand Alliance, 10, 13, 18, 37, 38, 39, 47, 49, 50, 92; end of, 82
Grand Hôtel, 168
Gray, Gordon, 141
Graziani, Rodolfo, 126
Graziano, Rocky, 101
Great Britain, 19, 63, 93, 172, 231; and détente, 221; and European integration, 114, 238, 252, 263, 313–14; and insurrection in Italy, 99; and Italian elections, 107, 109; Labor Party in, 239, 241, 242; and Opening to the Left in Italy, 239, 241
Greece, 143, 282, 316, 332
Green, William, 414 (n. 40)
Greene, Graham: *The Quiet American*, 317
Greshman, Carl, 377
Grew, Joseph, 66

ism; Gramsci, Antonio; Marxism; Mass culture; PCF; PCI; Postmodernism; Psychological warfare; Soviet Union; Thorez, Maurice; Togliatti, Palmiro; United States

International Confederation of Trade Unions, 184

Intervention. *See* CIA; Psychological warfare; United States

Iran, 204, 247, 368

IRBMs (Intermediate Range Ballistic Missiles), 231, 373–74

Ireland, 103

IRI (Istituto per la Ricostruzione Industriale), 73

Israel, 231, 260, 265, 332

Italian American Labor Council, 68

Italy, 2, 20, 21; bourgeoisie in, 17, 18, 19; contacts with U.S.S.R., 71–72; and decolonization, 67, 106, 143, 223–24; economic downturn in 1970s, 302, 315, 334, 347; economic growth in, 249, 265; and European integration, 114, 120–21, 134, 214, 232, 394; and G-7 agreements, 335–36, 344–45; Marshall Plan in, 87–101 passim, 110–17; and Mediterranean vocation, 143, 223–24, 230–32, 265, 270, 331; monarchy in, 19; national identity of, 14–15, 32, 33, 37; nationalism in, 67, 131–33, 153, 176, 212, 221; in NATO, 100, 118, 119, 143–44, 212, 214–15, 223–24, 231, 332, 373; neutralism in, 118, 119, 131–32, 134–36, 145, 202, 219, 221–22, 224, 230–31, 238, 239, 340, 341, 344, 383, 392; 1946 elections in, 27; 1948 elections in, 91, 101–10; 1951 elections in, 132; 1953 elections in, 148–49, 150–51; 1958 elections in, 222; 1963 elections in, 242; 1976 elections in, 336; 1979 elections in, 346; partitocracy in, 73, 230; and peace treaty, 40, 65, 119; postwar democracy in, 31; postwar reconstruction of, 13, 75, 76; prestige and, 62, 64, 67, 107, 214, 223–24, 231–32, 270, 332, 333–34; psychological impact of World War II in, 44, 53, 59; Soviet myth in, 37, 40, 53, 55, 388; and Tri-

este dispute, 65, 67, 107, 214; and U.N., 119, 214; U.S. myth in, 37, 40, 41, 53; U.S. pressures resisted by, 143, 152–56, 176. *See also* Americanization; Anti-Americanism; Catholicism; Fascism; Modernization; PCI; Risorgimento; United States; Youth movements

Jackson, C. D., 146, 148, 205, 241

Jacobinism, 22, 23

James, Henry, 45

Japan, 61, 203

Jaspers, Karl, 183, 365

Jernegan, John, 239

Joan of Arc, 19, 21

John Paul II (Pope), 346

Johns Hopkins University, Bologna Center, 178–79

Johnson, Lyndon B., 267, 270, 289, 293, 295; administration, 260

Johnston, Eric, 28

John XXIII (Pope), 241

Joliot-Curie, Frédéric, 122, 131, 187, 437 (n. 82)

Jordan, 231

Jotti, Nilde, 350–51, 467 (n. 21)

Jouaux, Léon, 96

Joyce, Robert P., 179

Judt, Tony, 30, 32, 198

Julien, Claude: *Le nouveau Nouveau monde*, 246

Kampelman, Max, 377

Kanapa, Jean, 314, 316, 322, 337, 362

Keaton, Buster, 172, 453 (n. 87)

Kennan, George F., 1–4, 56, 57, 58, 207; and CCF, 182; and European integration, 100, 219; and Italy (postwar), 66, 69; and Long Telegram, 57, 78; and Marshall Plan, 74, 88, 394; and psy-war, 78; views of American society, 2–4, 159; views of Western European Communism, 2–3, 391; and youth movements, 294–95

Kennedy, John F., 223, 269, 295; and European integration, 238; myth of, 237, 271; and Opening to the Left in

Italy, 241–43, 447 (n. 122); and PCF, 271; and PCI, 238, 271

Kennedy, Robert, 289, 292, 296

Kennedy administration, 213, 237–43, 295; and Flexible Response, 238; and Multilateral Force, 238; and Opening to the Left in Italy, 238–43

Kesselring, Albert, 126

Khrushchev, Nikita, 188, 196, 197, 248, 303; visit to U.S., 236

Kiesinger, Kurt Georg, 263, 333

King, Martin Luther, Jr., 292–93

King in New York, A, 172

Kirilenko, Andrej, 309

Kirk, Alexander, 65, 66

Kirkpatrick, Jeanne, 57, 377

Kissinger, Henry: and de Gaulle, 298, 327; and détente, 317, 330, 394; and Eisenhower administration, 235; and Eurocommunism, 331, 335–36, 337, 368, 394; and European integration, 330, 394; and European politics, 341, 347, 391; and French politics, 325–27, 333, 335; and German Social Democrats, 333–35, 345; and Historic Compromise, 327, 328, 330–31, 332–33, 334–35, 336, 345; and Italian prestige, 332; PCI's view of, 336–37, 368, 470 (n. 74); views of U.S. society, 159

Koestler, Arthur, 181

Komer, Robert W., 239, 240, 395

Korean War, 108, 117, 118, 119, 121, 124, 125–27, 130, 176, 209, 426 (n. 5)

Kosygin, Aleksei, 308

Kravchenko, Victor, 187

Kriegel, Annie, 17, 96, 166, 233

Kristeva, Julia, 287, 363

Kroes, Rob, 7

Kuisel, Richard, 170, 244

Labor Newsreel, 174

Labor Party. *See* Great Britain

Lacan, Jacques, 349, 363

LaFollette, Suzanne, 59

Lang, Jack, 360, 381

Lange, Peter, 337

Laniel, Joseph, 149, 152, 154

La Pira, Giorgio, 115, 269; and pacifism, 133, 226, 238, 265, 375, 384, 441 (n. 25); and Vietnam, 267–68

Laski, Melvin, 184

Lavau, Georges, 381

Lazar, Marc, 402 (n. 2), 403 (n. 5)

LCGIL (Libera Confederazione Generale Italiana del Lavoro), 96, 100

Leaves of Grass, 190

Lebanon, 231, 235

Lecoeur, Auguste, 125, 126–27, 129, 189

Ledda, Romano, 287

Lefebvre, Henri, 50

Lefort, Claude, 287, 363

Lefranc, Pierre, 248

Léger, Fernand, 437 (n. 82)

Lenin, Vladimir Ilyich, 248, 296, 355

Leone, Giovanni, 331, 332

Le Pen, Jean-Marie, 373

Leroy, Roland, 277, 308, 356

Le Roy Ladurie, Emmanuel, 199

Letters to Italy campaign, 103, 104

Lettres françaises, Les, 46, 49, 172, 187, 188, 278, 286, 291, 410 (n. 97), 432 (n. 12); termination of, 361

Lévy, Bernard-Henri, 362, 378

Lewis, John, 292

Lewis, Sinclair, 42

Liaison des Etudiants Anarchistes, 179

Libération, 357

Lincoln, Abraham, 272

Lippman, Walter, 2

Lipset, Seymour Martin, 185, 192, 393

Lister, George, 239

Lockheed scandal, 318

Lodge, Henry Cabot, Jr., 201

Lollobrigida, Gina, 164

Lombardi, Riccardo, 267, 328

London, Arthur, 304, 361

Longo, Luigi, 37, 95, 96, 215, 263, 264, 418 (n. 29); and Prague Spring, 304, 306; and student movement, 265, 284; and U.S. society, 289

Lotta Continua, 279, 354, 355, 455 (n. 119)

Lotta Femminista, 350

Lovestone, Jay, 68

Luce, Clare Boothe: and anti-Americanism

319, 381, 384–85; and Americanization, 5–6, 135, 158, 360, 387; and American literature, 45–46, 49–50, 190, 271; and anti-Americanism, 4, 6–9, 11, 24, 38, 43, 49, 50, 71, 91–97, 100, 111, 123–27, 135–36, 145, 158, 166, 169–70, 173, 186, 193–96, 203–4, 207–8, 211, 225, 237, 238, 264–65, 302, 305–6, 307–8, 319–20, 346, 361, 373, 374, 377, 383–86, 390, 472 (n. 3); and austerity, 314, 323, 389; and Catholics, 25–26, 170, 261, 428 (n. 35); clashes with PCI, 200, 252, 312, 315–16, 322, 450 (n. 55); congresses of, 49, 189, 286, 349; and decline of Soviet model, 310, 314–15, 361, 375, 377, 383; and decolonization, 18, 84, 203–4, 245; and de Gaulle, 18, 21–22, 71, 134, 232–33, 249, 252, 253, 257, 261, 284, 285, 308, 413 (n. 37); and democratic centralism, 285, 299, 302, 307, 386–87; and de-Stalinization, 188–89, 197–200, 211–12, 438 (n. 110); and détente, 259, 307–8, 314, 321; and economic reconstruction/reform, 24–25, 73, 245–56, 382; and European integration, 101, 132, 215–17, 250, 263, 307, 309–10, 313–14, 316, 321–22, 372, 383; and existentialism, 50, 54, 135, 186–87; expulsion from government, 82–86; and extraparliamentarian Left, 300, 302; and Hungary, 197–98; ideological section of, 157; institutional power of, 5, 24–27, 72–73, 74, 99, 141, 143–44, 391–92; and insurrection, 83, 95–96, 97, 98, 108, 152; and intellectuals, 15, 28, 29, 31–33, 135, 161, 162, 186–91, 198–200, 265–66, 277–79, 285–87, 324, 361–64, 366, 377–78, 388; international influence of, 225, 229, 257, 268, 385; and Marshall Plan, 87, 89–97, 123; and mass culture, 33, 158, 164–65, 166–69, 170, 271–72, 288–89, 359, 387; and media (radio/TV), 279, 288, 359, 372; and middle class, 245, 303, 323–24, 391; nationalism of, 4, 8, 21–24, 50, 60, 64, 65, 66, 96, 97, 128–33, 144, 197, 212, 216, 260; and NATO, 260, 263, 305, 307,

316, 337, 340, 394; and neocapitalism, 245–54, 390; and 1956 elections, 232; and 1958 elections, 232; and 1962 elections, 233, 242; and 1968 elections, 284; and 1978 elections, 324, 346; and 1981 elections, 324; and pacifist campaigns, 122–36 passim, 144–45, 168, 176, 232, 257, 260, 373–74, 384–86; and polycentrism, 200, 252, 257, 270; in postwar government, 25–26; and propaganda, 125–29, 132–34, 135–36, 145, 207–8, 237, 320, 391–92; relations with Soviet Union, 5, 96, 130, 211, 259, 300, 321–22, 371, 375; and schools, 165, 169, 254, 386; and Social Democrats in Western Europe, 313–14; Soviet control of, 15, 22, 29, 33, 87–88, 91–92, 95–96, 122–23, 136, 217, 242, 362, 383, 385–86; Soviet funding of, 161, 308–9; and Soviet myth, 23, 28, 53–54, 97, 161, 165, 211–12, 248, 307; and U.S. mass culture, 158–69, 172, 291, 349, 360, 378; and U.S. politics in 1970s–90s, 319, 368–70; and Vietnam War, 258–61, 263–66, 359, 362, 387; and working class, 18–19, 96, 97, 164, 169, 171–72, 245, 248–49, 286, 378, 386, 389. *See also* Civil rights movement; Communist youth; Counterculture; Feminism; France; French Revolution; Human rights; Maoism; Marxism; PCF and PCI compared; Prague Spring; Resistance; Socialist Party (French): relations with PCF; Trotskyism; United States; Youth culture; Youth movements

PCF and PCI compared, 10–11, 13–33, 43–44, 47–48, 55, 186–91, 197–200, 215–16, 246–54, 263, 271–72, 277, 279–85, 314–16, 321–22, 323–24, 352, 356–61, 364–65, 368–69, 372–73, 375–76

PCI (Partito Comunista Italiano), 1; and ambivalent anti-Americanism, 39–43, 47, 51, 171–72, 190, 271–72, 289–93, 300, 317–19, 381, 384–85; and Americanization, 5–6, 135, 165, 168, 194, 356, 360, 379, 387; and American literature, 42–43, 47–48, 190, 271; and anti-

Americanism, 4, 6–11, 24, 38, 46–49, 77, 91–97, 100, 102, 109–10, 111, 123–27, 135–36, 158, 168, 186, 193–96, 203–4, 207–8, 211, 215, 226, 238, 250, 260, 264–65, 302, 305–6, 307–8, 340, 345, 346, 361, 367, 373–74, 377, 383–86, 390, 410 (n. 103), 472 (n. 3); attacks on Christian Democrats, 49, 71, 104–5, 125, 131, 134, 158, 208, 246, 250, 254, 264–65; and austerity, 323, 331, 335–36, 389; and Catholics, 27, 96, 373, 374–75; and center-left governments, 264–65; clashes with PCF, 200, 252, 312, 315–16, 322, 450 (n. 55); congresses of, 32, 104, 187, 199–200, 217, 269, 287–88; cultural commission of, 157, 163, 168, 169, 188, 190, 191, 250; and cultural hegemony, 11, 29, 32–33; and decline of Soviet model, 310, 315, 322, 361, 368, 375, 377, 383; and decolonization, 203–4, 225–26, 257; and "democratic alternative," 367; and democratic centralism, 199, 269, 284, 297, 299, 302, 307, 313, 343, 371, 386–87; and de-Stalinization, 188–89, 196–200, 211–12, 441 (n. 23); and détente, 259, 261–62, 307–8, 310–11, 313, 336–37; and "doppiezza," 23, 64, 74; and economic reconstruction/reform, 26–27, 73, 245–56, 323, 325, 382, 409 (n. 81); and European integration, 101, 132–33, 215–17, 246, 260, 261–63, 307, 309–10, 315–16, 371–72, 383, 427 (n. 32); expulsion from government, 82–86; and extraparliamentarian Left, 199, 265, 269, 284, 300, 302, 307, 324, 350; and Hungary, 197–98, 226, 377; institutional power of, 5, 24–27, 72, 73, 74, 99, 141, 143–44, 152–53, 335–36, 391–92; and insurrection, 83, 95–96, 98, 108, 284; and intellectuals, 5, 15, 28, 30–33, 135, 158, 161, 162, 168, 186–91, 196–200, 265–66, 277–79, 281, 285, 287–88, 323, 361, 364–66, 377, 388; international influence of, 84–85, 226, 238, 241, 257, 258, 259, 261, 310–18, 330, 333, 335, 375, 385, 450 (n. 55); and

Marshall Plan, 87, 89–97, 113, 116; and mass culture, 33, 163–64, 165–69, 170–71, 271–72, 288–89, 358–59, 379, 387; and media (radio/TV), 166, 279–80, 288–89, 358–59, 379; and middle class, 246, 254, 303, 323, 391; nationalism of, 4, 8, 16–24, 50, 55, 60, 64, 66, 69, 96, 97, 128–33, 212, 215–16, 260, 311; and NATO, 259, 263, 305, 307, 322–23, 330, 337, 394; and neocapitalism, 245–54, 280, 311, 366, 390; and neorealism, 80, 163, 166; and 1948 elections, 91, 101–10, 157; and 1953 elections, 149–51; and 1958 elections, 222; and 1968 elections, 304; and 1975 elections, 324; and 1976 elections, 336; and 1979 elections, 346; and Opening to the Left, 211, 217; and pacifist campaigns, 123–36 passim, 155, 217, 257, 260, 373, 384–86; and polycentrism, 200, 216, 217, 226, 257, 261, 303, 333; in postwar government, 26–27; and propaganda, 96–97, 104–5, 109, 126, 128–29, 135, 207–8, 262, 264, 329, 386, 391–92; and PSI in 1970s–80s, 367–68, 370–71; relations with Soviet Union, 5, 10, 96, 130, 211, 259; and schools, 163, 168, 254; and Social Democrats in Western Europe ("Westpolitik"), 261, 307, 313, 325, 335, 337, 387; Soviet control of, 15, 22, 29, 33, 87–88, 91–92, 95–96, 122–23, 136, 268, 383, 385–86, 403 (n. 5), 472 (n. 3); Soviet funding of, 107, 109, 123, 132–34, 161, 308–9; and Soviet myth, 23, 28, 55, 95, 96, 124, 161, 211–12, 248, 307; Soviet pressures resisted by, 24, 162–63, 217, 390, 472 (n. 3); and U.S. mass culture, 158, 168–69, 170–72, 289, 352, 358–60, 378–80; and U.S. politics in 1970s–90s, 317–18, 336–37, 367–70, 379; and Vietnam War, 257–69 passim, 387; view of Carter administration, 336–37, 470 (n. 74); and working class, 19, 96, 169, 171–72, 248–49, 346, 378, 386, 389; and Yugoslavia, 69. *See also* Civil rights movement; Communist youth; Counterculture; Feminism;

Human rights; Italy; Maoism; Marxism; PCF and PCI compared; Prague Spring; Resistance; Socialist Party (Italian): unity with PCI; Terrorism; Trotskyism; United States; Youth culture; Youth movements

PDS (Partito Democratico della Sinistra), 371, 379, 396–97; and NATO, 379

Pearson, Drew, 103

Pecchioli, Ugo, 343

Peggio, Eugenio, 217, 251, 262

Pella, Giuseppe, 130–31, 155, 156, 221

Pensée, La, 188–89

Perle, Richard, 377

"Permanent revolution" (U.S.), 53, 78, 87, 292, 388

Pertini, Sandro, 397

Pesenti, Antonio, 26, 76

Pesenti, Jacques, 357

Pétain, Philippe, 128

Petruccioli, Claudio, 259, 280

Picasso, Pablo, 31, 45, 122, 189, 199, 266, 437 (n. 82)

Pinay, Antoine, 152, 176, 204, 219–20

Pintor, Giaime, 409 (n. 91)

Pipes, Richard, 377

Pius XII (Pope), 20, 21, 103

Platone, Felice, 166–67

Pleven, René, 118, 128. *See also* EDC

Plissonnier, Gaston, 362

Plyoushch, Leonid, 361

Point IV Program, 117

Poland, 71, 92, 373; Solidarity movement in, 368, 372, 470 (n. 73)

Poletti, Charles, 101

Policy Planning Staff (U.S.), 2, 99, 118, 422 (n. 66); Policy Planning Council, 256; and political warfare, 108, 139

Politecnico, Il, 42, 47, 48, 50, 411 (n. 113)

Political warfare. *See* Psychological warfare

Pompidou, Georges, 294, 319, 321, 327

Ponomariov, Boris, 310

Pons, Silvio, 313, 470 (n. 73)

Pop art, 277

Popular Democratic Front (Italy), 102–10 passim

Popular Front (France), 14–15, 29

Portelli, Alessandro, 293

Portugal, 93, 119, 316, 332; and "Carnation Revolution," 316, 332–33

Portuguese Communist Party, 316

Positivism (Italy), 48

Postmodernism, 363–64, 365, 375–76, 388; and U.S. academia, 363

Potere Operaio, 279

Poujade, Pierre, 255

Powers, Gary, 236

Pragmatism (U.S.), 53, 56

Prague Spring, 70, 198, 281, 284, 309; Club 231 in, 304; and PCF, 261, 263, 270, 285, 297–98, 302–6, 320–21; and PCF-PCI condemnation of Soviet intervention, 304–8; and PCF-PCI reconciliation with Soviet Union, 308; and PCI, 261, 262, 285, 297–98, 302–6, 320–21; and PSU, 299

Pratolini, Vasco, 199

Pravda, 161

Prenant, Marcel, 188

Presley, Elvis, 171, 358

Preuves, 183, 185

Prévert, Jacques, 199

Prezzolini, Giuseppe, 34

PRI (Partito Repubblicano Italiano), 108, 222, 328

Pro-Americanism (in public opinion): in France, 145, 254, 369–70, 381; in Italy, 143, 145, 168, 254, 381

Productivity, 111

Progresso italo-americano, Il, 103

Propaganda, 96–97

PSIUP (Partito Socialista Italiano di Unità Proletaria), 299

PSU (Parti Socialiste Unifié), 242, 298–99

Psychological Strategy Board, 134, 135–36, 137, 141, 149, 150, 154, 201, 205, 207, 220, 392. *See also* Psychological warfare

Psychological warfare, 10, 86, 101, 136–56; code "Cloven," 141; code "Clydesdale," 141, 155; code "Demagnetize," 141; code "Midiron," 141, 143; and diplomatic action, 201–2; and European integration, 139–41, 142; and intellectuals in France and Italy, 160–61; and LENAP, 147, 154; as "political warfare," 108–9

Purges: in postwar France and Italy, 24, 29

Quaderni rossi, 278
Quaderni piacentini, 278
Quasimodo, Salvatore, 437 (n. 82)
Quinzane, La, 170

Radical Party: in France, 25; in Italy, 351, 356, 366, 467 (n. 21)
Radio Free Europe, 342
Radio Moscow, 161
RAI (Radio Televisione Italiana), 174, 177, 288, 358
Ramadier, Paul, 83, 84, 114
Ramette, Arthur, 167
Ramparts, 184
Rapports France-Etats-Unis, 111
Rassemblement Démocratique Révolutionnaire, 115
Rassemblement du Peuple Français, 130
RDF (Radio Diffusion France), 174, 177
Reader's Digest, 191
Reagan, Ronald, 367–70; administration, 377, 384
Reale, Eugenio, 95, 199
Realism, socialist, 48, 187, 189, 191
Réalités, 111
Red Army, 23, 37
Red Scare. *See* McCarthyism
Reinhardt, Frederick, 237, 240, 255, 267
Remington-Rand France and Frigidaire, 251
Re Nudo, 357
Repetto, Margherita, 352
Repubblica, La, 359
Republican Party (U.S.), 205–6, 300, 368, 369, 376
Resistance: in France and Italy during World War II, 16, 17, 18, 21, 25, 26, 30, 37
Resnais, Alain, 289
Reuther, Victor and Walter, 240

Revel, Jean-François, 396; *Ni Marx, ni Jesus*, 293–94
Révolution, 362
Reynaud, Paul, 128
Ridgway, Matthew, 126–27, 135, 144, 145, 386
Riesman, David: *The Lonely Crowd*, 192, 252
Rinascita, 19, 94, 95, 124, 133, 170, 172, 277, 284, 289, 322, 350, 355, 411 (n. 113)
Rioux, Jean-Pierre, 18
Risi, Dino: *Il sorpasso*, 253
Risorgimento, 19, 21, 29, 55
Riva, Valerio, 472 (n. 3)
Robeson, Paul, 95
Rocard, Michel, 299
Rochet, Waldeck, 252, 258, 290; and European integration, 263; and Prague Spring, 304, 306; and Vietnam, 265; and youth movements, 282, 284
Rockefeller, John, 45
Rockefeller, Nelson A., 146, 201, 235, 249
Rockefeller Foundation, 184
Rocky, 379
Rodano, Franco, 323, 366
Roger, Philip, 43
Rolland, Jacques-François, 199
Rolland, Roman, 122
Romagnoli, Luciano, 249
Romain, Jules, 181
Romania, 72
Rony, Jean, 315
Roosevelt, Franklin Delano, 20, 36, 39, 63, 272
Roosevelt, Theodore, 7
Rosenberg, Julius and Ethel, 148, 186–87
Rossanda, Rossana, 287–88
Rossellini, Roberto: *Open City*, 79, 80
Rostow, Walt, 56
Roudy, Yvette, 348
Rousset, David, 187
Roy, Claude, 46, 80, 199
Rubin, Barry, 281
Rumor, Mariano, 115, 328, 331, 332, 464 (n. 100)
Rumsfeld, Donald, 359

211, 242, 245, 264, 299, 300, 303, 315, 321–22, 324, 327, 336, 362, 367, 368, 369, 372–73, 381. *See also* Mitterrand, François

Socialist Party (Italian) (PSIUP, PSI), 20, 27, 68, 115–16; and anti-Americanism, 105, 163, 215, 239, 328; and anticommunism, 367; in center-left governments, 264, 288; and European integration, 215, 240; and feminism, 351–52, 467 (n. 21); and neutralism, 240, 267; and Opening to the Left, 211, 222, 224, 238–43, 395; and pacifism, 71, 123; pro-Americanism of, 343, 366, 367, 369, 374; and Third World, 269; unity with PCI, 71, 96, 102, 105, 155, 226. *See also* Nenni, Pietro

Social sciences (U.S.): influence of, in France and Italy, 192, 364–65

Sogno, Edgardo, 139

Solidarity movement. *See* Poland

Solzhenitsyn, Aleksandr: *The Gulag Archipelago*, 361, 365; *One Day in the Life of Ivan Denisovich*, 286

Sonnenfeldt, Helmut, 326

South East Asian Treaty Organization, 208

Soviet Union, 1, 93, 157, 330; alliance with Nazi Germany, 16, 29; anti-Americanism in, 8, 193, 272; and cultural propaganda, 161, 162, and de Gaulle, 38, 62, 71, 232, 268; and de-Stalinization, 196–200, 209; and Fordism, 41; France and Italy influenced by, 13–14, 70–71, 72; and Franco-Russian Treaty of 1944, 38, 39, 62, 70–71, 72; and Hungary, 197–98, 209, 303, 309; and Italian elections, 106–7, 109; and Marshall Plan, 88, 91, 101; and Mitterrand, 268; myth of, in French and Italian Left, 8, 36, 54–55, 107, 388; and 1950s détente, 206, 209–10, 236, 256; and 1960s détente, 237, 256, 272, 308; and 1970s détente, 11, 317; and 1980s détente, 370; and pacifist campaigns, 122–23, 131, 151, 208; propaganda of, 207, 248; recognizes government of Italy, 70, 71–72; and Soviet appeal in

Third World, 209–10; and Twentieth CPSU Congress, 196–97; and Vietnam War, 258. *See also* Eurocommunism; Human rights; PCF; PCI; Prague Spring; Red Army; Sino-Soviet split

Soviet Writers Congress, 48

Spaghetti Westerns, 289

Spain, 241, 316, 332, 333, 344

Spellman, Francis (Cardinal), 103

Spengler, Oswald, 2, 365

Spielberg, Stephen, 376

Spini, Giorgio, 178

Spire, Antoine, 315

Spriano, Paolo, 266, 365

Springsteen, George, 294

Sputnik, 193, 235

Stalin, Joseph, 39, 55, 96, 172, 198, 209, 248; and French and Italian Communists, 22–23, 71, 95–96, 98, 131; and peace appeal of 1952, 131, 134; and Picasso, 189; purges by, 16; and Stalinism, 196–200, 314

Stalinism. *See* Soviet Union: and de-Stalinization; Stalin, Joseph

State Department: and cultural activities, 179–80; and EEC, 213; and Historic Compromise, 337, 342, 344; and Italian elections, 101–2, 103; and Marshall Plan, 112; and NATO, 119; and psy-war, 146

Steinbeck, John, 42, 44

Stendhal, 33

Stettinius, Edward, 64, 67

Stevenson, Adlai E., 180

Stiglitz, Joseph, 389–90, 396

Stil, André, 126

Stockholm Peace Appeal, 8–9, 122–23, 132, 181, 206, 373, 385–86

Structuralism, 361, 363, 364

Students for a Democratic Society, 289

Sturzo, Luigi (Don), 74

Suez crisis, 223, 225, 227, 228, 230, 234, 235

Suslov, Mikhail, 122, 309

Sweden, 263

Talenti, Pier, 328

Tarchiani, Alberto, 61, 62, 76, 106, 107, 345

Tardini (Monsignor), 62

Tasca, Henry J., 73, 74, 152, 222

Tati, Jacques: *Jour de fête*, 111; *Mon oncle*, 252; *Playtime*, 252

Tatò, Antonio, 323, 367

Tempo Presente, 184, 199

Temps modernes, Les, 29, 30, 54, 114, 170, 183, 252

Temps présent, 25, 26

Tendence Syndicale Révolutionnaire Fédéraliste, 179

Terracini, Umberto, 85, 91–92, 96, 304, 305, 312

Terrorism: in Germany, 291; in Italy, 284, 291, 303, 305, 317–18, 354, 386; and PCI, 312, 317–18, 322, 324, 346; and Red Brigades, 312, 324, 346, 355; and U.S., 317–18, 322. *See also* Moro, Aldo

Thibau, Jacques, 318

Tho, Le Duc, 258

Thoreau, Henry David, 42

Thorez, Maurice: and anti-Americanism, 93–96, 128, 158, 164–65, 403 (n. 1); and Catholics, 25–26; death of, 306; and de Gaulle, 18, 233; and de-Stalinization, 197–200, 211; and expulsion from government, 83–86, 409 (n. 80); and grandeur, 16; and insurrection, 98; and intellectuals, 31, 49, 164–65, 189; and Marshall Plan, 93–94; and mass culture, 158, 165, 171; moderation toward U.S., 39; and nationalism, 22, 130; and pacifism, 130, 136, 426 (n. 5); and PCI, 70; personality cult of, 18–19, 198; in postwar government, 14–15, 25; and Socialists, 225; and Stalin, 22, 23, 95; and state bureaucracy, 24–25; and U.S. aid, 91–92; in U.S.S.R., 131

Thorez-Vermeersch, Jeannette, 305

Tillon, Charles, 25, 122, 128, 130, 142, 287

Time, 183

Tito (Josip Broz)/Titoism, 128, 130

Tocqueville, Alexis de, 33, 191

Togliatti, Palmiro, 1, 62, 70, 71, 166, 366, 402 (n. 1), 447 (n. 122); and anti-Americanism, 1–4, 51, 85, 94–96, 105, 135, 163, 208, 226; assassination attempt against, 108; and Catholics, 133; cooperation with U.S., 39; death of, 306; and de-Stalinization, 196–200; and détente, 211; and "doppiezza," 23; and European integration, 216; and expulsion from government, 83–86; and Hungary, 197, 226; and insurrection, 98, 102; and intellectuals, 28, 31–33, 48, 163, 187–88, 189–90, 287; and Marshall Plan, 93, 96; and mass culture, 167; and nationalism, 17–18, 22; and 1948 elections, 102, 103–4, 105; and Opening to the Left, 240–41; and pacifism, 124, 130, 133, 136; and polycentrism, 197, 200, 303; in postwar government, 14–15, 26, 27; and propaganda, 109; and Stalin, 22, 23, 131; and U.S. aid, 91–92; and Vietnam War, 257–58; *Yalta Memorandum* of, 278, 287

Tönnies, Ferdinand, 2

Tortorella, Aldo, 366

Toscanini, Arturo, 101

Totalitarianism, 58, 286, 362–63, 377–78

Totò, 164

Touraine, Alain, 281, 378, 396

Trentin, Bruno, 254

Trieste dispute, 18, 65, 67, 69, 71, 131, 155

Trilling, Lionel, 159, 192

Trombadori, Antonello, 200

Trotskyism: in France, 259, 275, 277, 278, 363; in Italy, 259, 277, 279, 364

Truman, Harry S., 36, 128, 148, 427 (n. 23), 429 (n. 55); and France, 64; and Italy, 63, 66; targeted by PCF and PCI, 94, 129; Truman Doctrine, 62, 78, 85, 93

Truman administration, 60; and psy-war, 136–47, 160

Turkey, 332

Turner, Ted, 376

Tyler, William, 241, 434 (n. 43)

UDI (Unione delle Donne Italiane), 195, 350, 351

UIL (Unione Italiana del Lavoro), 96, 100, 144

Union Démocratique pour la Paix et la Liberté, 139

logical warfare; USIS; Vietnam; Youth culture; Youth movements

UNRRA (United Nations Relief and Recovery Administration), 75

Urban, George, 339–40

URSS et nous, L', 314, 315, 362

USIA (United States Information Agency), 147, 149, 177. *See also* USIE; USIS

USIE (United States Information and Education), 137, 141, 147

USIS (United States Information Service)/ U.S. cultural exchange programs, 80, 81–82, 147; and Eurocommunism, 342; and intellectuals, 185; and Marshall Plan, 110–11; and Office of Information and Cultural Affairs, 82, 178–80; and propaganda in France and Italy, 138–39, 168, 173–77, 210, 439 (n. 3); raided by PCF, 176; reduced activity of, 269

Utopian views. *See* PCF: and Soviet myth; PCI: and Soviet myth; United States: and anticommunism

Vailland, Roger, 199

Valenti, Jack, 267, 270

Valletta, Vittorio, 76

Vance, Cyrus, 339, 341

Vanoni, Ezio, 155

Vatican: and Italian elections, 102, 103–4, 109, 421 (n. 57); and Kennedy administration, 241; and Marshall Plan, 94; *Mater et Magistra*, 248; and PCI, 373; welcomes U.S. influence, 62, 103, 332–33. *See also* Catholicism

Veil, Simone, 348

Veltroni, Walter, 379

Vercors (Jean Bruller), 80, 187, 199, 266, 362

Vernant, Jean-Pierre, 278

Vernes, Jacqueline, 247

Vichy regime, 17, 24, 31

Vico, Giambattista, 366

Vie Nuove, 96, 164, 171, 172, 194, 276

Vie ouvrière, La, 167

Vietnam, 308, 330, 362, 375; Vietnam War, 10, 11, 245, 256–72 passim, 295, 296, 299, 307–8, 317, 325, 355, 356; war

with France, 84, 118, 119, 124, 154, 203, 209

Vietnam Party of Workers, 258

Vincent, Madeleine, 348

Vinson, Fred, 75, 76

Vital Center, 57, 60, 181, 184, 192, 218, 237, 395

Vittorini, Elio, 42, 47–48, 50, 187, 188, 287, 437 (n. 82)

Voice of America, 102–3, 110, 138, 173, 177

Volpe, John, 328, 342

Volpi, Giuseppe, 37

Wagnleitner, Reinhold, 173

Walesa, Lech, 368, 470 (n. 73)

Wall, Irwin, 82, 197

Wall, Matthew, 414 (n. 40)

Wallace, Henry A., 57, 75

Wallon, Henri, 199

Walmsley, Walter, 142

Weber, Max, 2

Welles, Sumner, 1

Wells, Orson, 172, 453 (n. 87)

West Bengal, 389

Western European Union, 213, 220

White, Theodore, 110

Whitman, Walt, 42, 190, 271, 272

Whyte, William H.: *The Organization Man*, 192, 252

Wilder, Billy, 79

Williams, William Appleman, 295

Wilson, Woodrow/Wilsonianism, 44, 56, 368–69, 377

Wisner, Frank, 139

World Committee of Peace Partisans, 123, 124, 256; World Congress of Peace Partisans sessions, 122, 125, 131, 181, 186

World Congress against Fascism and Imperialist War, 122

World Federation of Trade Unions, 216

Wright, Richard, 49

YMCA, 166

Yom Kippur War, 332

Young Americans for Freedom, 296

Youth culture: in France, 158, 171, 276, 356–58, 378–79; in Italy, 170, 171, 276,

354–55, 378–79; and PCF, 171, 277; and PCI, 171, 276, 277, 354–58; in U.S., 169–70, 171, 276, 297, 356–58

Youth movements: and Algerian war, 225, 275, 278; and Americanization, 273–75, 281–82, 284, 293–94, 302, 356–57, 387–88, 396; and anti-Americanism, 275, 279, 386; in France, 273–85, 290–91, 294–301, 356–57; in Italy, 265, 273–85, 290–91, 354–55, 357; libertarian traits of, 274–75, 278, 281–82, 290–91, 396; and PCF, 270, 273, 275, 279–85, 297–300, 356–57, 359, 386, 387; and PCI, 273, 275, 279–85, 297–300, 304, 354–55, 386, 387; and students in France, 254, 265, 268, 274–76, 279–85; and students in Italy, 254, 274–76, 279–85; and students in U.S., 11, 273–75, 281–82, 325, 359; and Third Worldism, 275, 279; U.S. government and, 294, 296–97; and Vietnam War, 275, 279–80, 359; and workers, 276, 280. *See also* Civil rights movement; Counterculture; *Gauchisme*; "Hot Autumn of 1969"; Maoism; May 1968 movement; New Left; Terrorism; Trotskyism

Yugoslavia, 44, 65, 130, 143, 263. *See also* Trieste dispute

Zaslavsky, Victor, 196, 472 (n. 3)
Zeffirelli, Franco, 342, 360
Zeldin, Theodore, 55
Zellerbach, David, 226, 239
Zhdanov, Andrei/Zhdanovism, 48, 85, 162, 187, 189, 190; and Cominform, 95; and PCF, 92

THE NEW COLD WAR HISTORY

Alessandro Brogi, *Confronting America: The Cold War between the United States and the Communists in France and Italy* (2011).

Gregg Brazinsky, *Nation Building in South Korea: Koreans, Americans, and the Making of a Democracy* (2007).

Vladislav M. Zubok, *A Failed Empire: The Soviet Union in the Cold War from Stalin to Gorbachev* (2007).

Stephen G. Rabe, *U.S. Intervention in British Guiana: A Cold War Story* (2005).

Christopher Endy, *Cold War Holidays: American Tourism in France* (2004).

Salim Yaqub, *Containing Arab Nationalism: The Eisenhower Doctrine and the Middle East* (2003).

Francis J. Gavin, *Gold, Dollars, and Power: The Politics of International Monetary Relations, 1958–1971* (2003).

William Glenn Gray, *Germany's Cold War: The Global Campaign to Isolate East Germany, 1949–1969* (2003).

Matthew J. Ouimet, *The Rise and Fall of the Brezhnev Doctrine in Soviet Foreign Policy* (2003).

Pierre Asselin, *A Bitter Peace: Washington, Hanoi, and the Making of the Paris Agreement* (2002).

Jeffrey Glen Giauque, *Grand Designs and Visions of Unity: The Atlantic Powers and the Reorganization of Western Europe, 1955–1963* (2002).

Chen Jian, *Mao's China and the Cold War* (2001).

M. E. Sarotte, *Dealing with the Devil: East Germany, Détente, and Ostpolitik, 1969–1973* (2001).

Mark Philip Bradley, *Imagining Vietnam and America: The Making of Postcolonial Vietnam, 1919–1950* (2000).

Michael E. Latham, *Modernization as Ideology: American Social Science and "Nation Building" in the Kennedy Era* (2000).

Qiang Zhai, *China and the Vietnam Wars, 1950–1975* (2000).

William I. Hitchcock, *France Restored: Cold War Diplomacy and the Quest for Leadership in Europe, 1944–1954* (1998).